Ninth Edition

Essentials of Children's Literature

Kathy G. Short
University of Arizona

Carol Lynch-Brown
Florida State University

Carl M. Tomlinson
Northern Illinois University

330 Hudson Street, NY, NY 10013

Editorial Director: Kevin M. Davis
Portfolio Manager: Drew Bennett
Content Producer: Yagnesh Jani
Portfolio Management Assistant: Maria Feliberty
Development Editor: Jill Ross
Executive Product Marketing Manager: Christopher Barry
Executive Field Marketing Manager: Krista Clark
Procurement Specialist: Deidra Smith
Cover Design: Carie Keller, Cenveo
Cover Art: Shaun Tan
Printer/Binder: LSC Communications, Inc.
Cover Printer: LSC Communications, Inc.
Editorial Production and Composition Services: iEnergizer Aptara®, Ltd.
Full-Service Project Manager: iEnergizer Aptara®, Ltd.
Text Font: Times LT Pro, 10/12

Text and illustration credits are located on pages 315–316.

Library of Congress Cataloging-in-Publication Data

Names: Short, Kathy Gnagey, author. | Lynch-Brown, Carol, author. | Tomlinson, Carl M., author.
Title: Essentials of children's literature/Kathy G. Short, Carol Lynch-Brown, Carl M. Tomlinson.
Description: Ninth edition. | New York : Pearson, 2017. | Includes bibliographical references and index.
Identifiers: LCCN 2017001632 | ISBN 9780134532592 (pbk.) | ISBN 0134532597 (pbk.)
Subjects: LCSH: Children's literature—Study and teaching (Higher) | Children's literature—History and criticism. | Children's literature—Bibliography.
Classification: LCC PN1009.A1 L96 2017 | DDC 809/.892820711—dc23 LC record available at https://lccn.loc.gov/2017001632

4 18

ISBN-13: 978-0-13-453259-2
ISBN-10: 0-13-453259-7

A Story Is a Doorway

A story is a doorway
That opens on a wider place.
A story is a mirror
To reflect the reader's face.

A story is a question
You hadn't thought to ponder,
A story is a pathway,
Inviting you to wander.

A story is a window,
A story is a key,
A story is a lighthouse,
Beaming out to sea.

A story's a beginning,
A story is an end,
And in the story's middle,
You just might find a friend.

—Richard Peck

Brief Contents

Detailed Contents

Features

Figures and Tables

Figures

Tables

About the Authors

Kathy G. Short teaches graduate courses in children's literature, inquiry, and curriculum at the University of Arizona and taught elementary school in Indiana and Ohio. Her books include *Teaching Globally: Reading the World through Literature, Critical Content Analysis of Children's and Young Adult Literature, Essentials of Young Adult Literature, Creating Classrooms for Authors and Inquirers, Literature as a Way of Knowing,* and *Stories Matter: The Complexity of Cultural Authenticity*. She is director of Worlds of Words (www.wowlit.org), an initiative to encourage intercultural understanding through literature. She served on the Caldecott Committee and as president of NCTE and USBBY.

Carol Lynch-Brown taught graduate and undergraduate courses in children's and young adult literature, reading, and language arts education at Florida State University. She was a teacher in elementary school and middle school in St. Paul and Minneapolis public schools and taught English in French public schools. She coauthored, with Carl M. Tomlinson, *Essentials of Young Adult Literature,* second edition, published by Pearson in 2010, and is a former editor of *The Reading Teacher,* a journal of the International Reading Association.

Carl M. Tomlinson taught graduate and undergraduate courses in children's literature and language arts at Northern Illinois University. He was an elementary and middle school teacher in Thomasville, Georgia, public schools, and taught classes in English in Norway. He coauthored with Carol Lynch-Brown *Essentials of Young Adult Literature,* second edition, published by Pearson in 2010, and is the editor of *Children's Books from Other Countries,* published by USBBY and Scarecrow Press in 1998.

Preface

Essentials of Children's Literature is a brief, affordable, yet comprehensive textbook with rich resources—a true compendium of information about children's literature. It is tailored to a survey course in children's literature but is also suitable as a companion text in an integrated language arts course because of its brevity and affordability.

The primary focus of a survey course in children's literature should be reading children's books, not reading an exhaustive textbook *about* children's books. Students in such a course need direct experience with books—reading independently, reading aloud, discussing, writing, comparing, criticizing, evaluating, and connecting to their lives, as well as exploring ways of sharing books with children.

Our goal is to invite students into story worlds and to help them develop an identity as readers, and that can only occur through experiencing the pleasure and excitement of reading many excellent books. At the same time, a body of knowledge about literature and about engaging children with literature is needed—that knowledge can be conveyed most efficiently through a textbook. *Essentials of Children's Literature* presents this body of knowledge in a clear, concise, direct narrative along with brief lists, examples, figures, and tables, thus freeing time for involvement with literature.

New to This Edition

Although much has changed in the field of children's literature, the ninth edition of *Essentials of Children's Literature* remains, in essence, true to our initial concept—a comprehensive but brief alternative to compendium textbooks. Our goal in revising this edition was to make it as current as possible to reflect new trends and titles and to produce a brief text without sacrificing content. We have added many new children's book titles and retained older titles most likely to be known and appreciated by students. Features within chapters—Milestones, Excellent Books to Read Aloud, Notable Authors and Illustrators, and Invitations for Further Investigation—have been updated to include important developments, recent outstanding children's titles, new creators of children's books, and current issues and topics related to the field. We have reorganized some of the content and moved sections from one chapter to another to create a stronger structure and flow to the text. We have also integrated many global and multicultural titles and authors throughout all chapters.

One important change is to separate the discussion of illustration and visual elements into its own chapter. Illustration is playing an increasingly significant role in all books, not just picturebooks, across genres and formats, including novels. The increasing richness of excellent graphic novels indicates the ways in which children's books reflect the strong visual culture of modern society. Another change is moving biography into the chapter with informational books, a shift in alignment with the definition of nonfiction in the Common Core State Standards. Other connections to the standards are integrated across chapters, including a focus on a specific literary element and a reader connection in each genre chapter to encourage close reading, a discussion of text complexity, an in-depth discussion of the features of informational books, and an analysis of how the standards connect to the use of literature in classrooms. In addition, the Invitations for Further Investigation provide suggestions for close reading and text analysis related to the focus of that chapter. In addition, we have integrated more connections to libraries and classrooms into chapters.

Revisions to individual chapters include the following.

Chapter 1: Learning about Story and Literature

- Updated research on trends in voluntary reading within the U.S.
- Revision of the identified landmark studies on literature and reading

Chapter 2: Learning about Children and Literature

- New examples of children's books appropriate for the stages of children's development
- Updated research on reading interests and evaluation of text complexity
- Additional information on book awards, review journals, and professional organizations from the fields of education, library science, and literary criticism

Chapter 3: Learning about Literature

- Careful discussion of close reading and reader response theory
- Balance of old and new book examples for the literary elements

Chapter 4: Illustration and Visual Elements

- A new chapter on illustration across all genres and formats
- Discussion on the role of visual elements, artistic media, artistic styles, and book design across different types of books, including picturebooks, novels, and graphic novels
- Updated Guide to Illustrations to reflect current trends in illustration

Chapter 5: Picturebooks and Graphic Novels

- An expanded discussion of graphic novels, including evaluation and selection criteria, historical overview, trends, and recommended titles
- Updated titles of picturebooks in the chapter and in the recommended lists, including addressing picturebooks for older readers and postmodern picturebooks

Chapter 6: Poetry

- Updated examples of poems and types of poetry books and recommended books

Chapter 7: Traditional Literature

- Discussion of the social function of folklore and the critiques of these stories from feminist scholars
- Updated recommended book lists

Chapter 8: Fantasy and Science Fiction

- Revised discussion of fantasy and science fiction as related but separate genres
- Updated types of fantasy to reflect current trends and titles for recommended book lists

Chapter 9: Realistic Fiction

- Updated themes and types of realistic fiction to reflect current trends, particularly in relation to gender identity
- Updated titles of recommended books

Chapter 10: Historical Fiction

- Moved biography to Chapter 11, Nonfiction: Biography and Informational Books
- Reorganized the discussion of types of historical fiction around themes rather than historical periods
- Updated titles of recommended books and inclusion of information on the time period and place in each book

Chapter 11: Nonfiction: Biography and Informational Books

- Chapter covers all nonfiction and includes both biography and informational books with a separate discussion of the criteria for evaluation, features, and types of books for the two types of nonfiction
- Expanded discussion of the features and structures of informational books
- Updated recommended book lists

Chapter 12: Literature for a Diverse Society

- Updated statistics and current trends related to cultural diversity within classrooms and within children's books
- Added a new section on Arab American and Persian American literature
- Updated recommended book lists for multicultural and international literature

Chapter 13: Literature in the Curriculum

- Updated discussion on the influence of the Common Core State Standards on the use of literature in classrooms and libraries
- Updated research studies on literature and reading and literature and writing
- Moved section on censorship into this chapter
- Integration of curriculum connections to libraries and classrooms

Chapter 14: Engaging Children with Literature

- Updated discussion of digital books and e-books and a new section on book apps
- Integration of engagements related to libraries and classrooms

Appendices

- Appendix A, Children's Book Awards, updated to include award winners and honor books for the years 2000–2016
- Appendix B, Professional Resources, updated to reflect the latest titles and editions
- Appendix C, Children's Magazines, updated to include new magazines and to reflect current magazine content, intended audience, website, and ordering information

Instructor's Manual and Test Bank

The instructor's manual features multiple syllabi of typical survey courses in children's literature. The test bank includes multiple-choice, matching, fill-in-the-blank, short answer, and essay questions. This supplement has been written by the text authors and is available for download at www.pearsonhighered.com.

Acknowledgments

We gratefully acknowledge the reviewers of the ninth edition: Lee Allen, University of Memphis; Janet Hilbun. Ph.D., University of North Texas; Roxanne Owens, DePaul University; Stephanie D. Reynolds, University of Kentucky; Judith Ann Stechly, West Liberty University; and Erika J. Travis, California Baptist University.

We are indebted to Shaun Tan for the cover art of this edition of *Essentials of Children's Literature*. His art underscores the power of community as readers travel together into a story world and the wonder that results from dialogue within the imaginary landscape of story.

Part 1

Children and Literature

Part 1 introduces you to the field of children's literature. These chapters will support you in learning how to read, select, and evaluate children's books.

Chapter 1 defines children's literature and examines the role of story and books in the lives of children. Stories fill our daily lives as the way in which we make sense of our experiences. Literature thus plays an essential role of inviting children into new experiences that provide them with important connections and understandings that go beyond entertainment and instruction. Overlooking this personal purpose for reading has personal and societal implications.

Chapter 2 emphasizes the need to know both children and books, so you can connect children with books that are significant in their lives and learning. Knowing children includes general guidelines for the types of literature likely to appeal to children as they develop from year to year, strategies for determining children's reading interests, and the factors to consider in evaluating text complexity. Knowing books involves building a knowledge of resources for book selection, including review journals, professional websites, and major awards, to select a balance and variety of books, as well as to understand why some children resist reading.

Approaches to studying and interpreting literature and elements of fiction are discussed in Chapter 3 related to written text. Chapter 4 explores the visual elements of illustrations across different types of books with a focus on picturebooks and graphic novels. The visual images in books are also essential in establishing elements of fiction, such as character, action, and setting.

Examples of notable books are provided throughout this text, but we do not include lengthy plot summaries or book reviews. We believe that more is gained from reading and discussing children's books themselves than reading *about* the books in a lengthy text.

Chapter 1

Learning about Story and Literature

The First Book

Open it.
Go ahead, it won't bite.
Well . . . maybe a little
More a nip, like. A tingle.
It's pleasurable, really.
You see, it keeps on opening.
You may fall in.
Sure, it's hard to get started.
Remember learning to use
Knife and fork? Dig in:
You'll never reach the bottom.
It's not like it's the end of the world—
just the world as you think
you know it.

—Rita Dove

A child leans forward, head cupped in hands, eyes wide with anticipation, listening to a story. Whether that child is seated beside an open fire in ancient times, on a rough bench in a medieval fairground, or on the story rug in a modern-day classroom or library, this image signals the same message—children love a good story.

Definition of Children's Literature

As you interact with children, whether your role is that of a teacher, librarian, or parent, you will have many opportunities to invite children to engage with good books. This text will help you become acquainted with the literature written for children from birth through early adolescence, and with the criteria to consider in selecting the best books for a particular child or a specific curricular need at just the right moment.

Children's books, first and foremost, are literature. Literature is not written to teach something, but to illuminate what it means to be human and to make the most fundamental experiences of life accessible—love, hope, loneliness, despair, fear, and belonging. Literature is the imaginative shaping of experience and thought into the forms and structures of language. Children read literature to experience life, and their experiences inside the world of a story challenge them to think in new ways about their lives and world.

More specifically, ***children's literature*** is defined as high-quality trade books for children from birth to early adolescence, covering topics of relevance and interest to children through prose and poetry, fiction and nonfiction. They are the books that children see as reflecting their life experiences, understandings, and emotions. This definition contains key concepts that will help you find your way around the 350,000 children's titles published in the last decade and currently in print (*Books In Print*, 2016) and the more than 29,000 new children's titles published annually in the U.S. (*Library and Book Trade Almanac*, 2015), as well as the many thousands of children's books published worldwide each year. In addition, children's books are now published in a range of electronic formats, including interactive digital books, e-readers, and apps for smartphones and tablets. These formats are not in competition with print books but instead offer different experiences and potentials for children to connect with literature.

Content

Children's books include the full range of childhood experiences from the difficult to the exciting. Whether these experiences are set in the past, present, or future, they need to be relevant to children today. The content of children's books includes amazingly diverse and interesting topics, including global cultures, space exploration, dinosaurs, and world records. This content can be expressed in prose or poetry. If the literary work is prose, it can be in the form of fiction (an invented narrative), nonfiction (a factual narrative), or a combination of the two.

The way in which this content is treated in books matters to children. Childhood stories that are forthright, humorous, or suspenseful are appealing to young readers; stories *about* childhood that are nostalgic or overly sentimental are written for adults looking back fondly at childhood. Content that authentically reflects diverse cultural experiences avoids damaging stereotypical images. And stories that show children in the midst of natural and human-made disasters contain some hint of hope for a better future, instead of only depicting the hopelessness and despair of the moment. An element of hope does not mean that stories must contain "happy endings," where all turns out well. Many children have experienced difficult life situations and know that a happy ending is not always possible; at the same time, some element of hope is essential to their survival and well-being as humans in the process of "becoming."

Teachers and librarians distinguish between the terms *textbook* and *trade book*. A ***textbook***, by design and content, is for the purpose of instruction, such as the basal readers and leveled books used in many classrooms for reading instruction or the content area books used in schools to teach science and history. In contrast, a ***trade book***, by design and content, tells a story to engage and intrigue children as readers and encourage new understandings. Trade books are often referred to as *library books* or "real" books. The books highlighted in this text are trade books, not textbooks.

Quality

Not all trade books aimed at young readers are worth close attention. Books ranging in quality from excellent to poor are readily available in bookstores and libraries as well as online. Racks of children's books can be found in department stores, drugstores, and even grocery stores.

Quality in writing and illustration has to do with originality and importance of ideas, imaginative use of language and image, and beauty of literary and artistic style that enable a work to remain fresh, interesting, and meaningful for many years. The best children's books offer enjoyment as well as memorable characters and situations and valuable insights into the human condition. These books have permanent value and stay in our memories.

This is not to say that books of good-but-not-great quality, such as series books, do not have value. These books do not win literary prizes, but they are enjoyed by young readers and encourage more reading and the development of fluency. They are excellent choices for independent reading but not for reading aloud to children. Read-alouds should challenge readers to consider new possibilities rather than focus on the easy and enjoyable books they are already reading on their own.

Many recent so-called children's books are nothing more than advertisements for film and television characters and associated products, such as candy, clothing, and toys. These books represent the low end of the quality spectrum and focus on the child as a consumer, rather than as a reader and human being.

The Value of Story in Making Meaning of Our Lives

Although this text focuses on literature, books connect to broader notions of story as meaning-making. Stories of all kinds are woven so tightly into the fabric of our everyday lives that it's easy to overlook their significance in framing how we think about ourselves and the world. They fill every part of life as we talk about events and people, read books, browse online news reports, send text messages, listen to music, watch video clips, check in with friends on Facebook, and catch up on a favorite television show. We live storied lives.

Stories are thus much more than a book—they are the way our minds make sense of our lives and world. Stories allow us to move from the chaotic "stuff" of daily life into understanding (Rosen, 1986). An endless flow of experiences surrounds us on a daily basis, so we create stories to impose order and coherence on those experiences and to work out their significance. Stories provide a means of structuring and reflecting on our experiences. We tell our stories to invite others to consider our meanings and to construct their own meanings, as well as to better understand those experiences ourselves. We listen to other's stories to try on another perspective or way of thinking about the world (Short, 2012).

Story is thus a mode of knowing—one of the primary ways in which we think and construct meaning from our experiences (Gottschall, 2012). Our views of the world are a web of interconnected stories: a distillation of all the stories we have shared. This web of stories becomes our interpretive lens for new experiences and is culturally based. Our human need to story about our experiences may be universal—but there is no one way to tell stories. Our stories are always interwoven with the stories that exist within our own communities, both in content and in the style and structure of the telling. All children come to school with stories, although the types of stories that they are familiar with and the ways in which they tell stories may be quite different from school norms.

We also construct stories to make sense of information. Theories are just bigger stories. Scientists create a theory by using current information to tell a story that provides an explanation of a natural phenomenon, such as reasons for black holes in outer space. These stories change over time as new information and perspectives become available. A story is thus a theory of something—what we tell and how we tell it reveals what we believe (Bruner, 1990).

Story is at the heart of who we each are as human beings and who we might become. Books for young children are often viewed as "cute" or as instructional lessons rather than recognizing their broader role as stories that children use to understand themselves and the world. The values of literature for children are interwoven with story as meaning making.

The Value of Literature in Children's Lives

Descriptions of children's literature in elementary schools and libraries typically focus on how to *use* children's books to teach something else. Literature is viewed as a material that is used to teach reading, math, science, social studies, or comprehension skills and writing strategies. We are often so focused on using literature to enhance academic learning that we lose sight of literature as having value in and of itself for children's lives (Wolf, Coats, Enciso, & Jenkins, 2011).

Enjoyment

First and foremost, good books offer enjoyment. Those of you who read widely as children will never forget the stories that were so funny that you laughed out loud, the poem that was so lilting that you chanted it from memory, the mystery that was so scary that your heart thumped with apprehension, and the characters who became your best friends or family. These positive early experiences often lead to a lifetime of reading to fulfill personal purposes and enjoyment.

Personal and Cultural Identity

Stories that are embedded in our communities and that are handed down from one generation to the next connect us to our past, to the roots of our cultural identities, and to the human condition. Readers grow in their identities by finding themselves and their families and communities within books and exploring the multiple connections of their identities, including race, ethnicity, nationality, gender, religion, language, disability, region, family structures, and social class.

Stories are also the repositories of culture. Knowing the tales, characters, and expressions that are part of our heritage supports us in becoming culturally literate. In addition, stories based on events in the past provide a connection to the people, both ordinary and extraordinary, who made the history that still influences us today.

Imagination and Transformation

By seeing the world through new perspectives and considering ways of living other than their own, children are encouraged to think creatively and divergently. Stories can provide children with alternative pathways for understanding their past or imagining their future. As children enter a world through stories that differ from the present, they develop their imaginations and are inspired to overcome obstacles, consider different viewpoints, and formulate personal goals. They transform their understandings of the possibilities for themselves and the world.

Often, story characters are placed in situations that require them to make difficult life decisions. As a story unfolds and a character's decision and the consequences of that choice become apparent, readers can critically consider their decisions and develop their own moral concepts and values.

Knowledge and Insights

Good books offer information and wisdom and so combine the heart and mind, reason and emotion. Informational books provide factual knowledge within a social context using a narrative arc to engage readers, whereas fiction and poetry offer insights into life along with information. When a story is so convincingly written that readers feel as though they have lived through an experience or in the place and time of that story, that book has given them a valuable personal experience that takes them beyond the constraints of their current lives. These experiences encourage children to view situations from perspectives other than their own.

Understanding and Empathy

Literature helps children gain an appreciation for the universality of human needs across history and place, which makes it possible for them to understand what connects us as human beings as well as what makes each of us unique. Living someone else's life through a story can help children develop a sense of social justice and a greater capacity to empathize with others. All children can benefit from stories that immerse them into the lives of characters who struggle with difficult circumstances or whose lives differ from theirs because of culture or geography. Literature plays an essential role in building intercultural understanding as children immerse themselves in the lives and thinking of characters within global cultures. Likewise, children can relate on a more personal level with the events and people of history when reading historical fiction that focuses on characters who are their own age.

Literary and Artistic Preferences

Another valuable result of children's interactions with literature is that they come to recognize the literary and artistic styles of many authors and illustrators. Children who read regularly from a wide array of books develop personal preferences for types of books and favorite authors and illustrators. Personal interest as expressed through self-selection of reading materials creates a sense of engagement that is critical to becoming a lifelong reader.

The more children know about their world, the more they discover about themselves—who they are, what they value, and what they stand for. These insights alone are sufficient to warrant making good books an essential part of a child's experiences.

The Value of Literature for Children's Learning

In addition to these roles within children's personal lives, literature is of tremendous value for academic learning. Literature provides interesting texts that support children in learning about text structures, literary elements, and reading/writing strategies and in exploring concepts and perspectives in science and social studies.

Reading and Writing

Reading, like any other process, improves by engaging in the actual "doing" of that process, not just learning *about* it. Regular reading of excellent literature can foster language development and help young children learn to read and value reading. Reading is devalued if children only read beginning reading materials that aren't worth the effort of reading them, and if we don't read aloud from books that engage their interest and minds.

Reading aloud to children at home and in classrooms and libraries greatly benefits children's acquisition of reading strategies and their attitudes toward reading. The landmark study *Becoming a Nation of Readers* (Anderson, Hiebert, Scott, & Wilkinson, 1985) found that the most important factor for building the knowledge that leads to success in reading is reading aloud to children. This report also noted that the greatest gains in vocabulary, fluency, and comprehension came from independent reading by children. So the two most important engagements we can provide on a daily basis are to read excellent literature aloud and to schedule time for independent reading of free-choice materials and books. Table 1.1 provides a summary of several landmark studies examining children's engagement with literature.

By listening to and reading excellent literature, children are exposed to rich vocabulary and excellent writing styles, which serve as good mentor texts for their own speaking and writing voices. Books that use particular literary devices such as dialogue and detailed description provide demonstrations of options for writing.

Government policies have a tremendous effect on the teaching of reading and writing and thus on the use of literature within literacy instruction. The specific policies change over time, with the Common Core State Standards and new performance assessments most recently affecting classrooms. Connections to these standards have been integrated throughout the chapters in this book but are addressed in depth as part of text complexity in Chapter 2 and the political context of reading in Chapter 13.

Literature across the Curriculum

Literature across the curriculum refers to using literature as teaching materials in social studies and history, science, health, the arts, and mathematics. Many trade books contain information that is relevant to the topics, issues, and themes that are explored in schools. Moreover, this information is often presented through captivating, beautifully illustrated narratives that are interesting and are more comprehensible and memorable. When using literature across the curriculum, children are not confined to a dry, pedantic textbook as the sole resource. Using several sources of information provides fuller factual coverage of topics and leads to more informed consideration of issues and perspectives. The abundance of well-written informational books for children provides rich resources for inquiries in the content areas and can be paired with fiction to engage children's interest and deepen their conceptual understandings and provide them with an explanation of the *why* behind facts.

Appreciation and Visual Culture

Illustrations in children's books are appreciated for their narrative value in telling the story and for their aesthetic value as art. Books provide a means of understanding art as a meaning-making process and

Table 1.1 Landmark Studies on Literature and Reading

Researcher(s)	Participants	Findings
Krashen (2011)	Meta-analysis of 83 studies	Reports on the positive impact of free reading on language acquisition and reading achievement across 83 published studies
Sipe (2008)	K–2 classrooms	Research on children's discussions of read-alouds led to the development of a system to describe children's literary understandings
Brooks (2006)	Middle school students	Study examined the influence of culturally relevant literature on the responses of African-American middle school girls
Eeds & Wells (1989)	Fifth-grade classrooms	Study of literature discussion groups led to a description of the features of "grand conversations" around books
Carlsen & Sherrill (1988)	College students who become committed readers	Conditions that promote a love of reading include freedom of choice in reading material, availability of books and magazines, family members who read aloud, role models and peers who value reading, sharing and discussing books, owning books, availability of libraries and librarians
Atwell (1987)	Middle-grade students	Long-term teacher research study detailing the curriculum and student interactions in reading/writing workshop
Eldredge & Butterfield (1986)	A total of 1,149 beginning readers in 50 classrooms	Use of children's literature to teach reading has a greater positive effect on reading achievement and attitudes than basal readers
Fielding, Wilson, & Anderson (1986)	Middle-graders	Students who read a lot at home show larger gains on reading achievement tests
Hickman (1981)	Fifth-grade classroom	Participant observation in a classroom to understand the complexity of teacher moves and student responses to literature
Applebee (1978)	Children ages 2 to 17	Children's sense of story grows as they mature; hearing and reading literature positively affects language development
Durkin (1966)	Children who read before attending school	Children who learned to read before school were read to regularly from the age of 3 and frequently were writing before reading

appreciating art for its own sake. By calling attention to striking illustrations in reading aloud, you highlight the value of art as visual culture. Children gain an understanding of visual images by discussing an artist's style, medium (watercolor, pastels, etc.), and use of color, line, and shape, as well as by using books as demonstrations of media and techniques for their own artwork.

In addition, children can learn to critically read visual images through interactions with books and so develop their knowledge of visual literacy. Visual literacy is essential to acquiring the ability to critique the pervasive images that surround children constantly in commercials, films, video games, and the Internet.

So Why Is the Reading of Literature at Risk in Our Society?

Given the significant values of story and literature, an obvious assumption is that engaging in personal reading is valued in our society. Research indicates that the opposite is true and that voluntary reading is at risk. Newspaper headlines put a spotlight on illiteracy—the number of people who cannot read and write at the levels needed to function in society—when the much bigger problem is aliteracy, the number of people who can read and choose not to. They read work-related materials, but reading books for personal purposes is not a regular part of their daily lives.

Voluntary reading of literature in the U.S. has been monitored by the National Endowment for the Arts (NEA) since 1982. After years of steady decline in voluntary reading across all age groups, particularly young adults ages 18–24, the NEA report in 2008 showed a rise in adults reading literature, but that number has again declined in the 2012 report. During 2012, 47 percent of Americans reported reading at least one work of literature and 54.6 percent read at least one book of any type, including informational, not related to school or work. A slight rise in reading books among 18–24-year-olds did occur between 2008 and 2012, and although the numbers declined for literary texts, the overall numbers show a slight rise, indicating more reading of informational books. The U.S. population now breaks into almost equally sized groups of readers and nonreaders, not because the nonreaders cannot read but because they are choosing not to read books, either electronic or print.

On a positive note, researchers at the PEW Research Center (Zickuhr, Rainie, & Purcell, 2013) found that although Americans ages 16–29 are heavy technology users, with almost all reporting that they are online on a regular basis, they also read and borrow printed books and value libraries. Readers in this age group report increased use of e-books (25 percent), but their print reading remains steady. They access the online services of libraries and are just as likely as older adults to visit the library, borrow print books, browse the shelves, and use research databases. They are also more likely to ask for assistance from librarians and express the need for separate teen hangout spaces in libraries.

The NEA's 2007 report found a correlation between the decline in reading and increased participation in electronic media, including the Internet, video games, and portable digital devices. This correlation is a concern because reading books supports the development of the focused attention and contemplation essential to complex communication and insight. The report also noted that the percentage of 17-year-olds who read nothing for pleasure doubled over a 20-year period, whereas the amount they read for school (15 or fewer pages a day) stayed the same. There was also a significant decline from childhood to adolescence from 54 percent to 22 percent for those who read almost daily for pleasure. College attendance is no longer a guarantee of active reading habits; one in three college seniors read nothing for pleasure in a given week. Many high school and college students stop reading for personal purposes because reading becomes associated with textbooks and schoolwork—hardly motivating reading!

The NEA 2007 report details the consequences of the loss of reading for personal purposes, noting that voluntary reading correlates strongly with academic achievement in reading and that proficient readers have more financially rewarding jobs and opportunities for career growth. Literary readers are three times more likely than nonreaders to visit museums, attend plays or concerts, and create artwork, and twice as likely to exercise, volunteer, and vote. The greater academic, professional, and civic benefits associated with higher levels of reading point to the significance of your role as a parent, teacher, or librarian in the lives of children.

Books do change lives for the better, but *you* need to be a reader to engage children as readers. Many of you are likely among those college students who stopped reading because of the lack of relevance in teacher-selected reading materials, dull textbooks, boring instructional practices, lack of time, peer pressure, past failures, a preference for electronic media, and a perception of reading as hard work. Because of the heavy load of course work and textbook reading, you are much more likely to watch television or YouTube videos and surf the Internet, activities that require passive participation, when you have free time. One of our goals is for you to rediscover the joys of reading for pleasure and gain insight through reading lots of children's books—graphic novels and novels in verse, fantasy in new worlds and fiction about the past, information about the world, and fiction about the struggles of daily life. If you are to immerse children in reading good books that add to their lives, you need to find those books for your life as well.

As you learn *about* literature in this textbook, be sure to immerse yourself in books you find compelling. Read picturebooks and novels, fiction and nonfiction, stories and poems, to reclaim these values for yourself and for the children with whom you will interact. We kept this textbook concise with invitations to encourage you to reclaim your reading life. We want you to experience books as adding value to the quality of your life.

Invitations for Further Investigation

- Document the stories that you tell across a single day and note the different ways in which you tell those stories. Share your data with a small group and create a list of roles that stories play in your lives.
- Create a timeline of stories that you remember from your childhood at home and at school. What kinds of stories were significant (oral, written, film, etc.)? What specific stories do you remember

interacting with over and over? Were there memorable people with whom you interacted around these stories? Why were those stories important to you as a child? Write or draw one of your literacy memories to share with class members.

- Reflect on your reading life as an adult. What types of books or materials do you currently read as an adult? If you do not read for pleasure, trace why reading does not play a role in your life and when you stopped reading for pleasure.
- Read one of the landmark studies and reflect on the significance of this study for the role of literature for children. Another option is to divide into small groups with each group reading and discussing one landmark study. Then form a new group with one person representing each study to examine insights across studies. Brainstorm implications for your work as a parent, librarian, or educator.

References

Anderson, R. C., Hiebert, E. H., Scott, J. A., & Wilkinson, I. A. G. (1985). *Becoming a nation of readers: The report of the Commission on Reading.* Washington, DC: National Institute of Education.

Applebee, A. N. (1978). *The child's concept of story.* Chicago, IL: University of Chicago.

Atwell, N. (1987). *In the middle.* Portsmouth, NH: Heinemann.

Bogart, D. (Ed.). (2015) *Library and book trade almanac* (60th ed.). Medford, NJ: Information Today.

Books in print. (2016). Amenia, NY: Grey House Publishing.

Brooks, W. (2006). Reading representations of themselves: Urban youth use culture and African American textual features to develop literary understandings. *Reading Research Quarterly, 41*(3), 372–392.

Bruner, J. (1990). *Acts of meaning.* Cambridge, MA: Harvard University Press.

Carlsen, G. R., & Sherrill, A. (1988). *Voices of readers: How we come to love books.* Urbana, IL: NCTE.

Dove, R. (2013). The first book. In C. Kennedy (Ed.), *Poems to learn by heart.* New York: Hyperion.

Durkin, D. (1966). *Children who read early.* New York: Columbia Teachers College Press.

Eeds, M. & Wells, D. (1989). Grand conversations: An exploration of meaning construction in literature study groups. *Research in the Teaching of English, 23*(1), 4–29.

Eldredge, J. L., & Butterfield, D. (1986). Alternatives to traditional reading instruction. *The Reading Teacher, 40,* 32–37.

Fielding, L. G., Wilson, P. T., & Anderson, R. C. (1986). A new focus on free reading: The role of trade books in reading instruction. In T. Raphael (Ed.), *The contexts of school-based literacy* (pp. 149–160). New York: Random House.

Gottschall, J. (2012). *The storytelling animal: How stories make us human.* Boston: Houghton.

Hickman, J. (1981). A new perspective on response to literature: Research in an elementary school setting. *Research in the Teaching of English, 15*(4): 343–354.

Krashen, S. (2011). *Free voluntary reading.* Chicago: Libraries Unlimited.

National Endowment for the Arts (2012). *How a nation engages with art.* Retrieved from www.arts.gov/sites/default/files/highlights-from-2012-sppa-revised-oct-2015.pdf.

National Endowment for the Arts. (2008). *Reading on the rise.* Retrieved from https://www.arts.gov/sites/default/files/ReadingonRise.pdf.

National Endowment for the Arts. (2007). *To read or not to read.* Research Division Report #47. Washington, DC: National Endowment for the Arts.

Rosen, H. (1986). *Stories and meanings.* London, England: NATE.

Short, K. (2012). Story as world making. *Language Arts, 90*(1), 9–17.

Sipe, L. (2008). *Storytime: Young children's literary understanding in the classroom.* New York: Teachers College Press.

Wolf, S., Coats, K., Enciso, P., & Jenkins, C. (2011). *Handbook of research on children's and young adult literature.* New York: Routledge.

Zickuhr, K., Rainie, L., & Purcell, K. (2013). *Younger Americans' library habits and expectations.* Washington, DC: PEW Research Center. http://libraries.pewinternet.org/2013/06/25/younger-americans-library-services/.

Chapter 2

Learning about Children and Literature

My Book!

I did it!
I did it!
Come and look
At what I've done!
I read a book!
When someone wrote it
Long ago
For me to read,
How did he know
That this was the book
I'd take from the shelf
And lie on the floor
And read by myself?
I really read it!
Just like that!
Word by word,
From first to last!
I'm sleeping with
This book in bed,
This is the FIRST book
I've ever read!

—David L. Harrison

You can engage children as readers by placing books in their hands that interest them and are appropriate for their reading abilities as well as challenge them as inquirers. Finding the right book at the right time is always a combination of knowing the child and knowing the books. This intersection of books and readers depends on building your knowledge of children and developing your strategies for selecting books.

Connecting Children with Books: Know the Child

The most important task you face in connecting children with books is getting to know their interests, households and families, friends, social activities, hopes for the future, and the kind of books they select in free-choice situations. Children's interests are one of the most powerful forces of engagement available to you. Because books are available on almost every topic conceivable and written at varying degrees of difficulty, you should be able to assemble a collection of books from which children can make satisfying selections.

You will also want to have a grasp of children's reading and listening levels. Young children, in particular, are able to listen to and comprehend more difficult material than they can read and comprehend. For these children, you can read aloud more challenging books while providing a choice of easier reading material for independent reading.

Considering the Age-Level Characteristics of Children

Helping children find books involves first considering general factors such as the types of books and topics appropriate for children of a particular age level. Children's physical, cognitive, language, and moral development are important considerations, as is their developing concept of story. Personal and cultural factors also need to be considered, such as a child's interests, experiences, and reading ability. Knowing children's general reading preferences provides some guidance in book selection, but there is no substitute for personally knowing each child in deep and meaningful ways.

Ages 0–2 In choosing books for infants, be sure to consider the practical aspects of physical development, such as how well babies can see the illustrations and how long they will sit still for a book experience. Often these books are collections of nursery rhymes, concept books, board books, and interactive books. Common features of these book types and formats are simplicity of content or story; repetitive text or language patterns; clearly defined, brightly colored illustrations, usually on a plain background; and physical durability. Opportunities for the child to participate or interact with the book are especially important to young children who like to remain active.

A classic example of a book for children ages 0–2 is Dorothy Kunhardt's interactive book *Pat the Bunny* (1962/2001), whereas a more recent example is *Hello Baby!* by Mem Fox (2009), illustrated by Steve Jenkins, composed of rhymes in a call-and-response between the adult and child. The best baby books, whether wordless or with brief text, invite the reader and listener to "talk" their way through the book, which promotes oral language development—a child's first step toward literacy.

Ages 2–4 Many of the book types enjoyed by babies are also enjoyed by toddlers, but with slight differences in emphasis. Nursery rhymes are often committed to memory by toddlers. Concept books now include letters (ABC books), numbers (counting books), and more complex concepts such as opposites. Word books, another type of concept book that encourages labeling, promote vocabulary development in creative ways. Herve Tullet's *Press Here* (2010) is an excellent example of a book that encourages young children's imaginative play as they are invited to press, poke, shake, and blow on pages and then turn the page to find out what happens next.

Picture storybooks that appeal to this age group feature simple plots, illustrations that help carry the story, and characters who exhibit the physical skills (running, whistling, buttoning clothes, tying shoes) that 2–4-year-olds take pride in accomplishing. A perennial favorite, *Owen* by Kevin Henkes (1993), and a more recent book, *Mine!* by Susie Jin (2016), feature protagonists who overcome problems typical of children at this age. Children also enjoy wordless books because they can "read" the pictures and enjoy the books independently and folktales because of their relatively simple plots, repetitive aspects, and two-dimensional, easy-to-understand characters.

Ages 4–7 Increasing independence and enthusiasm for finding out about the world are characteristics of 4–7-year-olds. Stories in which children interact with other children, spend time away from home, begin school, and learn interesting facts are popular. Picture storybooks, folktales, and informational picturebooks are at the heart of literature experiences during these years, as reflected in the appeal of Philip and Erin Stead's *Lenny & Lucy* (2015) and Hazel Hutchins and Kady Denton's *A Second Is a Hiccup* (2007).

Most children become emergent readers at this age level. Easy-to-read books and predictable books make use of familiar words, word and sentence patterns, illustration clues, and rhyme to make the text easier to read. Often these books appear in a series. Books for beginning readers should connect to children's interests, experiences, and reading abilities to support them in their initial reading experiences. The classic, easy-to-read Frog and Toad series by Arnold Lobel has been enjoyed by young children for more than 40 years and can be used alongside more recent series like Mo Willem's Elephant & Piggie books and Wong Herbert Yee's Mouse and Mole books.

Ages 7–9 Most 7- to 9-year-old children become readers as they are beginning to understand and accept others' perspectives, recognize that life and people do not fit into neat categories, and develop an understanding of time in the past and future. They also start to assert their growing abilities to meet their own needs. With these skills, they enjoy reading or listening to books about the lives of children of the past and present in picturebooks, transitional books, and some novels. Fittingly, these books often center on the adventures of young characters within their neighborhoods and communities, such as Monica Brown's Lola Levine series, Nikki Grimes's Dyamonde Daniel series, Sara Pennypacker's Clementine series, and Annie Barrows' Ivy and Bean series.

Ages 9–14 With their rapidly developing physical and mental skills and abilities, 9–14-year-olds are ready for more complicated story plots, including such devices as flashback, symbolism, and dialects of earlier times or diverse cultures. Both historical fiction and science fiction, which are set in the distant past and the distant future, respectively, are understood and enjoyed. They also enjoy stories about their peers who are growing up, asserting themselves, using their newfound skills, moving toward independence, and meeting challenges, as in survival stories. They are better able to recognize the legitimacy of opinions, values, and lifestyles different from their own and so enjoy stories that present alternative points of view, nontraditional characters, and moral dilemmas. Recent examples include *Inside Out and Back Again* (historical fiction, Vietnamese immigrant) by Thanhha Lai (2011), *The Arrival* (fantasy, wordless novel, immigrant) by Shaun Tan (2007), and *Rain Reign* (realistic fiction, Asperger's syndrome) by Ann Martin (2014).

Considering Research on Children's Reading Interests

Research studies on reading interest, preference, and choice provide useful information for selecting books for collections and children. These studies attempt to infer what children like to read. Generally, a ***reading interest*** suggests a feeling one has toward particular reading material; a ***reading preference*** implies making a forced choice from two or more options; a ***reading choice*** study investigates the materials that children select to read from a specific collection. These studies do not always provide an opportunity for children to express their interests; instead, they are required to select from the books offered by the researcher. Although findings from this body of research can be useful, the results reflect the reading interests of groups of students, not individuals.

Many studies of children's reading interests have been conducted during the past 50 years (Davila & Patrick, 2010). Differences in the choices offered to children and in the ways data were gathered make generalization difficult, but patterns include these:

- There are no significant differences between the reading preferences of boys and girls before age 9 and between avid readers of all ages. The greatest differences in reading preferences of boys and girls occur between ages 10 and 13, a result of socialization and media images.
- Boys and girls in the middle grades (ages 10 to 13) share a pronounced preference for mysteries and scary stories, along with humor, adventure, and animals.
- Preferences of boys in the middle grades include nonfiction, adventure, sports, science fiction, war or spy stories, and crime investigation, while the preferences of girls include fantasy stories, animal stories, romance, and realistic stories about people.

Certain characteristics of books may matter as much to a young reader as the topic. The patterns across studies (Davila & Patrick, 2010; Langerman, 1990; Strommen & Mates, 2004; Worthy, Moorman, & Turner, 1999) include the appeal of:

- Short books or books with short sections or chapters
- Picturebooks, illustrated books, comic books, and novels in which illustrations are interspersed throughout the book
- Books in a series or by the same author
- Episodic plots or progressive chronological plots that can be easily followed
- A quick start to the story with action on the first or second page to hook the reader
- Rapid introduction to main characters and a focus on only a few main characters
- Characters that are the age of the reader or slightly older
- Books based on movies and television and books connected to different types of multimedia formats

In addition, trivia books such as *Guinness World Records,* sports statistics books, joke books, and guides for video and computer games are appealing to some readers. Although you will want to encourage children to read books of excellent quality, the first step is to create an enthusiasm about books and reading; hence, start with high-appeal books. Once children are willing readers, you can booktalk and read aloud excellent books that they will come to love and want to read. The biggest factor that negatively affects children's attitudes toward reading is limiting their choices of reading materials, so your role is to provide as many options as possible from which children can find the books that meet their interests (Davila & Patrick, 2010).

These studies support adults in making general predictions about the types of books students of a certain age might enjoy, but general reading preferences do not capture individual reading interests. Because most teachers and librarians work with particular children over an extended period, they can learn the interests of each child and gain the knowledge needed to successfully match children with books.

Discovering Reading Interests of Individual Children

Learning children's reading interests can be accomplished by observing and keeping a record of their choices of books from the classroom collection or from the school library media center. You can also learn about children's interests through their free-choice writing and journal writing or by directly asking children to list their interests or the types of books they like to read in whole-class sharing and in one-to-one conferences. The following questions might start a dialogue with a child:

1. Who lives in your household? Tell me about each person.
2. What are your favorite things to do? at school? at home?
3. What are you good at doing? Tell me about it.
4. What would you like to learn more about?
5. What do you like to spend most of your free time doing? What do you do after school? on weekends?
6. Do you like fiction (stories) or nonfiction (information books) or both?
7. What kinds of stories do you like to hear?
8. Which topics do you enjoy reading about in information books?
9. Are there some kinds of books you don't enjoy reading? If so, why?
10. Tell me about a book that you especially enjoyed and why you enjoyed it.

Yet another way to keep current on students' reading interests is to conduct ***reading interest inventories*** several times a year. These steps are one way to conduct a reading interest inventory:

1. Collect 30–40 appropriate books that are new to children and represent a wide variety of genres and topics.
2. Number the books by inserting paper markers with numbers at the top.
3. Note the number and genre of each book on a master list.
4. Design a response form for children (Would You Like to Read This Book?) that asks them to circle yes or no next to each number.

5. Place the books in numerical order on tables and shelves.
6. Give children 20–30 minutes to make the circuit, browse the books, and mark their response forms.
7. Collect and tally their responses, and compare them with your master list to arrive at the types of books that seem to most interest children.

Reading interest inventories provide helpful information about children's current interests and introduce new genres, topics, and books. Many children will discover a book that they want to read from the books set out in this manner. Common sense tells us that children will engage more vigorously in reading or learning something that interests them than something that they find boring. Interest generates engagement, so introducing good books on topics that satisfy their individual interests is essential.

Evaluating Text Complexity

The readability and conceptual difficulty of books is another consideration in selecting books to meet the reading needs of children. ***Readability*** is an estimate of a text's difficulty based on vocabulary (common versus uncommon words) and sentence structure (short, simple sentences versus long, complex sentences). ***Conceptual difficulty*** is related to the complexity of ideas in the book and how these ideas are presented. Symbolism and lengthy description contribute to the complexity of ideas, just as the use of flashback contributes to the complexity of the plot.

Children's reading levels differ greatly at the same age or grade level, making it important to provide materials of varying difficulty. Assessing the difficulty of reading materials is helpful; however, for independent, leisure reading, children should be encouraged to read books of interest to them regardless of level, so long as they are capable of comprehending the material and want to read it. As adults, we would not appreciate being told that we cannot read a book because someone else thinks it's too easy for us. We should respect the rights of children to select their own books for leisure reading if our goal is that they become lifelong readers. Their selections for personal reading are balanced with teachers' selections of complex texts for instructional purposes.

The Common Core State Standards (CCSS) focus attention on ***text complexity*** and the need for children to engage with texts that gradually increase in difficulty of ideas and textual structures. This focus on rigor in reading is based on the goal that children understand the level of texts necessary for success in college and careers by the time they graduate from high school. Table 2.1 lists the three dimensions of text complexity as defined in the CCSS (National Governors Association Center for Best Practices & Council of Chief State School Officers, 2010).

Considering all three dimensions of text complexity, instead of relying only on quantitative formulas to level texts, such as the Lexile levels, is essential. Readability formulas may be helpful in selecting books but have drawbacks. Although sentence length and word choice are important, a child's knowledge or interest in a topic cannot be factored into a formula. The formulas also have difficulty measuring conceptual difficulty, the complexity of the ideas in a book, and how these ideas are presented. Symbolism, abstraction, and figurative language contribute to the complexity of ideas, just as the use of nonlinear plots or shifting points of view contribute to the complexity of the plot. *Skellig* (Almond, 1999) is a novel of magical realism in which two children become involved with an otherworldly being hidden in a garage. The text has easy vocabulary and short sentences with a readability of around grade 3.5. Yet the concepts of spirituality, faith, and prejudice cast the conceptual level of this novel at a higher level, making it more appropriate for students who are 11–15, depending on the background of the specific child. Another example is John Steinbeck's *The Grapes of Wrath* (1939), which scores at a second to third grade level on quantitative measures because of the use of familiar words and short sentences in the dialogue. Teachers, however, note that the many layers of meaning and mature themes indicate that this book is meant for grades 6 and above.

Information on readability can be found on some book covers and most online data bases list Lexile reading levels. You can estimate difficulty by selecting a page of uninterrupted text, reading the first sentence, counting the words in the sentence, and seeing if this length appears to be typical of the rest of the page. The page can then be read for word difficulty, noting the frequency of words children will likely not know.

The CCSS include a list of Text Exemplars consisting of stories, poems, and informational texts at each grade level. Excerpts from these texts are provided to help teachers and librarians explore text complexity. This list is not a core reading list of books for children; instead, the texts are exemplars to use in understanding text complexity to make more effective selections for children. Children should never be limited to reading only the books on these lists because many are dated classics that do not reflect the multicultural or global nature of children's lives.

Table 2.1 Common Core State Standards: The Three Dimensions of Text Complexity

Qualitative Dimensions of Text Complexity	Informed Decisions by Adults on Text Difficulty Based on Their Judgments about the Influences of the Text on a Reader
Levels of Meaning and Purpose	Determining complexity based on how many layers of meaning are in the text and whether the purpose of the text is implicit or clearly stated.
Structure	Examining if the text is organized around a simple, well-marked conventional structure that readers will quickly recognize or a structure that is unusual and seldom used.
Language Conventionality and Clarity	Examining whether the text uses clear contemporary language or relies on figurative, ambiguous, archaic, academic, or unfamiliar language.
Knowledge Demands	Evaluating assumptions about the life experiences and knowledge that readers will bring to a particular text.
Quantitative Dimensions of Text Complexity	**Computerized readability formulas that rate a text on word familiarity, word length, and sentence length**
Readability Formulas	Fry Readability Graph, the Dale-Chall Readability Formula, the Lexile Framework, the Accelerated Reader ATOS formula, and Coh-Metrix.
Lexile Framework	Recommended by the CCSS (www.lexile.com) but does not provide accurate levels for K–1, poetry, and complex narrative fiction for young adults (Schnick, 2000).
Reader and Task Considerations	**The fit between a text and a specific reader who is engaging in a particular task with that text**
Experiences and Strategies of a Reader	Cognitive abilities, motivation, interest, knowledge, and experiences of readers.
Task	The activity or experience a reader is asked to engage in with a particular text.

Connecting Children with Books: Know the Books

If you read children's books regularly and are familiar with a wide variety of genres as well as informed about recently published books, you are more likely to know the right book for the right moment and purpose in a child's life. Reading widely also allows you to share your reactions to a book with children and engage with them as a reader, rather than as an expert. Other ways to become familiar with a variety of books include sharing information about books with colleagues, reading book reviews, and consulting award lists. Resources you can use in developing knowledge of books and reference sources are integrated throughout the chapters in this text.

After you read a number of books from a genre, particularly notable examples, you will develop a framework for thinking about that type of book as you encounter new books. You will also develop a sense of how to evaluate the ways in which authors use literary and visual elements within particular genres. Criteria for evaluating literary and visual elements of literature within specific genres are discussed throughout the chapters, so you can gradually develop your own understandings and internal sense of these criteria.

Balance and Variety in Book Selections

In your work with children, you need to know many kinds of books, because children have a wide range of reading abilities and interests. You have your own reading preferences but need to go beyond those interests to gain familiarity with many types of books, including picturebooks, easy-to-read books, short chapter books, longer novels, and books of prose, poetry, fiction, and nonfiction. Balance among the *genres of literature* as well as *variety in topics* are essential. The chapters in this text will help you build this range and balance.

The books available for independent reading and chosen as read-alouds also need to be varied to challenge children and enhance their language and cognitive development. The *mood* of the books should include stories that are sad, humorous, silly, serious, reflective, boisterous, suspenseful, and scary. A steady diet of light, humorous books might appeal to children at first, but eventually, the sameness will become boring. Reading aloud books with the same predominant emotion ignores the rapid change and growth in personal lives and choices that are the hallmark of youth.

A balance between male and female main characters over the course of a year is necessary to meet the needs of children and to help members of each gender understand more fully the perspectives, problems, and feelings of members of other genders. Classroom and school library collections need to have a wide range of topics with a balance of male and female main characters. In addition, understanding and empathy for people with physical, emotional, mental, and behavioral disabilities can be gained through portrayals in books, and children with disabilities can encounter characters like themselves.

The representation of people of color as main characters is essential to present a realistic view of society and to challenge stereotypes. Through well-written ***multicultural literature,*** children of color can see characters from backgrounds similar to their own in leading roles. Characters with whom one can identify permit a deeper involvement in literature and help children understand situations in their own lives. Children need to see that someone from a different race, ethnic group, or religion has many of the same needs and feelings as they do, as well as recognize and value differences in experiences and cultural views. Literature by and about people different from oneself can develop an appreciation for difference as a resource, not a problem.

Global and international literature, literature from nations and regions of the world, should also be included in read-aloud choices and in book collections in order to encourage the development of global understanding. Through reading or listening to books about the lives of children from global cultures, children will experience cultural literacy on a worldwide basis.

Finding this range of books and staying current with new releases involves familiarity with the major book awards and review journals, as well as attending professional conferences to meet authors and illustrators and attend sessions on literature. These resources will allow you to locate the best in books being published for children and books that meet specific needs for diversity in collections.

Book Awards

Book award programs have been established to elevate and maintain the literary and artistic standards of children's books and honor the authors whose work is judged by experts in the field to have the greatest merit. These awards provide you with one source for selecting excellent works of literature to share with children. These awards are sometimes critiqued as recognizing books that appeal to literary critics rather than to children as readers and as reflecting societal biases of race, class, and gender within mainstream culture.

Table 2.2 lists the major awards for children's books in the United States, Canada, and England. The winners of these major children's book awards and other awards for specific genres or topics are found in Appendix A.

Some book award programs involve children in the selection process. The Children's Choices Project, cosponsored by the International Literacy Association (ILA) and the Children's Book Council, features new books selected by children around the country. The list of winners is available at www.literacyworldwide.org and www.cbcbooks.org. The ILA website also contains an annual list of winners for the Teachers' Choices Project. Teachers read and vote for recently published books worthy of use in the classroom, then develop the Teachers' Choices Booklist.

Most states also have their own children's choice awards and programs. Usually, a ballot of book titles is generated for certain age ranges, based on nominations from teachers, librarians, or children, and this list is circulated across the state for children to vote on their favorites. More information on state children's book awards and programs, including websites for many of the state programs, can be found at www.childrensbooks.about.com/cs/stateawards.

Table 2.2 Major U.S., Canadian, and British Children's Book Awards

Award/Country	Period	For/Year Established
Newbery Medal/U.S.	Annual	The most distinguished contribution to children's literature published in the previous year. Given to a U.S. author. Established 1922.
Caldecott Medal/U.S.	Annual	The most distinguished picturebook for children published in the previous year. Given to a U.S. illustrator. Established 1938.
National Book Award for Young People's Literature/U.S.	Annual	Outstanding contribution to children's literature in literary merit published in the previous year. Given to a U.S. writer. Established 1996.
Coretta Scott King Awards for Writing and for Illustration/U.S.	Annual, two awards	Outstanding contribution to literature for children and young people by an African American author and illustrator published in the previous year. Established 1970 (author award)/1974 (illustrator award).
Pura Belpré Awards for Writing and Illustration/U.S.	Annual, two awards	Writing and illustration in a work of literature for youth published in the previous year by a Latino writer and illustrator whose work portrays, affirms, and celebrates Latino cultural experiences. Established 1996.
Governor General's Literature for Children Award for Writing/Canada	Annual	Best book for children published in the previous year. Separate prizes for works in English and French. Established 1987.
Governor General's Literature for Children Award for Illustration/Canada	Annual	Best illustration in a children's work published in the previous year. Separate prizes for works in English and French. Established 1987.
Carnegie Medal/England	Annual	The most distinguished contribution to children's literature first published in the United Kingdom in the previous year. Given to an author. Established 1936.
Kate Greenaway Medal/England	Annual	The most distinguished picturebook for children first published in the United Kingdom in the previous year. Given to an illustrator. Established 1956.

Review Journals

Journals that review children's books and feature current topics in the field of children's literature are an important source of information. Professional teacher journals on literacy for elementary teachers, such as *The Reading Teacher* (www.literacyworldwide.org) and *Language Arts* (www.ncte.org), have columns that review new children's books. *The Journal of Children's Literature* (www.childrensliteratureassembly.org), a journal dedicated to children's literature and those involved in it, also has review sections of new children's books. In addition, these journals contain articles discussing effective strategies for incorporating literature into reading and content-area instruction and for bringing children and books together.

The following review journals offer evaluative reviews and suggested age ranges for books. The reviews primarily come from the perspectives of librarians and literary critics. These journals are readily available in most university libraries, as well as some school and public libraries.

- ***Booklist*** (www.ala.org/offices/publishing/booklist) reviews current print and nonprint materials for children and adults that are worthy of consideration for purchase by public libraries and school media centers. A free online version is available at www.booklistonline.com.
- ***The Bulletin of the Center for Children's Books*** (bccb.lis.illinois.edu) reviews current children's books, assigning a recommendation code to each.
- ***The Horn Book Magazine*** (www.hbook.com) includes reviews of high-quality children's books. The Newbery and Caldecott acceptance speeches are featured in the July/August issue annually.

- ***Kirkus Reviews*** (www.kirkusreviews.com) annually reviews approximately 5,000 titles of prepublication books for adults and children through a critical lens.
- ***School Library Journal*** (www.schoollibraryjournal.com) includes both negative and positive reviews of most children's books published along with articles of interest to school librarians.

Professional Associations and Websites

Major professional associations that have strong connections to the field of children's literature and provide a range of services, projects, and resources include:

- **Association for Library Service to Children** (ALSC; www.ala.org/alsc) is a division of the American Library Association and provides services to librarians and media specialists and supports major book awards in children's literature. The counterpart for librarians serving teens is YALSA, the **Young Adult Library Service Association** (www.ala.org/yalsa).
- **American Association of School Librarians** (AASL; www.ala.org/aasl) is a division of ALA and the only national organization focused on school librarians and their role as educational leaders.
- **International Literacy Association** (ILA; www.literacyworldwide.org) offers services to teachers of language, literacy, and literature. The Children's Literature and Reading Special Interest Group (clrsig.org) at ILA has a website, awards, activities, and journal, *The Dragon Lode*.
- **National Council of Teachers of English** (NCTE; www.ncte.org) addresses teaching and research in language and literature from preschool through college. The Children's Literature Assembly (www.childrensliteratureassembly.org) at NCTE promotes literature in the lives of children, supports awards, provides a forum for exchange among teachers of children's literature, and publishes the *Journal of Children's Literature*.
- **Children's Literature Association** (ChLA; www.childlitassn.org) has members from the field of literary criticism and addresses criticism, research, and teaching of children's literature through its journal, the *Children's Literature Association Quarterly*.
- **United States Board of Books for Young People** (USBBY; www.usbby.org) consists of publishers, authors, educators, and librarians who promote the use of literature to build international understanding and the right of all children to have books in their own language and culture. The U.S. national section is part of the international organization, IBBY (www.ibby.org) which publishes *Bookbird: A Journal of International Children's Literature.*

The following websites are helpful in locating professional information about children's literature:

- **Children's Book Council** (CBC; www.cbcbooks.org). This nonprofit association of children's book publishers offers book-related literacy materials for children and information on National Children's Book Week in May.
- **Children's Literature Comprehensive Database** (www.clcd.com). This independent media site gathers reviews from a range of journals and websites for each book and provides readability ratings for books.
- **Cooperative Children's Book Center** (CCBC; www.education.wisc.edu/ccbc). This children's literature research library site provides information about collections, events, and publications. CCBC publishes an annual report of trends in children's literature and recommended books.
- **Worlds of Words** (wowlit.org). This initiative focuses on the use of literature to build intercultural understanding and includes a searchable data base, an online book review journal that highlights cultural authenticity, an online journal of classroom vignettes about global literature, book lists and resources, and a blog of current issues.

Connecting Resistant Readers with Books: Know the Books *and* the Readers

Children and adolescents resist or reject reading for many reasons. Reaching these ***resistant readers*** who can read but choose not to requires you know books as well as those readers in order to find just the right books. Because children resist reading for different reasons, the types of books you offer them also need to vary.

Some children who have strong comprehension and few difficulties in decoding and fluency at third or fourth grade may still have decided that they do not like to read and so rarely read a book. With little or no reading engagement, these children eventually start to struggle as readers. Sometimes they perceive the books they are forced to read in school as irrelevant to their lives and boring. They may lack encouragement at home and school to read for personal purposes. They seldom or never go to public or school libraries to select books for their reading enjoyment because the emphasis in school is almost exclusively on learning isolated skills. Often their parents and teachers do not serve as reading role models or foster a love of reading because their focus is on raising test scores to the detriment of other aspects of reading. These children desperately need books that relate closely to their interests and lives in all kinds of formats.

Some children become discouraged because they struggle with reading from the earliest grades. Most can decode, but this skill remains a conscious cognitive act rather than an automatic process so they can focus on meaning. The act of concentrating on decoding words slows their reading rate and fluency, hampers their ability to make sense of the text, and tires them mentally. Others in this group are fluent decoders who have difficulty comprehending what they read. Experiencing ridicule by their peers and embarrassment in class for their reading difficulties has taught them to avoid reading whenever possible. These are the children for whom regular immersion in reading whole books for pleasure is especially important to develop reading fluency. They need books that are more supportive, such as easy-to-read books, transitional chapter books, graphic novels, and informational books heavy in visuals.

Some children resist reading because the books they encounter do not depict their lives or the lives of those who are significant to them in their families and communities. Children's books are more multiculturally and globally diverse today than in the past, but books that reflect the true range of cultural diversity in our society are still underrepresented in the broader body of children's books. Unless you make a conscious effort to search for books reflecting a range of cultural identities, children may not find themselves in books and therefore resist reading because they see these books as threatening and demeaning to their identities and irrelevant to their lives.

Students learning English as a second language sometimes struggle with reading because they lack strong vocabularies and well-developed sentence structures in English to draw on when encountering English language texts. They are often asked to read texts that portray unfamiliar experiences and cultural norms and thus avoid reading whenever possible. This group is large and growing- so you need to be familiar with predictable books, concept books, and wordless books, as well as books from a range of global cultures.

Boys who resist reading may do so in part because of the preponderance of female teachers in U.S. schools (75 percent in grades K–12), who tend to select reading materials that do not always appeal to boys (Brozo, 2010). Their resistance to reading also may stem from the perception that reading, because it is quiet and passive, is a female activity, or because teachers ask them to read silently from fiction when they prefer to interact socially with peers around an informational book. On average, boys exhibit more difficulty in reading and other language areas than girls. Some boys are avid readers, but of materials that schools do not traditionally recognize, such as magazines, Internet websites, and informational books. Informative sources about boys and reading are *Reading Don't Fix No Chevys: Literacy in the Lives of Young Men* (Smith & Wilhelm, 2002); *Teaching Reading to Black Adolescent Males: Closing the Achievement Gap* (Tatum, 2005); and *Connecting Boys with Books 2: Closing the Reading Gap* (Sullivan, 2009).

By connecting books with readers, you can inspire young people to engage with reading and to become aware of its power to inform, entertain, educate, and transform as well as help them develop the habits of lifelong readers.

Invitations for Further Investigation

- Conduct a reading interest inventory with a group of children. Analyze your findings, and suggest appropriate titles to children for independent reading from books available in the school or library.
- Observe and document the reading habits and literary selections of three children over a period of several weeks. Select one avid reader, one typical reader, and one resistant reader for your observations.
- Create a list of favorite books that you remember reading as a child, and use a data base to look up the Lexile ratings for those texts. Consider the quantitative ratings for these books and how they match with when you actually read them as a child. Which factors in your own characteristics as a reader influenced your ability to read and understand these books?

- Explore a book review journal or website that interests you, and provide a description of the resources and services available on that site for class members.
- Locate your state's children's choices book award, and read some of the current nominees or recent winners of the award. Evaluate their student appeal, literary quality, complexity, curricular value, and illustration quality.

References

Almond, D. (1999). *Skellig.* New York: Delacorte.

Brozo, W. G. (2010). *To be a boy, to be a reader: Engaging teen and preteen boys in active literacy*. Newark, DE: International Reading Association.

Davila, D., & Patrick, L. (2010). Research directions: What children have to say about their reading preferences. *Language Arts, 87*(3), 199–210.

Fox, M. (2009). *Hello baby!* Jenkins, S. (Illus.). New York: Beach Lane.

Harrison, D. L. (1993). My book! In D. L. Harrison (Ed.), *Somebody catch my homework.* Lewin, B. (Illus.). Honesdale, PA: Boyds Mills.

Henkes, K. (1993). *Owen.* New York: Greenwillow.

Hutchins, H. (2007). *A second is a hiccup: A child's book of time*. Denton, K. (Illus.). New York: Scholastic.

Jin, S. (2016). *Mine!* New York: Simon & Schuster.

Kunhardt, D. (1962/2001). *Pat the bunny.* New York: Golden.

Lai, T. (2011). *Inside out and back again.* New York: HarperCollins.

Langerman, D. (1990). Books and boys: Gender preferences and book selection. *School Library Journal 36*(3), 132–136.

Martin, A. (2014). *Rain reign.* New York: Feiwel and Friends.

National Governors Association Center for Best Practices & Council of Chief State School Officers. (2010). *Common Core State Standards for English language arts and literacy in history/social studies, science and technical subjects.* Washington, DC: Authors. Available from http://www.corestandards.org/

Schnick, T. (2000). *The Lexile framework: An introduction for educators.* Durham, NC: MetaMetrics.

Smith, M. W., & Wilhelm, J. D. (2002). *Reading don't fix no Chevys: Literacy in the lives of young men.* Portsmouth, NH: Heinemann.

Stead, P. (2015). *Lenny & Lucy*. E. Stead (Illus.). New York: Roaring Brook.

Steinbeck, J. (1939). *The grapes of wrath.* New York: Viking.

Strommen, L., & Mates, B. (2004). Learning to love reading: Interviews with older children and teens. *Journal of Adolescence and Adult Literacy, 48*, 188–200.

Sullivan, M. (2009). *Connecting boys with books 2: Closing the reading gap.* Chicago: American Library Association.

Tan, S. (2007). *The arrival.* New York: Scholastic.

Tatum, A. (2005). *Teaching reading to black adolescent males: Closing the achievement gap.* Portland, ME: Stenhouse.

Tullet, H. (2010). *Press here*. New York: Handprint.

Worthy, J., Moorman, M., & Turner, M. (1999). What Johnny likes to read is hard to find in school. *Reading Research Quarterly 34*(1), 12–27.

Chapter 3

Learning about Literature

Archeology of a Book

Remove
my words.
Remove
my art.
My story unravels
back
to the start.
Remove
my pages,
spine,
design.
What's left?
An idea
in the author's
mind.

—Betsy Franco

The ways in which you interact with children around literature can either encourage them to eagerly share their connections and engage in dialogue with each other or cause them to lose confidence in their abilities to construct the "right" interpretation. When you provide an opportunity for children to share their connections to a book, you respect their voices and experiences. They can then be encouraged to critique their initial interpretations through dialogue and searching for evidence in the text. Discussions around literature are supported by an understanding of literary elements as they play out in text and image in picturebooks and novels. These understandings are particularly significant for you in learning to evaluate the quality of literature for children and developing a language for talking about literature.

Approaches to Studying and Interpreting Literature

The scholarly study of literature focuses on the construction of meaning by authors and readers for a particular piece of literature. These approaches recognize literature as a discipline and separate course of study, a common focus in high schools and universities. What is often overlooked in elementary contexts is that literature is itself a content area—a way of knowing the world that differs from other ways of knowing such as science or history. Instead, literature in elementary classrooms is usually viewed as a material used to teach reading, math, science, or social studies.

Although teachers of literature in secondary schools and universities view literature as a field of study, their focus has often been on teaching the formal art of words and texts and introducing students to the classics and a literary heritage rather than on readers experiencing literature as life. When readers subject a work to deep analysis through exact and careful reading, it is referred to as ***New Criticism*** or ***close reading***. In this approach, the analysis of the words and structure of a work is the focus; the goal is to find the "correct" interpretation.

Close reading dominated literature classrooms until the 1960s, but many teachers continue to use this method today. This approach takes the view that there is one correct interpretation of any work of literature, and reading is a process of taking from the text only what was put there by the author. Successful readers of literature are determined by how closely their interpretations match the "authorized" interpretation. Students' responses are thus limited to naming (or guessing) the "right" answers to teachers' questions.

Many of you experienced this approach as students and know the frustration and apathy that can result from trying to replicate the teacher's interpretation. You may have even been one of many readers who did not bother with reading the actual book and instead consulted study guides or online resources. Close reading approaches do not encourage children to see reading as relevant to their lives or help children develop confidence in their abilities to construct meaning. Often these experiences are so painful that children stop reading books except to complete school assignments.

Louise Rosenblatt introduced ***reader response theory*** or the ***transactional view of reading*** in 1938. She asserted that what the reader brings to the reading act—his or her world of experience, personality, cultural views, and current frame of mind—is just as important in interpreting the text as what the author writes. Reading is thus a fusion of text and reader. Consequently, the meaning of a text will vary from reader to reader and, indeed, from reading to reading of the same text by the same reader. You may have experienced discussing a book with friends only to discover that they have interpreted the same book quite differently. Rosenblatt (1978) argues that although the text guides possible interpretations, a range of personal interpretations is valid and desirable as long as readers can support an interpretation by citing evidence from the text and their own lives.

Readers bring connections from their worlds of experience to a book, including (1) knowledge of various genres and literary forms gained from previous reading that helps them understand new, similar books; (2) social relationships that help them understand and evaluate characters' actions and motivations; (3) cultural knowledge that influences their attitudes toward self and others and their responses to story events; and (4) knowledge of the world or topic that can deepen readers' understanding of a text and enrich their response (Beach & Appleman, 2016).

Another aspect of Rosenblatt's theory is her focus on the importance of the stance that readers choose related to their purpose for reading. An efferent stance focuses the reader on taking knowledge or information from the text, whereas an aesthetic stance engages the reader in living through a literary experience and immersion into the world of the story. Whether people read efferently or aesthetically depends on what they are reading (e.g., a want ad versus a mystery novel) and why they are reading it (e.g., for information versus for pleasure). The problem is that many teachers encourage an efferent stance by asking questions on specific details in a book, and readers are so preoccupied with reading for those details that they fail to engage with or understand the story itself.

Rosenblatt's view of reading has important implications for the way you encourage children to respond to literature. Children first need an opportunity for personal response to literature as they make connections between their lives and the text to construct their initial interpretations. The first discussion of a book involves sharing these personal connections. If children are initially asked to answer literal-level questions or provide book summaries or reports, they read for the details but miss the story. When children are asked to start with literal comprehension and then move to higher levels of thinking, their understandings and interest in a book are inhibited. If you participate in adult book groups, you probably have experienced understanding the big issues in a book while forgetting specific details of names or events that are clarified in the process of group discussion.

Many educators have misunderstood Rosenblatt's theories and believe that reader response only promotes personal connections and so lacks rigor. Instead of an either/or approach, Rosenblatt (1991) points out that teachers and students can engage in close textual analysis of particular aspects of the text *after* first creating personal meaning and significance from their reading. She argues that personal response is essential but not sufficient. Children need to move from sharing personal responses into dialogue where they critique their individual responses by returning to the text and their lives for evidence to support their interpretations and deepen their understandings. This approach honors the individual voices of readers while also holding them responsible to the group and remaining open to other interpretations. As they examine their interpretations, they can also take on the lens of particular literary theories, such as feminist criticism, critical race theory, or postcolonialism, to ask difficult questions of themselves and the text.

The Common Core State Standards encourage a return to ***close reading*** with a focus on careful text analysis and an initial emphasis on literal comprehension, viewing personal response as interfering with comprehension. The assumption that close reading is in opposition to reader response is a misconception because readers still engage in careful textual analysis after sharing personal connections to search for evidence related to their interpretations. The danger of only focusing on text analysis is that readers will again be subjected to guessing the teacher's mind to find "correct" interpretations and move away from personal significance and dialogue.

Close reading highlights "reading between the four corners of the page" and text-dependent questions so that readers attend to what the text says and how it says that, rather than what a text means to a reader. Fisher and Frey (2014) believe that discussion should begin by asking, "What does the text say?" followed by asking, "How does the text work?" Only after discussing these questions in depth is the reader allowed to consider, "What does the text mean?" Rosenblatt (1938) argues that this final question is where readers both begin and end a reading event. By first considering what a text means, a purposeful context is provided for readers to consider evidence within the text and the literary devices that support meaning-making.

The literary elements provide a way to heighten your awareness of literary criticism and provide a shared vocabulary for talking with children about books. These literary terms are tools for initiating and sustaining conversations about literature. By using these terms in your talk, you help children acquire a literary vocabulary and support them in meeting the text analysis standards highlighted in the Common Core. Note that this chapter focuses on how the literary elements play out in written text, and Chapter 4 discusses how these elements are developed by visual images in books.

Elements of Fiction

Learning to evaluate children's books can best be accomplished by reading as many excellent books as possible. Gradually, you will develop the ability to make judgments on the merits of individual books. Discussing your responses to these books with others and listening to their responses will help you become more critical. Understanding the different parts, or elements, of a piece of fiction and how they work together can help you become more analytical about literary works; and this, too, can improve your evaluation of literature. The elements of fiction are discussed separately in the following sections, but it is the unity of these elements that produces the story. The elements of nonfiction literature are discussed in Chapter 11.

Plot

The events of the story and the sequence in which they are told constitute the *plot*. The plot is what happens in the story, so it is an important element of fiction for children. Often, adults believe that a story for children only needs to present familiar, everyday activities—the daily routines of life. Two- and 3-year-olds enjoy hearing these narratives, but by age 4, children want more excitement in books. A good plot produces conflict to build the excitement and suspense that are needed to keep the reader involved.

The nature of the ***conflict*** within the plot can arise from different sources. The basic conflict may occur within the main character, called ***person-against-self***. The main character struggles against inner drives and personal tendencies to achieve some goal or overcome a traumatic event, such as the death of a mother in *City Boy* by Jan Michael (2009). In this book, Sam loses his sense of identity when he is forced to move from the city to a rural village in Malawi and lashes out at family and friends while struggling with his own internal conflict. In Katherine Paterson's *The Great Gilly Hopkins* (1978), Gilly's goal is to escape foster care by finding her mother, an indication of her inner struggle to cope with her longings and fears as she schemes against anyone who shows her friendship or caring.

Another conflict is the struggle of a character with the forces of nature. This conflict is called ***person-against-nature*** and is often exemplified in survival novels such as *Hatchet* by Gary Paulsen (1987), in which Brian's plane goes down in the wilderness, and *Eight Days: A Story of Haiti* by Edwidge Danticat (2010), about a young boy struggling to survive in a hurricane. In Dan Gemeinhart's *The Honest Truth* (2015), Mark learns that his cancer has reoccurred, and he runs away to achieve his dream of climbing to the top of Mount Rainier. His conflict is both within himself and with nature when he is caught in a blinding snowstorm.

In other stories, the source of the conflict is between two characters. Conflicts with peers, problems with siblings, and rebellions against an adult are ***person-against-person*** conflicts. This type of plot occurs in Max's conflict with his mother in *Where the Wild Things Are* by Maurice Sendak (1963), and Auggie's interactions with a bully who makes fun of his severe facial deformities in R. J. Palacio's *Wonder* (2012). Issues of gender expression and bullying are at the heart of the conflict in *Morris Micklewhite and the Tangerine Dress* by Christine Baldacchino and Isabelle Malenfant (2014), when Morris faces the taunts of classmates because he likes wearing the tangerine dress from the dress-up center.

Stories for children presenting the main character in conflict with society could involve the environment being destroyed by new technology in a future world, children caught up in a political upheaval or war, or children struggling against societal expectations or discriminatory laws. This conflict of ***person-against-society*** occurs in Andrea Davis Pinkney's *The Red Pencil* (2014) at multiple levels. Amira struggles against society to survive when her village is attacked during a civil war in Darfur, Sudan, and to challenge societal expectations of her as a female. In Sharon Draper's *Stella by Starlight* (2015), Stella resists the discrimination she faces as an African American resulting from segregation laws and the intolerance of white racists in the 1930s segregated South.

In some stories, the protagonist faces ***multiple conflicts*** in which, for example, a character may be in conflict with society and also in a conflict with self. In Jean Craighead George's *Julie of the Wolves* (1972), Julie/Miyax rebels against the societal changes that threaten the wildlife in her native Alaska while at the same time seeking to resolve her own conflicting thoughts about her Inuit traditions and modern society.

Plots are constructed in many different ways. The most common plot structures in children's stories are ***chronological plots***, which cover a particular time and relate the events in order within that time period instead of moving back and forth across time. The events in *Charlotte's Web* by E. B. White (1952) take place over the course of months, while *Last Stop on Market Street* by Matt de la Peña and Christian Robinson (2015) follows the chronology of a single day.

Two distinct types of chronological plots are progressive plots and episodic plots. In books with ***progressive plots***, the first few chapters are the exposition, in which the characters, setting, and basic conflict are established. Following the expository chapters, the story builds through rising action to a climax. The climax occurs, a satisfactory conclusion (or dénouement) is reached, and the story ends. Figure 3.1 suggests how a progressive, chronological plot might be visualized in a book like *Charlotte's Web*, where Fern, Wilbur, and the conflict of saving Wilbur's life are introduced in the first few chapters, followed by the rising action of the friendship between Charlotte and Wilbur and Charlotte's attempts to save Wilbur's life. The climax occurs at the fair, where Wilbur's fame ensures his survival but also leads to Charlotte's death after she lays an egg sac. The dénouement brings a satisfactory conclusion when Charlotte's children are born and several remain with Wilbur.

An ***episodic plot*** ties together separate short stories or episodes, each an entity with its own conflict and resolution. These episodes are typically unified by the same cast of characters and the same setting, and each episode composes a chapter. Although the episodes are usually chronological, time relationships between episodes may be nonexistent or loosely connected by "during that same year" or "later." Chapter books with an episodic plot structure include *Ramona Quimby, Age 8,* by Beverly Cleary (1981), about

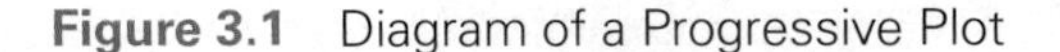

Figure 3.1 Diagram of a Progressive Plot

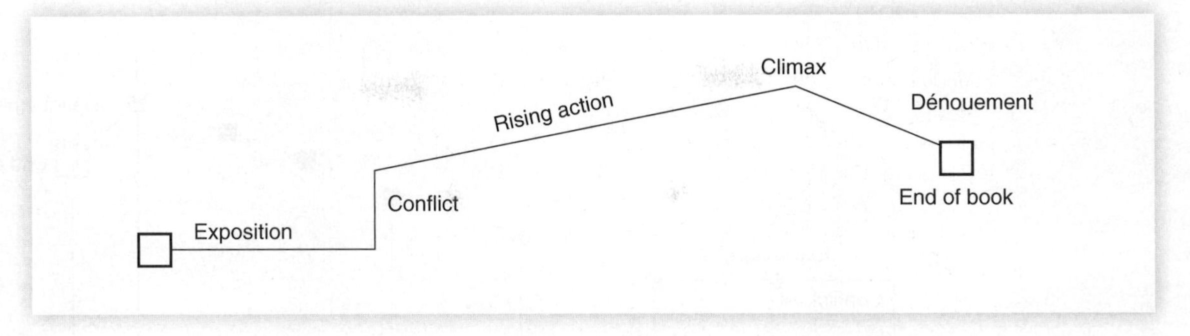

events in Ramona's life at home and school as a third-grader, and *Bo at Ballard Creek* by Kirkpatrick Hill (2013), which details various adventures in the life of a young girl in a 1930s Alaska gold-mining town. Because episodic plots are less complex, they tend to be easier to understand and often involve recounting humorous escapades, so readers who are transitioning to chapter books often find these plots appealing. Many easy-to-read books for beginning readers are structured in this way, such as *Frog and Toad Are Friends* by Arnold Lobel (1970). Figure 3.2 suggests how a chronological, episodic plot might be visualized, with each adventure of characters like Frog and Toad having its own rising action, climax, and resolution.

Authors use a ***flashback*** to convey information about events that occurred earlier, often before the beginning of the first chapter. The chronology of events is disrupted, and the reader is taken back to an earlier time. Flashbacks can occur more than once and in different parts of a story and are most frequent in novels. The use of a flashback permits authors to begin the story in the midst of the action but later fill in the background for fuller understanding of present events. You can help students understand this plot structure by reading aloud books such as *The Thing about Jellyfish* by Ali Benjamin (2015), in which Suzy flashes back to scenes and painful memories from her longtime friendship with Franny as she struggles to cope with the breakdown of that friendship and Franny's accidental death. In picturebooks, flashback memories are often signaled by sepia-toned illustrations that contrast with full-color illustrations of the present, as in *So Far from the Sea* by Eve Bunting and Chris Soentpiet (1998), in which a family visits the site where the grandfather was imprisoned in a Japanese American internment camp. The same strategy of sepia tones for the past is used in the graphic novel *Sisters* by Raina Telgemeier (2014) to signal flashbacks to memories showing the evolution of a battle between two sisters.

Class discussion can focus on the sequence of events and why the author has chosen to relate the events in this manner. Figure 3.3 illustrates the structure of a flashback in a book in which some events occurred before the beginning of the book.

More children's novels are appearing with new plot formulations such as ***complex multiple plots***, in which the traditional chronology is replaced by nonlinear plots that occur simultaneously or in a seemingly unconnected sequence. In Louis Sachar's *Holes* (1998), a humorous mystery and survival story, two apparently unrelated stories set in two different time periods are developed yet are gradually revealed to be connected to one another through the unraveling of the mystery. Pam Muñoz Ryan's *Echo* (2015) has a fairy-tale beginning that is the prelude to three historical stories during World War II in different settings that revolve around the healing power of music. The stories are initially connected only by a harmonica that travels to each location, until the conclusion reveals the intertwined fate of the protagonists from each story.

Figure 3.2 Diagram of an Episodic Plot

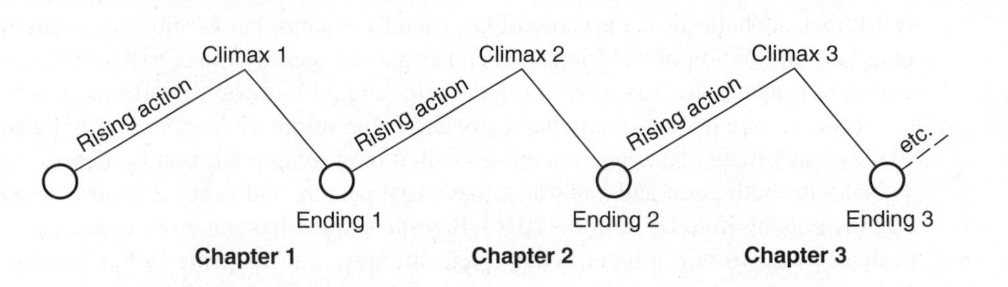

Figure 3.3 Diagram of a Flashback

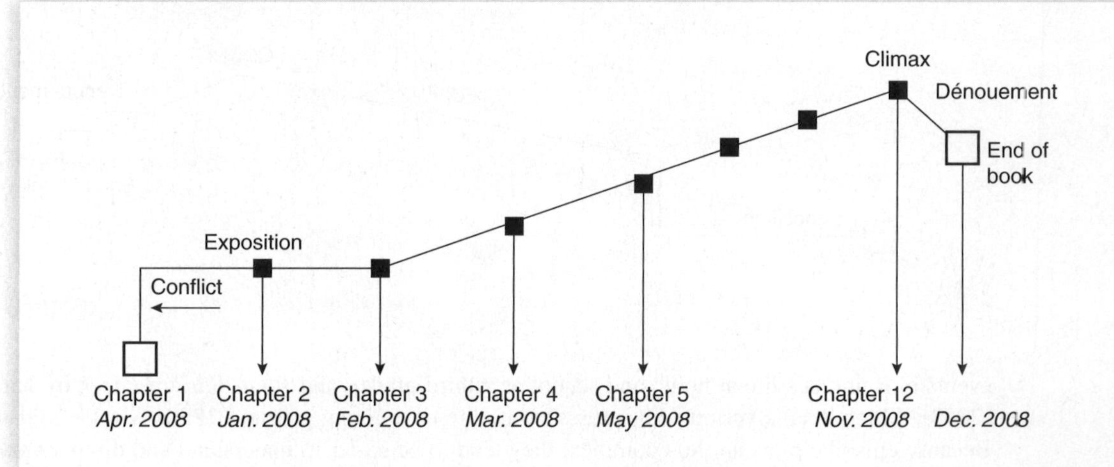

A stylistic plot device that prepares readers for coming events is ***foreshadowing***. This device gives clues to a later event, possibly even the climax of the story. For example, the first illustration of Max's bedroom in *Where the Wild Things Are* by Maurice Sendak shows a picture of a "wild thing" on the wall, whereas the classic *Tuck Everlasting* by Natalie Babbitt (1975) uses a detailed description of the long yellow road in the first chapter to foreshadow the long life journey of the Tuck family members.

You will find that plot is an important element to all readers, but especially to young readers, who enjoy fast-moving, exciting stories. A well-constructed plot contributes substantially to children's acceptance and enjoyment of stories.

Characters

Memorable characters populate the world of children's literature. You may fondly remember characters such as Charlotte the spider, Frances the badger, Mike Mulligan the steam shovel, Harry Potter, and Peter and his dog, Willie.

Characters, the "actors" in a story, are vital to the enjoyment of a story. A well-portrayed character can become a friend, a role model, or a temporary parent. Although young readers enjoy exciting events, the characters involved in those events must matter or the events no longer seem significant. How characters are depicted and developed in the course of the story is important to readers, who can get to know a character through characterization and character development.

Characterization refers to the way an author helps the reader know a character. The most obvious way is for the author to describe the character's physical appearance and personality. Portraying a character's emotional and moral traits or revealing a character's relationships with others are more subtle and effective techniques. In the most convincing characterizations, the character comes alive through a combination of actions and dialogue, the responses of other characters, and the narrator's descriptions.

Character development refers to the changes the character undergoes during the course of events in the story. If a character experiences significant, life-altering events, readers expect that the character will somehow be different as a result of those events. Bud runs away from both an orphanage and his foster family in *Bud, Not Buddy* (1999) by Christopher Paul Curtis to search for his real father during the Great Depression. He encounters danger and violence as well as kindness in a journey that changes his sense of identity and hopes for the future. In Ali Benjamin's *The Thing about Jellyfish*, Suzy researches a rare jellyfish that she believes is the cause of her friend's death as her flashbacks reveal that her grief is also guilt over her humiliation of her friend. When her plan to secretly travel to Australia to consult with a jellyfish expert falls apart, she has to face both the grief and guilt in ways that transform her as a person.

Usually one or two main characters and some minor characters are included in books for children. Ideally, each main character, sometimes called the ***protagonist,*** is fully described and is a complex individual with both good and bad traits, like a real person, and is considered a ***round character***. In *Raymie Nightengale* by Kate DiCamillo (2016), Raymie's father has run away with a dental hygienist and Raymie is determined to win a local beauty pageant, sure that his pride in her success will bring him home. Raymie is presented as a complex character with strengths and weaknesses who develops new friendships in her search for meaning as she tries to make sense of the world around her. In *Inside Out and Back Again* by Thanhha Lai (2011), the protagonist, a Vietnamese refugee in Alabama, is presented as a round, complex character dealing with the many challenges of immigration, but retaining a continued connection to and love of her own country. Kevin Henkes is the master of depicting round characters, like Lilly with her purple plastic purse (2006), in picturebooks through dialogue and visual images using body language and facial expressions to convey their changing emotions and personalities.

Minor, or ***secondary, characters*** may be described in a partial or less complete manner. The extent of description depends on what the reader needs to know about the character for a full understanding of the story. Some of the minor character's traits are described fully, whereas other facets of the character's personality may remain obscure. Because the purpose is to build the story and make it comprehensible, fragmentary knowledge of a minor character may suffice. In *The Small Adventure of Popeye and Elvis* by Barbara O'Connor (2009), the secondary character Elvis has an attitude of adventure that brings excitement into Popeye's boring small-town world. Popeye's life with his grandmother is described in depth, while Elvis is a temporary resident who soon moves on, leaving Popeye with the realization that life can be better with imagination and a friend. Parents are often secondary characters, such as Michael's mother in *Skellig* by David Almond (1999), who moves believably between frustration and sympathy for Michael as the family deals with a very sick baby but who is too distracted to be fully present in his life.

Occasionally, an author will insert a ***flat character***, a character described in a one-sided or underdeveloped manner. Although such people do not exist in real life, they may be justified within a story to propel the plot. For example, in Sara Pennypacker's *Pax* (2016), Peter's father forces him to abandon Pax, his pet fox found on the day of his mother's funeral. The father enlists in the military, which eliminates him from Peter's life, allowing the story to focus on the journey that Pax and Peter undertake from opposite directions to find each other. The father is a flat stereotype of an adult, unfeeling to his child's needs, but is never developed enough to get a sense of his motivations. Sometimes the character is all evil or all frivolous; for instance, folktales typically use flat characters, such as witches or wizards, as symbols of good and evil.

In some stories, a flat character plays the role of ***character foil,*** a person in direct juxtaposition to another character (usually the protagonist) who serves to highlight the characteristics of the other individual. A character foil may occur as a flat or round character. The character or force that is in direct opposition to the main character is called the ***antagonist***. In R. J. Palacio's *Wonder*, Julian is a bully who is an unrelenting antagonist, lacking Auggie's kindness and courage and challenging the definition of who is considered "normal." In *Now Is the Time for Running* by Michael Williams (2011), Deo encounters a greedy farmer and a drug dealer who serve as antagonists as he flees his home in Zimbabwe and looks for a place of safety in South Africa.

The main characters in an excellent work of fiction are rounded, fully developed characters who undergo change in response to life-altering events. Because children generally prefer personified animals or children of their own age or slightly older as the main characters, authors of children's books often face a dilemma. Although in real life children usually have restricted freedom of action and decision making within the confines of a family, the author can develop a more vivid and exciting story if the main characters are on their own. Thus, in many children's novels, parents are absent, preoccupied with their own lives, or no longer living, as in Cornelia Funke's *The Thief Lord* (2001), in which two orphaned brothers run away from a cruel aunt and uncle, hiding in Venice, where they join a gang of street children. The boys have adventures that would not occur without the absence of caring adults. Situations with absent adults also allow authors to focus on one aspect of life, enabling readers to understand this facet of life more clearly.

Setting

The time and place in which the story occurs constitute the ***setting***. As you read a range of books, you will notice that the setting's importance varies by genre. In historical fiction, the authentic re-creation of the period is essential to the comprehension of the events. In this situation, the setting, fully described in both time and place, is called an ***integral setting***. The story would not be the same if placed in another setting. *The War That Saved My Life* by Kimberly Brubaker Bradley (2015) is set in England during World War II, where the forced evacuation of children from London to the countryside allows Ada to escape her abusive mother and experience healing and compassion. Both the specific time period and the details of life in a squalid London flat and in a friendly country village are essential to the plot and character development as Ada learns to trust and experiences home for the first time.

By contrast, the setting in folktales is often vague and general. For example, "long ago in a cottage in the deep woods" is meant to convey a universal, timeless tale, one that could have happened anywhere and anytime except the present or recent past. This type of setting is called a ***backdrop setting*** and is used to set the stage and the mood.

Theme

The literary themes of a story are the underlying meanings or significance. Although the ***theme*** is often seen as the message or moral of the story, you will notice that it can just as easily be an aesthetic understanding, such as an appreciation for nature or a viewpoint on a societal issue. To identify the theme, consider the author's purpose in writing the story or what the author is saying through this story along with your own thinking about how this book connects to larger understandings of life.

A theme is usually better expressed by means of a complete sentence than by a single word. For example, children often suggest that friendship is a theme in *Charlotte's Web* by E. B. White. A better statement of the theme is, "Friendship is one of the most satisfying things in the world," as Wilbur tells us in the story. The single word *friendship* may be a topic within the story, but it is not an expression of a theme. Similarly, the phrase "race relations during the Jim Crow era" incompletely expresses the theme of *Stella by Starlight* by Sharon Draper. In the segregated South during the Depression, Stella and her brother witness the Ku Klux Klan burning a cross on a starry night, intensifying the fear that envelops her community. Stella's desire to become a writer is matched by her father's determination to vote. In a powerful scene, the entire black community accompanies three registered black voters to the polling location, waiting silently. "Community as the source of strength and protection in facing injustice" more clearly reflects the theme.

Themes in children's books should be worthy of children's attention and convey important life understandings. A theme should not overpower the plot and characters of the story—children read fiction for enjoyment, not enlightenment. If the theme is expressed in a heavy-handed, obvious fashion, then the pleasure of the reading experience is diminished. Likewise, overly "teachy" or didactic themes detract from a reader's enjoyment.

A well-written book may convey a moral message, but it should also tell a good story from which the message evolves so that the theme is subtly conveyed to the reader. The graphic novel *Roller Girl* by Victoria Jamieson (2015) reflects the excitement of Astrid's obsession with roller derby, while raising themes of individuality and the tensions that test friendships. The elderly zookeeper in Philip and Erin Stead's *A Sick Day for Amos McGee* (2010) has a clockwork life of daily care for zoo animals, until one day he stays home sick and the animals come to care for him, quietly conveying a message about caring and reciprocity as the heart of friendship.

Some adults write stories to teach morality lessons rather than for children's pleasure. Although stories of this sort are associated with the thinly disguised religious tracts in the early history of children's literature, some current authors use children's literature as a platform to preach about drug abuse, animal rights, and other contemporary issues. If the literary quality of these so-called problem novels is weakened, then the story and characters become secondary to the issue or problem. However, when moral values are embedded within the fabric of a powerful story, children can develop a sense of right and wrong without feeling as if they are being indoctrinated.

Style

Style is the way an author tells the story and focuses on the writing itself, as opposed to the content of the book. Because the style must suit the content of the particular book, the two are intertwined.

Different aspects of style are considered in evaluating a work of fiction. Most obviously, you can look at the ***words*** chosen to tell the story and whether they are long or short, common or uncommon, rhyming or melodic, boring and clichéd or rich and challenging, unemotional or emotional, standard dialect or regional/minority dialect. The words should be appropriate to the story; so ask yourself, Why did the author choose these words? What effect was the author trying to achieve?

The ***sentences*** may also be considered as to whether they read easily and flow without the reader needing to reread to gain the meaning of the text. Sometimes an author chooses to limit the word choices in a book for beginning readers. Yet in the hands of a gifted writer, the sentences will remain melodic, varied in length and structure, and enjoyable to read and hear as in Arnold Lobel's Frog and Toad stories, Mo Willem's Elephant & Piggie books, and Annie Barrows's Ivy and Bean series.

The ***organization*** of the book may be considered by noting the paragraphs and transitions, length of chapters, headings and chapter titles, preface, endnotes, prologue, epilogue, and length of the book. For the beginning reader, whether a story is divided into chapters is important. After years of looking at, listening to, and reading books without chapters, it is quite an accomplishment for a 6-year-old to move up to so-called chapter books, even if each chapter is only three pages long.

Chapter titles can provoke interest in what will follow as well as provide the reader with clues to predict story events. Some books provide a ***prologue,*** an introductory statement telling events that precede the start of the story, or an ***epilogue,*** a concluding statement telling events that occur after the story has ended. *Shadow on the Mountain* by Margi Preus (2012) is a historical fiction novel about the resistance movement in Norway during World War II. The novel begins with a pronunciation guide to Norwegian names, a map of the setting, and a prologue that provides a brief overview of the Nazi invasion of Norway. Each section of the novel is framed by a famous quote from that period. The end of the book has an Author's Note that identifies the actual historical events and people, sections on code breaking and invisible ink, a collection of historical photographs, a time line, and further readings.

Authors vary the organization of a book in interesting ways to engage readers. Pam Muñoz Ryan's *Echo* is a historical fiction novel set in World War II framed by a magical tale in an enchanted forest that both begins and ends the book, establishing the structure of a story within a story. *Finding Winnie* by Lindsay Mattick and Sophie Blackall (2015) is framed around a mother telling a bedtime story to her son as a technique to introduce two historical stories, one about a Canadian soldier adopting a baby bear and the other about that bear's inspiration for Winnie the Pooh. The book ends with the child and his mother looking at an album that then becomes an epilogue with a facsimile album of photos and records documenting the major events of both stories.

Point of view is another aspect of an author's style. If the story is told through the eyes and voice of a ***third-person narrator*** (the use of *he, she, it*), then the reader can know whatever the narrator knows about the events of the story. In many stories, the narrator is ***omniscient*** and can see into the minds of all characters and be at many places at the same time. Sharon Draper's *Stella by Starlight* uses an omniscient point of view to provide a perspective broader than young Stella's because much of life in the segregated South is beyond her understanding. The same omnificent point of view is presented in the words and images of Philip and Erin Stead's *A Sick Day for Amos McGee* to convey the feelings and actions of both Amos and the animals.

Other stories are narrated from the perspective of only one character in the story. The story is still told in third person, but the reader knows only what that particular character can see and understand. This latter technique is called ***limited omniscient*** point of view. Beverly Cleary's *Dear Mr. Henshaw* (1983) is a realistic story told from the perspective of Leigh, a boy troubled by family difficulties and changes at school who corresponds with an author. In *Raymie Nightengale* by Kate DiCamillo, the reader sees and understands only through Raymie, a viewpoint essential to conveying her confusion in making sense of her father's actions and her changed world.

Other times, authors choose to tell the story through a ***first-person narrator*** (the use of *I*), generally the main character of the story. The reader gains a sense of closeness to the main character but is not privy to any information unavailable to this character. Some authors accomplish a first-person point of view by writing the book as a series of letters or diary entries by the main character, a technique used in Sally Nicholls' *Ways to Live Forever* (2008), in which Sam, in the last stages of leukemia, writes a collection of journal entries, lists, and questions. Another strategy is narrative poems composed by characters, a technique used by Helen Frost in *Spinning Through the Universe* (2004) in which fifth-grade students tell their stories through first-person poems. Occasionally, a story is told in first person through the eyes of a minor character, such as Robert Lawson's *Ben and Me* (1939/2010), in which a mouse tells the story of Ben Franklin.

A ***shifting point of view*** permits the reader to see events from different characters' points of view. When the point of view shifts, the author must carefully cue readers to the changing point of view as Dan Gemeinhart does in *The Honest Truth*, signaling the shift from Mark's first-person perspective to his friend Jess's voice by changing how her chapters are numbered and putting her voice in italics. *Wonder* by R. J. Palacio uses shifting first-person perspectives, dividing the novel into eight sections that are clearly marked by whose voice frames that section. Although shifting narrators can be demanding for young readers, *A Tale of Two Beasts* by Fiona Robertson (2015) is divided in half, with the first half from the little girl's perspective and the second from the beast's perspective. The strategy of combining words and images to tell the same story from both perspectives and first telling the story from the familiar perspective of a child is effective in engaging young children.

This shifting point of view occurs in books written in third-person omniscient narrators, not just first person voices. In *Pax*, Sara Pennypacker uses an omniscient voice to move between the two stories of Pax and Peter, putting each chapter title on a silhouette of a boy or a fox to indicate whose story is the focus of that chapter and also cuing the reader by including the character's name in the first sentence of each chapter.

Symbolism is an artistic invention that authors use to suggest invisible or intangible meanings by analogy to something else through association, resemblance, or convention. Often, a symbol—a person, object, or situation—represents an abstract or figurative meaning in the story in addition to its literal meaning. Some symbols are universal and can be found repeatedly in literary works; others may be particular to the story. For example, a farm usually represents love and security in literature, as in E. B. White's *Charlotte's Web*. Children often read on a literal level but can be helped to note more obvious symbols in the books they are reading. If the symbolic feature recurs in the story, such as the number 3 in folktales, it is referred to as a ***motif***.

A story for children must be more than a plot and a character study; a story must integrate all the elements of fiction into a pleasing whole. In drawing together these elements in words and images, authors create new worlds for young readers. Although familiarity with literary elements is critical to building your knowledge, they represent only one aspect of the knowledge you need to understand literature as a discipline. The next chapter focuses on the visual elements of images. Each of the genre chapters in Part II includes knowledge about genres, notable books, authors and illustrators, and significant themes and topics. Note that Chapter 11 discusses the literary elements and text structures of nonfiction.

Invitations for Further Investigation

- Revisit a book that you remember loving as a child. Before you reread the book, write about your remembered response and connections to that book—what was it about the book that was significant for you as a child? Reread the book, and write about your response as an adult. Compare the two responses.
- Read a multilayered novel as a class, such as *Skellig* (Almond, 1999), *The Thing about Jellyfish* (Benjamin, 2015), or *Pax* (Pennypacker, 2016), and share your responses and connections. After your discussion, revisit the book with each small group taking on a different literary element to analyze how that element plays out in the novel. Develop a visual diagram or image to share your insights with the other groups.

References

Almond, D. (1999). *Skellig.* New York: Delacorte.

Babbitt, N. (1975). *Tuck everlasting.* New York: Farrar.

Baldacchino, C. (2014). *Morris Micklewhite and the tangerine dress.* Malenfant, I. (Illus.). Toronto: Groundwood.

Beach, R., & Appleman, D. (2016). *Teaching literature to adolescents.* New York: Routledge.

Benjamin, A. (2015). *The thing about jellyfish.* New York: Little Brown.

Bradley, K. B. (2015). *The war that saved my life.* New York: HarperCollins.

Bunting, E. (1998). So far from the sea. Soentpiet, C. (Illus.). New York: Harcourt.

Cleary, B. (1981). *Ramona Quimby, age 8.* Tiegreen, A. (Illus.). New York: Morrow.

Cleary, B. (1983). *Dear Mr. Henshaw.* Zelinsky, P. (Illus.). Orlando, FL: Harcourt.

Curtis, C. P. (1999). *Bud, not Buddy.* New York: Delacorte.

Danticat, D. (2010). *Eight days: A story of Haiti.* Delinois, A. (Illus.). New York: Orchard.

de la Peña, M. (2015). *Last stop on Market Street.* Robinson, C. (Illus.). New York: Putnam.

DiCamillo, K. (2016). *Raymie Nightengale.* Somerville, MA: Candlewick.

Draper, S. (2015). *Stella by starlight.* New York: Atheneum.

Fisher, D., & Frey, N. (2014). *Text-dependent questions, grades K-5.* Thousand Oaks, CA: Corwin.

Franco, B. Archeology of a book. In S. Vardell & J. Wong (Eds.), *The poetry Friday anthology.* Princeton, NJ: Pomelo.

Frost, H. (2004). *Spinning through the universe.* New York: Farrar, Straus & Giroux.

Funke, C. (2001). *The Thief Lord.* New York: Scholastic.

Gemeinhart, D. (2015). *The honest truth.* New York: Scholastic.

George, J. C. (1972). *Julie of the wolves.* Schoenherr, J. (Illus.). New York: Harper.

Henkes, K. (2006). *Lily and the purple plastic purse.* New York: Greeenwillow.

Hill, K. (2013). *Bo at Ballard Creek.* Pham, L. (Illus.). New York: Holt.

Jamieson, V. (2015). *Roller Girl.* New York: Penguin.

Lai, T. (2011). *Inside out and back again.* New York: Harper.

Lawson, R. (1939/2010). *Ben and me: A new and astonishing life of Benjamin Franklin as written by his good mouse Amos.* New York: Little Brown.

Lobel, A. (1970). *Frog and toad are friends.* New York: Harper.

Mattick, L. (2015). *Finding Winnie: The true story of the world's most famous bear*. Blackall, S. (Illus.). New York: Little, Brown.
Michael, Jan. (2009). *City boy*. New York: Clarion.
Nicholls, S. (2008). *Ways to live forever*. New York: Scholastic.
O'Connor, B. (2009). *The small adventure of Popeye and Elvis*. New York: Farrar, Straus & Giroux.
Palacio, R. J. (2012). *Wonder*. New York: Knopf.
Paterson, K. (1978). *The great Gilly Hopkins*. New York: HarperColllins.
Paulsen, G. (1987). *Hatchet*. New York: Bradbury.
Pennypacker, S. (2016). *Pax*. New York: HarperCollins.
Pinkney, A. D. (2014). *The red pencil*. Evans, S. (Illus.). New York: Little, Brown.
Preus, M. (2012). *Shadow on the mountain*. New York: Abrams.
Robertson, F. (2015). *A tale of two beasts*. New York: Kane/Miller.
Rosenblatt, L. (1938). *Literature as exploration*. Chicago: Modern Language Association.
Rosenblatt, L. (1978). *The reader, the text, the poem*. Carbondale: Southern Illinois University.
Rosenblatt, L. (1991). Literature—S.O.S.! *Language Arts, 68,* 444–448.
Ryan, P. M. (2015). *Echo*. New York: Scholastic.
Sachar, L. (1998). *Holes*. New York: Farrar.
Sendak, M. (1963). *Where the wild things are*. New York: HarperCollins.
Stead, P. (2010). *A sick day for Amos McGee*. Stead, E. (Illus.). New York: Roaring Brook.
Telgemeier, R. (2014). *Sisters*. New York: Scholastic.
White, E. B. (1952). *Charlotte's web*. Williams, G. (Illus.). New York: Harper.
Williams, M. (2011). *Now is the time for running*. New York: Little, Brown.

Illustration and Visual Elements

Cloudscape

I found a journal from sky once.
One page was titled:
Cursive in Prussian blue.
It was filled with scripts of air,
a wash of watercolor,
a flake-white calla lily,
talk of blooms and blossoms
fit for a museum; so gallant,
so lovely a brushwork of
space on canvas; sky said:
"Life, meet art." And
"Art, meet life."
In the center of the day,
each day, are lines upon a canvas,
an abstract image that floats
like a spirit somewhere
down around the heart
and out from fingertips.
Sky told me so.

—Rebecca Kai Dotlich

Illustrations and visual images have become increasingly significant in children's books across genres, formats, and age levels, so you need to understand the visual elements as well as the literary elements to evaluate the quality of literature. It's immediately evident that illustrations and book design are essential to meaning in picturebooks and graphic novels, but they are also playing a more significant role in novels and series books through drawings, margin sketches, and occasional full-page illustrations. As you explore how "pictures mean," you will be able to more effectively select and discuss books with children.

Books with strong visual images hold special appeal and meaning to children because they are immersed in a visual culture in which images are central to their representations of the world. This visual way of life influences what children know and how they think and feel about the world. A visual image is no longer limited to a specialized form of expression in an art class or a museum, but is instead an essential form of daily communication reflecting diverse ways of knowing (Duncum, 2002).

Visual Elements

Understanding the role of illustrations and book design in children's books begins with knowing the ***visual elements,*** the basic elements that reflect the choices made by illustrators as they decide what and how to illustrate the story, how to move the illustrations from page to page, and how to design the visual packaging of the book. These visual elements are line, shape, color, light, space, perspective, and texture as they come together to create a composition. Knowledge of these elements is essential to understanding the ways in which "pictures mean" as visual texts in children's books, just as literary elements are essential to understanding a written text.

The illustrations in picturebooks and graphic novels often contain details regarding setting, tone, plot, and characters that are not available in the written text. Children need to be able to use the visual elements along with the literary elements to create meaning and analyze their interpretations of a book. The same is true for you.

Line and Shape

Lines are the continuous stroke marks in a picture that define shapes and create texture. Artists may choose to use lines that are dark or pale, heavy or light, solid or broken, wide or thin, straight or curved. The lines may be mostly ***vertical, horizontal,*** or on a ***diagonal***. In pictures of the ocean and open prairies, the lines are predominantly horizontal to give an impression of calm and tranquility. If the ocean is stormy, then the lines are more likely diagonal and upward moving, suggesting action or emotion. The lines may be vertical on a sailboat mast or a tall tree to convey stability and strength. An ***implied line*** is not an actual stroke mark, but an arrangement of objects to create the illusion of a line, such as a row of trees along a pathway, to encourage the reader's eye to move to a focal point in the illustration. Each of these choices results in a different visual effect and can help set a different mood.

Lines should help create and convey the meaning and the feeling of the story. David Shannon's jagged, diagonal lines in *No, David!* convey the constant motion of an exuberant toddler and the resulting chaos (Illustration 1, p. 46), while the zigzag diagonal line of the viper signals attack in *Nic Bishop Snakes* (Illustration 13, p. 49). Anthony Emerson's landscape uses horizontal lines to suggest peace and tranquillity in *Songs of Shiprock Fair* (Illustration 7, p. 48). Those same calming horizontal lines of frogs drifting silently on lily pads in David Wiesner's *Tuesday* create an eeriness that is humorous rather than threatening (Illustration 2, p. 46).

The flamingo in *Flora and the Flamingo* by Molly Idle has a strong vertical line to suggest balance and agility (Illustration 6, p. 47). The diagonal placement of Flora and the flamingo and their line of sight creates an *implied line* that focuses readers on the flamingo's irritation with Flora, while Chris Raschka uses the implied line of sight between the child and grandmother in *The Hello, Goodbye Window* to signal a loving, intimate interaction (Illustration 3, p. 46).

Shape, or the spatial forms of a picture, is produced by lines and areas of color joining and intersecting to suggest outlines of forms. Shapes can be simple or complex, large or small, clearly defined or amorphous, and rigid (geometric shapes) or flexible (organic shapes). Shape helps to create moods and carry messages. Distinctly outlined figures can project security, reality, or permanence, whereas broken or thin outlines might suggest instability, make-believe, or transience. The proportion of one object to another in an illustration and the spaces surrounding the shapes carry nonverbal messages—the bigger, the more important.

In *A Nation's Hope*, Kadir Nelson signals the importance of Joe Louis in relation to the victorious German boxer by emphasizing Louis's size, even though he is sprawled in defeat (Illustration 4, p. 47), signaling to viewers which boxer to empathize with. The empty white space surrounding Flora and the flamingo focuses our attention on the interactions between the two characters (Illustration 6, p. 47), whereas the black lines around the characters in *Songs of Shiprock Fair* project the security and pleasure of a ride high in the sky (Illustration 7, p. 48). Bob Staake digitally composes and contrasts shapes into a geometric balance that has a strong narrative purpose in *Bluebird* (Illustration 5, p. 47).

Color and Light

Color involves a consideration of hue and intensity. ***Hue*** is the color itself, with predominant colors ranging from the cool end of the spectrum (the blues, greens, and gray-violets) or from the warm end (the reds, oranges, and yellows). The colors may be bright and intense or pale and dull (that is, more or less saturated) and range from diaphanous to opaque. The colors must complement the text, as in the use of cool, muted grays and blues to convey loneliness and threat in *Bluebird* (Illustration 5, p. 47) and the rich blues and greens that create a surreal mood in *Tuesday* (Illustration 2, p. 46). In contrast, the warm, glowing colors of *The Hello, Goodbye Window* project an emotionally warm mood and setting for a child's day with grandparents (Illustration 3, p. 46).

If the events and mood change during the story, then the colors will change to reflect and signal that shift. In *Bluebird,* the initial gloomy grays of the boy's loneliness give way to warm blues as the bluebird brings companionship into his life, only to turn into the darkness of threat and loss in Illustration 5 when bullies accidentally kill the bird. Sometimes illustrators choose not to use color or use color to focus our attention, such as Jiang Hong Chen's use of red in *The Magic Horse of Han Gan* to draw our attention to the warrior (Illustration 9, p. 48).

The amount of ***light and dark*** that artists use in an illustration is known as ***value*** and combines with color to bring a sense of drama and a three-dimensional effect to the illustrations. The illustration of the woman asleep in her chair indicates the flickering light of a television that provides shadows and establishes that this event is occurring at night (Illustration 2, p. 46), while the shadows and Louis's gleaming body in *A Nation's Hope* indicate the presence of spotlights on the boxing ring (Illustration 4, p. 47).

Space and Perspective

Space refers to the distance from one point to another in illustrations, with some illustrations appearing shallow with little depth and others creating the illusion of deep space. The father and daughter in *Knuffle Bunny* by Mo Willems are in the foreground, highlighted with color, while the buildings behind them in sepia tones create depth and background. The two are also in the center of the page, the point of greatest attention (Illustration 8, p. 48). The use of negative space or blank space can highlight characters as in *Flora and the Flamingo* (Illustration 6, p. 47). The oversize art of *The Magic Horse of Han Gan* fills the page to underscore the tale's drama and epic scale (Illustration 9, p. 48).

Perspective is an aspect of space used by illustrators to highlight particular details in their visual images. Perspective creates the point of view from which an artist observes a scene and gives a sense of action by varying perspectives from faraway views to close-ups and from a bird's-eye view looking down at a scene, a worm's-eye view looking up, or at eye level looking straight at the scene. Kadir Nelson is a master of using perspectives that range from extreme close-ups to faraway panoramic spreads. In *A Nation's Hope*, the reader is positioned below the stage looking up and at a dramatic angle that provides a close-up of the fallen Joe Louis (Illustration 4, p. 47). The extreme close-up of the viper in *Nic Bishop Snakes* indicates our imminent doom, as there is no chance of escape before the viper strikes (Illustration 13, p. 49).

Perspective is particularly important within the panels in graphic novels because they establish relationships between characters and their settings to elicit an affective response. In Raina Telgemeier's *Sisters*, the perspective moves between the view of the mother and that of the children as the argument unfolds, while *Bluebird* moves from a close-up to a distance to capture characters' emotions (Illustrations 11 and 5, pp. 49 and 47).

Texture

The tactile surface characteristics of pictured objects compose the ***texture*** of a picture. The reader's impression of how a pictured object feels is its texture. Sometimes young children will reach out to touch the surface of an illustration expecting to physically feel texture. Texture can also be implied through crosshatching or the use of feathery lines for hair as occurs in *The Magic Horse of Han Gan* (Illustration 9, p. 48). Textures may be rough or slick, firm or spongy, hard or soft, jagged or smooth. The effects of texture can offer a greater sense of reality, as in *Parrots over Puerto Rico* where Susan Roth creates fluttery, textual collages of paper to bring the parrots alive (Illustration 10, p. 48).

Composition

Composition refers to the arrangement of all of these visual elements and the way in which the visual elements relate one to the other and combine to make the picture. Many artists arrange each illustration around a single focal point, which is often a key to understanding composition. The artist decides on proportion, movement, balance, harmony, and dissonance within the various elements to produce the desired visual impact. The total effect should not overpower the story but rather extend and enrich the meaning and mood of the text. In *Knuffle Bunny: A Cautionary Tale,* Mo Willems places the main characters at the center of the illustration and then emphasizes them by using color against a nearly monochromatic sepia background. He draws the pair holding hands and sharing a loving look, and he places them in a calm, sunny, urban setting that is a digitally altered photograph. The use of white space and the placement of the tree also serve to focus attention on the pair, as does the directionality of their eyes toward each other (Illustration 8, p. 48). Although it is not mentioned in the text, the little girl is clutching her stuffed rabbit. This composition indicates that the story will be about a happy little girl who trusts her father and that what happens to them could actually occur in the real world.

The details in the illustrations should not conflict with those in the text, but they can add another story line and additional details, emotions, and events. Children are keenly observant of contradictions between the text and illustrations (e.g., a character or object missing from the illustration) and find them distracting. Although children accept illustrations that are varied in visual elements and artistic styles, they have little tolerance for inaccuracies.

Graphic novels bring in additional visual elements and conventions because the text must be conveyed economically through speech bubbles, thought bubbles, narrative boxes, and sound effects that are embedded into the illustration panels. The relationships between text and illustration are complex since the text rarely stands alone in a graphic novel. Certain elements such as line are important to show motion, and facial expressions are essential to inferring a character's inner thoughts and motives. The key resources used by readers in the visual design of an illustration in a graphic novel are perspective, facial expressions, color, and layout (Connors, 2012).

Readers of graphic novels visually begin in the top left panel and read left to right, top to bottom but spend a great deal of time carefully studying the interactions of text and visual image within each panel and moving back and forth between panels on a page. Graphic novels require the reader to be willing to linger on a page and to carefully study the composition of images within each panel and page (Pantaleo, 2011). They are not a quick, easy read but are engaging and appealing for children because of their reliance on visual image and dialogue.

Artistic Media

Artistic media are the materials and technical means used by artists to create pictures. ***Technique*** refers to *how* an illustrator uses a particular material, like watercolor. Although the variety of techniques and materials used by book illustrators is virtually unlimited, some of the more common media found in children's books are:

- ***Drawing:*** Pen and ink, colored pencils, pastels, charcoal pencils, scratchboard. The oil pastels in *The Hello, Goodbye Window* combine with watercolors to create loose, energetic depictions of a biracial family (Illustration 3, p. 46), while the colored pencils in *Flora and the Penguin* create delicate flowing lines with a limited color palette (Illustration 6, p. 47). Raina Telgemeier uses a range of drawing strategies in her graphic novel, starting with pencil drawings that are then inked over with India ink and scanned to digitally add borders, lettering, and color (Illustration 11, p. 49). Another drawing technique is scratchboard, where artists like Beth Krommes scratch white lines through the surface of a special paper with a black coating and then add color into the scratched areas using an oil pigment. Simple line drawings are frequently used in middle grade novels for context and character development as in the Wimpy Kid series by Jeff Kinney. Peter Sis used pen and ink pointillist drawings in the novel *The Dreamer* (2010) to create scenes of whimsy and introspection reflecting the imaginative mind of Pablo Neruda.

- ***Collage:*** An assemblage of materials such as real objects, cut or torn paper, fabric, and clay. Susan Roth's textural collages of cut paper create ruffly feathered parrots ((Illustration10) along with textured papers and fabric for trees, people and other objects. Steve Jenkins uses cut papers to assemble his dazzling animal collages in his many informational books, while Lois Ehlert often uses found objects to construct collages in concept books for young children.

- ***Printmaking:*** Woodcuts, linoleum prints, lithography, etching. Erin Stead (2010) has used a range of printmaking techniques, ranging from woodblock printing in *A Sick Day for Amos McGee* to carbon transfer printing and linoleum printing in other picturebooks. Arthur Geisert is known for a related medium, etching, where he draws a design on a waxed metal plate and dips the plate in acid. The acid eats thin lines into the metal that is used as an inked plate for printing.

- ***Photography:*** Black and white, color. Nic Bishop's close-up photographs of snakes are sharply focused, well composed and expertly lighted to support the factual nature of the book's content and to engage readers who feel as though the snake is poised and ready to jump off the page (Illustration 13, p. 49). Photographs are often used in concept books to help young children make the connection to their world.

- ***Painting:*** Oils, acrylics, watercolors, gouache, tempera. An opaque surface is produced by oils, acrylics, tempera, and gouache paints, which can give brilliant, rich colors and a solid appearance such as in Kadir Nelson's oil paintings on wood (Illustration 4, p. 47). Watercolors are more transparent and prized for the luminosity achieved by the white paper surface shining through the paint. Differences in watercolor techniques are apparent in comparing the illustrations of David Wiesner and Chris Raschka (Illustrations 2 and 3, p. 46). The tools with which the artist applies the paint affect its look and can be as varied as brushes, airbrushes, and sponges to apply paint. The bold colors in David Shannon's acrylic illustration from *No, David!* enhance the chaotic scene and the character's ebullient personality—a close look at the painting reveals the artist's actual brush strokes (Illustration 1, p. 46).

- ***Digital and mixed media:*** Digital painting, digital application of color to hand-drawn art, digital manipulation of images. Using software, drawing pads, and scanners, artists achieve unique artistic effects. In *Knuffle Bunny,* Mo Willems used a computer to color his hand-drawn characters, create the sepia tone of the background photographs, and remove unwanted items from the photographs (Illustration 8, p. 48). Multimedia techniques are a strong trend, with many artists combining media to achieve the desired effect, often using digital scans to combine and manipulate different parts of an illustration that have been created in various media to create an effective illustration. *Bluebird* is an example of an illustration that is completely digitally created through the use of Photoshop (Illustration 5, p. 47).

Brief explanations of the artist's techniques and materials are often included in the copyright information, on the dust jacket, or in an illustrator note. See the column of "Artistic Style: Media" in the Guide to Illustrations for examples of illustrations in a range of mediums.

Artistic Styles

Children can identify the distinctive features of their favorite illustrators, like Mo Willems or David Shannon. Although the style of a picture is individual to each artist, artwork in general can be grouped by style similarities. Five broad categories of artistic styles recognized in the Western world are realistic, impressionistic, expressionistic, abstract, and surrealistic. Another set of categories relate to styles that reflect traditional ways of creating visual images within a specific cultural group. Although an artist's works seldom fit neatly into one single art style, facets of these styles may be merged into the artist's personal expression of the world.

- ***Realistic art*** represents natural forms and provides accurate representations without idealization. Kadir Nelson's photographically realistic oil paintings and Molly Idle's delicate flowing drawings reflect the range of realistic art (Illustrations 4 and 6, p. 47).

- ***Impressionistic art*** depicts natural appearances of objects by rendering fleeting visual impressions with an emphasis on light. Chris Raschka's swirling lines, thick strokes, dabs of color, and use of white space create impressionistic depictions of a loving biracial family (Illustration 3, p. 46).

- ***Expressionistic art*** communicates an emotional experience more than an external reality. The artist draws attention to the central message by exaggeration and by eliminating competing details. David

Shannon distorts the figure of the boy to emphasize his noisy exuberance and keeps background details to a minimum in *No, David!* (Illustration 1, p. 46).

- ***Abstract art*** uses intrinsic geometric forms and surface qualities with little direct representation of objects to emphasize mood and feeling. Some abstract art is considered ***graphic design,*** adapted from the field of commercial art, as seen in Bob Staake's circle-and-square artwork with vertical lines punctuated by geometric shapes in blues and grays to portray an impressive range and depth of emotions (Illustration 5, p. 47).
- ***Surrealistic art*** emphasizes the subconscious by juxtaposing incongruous dreamlike and fantasy images with realistic ones. David Wiesner juxtaposes the realistic image of a woman asleep in front of the TV with frogs drifting silently on an eerie escapade imbued with mystery (Illustration 2, p. 46).
- ***Folk art,*** usually seen in picturebooks set in the distant past or in rural societies, is often representative of the artistic style prevalent in the culture of that story and is frequently found in traditional literature. Folk art thus varies by culture but typically involves flat, stylized figures as found in Anthony Emerson's paintings of a modern-day fair on the Navajo Nation, using vibrant colors evocative of the Southwest (Illustration 7, p. 48).
- ***Cartoon art*** often features rounded figures, exaggerated action, and simplified backgrounds. Peggy Rathmann's humorous illustrations are reminiscent of those found in comic books (Illustration 12, p. 49). Many graphic novels are based in sophisticated cartoon styles, such as those used by Raina Telgemeier (Illustration 11, p. 49).
- ***Cultural styles*** developed over time within the traditions of particular global cultures, such as the use of simplified forms and bright colors in African art and painting on silk and rice papers with flat designs for scenes in traditional Japanese art. These styles are particularly important in traditional literature or picturebooks of historical time periods dominated by that style within a culture. Modern artists from these cultures use a wide range of styles but may embed specific cultural elements from traditional styles into their illustrations. *The Magic Horse of Han Gan* is the legend of a ninth-century classic Chinese artist, so the illustrator used a traditional style of painting on brown silk (Illustration 9, p. 48). In the fantasy novel *Where the Mountain Meets the Moon* (2009), Grace Lin (2009) includes full-page illustrations in blues, reds, greens, and luminous golds influenced by traditional Chinese art, a choice that is in keeping with the integration of folktales throughout the fantasy.

Book Design

Book design is the artful orchestration of all components of a book into a coherent whole to create a broad architectural plan for the book (Lambert, 2015). Children's books are more than text and pictures, with the narrative often starting on the cover and including the endpapers and title page and finishing beyond the last page of the book on the back cover. The design includes a range of paratextual features:

- The ***dust jacket*** is a removable paper cover wrapped around the book for protection as well as to attract readers and inform them about the book, author, and illustrator. Marketing departments often spend a great deal of time designing a cover to have the most visual appeal in drawing the reader's eye in a display and encouraging the purchase of the book.
- The ***covers*** of a book are usually made of two boards, which make the book more durable and allow it to stand on a shelf. When no dust jacket is on a book, the front cover provides a first impression of the story. Some contain an embossed design related to the story focus and others are a particular color significant to the book. Still others contain a completely different image, such as *A Nation's Hope*, in which taking off the dust jacket reveals a close-up of Joe Louis's face.
- The ***title*** is usually first seen on the dust jacket or front cover along with an illustration to communicate the nature of the story to readers. Many titles suggest the topic of the story and help readers decide whether to read the book. Sometimes the title is found on the spine or back cover to allow the cover illustration to have maximum impact, a strategy used for *Parrots over Puerto Rico* (Illustration 10, p. 49).
- The ***endpapers*** are the pages glued to the inside front and back boards of the cover, and the ***flyleaf*** is the page facing each endpaper. The endpaper and flyleaf are often used to provoke curiosity in the reader for what follows, to set a mood, to evoke an affective response in preparation for the story. The endpapers

act as a visual prologue and epilogue in Bob Staake's *Bluebird,* which opens with a bluebird circling over the city and ends with the boy waving as he looks up into the clouds.

- The ***title page*** tells the book's full title, the names of the author(s) and illustrator(s); and the name and location of the publisher. Occasionally, a book will include a ***frontispiece,*** an illustration facing the title page, which is intended to establish the tone and to entice the reader to begin the story. *Bluebird* contains an elegant title sequence of panels that establishes a dialogue between the blue and gray tones of the story and includes the book's title on a billboard.

- On the reverse side of the title page, called the ***verso*** of the title page, is the ***publishing history*** of the book. On this page is the copyright notice, a legal right giving the holder permission to produce and sell the work. The copyright is indicated by the international symbol ©, followed by the name of the person(s) holding the copyright and the date it takes effect, which is the year the book is first published, along with dates of later publications. *The Magic Horse of Han Gan* includes information on the original publication in France and translation into English. The country in which the book was printed, the number assigned to the book by the Library of Congress, the International Standard Book Number (ISBN), and the edition of the book are also included. Many publishers include cataloguing information for libraries, a very brief annotation of the story, and a statement on the media and techniques used in the illustrations.

- The title page typically presents the ***typeface,*** the style of print, used throughout the book. The size and legibility of the typeface must be suited to the book's intended audience. Books for the young child who is just learning to read should have large, well-spaced print for easy eye scanning, as found in *Knuffle Bunny*. The print style for an easy-to-read book should be a somewhat larger-than-average standard block print with easily distinguishable and recognizable uppercase and lowercase letters. Legibility is diminished when background colors are used behind the text, leaving insufficient contrast for easy reading.

- The size, shape, and darkness of the ***print type*** can be heavy and strong, as in *The Hello, Goodbye Window*, or light and willowy as in the legend *The Magic Horse of Han Gan*. The choice of print type should enhance the overall visual message of the illustrations and fit the visual style and mood. The placement of the print on the pages in relation to the illustrations can subtly guide the reader and become a functional part of the story. The selection of large heavy print for "ENOUGH" in *Sisters* leaves no doubt as to the tone of the mother's response. The print type can also be in a particular color, as occurs in *The Dreamer*, where the green ink of Peter Sis's visual images is also reflected in the print type.

- Unusual ***print styles*** are sometimes selected, such as script print to give the impression of handwriting in a book with diary entries. Some illustrators choose to hand-letter the text as part of the design, as found in the classic *Millions of Cats* by Wanda Gág (1928). Print styles in graphic novels vary to signal different elements on the same page, such as narrative boxes, speech and thought bubbles, and sound effects.

- The ***page layout*** can vary from illustrations being placed one on a page, to on facing pages, on alternating pages, or on parts of pages. A picture that extends across the two facing pages is called a ***double spread*** and gives the effect of motion, drawing the eye to the next page. It can also give a feeling of grandeur, openness, and expansiveness. Sometimes, a picture will begin on a right-hand page and spill over to the following page, the reverse side, as found in *A Nation's Hope* (Illustration 4, p. 47). This offers a strong sense of continuity from one part of the story to the next. Layout also includes the placement of the written text relative to the illustrations, ranging from formal layouts with the text on a separate page or white space or informal with the words placed into the visual image as in *No, David!* (Illustration 1, p. 46).

- Some pictures have a ***border*** that frames an illustration to distance the reader from the action, lend a sense of order to the story, or make the mood more formal. The border itself may be a simple line or a broad, ornately decorated ribbon of information or another story line. The border can repeat images or symbols connected to the meaning of the story. Molly Idle uses a delicate pink blossom border at the top of the page to suggest a curtain framing, but not containing, the dance of Flora and the flamingo (Illustration 6, p. 47), whereas Peggy Rathmann uses a line border that can't quite contain the exuberance of Gloria, who breaks outside the border (Illustration 12, p. 49).

- The arrangement of ***panels*** on a page is essential to meaning in a graphic novel and is increasingly being used in picturebooks. The three horizontal frames in *Bluebird* show the unfolding of a key plot element and so are given equal space, including a moment of frozen disbelief (Illustration 5, p. 47). Pages with frames to carry the action forward alternate with full-page spreads that encourage the reader to slow down and experience the story. Raina Telgemeier uses a 2-2-1 arrangement of panels to depict the quickly unfolding argument followed by a larger panel showing the resolution (Illustration 11, p. 49). A series of small panels in a row is often used to show quick shifts in action, whereas larger panels provide a focal point, inviting the reader to slow down and stay within that panel longer. Panels can be different sizes and shapes and include characters and objects that break the frame to signal intensity.

- An important aspect of design in novels is ***chapter openers***, in which an illustrator creates visual images related to that chapter's theme and contents. Grace Lin creates delicate drawings as chapter openers in *Where the Mountain Meets the Moon* that have the look of woodblock prints. In *The Doldrums*, Nicholas Gannon (2015) creates drawings on brown-toned pages to separate the three parts of the books as well as small sketches as chapter openers to indicate an object or place of significance in that chapter.
- ***Paper*** is another part of the book makeup. The paper should be thick enough to be durable and can involve the use of textured or colored paper to enhance the story. The novel *Pax* by Sara Pennypacker (2016) is printed on textured cream-color papers with untrimmed deckle edges that fit the fablelike nature of the story. Similarly, the shape of the pages should be in keeping with the story or concept, particularly if it is unique or unusual, such as occurs with the ingenious flaps in *Flora and the Flamingo* that facilitate the dynamic pacing of the dance of the two characters.
- The ***size and orientation*** of the book is an important design feature. Large picturebooks are well suited for reading aloud to a class. Smaller picturebooks are usually not satisfactory choices for class read-alouds but support interaction with one child. *Parrots over Puerto Rico* is oriented vertically and opens calendar-style to make the most of the tall trees and the soaring parrots, whereas *The Magic Horse of Han Gan* is oriented horizontally to depict the racing horses and battles.
- ***Book binding,*** or the way the pages are held together, determines a book's durability. Books may be bound in hardcover, paperback, or some special-purpose material. Books for babies are frequently bound in sturdy cardboard or vinyl to withstand the dual role of toy and book. Carefully open the book at its midpoint to determine whether the binding of a hardcover book is glued or sewn. Stitches in the gutter of the book can be seen in a book binding that is sewn. Sewn bindings last much longer than glued ones. Durability relative to cost is the usual trade-off in selecting paper or hardcover bindings for classroom or school libraries, with the cost of hardcover books justified for fairly heavy use.

Observing the Role of Illustrations in Books

The role of illustrations in books can best be understood as the intersection of visual elements, artistic styles, and artistic media with literary elements (e.g., character, setting, theme, plot). These roles vary in importance, depending on the type of book. In wordless picturebooks, the illustrations tell the whole story; in picture storybooks, they tell part of the story; in graphic novels, the visual images are the central focus with the text embedded within those images; in illustrated books, they provide context to enhance the reader's engagement and understanding.

The Guide to Illustrations starts on page 44, and gives a brief analysis of each illustration and how it contributes to the story. To better understand the examples, locate the books from which the illustrations were taken and use the guide as an aid to understanding how artistic styles, visual elements, and elements of fiction contribute to each story's meaning. For example, in David Shannon's *No, David!* (Illustration 1, p. 46), a pajama-clad little boy, instead of quietly preparing for sleep, careens off his bed imagining that he is a superhero. His mother's presence is found only in her words, "Settle down!" For child and adult reader alike, the boy's exaggerated expression and motion provide humor. Shannon's use of an expressionistic style, bold colors, and jagged, diagonal lines emphasize the child's energy, motion, and zest for life. Seen from his mother's perspective, however, these same artistic attributes could be interpreted as emphasizing the child's mischievousness and disobedience.

The key to understanding and appreciating the role of illustrations in picturebooks is to look carefully at illustrations for the messages they contain. You need to be able to "read" the ways in which pictures "mean." Table 4.1 offers tips about what to look for as you read illustrations, particularly within picture storybooks.

Graphic novels require additional strategies for reading illustrations in that the reader must make connections between the images and the text (captions or speech balloons) and must create links between each panel and the page as a whole. Children must "read between the panels" to figure out what has occurred between one panel and the next (Connors, 2012). This ability is vital in a multimodal world where readers are constantly moving between images on the Internet and video games and need to fill in the gaps of what has occurred between those images to create meaning.

Table 4.1 How Illustrations Contribute to Picturebook Stories: A Summary

Artistic and Literary Aspects		Contributions of Illustrations to Stories
Literary Elements	Plot	Convey story events not in the text.
	Character	Show characters not in the text; contribute to characterization by showing physical appearance and actions.
	Setting	Show the setting and time period. Indicate the passing of time in a day or seasons.
	Theme	Accentuate the book's theme. Indicate the theme in wordless books.
	Style	Show author's stance toward the protagonist by viewing the world from the protagonist's perspective. Support a book's literary style to faithfully represent an era or culture.
Visual Elements	Line	Indicate motion or action, story mood (e.g., calm vs. agitated), aspects of plot (e.g., real vs. dreamed), and character (e.g., fragile vs. strong).
	Color	Indicate characters' emotions and personalities, story mood, and aspects of setting (e.g., lush vs. arid, cold vs. warm).
	Shape and space	Indicate what is most important by relative size. Emphasize contrast by juxtaposing large and small objects. Use of blank space to highlight an object or show isolation.
	Perspective and light	Create a sense of drama and action by taking points of view from above, from below, or at eye level. Use of a light source to focus attention or to establish time of day and reality.
	Texture	Intensify a sense of character or setting by indicating the feel of objects or surroundings.
	Composition	Focus the eye on what is most important (usually in the center). Indicate a character's perspective (how the character sees the world).
Artistic Styles	Realistic	Emphasize that information in nonfiction is real and that realistic fiction could be true or based on fact.
	Impressionistic	Contribute to settings through light-filled scenes of nature.
	Expressionistic	Express characters' feelings and emotions through exaggeration.
	Abstract	Emphasize basic, shared traits of characters; create a nonspecific setting.
	Surrealistic	Help connect characters' conscious and unconscious thoughts, emotions, and concerns.
	Folk	Establish and develop settings in the past or in particular cultural traditions.
	Cartoon	Provide humor through exaggeration of character appearance and actions.
	Cultural	Provide connections to traditions that developed over time within particular cultures.

Guide to Illustrations

	Source of Book Illustration	Artistic Style; Media	Visual Elements	Elements of Fiction in Illustrations
1	Shannon, David. *No David!* Scholastic, 1998.	Expressionist, acrylic paint, colored pencil	Line, shape, color, double-page spreads	Character, plot, mood, theme, style
2	Wiesner, David. *Tuesday*. Clarion, 1981.	Surrealist; watercolors, wordless	Line, color, perspective, light and dark	Mood, plot, setting
3	Juster, Norton. *The Hello, Goodbye Window*. Illustrated by Chris Raschka. Hyperion, 2005.	Impressionistic; oil pastels, pen and ink, watercolor	Composition, color, line, shape	Character, setting, mood, style
4	de la Peña, Matt. *A Nation's Hope.* Illustrated by Kadir Nelson. Dial, 2011.	Photographically realistic; oil paints on wood	Perspective, space, color	Character, setting, mood, theme
5	Staake, Bob. *Bluebird*. Schwartz & Wade, 2013.	Abstract/graphic design; digital (Photoshop), wordless	Shape, color, line, panels, composition, book design	Character, mood, plot, theme, setting
6	Idle, Molly. *Flora and the Flamingo*. Chronicle, 2013.	Realistic; colored pencil, flaps, wordless	Color, line, space, composition, border	Character, plot, mood, setting, theme, style
7	Tapahonso, Luci. *Songs of Shiprock Fair*. Illustrated by Anthony Chee Emerson. Kiva, 1999.	Folk art; opaque paint	Line, shape, color	Plot, mood, setting

Guide to Illustrations

	Source of Book Illustration	Artistic Style; Media	Visual Elements	Elements of Fiction in Illustrations
8	Willems, Mo. *Knuffle Bunny: A Cautionary Tale*. Hyperion, 2004.	Cartoon/ realistic; pen and ink, digital photography, computer	Line, color, composition	Character, setting, mood, theme
9	Chen, Jiang Hong. *The Magic Horse of Han Gan*. Enchanted Lion, 2006.	Realistic, oil paints on silk paper; traditional Chinese classic style	Line, color, space, texture, endpapers, title page	Character, plot, mood, theme, setting
10	Roth, Susan and Trumbore, Cindy. *Parrots over Puerto Rico*. Lee & Low, 2013.	Realistic; paper and fabric collages	Texture, perspective, book/page orientation, composition	Setting, plot
11	Telgemeier, Raina. *Sisters*. Scholastic, 2014.	Cartoon; graphic narrative; pencil, India ink, digital coloring and panels	Line, perspective, color, panels and frames	Character, plot, mood, theme, setting
12	Rathmann, Peggy. *Officer Buckle and Gloria*. Putnam, 1995.	Cartoon; watercolors, pen and ink	Line, composition, endpapers	Plot, character, theme, mood
13	Bishop, Nic. *Nic Bishop Snakes*. Scholastic, 2012.	Realistic; photography	Line, space, perspective, texture	Character, setting

SETTLE DOWN!
1
3
2

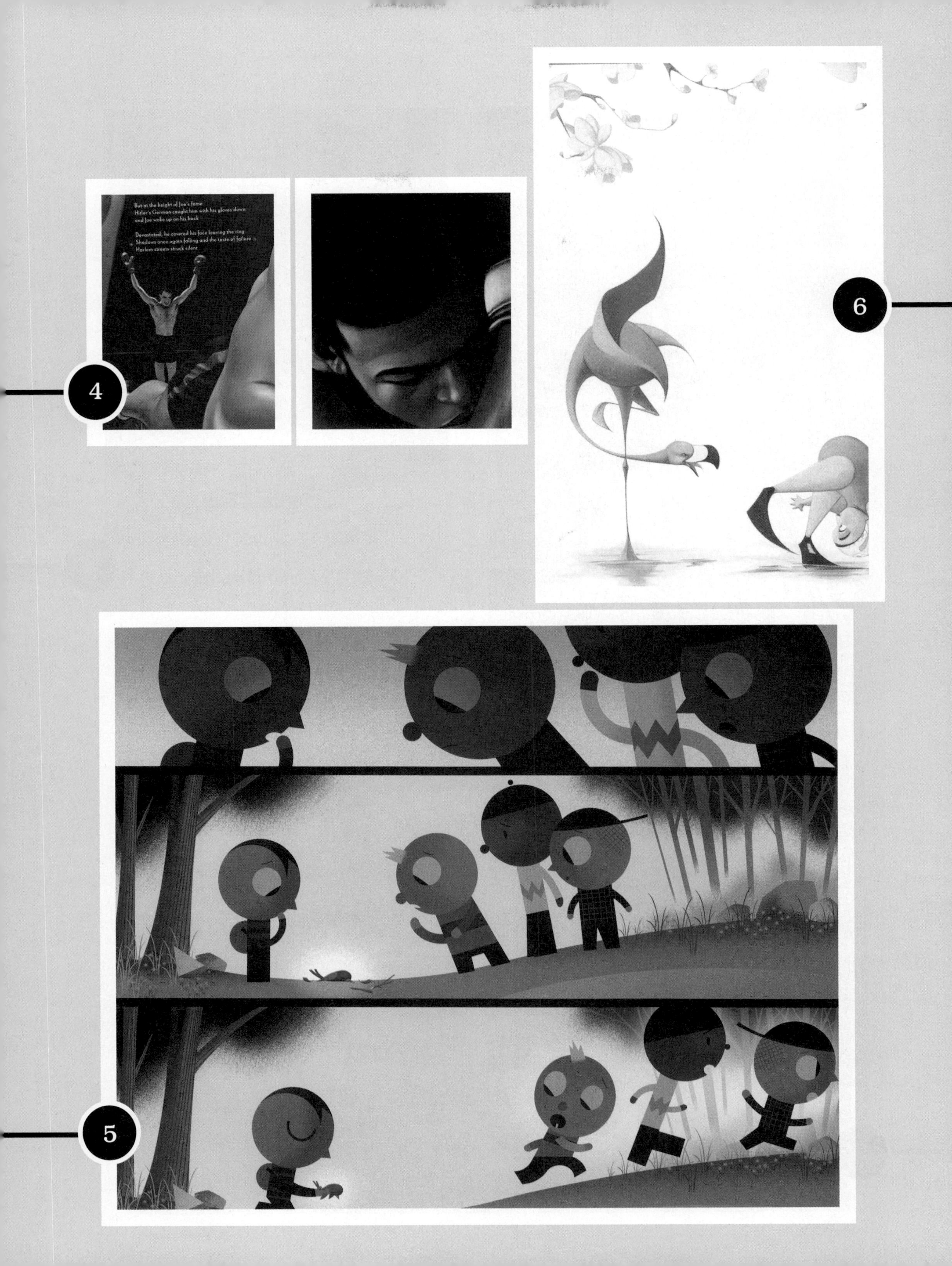
4
But at the height of Joe's fame
Hitler's German caught him with his gloves down
and Joe woke up on his back
Devastated, he covered his face leaving the ring
Shadows once again falling and the taste of failure
Harlem streets struck silent
6
5

7

8

9

10
MOM, CAN WE GO TO McDONALD'S?
PLEEEASE?! I'LL DIE IF I HAFTA EAT ANOTHER CUP O' NOODLES.
ME TOO!
I WANT WENDY'S!
NO, McDONALD'S!
WENDY'S!
McDONALD'S
ENOUGH!!
I WOULD'VE VOTED FOR BURGER KING, MYSELF....
11

12

13

Explorations of visual imagery in children's books are important not only in creating deeper understandings of those books but also in providing the tools children need to develop awareness of how and why they are influenced by images in everyday life. Their explorations of the contexts of those images as social practices facilitates both a critique of the negative effects of images in conveying societal stereotypes and biases and the use of images as tools for transformative thinking and action. Studying the ways in which visual images create meaning within books provides children with the tools they need to develop critical consciousness and construct their own positions on important social issues and questions.

Invitations for Further Investigation

- Read Molly Bang's *Picture This: How Pictures Work* (2016) about the elements that make up a picture and the ways images work to tell a story that engages the emotions. Apply her principles of color, line, and shape to create a scary picture using simple geometric shapes and four basic colors (red, black, white, and purple).
- Investigate the ways in which illustrators use visual images to raise questions about common social practices. You might start by exploring Anthony Browne's books, particularly *Piggybook* (1990), *Zoo* (1983), and *Voices in the Park* (2001), to examine the use of visual images and symbolism to raise critical issues.
- Gather a set of 8–10 picturebooks and create a three-column chart to document the design decisions for each book (see chapter for a list of design features) and how those decisions relate to each book's meaning (e.g., size and orientation of book, dust jacket, endpapers, title page). Select one of these picturebooks to share with children, using suggested questions from Lambert (2015) to encourage children to make observations about the paratextual features in the design.
- Examine a graphic novel by Raina Telgemeier, and document the different ways in which text is embedded into the visual images/panels and the different roles of these text features. Also look closely at several pages to determine what needs to be read "between the panels" to figure out what occurred between one panel and the next.
- Gather a set of middle-grade novels published in the past 2–3 years, and examine the types of visual images and illustrations as well as their purpose. Compare these novels to ones published 10–20 years ago to identify changes over time in the use of visual images.

References

Bang, M. (2016). *Picture this: How pictures work.* San Francisco: Chronicle.

Bishop, N. (2012). *Nic Bishop snakes.* New York: Scholastic.

Browne, A, 1983). *Zoo.* New York: Knopf.

Browne, A. (1990). *Piggybook.* New York: Knopf.

Browne, A. (2001). *Voices in the park.* New York: Knopf.

Chen, J. H. (2006). *The magic horse of Han Gan.* New York: Enchanted Lion.

Connors, S. (2012). Weaving multimodal meaning in a graphic novel reading group. *Visual Communication, 12*(1), 27–53.

de la Peña, M. (2011). *A nation's hope: The story of boxing legend Joe Louis.* Nelson, K. (Illus.). New York: Dial.

Dotlich, R. K. (2012). Cloudscape. In J. Corcoran (Ed.), *Dare to dream . . . change the world.* Tulsa, OK: Kane Miller.

Duncum, P. (2002). Visual culture art education: Why, what and how. *International Journal of Art and Design Education, 21*(1), 14–23.

Gág, W. (1928). *Millions of cats.* New York: Coward-McCann.

Gannon, N. (2015). *The doldrums.* New York: Greenwillow.

Idle, M. (2013). *Flora and the flamingo.* San Francisco: Chronicle.

Juster, N. (2005). *The hello, goodbye window.* Raschka, C. (Illus.). New York: Hyperion.

Lambert, M. D. (2015*). Reading picture books with children.* Watertown, MA: Charlesbridge.

Lin, G. (2009). *Where the mountain meets the moon.* New York: Little, Brown.

Pantaleo, S. (2011). Grade 7 students reading graphic novels: "You need to do a lot of thinking." *English in Education, 45*(2), 113–131.

Pennypacker, S. (2016). *Pax.* Klassen, J. (Illus.). New York: HarperCollins.

Rathmann, P. (1995). *Officer Buckle and Gloria.* New York: Putnam.

Roth, S., & Trumbore, C. (2013). *Parrots over Puerto Rico*. New York: Lee & Low.

Ryan, P. M. (2010). *The dreamer*. Sis, P. (Illus.). New York: Scholastic.

Shannon, D. (1998). *No, David!* New York: Scholastic.

Staake, B. (2013). *Bluebird*. New York: Schwartz & Wade.

Stead, P. (2010). *A sick day for Amos McGee*. Stead, E. (Illus.). New York: Roaring Brook.

Tapahonso, L. (1999). *Songs of Shiprock Fair*. Emerson, A. C. (Illus.). Walnut, CA: Kiva.

Telgemeier, R. (2014). *Sisters*. New York: Scholastic.

Wiesner, D. (1981). *Tuesday*. New York: Clarion.

Willems, M. (2004). *Knuffle bunny: A cautionary tale*. New York: Hyperion.

Part 2

Categories of Literature

The purpose of this text is to introduce you to literature as a discipline so that you become familiar with genres, literary and visual elements, evaluation and selection criteria, critical issues, and resources, along with reading widely from children's books. A literature curriculum can be organized by genre, theme or topic, author or illustrator, literary or visual elements, or notable books. The chapters in Part II focus on genre to encourage you to read broadly, but within that genre structure, each chapter is organized around themes and topics and includes discussions of literary elements and lists of authors, illustrators, notable books, and awards.

Genre provides a context for you to learn about the various types of books and their characteristics, such as historical fiction, fantasy, poetry, etc. The goal is to expose you to a wide variety of literature and to explore the evaluation and selection criteria for excellent books within each genre as well as the types of formats found within genres.

Theme or ***topic*** focuses attention on a book's meaning and is the primary approach used in classrooms and libraries. Organizing a set of books around particular themes, such as alienation and acceptance by peers encourages critical thinking and in-depth consideration of issues along with thoughtful connections across books. Organizing books by topics, such as pets or World War II, can help children find books of interest for independent reading but is less useful for in-depth discussion. The chapters encourage you to explore both themes and topics.

An ***author*** or ***illustrator*** approach involves organizing books around the people who create books and becoming familiar with their books, creative processes, and life experiences. A list of notable authors and illustrators for each genre is included in the chapters, and you are encouraged to inquire into the life and work of people whose books intrigue you.

Literary and visual elements, presented in Chapters 3 and 4, are another way to organize a literature curriculum. Literary devices are particular techniques used by authors for a special effect, such as irony, symbolism, or parody. Illustrators vary their techniques with a particular medium like watercolor or element like color to draw the reader's attention to a character. Each genre chapter highlights a particular literary element to provide an opportunity for you to revisit these elements and explore them in greater depth. Examining these elements will give you a better understanding of creating books and are essential to engaging in close textual analysis.

Organizing around ***notable books*** involves an in-depth focus on award-winning books or exemplary classic or contemporary books. The emphasis is on reading a few books closely and engaging in discussions with other readers about personal connections and significant issues, and then analyzing the features that contribute to their excellence, such as their relevance to readers, unique perspectives or insights, memorable characters, or illustration style. Each chapter includes a list of recommended books for reading aloud, a reader connection that encourages you to interact closely with a set of books, and references to award lists that you can consult. You are encouraged to engage in literature discussions around an

Table 5.1 Genres and Topics of Children's Literature

	Prose				
	Fiction				Nonfiction
	Fantasy		Realism		
Poetry (Ch. 6)	**Traditional Literature (Ch. 7)**	**Fantasy and Science Fiction (Ch. 8)**	**Realistic Fiction (Ch. 9)**	**Historical Fiction (Ch. 10)**	**Informational Books and Biographies (Ch. 11)**
Nursery rhymes Lyric poems Narrative poems	Myths Epics and legends Folktales Fables Religious stories	Modern folktales and mythology Animal fantasy Miniature worlds Unusual characters and strange situations Suspense and the supernatural Historical fantasy Quests and imagined worlds Science fiction	Families Peers Physical, emotional, mental, and behavioral challenges Local and global communities Animals Sports, mystery, and adventure Gender and sexuality Difficult life situations	Mystery and adventure Forced journeys of transformation Fear and intolerance Resistance and challenge to injustice Facing adversity through relationships Ingenuity and innovation	Biography Biological science Physical science Applied science Social science Humanities

exemplary book or set of books for each genre to deepen your understandings and ability to evaluate literature.

Chapters 6 through 11 focus on literary genres. An overview of the genres, subtopics, and their relationships to one another is displayed in Table 5.1. Understanding genre characteristics builds a frame of reference of a particular genre and can facilitate comprehension. Many authors are playing with the traditional boundaries of a genre, and knowledge of the traditional literary forms helps you understand what authors are doing and gain new understandings from this shift.

Authors have been experimenting with books that blend characteristics of several genres, so that genre boundaries are increasingly blurred. Novels written in verse form, usually free verse, are occurring with greater frequency across genres, such as in Karen Hesse's *Out of the Dust,* awarded the Newbery Medal and the Scott O'Dell Award for Historical Fiction. Novels in verse are listed under their particular narrative genre, such as historical fiction, rather than in the chapter about poetry. Books of magical realism combine realism and fantasy to offer new ways to perceive the world, as in *Skellig* by David Almond, and are included in fantasy. Historical fantasy blends historical fiction and modern fantasy, as Rebecca Stead does in *When You Reach Me* with moving time frames; these books are included in the fantasy chapter.

Other blended genres include works of fictionalized biography and informational books that contain elements of fiction and nonfiction, as in Russell Freedman's *Confucius: The Golden Rule* and David Macaulay's *Mosque*. These blended-genre works offer readers new perspectives and heighten the interest of readers. Another trend is multigenre books in which several distinct genres are included in the same book, such as poetry along with a separate box of information on each page as in *Where in the Wild?* by David Schwartz and Yael Schy or that combine biography with a collection of poems as in *Enormous Smallness* by Matthew Burgess and Kris DiGiacomo (2015) about the life and poems of e.e. cummings. The Magic School Bus series by Joanna Cole and Bruce Degen is a well-known example of multigenre.

Chapters 5 and 12 diverge from the organization of genre and present books that go across genres around a particular focus. Chapter 5 focuses on picturebooks and graphic novels, defined by their integration of word and image as essential to the narrative. These books actually fit into a range of genres but are grouped together because of their distinctive format and to highlight the types of books appropriate for young children. This chapter emphasizes the format of a book, rather than a genre. Chapter 12 is organized by culture and goes across genres to overview current issues, trends, and recommended books that are multicultural and international to highlight the importance of these areas. Although multicultural and international books have been placed in a separate chapter for emphasis, multicultural and international titles are integrated into all of the genre chapters.

The special features in each chapter of Part II include a Milestones feature that gives an overview of the history of the development of each genre. The lists of Notable Authors familiarize you with well-known creators of literature and helps you make choices for in-depth author studies, just as the Excellent Books to Read Aloud features provide help in selecting good read-alouds. The Invitations for Further Investigation suggest aspects of each chapter's content for in-depth study, issues for discussion, and literature-related inquiries. Reader Connections suggest a response engagement to encourage you to pursue your own questions within a set of books and to think collaboratively with peers.

The Recommended Books sections are lists of books at the end of each genre chapter. Our goal is to include the best books published in the past 10 years as well as a few older titles that continue to hold wide appeal. Titles in the Recommended Books lists are organized by the same topics as presented in the body of the chapter to make finding specific types of books easier. A brief list of films related to each genre follows the Recommended Books lists. Other recommended children's literature titles may be found in Appendix A (Children's Book Awards). Appendix C lists good magazines available for children. Information on the genre of plays in children's literature is found in Chapter 13.

Chapter 5

Picturebooks and Graphic Novels

Picture This

I'm the belle of the ball!
I'm the star of the show!
When you open a book
I'm the place your eyes go.
I'm colors and shapes.
I'm an actor on stage,
worth one thousand words
that just sit on the page!
I'm scattered throughout.
I'm the best part to see.
I know when you read
you are hoping for me!

—Laura Purdie Salas

In an era when picturebooks abound and invite children into the world of books, it is difficult to imagine a time when books had little or no illustrations. The picturebook is actually a product of the 20th century when different types of picturebooks developed in response to an awareness of the importance of early learning. The picturebook, however, is not just for young children. Many sophisticated and complex picturebooks are published for older readers because of their affinity for visual images resulting from their daily immersion into a world filled with images that are both global in scope and every day in practice. This same connection to visual image has led to the increasing popularity of graphic novels, building from the comic book tradition to sophisticated graphic narratives. Picturebooks and graphic novels provide a means of developing the ability to read and critique these images as well as to engage with a thought-provoking story.

Definition and Description

Picturebooks are not a genre but a format in which both words and illustrations are *essential* to the meaning of a story. The illustrations are integral to the reader's experience of the book and to the telling of the story. The recent move from the use of picture book as two words to the compound word picturebook reflects this integration of visual image and text. The illustrations can be symmetrical to the text by providing similar information, complementary with the text and image each doing different work, or counterpoint with the images providing alternative or contradictory information to the text (Nikolajeva & Scott, 2006). Picturebooks are written in all genres and typically are 32 pages long with illustrations on every page or every other page.

Where the Wild Things Are by Maurice Sendak is often cited as an exemplary picturebook because of the fusion of word and image into a seamless whole. Sendak's use of space conveys emotion and movement as the illustrations break out of their borders and take over the white space to signal the story's climax during Max's imaginary journey to the "wild things" and then shrink back within their borders when Max returns home to find his supper waiting for him. The dreamlike story setting is signaled through the subdued watercolor washes over delicate line drawings, while the crosshatched lines set up emotional tension that shifts across the pages.

Graphic novels are comics, a sequential art form that uses frames, words, and visual images to tell a story, but are distinctive due to a lengthy storyline that carries across the entire narrative within a book. In a graphic novel, the images *are* the text, they do not just support or enhance the text. Words are typically integrated within the images through speech or thought bubbles so that readers walk with characters and see their points of view. Graphic novels are a strong recent trend, initially for older readers, but their influence is now evident in picturebooks through large panels that convey the movement of the plot as seen in Bob Staake's *Bluebird.*

Illustrated books have occasional illustrations that break up or enhance the text, add interest, or depict specific incidents or settings. Illustrations in these books are not essential to understanding the story but provide context and bring visual interest for readers. Michael Foreman's middle grade novel, *The Tortoise and the Soldier*, tells a true story from World War I that includes full-page watercolors along with small watercolor vignettes and occasional sketches. These illustrations represent and enhance the text and provide context but do not add new information that is essential to understanding the story line, as would be true in a picturebook.

Illustrated books are increasingly prevalent, given the saturation of children's lives and surroundings with visual images. Their comfort with a complex interplay of words and images has encouraged authors of middle grade novels to integrate different types of illustrations, such as the cartoon drawings in the margins of Tom Angleberger's Origami Yoda books and the full-color illustrations and chapter openers in Grace Lin's *Where the Mountain Meets the Moon.* Transition chapter books aimed at a slightly younger audience use even more illustrations, some of which contain important context for the story.

Evaluation and Selection of Picturebooks and Graphic Novels

Children's first experiences with books must be enjoyable and meaningful to create an interest and involvement with literacy. Evaluation and selection of picturebooks involves a balance between what children naturally enjoy and invitations to extend their interests as readers. The following criteria will help you identify the best picturebooks:

- **Is the picturebook on a topic that children enjoy or find intriguing?** Avoid picturebooks that are *about* childhood through nostalgia or reminiscence of childhood. Overly sentimental books are for adults, not children.

- **Does the book avoid racial, ethnic, social class, or gender stereotyping in text and illustrations?** Subtle forms of stereotyping are often embedded within the illustrations of hairstyles, homes, or aspects of a character's appearance and context.
- **Is the language and writing style rich and varied but not so complicated as to be difficult for a child to understand?** New or unusual vocabulary should be incorporated within the context of interesting situations and complementary illustrations. Children do not need controlled vocabulary that is overly simplistic, but they do need to be able to make sense of the meaning of unfamiliar words. They also may struggle with making inferences essential to the story if those inferences are based in the perspectives and experiences of older youth or adults.
- **Are the illustrations appropriate in complexity to the age of the intended audience?** For example, in picturebooks for infants, relatively uncomplicated pages showing outlined figures against a plain background provide the most enjoyment. Unusual perspectives or page designs in which only parts of a figure are shown may not be readily understood by children younger than age 2.
- **Are the illustrations appropriate to the story?** The artistic style, medium, elements, and design should have a close fit with the meaning of the story. Collage, for example, is often not as effective in capturing facial expressions as oil paintings and so might not be a good choice for a story centered on a child's emotions. Also consider whether the illustrations overpower the text or work with the text in telling a story.
- **Does the book offer connections for both children and adults in a read-aloud experience?** Picturebooks read aloud by parents, teachers, and librarians should offer something to both listener and reader and promote interaction. Multiple layers of meaning, child and adult perspectives, and humor are sources of enjoyment in books that adults willingly read and reread to children.
- **Is the amount of text on a page appropriate to the child audience?** The amount of text on the pages of a picturebook determines how long it will take to read, with long texts usually intended for older audiences. Children's willingness to listen to stories grows with experience, which may result in a young child who has been read to regularly having a longer attention span than an older child with no story experience.

The illustrations in graphic novels play a different and often more complex role and are typically for older readers. The evaluation criteria for picturebooks are applicable to graphic novels since, like picturebooks, the visual images are essential to the telling of the story. Pagliaro (2014) suggests these additional criteria to consider in examining how the visual images provide narrative information in graphic novels:

- **Do the images provide important information about the character, plot, and setting without extensive explanation?** Graphic novels contain a narrator voice in a box at the top of a panel or use dialogue to provide background information on a character's emotions, key plot elements, or the context of the story. Some use of these conventions is appropriate, but this information should primarily be integrated into the visual images. Do the images *show* this context or are you *told* by the text?
- **Does the structure of the page fit the tone of the story?** Graphic novels use an arrangement of panels on the page that can vary in size, color, and shape to convey mood or action. Panels that are asymmetrical and irregular, for example, can signal a chaotic scene. Scenes in which the characters break outside the frame can signal strong emotions or actions. The structure also includes different comic conventions for signaling emotions, imagination, thoughts, dialogue, sounds, etc.
- **Is the dialogue contained within speech and thought bubbles authentic to the characters?** Graphic novels make extensive use of dialogue to develop characters, establish setting, and convey action, and that dialogue can sometimes become awkward and explanatory rather than true dialogue. Dialogue between characters should be appropriate to the age and cultural background of the character.

Several key awards provide access to outstanding picturebooks and graphic novels. The most prestigious illustrator award in the U.S. is the Caldecott Medal, which typically goes to a picturebook, although several graphic novels have recently been recognized. The equivalent award in Great Britain is the Kate Greenaway Medal; in Canada, the Governor General's Award for Illustration; and in Australia, the Picturebook of the Year Award (see Appendix A). Another source of excellent picturebooks is "The *New York Times* Best Illustrated Children's Books of the Year," released annually in early November. The Will Eisner Comic Industry Awards includes the categories of Best Publication for Early Readers, Kids, and Young Adults.

Excellent Picturebooks to Read Aloud

Agee, Jon. *It's Only Stanley.* Ages 6–8.
Alakija, Polly. *Counting Chickens.* Ages 2–5.
Brown, Monica. *Maya's Blanket/La manta de Maya.* Illustrated by David Diaz. Ages 5–9.
Brown, Peter. *Mr. Tiger Goes Wild.* Ages 3–7.
DiCamillo, Kate and Alison McGhee. *Bink & Gollie.* Illustrated by Tony Fucile. Ages 5–8.
Henkes, Kevin. *Waiting.* Ages 3–6.
Klassen, Jon. *I Want My Hat Back.* Ages 6–9.
Lipan, Sabine. *Mom, There's a Bear at the Door.* Illustrated by Manuela Olten. Ages 4–7.
Mahy, Margaret. *Bubble Trouble.* Illustrated by Polly Dunbar. Ages 4–8.
Murray, Diana. *City Shapes.* Illustrated by Bryan Collier. Ages 3–6.
Shannon, David. *Duck on a Tractor.* Ages 4–8.
Stead, Phillip. *A Sick Day for Amos McGee.* Illustrated by Erin Stead. Ages 5–8.
Stein, David. *Interrupting Chicken.* Ages 3–7.
Willems, Mo. *That Is NOT a Good Idea.* Ages 3–8.

Historical Overview of Picturebooks and Graphic Novels

Orbis Pictus (The World in Pictures), an ABC book written and illustrated by John Amos Comenius in Moravia in 1657, is considered the first children's picturebook. Comenius was the first to emphasize using pictures to explain and expand the meaning of the text in books for young people. Because early books were rare and prohibitively expensive, very few children had access. Moreover, until well into the 1800s, Europeans and Americans believed that books were for the serious business of educating and soul saving—not enjoyment! Today's full-color, beautifully illustrated books resulted from the following:

- Technological advances in color printing made high-quality illustrations more affordable. More recent technologies have facilitated the printing of engineered books with flaps, foldouts, and other movable parts.
- A more understanding attitude toward childhood evolved. During the1800s, society began to accept childhood as a time for playing and learning, and the economy could support the leisure time these activities require for a child.
- Higher standards of excellence in picturebook illustration developed through the beauty and charm of 19th-century illustrators Randolph Caldecott, Kate Greenaway, and Walter Crane, gaining the attention of the general public.
- The establishment of national awards for excellence in children's book illustration in the 20th century encouraged more artists to enter the field.
- The growth of public school systems and public and school library systems increased the demand for books. In addition, reading came to be recognized as one of the child's best tools for learning and entertainment.
- Recent technologies have encouraged a move to mixed-media and digital illustrations. Illustrators can use a range of media for different elements of an illustration that are scanned into a computer and layered with additional digital manipulations to create the final illustration.

Today, the picturebook is well established, with an ever-widening audience and a focus on multicultural and global themes on issues such as the effects of war, poverty, immigration, and environmental destruction on the lives of children. Greater diversity in book design and in illustration styles and mediums as well as ways of telling stories is evident. A trend of the 1990s was to publish picturebooks with high levels of conceptual difficulty and artistic sophistication intended for middle-grade students.

MILESTONES in the Development of Picturebooks

Date	Event	Significance
1484	*Aesop's Fables,* illustrated by William Caxton	One of the first-known illustrated books enjoyed by children
1657	*Orbis Pictus,* written and illustrated by John Amos Comenius	Considered the first picturebook for children
1860–1900	Golden Age of book illustration in England, led by Randolph Caldecott, Walter Crane, and Kate Greenaway	Increased stature, popularity, and appreciation of picturebooks
1902 and 1928	*The Tale of Peter Rabbit* by Beatrix Potter and *Millions of Cats* by Wanda Gág	Early important modern picture storybooks in England and the U.S.
1938	First Caldecott Award for illustration in children's books in the U.S.	Promoted excellence in illustration and encouraged talented artists to illustrate picturebooks
1940	*Pat the Bunny* by Dorothy Kunhardt	One of the first books for babies; began the move to different types of picturebooks for different ages
1957	*The Cat in the Hat,* written and illustrated by Dr. Seuss, and *Little Bear,* written by Else Minarik and illustrated by Maurice Sendak	Introduced easy-to-read books
1966	Hans Christian Andersen Illustrator's Award established	Highest international recognition of an illustrator for a body of work
1967	*A Boy, a Dog, and a Frog,* illustrated by Mercer Mayer	Popularized wordless books
1990	*Color Zoo* by Lois Ehlert wins a Caldecott Honor Award	Recognition of engineered books
1991	*Black and White* by David Macaulay wins Caldecott Medal	Influence of postmodernism and acceptance of nontraditional picturebook formats
1992	*Maus II* by Art Spiegelman wins the Pulitzer Prize; Bone series by Jeff Smith	Graphic novels receive recognition as a literary form and graphic novels for children gain attention
2006	First Theodor Seuss Geisel Award	Promoted excellence in books for beginning readers

The past 10 years has witnessed the tremendous growth of the graphic novel, a novel-length comic book originally created for adults that now includes books for children. Comic books began as a repackaging of Sunday comic strips into serial paperbacks and became a massive industry with the introduction of Superman in 1938. Severe criticism of comic books as the cause of antisocial behavior led to a code of standards in 1954 that resulted in many artists and writers leaving the comic book industry. They created alternative comics that moved away from serial paperbacks to independently bound books that are today's graphic novels. Will Eisner, a leading graphic artist, popularized the term "graphic novel" and wrote *Graphic Storytelling and Visual Narrative.* When Art Speigelman won the 1992 Pulitzer Prize for *Maus II* (1991), graphic novels gained status as a literary form and became widely available in libraries but only recently have been accepted as reading materials in classrooms.

Types of Picturebooks

Today's picturebooks differ in intended audience, purpose, format, and relative amount of text and illustration. These differences are not absolute, but picturebooks can be grouped according to characteristics into several specific types. Although overlap between types is inevitable, the following kinds of picturebooks are organized here by the intended age of the audience from youngest to oldest. Note that poems, nursery

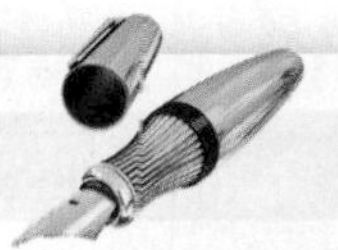

Notable Illustrators of Picturebooks and Graphic Novels

Peter Brown, author/illustrator. Picturebooks celebrating imagination and self-expression using animals as main characters in multimedia illustrations. *Mr. Tiger Goes Wild, Children Make Terrible Pets; Creepy Carrots.* www.peterbrownstudio.com/

Eric Carle, author/illustrator. Picturebooks and concept books with interactive formats. *The Grouchy Ladybug; The Very Hungry Caterpillar.* www.eric-carle.com

Kevin Henkes, author/illustrator. Family picturebooks featuring mice and stories from a young child's view. *Lilly's Purple Plastic Purse; Kitten's First Full Moon; Waiting.* www.kevinhenkes.com

Jon Klassen, Canadian author/illustrator. Dry wit and deadpan humor combine with earth-tone digital illustrations in suspense-filled picturebooks. *I Want My Hat Back; This is Not My Hat; We Found a Hat; Sam & Dave Dig a Hole; The Dark.* http://jonklassen.tumblr.com/

Barbara Lehman, illustrator. An uncluttered cartoon style in wordless picturebooks that blend real and imagined worlds. *The Red Book; The Secret Box; The Plan.* www.barbaralehmanbooks.com/

Liniers, Argentine cartoonist. Quiet stories of childhood and imagination in graphic narratives for young children. *The Big Wet Balloon; Written and Drawn by Henrietta.*

Helen Oxenbury, author/illustrator. British watercolorist known for baby books in board book format. *I Can; I See; I Touch; I Hear; Ten Little Fingers and Ten Little Toes.*

Chris Raschka, illustrator. Spare, expressionist watercolors and brief texts elegantly capture mood. Two-time Caldecott medalist. *Yo! Yes?; The Hello, Goodbye Window; A Ball for Daisy.*

Christian Robinson, illustrator. Creates paint-and-collage artwork featuring multicultural figures immersed in daily life. *Last Stop of Market Street; A School's First Day of School.* http://theartoffun.com/

Robert Sabuda, pop-up book artist and paper engineer. Intricate award-winning pop-up books based in children's classics, folklore, and prehistorical animals. Often works with Matthew Reinhart. *The Little Mermaid*; *The White House.* www.robertsabuda.com/

Laura Vaccaro Seeger, author/illustrator. Concept and beginning reader books with bold lines, bright colors, and die-cuts. *First the Egg; One Boy; Lemons Are not Red; I Used to Be Afraid.* www.studiolvs.com

Brian Selznick, author/illustrator. Period detail and unusual perspectives in groundbreaking picturebooks for older readers. *The Invention of Hugo Cabret; Wonderstruck, The Marvels.* www.theinventionofhugocabret.com

Maurice Sendak, author/illustrator. Explores the dreams and imagination of children in complex picture storybooks. Caldecott Medal for *Where the Wild Things Are; Outside Over There.*

Peter Sís, author/illustrator. Intricate pen and ink and watercolor illustrations in picture book biographies for older readers. *The Wall; The Pilot and the Little Prince.* www.petersis.com

Philip and Erin Stead, author/illustrators. Picturebooks that capture the longings of children. Erin is an illustrator who uses printing techniques and Philip is both an author and illustrator who uses a range of media. *A Sick Day for Amos McGee; Lenny & Lucy; A Home for Bird.* https://erinstead.com/ and https://philipstead.com/

Herve Tullet, French author/illustrator. Interactive touch-and-feel board books that capture the imagination of young children. *Press Here; Mix It Up*! www.herve-tullet.com/

Sara Varon, illustrator and comics artist. Wordless graphic novels that focus on the nature of friendship, using a range of characters. *Robot Dreams; Bake Sale; Chicken and Cat.* www.chickenopolis.com/

David Wiesner, author/illustrator. Wordless fantasy stories and postmodern picture books. Three-time Caldecott medalist. *Tuesday; Flotsam; The Three Pigs; Art and Max; Mr. Wuffles.* www.hmhbooks.com/wiesner

Mo Willems, author/illustrator. Picture books for preschoolers featuring minimalist childlike art, humor, and action. *Don't Let the Pigeon Drive the Bus!; Knuffle Bunny: A Cautionary Tale, That Is NOT a Good Idea; Waiting Is Not Easy.* www.mowillems.com

Salina Yoon, author/illustrator. Interactive board books and simple picturebooks on a child's view of friendship. *Kaleidoscope; Penguin and Pinecone.* www.salinayoon.com/

rhymes, and songbooks in picturebook format are included in the chapter on Poetry. Because picturebooks are a format that goes across genres, relevant picturebooks are included in each of the fiction chapters and in the nonfiction chapter.

Baby Books

Baby books are simply designed, brightly illustrated, durable picturebooks intended for children ages 0–2, such as *Global Baby Bedtimes* by Maya Ajmera. Safety is ensured by rounded corners, nontoxic materials, washable pages, and no loose attachments. The types of baby books are based on the material used in their construction, like vinyl, cloth, or heavy, laminated cardboard. These books have little or no text with simple, clear illustrations that are easy to label, such as the classic *Goodnight Moon* by Margaret Wise Brown, which many parents have read over and over and over again. Their content, which deals with the objects and routines that are familiar to the infant and toddler, is presented mainly in the illustrations. The best baby books, like those produced by Helen Oxenbury, are thoughtfully designed to emphasize patterns and associations that promote dialogue between the caregiver and the young child.

Interactive Books

Interactive books are picturebooks that invite a child's verbal or physical participation as the book is read. These books ask the child direct questions, invite unison recitation of chants or repeated lines, encourage clapping or moving to the rhythm of the words, or require the child to touch or manipulate the book or find objects in the illustrations. The intended audience is usually children ages 2–6, and the books are seen as an extension of their world of play. One classic example is Dorothy Kunhardt's *Pat the Bunny*, which incorporates textures for the child to touch. A recent example is *Press Here*, by Herve Tullet, which invites readers to press the dots, shake the pages, tilt the book, and then turn the page to see what magic has unfolded.

Engineered Books

Sometimes called toy books, ***engineered books*** use paper that has been cut, folded, and constructed to provide pop-up, see-through, movable, foldout, or three-dimensional illustrations. Engineered books can be found for all ages, with the simpler types of engineering for young children, such as pages of varying widths or drilled holes for see-through effects as in Eric Carle's classic *The Very Hungry Caterpillar* or Laura Seeger's *I Used to Be Afraid.* Others have fragile or elaborate pop-up features, such as Robert Sabuda's amazing pop-up version of *The Little Mermaid* and his behind-the-scenes tour of *The White House*, which delight older children and adults.

Wordless Books

Wordless books depend entirely on carefully sequenced illustrations to present the story. With either no text or text on only one or two pages, the illustrations must carry the narrative, as in Jerry Pinkney's *The Lion and the Mouse* and Chris Raschka's *A Ball for Daisy,* both Caldecott Medal winners. The recent increase in excellent wordless books has led to many awards and an avid audience. These books are also called pictorial texts or visual narratives rather than the more negative term of "wordless."

Wordless books are often viewed as appropriate for young emergent readers or English language learners, but many sophisticated wordless books exist for older readers, such as Bob Staake's *Bluebird* and Shaun Tan's *The Arrival.* When children "read" these illustrations in their own words, they benefit from the book's visual story structure in several ways:

- They develop a concept of story as a cohesive narrative with a beginning and an end.
- They learn the front-to-back, left-to-right page progression in reading.
- They explore the complexity of visual images in telling a story.
- They use language inventively to tell a story, promoting language development.
- They understand that stories can be found in themselves, not just in books, and can create multiple stories to interpret the illustrations both orally and in writing.

Alphabet Books

The ***alphabet*** or ***ABC book*** presents the alphabet letter by letter to acquaint young children with the shapes, names, and sounds of the letters. Many are organized around a particular theme as the nature walk in Hannah Viano's *B is for Bear: A Natural Alphabet.* Others use a device, such as finding objects beginning with a featured letter in an illustration, to give their books cohesion. In choosing an ABC book, consider the appropriateness of the theme or device for children, whether both uppercase and lowercase letters are displayed, and the use of a simple, easy-to-read style of print.

Some ABC books are intended for emergent readers, whereas others use the alphabet as a device for presenting information or wordplay, and so the intended audience is older children who already know the alphabet. In *Once upon an Alphabet* by Oliver Jeffers, each letter gets its own story in an inventive collection of interlocking four-page tales of humor and intrigue.

Counting Books

The ***counting book*** presents numbers, usually 1 through 10, to acquaint young children with the numerals and their shapes (1, 2, 3), the number names (one, two, three), the sense of what quantity each numeral represents, and the counting sequence. Anthony Browne's *One Gorilla* uses large close-up watercolor illustrations of primates for a lesson in both science and counting, whereas Polly Alakija's *Counting Chickens* engages readers in a narrative about counting farm animals within a small village in Nigeria.

As with alphabet books, themes or devices are used to make counting books more cohesive and interesting. Specific considerations include the appeal to children of the theme and objects chosen to illustrate the number concepts and the clarity with which the illustrator presents the concept of number. Some counting books are meant for older readers, either because of the sophistication of the number concepts or the use of counting as an organizing structure to present themes or information aimed at older readers, as in *Ten Birds* by Cybele Young, a celebration of individuality and creativity through the actions of ten small birds trying to figure out how to cross the river.

Illustrators often fill their alphabet and counting books with unusual and intriguing objects for children to name and count, such as aardvarks or barracudas, inviting children to pick up interesting information and vocabulary. You will be in the best position to decide whether the novelty of these objects will be motivating or confusing to a particular child.

Concept Books

A ***concept book*** is a picturebook that explores or explains an idea or concept (e.g., opposites), an object (e.g., a train), or an activity (e.g., working) rather than telling a story. Many concept books have no plot but use repeated elements in the illustrations and text to tie the book together. Concept books are a form of informational book that focuses on a specific concept appropriate for young children, such as Lizi Boyd's *Big Bear Little Chair* that explores opposites through visual narratives and Diana Murray's *City Shapes* that depicts shapes found during a walk in the city. The concepts are not necessarily simplistic, as in *More* by I. C. Springman, which explores excessive materialism through the antics of a magpie who hoards too much stuff and the mice who show that less is more. Limited text and clearly understood illustrations encourage children's exploratory talk about the concepts, objects, and activities.

Alphabet and counting books are considered concept books about numbers and letters. They also are often organized around important concepts, such as George Shannon's *One Family*, both a counting book and a book that celebrates families in all of their complexity. Another variety of concept book popular with 2- to 4-year-olds is the ***naming book,*** which presents simple pictures of people, animals, and objects that are labeled for young children to identify, such as *The Big Book of Words and Pictures* by Ole Konnecke.

Picture Storybooks

The most common type of picturebook is ***picture storybooks***, in which a story is told through both words and pictures. Text and illustration occur with equal frequency, and both are in view on most double spreads. The term *picturebook* is usually associated with this type of book, which includes enduring favorites, such as Maurice Sendak's *Where the Wild Things Are* and Chris Van Allsburg's *Jumanji.* Recent examples that are Caldecott Medal winners include Jon Klassen's *This Is Not My Hat* and Philip and Erin Stead's *A Sick Day for Amos McGee.* Unlike concept books and easy-to-read books where the illustrations mirror or complement what is already in the words, the illustrations in picture storybooks often contradict the words or provide alternative interpretations or story lines.

The text of most picture storybooks is meant to be read aloud to 4- to 7-year-olds, at least for the first time or two, and often includes challenging language. Many of the best picture storybooks are also read and enjoyed independently by children 8 years old and up. Picture storybooks reflect a range of genres and reader audiences, and examples are included in all of the genre chapters. The recommended picture storybooks in this chapter focus on books for young children.

Predictable Books and Word Play

Predictable, or ***pattern, books*** have repeated language patterns, story patterns, or familiar sequences that encourage children to chime in on repeating phrases as found in Bill Martin Jr. and Eric Carle's perennial favorite *Brown Bear, Brown Bear, What Do You See?* and Emily Gravett's *Monkey and Me*. These books support readers through meaning and illustration clues and the use of repeating refrains or phrases. Some predictable books use language regularities and repeat certain phonological features, as in *Look!* by Jeff Mack, which uses only two words, "look" and "out," within expressive illustrations to convey a story about the pleasures of reading. Others repeat a phrase throughout the book as in Denise Fleming's *Sleepy, Oh So Sleepy*, in which animal mothers use the title phrase to quietly lull their babies to sleep.

Predictable books often also engage in fun wordplay, such as in Alison Paul's *The Plan*, in which an interaction between father and daughter takes the form of a word game using 20 simple, well-chosen words that shift one letter at a time for each new word. Michael Escoffier's *Where's the Baboon?* uses a riddle format to engage readers in finding one word embedded within another.

Easy-to-Read Books

Easy-to-read books help the beginning reader read independently with success. These books have limited text on a page, large print, double-spacing, short sentences, and often are published as a series. Illustrations vary from every page to every other page and are symmetrical or redundant with the text to support readers in figuring out the words. Language is often, but not always, controlled, and words are short and familiar. Kevin Henke's *Penny and Her Marble* explores the emotional world of childhood guilt, whereas Mo Willems's *Waiting Is Not Easy!* focuses on friendship and tells the story in dialogue balloons. Easy-to-read books can be used with any child who is an emergent reader, but the audience is usually 5- to 7-year-olds.

The easy-to-read book differs in appearance from the picture storybook in several obvious ways. Because they are intended for independent reading, they do not have to be seen from a distance, so are smaller, the text takes up a greater proportion of each page, and the book is often divided into short chapters. *Billy & Milly, Short & Silly* by Eve Feldman plays with this format, telling 13 short stories of the adventures of two friends with only three or four words in each story. These books are considered picturebooks in that they rely on the illustrations to carry the story line, with the text and illustrations mirroring each other as complementary to facilitate emergent readers.

The importance of easy-to-read books was recognized with the establishment of the Theodor Seuss Geisel Award in 2004. This annual award, named for the renowned Dr. Seuss and sponsored by the American Library Association, is given to the author and illustrator of the most distinguished American book for beginning readers. Mo Willems has won this award multiple times for his Elephant and Piggy series, as has Tedd Arnold for his Fly Guy series. Theodor Seuss Geisel believed that easy-to-read books, with their limited vocabulary, could engage young readers with imagination and creativity instead of forcing them to read the pedantic stories found in many early reading materials. These award winners are excellent examples of books that invite children to eagerly engage as readers.

Transitional Books

Transitional books are books for children who can read but have not yet become fluent readers and lie somewhere between picturebooks and full-length novels. They typically have an uncomplicated writing style and vocabulary, illustrations on about every third page, division of text into short chapters, slightly enlarged print, and an average length of 100 pages. Even though the illustrations are not essential to the telling of the story in the same way as a picturebook, they do contain details of setting and character that are not included in the text.

The Carver Chronicles and Nikki and Deja books by Karen English and the Lola Levine books by Monica Brown reflect a trend toward more multicultural content. Books for the transitional reader usually occur in a series, as Donald J. Sobol's much-loved Encyclopedia Brown books and the more recent Ivy and Bean series by Annie Barrows and Mercy Watson series by Kate DiCamillo. The No. 1 Car

Spotter series and the Anna Hibiscus series by Atinuke based on her Nigerian childhood provide a global connection.

The Center for Children's Books at the University of Illinois at Urbana–Champaign established the Gryphon Award for transitional books in 2004. This prize is given to fiction or nonfiction that best exemplifies qualities that successfully bridge the gap in difficulty between picturebooks and full-length books. The 2015 winner, Karen English's *Skateboard Party*, is a school/family story involving mischief and procrastination, reflecting the range of life experiences depicted in transitional books.

Picturebooks for Older Readers

Picturebooks for older readers are generally more sophisticated, abstract, or complex in themes, stories, and illustrations and are suitable for children aged 10 and older. This type of picturebook began to appear in the 1970s in response to increasingly visual modes of communication. Peter Sís' autobiographical *The Wall: Growing Up Behind the Iron Curtain* about the loss of freedom in Czechoslovakia has aspects of picturebooks and graphic novels with serious content and factual history aimed at older readers. Brian Selznick's *The Invention of Hugo Cabret* is a groundbreaking book that blurs genres, winning the Caldecott as a picturebook even though it is more than 500 pages long. The book contains long sequences of black-and-white illustrations without any text between sections of text that do not have illustrations. Because the illustrations are essential to the telling of the story, the book is considered a picturebook, although it also has characteristics of a graphic novel or stills from a film presented in a slow motion sequence.

Picturebooks for older readers lend themselves to use across the content areas in the middle- and high-school curriculum, including social studies, science, and language arts (Albright, 2002). These uses for older readers include:

- Read-alouds to introduce and supplement textbook units of instruction.
- Text sets (several books on the same topic or theme) for small groups to read and discuss in class and to provide background for a novel, event, or time period.
- Models of excellent writing to use in minilessons and writing inquiries.
- Source of humor and interest in a topic, and as a way to provoke discussion, which can result in a deeper understanding of the content.
- Demonstration of practical applications of difficult concepts.
- Factual content that reinforces or adds to that found in textbooks.
- Source of different perspectives on issues and historical events, particularly those of underrepresented groups.

The traditional notion that picturebooks are only for younger children no longer applies. Although some adults may persist in guiding older children away from picturebooks, you will find picturebooks offer an effective way to thoughtfully engage children of all ages.

Postmodern Picturebooks

Another recent trend is that authors and illustrators are playing with multiple storylines, voices, and perspectives to create ***postmodern picturebooks*** that are exciting because of their unpredictability. These books reflect the fragmented and multimodal nature of modern society, with frequent changes in attitudes, styles, and knowledge: everything is constantly shifting. This uncertainty is used in picturebooks to create playful, unexpected, and sometimes cynical books that delight in breaking the rules of convention and giving greater power to the reader. Most are meant for older readers because of their sophistication, sarcasm, and reference to other texts.

David Wiesner's *The Three Pigs* is viewed as an exemplar of postmodern picturebooks. This book is *not* a traditional folktale—his pigs step off the page of the book to peer at the reader and fold up the page to create a paper airplane to fly into other stories. The characteristics of postmodern picturebooks (Goldstone, 2004) include:

- **Multiple storylines.** The text may move back and forth in time, jumble up time, or interrupt a story that then goes in multiple directions, as occurs when Wiesner's pig steps off the page. In Emily Gravett's *Wolves,* the text reads like a simple information book on wolves, but the illustrations reveal a different narrative as a menacing wolf looms over the rabbit immersed in reading information on the eating habits of wolves.

- **Multiple perspectives and page planes.** Different characters may tell their side of the story or the narrator's story may be interrupted by characters, as in Melanie Watt's *Chester,* in which the cat changes the author's story about a mouse. Multiple planes can be revealed in the illustrations where the characters break outside the surface plane of the page and move into the reader's space or suddenly move underneath or above the page. Wiesner's pigs talk to each other, to the reader, and to themselves, as they step off pages, fold up pages, and look behind and over pages.
- **Irony and contradiction.** A sarcastic or mocking tone can be found in fractured and spoofed fairy tales, as in Diane and Christian Fox's *The Cat, the Dog, Little Red, the Exploding Eggs, the Wolf, and Grandma* (2014), in which Cat attempts to read the familiar folktale to Dog who continuously interrupts with his own interpretations and questions. This tone can also occur through discrepancies, unexpected elements, and other storylines in the illustrations, to the point that the illustrations may purposefully completely contradict the text.
- **Uncovering the artistic process of bookmaking.** The act of making the book is revealed by having the characters argue with the illustrator or author, or the author and illustrator may argue with each other as in *Chloe and the Lion* by Mac Barnett and Adam Rex. Sometimes readers are invited to step into a story world but are spoken to by the characters about creating the story, as occurs in Mordicai Gerstein's *A Book* and in Richard Byrne's *This Book Just Ate My Dog!*, in which a girl's dog disappears into the gutter of the book. These metafictive elements reveal the roles of authors and illustrators and often bring them directly into the book.

These same characteristics are also used to create postmodern novels, as in Kate DiCamillo's *The Tale of Despereaux* with its multiple parallel stories and a narrator who directly addresses the reader.

Graphic Novels

Graphic novels are novel-length books that feature illustrations in panels with words integrated into speech bubbles or captions. The multiple images on each page are separated into panels divided by a black line to create frames. These graphic narratives have become so popular that they are found across all genres and are incorporated throughout the genre chapters and marked with a "GR" in recommended book lists. Many graphic novels contain content directed to the experiences of older readers, but a recent trend is aimed at young readers. Their positioning between picturebooks and novels was evident in 2015 when Cece Bell's memoir, *El Deafo*, received a Newbery Honor for writing and Mariko Tamaki's *This One Summer* received a Caldecott Honor for illustration.

Graphic novels are highly appealing because of their dependence on visuals and dialogue, availability as a series, and close ties to popular culture such as films and comic-book superheroes. They are action-oriented with attention-grabbing graphics. Nathan Hale's Hazardous History series engages readers in history, whereas Barry Deutsch's Hereville series is a superhero tale of a young Orthodox Jew. The Babymouse series by Jennifer Holm and illustrated by her brother, Matthew Holm, is appropriate for younger readers. Another trend is graphic novels based on a best-selling series that already exists as chapter books, such as Rick Riordan's Percy Jackson books or Ann Martin's Babysitter Club books. An excellent site for locating reviews and lists of graphic novels is No Flying No Tights (www.noflyingnotights.com).

Manga is a form of comic book that originated in Japan for older readers and is often based on anime, films, and television shows that are animated. Most are for older readers, but there are Pokémon and Dragon Ball Z manga for younger children as well as Kiyohiko Azuma's Yotsuba&! series about a young child's misconceptions of the world. Manga use highly stylized artwork with exaggerated eyes and spiked hair.

During the 20th century, the picturebook developed as a genre, diversified to meet the demands of an ever-expanding audience and market, and improved as a result of printing technology. As researchers came to realize the connections between positive early experiences with good literature, reading, and school success, new types of picturebooks were developed. Graphic novels have gained prominence as publishers realize their appeal for older visually oriented readers. Today, high-quality picturebooks and graphic novels on nearly every imaginable topic can enrich the lives and imaginations of children of all ages.

Invitations for Further Investigation

- Select a picture storybook appropriate for a particular group of children. Read the book aloud and invite children to share their connections and responses. Ask how the illustrations contribute to their understandings of the story. If possible, share several books by the illustrator so students can identify patterns (see Table 4.1).
- Read a graphic novel, and keep a record of the strategies you use to engage with the story. Compare your strategies with those noted in Rudiger's (2006) "Graphic Novels 101: Reading Lessons." Or use Pagliaro's (2014) Rubric of Literary Merit in Graphic Novels 2.0 to learn how to read and evaluate a graphic novel.
- Read several postmodern picturebooks along with the article by Goldstone (2004). Identify the postmodern features of these books and consider their appeal for older readers.

References

Albright, L. K. (2002). Bringing the Ice Maiden to life: Engaging adolescents in learning through picturebook read-alouds in content areas. *Journal of Adolescent and Adult Literacy, 45*(5), 418–428.

Burgess, M. (2015). *Enormous smallness*. DiGiacomo, K. (Illus.). New York: Enchanted Lion.

DiCamillo, K. (2003). *The tale of Despereaux*. Somerville, MA: Candlewick.

Eisner, W. (2008). *Graphic storytelling and visual narrative*. New York: W. W. Norton.

Foreman, M. (2015). *The tortoise and the soldier*. New York: Holt.

Goldstone, B. (2004). The postmodern picturebook. *Language Arts, 81*(3), 196–204.

Grace, L. (2009). *Where the mountain meets the moon*. New York: Little, Brown.

Nikolajeva, M., & Scott, S. (2006). *How picturebooks work*. Mahwah, NJ: Routledge.

Pagliaro, M. (2014). Is a picture worth a thousand words? Determining the criteria for graphic novels with literary merit. *English Journal, 103*(4), 31–45.

Rudiger, H. M. (2006). Graphic novels 101: Reading lessons. *Horn Book Magazine, 82*(2), 126–134.

Salas, L. P. (2011). Picture this. In L. P. Salas, *Bookspeak!* New York: Houghton Mifflin Harcourt.

Speigelman, A. (1991). *Maus II: A survivor's tale: And here my troubles began*. New York: Pantheon.

Recommended Picturebooks

Ages indicated refer to approximate concept and interest levels.

Board Books

Ajmera, Maya. ***Global Baby Bedtimes.*** Charlesbridge, 2015. Ages 0–3.

Ajmera, Maya, and Global Fund for Children. ***Global Babies***. Charlesbridge, 2007. Ages 0–2.

Brown, Margaret Wise. ***Goodnight Moon.*** Illus. Clement Hurd. Harper, 1947. Ages 0–3.

Deneux, Xavier. ***Homes (Touchthinklearn).*** Chronicle, 2016. Ages 2–4. (France)

Fox, Mem. ***Hello Baby!*** Illus. Steve Jenkins. Beach Lane, 2009. Ages 1–3.

Henderson, Kathy. ***Look at You! A Baby Body Book***. Illus. Paul Howard. Candlewick, 2007. Ages 2–4. (Interactive)

Light, Steve. ***Boats Go.*** Chronicle, 2015. Ages 0–2.

Lobel, Anita. ***Hello, Day!*** Greenwillow, 2008. Ages 2–4.

Oxenbury, Helen. ***I Can.*** Walker, 2000. Ages 0–3. Also ***I See; I Touch; I Hear*** (2000).

Smith, Monique. ***My Heart Fills with Happiness.*** Illus. Julie Flett. Orca, 2016. Ages 1–4.

Snyder, Betsy. ***I Can Dance.*** Chronicle, 2015. Ages 0–2.

Wildsmith, Brian. ***Brian Wildsmith's Animal Colors***. Star Bright, 2008. Ages 1–3.

Yoon, Salina. ***One, Two, Buckle My Shoe: A Counting Nursery Rhyme***. Robin Corey, 2011. Ages 1–3. Also ***Kaleidoscop***e (2012).

Young, Cybele.***Out of the Window.*** Groundwood, 2013. Ages 2–4. (Canada)

Ziefert, Harriet. ***Who Said Moo?*** Illus. Simms Taback. Blue Apple, 2010. Ages 1–3.

Interactive Books

Chwast, Seymour. ***Seymour Chwast Says—Get Dressed!*** Appleseed, 2012. Ages 2–6. (Flaps)

Fox, Mem. ***Ten Little Fingers and Ten Little Toes.*** Illus. Helen Oxenbury. Harcourt, 2008. Ages 3–5. (Australia)

Horacek, Petr. ***The Fly.*** Candlewick, 2015. Ages 3–6.

Kunhardt, Dorothy. ***Pat the Bunny.*** Golden, 2001 (1940). Ages 2–4.

Manceau, Edouard. ***Look!*** Owlkids, 2015. Ages 2–5.

Matheson, Christie. ***Tap the Magic Tree.*** Greenwillow, 2013. Ages 2–6. Also ***Touch the Brightest Star*** (2015).

Rotner, Shelley. ***Whose Eye Am I?*** Holiday House, 2016. Ages 4–8.

Tullet, Herve. ***Press Here.*** Handprint, 2010. Ages 3–6. Translated from French. Also ***Mix It Up!*** (2014).

Yee, Wong H. ***Who Likes Rain?*** Holt, 2007. Ages 3–6.

Engineered Books

Campbell, Rod. ***Dear Zoo: A Lift-the-Flap Book.*** Little Simon, 2007 (1982). Ages 1–4.

Carle, Eric. ***The Very Hungry Caterpillar.*** Philomel, 1968. Ages 4–6. (Die-cut pages)

Carter, David. ***White Noise.*** Little Simon, 2009. Ages 6–12. (Pop-up)

Dieudonné, Cléa. ***Megalopolis and the Visitor from Outer Space.*** Thames & Hudson, 2016. Translated from French. (Vertical folding panorama)

Graves, Keith. ***The Monsterator.*** Roaring Brook, 2014. Ages 5–9. (Split pages)

Gravett, Emily. ***The Rabbit Problem.*** Simon & Schuster, 2010. Ages 5–8. (Pop-up)

Hacohen, Dean. ***Who's Hungry?*** Illus. Sherry Scharschmidt. Candlewick, 2015. (Die-cut pages)

Idle, Molly S. ***Flora and the Peacocks.*** Chronicle, 2016. Ages 3–7. (Lift-the-flap)

Jenkins, Steve. ***Animals Upside Down: A Pull, Pop, Lift & Learn Book!*** Houghton Mifflin Harcourt, 2013. Ages 5–9. (Pop-up)

Polhemus, Coleman. ***The Crocodile Blues.*** Candlewick, 2007. Ages 3–7. (Lift-the-flap)

Sabuda, Robert. ***The Little Mermaid.*** Little Simon, 2013. Ages 9–12. (Pop-up)

Sabuda, Robert. ***The White House.*** Scholastic, 2016. Ages 7–10. (Pop-up)

Seeger, Laura Vaccaro. ***First the Egg.*** Roaring Brook, 2007. Ages 3–5. (Die-cut pages)

Seeger, Laura Vaccaro. ***I Used to Be Afraid.*** Roaring Brook, 2015. Ages 3–6. (Die-cut pages)

Teckentrup, Britta. ***Tree: A Peek-Through Picture Book.*** Doubleday, 2015. Ages 3–6. (Die-cut pages) (Germany)

Walsh, Melanie. ***Living with Mom and Living with Dad.*** Candlewick, 2012. Ages 2–6. (Lift-the-flap)

Wordless Books

Becker, Aaron. ***Journey.*** Candlewick, 2013. Ages 2–6. Also ***Quest*** (2014) and ***Return*** (2016).

Boyd, Lizi. ***Inside Outside.*** Chronicle, 2013. Ages 2–6. Also ***Flashlight*** (2014).

Cole, Henry. ***Spot, the Cat.*** Little Simon, 2016. Ages 3–8.

Colon, Raul. ***Draw!*** Simon & Schuster, 2014. Ages 4–8.

Devernay, Laetitia. ***The Conductor.*** Chronicle, 2011. Ages 5–9. (France)

Frazee, Marla. ***The Farmer and the Clown.*** Beach Lane, 2014. Ages 3–6.

Geisert, Arthur. ***Thunderstorm.*** Enchanted Lion, 2013. Ages 4–8.

Guojing. ***The Only Child.*** Schwartz & Wade, 2015. Ages 5–12. (China)

Idle, Molly. ***Flora and the Flamingo.*** Chronicle, 2013. Ages 3–6. Also ***Flora and the Penguin*** (2014).

Judge, Lita. ***Red Sled.*** Atheneum, 2011. Ages 3–7.

Kuhlmann, Torben. ***Moletown.*** Northsouth, 2015. Ages 4–8. (Germany)

Lawson, Jon. ***Sidewalk Flowers.*** Groundwood, 2016. Ages 4–7. (Canada)

Lee, Suzy. ***Wave.*** Chronicle, 2008. Ages 5–8. Also ***Shadow*** (2010) and ***Mirror*** (2010). (Korea)

Lehman, Barbara. ***The Secret Box.*** Houghton Mifflin, 2011. Ages 4–8. Also ***The Red Book*** (2004).

McPhail, David. ***No!*** Roaring Brook, 2009. Ages 4–8.

Pinkney, Jerry. ***The Lion & the Mouse.*** Little, Brown, 2009. Ages 3–6.

Raschka, Chris. ***A Ball for Daisy.*** Schwartz & Wade, 2011. Ages 5–8.

Staake, Bob. ***Bluebird.*** Schwartz & Wade, 2013. Ages 6–10.

Tolman, Marije and Ronald. ***The Tree House.*** Lemniscaat, 2010. Ages 4–8. (Netherlands). Also ***The Island*** (2012).

Wiesner, David. ***Mr. Wuffles!*** Clarion, 2013. Ages 4–8. Also ***Flotsam*** (2006) and ***Tuesday*** (1991).

Yum, Hyewon. ***Last Night.*** Farrar, 2008. Ages 3–6.

Alphabet Books

Caldicott, Chris. ***World Food Alphabet.*** Frances Lincoln, 2015. Ages 5–9.

Cooper, Elisha. ***8, An Animal Alphabet.*** Orchard, 2015. Ages 4–10.

Isol. ***Daytime Visions: An Alphabet.*** Enchanted Lion, 2016. Ages 3–8. (Argentina)

Jay, Alison. ***ABC: A Child's First Alphabet Book.*** Dutton, 2003. Ages 4–7.

Jeffers, Oliver. ***Once upon an Alphabet.*** Philomel, 2014. Ages 6–10.

Johnson, Stephen. ***Alphabet School.*** Simon & Schuster, 2015. Ages 4–8.

Krans, Kim. ***ABC Dream.*** Random House, 2016. Ages 5–8.

Lobel, Anita. ***Playful Pigs from A to Z.*** Knopf, 2015. Ages 3–6.

Martin, Bill, and John Archambault. ***Chicka Chicka Boom Boom.*** Illus. Lois Ehlert. Simon & Schuster, 1989. Ages 3–6.

McGuirk, Leslie. ***If Rocks Could Sing: A Discovered Alphabet.*** Tricycle, 2011. Ages 4–8.

Sierra, Judy. ***The Sleepy Little Alphabet.*** Illus. Melissa Sweet. Knopf, 2009. Ages 3–6.

Viano, Hannah. ***B Is for Bear: A Natural Alphabet.*** Little Bigfoot, 2015. Ages 3–8.

Woop Studios. ***A Zeal of Zebras: An Alphabet of Collective Nouns.*** Chronicle, 2011. Ages 5–10.

Counting Books

Alakija, Polly. ***Counting Chickens.*** Frances Lincoln, 2014. Ages 2–5. (Nigeria)

Browne, Anthony. ***One Gorilla: A Counting Book.*** Candlewick, 2012. Ages 3–8. (UK)

Cotton, Katie. ***Counting Lions: Portraits from the Wild.*** Illus. Stephen Walton. Candlewick, 2015. Ages 4–10. (Global)

Hines, Anna Grossnickle. ***1, 2, Buckle My Shoe.*** Harcourt, 2008. Ages 2–5.

Jay, Alison. ***123: A Child's First Counting Book.*** Dutton, 2007. Ages 4–7.

Martin, Bill, Jr. ***Ten Little Caterpillars.*** Illus. Lois Ehlert. Beach Lane, 2011. Ages 3–6.

McLimans, David. ***Gone Fishing: Ocean Life by the Numbers.*** Walker, 2008. Ages 6–9.

Medina, Juana. ***1 Big Salad.*** Viking, 2016. Ages 2–4.

Menotti, Andrea. ***How Many Jelly Beans***? Illus. Yancey Labat. Chronicle, 2012. Ages 4–8.

Morales, Yuyi. ***Just a Minute: A Trickster Tale and Counting Book.*** Chronicle, 2003. Ages 6–8. (Mexico)

Nagara, Innosanto. ***Counting on Community.*** Seven Stories, 2015. Ages 2–5.

Seeger, Laura Vaccaro. ***One Boy.*** Roaring Brook, 2008. Ages 3–8. (Die-cut windows)

Young, Cybele. ***Ten Birds.*** Kids Can Press, 2011. Ages 6–9. (Canada)

Concept Books

Ajmera, Maya. ***What We Wear: Dressing Up Around the World.*** Charlesbridge, 2012. (Global). Also ***Healthy Kids*** (2013).

Badescu, Ramona. ***Pomelo's Opposites.*** Illus. Benjamin Chaud. Enchanted Lion, 2013. Ages 4–6. Translated from French.

Bernhard, Durga. ***While You Are Sleeping: A Lift-the-Flap Book of Time Around the World.*** Charlesbridge, 2011. Ages 5–8. (Global)

Blexbolex. ***Seasons.*** Trans. Claudia Bedrick. Enchanted Lion, 2010. Ages 5–12. (France)

Boyd, Lizi. ***Big Bear Little Chair.*** Chronicle, 2015. Ages 3–7.

Coat, Janik. ***Hippopposites.*** Appleseed, 2012. Ages 2–5. Translated from French.

Coffelt, Nancy. ***Big, Bigger, Biggest.*** Holt, 2009. Ages 3–7.

Cottin, Menena. ***The Black Book of Colors.*** Illus. Rosana Faria. Trans. Elisa Amado. Groundwood, 2008. Ages 5–8. (Mexico)

Ehlert, Lois. ***Color Zoo.*** Lippincott, 1989. Ages 3–6.

Gravett, Emily. ***Orange Pear Apple Bear.*** Simon & Schuster, 2007. Ages 2–4. (UK)

Hutchins, Hazel. ***A Second Is a Hiccup: A Child's Book of Time.*** Illus. Kady M. Denton. Scholastic, 2007. Ages 3–7.

Konnecke, Ole. ***The Big Book of Words and Pictures***. Gecko Press, 2012. Ages 2–5. (Germany)

Konrad, Marla Stewart. ***Grand.*** Tundra, 2010. Ages 4–6. (Global)

Marnada, Mineko. ***Which Is Round? Which Is Bigger?*** Kids Can, 2013. Ages 4–6. (Japan)

Martins, Isabel, and Bernardo Carvalho. ***The World in a Second.*** Enchanted Lion, 2015. Ages 4–8. Translated from Portuguese.

Messner, Kate. ***Over and Under the Snow***. Illus. Christopher S. Neal. Chronicle, 2011. Ages 4–8.

Murray, Diana. ***City Shapes.*** Illus. Bryan Collier. Little, Brown and Company, 2016. Ages 3–6.

Na, Il Sung. ***The Opposite Zoo.*** Knopf, 2016. Ages 2–4. (Korea)

Ogburn, Jacqueline. ***Little Treasures: Endearments from Around the World.*** Houghton, 2011. Ages 4–8. (Global)

Onyefulu, Ifeoma. ***Deron Goes to Nursery School.*** Frances Lincoln, 2015. Ages 3–5. (Ghana)

Padmanabhan, Manjula. ***I Am Different! Can You Find Me?*** Charlesbridge, 2011. Ages 6–9. (India)

Sayre, April. ***Raindrops Roll***. Beach Lane, 2015. Ages 3–8.

Seeger, Laura Vaccaro. ***Green.*** Roaring Brook, 2012. Ages 3–7. Also ***Lemons Are Not Red*** (2004).

Shannon, George. ***One Family.*** Illus. Blanca Gomez. Ages 4–7. (Counting)

Springman, I. C. ***More.*** Illus. Brian Lee. Houghton, 2012. Ages 4–9.

Stangl, Katrin. ***Strong as a Bear.*** Enchanted Lion, 2016. Ages 2–5. Translated from German.

Steggall, Susan. ***Red Car, Red Bus.*** Frances Lincoln, 2014. Ages 2–5. (UK)

Thong, Roseanne. ***Green Is a Chile Pepper: A Book of Colors.*** Illus. John Parra. Chronicle, 2014. Ages 4–7.

Underwood, Deborah. ***The Loud Book.*** Houghton, 2011. Ages 4–8. Also ***The Quiet Book*** (2010).

Picture Storybooks

Note: The picture storybooks included here highlight the experiences of young children. Other picturebooks relevant to a specific genre and older audiences are included in the genre chapters.

Agee, Jon. ***Nothing.*** Hyperion, 2007. Ages 4–8. Also ***Terrific*** (2005). Ages 5–8.

Agee, Jon. ***It's Only Stanley.*** Dial, 2015. Ages 6–8.

Ahlberg, Allan. ***The Pencil.*** Illus. Bruce Ingman. Candlewick, 2008. Ages 4–7. (UK)

Antony, Steve. ***Green Lizards vs. Red Rectangles.*** Scholastic, 2015. Ages 3–5.

Bagley, Jessixa. ***Boats for Papa.*** Roaring Brook, 2015. Ages 4–8.

Barasch, Lynne. ***First Come the Zebra.*** Lee & Low, 2009. Ages 5–9. (Kenya)

Barnett, Mac. ***Extra Yarn.*** Illus. Jon Klassen. Balzer, 2012. Ages 5–9.

Barnett, Mac. ***Sam & Dave Dig a Hole.*** Illus. Jon Klassen. Candlewick, 2014. Ages 4–8.

Bean, Jonathan. ***At Night.*** Farrar, 2007. Ages 5–7.

Black, Michael Ian. ***Chicken Cheeks.*** Illus. Kevin Hawkes. Simon & Schuster, 2009. Ages 4–8.

Bley, Anette. ***A Friend***. Translated from German. Kane/Miller, 2009. Ages 4–10.

Brown, Peter. ***Mr. Tiger Goes Wild.*** Little, Brown, 2013. Ages 3–7. Also ***Children Make Terrible Pets*** (2010).

Burningham, John. ***Edwardo: The Horriblest Boy in the Whole Wide World.*** Knopf, 2007. Ages 4–8. (UK)

Burningham, John. ***The Way to the Zoo.*** Candlewick, 2014. Ages 2–5. (UK)

Carle, Eric. ***The Grouchy Ladybug.*** Crowell, 1971. Ages 5–7. Also ***The Very Busy Spider*** (1984).

Carle, Eric. ***Friends.*** Philomel, 2013. Ages 3–6.

Charlip, Remy. ***A Perfect Day.*** Greenwillow, 2007. Ages 4–7.

Chen, Zhiyuan. ***Artie and Julie.*** Heryin, 2008. Ages 6–9. (Taiwan)

Coffelt, Nancy. ***Fred Stays with Me!*** Illus. Tricia Tusa. Little, Brown, 2007. Ages 5–7.

Cole, Brock. ***Good Enough to Eat.*** Farrar, 2007. Ages 4–8.

Cole, Henry. ***On Meadowview Street.*** Greenwillow, 2007. Ages 5–8.

Cronin, Doreen. ***Click, Clack, Moo: Cows That Type.*** Illus. Betsy Lewin. Simon & Schuster, 2000. Ages 4–7.

Cronin, Doreen. ***Diary of a Fly.*** Illus. Harry Bliss. HarperCollins, 2007. Ages 3–8.

Cronin, Doreen. ***Smick!*** Illus. Juana Medina. Viking, 2015. Ages 2–8.

Cunnane, Kelly. ***For You Are a Kenyan Child.*** Illus. Ana Juan. Atheneum, 2006. Ages 5–8. (Kenya).

Daywalt, Drew. ***The Day the Crayons Quit.*** Illus. Oliver Jeffers. Philomel, 2013. Ages 3–7.

Deacon, Alexis. ***I Am Henry Finch.*** Illus. Viviane Schwarz. Candlewick, 2015. Ages 6–8. (UK)

de la Peña, Matt. ***Last Stop on Market Street***. Illus. Christian Robinson. Putnam's, 2015. Ages 4–7.

DiCamillo, Kate. ***Louise, the Adventures of a Chicken.*** Illus. Harry Bliss. HarperCollins, 2008. Ages 5–8.

Dillon, Leo, and Diane Dillon. ***Jazz on a Saturday Night.*** Scholastic, 2007. Ages 5–9.

Dodds, Dayle. ***The Prince Won't Go to Bed!*** Illus. Krysten Brooker. Farrar, 2007. Ages 3–6.

Dubuc, Marianne. ***In Front of My House.*** Translated from French. Kids Can, 2010. Ages 6–9. (Canada)

Dunrea, Olivier. ***Gemma and Gus***. Houghton, 2015. Ages 3–5. Also ***Gossie*** (2002).

Falconer, Ian. ***Olivia and the Fairy Princess.*** Atheneum, 2012. Ages 4–7. Also ***Olivia*** (2000).

Foreman, Jack. ***Say Hello***. Illus. Michael Foreman. Candlewick, 2008. (UK)

Frazee, Marla. ***A Couple of Boys Have the Best Week Ever.*** Harcourt, 2008. Ages 5–8.

Freeman, Don. ***A Pocket for Corduroy.*** Viking, 1978. Ages 3–5.

Fromental, Jean-Luc. ***Oops!*** Illus. Joelle Jolivet. Translated from French. Abrams, 2010. Ages 5–10. (France)

Gág, Wanda. ***Millions of Cats.*** Coward-McCann, 1928. Ages 4–6.

Graham, Bob. ***The Silver Button.*** Candlewick, 2013. Ages 4–6. (Australia)

Gray, Kes. ***Frog on a Log?*** Illus. Jim Field. Scholastic, 2015. Ages 3–7.

Grey, Mini. ***Traction Man Meets Turbodog.*** Knopf, 2008. Ages 5–7. (UK)

Hall, Michael. ***Red: A Crayon's Story.*** HarperCollins, 2015. Ages 4–8.

Hamilton, Kersten. ***Red Truck.*** Illus. Valeria Petrone. Viking, 2008. Ages 3–5.

Harper, Charise. ***When Randolph Turned Rotten.*** Knopf, 2007. Ages 3–7.

Harrington, Janice. ***The Chicken-Chasing Queen of Lamar County.*** Illus. Shelley Jackson. Farrar, 2007. Ages 5–7.

Harris, Robie. ***Maybe a Bear Ate It!*** Illus. Michael Emberley. Orchard, 2008. Ages 3–8.

Henkes, Kevin. ***Lilly's Big Day.*** Greenwillow, 2006. Ages 4–7. Also ***Lilly's Purple Plastic Purse*** (1996).

Henkes, Kevin. ***Waiting.*** Greenwillow, 2015. Ages 3–6. Also ***Kitten's First Full Moon*** (2004).

Hest, Amy. ***The Dog Who Belonged to No One.*** Illus. Amy Bates. Abrams, 2008. Ages 3–6.

Isadora, Rachel. ***Yo, Jo!*** Harcourt, 2007. Ages 4–7.

Jeffers, Oliver. ***The Incredible Book Eating Boy.*** Philomel, 2007. Ages 4–8.

Jenkins, Emily. ***What Happens on Wednesdays.*** Illus. Lauren Castillo. Farrar, 2007. Ages 4–6.

Jin, Susie L. ***Mine!*** Simon & Schuster, 2016. Ages 2–5.

Juster, Norton. ***The Hello, Goodbye Window.*** Illus. Chris Raschka. Hyperion, 2005. Ages 4–7.

Kajikawa, Kimiko. ***Tsunami!*** Illus. Ed Young. Philomel, 2009. Ages 4–7. (Japan)

Kimmel, Elizabeth. ***The Top Job.*** Illus. Robert Neubecker. Dutton, 2007. Ages 5–8.

Klassen, Jon. ***I Want My Hat Back***. Candlewick, 2011. Ages 6–9. Also ***This Is Not My Hat*** (2012) and ***We Found a Hat*** (2016). (Canada).

Kohara, Kazuno. ***Ghosts in the House!*** Roaring Brook, 2008. Ages 3–7.

Kolar, Bob. ***Big Kicks.*** Candlewick, 2008. Ages 4–8.

Krauss, Ruth. ***The Growing Story.*** Illus. Helen Oxenbury. HarperCollins, 2007. Ages 3–5.

Larochelle, David. ***The End.*** Illus. Richard Egielski. Scholastic, 2007. Ages 4–8.

Larsen, Andrew. ***See You Next Year.*** Illus. Todd Stewart. Owlkids Books, 2015. Ages 3–6.

Lee, Hyun Young. ***Something for School***. Kane/Miller, 2008. Ages 4–8. Translated from Korean.

Lipan, Sabine. ***Mom, There's a Bear at the Door***. Illus. Manuela Olten. Eerdmans, 2016. Ages 4–7. Translated from German.

Lipp, Frederick. ***Running Shoes.*** Illus. Jason Gaillard. Charlesbridge, 2008. Ages 6–9. (Cambodia)

Madison, Alan. ***Velma Gratch and the Way Cool Butterfly.*** Illus. Kevin Hawkes. Random, 2007. Ages 5–8.

Mahy, Margaret. ***Bubble Trouble.*** Illus. Polly Dunbar. Clarion, 2009. Ages 4–8. (New Zealand)

Manning, Maurice. ***Laundry Day***. Clarion, 2012. Ages 5–9.

McCarty, Peter. ***Chloe.*** Balzer + Bray, 2012. Ages 3–6.

Nakagawa, Chihiro. ***Who Made This Cake?*** Illus. Junji Koyose. Front Street, 2008. Ages 3–5. (Japan)

Nevius, Carol. ***Baseball Hour.*** Illus. Bill Thomson. Cavendish, 2008. Ages 7–9.

O'Malley, Kevin. ***Gimme Cracked Corn & I Will Share.*** Walker, 2007. Ages 7–9.

Park, Linda Sue. ***Xander's Panda Party.*** Illus. Matt Phelan. Clarion, 2013. Ages 3–5.

Parker, Danny. ***Parachute.*** Illus. Matt Ottley. Eerdmans, 2016. Ages 4–8. (Australia)

Pennypacker, Sara. ***Pierre in Love.*** Illus. Petra Mathers. Scholastic, 2007. Ages 4–7.

Perkins, Lynne Rae. ***Pictures from Our Vacation.*** Greenwillow, 2007. Ages 5–7.

Pizzoli, Greg. ***The Watermelon Seed.*** Disney/Hyperion, 2013. Ages 3–5.

Rathmann, Peggy. ***Officer Buckle and Gloria.*** Putnam, 1995. Ages 6–8.

Rex, Adam. ***School's First Day of School.*** Illus. Christian Robinson. Roaring Brook, 2016. Ages 5–7.

Reynolds, Aaron. ***Creepy Carrots!*** Illus. Peter Brown. Simon & Schuster, 2012. Ages 4–7.

Richardson, Justin, & Peter Parnell. ***And Tango Makes Three.*** Illus. Henry Cole. Simon & Schuster, 2005. Ages 5–8.

Roberton, Fiona. ***A Tale of Two Beasts.*** Hodder, 2015. Ages 5-8. (UK)

Rocco, John. ***Blackout.*** Hyperion, 2012. Ages 5–8. Also ***Blizzard*** (2014).

Rohmann, Eric. ***My Friend Rabbit.*** Roaring Brook, 2002. Ages 4–8.

Santat, Dan. ***The Adventures of Beekle.*** Little, Brown, 2014. Ages 3–7.

Santat, Dan. ***Are We There Yet?*** Little, Brown, 2016. Ages 5–8.

Scanlon, Elizabeth. ***All the World.*** Illus. Marla Frazee. Beach Lane, 2009. Ages 3–6.

Schwartz, Amy. ***Starring Miss Darlene.*** Roaring Brook, 2007. Ages 5–7.

Scieszka, Jon. ***Cowboy & Octopus.*** Illus. Lane Smith. Viking, 2007. Ages 5–10.

Scieszka, Jon. ***Welcome to Trucktown!*** Illus. David Shannon, Loren Long, David Gordon. Simon & Schuster, 2008. Ages 3–7. Also ***Robot Zot!*** (2009).

Seeger, Laura V. ***What If?*** Roaring Brook, 2008. Ages 5–9.

Sendak, Maurice. ***Where the Wild Things Are.*** Harper, 1963. Ages 5–7.

Shannon, David. ***No, David!*** Scholastic, 1998. Ages 2–5.

Shannon, David. ***Duck on a Tractor.*** Scholastic, 2016. Ages 4–8.

Sheth, Kashmira. ***Tiger in My Soup.*** Illus. Jeffrey Ebbeler. Peachtree, 2013. Ages 4–7.

Shulevitz, Uri. ***Dusk.*** Farrar, 2013. Ages 4–8.

Smith, Lane. ***It's a Book.*** Roaring Brook, 2010. Ages 8–11. Also ***Grandpa Green*** (2011).

Snicket, Lemony. ***The Dark.*** Illus. Jon Klassen. Little, Brown, 2013. Ages 3–7.

Stead, Philip. ***A Sick Day for Amos McGee.*** Illus. Erin Stead. Roaring Brook, 2010. Ages 5–8.

Stead, Philip. ***A Home for Bird.*** Roaring Brook, 2012. Ages 3–8.

Stead, Philip. ***Lenny & Lucy.*** Illus. Erin E. Stead. Roaring Brook, 2015. Ages 4–8.

Stein, David. ***Interrupting Chicken.*** Putnam, 2010. Ages 3–7.

Teckentrup, Britta. ***Grumpy Cat.*** Boxer, 2008. Ages 2–5. (Germany)

Thompson, Lauren. ***Polar Bear Morning.*** Illus. Stephen Savage. Scholastic, 2013. Ages 2–5.

Viva, Frank. ***Along a Long Road.*** Little, Brown, 2011. Ages 5–8. (Canada)

Wells, Rosemary. ***Yoko Writes Her Name.*** Hyperion, 2008. Ages 3–7.

White, Dianne. ***Blue on Blue.*** Illus. Beth Krommes. Beach Lane, 2014. Ages 2–6.

Wiesner, David. ***Art & Max.*** Clarion, 2010. Ages 4–10.

Willems, Mo. ***Don't Let the Pigeon Drive the Bus!*** Hyperion, 2003. Ages 4–7.

Willems, Mo. ***Knuffle Bunny: A Cautionary Tale.*** Hyperion, 2004. Ages 3–5.

Willems, Mo. ***That Is NOT a Good Idea!*** Balzer + Bray, 2013. Ages 3–8.

Williams, Karen Lynn, and Khadra Mohammed. ***My Name Is Sangoel.*** Illus. Catherine Stock. Eerdmans, 2009. Ages 7–9. (Sudan/U.S.)

Yolen, Jane. ***What to Do With a Box.*** Illus. Chris Sheban. Creative Editions, 2016. Ages 3–8.

Yoon, Salina. ***Penguin and Pinecone.*** Walker, 2012. Ages 3–7.

Zagarenski, Pamela. ***The Whisper.*** Houghton Mifflin Harcourt, 2015. Ages 4–8.

Predictable Books and Word Play

Bernstrom, Daniel. ***One Day in the Eucalyptus, Eucalyptus Tree.*** Illus. Brenden Wenzel. HarperCollins, 2016. Ages 3–8.

Brown, Monica. ***Maya's Blanket/La manta de Maya.*** Illus. David Diaz. Children's Book Press, 2015. Ages 5–9. Bilingual.

Bunting, Eve. ***Hurry! Hurry!*** Illus. Jeff Mack. Harcourt, 2007. Ages 3–6.

Escoffier, Michael. ***Where's the Baboon?*** Illus. Kris DiGiacomo. Enchanted Lion, 2015. Ages 5–12. Translated from French.

Fleming, Denise. ***The Cow Who Clucked.*** Holt, 2006. Ages 3–6.

Fleming, Denise. ***Sleepy, Oh So Sleepy.*** Holt, 2010. Ages 2–5.

Goetz, Steve. ***Old MacDonald Had a Truck.*** Illus. Eda Kaban. Ages 3–6.

Gravett, Emily. ***Monkey and Me.*** Simon & Schuster, 2008. Ages 4–6. (UK)

Mack, Jeff. ***Look!*** Philomel, 2015. Ages 2–5.

MacLennan, Cathy. ***Chicky Chicky Chook Chook.*** Boxer, 2007. Ages 3–6. (Zimbabwe)

Martin, Bill, Jr. ***Brown Bear, Brown Bear, What Do You See?*** Illus. Eric Carle. Holt, 1983. Ages 3–6.

Meisel, Paul. ***See Me Run***. Holiday, 2011. Ages 5–7. I Like to Read series.

Patricelli, Leslie. ***Higher! Higher!*** Candlewick, 2009. Ages 3–7.

Paul, Alison. ***The Plan.*** Illus. Barbara Lehman. Houghton Mifflin Harcourt, 2015. Ages 4–8.

Rohmann, Eric. ***A Kitten Tale.*** Knopf, 2008. Ages 2–4.

Ryan, Candace. ***Moo Hoo.*** Illus. Mike Lowery. Walker, 2012. Ages 4–8.

Smith, Lane. ***There Is A Tribe of Kids.*** Roaring Brook, 2016. Ages 3–7.

Swanson, Susan. ***The House in the Night.*** Illus. Beth Krommes. Houghton, 2008. Ages 3–7.

Wickenburg, Susan. ***Hey Mr. Choo-Choo, Where Are You Going?*** Illus. Yumi Heo. Putnam, 2008. Ages 3–6.

Wild, Margaret. ***Piglet and Papa.*** Illus. Stephen M. King. Abrams, 2007. Ages 3–5. (Australia)

Wood, Audrey. ***The Napping House.*** Illus. Don Wood. Harcourt, 1984. Ages 3–7.

Easy-to-Read Books (Series books)

Adler, David A. ***Don't Throw It to Mo!*** Illus. Sam Ricks. Penguin, 2015. Ages 4–7.

Arnold, Tedd. ***Prince Fly Guy.*** Cartwheel, 2015. Ages 5–8.

Bang-Campbell, Monika. ***Little Rat Makes Music.*** Illus. Molly Bang. Harcourt, 2007. Ages 5–7.

Brown, Marc T. ***Arthur Turns Green.*** Little Brown, 2011. Ages 4–8.

Cammuso, Frank, and Jay Lynch. ***Otto's Orange Day.*** Illus. Frank Cammuso. TOON, 2008. Graphic novel. Ages 5–7.

Cowley, Joy. ***Snake and Lizard.*** Illus. Gavin Bishop. Kane/Miller, 2008. Ages 6–9. (New Zealand)

Davis, Eleanor. ***Stinky: A Toon Book.*** Toon, 2008. Ages 5–8.

DiCamillo, Kate, and Alison McGhee. ***Bink & Gollie.*** Illus. Tony Fucile. Candlewick, 2010. Ages 5–8.

Dunrea, Olivier. ***Gossie & Gertie.*** Houghton Mifflin Harcourt, 2014. Ages 5–8.

Feldman, Eve. ***Billy & Milly, Short & Silly.*** Illus. Tuesday Mourning. Putnam, 2009. Ages 5–7.

Fenske, Jonathan. ***A Pig, a Fox, and a Box.*** Penguin, 2015. Ages 5–8.

Greene, Stephanie. ***Princess Posey and the First Grade Parade.*** Illus. Stephanie Sisson. Putnam, 2010. Ages 6–8.

Harper, Jessica. ***Uh-Oh, Cleo.*** Illus. Jon Berkeley. Putnam, 2008. Ages 5–8.

Hayes, Geoffrey. ***Benny and Penny in the Big No-No!*** Toon, 2009. Graphic novel. Ages 5–7.

Henkes, Kevin. ***Penny and Her Marble.*** Greenwillow, 2013. Ages 5–8.

Hoberman, Mary Ann. ***Very Short Fables to Read Together.*** Illus. Michael Emberley. Little, Brown, 2010. Ages 5–7.

Kang, Anna. ***You Are (Not) Small.*** Illus. Christopher Weyant. Two Lions, 2014. Ages 4–8.

Kvasnosky, Laura McGee. ***Zelda and Ivy: The Runaways.*** Candlewick, 2006. Ages 5–8.

Lin, Grace. ***Ling & Ting: Not Exactly the Same!*** Little Brown, 2010. Ages 5–8.

Lobel, Arnold. ***Frog and Toad Together.*** HarperColllins, 1972. Ages 5–8. Also ***Owl at Home*** (1975).

McMullan, Kate. ***Pearl and Wagner: One Funny Day.*** Dial, 2009. Ages 5–8.

Rylant, Cynthia. ***Henry and Mudge and the Great Grandpas.*** Illus. Suçie Stevenson. Simon & Schuster, 2005. Ages 5–7.

Rylant, Cynthia. ***Mr. Putter & Tabby Turn the Page.*** Illus. Arthur Howard. Houghton Mifflin Harcourt, 2014. Ages 6–8.

Schaefer, Carole L. ***Monkey and Elephant Go Gadding.*** Illus. Galia Bernstein. Candlewick, 2014. Ages 6–8.

Schneider, Josh. ***Tales for Very Picky Eaters.*** Clarion, 2011. Ages 5–9.

Seeger, Laura. ***Dog and Bear: Two Friends, Three Stories.*** Roaring Brook, 2007. Ages 4–7.

Smith, Jeff. ***Little Mouse Gets Ready.*** Toon, 2009. Graphic novel. Ages 4–7.

Willems, Mo. ***Waiting Is Not Easy!*** Hyperion, 2014. Ages 6–8.

Yee, Wong Herbert. ***Mouse and Mole: Fine Feathered Friends.*** Houghton, 2009. Ages 5–8.

Transitional Books (Series books)

Alvarez, Julía. ***How Tia Lola Ended Up Starting Over.*** Knopf, 2011. Ages 8–11.

Atinuke. ***Anna Hibiscus.*** Illus. Lauren Tobia. Kane Miller, 2007. Ages 5–8. (Nigeria)

Atinuke. ***The No. 1 Car Spotter.*** Illus. Warwick Cadwell. Kane Miller, 2010. Ages 7–10. (Nigeria)

Barrows, Anne. ***Ivy + Bean Take the Case.*** Illus. Sophie Blackall. Chronicle, 2013. Ages 6–9.

Benton, Jim. ***Franny K. Stein, Mad Scientist: Lunch Walks among Us.*** Simon & Schuster, 2003. Ages 6–9.

Brown, Monica. ***Lola Levine Is Not Mean!*** Illus. Angela Dominguez. Little, Brown, 2015. Ages 6–10.

Cronin, Doreen. ***The Chicken Squad: The First Misadventure.*** Illus. Kevin Cornell. Atheneum, 2014. Ages 6–9.

DiCamillo, Kate. ***Mercy Watson Goes for a Ride.*** Illus. Chris Van Dusen. Candlewick, 2006. Ages 6–9.

English, Karen. ***Nikki & Deja: Birthday Blues***. Illus. Laura Freeman. Clarion, 2009. Ages 6–10.

English, Karen. ***Skateboard Party.*** Illus. Laura Freeman-Hines. Houghton Mifflin Harcourt, 2014. Ages 6–10.

Fine, Anne. ***Jamie and Angus Together.*** Illus. Penny Dale. Candlewick, 2007. Ages 5–7. (UK)

Grimes, Nikki. ***Make Way for Dyamonde Daniel.*** Illus. R. Gregory Christie. Putnam, 2009. Ages 6–9.

Hale, Shannon. ***The Princess in Black.*** Illus. LeUyen Pham. Candlewick, 2014. Ages 5–8.

Harper, Charise. ***Just Grace.*** Houghton, 2007. Ages 7–9.

Hartnett, Sonya. ***Sadie and Ratz.*** Illus. Ann James. Candlewick, 2008. Ages 5–8.

Kerrin, Jessica. ***Martin Bridge in High Gear!*** Illus. Joseph Kelly. Kids Can, 2008. Ages 7–10.

McKay, Hilary. ***Lulu and the Dog from the Sea.*** Illus. Priscilla Lamont. Whitman, 2011. Ages 7–9.

Murphy, Sally. ***Pearl Verses the World***. Illus. Heather Potter. Candlewick, 2011. Ages 8–12. (Australia)

Roberts, Ken. ***Thumb and the Bad Guys.*** Illus. Leanne Franson. Groundwood, 2009. Ages 8–11. Series. (Canada)

Scieszka, Jon. ***Marco? Polo!*** Illus. Adam McCauley. Viking, 2006. Ages 7–10. Time Warp Trio series.

Sobol, Donald J. ***Encyclopedia Brown: Boy Detective.*** Illus. Leonard Shortall. Bantam, 1985. Ages 7–10.

Sternberg, Julie. ***Like Pickle Juice on a Cookie***. Amulet, 2011. Ages 7–10.

Warner, Sally. ***EllRay Jakes Is Not a Chicken!*** Illus. Jamie Harper. Viking, 2011. Ages 7–11.

Picture Books for Older Readers

Cole, Tom. ***Wall.*** Candlewick, 2014. Ages 7–10. (Germany)

Davies, Nicola. ***The Promise.*** Illus. Laura Carlin. Candlewick, 2014. Ages 7–10. (UK)

de la Peña, Matt. ***A Nation's Hope: The Story of Boxing Legend Joe Louis***. Illus. Kadir Nelson. Dial, 2011. Ages 8–11. (Germany/U.S.)

Greder, Armin. ***The Island***. Allen & Unwin, 2008. Ages 9–12. (Australia)

Johnson, D. B. ***Magritte's Marvelous Hat: A Picture Book.*** Houghton, 2012. Ages 7–10.

Kuhlmann, Torben. ***Lindbergh: The Tale of a Flying Mouse.*** North-South, 2014. Ages 8–11. Translated from German.

Lanthier, Jennifer. ***The Stamp Collector***. Illus. Francois Thisdale. Fitzhenry, 2013. Ages 9–12. (China)

Lewis, J. Patrick. ***And the Soldiers Sang.*** Illus. Gary Kelley. Creative, 2011. Ages 9–12.

Milway, Katie Smith. ***One Hen: How One Small Loan Made a Big Difference.*** Illus. Eugenie Fernandez. Kids Can, 2008. Ages 9–12. (Ghana)

Reibstein, Mark. ***Wabi Sabi***. Illus. Ed Young. Little, Brown, 2008. Ages 7–11. (Japan)

Rumford, James. ***Silent Music: A Story of Baghdad***. Roaring Brook, 2008. Ages 6–10. (Iraq)

Selznick, Brian. ***The Invention of Hugo Cabret.*** Scholastic, 2007. Ages 9–12. Also **Wonderstruck** (2011) and ***The Marvels*** (2015).

Sís, Peter. ***The Wall: Growing Up Behind the Iron Curtain.*** Farrar, 2007. Ages 9–14. (Czechoslovakia)

Sís, Peter. ***The Pilot and the Little Prince: The Life of Antoine de Saint-Exupery.*** Farrar, 2014. Ages 7–12. (France)

Tan, Shaun. ***Rules of Summer.*** Arthur A. Levine Books, 2014. Ages 7–12. (Australia)

Thurber, James. ***The Tiger Who Would Be King***. Illus. JooHee Yoon. Enchanted Lion, 2015. Ages 9–12.

Van Allsburg, Chris. ***Jumanji.*** Houghton, 1981. Ages 6–10. Also ***The Polar Express*** (1995).

Watt, Melanie. ***Bug in a Vacuum.*** Tundra Books, 2015. Ages 6–10.

Postmodern Picture Books

Barnett, Mac. ***Chloe and the Lion.*** Illus. Adam Rex. Hyperion, 2012. Ages 6–9.

Browne, Anthony. ***Voices in the Park.*** DK Ink, 1998. Ages 6–10. (UK)

Byrne, Richard. ***This Book Just Ate My Dog!*** Henry Holt, 2014. Ages 4–7.

Chin, Jason. ***Redwoods***. Flash Point, 2009. Ages 6–9.

Fox, Diane. ***The Cat, the Dog, Little Red, the Exploding Eggs, the Wolf, and Grandma.*** Illus. Christyan Fox. Scholastic, 2014. Ages 5–9.

Gerstein, Mordicai. ***A Book***. Roaring Brook, 2009. Ages 6–9.

Gravett, Emily. ***Wolves.*** Simon & Schuster, 2006. Ages 6–9. (UK)

Ji, Zhaochua. ***No! That's Wrong!*** Kane/Miller, 2008. Ages 6–8. Translated from Chinese.

Lehrhaupt, Adam. ***Warning: Do Not Open This Book!*** Illus. Matthew Forsythe. Simon & Schuster, 2013. Ages 3–7.

Macaulay, David. ***Black and White.*** Houghton, 1990. Ages 7–10.

Rayner, Catherine. ***Ernest, the Moose Who Doesn't Fit.*** Farrar Straus Giroux, 2009. Ages 2–6.

Scieszka, Jon. ***The Stinky Cheese Man & Other Fairly Stupid Tales***. Illus. Lane Smith. Viking, 1992. Ages 7–10. Also ***The True Story of the 3 Little Pigs*** (1989).

Scieszka, Jon, and Mac Barnett. ***Battle Bunny.*** Illus. Matthew Myers. Simon & Schuster, 2013. Ages 6–10.

Watt, Melanie. ***Chester.*** Kids Can, 2007. Ages 5–8. (Canada)

Wiesner, David. ***The Three Pigs.*** Clarion, 2001. Ages 6–12.

Graphic Novels

Azuma, Kiyohiko. ***Yotsuba&!. 1.*** Yen Press, 2009. Ages 8–11.

Bell, Cece. ***El Deafo.*** Amulet, 2014. Ages 8–12.

Brown, Don. ***Drowned City: Hurricane Katrina & New Orleans.*** Houghton Mifflin Harcourt, 2015. Ages 11–15.

Cammuso, Frank. ***Knights of the Lunch Table, Book 1.*** Scholastic, 2008. Ages 9–13.

Dembiki, Matt, editor. ***Trickster: Native American Tales.*** Fulcrum, 2010. Ages 10–14.

Gaiman, Neil. ***Coraline: Graphic Novel.*** Illus. P. Craig Russell. HarperCollins, 2008. Ages 9–12.

Gownley, Jimmy. ***Amelia Rules! What Makes You Happy.*** ibooks, 2004. Ages 8–12.

Hale, Nathan. ***The Underground Abductor.*** Amulet, 2015. Ages 8–13.

Hatke, Ben. ***Zita the Spacegirl: Far from Home***. First Second, 2010. Ages 9–12.

Hayes, Geoffrey. ***Benny and Penny: In Just Pretend.*** TOON, 2008. Ages 4–6.

Holm, Jennifer. ***Babymouse: Bad Babysitter.*** Illus. Matthew Holm. Random, 2015. Ages 8–10.

Holm, Jennifer L. ***Sunny Side Up.*** Illus. Matthew Holm. Graphix, 2015. Ages 9–11.

Kibuishi, Kazu, editor. ***Explorer: The Lost Islands.*** Amulet, 2013. Ages 7–12.

Lat. ***Kampung Boy.*** First Second, 2006. Ages 9–14. Autobiography. (Malaysia; Muslim)

Liniers. ***The Big Wet Balloon.*** TOON, 2013. Ages 4–7. (Argentina)

Liniers. ***Written and Drawn by Henrietta.*** TOON, 2015. Ages 7–9. (Argentina)

Morse, Scott. ***Magic Pickle.*** Scholastic, 2008. Ages 7–9.

Neri, Greg. ***Yummy: The Last Days of a Southside Shorty.*** Illus. Randy DuBurke. Lee & Low, 2010. Ages 10–14.

O'Malley, Kevin. ***Captain Raptor and the Space Pirates.*** Illus. Patrick O'Brien. Walker, 2007. Ages 5–9.

Phelan, Matt. ***The Storm in the Barn.*** Candlewick, 2009. Ages 11–14.

Siegel, Siena. ***To Dance: A Ballerina's Graphic Novel.*** Illus. Mark Siegel. Simon & Schuster, 2006. Ages 10–14.

Smith, Jeff. ***Bone: Out from Boneville.*** Graphix, 2015. Ages 9–14.

Steinberg, D. J. ***Sound Off!*** Illus. Brian Smith. Grosset, 2008. Ages 8–10.

Tamaki, Mariko. ***This One Summer.*** Illus. Jillian Tamaki. First Second, 2014. Ages 12–16. (Canada)

Tan, Shaun. ***The Arrival.*** Scholastic, 2007. Ages 12–18. Wordless. (Australia)

Telgemeier, Raina. ***Sisters.*** Graphix, 2014. Ages 10–15.

Varon, Sara. ***Robot Dreams.*** First Second, 2007. Ages 8–14.

Winick, Judd. ***Hilo. Book 1, The Boy Who Crashed to Earth.*** Random House, 2015. Ages 7–12.

Yang, Gene L. ***American Born Chinese.*** First Second, 2006. Ages 12–16. (Chinese American)

Related Films, Videos, and DVDs

Bink & Gollie: Two for One. (2013). Authors: Kate DiCamillo and Alison McGhee & Illustrator: Tony Fucile (2010). 14 minutes.

Children Make Terrible Pets. (2011). Author/illustrator: Peter Brown (2010). 6 minutes.

Each Kindness (2014). Author: Jacqueline Woodson & Illustrator: E. B. Lewis (2012). 8 minutes.

Hugo. (2012). Author/illustrator: Brian Selznick (2007). 126 minutes.

Jumanji. (1995). Author/illustrator: Chris Van Allsburg (1981). 104 minutes.

Last Stop on Market Street. (2016). Author: Matt de la Peña & Illustrator: Christian Robinson (2015). 10 minutes.

That Is NOT a Good Idea! (2015). Author/illustrator: Mo Willems (2013). 7 minutes.

This Is Not My Hat. (2014). Author/illustrator: Jon Klassen (2012). 5 minutes.

Chapter 6

Poetry

What's a Poem?

A whisper,
a shout,
thoughts turned
inside out.

A laugh,
a sigh,
an echo
passing by.

A rhythm,
a rhyme,
a moment
caught in time.

A moon,
a star,
a glimpse
of who you are.

—Charles Ghigna

Poetry is a natural beginning to literature for young children and an enjoyable literary form for all ages. In their earliest years, children acquire language and knowledge of the world around them through listening and observing. Poetry is primarily an oral form of literature that draws heavily on the auditory perceptions of listeners and so is ideally suited to young children. Throughout elementary and middle school, poetry that relates to topics and issues explored in the classroom or library can be shared, providing a flash of humor or a new perspective on a difficult life issue.

Definition and Description

Poetry is the concentrated expression of ideas and emotions through precise and imaginative words carefully selected for their sonorous and rhythmical effects. Originally, poetry was oral, recited by minstrels as they traversed the countryside, sharing poems and songs with listeners of all ages. The musicality of poetry makes it an especially suitable literary form to read aloud.

Children often believe that rhyme is an essential ingredient of poetry, yet some types of poetry do not rhyme. What distinguishes poetry from prose is the concentration of thought and emotion expressed in succinct, exact, and beautiful language as well as an underlying pulse or rhythm and the arrangement of the words. Children enjoy the perfectly captured image in words and listening to the beat of the rhythm as you read a poem aloud to invite their participation and reflection.

Not all rhyming, rhythmical language merits the label of poetry. ***Verse*** is a language form in which thoughts or stories are told succinctly in rhyme with a distinct beat or meter. Mother Goose and nursery rhymes are good examples of well-known, simple verses. And, of course, ***jingle,*** a catchy repetition of sounds heard so often in commercials, is a constant in our lives. The most important feature of verses and jingles is their strong rhyme and rhythm with light or silly content. Although verses and jingles are enjoyable, poetry enriches children's lives by giving new insights and fresh views on life's experiences and inviting strong emotional responses.

A strong recent trend is ***novels in verse,*** which are novel-length narratives told through poetic language, instead of prose, usually some type of free verse. These novels in verse focus less on the structure or individuality of single poems that relate to each other, as found in a themed poetry collection, and more on the use of the verse format to serve the structure of a novel in telling a particular story, such as Thanhha Lai's *Inside Out & Back Again* (2011). The verses in these novels work together to create character development and setting, convey a story, and establish a strong voice. Novels in verse are thus not included in this chapter but are integrated into the genre chapters.

The term *poetry* is used in this chapter both to refer to a form of language that can evoke great depth of feeling and provoke new insights through imaginative and beautiful language and to refer to favorite verses of childhood.

Types of Poetry Books

Poetry touches our minds and hearts by drawing on all of our senses. Children respond to poetry, even though the themes that move them may differ from those that move adults. A wide variety of poetry books is available. As you select books of poetry in classrooms and libraries to use as bridges between activities, materials for reading, and literature for enjoyment, you need to become familiar with the types of poetry books, including nursery rhymes, comprehensive anthologies, themed anthologies and poet collections, and single illustrated poems in picturebook formats.

Mother Goose, Nursery Rhymes, and Songs

Mother Goose and ***nursery rhymes*** are richly illustrated collections of traditional verse. Often, a familiar illustration is all a child needs to recite a well-loved verse. Collected nursery rhymes first appeared in Charles Perrault's *Tales of Mother Goose* in France in the 1700s. Many of the rhymes were not initially intended for children but repeated by adults as a secret commentary on life and politics. This history is shared along with rhymes in Katherine Govier's collection, *Half for You and Half for Me*.

Nursery rhymes are part of children's literary heritage and serve as a wonderful introduction to the world of literature. In Western societies in which countless allusions are made every day to characters and situations in nursery rhymes, knowledge of this literature is a mark of being culturally literate. Other cultures have their own collections of nursery rhymes, such as Magdeleine Lerasle's *Songs from a Journey with a Parrot: Lullabies and Nursery Rhymes from Brazil and Portugal*.

Because so many of these verses exist, the better collections include large numbers of rhymes organized around themes or topics and indexed by titles or first lines as found in *The Arnold Lobel Book of Mother Goose* and David McPhail's *My Mother Goose*. Cultural connections can be expanded by global collections, such as *My Village: Rhymes from around the World* by Danielle Wright and *Over the Hills and Far Away* by Elizabeth Hammill. Modern versions of rhymes can be found in *Nursery Rhyme Comics,* edited by Chris Duffy, in which cartoonists give their take on traditional rhymes, and *Spinster Goose* by Lisa Wheeler, which satirizes traditional rhymes with a focus on the consequences of bad behavior.

Nursery songs are beautifully illustrated collections of traditional and modern verses with musical notation. Melody emphasizes the innate musicality of these verses and turns some verses into games ("Ring around the Roses") and others into lullabies ("Rock-a-Bye Baby") and finger plays ("Eensy, Weensy Spider"). Collections of songs, like Miles van Hout's *Twinkle, Twinkle, Little Star,* appeal to young children. Single illustrated versions of familiar songs provide innovative interpretations, such as the two picturebook versions of *Hush, Little Baby* by Brian Pinkney and Marla Frazee, and cultural adaptations like Kabir Sehgal's *The Wheels on the Tuk Tuk*, set in India.

Anthologies of Poetry

A large, comprehensive ***anthology of poetry*** for children is a must in every classroom and library. Anthologies should be organized by subject for easy retrieval of poems appropriate for any occasion, along with indexes of poets and titles or first lines. Works by contemporary and traditional poets can be found in most anthologies; they appeal to a wide age range, providing nursery rhymes for toddlers as well as longer, narrative poems for older readers. Examples include *The Random House Book of Poetry for Children,* edited by Jack Prelutsky, and *The Bill Martin Jr. Big Book of Poetry,* edited by Bill Martin Jr. and Michael Sampson.

Themed Poetry Anthologies and Poet Collections

Themed poetry books contain a range of poems around a specific focus. Some are ***themed anthologies*** in which the poems have been selected by a compiler from different poets around a topic or poetic form, such as *Amazing Places* selected by Lee Bennett Hopkins and *Beastly Verse* selected by JooHee Yoon. The biggest trend in poetry is ***themed poet collections*** containing poems on a topic or poetic form by one poet, such as Joyce Sidman's *Winter Bees and Other Poems of the Cold* and Marilyn Singer's *Echo Echo: Reverso Poems about Greek Myths*. These anthologies and poet collections are often beautifully illustrated and support classroom inquiries and library story programs. A recent trend is multigenre collections that combine poetry and information around topics in science and history, such as Sidman's book on the natural world during winter and J. Patrick Lewis's *When Thunder Comes: Poems for Civil Rights Leaders*.

Single Illustrated Poems

Single illustrated poems in a picturebook format make poetry more appealing and accessible for children. Because poetry is often an expressive reflection on life, the illustrations play a different role than in picture storybooks that focus on telling a story through word/image relationships. Poetry picturebooks are often lyrical, with illustrations that use repetitive visual elements and structures or abstract visual symbols and metaphors. *My People,* with photographs by Charles Smith, is a visual metaphor of Langston Hughes's classic poem, whereas Ed Young's *Should You Be a River* uses torn-paper and nature-photograph collages to create visual compositions of shapes and images around a theme of unconditional love.

Evaluation and Selection of Poetry

The criteria to keep in mind in evaluating a poem for use with children are as follows:

- **Does the poet use authentic, fresh, and imaginative language and images to express ideas and emotions?** Because poetry conveys the essence of an idea or experience, the poet's use of language must be careful and original.

- **Does the poem convey ideas and emotions in ways that encourage children to perceive ordinary things through a new perspective?** Poems should invite readers to view familiar experiences and everyday objects through a new lens.
- **Does the poem present the world through a child's perspective and life experiences? Does the poet avoid preaching to children and looking back at childhood with nostalgia?** Some poets make comparisons that are based on adult views and life experiences, rather than a child's perspective. Adult perspectives can take the form of nostalgia about childhood or the view that children's behavior is "cute" or needs to be corrected.
- **What is the quality of the poems selected around a specific theme within an anthology or collection? Do the selected poems provide a range of perspectives for that theme?** Anthologies organize poems around themes and topics; therefore, the range of poems and perspectives included in each theme need to be examined.
- **What is the relationship of the illustrations and visual images to the mood and content of the poems?** The illustrations that are created for each poem should reflect the content and tone or mood of the poem.

In selecting poems to read aloud to children, start with the Golden Age poets in the Milestones feature, the list of Notable Authors of Poetry, and poets who have won the National Council of Teachers of English (NCTE) Excellence in Poetry for Children. The NCTE Award recognizes the body of writing of living U.S. poets whose poetry has contributed substantially to children's lives. The NCTE award committee also names an annual Notable Poetry List. In addition, the Poetry Foundation established a Young People's Poet Laureate in 2006. Jack Prelutsky, Mary Ann Hoberman, J. Patrick Lewis, Kenn Nesbitt, and Jacqueline Woodson each served two-year terms. The Lee Bennett Hopkins Poetry Award is given annually to an American poet or anthologist for the most outstanding new book of poetry for children.

Although more poetry for children is being written, published, and enjoyed, you may feel uncertain about how to select poems for children. By learning about children's preferences in poetry and exploring well-known poems and poets, you can become more confident about selecting poems that engage children.

Children's Poetry Preferences

The findings from surveys of children's poetry preferences can be helpful in guiding initial poetry selections. Fisher and Natarella (1982) surveyed primary-grade children and their teachers, whereas Terry (1974) and Kutiper and Wilson (1993) studied intermediate-grade children. Abrahamson (2002) and McNair (2012) summarize these findings as highlighting:

- A preference for narrative poems over lyric poems and modern over classics.
- An enjoyment of limericks and dislike of haiku.
- A preference for poems with pronounced sound patterns, especially poems that rhyme or have a regular, distinctive rhythm.
- An interest in humorous poems, poems about animals, and poems about enjoyable, familiar experiences.
- Primary grade children prefer poems about strange and fantastic events, animals, and children. Older children prefer poems on humor, familiar experiences, unusual people, moments of crisis, and social issues.
- Figurative language in poetry can be initially confusing to children and interfere with their attempts to understand the poems.

Children's appreciation of poetry can be broadened and deepened by starting with the kinds of poems that they enjoy and then sharing other types of poetry. An interesting selection of rhyming, narrative poems with distinct rhythms about humorous events and familiar experiences is a good starting point. After reading humorous poets such as Jack Prelutsky and Shel Silverstein, you can select poems from notable poets that move children from light verse into poems with high-quality language and poetic arrangements. Children need exposure to an array of poetry and poets that build on their interests.

The Significance of Style and Word Choice in Poetry

Just as with a work of fiction, the elements of a poem should be considered to understand and evaluate the poem. Each of these parts—meaning, rhythm, sound patterns, figurative language, and sense

NCTE Excellence in Poetry for Children Award Winners

1977	David McCord	1993	Barbara J. Esbensen
1978	Aileen Fisher	1997	Eloise Greenfield
1979	Karla Kuskin	2000	X. J. Kennedy
1980	Myra Cohn Livingston	2003	Mary Ann Hoberman
1981	Eve Merriam	2006	Nikki Grimes
1982	John Ciardi	2009	Lee Bennett Hopkins
1985	Lilian Moore	2011	J. Patrick Lewis
1988	Arnold Adoff	2013	Joyce Sidman
1991	Valerie Worth	2015	Marilyn Singer

imagery—work together to express ideas and feelings. Emotion, imagery, and the music of poetry are at the heart of poems that touch our hearts and minds.

- ***Meaning*** is the underlying idea, feeling, or mood conveyed through the poem. Poetry is a form of communication in which a poet chooses to express emotions and thoughts through the choice and arrangement of words.
- ***Rhythm*** is the beat or regular cadence of the poem. Poetry is an oral form of literature that often relies on rhythm to help communicate meaning. A fast rhythm is effected through short lines; clipped syllables; sharp, high vowel sounds, such as the sounds represented by the letters *a, e,* and *i;* and abrupt consonant sounds, such as the sounds represented by the letters *k, t, w,* and *p.* A fast rhythm can provide the listener with a feeling of happiness, excitement, drama, and even tension and suspense. A slow rhythm is effected by longer lines, multisyllabic words, full or low vowel sounds such as the sounds represented by the letters *o* and *u,* and resonating consonant sounds such as the sounds represented by the letters *m, n,* and *r.* A slow rhythm can evoke languor, tranquillity, inevitability, and harmony, among other feelings. A change in rhythm during a poem signals the listener that a change in meaning is coming.

The following poems reflect the use of rhythm to either communicate the dizzy and increasing speed of a merry-go-round or the calm and quiet of summer.

Merry-Go-Round

I climbed up on the merry-go-round.
And it went round and round.
I climbed up on a big brown horse,
And it went up and down.
Around and round
And up and down,
Around and round
And up and down.
I sat high up
On a big brown horse
And rode around
On the merry-go-round
And rode around
On the merry-go-round
I rode around
On the merry-go-round
Around
And round
And
Round....

—Dorothy Baruch

Slowly

Slowly the tide creeps up the sand.
Slowly the shadows cross the land.
Slowly the cart-horse pulls his mile,
Slowly the old man mounts the stile.

Slowly the hands move round the clock.
Slowly the dew dries on the dock.
Slow is the snail—the slowest of all
The green moss spreads on the old brick wall.

—James Reeves

- ***Sound patterns*** are made by repeated sounds and combinations of sounds in the words. Words, phrases, or lines are sometimes repeated in their entirety. Also, parts of words may be repeated through different sound devices:
    - ***Rhyme*** occurs when the ends of words (the last vowel sound and any consonant sound that may follow it) have the same sounds, such as *fat, vat,* and *brat* or *hay, they, stray,* and *obey.*
    - ***Assonance*** is a pattern where the same vowel sound is heard repeatedly within a line or a few lines of poetry, such as *hoop, gloom, moon, moot,* and *boots.*
    - ***Alliteration*** is a pattern in which initial consonant sounds are heard frequently within a few lines of poetry, such as *ship, shy,* and *shape.*
    - ***Consonance*** is similar to alliteration but usually refers to a close juxtaposition of similar final consonant sounds, as in fla*k*e, chu*ck,* and stro*k*e.
    - ***Onomatopoeia*** is the device in which the sound of a word imitates its real-world sound, such as *buzz* for the sound of a bee and *hiss* for a snake's sound.
- ***Figurative language*** involves comparing or contrasting one object, idea, or feeling with another one and occurs in these forms:
    - A ***simile*** is a direct comparison, typically using *like* or *as* to point out similarities. The familiar poem "The Star" includes a simile comparing a star to a diamond.

The Star

Twinkle, twinkle little star,
How I wonder what you are!
Up above the world so high,
Like a diamond in the sky.

—Jane Taylor

- A ***metaphor*** is an implied comparison without a signal word to evoke the similarities. In "The Night Is a Big Black Cat," the metaphor implies a comparison between the night sky and a black cat.

The Night Is a Big Black Cat

The Night is a big black cat
The Moon is her topaz eye,
The stars are the mice she hunts at night,
In the field of the sultry sky.

—G. Orr Clark

- ***Personification*** is giving human qualities to animals or objects for the purpose of drawing a comparison between the animal/object and human beings. Poets might say that lightning is dancing across the sky, an alarm clock is yelling at me, or flowers are begging for water.
- ***Hyperbole*** is an exaggeration to highlight reality or to point out ridiculousness. Hyperbole appeals to children's strong sense of the absurd, such as saying that a boy is walking slower than a snail or a child's stomach is a bottomless pit.

- ***Sense imagery*** is the way in which a poet plays with the five senses in descriptive and narrative language. *Sight* may be awakened through the depiction of beauty; *hearing* may be evoked by the sounds of a city street; *smell* and *taste* may be recalled through the description of a fish left too long in the sun; and *touch* can be sensitized through describing the gritty discomfort of a wet swimsuit caked with sand from the beach. After listening to a poem, you can invite children to think about which senses the poet is appealing to.

These elements of poetry can help you select varied types of poems and engage in dialogue with children. However, little is gained by teaching these elements separately as skills to memorize or to use for poetic analysis—both have created a dislike of poetry for many children. You can encourage appreciation of poetry by selecting poems carefully, reading them aloud well, and sharing poems in enjoyable ways.

Historical Overview of Poetry

Poetry for children began centuries ago in the form of nursery rhymes and lullabies that were recited to babies and toddlers and passed along through oral tradition. The earliest collection of nursery rhymes that survives today is *Tommy Thumb's Pretty Song Book* (1744), containing familiar rhymes such as "Hickory Dickory Dock." The term *Mother Goose* was first used in France by Charles Perrault (1697) to refer to his collection of fairy tales. Later editions contained nursery rhymes, which were so popular that Mother Goose became a general name for nursery rhymes. For many children, nursery rhymes and poems are their first experiences with literature and so come to symbolize the reassuring sounds of childhood.

Poems with a moral and religious bent were shared with obvious didactic intent, reflecting the strict attitude toward the rearing of children prevalent in the Western world from the Middle Ages to the late 1800s. Fear of death and punishment was used to gain obedience to authority in Ann and Jane Taylor's *Original Poems, for Infant Minds, by Several Young Persons* (1804). The Golden Age of Poetry for

MILESTONES in the Development of Poetry

Date	Poet	Landmark Work	Country	Characteristic
1846	Edward Lear	*A Book of Nonsense*	England	Father of nonsense poetry, limericks
1872	Christina Rossetti	*Sing Song*	England	Poems on children and the small things around them
1885	Robert Louis Stevenson	*A Child's Garden of Verses*	England	Descriptive poems of childhood memories
1896	Eugene Field	*Poems of Childhood*	U.S.	Poems reflecting on children and child life
1902	Walter de la Mare	*Songs of Childhood*	England	Musical and imaginative poetry
1922	A. A. Milne	*When We Were Very Young*	England	Humorous poems observing a child's world
1926	Rachel Field	*Taxis and Toadstools*	U.S.	Poems about the everyday world through a child's eyes
1932	Langston Hughes	*The Dream Keepers and Other Poems*	U.S.	Celebration of African American experiences
1974	Shel Silverstein	*Where the Sidewalk Ends*	U.S.	Humorous poems that comment on urban life
1982	Nancy Willard	*A Visit to William Blake's Inn*	U.S.	Recognition of poetry by the Newbery Award
1989	Paul Fleischman	*Joyful Noise*		

children, the 1850s through the 1920s, moved away from moralistic poetry to poems about the beauty of life and nature; poems of humor, nonsense, and word play; and imaginative poems on life from a child's perspective. Much of the Golden Age poetry retains its appeal today, including favorite poems from *A Child's Garden of Verses* (1885) by Robert Louis Stevenson.

In the 1960s and 1970s, the trend toward realism in children's literature was reflected in protest poetry, poems about girls in nontraditional roles, and irreverent poems. Adults became fair game for ridicule and mockery, and poets from diverse cultures were more frequently published. Poems became more popular in classrooms beginning in the 1980s. Publishers presented single poems and collections in beautifully illustrated book formats, and several poetry books received the Newbery, indicating greater recognition of poetry for young people. An increase in anthologies of poems by and about people of color, such as *Pass It On,* edited by Wade Hudson, and *Cool Salsa,* edited by Lori Carlson, appeared in the 1990s. This increased publication also resulted in greater attention to earlier African American poets, such as Paul Laurence Dunbar and Langston Hughes.

Recent trends include novels in verse, themed poetry collections, multigenre books that combine poetry with informational text, and poetry focusing on science and history (Lowery, 2016). Authors such as Karen Hesse, Helen Frost, Jacqueline Woodson, Kwame Alexander, and Margarita Engle have become known for their use of poetry to create fiction and memoir that are referred to as novels in verse.

Poetry Types and Forms

Poetry can be classified in many ways; one way is to consider two main types that generally differ in purpose. ***Lyric poetry*** captures a moment, a feeling, or a scene and is descriptive in nature, whereas ***narrative poetry*** tells a story or includes a sequence of events. This example is a lyric poem.

Night Creature

I like
the quiet breathing of the night,

the tree talk
the wind-swish
the star light.

Day is
glare-y
loud
scarey.
Day bustles.

Night rustles.
I like
night.

—Lilian Moore

Although many narrative poems are quite lengthy in telling a story, the next selection is a very succinct narrative:

Traditional American Rhyme

Algy saw a bear.
The bear saw Algy.
The bear grew bulgy.
The bulge was Algy.

Poetry can also be categorized by its ***poetic form,*** which refers to the way the poem is structured or put together. ***Couplets, tercets, quatrains,*** and ***cinquains*** refer to the number (two, three, four, and five) of lines of poetry in a stanza—a set of lines of poetry grouped together and that usually rhyme, though the rhyme scheme may vary. These poetic forms may constitute an entire poem, or a poem may comprise a few stanzas of couplets, tercets, and so on. "Higglety, Pigglety, Pop!" is an example of the cinquain poetic form in a traditional nursery rhyme.

Higglety, Pigglety, Pop!

Higglety, pigglety, pop!
The dog has eaten the mop.
The pig's in a hurry,
The cat's in a flurry,
Higglety, pigglety, pop!

—Samuel Goodrich

Other specific poetic forms frequently found in children's poetry are limericks, ballads, haiku, sijo, free verse, and concrete poetry. Paul Janeczko's *A Kick in the Head* contains examples of poetic forms along with brief explanations of the form.

A ***limerick*** is a humorous one-stanza, five-line verse form (usually a narrative), in which lines 1, 2, and 5 rhyme and are of the same length and lines 3 and 4 rhyme and are of the same length but shorter than the other lines. The following is an example of a limerick by Edward Lear, the poet who popularized this poetic form in the 19th century.

Limerick

There was an Old Person whose habits,
  Induced him to feed upon Rabbits;
When he'd eaten eighteen,
He turned perfectly green.
  Upon which he relinquished those habits.

—Edward Lear

A ***ballad*** is a fairly long narrative poem of popular origin, usually adapted to singing. These traditional story poems are often romantic or heroic, such as "Robin Hood" or "John Henry."

Haiku is a lyric unrhymed poem of Japanese origin with 17 syllables, arranged on three lines with a syllable count of five, seven, and five. Haiku is highly evocative poetry that frequently espouses harmony with and appreciation of nature.

One long crack in the
pavement—an endless freeway
for commuting ants

—Myra Cohn Livingston

Sijo is a traditional Korean poetry form with three lines, each with 14–16 syllables. The first line introduces the topic, the second develops the topic, and the third contains some kind of twist. The sijo in Linda Sue Park's *Tap Dancing on the Roof* focuses on many topics, including relationships and everyday moments.

Free verse is unrhymed poetry with little or light rhythm. Sometimes words within a line will rhyme. The subjects of free verse can be abstract and philosophical or humorous as the poet reflects on everyday situations.

My Mouth
  stays shut
    but
  food just
  finds
    a way
      my tongue says
  we are
    full today
    but
      teeth just
        grin

and
say
come in
i am always hungry
—Arnold Adoff

Concrete poetry is written and printed in a shape that signifies the subject of the poem. Concrete poems are a form of poetry that must be seen as well as heard to be fully appreciated. These poems do not usually have rhyme or definite rhythm; they rely mostly on the words, their meanings and shapes, and the way the words are arranged on the page to evoke images, as in the following example:

Help!

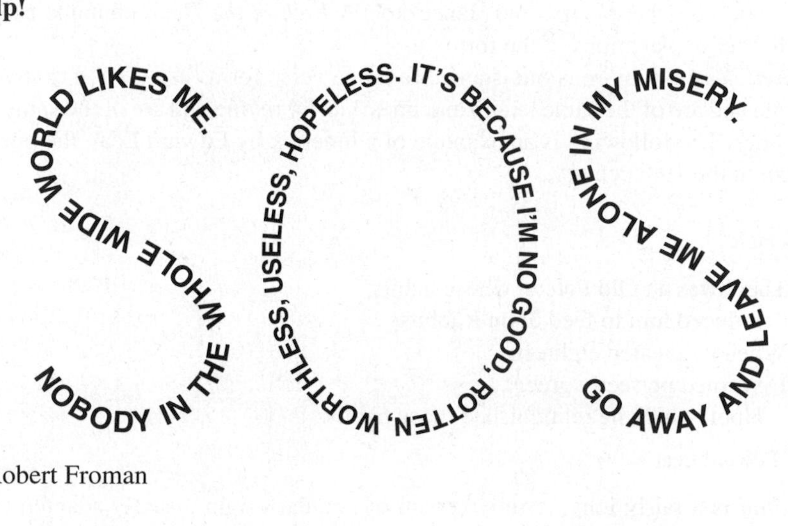

—Robert Froman

Reader Connections: Poetry in the Classroom

Young children delight in the sounds and language play of poetry—yet by fifth grade, students typically indicate that poetry is their least favorite genre. The cause of this huge shift is school. Poetry is the most misused genre in classrooms, often chosen for memorization and handwriting practice. Poetry tends to be neglected, seldom shared until the dreaded poetry unit comes along and children are bombarded with abstract poems that they are expected to analyze to uncover the "hidden meanings." The result is that children often build a lifelong dislike of poetry instead of engaging in experiences that create a lifelong love of poetry.

Reading Poetry Aloud

Because poetry was originally an oral form of literature and relies on musicality for its appeal to listeners, it should be introduced first and often in an oral form. Moreover, children's oral language is the basis for their acquisition of literacy, so listening to and saying poems provides a natural introduction to literature.

Poetry should be read aloud to children on a daily basis. Reading poetry aloud with expression is effective in drawing children's attention to literate language (Elster & Hanauer, 2002). Brief, positive encounters with one to three poems at a time are best. Too many poems in one sitting can overwhelm children or make the reading tedious. Introduce the poem before reading it aloud, either by tying the poem in with something else or by briefly telling why you chose the poem. Then state the title of the poem and the poet and begin to read. Because poetry tends to be brief and conceptually dense, reading the poem several times is often necessary for children to make connections and construct understandings. Learning to read poetry well involves:

- Read poetry for its meaning. Stress the meaning of the poem just as when reading a story. Pauses are determined by the meaning units in a poem, not the end of the lines.

Notable Authors of Poetry

Douglas Florian, poet and illustrator, blends wordplay, free flowing poems, interesting facts, and collage art to create picturebook collections. *Dinothesaurus; Poetrees; Poem Depot; Shiver Me Timbers!* www.douglasflorian.com

Helen Frost, poet of novels in verse and poetry picturebooks using photography to capture a moment in the life of birds or insects. *Room 214: A Year in Poems; Step Gently Out; Sweep Up the Sun.* www.helenfrost.net

Nikki Grimes, poet who celebrates the everyday lives of African American children. Novels in verse, *Words with Wings,* and themed poet collections, *Danitra Brown: Class Clown* and *Poems in the Attic.* www.nikkigrimes.com

Lee Bennett Hopkins, poet and award-winning anthologist of collections on a wide range of topics. *Amazing Faces; America at War; Sharing the Seasons; Jumping Off Library Shelves.* www.leebennetthopkins.com

Paul B. Janeczko, poet and anthologist of poetry that invites children to enjoy and learn about many different kinds of poetry. *A Poke in the I; A Foot in the Mouth; A Kick in the Head; Firefly July.* www.pauljaneczko.com

J. Patrick Lewis, poet who creates thematic collections of poetry, ranging from mathematics and civil rights to legendary creatures. *Bigfoot is Missing!; Harlem Hellfighters; When Thunder Comes; Edgar Allan Poe's Pies.* www.jpatricklewis.com

Marilyn Nelson, poet who uses a range of poetic forms from requiem to sonnets as reflections on African American history. *Sweethearts of Rhythm*; *A Wreath for Emmet Till;* and a memoir in verse, *How I Discovered Poetry.* www.blueflowerarts.com/marilyn-nelson

Joyce Sidman, award-winning poet of picturebook collections who uses poetic forms ranging from riddles to concrete poems in celebrations of nature. *Red Sings from Treetops; Dark Emperor; Winter Bees and Other Poems of the Cold.* www.joycesidman.com

Marilyn Singer, poet of picturebook collections on a variety of topics in science and history and the creator of a new poetic form, reverso. *Mirror Mirror: A Book of Reversible Verse*; *Rutherford B., Who Was He?: Poems about Our Presidents*; *Echo Echo: Reverso Poems about Greek Myths.* www.marilynsinger.net

- Do not overemphasize the beat of the poem. Doing so results in an annoying singsong effect. Let the poetic language provide the rhythm.
- Enunciate the poem clearly. Each sound and each syllable are important and need to be heard to be appreciated. Slow down your normal reading pace to give full value to each sound. Poetry requires a willingness to listen with an expectation that the sounds will be pleasing and meaningful.
- Poetry begs to be performed and dramatized. Try out different effects (using different voices, elongating words, singing, shouting, whispering, pausing dramatically) as you read poems aloud. Your voice is a powerful tool—you can change it from louder to softer to only a whisper; start at a deep, low pitch and rise to a medium and eventually high pitch; speak very quickly in a clipped fashion and then slow down and draw out the words. Sara Holbrook's *Wham! It's a Poetry Jam: Discovering Performance Poetry* (2002) offers suggestions for performing poetry.
- Some poems need to be read aloud a number of times for the meaning to be fully understood by listeners. Also, favorite poems can be enjoyed again and again, as children savor one more reading and linger over the musicality and word choice.
- Read poems in pairs that relate by theme or topic to put the poems in conversation with each other so that the ideas resonate and illuminate the experience of being in the poem.
- Make recordings of poems available along with the poem on a chart or in a book for children to listen to and read. Recordings of poets reading their poems aloud is found at www.childrenspoetryarchive.org.
- After reading a poem aloud, response can extend children's enjoyment through choral reading, discussion, art, drama, etc. Do not begin with analysis, but with responding to the emotional or imaginative aspects of the poem. Children can share how the poem made them feel or what it made them think about by discussing, "How did this poem make you feel? What meaning does this poem have for you?"
- Picturebooks that combine the life story of poets with a collection of their poems provide another way to engage children's interest. See Sally Derby's *Jump Back Paul* about Paul Laurence Dunbar and Matthew Burgess's *Enormous Smallness* about e. e. cummings.

Overanalyzing the form, figurative language, and meaning of poems has led to a dislike of poetry. Often, just reading and enjoying the poem is all that is needed. Other times, children can respond to the emotional impact of a poem. Once children have experience with a poem, a careful look at form is appropriate occasionally but only *after* they have an opportunity for personal response. Children can be asked to point out parts of the poem that they like and talk about why. They can also be encouraged to explore metaphor, imagery, and sensory language in a poem as they relate to the poem's meaning. An analysis of form and language can be integrated into minilessons as children write their own poetry and want to make their poems more effective. The major focus should always be on the meaning and emotional impact of a poem.

Choral Poetry Choral reading of poetry provides an opportunity to say and hear poems over and over again as a form of reader response. ***Choral poetry*** consists of orally interpreting the poem through your voice by saying a poem together as a group activity. These poems may be practiced and recited or read aloud. Children enjoy this way of experiencing poetry because they have a participatory role in the activity. Most poetry, intended to be listened to, is suitable for choral presentation. Selecting and arranging choral poems involves:

1. **Selection.** Initially, select short poems (from one to four stanzas) until children develop skill in reciting and performing poems. Humorous narrative poems are good first choices, leading to longer poems. Provide children with a copy of the poem.
2. **Arrangements.** Options for reading a poem chorally include unison, two or three part, solo voices, cumulative buildup, and simultaneous voices.
   - In *unison* choral speaking, children recite the poem together as a group. Two- or three-part choral poetry is usually based on arranging children into voice types (e.g., high, medium, low) to achieve different effects and by selecting lines of the poem for each group to recite or read.
   - *Solo* voices can be added to either of these presentations and are sometimes used for asking a question or making an exclamation.
   - Some poems lend themselves to *cumulative* presentations that build up, such as voices saying the first line, then two more joining in on the second, and then two more, gradually building to a crescendo until the entire group says the last line or stanza.
   - Poems can be presented by *simultaneous* recitation, which forms a presentation similar to a musical round. Group one begins the poem and recites it all the way through. When group one begins the third line, group two starts the first line, and the two groups recite simultaneously until the end. Other groups can, of course, be added.
   - Poetry selected and arranged for dramatic choral readings on a particular theme infuses an interesting variation into choral poetry. Paul Fleischman's *Joyful Noise: Poems for Two Voices* and Betsy Franco's *Messing Around on the Monkey Bars and Other School Poems for Two Voices* are collections of poetry written to be read aloud by two readers at once, one reading the left half of the page and one reading the right half as well as certain lines simultaneously. Another good source for poems that work well for choral reading is Paul Janeczko's *A Foot in the Mouth.*

   Many other variations can be developed for choral readings. Let imagination be your guide. Words and lines can be spun into ghostly moans, or barked, or sung, or repeated. Choreography adds visual impact, as do simple props. As soon as children learn that poems do not have to be read sedately exactly as written, they will find excitement and deeper meaning in poetry.
3. **Performance.** Incorporating action, gestures, body movements, and finger plays can produce interesting and enjoyable presentations. Many of these performances will be informal, with a focus on playing with various arrangements of a poem in a small or large group. More formal performances involve memorizing a well-loved poem, trying out various arrangements, and rehearsing the final arrangement for presentation to an audience.

Reading and Writing Poems with Children

Learning to Read Poetry Children enjoy reading poetry silently and aloud to others. Classroom libraries should have one or two comprehensive poetry anthologies for children to browse. In addition, classrooms need themed collections by a single poet, such as Douglas Florian's book of humor poems

Poem Depot: Aisles of Smiles, and collections of poems on a single topic, such as the poems about *Amazing Places* selected by Lee Bennett Hopkins. Children can make copies of favorite poems from these collections to develop personal anthologies, illustrating and arranging the poems in new and inventive ways. Introducing new poetry books occasionally will spark renewed interest in reading poetry. Consider these additional activities to encourage the reading of poetry:

- Children can take turns reading favorite poems to one another in pairs. Make video or audio recordings of these readings so they can watch or listen to their readings.
- Ask each child to select three poems by one poet (e.g., a Golden Age poet or an NCTE poet) and find something out about the poet; then place children in groups of five or six to tell briefly about the poet and read the three poems aloud. Paul B. Janeczko's *The Place My Words Are Looking For: What Poets Say About and Through Their Work* (1990) and Sylvia Vardell's *Poetry People* (2007) are excellent resources. Information about children's authors can also be found on many websites, including www.childrenslit.com.
- Invite children to find three poems on the same topic or theme, such as dinosaurs, baseball, or the value of friendship, to read aloud in small groups.
- Encourage children to find poems that are of the same poetic form (cinquains, limericks, etc.), or that exhibit similar poetic elements (rhyme, alliteration, onomatopoeia, etc.), or that have fast or slow rhythms. These poems can be used for reading aloud that day or week.
- Select a poem in small groups for a multimodal response by creating a Cin(E) Poem (Stuart, 2010). Children sketch a storyboard of the poem that integrates images with the language of the poem and then collect or create digital images, words, sounds, and music to construct a visual interpretation and experience of their poem to present.
- Excellent sites for ideas and resources for finding and sharing poetry with children are Sylvia Vardell's blog (poetryforchildren.blogspot.com), and the Young People's Laureate on the Poetry Foundation website (www.poetryfoundation.org/children).
- Georgia Heard (2012) and Paul Janeczko (2011) provide suggestions for encouraging students to read and appreciate poetry in order to address the Common Core State Standards.

Do	Don't
Read poetry aloud every day	Limit poetry choices to one or two poets or types of poems
Practice reading a poem before reading it aloud for the first time to children	Read poems in a singsong style
Choose poetry that appeals to children	Choose only classic traditional poems
Have a variety of poetry anthologies and themed poetry books available in classroom and library collections	Have a poetry marathon for days or weeks to make up for not sharing poetry regularly
Encourage children to recite, read, and write poems of all kinds	Force children to memorize and recite poems and write formula poems
Facilitate choral readings of poetry	Make analysis the focus of poetry study
Invite responses to poetry through art, music, and movement	Have children copy poems for handwriting practice
Feature a notable poet each month	Share from one or two poets
Begin and end each day or story time with a poem	Read poems only during the annual poetry unit

Learning to Write Poetry A rich poetry environment stimulates children's interest in writing their own poems. Children need to be familiar with poetry of many kinds and by many poets before they are asked to compose poems. The collection of poems *Inner Chimes: Poems on Poetry,* selected by Bobbye S. Goldstein, may be a natural starting place for helping children to develop a conceptualization of poetry. This collection contains poems by well-known children's poets about creating poetry. Other books that provide suggestions on poetry in the classroom are *Awakening the Heart* (1999) by Georgia Heard, *Poetry Aloud Here!* (2006) by Sylvia Vardell, and *Catch Your Breath* (2015) by Laura Purdie Salas.

One way to start writing poetry is through a collaborative effort. A group brainstorms ideas and composes the poem orally as you write the lines on chart paper. As children become comfortable with writing group poetry, they can branch off and compose poems in pairs or individually. Georgia Heard suggests list poetry and found poetry, created from different kinds of lists and pieces of print found on signs and scraps of paper, which provide fun ways to ease children into writing poetry.

Poetry is a form of communication, so encourage children to think of an idea, feeling, or event that matters to them. They should be reminded that poetry does not have to rhyme and that they may write about something of interest to them. Children's poetry follows no absolute rules; perfection of form should not be a goal. Other suggestions to encourage poetry writing include:

- Have children compile personal and class anthologies of their favorite poems. Another type of anthology is to collect poems that reflect their own identities and interests.
- Design bulletin boards with displays of children's poems as well as copies of poems by favorite poets. Children may also design posters, individually or in groups, to illustrate a favorite poem.
- Encourage children to model the works of professional poets by imitating a whole poem or specific techniques.
- Read aloud many poems of one poetic form; then analyze the form with children to reveal the characteristics of its structure. Quatrains, cinquains, haiku, concrete poems, and limericks can be used as models once children have an appreciation for poetry and for a specific poetic form. Share Joan Graham's *The Poem That Will Not End* (2014), a picturebook about a boy who writes poems in different forms, or two novels in verse, Helen Frost's *Room 214: A Year in Poems* (2014) and Tamera Wissinger's *Gone Fishing: A Novel in Verse* (2013), which end with descriptions of the poetry forms used in these novels.
- Other resources to encourage children to compose poems are Ralph Fletcher's *Poetry Matters: Writing a Poem from the Inside Out* (2002) and Jack Prelutsky's *Pizza, Pigs, and Poetry: How to Write a Poem* (2008).

Positive views of poetry can be developed by reading novels and picturebooks where the main characters use poetry to gain perspective on situations in their daily lives, such as Sharon Creech's *Love that Dog* (2001), Kevin Henkes's *The Year of Billy Miller* (2013), Robin Herrera's *Hope Is a Ferris Wheel* (2014), and Margaret McNamara's *A Poem in Your Pocket* (2015). These books can help children embrace poetry as having the potential to add significance to their lives as well.

Invitations for Further Investigation

- Create a self-portrait anthology by collecting poems that celebrate and explore the different aspects of who you are and what you are doing, thinking, and feeling. Open the anthology by selecting a signature poem that reflects your sense of self. Georgia Heard's *Songs of Myself* is a useful resource for this type of anthology.
- Share your collections of favorite poems, and select a poem as a small group to explore through the multimodal approach of Cin(E) Poetry (Stuart, 2010).
- Research nursery rhymes and their history within a particular global culture.
- Challenge the viewpoint that poetry is sentimental and irrelevant by locating poetry that provokes feelings and ideas about issues of social justice. Consider this role for poetry by reading about experiences with children (Ciardiello, 2010, or Damico, 2005) and collecting poems that address complex social issues.
- Pair sets of poems with each other or pair a poem with a picturebook, novel, or song so the ideas in these texts play off each other to provide different perspectives.
- Listen to recordings of poets reading their work on www.childrenspoetryarchive.org, and then select a poem to prepare and perform orally to a group of children or your peers.

References

Abrahamson, R. (2002). Poetry preference research. *Voices from the Middle, 10*(2), 20–22.

Adoff, A. (1992). My mouth. In A. Adoff, *Eats*. New York: HarperCollins.

Baruch, D. (1932). Merry-go-round. In D. Baruch, *I like machines*. New York: Harper.

Ciardiello, A. V. (2010). "Talking Walls": Presenting a case for social justice poetry in literacy education. *The Reading Teacher, 63*(6), 464–473.

Clark, G. O. (1983). The night is a big black cat. In J. Prelutsky (Ed.), *The Random House book of poetry for children.* Lobel, A. (Illus.). New York: Random House.

Creech, S. (2001). *Love that dog.* New York: HarperCollins.

Damico, J. (2005). Evoking hearts and heads: Exploring issues of social justice through poetry. *Language Arts, 83*(2), 137–146.

Elster, C. A., & Hanauer, D. I. (2002). Voicing texts, voices around texts: Reading poems in elementary school classrooms. *Research in the Teaching of English, 37*(1), 89–134.

Fisher, C. J., & Natarella, M. A. (1982). Young children's preferences in poetry: A national survey of first, second and third graders. *Research in the Teaching of English, 16*(4), 339–354.

Fletcher, R. (2002). *Poetry matters: Writing a poem from the inside out.* New York: HarperCollins.

Froman, R. (1974). Help! In R. Froman, *Seeing things*. New York: Crowell.

Frost, H. (2014). *Room 214: A year in poems.* New York: Square Fish.

Ghigna, C. (2003). What's a poem? In C. Ghigna (Ed.), *A fury of motion: Poems for boys.* Honesdale, PA: Boyds Mills.

Goodrich, S. (1983). Higglety, pigglety, pop! In J. Prelutsky (Ed.), *The Random House book of poetry for children.* Lobel, A. (Illus.). New York: Random House.

Graham, J. (2014). *The poem that will not end: Fun with poetic forms and voices.* Brooker, K. (Illus.). Las Vegas, NV: Two Lions.

Grimes, N. (2013). *Words with wings.* Honesville, PA: Boyds Mills.

Heard, G. (1999). *Awakening the heart: Exploring poetry in elementary and middle school.* Portsmouth, NH: Heinemann.

Heard, G. (2000). *Songs of myself: An anthology of poems and art.* New York: Mondo.

Heard, G. (2012). *Poetry lessons to meet the Common Core State Standards.* New York: Scholastic.

Henkes, K. (2013). *The year of Billy Miller.* New York: Greenwillow.

Herrera, R. (2014). *Hope is a ferris wheel.* New York: Amulet.

Holbrook, S. (2002). *Wham! It's a poetry jam: Discovering performance poetry.* Honesdale, PA: Boyds Mills.

Janeczko, P. B., selector. (1990). *The place my words are looking for: What poets say about and through their work.* New York: Bradbury.

Janeczko, P. B. (2011). *Reading poetry in the middle grades.* Portsmouth, NH: Heinemann.

Kutiper, K., & Wilson, P. (1993). Updating poetry preferences: A look at the poetry children really like. *The Reading Teacher, 47*(1), 28–35.

Lai, T. (2011). *Inside out & back again.* New York: Harper.

Lear, E. (1946). *The complete nonsense book.* New York: Dodd, Mead.

Livingston, M. C. (1997). One long crack. In M. C. Livingston, *Cricket never does.* New York: Simon & Schuster.

Lowery, R. (2016). Spotlight on poetry. *The Dragon Lode, 34*(2), 68–72.

McNair, J. (2012). Poems about sandwich cookies, jelly, and chocolate: Poetry in K-3 classrooms. *Young Children, 67*(4), 94–100.

McNamara, M. (2015). *A poem in your pocket.* New York: Schwartz & Wade Books.

Moore, L. (1988). Night creature. In de Regniers, B. S., *Sing a song of popcorn.* New York: Scholastic.

Prelutsky, J. (2008). *Pizza, pigs, and poetry: How to write a poem.* New York: Greenwillow.

Reeves, J. (1963). Slowly. In E. Blishen (Ed.), *Oxford book of poetry for children.* Oxford, England: Oxford University Press.

Salas, L. (2015). *Catch your breath: Writing poignant poetry.* Mankato, MN: Capstone Press.

Stuart, D. (2010). Cin(E) Poetry: Engaging the digital generation in 21st century response. *Voices from the Middle, 17*(3), 27–35.

Taylor, J. (1983). The star. In J. Prelutsky (Ed.), *The Random House book of poetry for children.* Lobel, A. (Illus.). New York: Random House.

Terry, A. C. (1974). *Children's poetry preferences: A national survey of upper elementary grades.* Urbana, IL: National Council of Teachers of English.

Vardell, S. (2006). *Poetry aloud here! Sharing poetry with children.* Chicago, IL: American Library Association.

Vardell, S. (2007). *Poetry people: A practical guide to children's poets.* Santa Barbara, CA: Libraries Unlimited.

Wissinger, T. W. (2013). *Gone fishing: A novel in verse.* Cordell, M. (Illus.). Boston, MA: Houghton Mifflin.

Recommended Poetry Books

Because poetry is usually of interest to a broad age group, entries of poetry books indicate age only for books mainly suitable for older readers. Books that are multigenre or global in origin or setting are also indicated.

Mother Goose, Nursery Rhymes, and Songs

Ada, Alma For and Campoy, Isabel, selectors. ***Muu, moo! Rimas de animals/Animal Nursery Rhymes.*** Illus. Vivi Escriva. Rayo, 2010. (Latin America)

Chorao, Kay, compiler. ***Rhymes 'Round the World.*** Dutton, 2009. (Global)

Duffy, Chris, editor. ***Nursery Rhyme Comics: 50 Times Rhymes from 50 Celebrated Cartoonists***. First Second, 2011.

Frazee, Marla. ***Hush, Little Baby.*** Harcourt, 2003.

Govier, Katherine. ***Half for You and Half for Me: Best-Loved Nursery Rhymes and the Stories Behind Them.*** Illus. Sarah Clement. Whitecap, 2014.

Hammill, Elizabeth, compiler. ***Over the Hills and Far Away: A Treasury of Nursery Rhymes.*** Candlewick, 2015.

Hout, Mies Van. ***Twinkle, Twinkle, Little Star.*** Lemiscaat, 2014. Translated from Dutch.

Lerasle, Magdeleine, compiler. ***Songs from a Journey with a Parrot: Lullabies and Nursery Rhymes from Brazil and Portugal.*** Illus. Aurelia Fronty. Secret Mountain, 2013. (Brazil)

Lobel, Arnold, selector. ***The Arnold Lobel Book of Mother Goose.*** Knopf, 1997.

McPhail, David. ***My Mother Goose.*** Roaring Book, 2013.

Morris, Jackie. ***The Cat and the Fiddle: A Treasury of Nursery Rhymes.*** Frances Lincoln, 2015.

Opie, Iona, editor. ***Mother Goose's Little Treasures.*** Illus. Rosemary Wells. Candlewick, 2007.

Orozco, José Luis, selector and translator. ***Diez Deditos and Other Play Rhymes and Action Songs from Latin America.*** Illus. Elisa Kleven. Dutton, 1997. (Latin America)

Pinkney, Brian. ***Hush, Little Baby.*** Greenwillow, 2006.

Sehgal, Kabir. ***The Wheels on the Tuk Tuk.*** Illus. Jess Golden. Beach Lane Books, 2015. (India)

Taylor, Jane. ***Twinkle, Twinkle, Little Star.*** Illus. Jerry Pinkney. Little, Brown, 2011.

Wheeler, Lisa. ***Spinster Goose.*** Illus. Sophie Blackwell. Atheneum, 2011.

Wright, Danielle. ***My Village: Rhymes from around the World***. Illus. Mique Moriuchi. Frances Lincoln, 2010. (Global)

Wright, Danielle. ***Korean Nursery Rhymes: Wild Geese, Land of Goblins and Other Favorite Songs and Rhymes.*** Illus. Helen Acraman. Tuttle, 2013. (Korea)

Anthologies of Poetry

Ferris, Helen, compiler. ***Favorite Poems Old and New.*** Illus. Leonard Weisgard. Doubleday, 1957.

Hall, Donald, editor. ***The Oxford Illustrated Book of American Children's Poems.*** Oxford University Press, 1999.

Hoberman, Mary Ann, compiler. ***Forget Me Nots: Poems to Learn by Heart***. Illus. Michael Emberley. Little Brown, 2012.

Kennedy, Caroline, selector. ***Poems to Learn by Heart.*** Disney/Hyperion Books, 2013.

Martin, Bill, Jr., and Michael Sampson, editors. ***The Bill Martin Jr. Big Book of Poetry.*** Simon & Schuster, 2008.

Prelutsky, Jack, editor. ***The Random House Book of Poetry for Children.*** Illus. Arnold Lobel. Random House, 1983.

Yolen, Jane, and Andrew Peters, collectors. ***Here's a Little Poem: A Very First Book of Poetry.*** Illus. Polly Dunbar. Candlewick, 2007.

Themed Poetry Anthologies

Berry, James, editor. ***Around the World in Eighty Poems.*** Illus. Katherine Lucas. Chronicle, 2002. (Global)

Carlson, Lori, editor. ***Red Hot Salsa: Bilingual Poems on Being Young and Latino in the United States.*** Holt, 2005. Ages 10–16. Also ***Cool Salsa*** (1994).

Cullinan, Bernice, and Deborah Wooten, editors. ***Another Jar of Tiny Stars: Poems by More NCTE Award–Winning Poets.*** Wordsong, 2009. Also ***A Jar of Tiny Stars*** (1995).

Giovanni, Nikki, editor. ***Hip Hop Speaks to Children: A Celebration of Poetry with a Beat.*** Illus. K. Balouch. Sourcebooks, 2008.

Goldstein, Bobbye S., editor. ***Inner Chimes: Poems on Poetry.*** Illus. Jane Breskin Zalben. Wordsong, 1992.

Greenberg, Jan, editor. ***Side by Side: New Poems Inspired by Art from Around the World.*** Abrams, 2008. Ages 11–15. (Global)

Heard, Georgia, editor. ***Falling Down the Page***. Roaring Brook, 2009.

Heard, Georgia, editor. ***The Arrow Finds Its Mark: A Book of Found Poems***. Illus. Antoine Guilloppe. Roaring Brook, 2012.

Hopkins, Lee Bennett, selector. ***Sharing the Seasons: A Book of Poems***. Illus. David Diaz. McElderry, 2010.

Hopkins, Lee Bennett, selector. ***Amazing Places.*** Illus. Chris Soentpiet. Lee & Low, 2015.

Hopkins, Lee Bennett, selector. ***Jumping Off Library Shelves***. Illus. Jane Manning. WordSong, 2015.

Hudson, Wade, editor. ***Pass It On: African American Poetry for Children.*** Illus. Floyd Cooper. Scholastic, 1993.

Janeczko, Paul B., editor. ***A Poke in the I: A Collection of Concrete Poems.*** Illus. Chris Raschka. Candlewick, 2000.

Janeczko, Paul B., editor. ***A Kick in the Head: An Everyday Guide to Poetic Forms.*** Illus. Chris Raschka. Candlewick, 2005.

Janeczko, Paul B., editor. ***A Foot in the Mouth: Poems to Speak, Sing, and Shout.*** Illus. Chris Raschka. Candlewick, 2009.

Janeczko, Paul B., selector. ***Firefly July: A Year of Very Short Poems.*** Illus. Melissa Sweet. Candlewick Press, 2014.

Janeczko, Paul B., selector. ***The Death of the Hat: A Brief History of Poetry in 50 Objects.*** Illus. Chris Raschka. Candlewick, 2015.

Nye, Naomi Shihab, editor. ***19 Varieties of Gazelle: Poems of the Middle East.*** HarperCollins, 2002. Ages 11–18.

Peterson, Katherine, selector. ***Giving Thanks: Poems, Prayers, and Praise Songs of Thanksgiving.*** Illus. Pamela Dalton. Chronicle, 2013.

Rochelle, Belinda, selector. ***Words with Wings: A Treasury of African American Poetry and Art.*** HarperCollins, 2001.

Yoon, JooHee, selector and illustrator. ***Beastly Verse.*** Enchanted Lion, 2015.

Themed Poet Collections

Adoff, Arnold. ***Roots and Blues: A Celebration***. Illus. R. Gregory Christie. Clarion, 2011.

Agee, Jon. ***Orangutan Tongs: Poems to Tangle Your Tongue.*** Disney/Hyperion, 2009.

Brooks, Gwendolyn. ***Bronzeville Boys and Girls.*** Illus. Faith Ringgold. HarperCollins, 2007.

Burgess, Matthew. ***Enormous Smallness.*** Illus. Kris DiGiacomo. Enchanted Lion, 2015. Poetry/biography.

Coombs, Kate. ***Water Sings Blue: Ocean Poems.*** Illus. Meilo So. Chronicle, 2012.

Derby, Sally. ***Jump Back, Paul: The Life and Poems of Paul Laurence Dunbar.*** Illus. Sean Qualls. Candlewick, 2015. Poetry/biography.

Durango, Julia. ***Under the Mambo Moon.*** Illus. Frabricio Vanden Broeck. Charlesbridge, 2011. (Latin America)

Elliott, David. ***In the Wild.*** Illus. Holly Meade. Candlewick, 2010. Also ***In the Sea*** (2012) and ***On the Wing*** (2014).

Fleischman, Paul. ***Joyful Noise: Poems for Two Voices.*** Illus. Eric Beddows. Harper, 1988. Also ***I Am Phoenix: Poems for Two Voices*** (1985).

Florian, Douglas. ***Dinothesaurus: Prehistoric Poems and Paintings.*** Atheneum, 2009.

Florian, Douglas. ***Poetrees.*** Beach Lane, 2010.

Florian, Douglas. ***Shiver Me Timbers!: Pirate Poems & Paintings.*** Beach Lane, 2012.

Florian, Douglas. ***Poem Depot: Aisles of Smiles.*** Penguin, 2015.

Fogliano, Julie. ***When Green Becomes Tomatoes.*** Illus. Julie Morstad. Roaring Brook, 2016.

Franco, Betsy. ***A Dazzling Display of Dogs: Concrete Poems***. Illus. Michael Wertz. Tricycle, 2011. Also ***A Curious Collection of Cats*** (2009).

Franco, Betsy. ***Messing Around on the Monkey Bars And Other School Poems for Two Voices***. Illus. Jessie Harland. Candlewick, 2009.

Frank, John. ***Lend A Hand: Poems About Giving.*** Illus. London Ladd. Lee & Low, 2014.

George, Kristine O'Connell. ***Emma Dilemma: Big Sister Poems***. Illus. Nancy Carpenter. Clarion, 2011.

Grady, Cynthia. ***I Lay My Stitches Down: Poems of American Slavery.*** Illus. Michele Wood. Eerdmans, 2012.

Greenfield, Eloise. ***Honey, I Love, and Other Love Poems.*** Illus. Leo & Diane Dillon. HarperCollins, 1978.

Greenfield, Eloise. ***The Great Migration: Journeys to the North.*** Illus. Jan Spivey Gilchrist. Amistad, 2011.

Grimes, Nikki. ***Danitra Brown: Class Clown.*** Illus. E. B. Lewis. HarperCollins, 2005.

Harley, Avia. ***African Acrostics: A Word in Edgeways***. Photos Deborah Noyes. Candlewick, 2009. (Africa)

Hines, Anna Grossnickle. ***Peaceful Pieces: Poems and Quilts about Peace.*** Holt, 2011.

Hines, Nikki. ***Poems in the Attic.*** Illus. Elizabeth Zunon. Lee & Low, 2015.

Hughes, Langston. ***Sail Away.*** Illus. Ashley Bryan. Atheneum, 2015.

Jiang, Emily. ***Summoning the Phoenix: Poems and Prose about Chinese Musical Instruments.*** Illus. April Chu. Shen's Books, 2013. Poetry/information. (China)

Kuskin, Karla. ***Green as a Bean.*** Illus. Melissa Iwai. HarperCollins, 2007.

Latham, Irene. ***Dear Wandering Wildebeest: And Other Poems from the Water Hole.*** Illus. Anna Wadham. Millbrook, 2014. Poetry/information. (Kenya)

Lear, Edward. ***His Shoes Were Far Too Tight.*** Selected by Daniel Pinkwater. Illus. Calef Brown. Chronicle, 2011.

Lewis, J. Patrick. ***Edgar Allan Poe's Pies: Math Puzzlers in Classic Poems***. Illus. Michael Slack. Harcourt, 2012.

Lewis, J. Patrick. ***When Thunder Comes: Poems for Civil Rights Leaders***. Illus. Jim Burke. Chronicle, 2013.

Lewis, J. Patrick. ***Harlem Hellfighters***. Illus. Gary Kelley. Creative Editions, 2014.

Lewis, J. Patrick, and Nesbitt, Kenn. ***Bigfoot Is Missing!*** Illus. Minalima Design. Chronicle, 2015.

Mora, Pat. ***Yum! Mmmm! Que rico!: America's Sproutings***. Illus. Rafael Lopez. Lee & Low, 2007.

Muth, Jon J. ***Hi, Koo!: A Year of Seasons.*** Scholastic, 2014.

Myers, Walter Dean. ***Blues Journey.*** Illus. Christopher Myers. Holiday, 2003. See also ***Jazz*** (2006).

Myers, Walter Dean. ***We Are America: A Tribute from the Heart.*** Illus. Christopher Myers. Harper, 2011.

Nelson, Marilyn. ***A Wreath for Emmett Till.*** Illus. Philippe Lardy. Houghton, 2005. Ages 12–18.

Nelson, Marilyn. ***Sweethearts of Rhythm: The Story of the Greatest All Girl Swinging Band in the World.*** Illus. Jerry Pinkney. Dial, 2009. Ages 10–14.

Oliver, Lin. ***Little Poems for Tiny Ears.*** Illus. Tomie DePaola. Nancy Paulsen, 2014.

Orgill, Roxane. ***Jazz Day: The Making of a Famous Photograph.*** Illus. Francis Vallejo. Candlewick, 2016.

Park, Linda Sue. ***Tap Dancing on the Roof: Sijo (Poems).*** Illus. Istvan Banyai. Clarion, 2007. (Korea)

Pasckis, Julie. ***Flutter & Hum: Animal Poems/Aleteo y zumbido: Poemas de animales.*** Holt, 2015. Bilingual.

Prelutsky, Jack. ***I've Lost My Hippopotamus.*** Illus. Jackie Urbanovic. Greenwillow, 2012.

Prelutsky, Jack. ***Stardines Swim High Across the Sky and Other Poems.*** Illus. Carin Berger. Greenwillow, 2012.

Raczka, Bob. ***Lemonade: And Other Poems Squeezed from a Single Word.*** Illus. Nancy Doniger. Roaring Brook, 2011.

Raczka, Bob. ***Wet Cement: A Mix of Concrete Poems.*** Roaring Brook, 2016.

Rasmussen, Halfdan. ***A Little Bitty Man and Other Poems for the Very Young.*** Illus. Kevin Hawkes. Candlewick, 2011. Translated from Danish.

Rosen, Michael J. ***The Maine Coon's Haiku and Other Poems for Cat Lovers.*** Illus. Lee White. Candlewick, 2015.

Ruddell, Deborah. ***Today at the Bluebird Cafe: A Branchful of Birds.*** Illus. Joan Rankin. M. K. McElderry, 2007.

Ruddell, Deborah. ***A Whiff of Pine, a Hint of Skunk: A Forest of Poems.*** Illus. Joan Rankin. M. K. McElderry, 2009.

Salas, Laura P. ***Bookspeak: Poems about Books.*** Illus. Josee Bisaillon. Clarion, 2011.

Schertle, Alice. ***Button Up! Wrinkled Rhymes.*** Illus. Petra Mathers. Harcourt, 2009.

Schmidt, Annie. ***A Pond Full of Ink.*** Illus. Sieb Posthuma. Eerdmans, 2014. Translated from Dutch.

Shange, Ntozake. ***We Troubled the Waters.*** Illus. Rod Brown. Collins, 2009. Ages 10–14.

Sidman, Joyce. ***Red Sings from Treetops: A Year in Colors.*** Illus. Pamela Zagarenski. Houghton Mifflin, 2009.

Sidman, Joyce. ***Dark Emperor & Other Poems of the Night.*** Illus. Rick Allen. Houghton Mifflin, 2010.

Sidman, Joyce. ***Winter Bees & Other Poems of the Cold.*** Illus. Rick Allen. Houghton Mifflin Harcourt, 2014. Poetry/information.

Silverstein, Shel. ***Where the Sidewalk Ends.*** Harper, 1974. Also ***The Light in the Attic*** (1981).

Singer, Marilyn. ***Mirror Mirror: A Book of Reversible Verse.*** Illus. Josee Masse. Dutton, 2010.

Singer, Marilyn. ***A Full Moon Is Rising.*** Illus. Julia Cairns. Lee & Low, 2011. Global journey.

Singer, Marilyn. ***Rutherford B., Who Was He?: Poems About Our Presidents.*** Illus. John Hendrix. Disney/Hyperion Books, 2013.

Singer, Marilyn. ***Echo Echo: Reverso Poems about Greek Myths.*** Illus. Josee Masse. Dial, 2015. Greece

Smith, Charles. ***28 Days: Moments in Black History that Changed the World.*** Illus. Shane Evans. Roaring Brook, 2015. Poetry/biography/information.

Thomas, Joyce Carol. ***The Blacker the Berry.*** Illus. Floyd Cooper. HarperColllins, 2008.

Wardlaw, Lee. ***Won Ton: A Cat Tale Told in Haiku.*** Illus. Eugene Yelchin. Holt, 2011.

Willard, Nancy. ***A Visit to William Blake's Inn: Poems for Innocent and Experienced Travelers.*** Illus. Alice and Martin Provensen. Harcourt, 1981.

Worth, Valerie. ***Animal Poems.*** Illus. Steve Jenkins. Farrar, 2007.

Yolen, Jane. ***Birds of a Feather.*** Photos Jason Stemple. Wordsong, 2011.

Single Illustrated Poems

Picturebooks with a single illustrated poem are listed here. Illustrated stories in verse and rhyme are included in Chapter 5, Picturebooks and Graphic Novels.

Argueta, Jorge. ***Salsa: Un poema para cocinar: A Cooking Poem.*** Illus. Duncan Tonatiuh. Groundwood, 2015. Indigenous (Mexico)

Bartoletti, Susan. ***Naamah and the Ark at Night.*** Illus. Holly Meade. Candlewick, 2011. Arabic ghazel verse form.

Carroll, Lewis. ***Jabberwocky.*** Illus. Christopher Myers. Jump at the Sun/Hyperion, 2007.

Fitch, Sheree. ***Night Sky Wheel Ride.*** Illus. Yayo. Tradewind, 2012. (Canada)

Frost, Helen. ***Step Gently Out.*** Photos Rick Lieder. Candlewick, 2012.

Frost, Helen. ***Sweep Up the Sun.*** Illus. Rick Lieder. Candlewick, 2015.

Hughes, Langston. ***My People.*** Photos Charles R. Smith Jr. Atheneum, 2009.

Hughes, Langston. ***The Negro Speaks of Rivers.*** Illus. E. B. Lewis. Disney/Jump at the Sun, 2009.

Janeczko, Paul, and J. Patrick Lewis. ***Birds on a Wire: A Renga 'round Town.*** Illus. Gary Lippincott. Wordsong, 2008.

Pendziwol, Jean. ***Once Upon a Northern Night.*** Illus. Isabelle Arsenault. Groundwood, 2013. (Canada)

Sidman, Joyce. ***Swirl by Swirl: Spirals in Nature.*** Illus. Beth Krommes. Houghton Mifflin, 2011.

Thayer, Ernest L. ***Casey at the Bat: A Ballad of the Republic Sung in the Year 1888.*** Illus. C. F. Payne. Simon & Schuster, 2003.

Yolen, Jane. ***On Bird Hill.*** Illus. Bob Marstall. Cornell Lab Publishing, 2016.

Young, Ed. ***Should You Be a River: A Poem About Love.*** Little, Brown, 2015.

Chapter 7

Traditional Literature

Once Upon a Time

The Storyteller came to town
To share his gifts sublime.
   Tell it again. Storyteller
   Tell it again.
Onceupona
Onceupona
Onceuponatime,
   Tell it again. Storyteller
   Tell it again.
Doors flew open to him.
Kings begged him not depart,
And children tucked his stories
In the pockets of their heart.
Tell it again. Storyteller
   Tell it again.
Onceupona
Onceupona
Onceuponatime.
Tell it again. Storyteller
   Tell it again.
He told of scary ghosts
And of witches who became toast,
Of knights of old
And outlaws bold.
Oh
Onceupona
Onceupona
Onceuponatime.
   Tell it again. Storyteller
   Tell it again.

—Bill Martin Jr. and Michael Sampson

Visual narratives on ancient cave paintings in Europe, Asia, and Australia indicate that humans had stories to tell long before they had a written language. For thousands of years, the best of these stories were preserved through the art of storytelling from one generation to the next. These stories survived because people enjoyed hearing them and used them to make sense of their lives and world. Our most ancient stories are folk literature, providing a priceless literary and cultural heritage that links us to our beginnings as thinking beings.

Definition and Description

Traditional literature is the body of ancient stories and poems that grew out of the oral tradition of storytelling before being eventually written down. Having no known or identifiable authors, these stories and poems are attributed to entire groups of people or cultures. Although traditional stories are often told as cultural or spiritual truths or may contain factual elements, most are not based in real historical events.

Because these stories have been preserved over time, they provide insights into the underlying values and beliefs of particular cultural groups and opportunities for comparisons across cultures. Most are considered imaginative stories that provide a window into human nature and cultural beliefs. These traditional stories also provide the basis for many works of modern literature and drama and so children need a strong background in these stories.

Folklore is still being created, particularly in cultures and countries where the oral tradition remains an important means of communication. In the United States, urban legends, jokes, and jump-rope rhymes are part of the constantly evolving body of modern folklore.

Evaluation and Selection of Traditional Literature

For thousands of years, people of all ages were the intended audience for traditional stories. In our contemporary society with its strong focus on scientific fact, these stories of the supernatural and magic are often relegated to children, even though they are still enjoyed by adults. Traditional literature includes several different types of stories, but because they were all shared orally for so long, they have many features in common.

- ***Plots*** are short, simple, and direct; countless oral retellings retained only the essentials to the telling of the story.
- ***Action*** is concentrated and fast paced, adding interest.
- ***Characters*** are two-dimensional and easily identified as good or bad.
- ***Settings*** are unimportant and vague ("Long ago in a land far away").
- ***Literary style*** is characterized by standard beginnings and endings ("Once upon a time"), ***motifs*** (recurring features such as the number 3), and repeated refrains ("Mirror, mirror, on the wall").
- ***Themes*** are limited (e.g., good overcomes evil, the small and powerless overcome the powerful, explanations for the ways of the world).
- ***Endings*** are almost always happy ("and they lived happily ever after").

The following criteria are important to evaluating traditional literature:

- **Does the tale reflect a narrative storytelling style?** A traditional tale should sound as though it is being told even though it is written down.
- **Does the tale preserve the sound and "feel" of the culture or country of its origin?** Techniques involve the use of distinctive speech patterns and the integration of terms or proper names common to the culture.
- **Do the illustrations match the tone of the text and help to capture the essence of the culture?** Some illustrators use traditional art forms or folk art, whereas others use a style that is more contemporary but that still captures the tone of the story and the cultural context.
- **Does the tale employ a rich literary style?** Children are fascinated by the chants, stylistic flourishes, and colorful vocabulary that are characteristic of masterful storytelling.

In evaluating collections of traditional literature, consider the number and variety of tales in the collection and the reference aids, such as a table of contents and index to help readers locate tales. One issue raised by some adults in evaluating traditional literature is that the gruesome violence in traditional stories will harm or traumatize children. Many traditional stories have been rewritten to omit the violence, as in the Disney versions of folktales. In a "softened" version of "Snow White," the evil stepmother is forgiven by the heroine or banished from the kingdom instead of dancing to her death in red-hot iron shoes, which was her fate in early Grimm versions. Critics of these softened versions argue that altering the stories robs them of their power, appeal, and psychological benefit to children, who are reassured that the evil force is gone forever and cannot come back to hurt them (Bettleheim, 2010; Zipes, 2013).

Another critique is that many traditional tales reflect male chauvinism and poor female role models, from ever-sinister stepmothers to ever-helpless princesses. These stories reflect the values of past societies and of the male collectors who selected which tales to immortalize in written form. In addition, the written stories became frozen in time instead of continuing to evolve through oral retellings to reflect societal changes as they had for thousands of years. Collections of traditional literature that depict girls and women in more diverse roles are available, but the issue of gender continues to be a concern in selecting a range of traditional literature to share with children.

The Significance of Plot in Traditional Literature

Because traditional literature highlights simple direct plots, these stories provide an opportunity to explore plot as a sequence of events that show characters in conflict. Traditional literature is all about plot and so provides the opportunity for children to develop deeper insights into plot as a literary element. Traditional literature uses chronological or time order in ***rising action,*** in which the events rise by building suspense to a peak or ***climax,*** and then quickly conclude with ***falling action.*** The conclusion is a ***closed ending,*** in which the reader is assured that all is well. These explorations of the patterns in plot can be made visible by having children create plot lines to depict the exposition (the initial explanation of the situation and character), the rising action of the events, the climax, and the denouement or ending after the climax.

In the traditional tale of "Hansel and Gretel," for example, the exposition introduces a poor woodcutter, his young children, and his second wife during a time of famine. The rising action begins with the decision to leave the children in the woods and continues through a series of events until the children are trapped in the witch's house. The climax occurs when Gretel shoves the witch into the oven and the two children escape. The falling action traces the children's journey home and reunion with their father, along with news of their stepmother's death. The family becomes rich from the witch's treasure, and everyone lives happily ever after, bringing the story to conclusion.

Historical Overview of Traditional Literature

The world's first stories grew out of the dreams, wishes, ritual chants, and retellings of the notable exploits of our earliest ancestors. Little can be said about the early history of this genre except that these stories existed in oral form for thousands of years.

Folklorists are intrigued by the startling similarity of traditional tales around the world. "Cinderella"-type tales, for example, can be found in every culture. One explanation is that the first humans created these stories, which they took with them as they moved around the globe. This theory is called ***monogenesis,*** or "single origin." Another theory credits the fundamental psychological similarity of humans for the similarity of their stories. ***Polygenesis,*** or "many origins," holds that early humans had similar longings and intentions, asked similar fundamental questions about themselves and the world, and created similar stories in response. Both theories have merit, and since the answer lies hidden in ancient prehistory, neither theory has prevailed.

The popularity of traditional literature with children has continued to grow, owing in part to a renewed interest in storytelling. Trends contributing to the popularity of this genre are the publication of single illustrated retellings of traditional literature, cultural variants of traditional tales from around the world, and traditional literature reflecting the cultural diversity of groups within North America.

Types of Traditional Literature

Classification of traditional literature can be confusing, particularly because scholars use different terms for certain types of traditional stories. Also, modern stories written by known authors in the style of the traditional ones, but not of ancient and unknown origin, are not "traditional" in the strict sense. These stories are considered fantasy because they did not originate orally and have an identified author, such as the tales created by Hans Christian Andersen, and so are included in the chapter on fantasy.

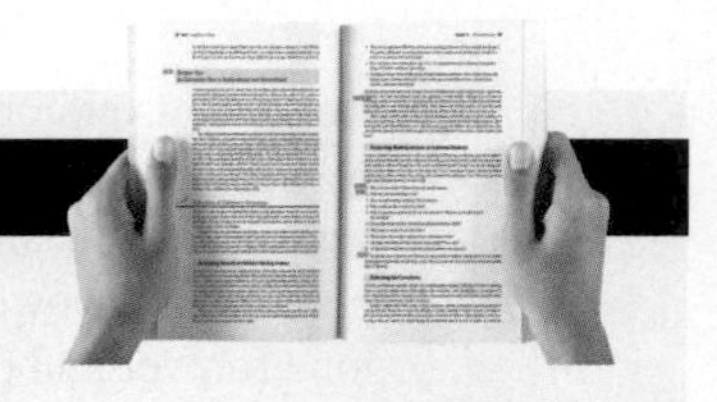

Excellent Traditional Literature to Read Aloud

Andrews, Jan. *When Apples Grew Noses and White Horses Flew: Tales of Ti-Jean.* Illustrated by Dusan Petricic. Ages 9–11. French-Canadian humorous fool tales.

Bryan, Ashley. *Can't Scare Me!* Ages 4–7. French Antilles trickster tale.

Chen, Jiang Hong. *The Magic Horse of Han Gan.* Ages 5–9. Chinese legend.

Emberley, Rebecca. *Chicken Little.* Illustrated by Ed Emberley. Ages 4–7. Aesop fable.

Fleischman, Paul. *Glass Slipper, Gold Sandal: A Worldwide Cinderella.* Illustrated by Julie Paschkis. Ages 6–10. Global folktale variants.

MacDonald, Margaret Read. *How Many Donkeys? An Arabic Counting Tale.* Illustrated by Carol Liddiment. Ages 4–7. Saudi wise fool tale.

Patel, Sanjay, & Haynes, Emily. *Ganesha's Sweet Tooth.* Ages 5–8. Hindu myth.

Pinkney, Jerry. *The Lion and the Mouse.* Ages 5–8. Aesop fable (wordless), set in Africa.

Riordan, Rick. *Percy Jackson's Greek Gods.* Illustrated by John Rocco. Ages 10–14. Greek myth.

The following terms are commonly used when referring to traditional literature:

- ***Traditional literature.*** The body of stories passed down from ancient times by oral tradition. The term ***folktales*** is sometimes used synonymously, but we use it as a subcategory of traditional literature.
- ***Retold tale.*** A ***version*** of a tale written in a style that will appeal to a contemporary audience but otherwise remains true to the ancient tale.
- ***Variant.*** A story that shares elements of plot or character with stories in the same "story family" but differs by culture. Some tales, such as "Cinderella," have hundreds of variants from around the world that originated in the ancient past. Modern variants in which an author uses these elements to create an original story in a new time and place are considered fantasy.

Myths

Myths are stories that recount and explain the origins of the world and the phenomena of nature. They are sometimes referred to as ***creation stories.*** The characters are mainly gods and goddesses, with occasional mention of humans, and the setting is high above Earth in the home of the gods. Although often violent, myths mirror human nature and the essence of our sometimes primitive emotions, instincts, and desires. Some folklorists believe that myths are the foundation of all other ancient stories. The best-known mythologies are of Greek, Roman, and Norse origin, but recent anthologies include the mythologies of Egypt and India. Many myths are published in collections like Katrin Tchana's *Changing Woman and Her Sisters* about goddesses from around the world and Rick Riordan's *Percy Jackson's Greek Gods.*

The complexity and symbolism often found in myths make them most appropriate for older children. Paul Fleischman and Julie Paschkis weave together the storylines from multiple global creation myths in *First Light, First Life*, an excellent example of a book aimed at a younger audience but enjoyed by readers of all ages.

Epics and Legends

Epics are long stories of human adventure and heroism recounted in many episodes, sometimes in verse. Epics are grounded in mythology, and their characters can be both human and divine. However, the hero is always human or, in some cases, superhuman, as were Ulysses and Beowulf. The setting is earthly but not always realistic. Because of their length and complexity, epics are more suitable for adolescents, but some have been adapted and shortened for younger audiences because of their compelling characters and events. A good example is "Beowulf," retold in three vividly illustrated versions by James Rumford, Gareth Hinds, and Nicky Raven.

Legends are stories based on real or supposedly real individuals and their marvelous deeds. Legendary characters such as King Arthur and Robin Hood and legendary settings such as Camelot are a tantalizing mix of

MILESTONES in the Development of Traditional Literature

Date	Event	Significance
Prehistory –1500s	Oral storytelling	Ancient stories as literature for the common people
500 B.C.E.	Aesop, a supposed Greek slave, wrote classic fables	Established the fable as a type of traditional literature
1484	*Aesop's Fables* published by William Caxton in England	First known publication of traditional literature
1500–1700	Puritan movement and chapbooks	Opposition to publication of traditional literature led to chapbooks to provide access
Late 1600s	Jean de la Fontaine of France adapted fables in verse form	Popularized the fable
1697	*Tales of Mother Goose* published by Charles Perrault in France	First written version of folktales
1700s	Romantic Movement	Traditional fantasy promoted and embraced in Europe
1812	Wilhelm and Jakob Grimm collected German *Nursery and Household Tales*	Popularized German folk literature
1851	Asbjørnsen and Moe collected *The Norwegian Folktales*	Popularized Nordic folk literature
1889–1894	Andrew Lang collected four volumes of world folktales	Growing popularity and knowledge of folktales worldwide
1894	Joseph Jacobs collected *English Fairy Tales* and adapted many tales for children	Popularized folk literature and made them accessible for children

realism and fantasy. Although the feats of these heroes defy belief today, in ancient times these stories were considered factual. Some legendary characters, such as Johnny Appleseed and John Henry, also appear in tall tales.

Folktales

Folktales are stories that grew out of the lives and imaginations of the people, or folk. Folktales have always been a favorite for children from age 3 and up. Folktales vary in content because of their original intended audiences. Long ago, the nobility and their courtiers heard ***castle stories*** of the heroism and benevolence of people like themselves—the ruling classes. In contrast, the ***cottage stories*** heard by the common people portrayed the ruling classes as unjust or hard taskmasters whose riches were fair game for quick-witted or strong common folk.

Some people use the terms ***folktale*** and ***fairy tale*** interchangeably. The majority of folktales have no fairies or magic characters, so to use one term in place of the other can be confusing and erroneous. Fairy tales are categorized here as a type of folktale that has magic characters such as fairies.

The following is a list of the most prevalent kinds of folktales. Note that some folktales have characteristics of two or more folktale categories.

Cumulative The ***cumulative tale*** uses repetition, accumulation, and rhythm to make an entertaining story out of the barest of plots. Because of its simplicity, rhythm, and humor, the cumulative tale has special appeal to young children, such as "The Gingerbread Man," with its runaway cookie and growing host of pursuers.

Humorous The ***humorous tale*** revolves around a character's incredibly stupid and funny mistakes. These tales are also known as ***noodleheads, sillies, drolls,*** and ***numbskulls.*** They have endured for their comic appeal and the laughter they evoke. Some famous noodleheads are the Norwegian husband who kept house (and nearly demolished it) and the Puerto Rican Juan Bobo who follows instructions too literally and goes from one disaster to another.

Beast The ***beast tale*** features talking animals and overstated action with occasional human characters, such as "Goldilocks and the Three Bears." Young children accept and enjoy these talking animals, and older children understand that the animals symbolize humans. Trickster tales are a type of beast tale that features an animal character who outsmarts others, such as Br'er Rabbit, Anansi the Spider, and Coyote.

Magic *Fairy tales* contain elements of magic or enchantment in characters, plots, or settings. Fairies, elves, pixies, witches, magicians, genies, and fairy godparents are pivotal characters, using magic objects or words to weave their enchantments. Talking mirrors, hundred-year naps, glass palaces, enchanted forests, thumb-sized heroines, and magic kisses are the stuff of magic tales, such as "The Princess and the Frog."

Pourquoi *Pourquoi tales* explain phenomena of nature as in "Why the Sun and Moon Live in the Sky." The word ***pourquoi*** is French for ***why,*** and these tales can be understood as explanations for the many "why" questions asked by early humans. The strong connection between these tales and myths is obvious, which is why some folklorists identify pourquoi tales as the simplest myths. However, deities play no role in pourquoi tales as they do in myths, and the setting in pourquoi tales is earthly, whereas the setting in myths is the realm of the gods.

Tall Tales *Tall tales* are highly exaggerated accounts of the exploits of persons, both real and imagined. Over time, as each teller embroidered on the hero's abilities or deeds, the tales became outlandishly exaggerated and were valued more for their humor and braggadocio than for their factual content. Well-known North American tall-tale heroes are Pecos Bill, Paul Bunyan, John Henry, and Johnny Appleseed. Lesser known but equally amazing are tall-tale heroines such as Sally Ann Thunder Ann Whirlwind Crockett.

Realistic *Realistic tales* are those whose characters, plot, and setting could conceivably have occurred. There is no magic in these tales, and any exaggeration is limited to the possible. Only a few realistic tales exist, including "Dick Whittington and His Cat."

Fables

The *fable* is a simple story that incorporates characters—typically animals—whose actions teach a moral lesson or universal truth with the moral stated at the end of the story. Fables appeal to adults as well as to children, for these stories are simple and wise. Moreover, their use of animals as symbols for humans have made them safe, yet effective, political tools. Perhaps because of their adult appeal, fables were put into print far earlier than other forms of traditional literature. Aesop's fables compose the best-known collection of fables in the Western world, but other collections include the Panchatantra tales from Persia; the Jataka tales from India; and the collected fables of Jean de la Fontaine from France.

Notable Retellers and Illustrators of Traditional Literature

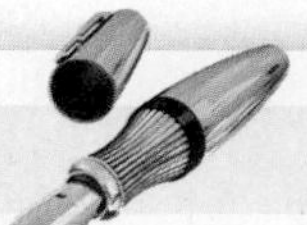

Ashley Bryan, illustrator and author of African traditional literature and African American spirituals. *Can't Scare Me!*; *Beautiful Blackbird; Ashley Bryan's African Tales, Uh-Huh; Let It Shine: Three Favorite Spirituals*. http://ashleybryancenter.org/

Trina Schart Hyman, reteller and illustrator of classic European folktales. *Little Red Riding Hood; The Sleeping Beauty; St. George and the Dragon.*

Margaret Read MacDonald, storyteller, collector, and reteller of global folklore. *Party Croc!; The Boy From the Dragon Palace; How Many Donkeys?; Give Up, Gecko!* www.margaretreadmacdonald.com/

George O'Connor, graphic novelist of Olympians series that retells classic Greek myths. *Athena: Grey-Eyed Goddess; Hades: Lord of the Dead.* www.olympiansrule.com

Jerry Pinkney, Caldecott medalist whose realistic watercolors invigorate folktales and fables. *The Grasshopper and the Ants*; *Noah's Ark; John Henry; The Lion and the Mouse.* www.jerrypinkneystudio.com/

Ed Young, illustrator and author of Chinese folklore and other global folklore. *Lon Po Po; Yeh-Shen; Seven Fathers; I, Doko: The Tale of a Basket.* www.edyoungart.com

Paul Zelinsky, illustrator whose realistic oil paintings provide insights into folktales. *Hansel and Gretel; Rapunzel; Rumpelstiltskin.* www.paulozelinsky.com/paul.html

Lisbeth Zwerger, illustrator from Vienna with a focus on translated European traditional literature. *Tales from Brothers Grimm; The Pied Piper of Hamlin, Aesop's Fables.*

Religious Stories

Stories based on religious writings or taken intact from religious manuscripts are considered to be ***religious stories.*** These stories may recount milestones in the development of a religion and its leadership, or they may present a piece of religious doctrine in narrative form, called ***parables.***

Scholars of religion, language, and mythology have found a definite thread of continuity from myth and folk narrative to early religious thinking and writing. Many of the stories, figures, and rituals described in the sacred scriptures of Christianity, Hinduism, and Buddhism, among other religions, have their roots in ancient mythology.

Regardless of whether religious stories are considered fact or fiction, these stories are rich with cultural and spiritual narratives and provide unique perspectives for readers. Indigenous scholars argue that much of their traditional literature is rooted in spiritual beliefs but have been mislabeled as legend. Because religion in the classroom is potentially controversial, some teachers and librarians do not feel comfortable sharing stories with religious connections. The consequence is that children miss characters, sayings, situations, and stories essential to understanding particular cultures.

Reader Connections: Storytelling in the Classroom

Given that traditional literature is rooted in oral tradition, telling these stories provides an effective and powerful means for engaging children with this literature. Children are attentive listeners when adults tell stories and quickly begin telling stories themselves. By bringing stories to life through personal expression and interpretation, storytellers establish a close communication with their audience and are a form of reader response.

Selection of a Story

To find stories for telling, read through collections of folktales and short stories until you find several you especially like. Consider these points:

- Good stories for telling usually have few characters (from two to five), high conflict, action that builds to a climax, and a quick conclusion that ties together all the threads of the story. Humorous elements are also worth seeking.
- Initially select short stories that are shorter than 10 minutes before moving to longer stories.

Good resources for teachers and students who want to tell stories are Pellowski's *The Storytelling Handbook* (2008), Freeman's *The Handbook for Storytellers* (2015), MacDonald's *Teaching with Story* (2013), and Bruchac's *Tell Me a Tale* (1997). Websites that provide stories and storytelling resources and tips include www.storyarts.org and www.storynet.org.

Preparation for Telling

Outline the story content in terms of the plot. Many storytellers note the title and source of the tale, the characters' names and story events, and any other information that may be helpful on an index card to consult quickly before telling a story. Another option is to tape yourself telling stories to use in refreshing your memory for retellings.

Tell the story aloud to yourself again and again. Do not memorize the story, but keep in mind the characters and sequence of main story events. Each time you tell the story, it will change a bit, becoming more and more your own story as you include personal touches. Some storytellers use simple props (a hat, stick-on mustache, or stuffed toy) or more elaborate ones (a mask, puppet, or costume). You can also tell stories with pictures or objects that you move around during the story.

Digital storytelling connects the age-old art of storytelling with children's digital worlds through the use of computer-based tools. Digital stories can be personal narratives, traditional tales, or historical recounts that combine computer-based images, text, recorded audio narration, video clips, photographs, drawings, and/or music to tell a brief story. Resources include Miller's *Make Me a Story* (2010), Ohler's *Digital Storytelling in the Classroom* (2013), the Center for Digital Storytelling (www.storycenter.org), and Educational Uses of Digital Storytelling (http://digitalstorytelling.coe.uh.edu).

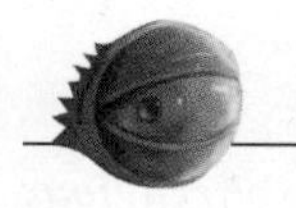

Invitations for Further Investigation

- Explore sexism in traditional literature and the subtle messages conveyed to children. Also examine less well-known tales that portray women as leaders rather than victims, such as Jane Yolen's *Not One Damsel in Distress.*
- Create plot lines to show the action in several folktales and discuss the patterns that emerge. Compare the patterns in plot lines in folklore from different cultures.
- Engage in a cross-cultural analysis of the "Cinderella" tale. Gather variants from around the world, including Asian, Western European, and American Indian cultures. Compare plot details, themes, and gender messages.
- Disney versions of fairy tales enjoy tremendous popularity and yet are negatively critiqued as stereotyped. Watch the video *Mickey Mouse Monopoly* or locate articles that critique Disney films and books. Use the stereotypes chart in Christensen (2002) to engage in your own analysis.
- Select, learn, and tell (not read) a folktale to a group of children, using props, if appropriate. Note the differences in telling and reading a story to a young audience.
- Select a folktale and create a digital telling of that story using the online websites for suggestions.

References

Bettelheim, B. (2010). *The uses of enchantment*. New York: Vintage.

Bruchac, J. (1997). *Tell me a tale*. San Diego, CA: Harcourt.

Christensen, L. (2002). Unlearning the myths that bind us. In *Reading, Writing and Rising Up* (pp. 39–51). Milwaukee, WI: Rethinking Schools.

Freeman, J. (2015). *The handbook for storytellers*. Chicago: American Library Association.

MacDonald, M. R. (2013). *Teaching with story*. Atlanta, GA: August House.

Martin, B., Jr. & Sampson, M. (2008). Once upon a time. In B. Martin Jr, *The Bill Martin Jr. big book of poetry*. New York: Simon & Schuster.

Miller, L. (2010). *Make me a story*. Portland, ME: Stenhouse.

Ohler, J. (2013). *Digital storytelling in the classroom*. Thousand Oaks, CA: Corwin.

Pellowski, A. (2008). *The storytelling handbook*. New York: Aladdin.

Zipes, J. (2013). *The irresistible fairy tale: The cultural and social history of a genre*. New York: Princeton University.

Recommended Traditional Literature

Ages refer to concept and interest levels. Formats other than novels will be coded as follows:

(**PB**) Picturebook
(**COL**) Short story collection
(**GR**) Graphic novel

Myths

d'Aulaire, Ingri, and Edgar Parin d'Aulaire. ***Norse Gods and Giants.*** Doubleday, 1967. (**COL**). Ages 8–10. (Norway)

Fleischman, Paul. ***First Light, First Life.*** Illus. Julie Paschkis. Holt, 2016. (**PB**). Ages 6–10. (Global)

Gerstein, Mordicai. ***I am Pan***. Roaring Brook, 2014. Ages 7–11. (Greece)

Hamilton, Virginia, reteller. ***In the Beginning: Creation Stories from Around the World.*** Illus. Barry Moser. Harcourt, 1988. (**COL**). Ages 9–12. (Global)

Karas, G. Brian. ***Young Zeus.*** Scholastic, 2010. (**PB**). Ages 5–8. (Greece)

Kimmel, Eric. ***The McElderry Book of Greek Myths.*** Illus. Pep Montserrat. M. K. McElderry, 2008. (**COL**). Ages 9–12. (Greece)

Marshall, James. ***Stories from the Billabong***. Illus. Francis Firebrace, Frances Lincoln, 2008. (**COL**). Ages 5–9. (Australian Aboriginal)

Menchú, Rigoberta, and Dante Liano. ***The Honey Jar.*** Translated by David Unger. Illus. Domi. Groundwood, 2006. (**COL**). Ages 9–12. (Guatemala/Mayan)

Napoli, Donna. ***Treasury of Norse Mythology.*** Illus. Christina Balit. National Geographic, 2015. (**COL**). Ages 9–14. (Norway)

O'Connor, George. ***Hades: Lord of the Dead***. First Second, 2011. (**GR**). Ages 10–14. Olympians series on Greek gods. Also **Ares: Bringer of War** (2015). (Greece)

Riordan, Rick. ***Percy Jackson's Greek Gods.*** Illus. John Rocco. Disney/Hyperion, 2014. (**COL**). Ages 10–14.

Tchana, Katrin Hyman. ***Changing Woman and Her Sisters.*** Illus. Trina Schart Hyman. Holiday, 2006. (**COL**). Ages 10–14. (Global)

Williams, Marcia. ***Ancient Egypt: Tales of Gods and Pharaohs.*** Candlewick, 2011. (**GR**). Ages 9–12. (Egypt)

Epics and Legends

Arni, Samhita. ***Sita's Ramayana.*** Illus. Moyna Chitraker. Groundwood, 2011. (**GR**). Ages 12–15. (India)

Chen, Jiang Hong. ***The Magic Horse of Han Gan.*** Translated by Claudia Zoe Bedrick. Enchanted Lion, 2006. (**PB**). Ages 5–9. (China)

Clayton, Sally. ***Rama and Sita: Path of Flames.*** Illus. Sophie Hersheimer. Frances Lincoln, 2010. Ages 9–12. (India)

Henderson, Kathy. ***Lugalbanda: The Boy Who Got Caught Up in a War.*** Illus. Jane Ray. Candlewick, 2006. (**PB**). Ages 9–12. (Iraq)

Hinds, Gareth. ***Beowulf.*** Candlewick, 2007. (**GR**). Ages 10–14. (U.K.)

Hinds, Gareth. ***The Odyssey***. Candlewick, 2010. (**GR**). Ages 12–15. (Greece)

Hodges, Margaret. ***Saint George and the Dragon.*** Illus. Trina Schart Hyman. Little, Brown, 1984. (**PB**). Ages 8–10. (U.K.)

Jules, Jacqueline. ***Never Say a Mean Word Again: A Tale From Medieval Spain.*** Illus. Durga Bernhard. Wisdom Tales, 2014. (**PB**). Ages 5–9. (Spain)

Laird, Elizabeth. ***Shahnameh: The Persian Book of Kings.*** Illus. Shirin Adl. Frances Lincoln, 2014. (**COL**). Ages 9–12. (Iran)

Lee, Tony. ***Excalibur: The Legend of King Arthur***. Illus. Sam Hart. Candlewick, 2011. (**GR**). Ages 11–15. (U.K.)

Mandell, Muriet. ***A Donkey Reads.*** Illus. Andre Letria. Star Bright, 2011. (**PB**). Ages 5–9. (Turkey)

Morpurgo, Michael. ***Sir Gawain and the Green Knight.*** Illus. Michael Foreman. Candlewick, 2015. Ages 10–13. (U.K.)

Morris, Gerald. ***The Legend of the King.*** Houghton Mifflin, 2010. Ages 10–14. Squire's Tales series. (King Arthur, U.K.)

Raven, Nicky. ***Beowulf.*** Illus. John Howe. Candlewick, 2007. Ages 10–14. (U.K.)

Rumford, James. ***Beowulf: A Hero's Tale Retold.*** Houghton Mifflin, 2007. Ages 10–14. (U.K.)

San Souci, Robert. ***Robin Hood and the Golden Arrow.*** Illus. E. B. Lewis. Orchard, 2010. (**PB**). Ages 6–9. (U.K.)

Souhami, Jessica. ***Rama and the Demon King: An Ancient Tale from India.*** Frances Lincoln, 2015. (**PB**). Ages 5–9. (India, The Ramayana)

Tonatiuh, Duncan. ***The Princess and the Warrior: A Tale of Two Volcanoes***. Abrams, 2016. (**PB**). Ages 6-10. (Mexico, Indigenous)

Watts, Irene N. ***Clay Man: The Golem of Prague.*** Illus. Kathryn E. Shoemaker. Tundra, 2009. Ages 9–12. (Czech Republic)

Wisniewski, David. ***Golem.*** Clarion, 1996. (PB). Ages 6–12. (Jewish legend, Czech Republic)

Folktales

Aardema, Verna. ***Why Mosquitoes Buzz in People's Ears.*** Illus. Leo & Diane Dillon. Dial, 1975. (**PB**). Ages 5–7. (Kenya)

Allen, Nancy. ***First Fire: A Cherokee Folktale.*** Illus. Sherry Rogers. Sylvan Dell, 2014. (**PB**). Ages 5–8. (Cherokee)

Andrews, Jan. ***When the Apples Grew Noses and White Horses Flew: Tales of Ti-Jean.*** Illus. Dusan Petricic. Groundwood, 2011. (**PB**). Ages 9–11. (French Canadian)

Aylesworth, Jim. ***The Mitten.*** Illus. Barbara McClintock. Scholastic, 2009. (**PB**). Ages 5–9. (Ukraine)

Aylesworth, Jim. ***My Grandfather's Coat.*** Illus. Barbara McClintock. Scholastic, 2014. (**PB**). Ages 4–9. (Yiddish folk song)

Brown, Marcia. ***Stone Soup.*** Scribner, 1975/1947. (**PB**). Ages 6–8. (France)

Bruchac, Joseph. ***The Hunter's Promise***. Illus. Bill Farnsworth. Wisdom Tales, 2015. (**PB**). Ages 6–8. (Abenaki)

Bruchac, James, and Joseph Bruchac. ***The Girl Who Helped Thunder and Other Native American Folktales.*** Illus. Stefano Vitale. Sterling, 2008. (**COL**). Ages 9–12. (American Indian)

Bryan, Ashley. ***Beautiful Blackbird.*** Atheneum, 2003. (**PB**). Ages 5–7. (Zambia)

Bryan, Ashley. ***Can't Scare Me!*** Atheneum, 2003. (**PB**). Ages 4–8. (St. Thomas)

Bunanta, Murti. ***The Tiny Boy and Other Tales from Indonesia.*** Illus. Hardiyono. Groundwood, 2013. (**COL**). Ages 8–12. (Indonesia)

Campoy, F. Isabel. ***Tales Our Abuelitas Told: A Hispanic Folktale Collection.*** Illus. Felipe Davalos. Atheneum, 2006. (**COL**). Ages 5–9. (Latino/global)

Dembicki, Matt, editor. ***Trickster: Native American Tales***. Fulcrum, 2010. (**GR, COL**). Ages 10–14. (American Indian)

Demi. ***The Hungry Coat.*** M. K. McElderry, 2004. (**PB**). Ages 5–9. (Turkey)

dePaola, Tomie. ***Strega Nona.*** Prentice Hall, 1975. (**PB**). Ages 5–8. (Italy)

Duffy, Chris (editor). ***Fairy Tale Comics.*** First Second, 2013. (**COL, GR**). Ages 7–10. (Europe)

Emberley, Rebecca. ***Chicken Little.*** Illus. Ed Emberley. Roaring Brook, 2009. (**PB**). Ages 4–7. (U.K.)

Flanagan, Liz. ***Dara's Clever Trap.*** Illus. Martina Peluso. Barefoot, 2014. (**PB**). Ages 6–8. (Cambodia)

Fleischman, Paul. ***Glass Slipper, Gold Sandal: A Worldwide Cinderella.*** Illus. Julie Paschkis. Holt, 2007. (**PB**). Ages 5–9. (Global)

Galdone, Paul. ***The Gingerbread Man.*** Clarion, 1975. (**PB**). Ages 4–6. See also ***The Little Red Hen*** (1973) and ***The Three Billy Goats Gruff*** (1973). (U.K.)

Gerson, Mary-Joan. ***Fiesta Femenina: Celebrating Women in Mexican Folktales.*** Barefoot, 2001. (**COL**). Ages 10–13. (Mexico)

Goble, Paul. ***The Girl Who Loved Wild Horses.*** Atheneum, 1978. (**PB**). Ages 4–8. (Plains Indian)

Goble, Paul. ***The Man Who Dreamed of Elk-Dogs & Other Stories from the Tipi.*** Wisdom Tales, 2012. (**COL**). Ages 9–11. (Blackfoot, Lakota, Assiniboin, Pawnee, and Cheyenne)

Goldman, Judy. ***Whiskers, Tails, & Wings: Animal Folktales from Mexico***. Illus. Fabricio V. Broeck. Charlesbridge, 2013. (**COL**). Ages 7–11. (Mexico, Indigenous)

Grimm, Jacob, and Wilhelm Grimm. ***Little Red Riding Hood.*** Illus. Sybille Schenker. Minedition, 2014. (**PB**). Ages 5–10. (Germany)

Grimm, Jacob, and Wilhelm Grimm. ***Little Red Riding Hood.*** Illus. Trina Schart Hyman. Holiday, 1982. (**PB**). Ages 6–8. (Germany)

Grimm, Jacob, and Wilhelm Grimm. ***Hansel and Gretel.*** Illus. Anthony Browne. Knopf, 1998 (1981). (**PB**). Ages 8–14. (Germany)

Hamilton, Virginia. ***The People Could Fly: The Picture Book.*** Illus. Leo Dillon. Knopf, 1985. (**PB**). Ages 8–12. (African American)

Hamilton, Virginia. ***Her Stories: African American Folktales, Fairy Tales, and True Tales.*** Illus. Leo & Diane Dillon. Scholastic, 1995. (**COL**). Ages 9–15. (African American).

Hamilton, Virginia. ***The Girl Who Spun Gold.*** Illus. Leo & Diane Dillon. Blue Sky, 2000. (**PB**). Ages 5–8. (West India)

Hamilton, Virginia. ***Bruh Rabbit and the Tar Baby Girl.*** Illus. James Ransome. Scholastic, 2003. (**PB**). Ages 5–7. (Gullah, South Carolina)

Hodges, Margaret, reteller. ***Dick Whittington and His Cat.*** Illus. Melisande Potter. Holiday, 2006. (**PB**). Ages 5–9. (U.K.)

Hurston, Zora Neale. ***Lies and Other Tall Tales.*** Illus. Christopher Myers. HarperCollins, 2005. (**PB**). Ages 7–10. (Southern U.S.)

Hyman, Trina Schart. ***The Sleeping Beauty.*** Little, Brown, 1977. (**PB**). Ages 5–8. (Germany)

Isadora, Rachel. ***The Twelve Dancing Princesses.*** Putnam, 2007. (**PB**). Ages 5–9. (Africa)

Janisch, Heinz. ***Fantastic Adventures of Baron Munchausen: Traditional and Newly Discovered Tales of Karl Friedrich Hieronymus van Munchausen.*** Translated by Belinda Cooper. Illus. Aljoscha Blau. Enchanted Lion, 2009. (**PB**). Ages 6–9. (Germany, tall tale)

Johnson-Davies, Denys. ***Goha the Wise Fool.*** Illus. Hany El Saed Ahmed and Hag Hamdy Mohamed Fattouh. Philomel, 2005. (**COL**). Ages 6–12. (Middle East)

Kellogg, Steven, reteller. ***Paul Bunyan.*** Morrow, 1984. (**PB**). Ages 6–8. Also ***Johnny Appleseed*** (1988) and ***Pecos Bill*** (1986). (United States, tall tales)

Kilaka, John. ***True Friends.*** Groundwood, 2006. (**PB**). Ages 5–9. (Tanzania)

Knutson, Barbara. ***Love and Roast Chicken: A Trickster Tale from the Andes Mountains.*** Carolrhoda, 2004. (**PB**). Ages 4–7. (Peru)

Laird, Elizabeth. ***The Ogress and the Snake and Other Stories from Somalia***. Illus. Shelley Fowles. Frances Lincoln, 2009. (**COL**). Ages 9–12. (Somalia)

Laird, Elizabeth. ***Pea Boy and Other Stories from Iran***. Illus. Shirin Adl. Frances Lincoln, 2010. (**COL**). Ages 9–12. (Iran)

Lesser, Rika. ***Hansel and Gretel.*** Illus. Paul Zelinsky. Dutton, 1999. (**PB**). Ages 5–8. (Germany)

Lester, Julius, reteller. ***The Tales of Uncle Remus: The Adventures of Brer Rabbit.*** Illus. Jerry Pinkney. Dial, 1987. (**COL**). Ages 7–9. (African American)

Lester, Julius, reteller. ***John Henry.*** Illus. Jerry Pinkney. Dial, 1994. (**PB**). Ages 8–10. (African American tall tale)

Louie, Ai-Ling. ***Yeh-Shen: A Cinderella Story from China.*** Illus. Ed Young. Philomel, 1982. (**PB**). Ages 7–9. (China)

Lunge-Larsen, Lise. ***The Hidden Folk: Stories of Fairies, Dwarves, Selkies, and Other Secret Beings.*** Illus. Beth Krommes. Houghton, 2004. (**COL**). Ages 6–12. (Northern Europe)

MacDonald, Margaret R. ***How Many Donkeys? An Arabic Counting Tale.*** Illus. Carol Liddiment. Whitman, 2009. (**PB**). Ages 3–6. (Middle East)

MacDonald, Margaret. ***The Boy from the Dragon Palace.*** Illus. Sachiko Yoshikawa. Whitman, 2011. (**PB**). Ages 4–8. (Japan)

MacDonald, Margaret. ***Give Up, Gecko!*** Illus. Deborah Melmon. Amazon Children's Pub, 2013. (**PB**). Ages 4–8. (Uganda)

MacDonald, Margaret. ***Party Croc!*** Illus. Derek Sullivan. Whitman, 2015. (**PB**). Ages 4–8. (Zimbabwe)

Marshall, James. ***Goldilocks and the Three Bears.*** Dial, 1988. (**PB**). Ages 5–7. (U.K.)

Martin, Rafe, reteller. ***The Rough-Face Girl.*** Illus. David Shannon. Putnam, 1992. (**PB**). Ages 8–10. (Mi'kmaq)

McDermott, Gerald. ***Monkey: A Trickster Tale.*** Harcourt, 2011. (**PB**). Ages 6–9. (India)

McGill, Alice. ***Way Up and Over Everything.*** Illus. Jude Daly. Houghton Mifflin, 2008. (**PB**). Ages 8–12. (African American)

Mollel, Tololwa. ***Subira Subira.*** Illus. Linda Saport. Clarion, 2000. (**PB**). Ages 5–10. (Tanzania)

Muth, Jon J. ***Stone Soup.*** Scholastic, 2003. (**PB**). Ages 4–8. (China)

Nshizuka, Koko. ***The Beckoning Cat.*** Illus. Roxanne Litzinger. (**PB**). Ages 6–9. Holiday, 2009. (Japan)

Onyefulu, Ifeoma. ***The Girl Who Married a Giant and Other Tales from Nigeria.*** Illus. Julia Cairns. Frances Lincoln, 2010. (**COL**). Ages 9–12. (Nigeria)

Paterson, Katherine. ***The Tale of the Mandarin Ducks.*** Illus. Leo and Diane Dillon. Lodestar, 1990. (**PB**). Ages 7–9. (Japan)

Perrault, Charles. ***Cinderella.*** Illus. Marcia Brown. Scribner, 1954. (**PB**). Ages 6–8. (France)

Perrault, Charles. ***Puss in Boots.*** Illus. Fred Marcellino. Farrar, 1990. (**PB**). Ages 6–8. (France)

Pinkney, Jerry. ***Little Red Riding Hood.*** Little. Brown, 2007. (**PB**). Ages 5–9. (Germany)

Powell, Patricia H. ***Frog Brings Rain/Ch'at Tó Yinílo'.*** Translated by Peter A. Thomas. Illus. Kendrick Benally. Salina Bookshelf, 2006. (**PB**). Ages 5–8. (Navajo)

Raecke, Renate. ***The Pied Piper of Hamelin.*** Illus. Lisbeth Zwerger. Minedition, 2014. (**PB**). Ages 5–9. (Germany)

Ramsden, Ashley. ***Seven Fathers***. Illus. Ed Young. Roaring Brook, 2011. (**PB**). Ages 6–9. (Norway)

San Souci, Robert. ***Sister Tricksters: Rollicking Tales of Clever Females.*** Illus. Daniel San Souci. August House, 2006. (**COL**). Ages 8–12. (Southern U.S.)

San Souci, Robert. ***As Luck Would Have It: From the Brothers Grimm.*** Illus. Daniel San Souci. August House, 2008. (**COL**). Ages 5–10. (Germany)

Scott, Nathan. ***The Sacred Banana Leaf: An Indonesian Trickster Tale.*** Illus. Radhashyam Raut. Tara, 2008. (**PB**). Ages 6–9. (Indonesia). Also ***The Great Race*** (2011).

Sellier, Marie. ***What the Rat Told Me: A Legend of the Chinese Zodiac.*** Illus. Catherine Louis and Wang Fu. North-South, 2009. (**PB**). Ages 6–9. (China)

Shelby, Anne. ***The Man Who Lived in a Hollow Tree.*** Illus. Cor Hazelaar. Atheneum, 2009. (**PB**). Ages 6–9. (Appalachian tall tale)

Singer, Isaac Bashevis. ***When Shlemiel Went to Warsaw and Other Stories.*** Translated by Elizabeth Shub. Illus. Margot Zemach. Farrar, 1968. (**COL**). Ages 8–10. (Jewish, Poland)

Smith, Chris. ***One City, Two Brothers.*** Illus. Aurélia Fronty. Barefoot Books, 2007. (**PB**). Ages 5–9. (Israel)

Stampler, Ann. ***The Rooster Prince of Breslov***. Illus. Eugene Yelchin. Clarion, 2010. (**PB**). Ages 6–9. (Ukraine)

Steptoe, John. ***Mufaro's Beautiful Daughters.*** Lothrop, 1987. (**PB**). Ages 6–8. (Zimbabwe)

Storace, Patricia. ***Sugar Cane: A Caribbean Rapunzel.*** Illus. Raúl Colón. Hyperion, 2007. (**PB**). Ages 9–12. (Caribbean)

Taback, Simms, reteller. ***This Is the House That Jack Built.*** Putnam, 2002. (**PB**). Ages 5–7. (Hebrew)

Tan, Shaun. ***The Singing Bones.*** Scholastic, 2016. (**COL**). Ages 12–18. (Germany)

Tatar, Maria. ***The Story of Little Red Riding Hood.*** Illus. Christopher Bing. Handprint, 2010. (**PB**). Ages 6–9. (Germany)

Tchana, Katrin. ***The Serpent Slayer and Other Stories of Strong Women.*** Illus. Trina Schart Hyman. Little, Brown, 2000. (**COL**). Ages 7–12. (Global)

Tarnowska, Wafa. ***The Arabian Nights.*** Illus. Carole Henaff. Barefoot, 2010. **(COL).** Ages 9–12. (Lebanon)

Taylor, Sean. ***The Great Snake: Stories from the Amazon.*** Illus. Fernando Vilela. Frances Lincoln, 2008. **(COL).** Ages 9–12. (Brazil)

Walser, David. ***The Glass Mountain.*** Illus. Jan Pienkowski. Candlewick, 2014. (**COL**). Ages 8–11. (Poland)

Weulersse, Odile. ***Nasreddine***. Illus. Rebecca Dautemer. Erdmans, 2013. Translated from French by Kathleen Marz. (**PB**). Ages 6–9. (Middle East)

Yolen, Jane. ***Not One Damsel in Distress: World Folktales for Strong Girls.*** Illus. Susan Guevara. Silver Whistle, 2000. (**COL**). Ages 8–13. (Global)

Young, Ed. ***Lon Po Po: A Red-Riding Hood Story from China.*** Philomel, 1989. (**PB**). Ages 7–9. (China)

Young, Ed. ***I, Doko: The Tale of a Basket.*** Philomel, 2004. (**PB**). Ages 5–9. (Nepal)

Zelinsky, Paul. ***Rapunzel.*** Dutton, 1997. (**PB**). Ages 5–8. (Germany) See also ***Rumpelstiltskin*** (1986).

Zemach, Harve. ***Duffy and the Devil.*** Illus. Margot Zemach. Farrar, 1973. (**PB**). Ages 6–8. (U.K.)

Zemach, Margot. ***It Could Always Be Worse.*** Farrar, 1977. (**PB**). Ages 6–8. (Jewish)

Zwerger, Lisbeth (editor, illustrator). ***Tales from the Brothers Grimm.*** Minedition, 2013. (**COL**). Ages 9–13. (Germany)

Fables

Brown, Marcia. ***Once a Mouse.*** Scribner, 1961. (**PB**). Ages 6–8. (India)

Burkert, Rand. ***Mouse & Lion.*** Illus. Nancy Ekholm Burkert. Michael di Capua Books, 2011. (**PB**). Ages 5–9. (Aesop)

Duffy, Chris (editor). ***Fable Comics.*** First Second, 2015. (**COL, GR**). Ages 6–10. (Global)

Husain, Shahrukh. ***The Wise Fool: Fables from the Arabic World.*** Illus. Micha Archer. Barefoot, 2011. (**COL**). Ages 6–9. (Arabic)

Naidoo, Beverley. ***Aesop's Fables.*** Illus. Piet Grobler. Frances Lincoln, 2011. (**COL**). Ages 6–9. (Aesop/ South African setting)

Pinkney, Jerry. ***The Lion and the Mouse.*** Little, Brown, 2009. (**PB**). Ages 5–9. (Aesop, wordless). Also ***The Tortoise and the Hare*** (2013).

Pinkney, Jerry. ***The Grasshopper and the Ants.*** Little, Brown, 2015. (**PB**). Ages 3–6. (Aesop)

Wormell, Christopher. ***Mice, Morals, & Monkey Business: Lively Lessons from Aesop's Fables.*** Running Press, 2005. (**COL**). Ages 5–8. (Aesop)

Religious Stories

Hao, K. T. ***Little Stone Buddha.*** Translated by Annie Kung. Illus. Giuliano Ferri. Purple Bear, 2005. (**PB**). Ages 4–7. (Buddhist)

Koralek, Jenny. ***The Story of Queen Esther.*** Illus. Grizelda Holderness. Eerdmans, 2009. (**PB**). Ages 6–9. (Jewish)

Muth, Jon. ***Zen Shorts.*** Scholastic, 2005. (**PB, COL**). Ages 5–9. See also ***Zen Socks*** (2015). (Buddhist)

Patel, Sanjay, and Haynes, Emily. ***Ganesha's Sweet Tooth.*** Chronicle, 2012. (**PB**). Ages 5–8. (Hindu)

Pinkney, Jerry. ***Noah's Ark.*** North-South, 2002. (**PB**). Ages 5–8. (Jewish/Christian)

Snyder, Laurel. ***The Longest Night: A Passover Story.*** Illus. Catia Chien. Schwartz & Wade, 2013. (**PB**). Ages 6–10. (Jewish/Egypt)

Stampler, Ann R. ***The Wooden Sword: A Jewish Folktale from Afghanistan.*** Illus. Carol Liddiment. Albert Whitman & Co., 2012. (**PB**). Ages 5–8. (Jewish/Afghanistan).

Wolf, Gita. ***The Enduring Ark.*** Illus. Joydeb Chitrakar. Tara Books, 2012. (**PB**). Ages 3 and up. (Indian retelling of Noah's Ark)

Young, Ed. ***Monkey King.*** HarperCollins, 2001. (**PB**). Ages 5–8. (Buddhist, China)

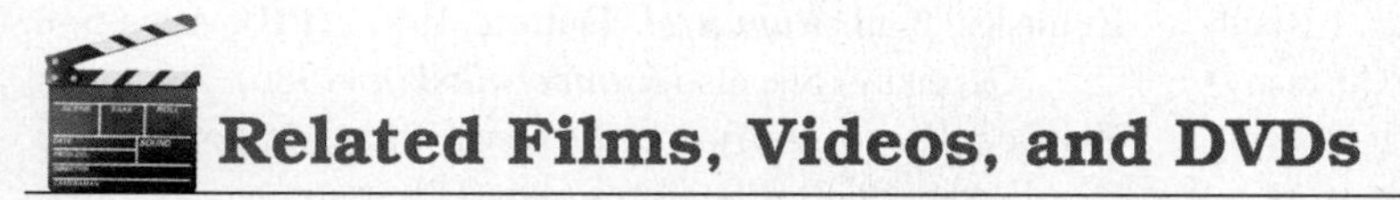

Related Films, Videos, and DVDs

American Tall Tales (includes ***John Henry, Swamp Angel***). (2006). Retellers: Julius Lester and Paul Zelinsky. Illustrators: Jerry Pinkney and Paul Zelinsky. 32 minutes.

Favorite Fairy Tales, Volume II (includes ***Rapunzel, Princess Furball***). (2006). Retellers: Paul Zelinsky and Charlotte Huck. Illustrators: Paul Zelinsky and Anita Lobel. 32 minutes.

Lon Po Po (2008). Reteller/Illustrator: Ed Young. 14 minutes.

Stone Soup (2011). Reteller/illustrator: Jon Muth. 12 minutes.

There Was an Old Lady Who Swallowed a Fly (2002). Illustrator: Simms Tabeck. 8 minutes.

Why Mosquitoes Buzz in People's Ears and Other Caldecott Classics (includes ***Why Mosquitoes Buzz in People's Ears; The Village of Round and Square Houses; A Story, A Story: An African Tale***). (2002). Retellers: Verna Aardema, Ann Grifalconi, and Gail Haley. Illustrators: Leo and Diane Dillon, Ann Grifalconi, and Gail E. Haley. 32 minutes.

Chapter 8

Fantasy and Science Fiction

Magic Words

In the very earliest time,
When both people and animals lived on earth,
a person could become an animal if he wanted to
and an animal could become a human being.
Sometimes they were people
and sometimes animals
and there was no difference.
All spoke the same language.
That was the time when words were like magic.
The human mind had mysterious powers.
A word spoken by chance
might have strange consequences.
It would suddenly become alive
and what people want to happen could happen—
all you had to do was say it.
Nobody could explain this:
That's the way it was.

—Anonymous Inuit Poet

Modern fantasy has its roots in traditional literature, from which motifs, characters, stylistic elements, and themes have been drawn. Many of the most well-known works of children's literature fall into the genre of fantasy. *Alice's Adventures in Wonderland, The Wonderful Wizard of Oz, Winnie-the-Pooh, Pippi Longstocking,* and *Charlotte's Web* immediately come to mind along with contemporary favorites such as *Harry Potter and the Sorcerer's Stone*. Science fiction books, particularly dystopias about future worlds such as *The Giver*, have enjoyed tremendous success. The creation of stories that are highly imaginative—yet believable—is the hallmark of this genre.

Definition and Description

Fantasy refers to stories in which the authors have created events, settings, or characters that are outside the realm of possibility. A fantasy is a story that cannot happen in the real world. In these stories, animals talk, objects come to life, monsters and giants walk the earth, heroines go to battle in imagined kingdoms, and young people fight to survive in epic battles. Fantasies are written by known authors, and this distinguishes the genre from traditional literature in which the tales are handed down through oral tradition and have no known author. Although the events could not happen in real life, fantasies often contain truths that help the reader understand today's world.

Science fiction is a closely related genre that features scientifically plausible or technologically possible developments that were imaginary at the time of publication, but could occur in the future. Futuristic novels, especially ***dystopias***, are popular as reflected in the success of the Hunger Games trilogy by Suzanne Collins.

Both fantasy and science fiction refuse to accept the world as it is, instead focusing on what could be or what might have been, and so are known as ***speculative fiction***. Both create new or different worlds that have internal consistency through rules invented by authors. The difference is that the made-up rules of imagined worlds in science fiction have limits based in science and technology. In contrast, fantasy employs magic with plots that cannot be explained rationally now or in the future.

The ***cycle*** or ***series format,*** in which one book is linked to another through characters and settings across multiple books, is a growing trend. Authors attempt to make each novel self-contained, but reading the entire series provides for more complex and in-depth experiences. The cycle format appeals to readers who become attached to characters and eagerly anticipate the next book. The cycle format can be found in the Inkheart trilogy by Cornelia Funke, the Shadow Children series by Margaret Peterson Haddix, and the Percy Jackson series by Rick Riordan.

Evaluation and Selection of Fantasy

The usual standards for fiction must be met by authors of fantasy, including believable and well-rounded characters who develop and change, well-constructed plots, well-described settings with internal consistency, a style appropriate to the story, and worthy themes. In addition, the following criteria apply specifically to fantasy:

- **Does the story have an internal logic and consistency that allows the impossible to seem real?** Authors of fantasy must persuade readers to open themselves to believing that which is contrary to reality, strange, whimsical, or magical. This believability is dependent on authors developing a strong internal logic and consistency to their fantasy world and story. Sometimes authors begin the story in a familiar modern setting with typical children before transitioning to the fantasy world, such as when Harry Potter leaves his ordinary life in London to get on the train at Platform 9¾ for transport to Hogwarts. Other fantasies begin in the imagined world but use well-described settings and consistent well-rounded characters to make this new reality believable as in J. R. R. Tolkien's *The Hobbit*. Either way, the plot, characters, and setting must be so well developed that the reader is able to suspend disbelief and accept the impossible as real.
- **Does the author provide a unique imaginative setting? How does the author move the setting beyond the realistic?** In some stories, the setting may move beyond the realistic in both time (moving to the past or future or holding time still) and place (imagined worlds); in other stories, only one of these elements (place or time) will go beyond reality. Moreover, a modern fantasy author's creation must be original. When the Harry Potter books gained tremendous popularity, other books with similar worlds of wizards and magic quickly appeared but were formulaic, failing to match the originality and imaginative power of the original books.

Excellent Fantasy to Read Aloud

Applegate, Katherine. *The One and Only Ivan.* Ages 9–12.
DiCamillo, Kate. *The Miraculous Journey of Edward Tulane.* Ages 8–12.
Graham, Bob. *April and Esme: Tooth Fairies.* Ages 5–8.
Law, Ingrid. *Savvy.* Ages 10–14.
Lin, Grace. *Where the Mountain Meets the Moon.* Ages 9–12.
Pennypacker, Sara. *Pax.* Ages 9–13.
Preus, Margi. *West of the Moon.* Ages 10–14.
Schlitz, Laura. *Splendor and Glooms.* Ages 9–12.
Stead, Rebecca. *When You Reach Me.* Ages 10–14.
Turk, Evan. *The Storyteller.* Ages 6–11.
Valente, Catherynne. *The Girl Who Circumnavigated Fairyland in a Ship of Her Own Making.* Ages 10–14.

The Significance of Theme in Fantasy

Theme, the key ideas that hold a story together and allow readers to construct insights into their lives and world, is of particular significance in fantasy. Theme unifies and illuminates a story, providing the "So what?" that allows a book to be more than just an enjoyable reading experience. Theme goes beyond the specific details of the story to focus on what it means to be human in a complex world (Lukens, 2012). The power of fantasy for many readers is that it's a safe place to explore an alternative world as a metaphor for life in their own world. Theme provides the metaphorical connection that encourages readers to consider "what if" and imagine a different way of living in their own world.

All books have a range of possible themes, because themes are constructed by readers as they interpret that book through the lens of their differing life experiences. ***Primary themes*** are highlighted throughout the book, whereas ***secondary themes*** are of lesser importance to the book but of significance to the lives of specific readers. Although fantasies often play with the theme of good versus evil, many have variations of this theme along with other themes. ***Explicit themes*** are directly stated by the author, often through the words of a character, whereas an ***implicit theme*** is implied through actions and events. These themes are not a single topic or concept like justice or evil, but a life understanding that raises issues and addresses complexity, such as the ways in which society treats those who are viewed as "different." Gathering a text set, such as Ingrid Law's *Savvy,* Merrie Haskell's *Handbook for Dragon Slayers*, Kate DiCamillo's *Flora & Ulysses,* Victoria Forester's *The Girl Who Could Fly,* and Okorafor Nnedi's *Akata Witch,* provides an opportunity to explore the complexities that surround societal views about girls and difference in more depth within and across books as well as to consider secondary themes in each book.

Historical Overview of Fantasy and Science Fiction

Imaginative literature appeared in the 18th century in stories intended as political satires for adults but enjoyed by children. *Gulliver's Travels* (1726) by Irish clergyman Jonathan Swift was published as an adult satire ridiculing the antics of the English courts. Gulliver travels to strange, imaginary places, such as the world of the six-inch Lilliputians, described in fascinating detail and with sufficient humor to appeal to a child audience.

In England in 1865, Charles Dodgson, an Oxford don who used the pen name Lewis Carroll, wrote *Alice's Adventures in Wonderland* about Alice's fantastic journey through a rabbit hole into an imaginary world. The absence of didacticism—replaced by humor and fantasy—resulted in the book's lasting appeal. Other fantasies that originated in England include *The Light Princess* (1867) and *At the Back of the North Wind* (1871) by George MacDonald and *Just So Stories* (1902) by Rudyard Kipling. This early development of modern fantasy in England was unrivaled by any other country and established the standard for the genre worldwide.

Fantasy continued to thrive in England, through noteworthy contributions such as *The Tale of Peter Rabbit* (1902) by Beatrix Potter, *The Wind in the Willows* (1908) by Kenneth Grahame, *The Velveteen Rabbit* (1922) by Margery Williams, *Winnie-the-Pooh* (1926) by A. A. Milne, *Mary Poppins* (1934) by

MILESTONES in the Development of Fantasy and Science Fiction

Date	Event	Significance
1726	*Gulliver's Travels* by Jonathan Swift (England)	An adult novel that became a model for children's fantasy adventures
1835	*Fairy Tales* by Hans Christian Andersen (Denmark)	First modern folktales
1864	*Journey to the Center of the Earth* by Jules Verne (France)	First science fiction novel (for adults)
1865	*Alice's Adventures in Wonderland* by Lewis Carroll (England)	First children's masterpiece of modern fantasy
1881	*The Adventures of Pinocchio* by Carlo Collodi (Italy)	Early classic personified toy story
1900	*The Wonderful Wizard of Oz* by L. Frank Baum (U.S.)	First U.S. modern fantasy for children
1908	*The Wind in the Willows* by Kenneth Grahame (England)	Early animal fantasy
1910	*Tom Swift and His Airship* by Victor Appleton (U.S.)	First science fiction novel for children
1926	*Winnie-the-Pooh* by A. A. Milne (England)	Early personified toy story
1937	*The Hobbit* by J. R. R. Tolkien (England)	Early quest adventure that remains popular
1950	*The Lion, the Witch and the Wardrobe* by C. S. Lewis (England)	Early quest adventure for children; first of the Narnia series
1952	*Charlotte's Web* by E. B. White (U.S.)	Classic U.S. animal fantasy
1953	*The Borrowers* by Mary Norton (England)	Classic little people fantasy
1962	*A Wrinkle in Time* by Madeleine L'Engle (U.S.)	Classic U.S. science fiction novel
1993	*The Giver* by Lois Lowry (U.S.)	Early dystopia; Newbery Medal
1998	*Harry Potter and the Sorcerer's Stone* by J. K. Rowling (England)	Best-selling quest fantasy series

Pamela Travers, *The Hobbit* (1937) by J. R. R. Tolkien, *The Lion, the Witch and the Wardrobe* (1950) by C. S. Lewis, and *The Borrowers* (1953) by Mary Norton.

Early books of fantasy from other countries include *The Adventures of Pinocchio* (1881) by Carlo Collodi from Italy and *Journey to the Center of the Earth* (1864) and *Twenty Thousand Leagues under the Sea* (1869) by the Frenchman Jules Verne, considered the first science fiction novels. Jean de Brunhoff from France wrote *The Story of Babar* (1937), the first book of a popular series about an elephant family.

Hans Christian Andersen, a Dane, published many modern folktales using the same literary elements as traditional tales, but he was the originator of most of his tales, for which his own life experiences were the inspiration. "The Ugly Duckling," "The Emperor's New Clothes," and "Thumbelina" are three of his most loved stories. His tales, published in 1835, are considered the first modern fairy tales. A century later, Swedish author Astrid Lindgren produced *Pippi Longstocking* (1945). Pippi, a lively, rambunctious, and strong heroine who throws caution to the wind, lives an independent life of escapades that are envied by children the world over.

The United States produced some outstanding fantasies, beginning with *The Wonderful Wizard of Oz* (1900) by L. Frank Baum, considered the first classic U.S. modern fantasy for children. Other landmark works are *Charlotte's Web* (1952) by E. B. White, the best-known and best-loved U.S. work of fantasy, and the Prydain Chronicles by Lloyd Alexander, a high fantasy series of an ordinary boy on a hero's quest.

Science fiction is based in the 19th-century novels of Jules Verne and H. G. Wells (*Time Machine,* 1895) for adults. It was not until the 20th century that science fiction began to be aimed specifically at children. In the early 1900s, the Tom Swift series by Victor Appleton (collective pseudonym for the Stratemeyer Syndicate), although stilted in style and devoid of female characters, can be considered the first science fiction for children. The success of the science fiction magazine *Amazing Stories,* launched in 1926, brought formal recognition to the genre of science fiction.

In 1963, Madeleine L'Engle's *A Wrinkle in Time*, considered a modern classic in science fiction, was awarded the Newbery Medal, after which many science fiction novels for children appeared. In the late 1960s and 1970s, the theme of mind control was popular in books such as John Christopher's Tripods trilogy and William Sleator's *House of Stairs* (1974). Space travel and future worlds were frequent science fiction topics in the 1980s.

Fantasy for children remains strong, especially in England and English-speaking countries. Although animal fantasies remain popular, the major trend is interweaving fantasy into history to create historical fantasies. Fractured folktales, traditional tales with a contemporary twist or a tale told from a new perspective, took on new popularity with *The True Story of the 3 Little Pigs* in the voice of A. Wolf by Jon Scieszka and Lane Smith. This blurring of traditional genres can also be seen in realistic mystery stories with supernatural elements, as in the popular mysteries of Mary Downing Hahn. One cultural shift is integrating myths and legends from non-Western cultures within fantasy, such as Chinese folklore in Grace Lin's *Where the Mountain Meets the Moon* and Russian Baba Yaga legends in Katherine Marsh's *The Door by the Staircase.*

Fantasy continues to be a popular genre, as evidenced by the extraordinary popularity of the Harry Potter series by J. K. Rowling, whose first novel was published in 1998, along with the recent success of dystopias such as the Hunger Games series by Suzanne Collins and the Divergent series by Veronica Roth.

Types of Fantasy

In fantasy, the distinctions between types are not totally discrete. These types of fantasy are a starting point for thinking about the variety of fantastic stories, motifs, themes, and characters created by authors. Additional categories could be listed, and some stories clearly fit in more than one category. Kate DiCamillo's *The Tale of Despereaux,* for example, could be categorized as a modern fairy tale or quest fantasy as well as an animal fantasy.

Fantasy Based in Folklore and Mythology

Modern folktales, or ***literary tales,*** are stories told in a form similar to that of a traditional tale with limited character description, strong conflict, fast-moving plot with a sudden resolution, vague setting, and, in some cases, magical elements. But these modern tales have a known, identifiable author who has written the tale in this form. The tales do not spring from the oral traditions and cultural heritage of a group of people but rather from the mind of one creator. This distinction does not matter to children, who delight in these tales.

The tales of Hans Christian Andersen are the earliest and best known of these modern tales. More recently, other authors, including Gail Carson Levine (*Ella Enchanted*) and Shannon Hale *(Princess Academy),* have become known for their modern folktales, whereas Anne Isaacs (*Swamp Angel*) creates modern tall tales. Their books provide feisty resourceful female characters in contrast to the old-fashioned, stereotyped view of male and female characters in traditional tales.

Fractured folktales are traditional folktales with a contemporary twist, as in Corey Schwartz's and Dan Santat's *The Three Ninja Pigs*, in which the pigs learn self-defense. and Susan Elya's and Susan Guevara's *Little Roja Riding Hood*, in which a bilingual Little Roja rides an ATV through the woods to save the day. Sometimes the tales are told from a new perspective, such as Zoe and R.W. Alley's *There's a Wolf at the Door*, providing the wolf's tale of woe in cartoon panels.

Some authors create imagined worlds based in mythology, such as Rick Riordan's Percy Jackson and the Olympian series where teens move into alternative worlds populated by characters from Greek mythology. King Arthur legends are another popular source, as in Philip Reeve's *Here Lies Arthur* and Kevin Crossley-Holland's *The Seeing Stone.* Recent books draw from a wider range of mythologies, including Japanese mythology in Margaret Dilloway's *Momotaro* and Indian mythology in Sarwat Chadda's *The Savage Fortress.*

Animal Fantasy

Animal fantasies are stories in which animals behave as human beings in that they experience emotions, talk, and have the ability to reason. Usually, the animals in fantasies retain many of their animal characteristics. In the best of these animal fantasies, the author interprets the animal for the reader in human terms without destroying the animal's integrity or removing it from membership in the animal world. For example, the fox character in Sara Pennypacker's *Pax* retains natural abilities of speed and intelligence to outsmart adversaries. At the same time, the reader sees human qualities, such as caring and love, through the fox's interactions with a boy and several fox companions.

Animal fantasies can be read to young children who enjoy the exciting but reassuring adventures in *The Tale of Peter Rabbit* by Beatrix Potter and Philip and Erin Stead's *A Sick Day for Amos McGee*. Many

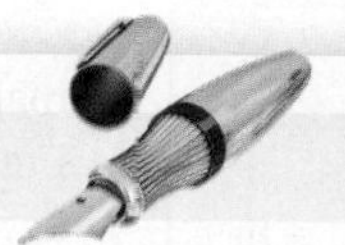

Notable Authors of Fantasy and Science Fiction

David Almond, British author noted for magical realism novels. *Skellig,* Carnegie Medal winner; *The Boy Who Climbed to the Moon; Mouse, Bird, Snake, Wolf.*

Kate DiCamillo, author of animal and toy fantasies. *The Tale of Despereaux* and *Flora & Ulysses,* Newbery Medals; *The Miraculous Journey of Edward Tulane;* the Mercy Watson series. www.katedicamillo.com

Neil Gaiman, British author of novels, graphic novels, and picturebooks featuring unusual characters in strange situations, such as *Coraline* and *The Graveyard Book,* winner of both the Newbery Medal and the Carnegie Medal. www.neilgaiman.com

Mini Grey, award-winning British author/illustrator of humorous picturebooks featuring action toys. *Traction Man and the Beach Odyssey; Into the Woods; Three by the Sea.*

Margaret Peterson Haddix, author of two popular fantasy series, the Shadow Children and the Missing, as well as numerous fantasy and science fiction novels. www.haddixbooks.com/

Shannon Hale, author of modern folktale novels. *Book of a Thousand Days; Princess Academy; Rapunzel's Revenge; The Princess in Black.* www.squeetus.com

Anne Isaacs, author of original tall tales featuring strong women. *Swamp Angel; Dust Devil; Meanwhile Back at the Ranch.* www.anneisaacs.com/

Gail Carson Levine, author of modern folktale novels with strong female characters. *Ella Enchanted; A Tale of Two Castles; Fairy Dust and the Quest for the Egg.* www.gailcarsonlevine.com

Grace Lin, author of fantasy quest novels integrating Chinese folklore. *Where the Mountain Meets the Moon; Starry River of the Sky; When the Sea Turned to Silver.* www.gracelin.com/

Lois Lowry, 1994 Newbery Medal for *The Giver,* a popular work of science fiction. Giver Quartet includes *Gathering Blue, Messenger,* and *Son.* www.loislowry.com

Nnedi Okorafor, Nigerian American writer of fantasy and science fiction set in Nigeria, including *The Shadow Speaker* and *Akata Witch.* www.nnedi.com

Philip Pullman, British creator of His Dark Materials fantasies, a trilogy comprising *The Golden Compass, The Subtle Knife,* and *The Amber Spyglass.* www.philip-pullman.com

J. K. Rowling, British author of the best-selling series about Harry Potter. *Harry Potter and the Sorcerer's Stone.* www.jkrowling.com

picturebooks for young children use animal characters to depict the normal interactions of families and friends, such as the mice in books by Kevin Henkes and the pig in the Olivia books by Ian Falconer.

Books for children in primary grades include somewhat longer stories, often in a humorous vein, such as Beverly Cleary's *The Mouse and the Motorcycle,* Richard Peck's *Secrets at Sea,* and the beloved pig in the Mercy Watson series by Kate DiCamillo. Enjoyable animal fantasies for the young reader often have easy-to-follow, episodic plots.

Fully developed fantasy novels with subtle and complex characterizations, such as *Charlotte's Web* by E. B. White, continue to be well loved by children. Recent favorites include *The Tale of Despereaux* by Kate DiCamillo about the interconnected tales of a mouse, princess, rat and servant girl, and *The One and Only Ivan* by Katherine Applegate about a gorilla on display in a shopping mall. A classic book with rich characterizations, *The Wind in the Willows* by Kenneth Grahame describes the life of animal friends along a riverbank using an episodic plot structure that works well for read-alouds. Larissa Theule's *Fat & Bones* is a recent episodic tale of dark humor where revenge and bravery jumble together during a feud on an isolated farm.

Although interest in animal fantasy peaks at age 8 or 9, many children and adults continue to enjoy well-written animal fantasies. In animal fantasies for older readers, an entire animal world is created, portraying the complexity of relationships and personalities within a community, such as found in *Watership Down* by Richard Adams and *The Amazing Maurice and His Educated Rodents* by Terry Pratchett.

Miniature Worlds

Young children are particularly drawn to fantasies that revolve around miniature worlds of small people or personified toys. Stories in which beloved toys are bought to life, often because of a child's belief, include classics such as *The Adventures of Pinocchio* by Carlo Collodi and the *Velveteen Rabbit* by Marjorie Williams. In these stories, a toy or doll becomes real to the human protagonist and, in turn, becomes real to the child reader (who has perhaps also imagined a toy coming to life). More recent toy stories include the doll world created by Ann Martin and Laura Godwin in The Doll People series. Emily Jenkins's *Toys Go Out* is part of a series that depicts toys who become friends with one another. In Kate DiCamillo's *The Miraculous Journey of Edward Tulane,* a vain china rabbit learns the power of love. Personified toy stories appeal to children of all ages, as reflected in the popularity of the Toy Story movies.

Children are fascinated by worlds inhabited by miniature people who have developed a culture of their own, such as the well-loved Borrowers books by Mary Norton. A fairy world that includes young tooth fairies in training is portrayed in Bob Grahame's picturebook, *April and Esme, Tooth Fairies.* In *Toby Alone,* the Tree is populated by a society of miniature people whose world is threatened by their lifestyle. These stories delight children because they identify with the indignities foisted on powerless little people and because the big people are invariably outdone by the more ingenious little people

Unusual Characters and Strange Situations

Some authors approach fantasy through reality but then go beyond reality to the ridiculous or exaggerated through unusual characters or strange situations, such as a boy sailing across the Atlantic Ocean in a giant peach (*James and the Giant Peach* by Roald Dahl) and a small-town girl who seems unremarkable, except when she flies (*The Girl Who Could Fly* by Virginia Forester).

Because these books are rooted in reality, they provide an entry for readers who are new to fantasy, along with an opportunity for children to explore their deepest fears and wishes. In *Tuck Everlasting,* Natalie Babbitt explores the theme of immortality and its consequences for a family who continually move in the real world to avoid discovery, whereas Katherine Applegate explores a child's right to know the truth in difficult family situations in *Crenshaw.* Guojing's *The Only Child*, a wordless graphic novel from China, captures the emotional life of a young child filled with loneliness and longing.

Magical realism, a blend of fantasy and realism, has the appearance of a work of realism but gradually introduces the fantastic as an integral, and necessary, part of the story. The fantastic is merged into these stories such that the distinction between realism and fantasy is blurred, often leaving the reader in some doubt as to what is real and what is fantasy. These stories have the feel of realism but also contain magical elements such as the supernatural creature that brings rain to a Dust Bowl farm in the wordless graphic novel *Storm in the Barn* by Matt Phelan, and the mysterious stranger who is something like a bird and something like an angel in David Almond's *Skellig.*

Suspense and the Supernatural

Many fantasies include some type of supernatural beings, such as ghosts, monsters, and witches. Ghost stories intrigue children, especially when the topic is treated humorously and reassuringly, such as the picturebook *Leo: A Ghost Story* by Mac Barnett and Christian Robinson or the ghosts who protect a young boy from an assassin in Neil Gaiman's *The Graveyard Book.* Ghosts can be fearful threats or helpful protectors, as is the ghost of Cynthia DeFelice's *The Ghost of Poplar Point,* who is angry about the disturbance of sacred grounds marking a massacre of Seneca Indians. Many mysteries involve solutions with some type of supernatural assistance.

Witches are often portrayed as the broom-wielding villains of both traditional and modern tales as in Frances Hardinge's *Well Witched,* in which three children discover that a witch has endowed stolen coins with strange powers. Although horror is typically associated with adolescent novels, scary stories have long been favorites of children as reflected in the ongoing popularity of R. L. Stine's Goosebumps and Fear Street books. In *A Monster Calls*, Patrick Ness draws on classic horror stories to create an emotional tale of nightmares and monsters in the life of a boy struggling with loss and fear.

Historical Fantasy

Historical fantasies are set in a specific historical period that is authentically represented, but to which some aspect of magic or the supernatural has been added, such as in the gothic thriller of kidnapping and magical imprisonment by Amy Schlitz, *Splendors and Glooms*, set in Victorian England. Ying Chang Compestine's *Secrets of the Terra-Cotta Soldier*, set in a small village in 1970s Communist China, revolves around a boy's interactions with a talking statue from ancient times. Historical fantasies must fully and authentically develop the historical setting, both time and place, just as in a book of historical fiction.

Time-travel fantasies are a type of historical fantasy in which a protagonist goes back or forward in time to a different era. A contrast between the two times is shown to readers through the modern-day protagonist's discoveries of earlier customs. In *Saving Lucas Biggs* by Marisa de los Santos and David Teague, a girl travels back in time to save her father, who has been sentenced to death for a crime he did not commit. Rebecca Stead's *When You Reach Me* plays with time in complex ways when Miranda, an ordinary 12-year-old girl in 1979 Manhattan who loves *A Wrinkle in Time*, receives mysterious notes set in the future. Time travel has also been used in easily accessible series books, such as the Time Warp Trio books by Jon Scieszka.

Quests and Imagined Worlds

Quest stories are adventure stories with a search motif that occur within an imagined alternative world. The quest may be pursuit for a lofty purpose, such as justice or love, or for a rich reward, such as a magical power or a hidden treasure. A recent trend is a focus on action-packed adventures, such as in the Septimus Heap series by Angie Sage and the Time Out of the Door adventures by Maureen McQuerry. Many recent books portray a world within a world, such as *Falling In* by Frances O'Roark Dowell, in which a sixth grader falls through the floor of a closet into a parallel universe, and Maureen McQuerry's *Beyond the Door*, in which an ordinary boy opens the door to find mythical strangers who take him on perilous adventures through time to challenge an ancient evil. Steampunk elements add to the adventure in S. E. Grove's *The Glass Sentence,* in which the Great Disruption of 1799 plunges the world into chaos and the continents into different times. This intricate fantasy, featuring maps of all kinds, sends a 13-year-old girl on a quest to rescue her uncle and save the world.

Steampunk includes the element of anarchy or rebellion (punk) within the social or technological aspects of the 19th-century Victorian era (the steam), thus fusing futuristic and antiquated elements. These novels usually feature steam-powered machinery in an alternative history or a postapocalyptic future where steam power has regained mainstream use, as in Kenneth Oppel's Airborn trilogy and Philip Reeve's Mortal Engines series, and so are sometimes labeled as science fiction dystopias.

Quest stories that are serious in tone with detailed worlds are called ***high fantasy.*** In high fantasies, an imaginary otherworld is fully portrayed: the society, its history, family trees, geographic location, population, religion, customs, and traditions. The conflict in these tales usually centers on the struggle between good and evil. *The Hobbit,* written by J. R. R. Tolkien in 1937, is one of the first of these high fantasies. Other examples are C. S. Lewis's Chronicles of Narnia series, Philip Pullman's His Dark Materials trilogy, and J. K. Rowling's Harry Potter series.

Many quest fantasies follow a structure found in traditional myths and described by Joseph A. Campbell (1949) as a ***monomyth*** or ***hero cycle.*** In this structure, the hero starts out in the ordinary world and receives a call to enter a strange, dangerous, supernatural world, facing daunting struggles against external forces and internal temptations. If the hero overcomes these trials, he or she receives a precious gift and must decide whether to return to the ordinary world or to remain in the supernatural world. If the hero chooses to return, he or she faces more trials on the return journey. After returning successfully, the hero shares the gift to improve the world. The hero cycle represents a journey of self-discovery and personal growth for the protagonist.

This cycle plays out in Catherynne Valente's *The Girl Who Circumnavigated Fairyland in a Ship of Her Own Making*, in which an ill-tempered girl is transported from her dull life in Omaha to the bizarre world of Fairyland. Once there, she accepts a quest to rescue the inhabitants from the rule-mad Marquess and becomes a heroine who is resourceful and brave. The initial quest ends with her trapped in Fairyland, so the journey of adventure and self-discovery continues in two more books.

Science Fiction

Science fiction is a form of imaginative literature that projects the future on the Earth or other planets based on scientific facts and principles; therefore, story elements in science fiction must have the appearance of scientific plausibility or technical possibility. Hypotheses about the future of humankind and the universe presented in science fiction appear possible to the reader because settings and events are built on extensions of known technologies and scientific concepts. As in fantasy, these alternative perspectives of reality are explored in a world that must maintain internal consistency, but science fiction must also meet this additional evaluation criteria:

- **Does the story appear to be scientifically plausible or technically possible?** The situations presented in scientific fiction should seem believable because the settings and events are extensions of known technologies and scientific concepts.

In novels of science fiction, such topics as mind control, genetic engineering, space technologies and travel, visitors from outer space, and future political and social systems all seem possible to the readers. Jeanne DuPrau's *The City of Ember* explores a future world in which an underground city is running out of supplies and electricity and the map to the surface has been lost. Although science fiction often takes on difficult social issues, some books use humor, particularly in tales of aliens from outer space who jet around the universe with human friends, such as Adam Rex's *Smek for President!* and M. T. Anderson's Pals in Peril series. Outer space and aliens are a frequent focus in graphic novels, such as Ben Hatke's *The Return of Zita, the Spacegirl,* and in series books, such as the Spaceheadz and Frank Einstein series by Jon Scieszka.

Science fiction fascinates many young people because they feature characters who must adjust to change and become new people. In addition, science fiction stories portray the world that young people might one day inhabit and so are sometimes called ***futuristic fiction.*** Many current futuristic fantasies focus on a ***dystopia,*** in which authors depict a dark future world of dehumanization and fear, such as found in the Hunger Games trilogy by Suzanne Collins and the 5th Wave trilogy by Rick Yancey. Most dystopias are written for an adolescent audience, but movies have extended their popularity to middle grade children. One of the first dystopias is *The Giver* by Lois Lowry, so the Giver Quartet provides a good entry point for children.

Worlds of magic and monsters and dystopian worlds of the future have great appeal to children. Their lively imaginations invite them into these worlds to explore the many different kinds of fantasies and to reach toward complex concepts and themes. This openness and delight in fantasy is not always appreciated by adults, some of whom see these books as dangerous to children's minds. Despite censorship challenges, fantasy and science fiction remain a popular genre that engages children as readers. These inspiring and thought-provoking stories invite us to become greater than we are—and that we hope to be.

Reader Connection: Journey Maps

Readers can explore the transformational journeys of heroes and heroines within fantasy by constructing ***journey maps***. Children create visual maps of a favorite character's journey to show literal as well as figurative transformations. By defining journeys metaphorically as movement across a pathway, many pathways can be considered, including physical, emotional, cultural, spiritual, cognitive, and psychological changes over time. Children can develop their own creative formats for the map, such as a road map, time line, graph, or the map of a character's heart or brain. *My Map Book* by Sara Fanelli provides creative examples of maps developed by a child mapping her face, tummy, neighborhood, and family. Most fantasy and science fiction involve journeys with quests in imaginary worlds and are particularly rich sources of transformative journeys that go far beyond a character moving from one place to another.

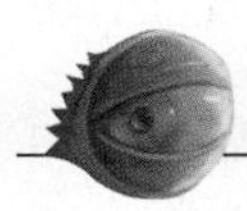

Invitations for Further Investigation

- Select a classic work of fantasy for children, such as *Alice's Adventures in Wonderland, Charlotte's Web, The Wonderful Wizard of Oz,* or *The Wind in the Willows.* Read the book and several articles of literary criticism. Present your perspectives and consider whether this book is still relevant for children today.
- Select a concept of significance to children, such as freedom, hope, beauty, or forgiveness, and put together a text set of three to five fantasies or science fiction books that focus on this concept. Discuss the books with other readers to identify the primary themes in each book and select excerpts from each book that explicitly or implicitly state the theme. Compare the ways in which the themes play out in these books, and list the secondary themes in each fantasy.
- Select a quest story from the recommended list, and work with a small group to create a journey map depicting the characters' journeys and transformations over time.

References

Campbell, J. A. (1949). *The hero with a thousand faces.* New York: Pantheon.

Fanelli, S. (1995). *My map book.* New York: HarperCollins.

Lukens, R. (2012). *A critical handbook of children's literature,* 9th ed. New York: Pearson.

Recommended Fantasy and Science Fiction Books

Ages indicated refer to concept and interest levels. Formats other than novels are coded as:
(PB) Picturebook
(NV) Novel in Verse
(COL) Short story collection
(GR) Graphic novel

Fantasy Based in Folklore and Mythology

Alley, Zoe. ***There's a Wolf at the Door***. Illus. R. W. Alley. Roaring Brook, 2008. (**PB, GR**). Ages 6–8. Also ***There's a Princess in the Palace*** (2010). (Interwoven folktales)

Almond, David. ***Mouse, Bird, Snake, Wolf***. Illus. Dave McKean. Candlewick, 2013. (**GR**). Ages 9–12. (U.K.)

Andersen, Hans Christian. ***The Snow Queen***. Illus. Bagram Ibatoulline. Harper, 2013. (**PB**). Ages 7–12. (Denmark)

Andersen, Hans Christian. ***Nightingale's Nest***. Illus. Nikki Loftin. Razorbill, 2014. Ages 9–12. (Denmark, magical realism)

Chadda, Sarwat. ***The Savage Fortress.*** Scholastic, 2012. Ages 11–14. (Indian mythology)

Crossley-Holland, Kevin. ***The Seeing Stone.*** Scholastic, 2001. Ages 12–16. (King Arthur, U.K.)

Daly, Niki. ***Thank You, Jackson***. Illus. Jude Daly. Frances Lincoln, 2015. (**PB**). Ages 5–7. (South Africa)

Dilloway, Margaret. ***Momotaro: Xander and the Lost Island of Monsters***. Illus. Choong Yoon. Hyperion, 2016. Ages 8–12. (Japanese)

Elya, Susan Middleton. ***Rubia and the Three Osos***. Illus. Melissa Sweet. Hyperion, 2010. (**PB**). Ages 3–7. (Mexican American retelling)

Elya, Susan Middleton. ***Little Roja Riding Hood***. Illus. Susan Guevara. Putnam, 2014. (**PB**). Ages 3–7. (Mexican American retelling)

Fleming, Candace. ***Clever Jack Takes the Cake.*** Illus. G. Brian Karas. Schwartz & Wade, 2010. (**PB**). Ages 5–9. (Fairy tale)

Gidwitz, Adam. ***A Tale Dark and Grimm***. Dutton, 2010. Ages 10–14. (Hansel and Gretel)

Hale, Shannon. ***Princess Academy.*** Bloomsbury, 2005. Ages 10–14.

Hale, Shannon. ***Book of a Thousand Days.*** Bloomsbury, 2007. Ages 11–15. (Grimm, Central Asia)

Hale, Shannon, and Dean Hale. ***Rapunzel's Revenge.*** Illus. Nathan Hale. Bloomsbury, 2008. (**GR**). Ages 10–14.

Haskell, Merrie. ***Handbook for Dragon Slayers***. Harper, 2013. Ages 10–14. (Arthurian legends)

Isaacs, Anne. ***Dust Devil***. Illus. Paul Zelinsky. Schwartz & Wade, 2010. (**PB**). Ages 6–9. Also ***Swamp Angel*** (1994) and ***Meanwhile Back at the Ranch*** (2014). (Tall tales)

Krishnaswami, Uma. ***The Girl of the Wish Garden: A Thumbelina Story***. Illus. Nasrin Khosravi. Groundwood, 2013. (**PB**). Ages 5–10. (Retelling, Iran/India)

Levine, Gail Carson. ***Ella Enchanted.*** HarperCollins, 1997. Ages 10–13. (Cinderella). Also ***A Tale of Two Castles*** (2011).

Levine, Gail Carson. ***Fairy Dust and the Quest for the Egg.*** Illus. David Christiana. Disney, 2005. Ages 8–11. (Peter Pan)

Lin, Grace. ***Where the Mountain Meets the Moon***. Little, Brown, 2009. Ages 9–12. (Chinese folklore). Also ***Starry River of the Sky*** (2014) and ***When the Sea Turned to Silver*** (2016).

Marsh, Katherine. ***The Door by the Staircase***. Illus. Kelly Murphy. Hyperion, 2016. Ages 8–12. (Russian)

McCoola, Marika. ***Baba Yaga's Assistant***. Illus. Emily Carroll. Candlewick, 2015. (**GR**). Ages 9–14. (Russian folklore)

McKissack, Patricia C. ***Porch Lies: Tales of Slicksters, Tricksters, and Other Wily Creatures.*** Illus. Andre Carilho. Random, 2006. (**COL**). Ages 8–11. (African American legends)

Mora, Pat. ***Doña Flor: A Tall Tale about a Giant Woman with a Great Big Heart.*** Illus. Raúl Colón Knopf, 2005. (**PB**) Ages 4–8. (Mexico, tall tale)

Preus, Margi. ***West of the Moon***. Amulet, 2014. Ages 11–14. (Norway)

Reeve, Philip. ***Here Lies Arthur.*** Scholastic, 2008. Ages 12–18. (King Arthur legend, U.K.)

Riordan, Rick. ***The Lightning Thief.*** Hyperion, 2005. Ages 10–15. Percy Jackson and the Olympians series. Also, ***The Lost Hero*** (2010) and ***The Hidden Oracle*** (2016). (Greek mythology)

Schwartz, Corey Rosen. ***The Three Ninja Pigs***. Illus. Dan Santat. G. P. Putnam's Sons, 2012. (**PB**). Ages 5–8.

Turk, Evan. ***The Storyteller***. Atheneum, 2016. (**PB**). Ages 3–11. (Morocco)

Ursu, Anne. ***Breadcrumbs.*** Illus. Erin McGuire. Walden Pond, 2011. Ages 9–12. (Snow Queen)

Animal Fantasies

Adams, Richard. ***Watership Down***. Scribner, 1972. Ages 12–15.

Appelt, Kathi. ***The Underneath.*** Atheneum, 2008. Ages 9–14. (Magical realism)

Appelt, Kathi. ***The True Blue Scouts of Sugar Man Swamp***. Atheneum, 2013. Ages 10–14.

Applegate, Katherine. ***The One and Only Ivan***. Illus. Patricia Catelao. Harper, 2012. Ages 8–12.

Brown, Peter. ***The Wild Robot***. Little, Brown and Company, 2016. Ages 7–11.

Bruchac, Joseph. ***Wabi: A Hero's Tale.*** Dial, 2006. Ages 10–15. (Abenaki)

Busby, Cylin. ***The Nine Lives of Jacob Tibbs***. Illus. Gerald Kelley. Knopf, 2016. Ages 8–12.

Cleary, Beverly. ***The Mouse and the Motorcycle.*** Morrow, 1965. Ages 7–11.

Deedy, Carmen. ***The Cheshire Cheese Cat: A Dickens of a Tale***. Illus. Barry Moser. Peachtree, 2011. Ages 9–12.

DiCamillo, Kate. ***The Tale of Despereaux.*** Illus. Timothy B. Ering. Candlewick, 2003. Ages 7–10.

DiCamillo, Kate. ***Flora & Ulysses: The Illuminated Adventures***. Illus. K. G. Campbell. Candlewick, 2013. Ages 8–12.

Grahame, Kenneth. ***The Wind in the Willows.*** Illus. E. H. Shepard. Scribner, 1908. Ages 8–12. (UK)

Grey, Mimi. ***Three by the Sea***. Knopf, 2011. (**PB**). Ages 5–8. (U.K.)

Horvath, Polly. ***Mr. and Mrs. Bunny—Detectives Extraordinaire***! Illus. Sophie Blackall. Schwartz & Wade, 2012. Ages 9-12. (Canada)

Jonell, Lynne. ***Emmy and the Incredible Shrinking Rat.*** Holt, 2007. Ages 8–11. Series.

Kuhlmann, Torben. ***Lindbergh: The Tale of a Flying Mouse***. North-South, 2014. (**PB**). Ages 8–12. (Germany)

Oppel, Kenneth. ***Darkwing***. Illus. Keith Thompson. HarperCollins, 2007. Ages 10–14. (Canada)

Park, Linda Sue. ***Forest of Wonders***. Illus. Jim Madsen. Harper, 2016. Ages 8–12.

Peck, Richard. ***Secrets at Sea: A Novel***. Illus. Kelly Murphy. Dial, 2011. Ages 8–12.

Pennypacker, Sara. ***Pax***. Illus. Jon Klassen. Balzer + Bray, 2016. Ages 9–13.

Potter, Beatrix. ***The Tale of Peter Rabbit.*** Warne, 1902. (**PB**). Ages 5–9. (U.K.)

Pratchett, Terry. ***The Amazing Maurice and His Educated Rodents.*** HarperCollins, 2001. Ages 12–16. (U.K.)

Seidler, Tor. ***Gully's Travels.*** Illus. Brock Cole. Scholastic, 2008. Ages 9–12.

Theule, Larissa. ***Fat & Bones: And Other Stories***. Illus. Adam Doyle. Carolrhoda, 2014. Ages 12–15.

White, E. B. ***Charlotte's Web.*** Illus. Garth Williams. Harper, 1952. Ages 8–11.

Miniature Worlds

Augarde, Steve. ***Winter Wood.*** David Fickling, 2009. Ages 10–14. (U.K.)

Black, Holly. ***Doll Bones***. Margaret K. McElderry Books, 2013. Ages 10–14.

De Fombelle, Timothy. ***Toby Alone***. Candlewick, 2009. Trans. Sarah Ardizzone. Ages 10–14. Translated from French.

DiCamillo, Kate. ***The Miraculous Journey of Edward Tulane.*** Illus. Bagram Ibatoulline. Candlewick, 2006. Ages 8–12.

Graham, Bob. ***April and Esme, Tooth Fairies***. Candlewick, 2010. (**PB**). Ages 5–8. (Australia)

Grey, Mini. ***Toys in Space***. Knopf, 2012. (**PB**). Ages 4–7. (U.K.)

Grey, Mini. ***Traction Man and the Beach Odyssey***. Knopf, 2012. (**PB**). Ages 5–8. (U.K.)

Jenkins, Emily. ***Toys Come Home: Being the Early Experiences of an Intelligent Stingray, A Brave Buffalo and a Brand-New Someone Called Plastic.*** Illus. Paul Zelinsky. Random, 2011. Ages 5–8.

Martin, Ann, and Laura Godwin. ***The Doll People.*** Illus. Brian Selznick. Hyperion, 2000. Ages 8–12. Also ***The Doll People Set Sail*** (2014).

Pratchett, Terry. ***The Wee Free Men.*** HarperCollins, 2003. Ages 10–15. (U.K.)

Unusual Characters and Strange Situations

Almond, David. ***Skellig.*** Delacorte, 1999. Ages 10–14. Also ***The Boy Who Climbed to the Moon*** (Candlewick, 2010). (U.K.)

Applegate, Katherine. ***Crenshaw.*** Feiwel & Friends, 2015. Ages 7–11.

Babbitt, Natalie. ***Tuck Everlasting.*** Farrar, 1975. Ages 10–14.

Banks, Angelica. ***Finding Serendipity.*** Illus. Stevie Lewis. Square Fish, 2016. Ages 8–12.

Barry, Dave, and Ridley Pearson. ***Peter and the Starcatchers.*** Hyperion, 2004. Ages 9-13.

Dahl, Roald. ***James and the Giant Peach.*** Knopf, 1961. Ages 8–11. (U.K.)

Deutsch, Barry. ***Hereville: How Mirka Caught a Fish.*** Amulet, 2015. Ages 8–13.

DiCamillo, Kate. ***The Magician's Elephant***. Illus. Yoko Tamaka. Candlewick, 2009. Ages 9–12.

Eagar, Lindsay. ***Hour of the Bees***. Candlewick, 2016. Ages 10–14. (Mexican American)

Forester, Victoria. ***The Girl Who Could Fly***. Feiwel & Friends, 2008. Ages 9–12.

Funke, Cornelia. ***The Thief Lord.*** Trans. Oliver Latsch. Scholastic, 2002. Ages 10–14. Translated from German.

Gonzalez, Christina Diaz. ***Moving Target.*** Scholastic, 2015. Ages 9–12.

Grabenstein, Chris. ***The Island of Dr. Libris.*** Yearling, 2016. Ages 9–13.

Graff, Lisa. ***A Tangle of Knots***. Penguin, 2013. Ages 8–12.

Guojing. ***The Only Child.*** Schwartz & Wade, 2015. (**PB**). Ages 5–9. (China, wordless)

Law, Ingrid. ***Savvy***. Dial, 2008. Ages 10–14. Also ***Scramble*** (2010) and ***Switch*** (2016).

Leeuwen, Joke van. ***Eep!.*** Gecko, 2010. Ages 9–12. Translated from Dutch.

Mass, Wendy. ***11 Birthdays.*** Scholastic, 2009. Ages 9–12. Also ***13 Gifts*** (2011).

Phelan, Matt. ***The Storm in the Barn***. Candlewick, 2009. (**GR**). Ages 10–14.

Reeve, Philip. ***No Such Thing as Dragons.*** Scholastic, 2009. Ages 9–12. (U.K.)

Shulman, Polly. ***The Grimm Legacy.*** Putnam's, 2010. Ages 12–15.

Tan, Shaun. ***Tales from Outer Suburbia.*** Scholastic, 2010. Ages 11–16. (Australia)

Tan, Shaun. ***Rules of Summer.*** Scholastic, 2014. (**PB**). Ages 6–12. (Australia)

Suspense and the Supernatural

Barnett, Mac. ***Leo: A Ghost Story.*** Illus. Christian Robinson. Chronicle, 2015. (**PB**). Ages 3–6.

Bell, Hilari. ***The Goblin Wood.*** EOS, 2003. Ages 11–16. Also ***The Goblin War*** (2011).

Bowles, David. ***The Smoking Mirror.*** IFWG, 2015. Ages 10–14. (Mexico)

Compestine, Ying Chang. ***A Banquet for Hungry Ghosts: A Collection of Deliciously Frightening Tales***. Holt, 2009. Ages 12–15. (China)

DeFelice, Cynthia. ***The Ghost of Poplar Point.*** Farrar, 2007. Ages 9–12. (Seneca Indians)

Delaney, Joseph. ***Revenge of the Witch: The Last Apprentice.*** Greenwillow, 2005. Ages 10–14. Series. Also ***Fury of the Seventh Son*** (2014). (U.K.)

DiPucchio, Kelly. ***Zombie in Love***. Illus. Scott Campbell. Atheneum, 2011. (**PB**). Ages 6–9.

Funke, Cornelia. ***Inkheart.*** Trans. Anthea Bell. Scholastic, 2003. Ages 12–18. Also ***Inkspell*** (2005) and ***Inkdeath*** (2008). Translated from German.

Gaiman, Neil. ***Coraline: Graphic Novel.*** Adapted by P. Craig Russell. HarperCollins, 2008. (**GR**). Ages 10–14. (U.K.)

Gaiman, Neil. ***The Graveyard Book.*** Illus. Dave McKean. HarperCollins, 2008. Ages 10–15. (U.K.)

Hahn, Mary Downing. ***The Ghost of Crutchfield Hall.*** Clarion, 2010. Ages 9–12.

Hardinge, Frances. ***Well Witched.*** HarperCollins, 2008. Ages 10–14.

Johnson, Hal. ***Fearsome Creature of the Lumberwoods: 20 Chilling Tales from the Wilderness.*** Illus. Tom Mead. Workman Publishing Co., 2015. Ages 10–13.

Jones, Diana Wynne. ***Earwig and the Witch***. Illus. Paul Zelinsky. Greenwillow, 2012. Ages 7–9.

Ness, Patrick. ***A Monster Calls.*** Illus. Jim Kay. Candlewick, 2011. Ages 11–14. (U.K.)

Nnedi, Okorafor. ***Akata Witch.*** Viking, 2011. Ages 12–15. (Nigeria)

Rohmann, Eric. ***Bone Dog***. Roaring Brook, 2011. (**PB**). Ages 6–9.

Stine, R. L., editor. ***Beware! R. L. Stine Picks His Favorite Scary Stories.*** HarperCollins, 2002. (**COL**). Ages 9–14.

Telgemeier, Raina. ***Ghosts.*** Graphix, 2016. (**GR**). Ages 9–12.

White, J. A. ***The Thickety: A Path Begins.*** Katherine Tegen Books, 2014. Ages 11–14.

Historical Fantasy and Time Travel

Avi. ***The Seer of Shadows.*** HarperCollins, 2008. Ages 9–14. (New York, 1865–1868)

Bell, Ted. ***Nick of Time***. St. Martins, 2008. Ages 10–14. (WWII, U.K.)

Compestine, Ying Chang. ***Secrets of the Terra-Cotta Soldier.*** Amulet, 2014. Ages 10–12. (China, 1970)

De Los Santos, Marisa. ***Saving Lucas Biggs.*** Harper, 2014. Ages 9–12. (Time travel)

Fox, Janet. ***The Charmed Children of Rookskill Castle.*** Viking, 2016. Ages 10–14. (Scotland, 1940)

Haddix, Margaret Peterson. ***Found.*** Simon & Schuster, 2008. Ages 10–14. Missing series (Time travel)

Nielsen, Jennifer. ***Mark of the Thief.*** Scholastic, 2015. Ages 10–14. (Ancient Rome)

Oppel, Kenneth. ***The Boundless.*** Simon & Schuster, 2014. Ages 9–14. (Canada, 1885)

Sands, Kevin. ***The Blackthorn Key.*** Aladdin, 2015. Ages 8–12. (London, 17th century).

Schlitz, Laura. ***Splendors and Glooms.*** Candlewick, 2012. Ages 9–13. (Victorian London, 1860)

Shulman, Polly. ***The Wells Bequest.*** Nancy Paulsen Books, 2013. Ages 10–14. (Time travel)

Stead, Rebecca. ***When You Reach Me.*** Wendy Lamb, 2009. Ages 10–14. (1979, New York)

Quests and Imagined Worlds

Alexander, Lloyd. ***The Book of Three.*** Holt, 1964. Ages 10–15. Prydain Chronicles.

Anderson, Jodi. ***My Diary from the Edge of the World.*** Aladdin, 2015. Ages 9–13.

Bruchac, Joseph. ***Dragon Castle.*** Dial, 2011. Ages 10–14. (Slovakia)

Bueno, Carlos. ***Lauren Ipsum: A Story about Computer Science and Other Improbable Things.*** No Starch Press, 2015. Ages 8–14.

Collins, Suzanne. ***Gregor the Overlander.*** Scholastic, 2003. Ages 9–14. Underland Chronicles.

Dowell, Frances O'Roark. ***Falling In.*** Atheneum, 2010. Ages 9–12.

Durham, Paul. ***The Luck Uglies.*** Illus. Petur Antonsson. Harper, 2015. Ages 9–13.

Flanagan, John. ***The Royal Ranger.*** Philomel, 2013. Ages 10–14. Rangers Apprentice series. Also ***The Outcasts*** (2011), Brotherband Chronicles. (Australia)

Grove, S. E. ***The Glass Sentence.*** Puffin, 2015. Ages 10–14.

Hale, Shannon. ***The Princess in Black***. Illus. LeUyen Pham. Candlewick, 2014. Ages 6–9.

Jones, Diana Wynne. ***House of Many Ways.*** Greenwillow, 2008. Ages 10–14.

LeGuin, Ursula. ***The Wizard of Earthsea.*** Parnassas, 1968. Ages 12–15.

Lewis, C. S. ***The Lion, the Witch and the Wardrobe.*** Macmillan, 1950. Ages 9–12. Chronicles of Narnia series. (U.K.)

Mackey, Heather. ***Dreamwood.*** Putnam, 2014. Ages 8–13.

McQuerry, Maureen. ***Beyond the Door.*** Amulet, 2014. Ages 10–14. Trilogy. (Celtic mythology)

Nielsen, Jennifer. ***The False Prince.*** Scholastic, 2012. Ages 8–14. Trilogy.

Oppel, Kenneth. ***Airborn.*** HarperCollins, 2004. Ages 11–14. Also ***Starclimbe***r (2009). (Canada)

Pratchett, Terry. ***Nation.*** HarperCollins, 2008. Ages 11–15. (U.K.)

Prineas, Sarah. ***The Magic Thief***. HarperCollins, 2008. Ages 9–12.

Pullman, Philip. ***The Golden Compass.*** Knopf, 1996. Ages 12–16. His Dark Materials trilogy. (U.K.)

Reeve, Philip. ***Mortal Engines.*** HarperCollins, 2003. Ages 12–18. Hungry Cities Chronicles. (U.K.)

Reeve, Philip. ***Larklight: A Rousing Tale of Dauntless Pluck in the Farthest Reaches of Space.*** Bloomsbury, 2006. Ages 10–15. (U.K.)

Rodda, Emily. ***The Key to Rondo***. Scholastic, 2007. Ages 9–12. (Australia)

Rowling, J. K. ***Harry Potter and the Sorcerer's Stone.*** Scholastic, 1998. Ages 9–13. (U.K.)

Sage, Angie. ***Magyk***. Katherine Tegen, 2005. Ages 9–12. Septimus Heap series. Also ***Pathfinder*** (2014). (U.K.)

Tolkien, J. R. R. ***The Hobbit.*** Houghton, 1937. Ages 12–18. Also the Lord of the Rings trilogy. (U.K.)

Turner, Megan Whalen. ***A Conspiracy of Kings.*** Greenwillow, 2010. Ages 11–18. Also ***The Thief*** (1997).

Valente, Catherynne. ***The Girl Who Circumvented Fairyland in a Ship of Her Own Making***. Feiwel & Friends, 2011. Ages 10–14. Trilogy.

Weston, Robert. ***Zorgmazoo.*** Razorbill, 2008. Ages 10–14. (**NV**)

Yep, Laurence. ***A Dragon's Guide to the Care and Feeding of Humans.*** Illus. Mary GrandPre. Crown, 2015. Ages 8–12.

Science Fiction

Anderson, M. T. ***He Laughed With His Other Mouths.*** Illus. Kurt Cyrus. Beach Lane, 2014. Ages 12–16.

Arntson, Steven. ***The Trap.*** Houghton Mifflin Harcourt, 2015. Ages 9–12. (Multiracial)

Boyce, Frank C. ***Cosmic.*** Walden Pond, 2008. Ages 10–14. (U.K.)

Collins, Suzanne. ***The Hunger Games***. Scholastic, 2008. Ages 12–15.

DuPrau, Jeanne. ***The City of Ember.*** Random House, 2003. Ages 10–14.

Farmer, Nancy. ***The House of the Scorpion.*** Simon & Schuster, 2002. Ages 12–18. (Mexico)

Haddix, Margaret Peterson. ***Under Their Skin.*** Simon & Schuster, 2016. Ages 8–13.

Hatke, Ben. ***The Return of Zita the Spacegirl.*** First Second, 2014. (**GR**). Ages 8–13.

Hatke, Ben. ***Little Robot.*** First Second, 2015. (**GR**). Ages 3–12.

L'Engle, Madeleine. ***A Wrinkle in Time.*** Farrar, 1962. Ages 11–15.

Lowry, Lois. ***The Giver.*** Houghton, 1993. Ages 11–15. Also ***Messenger*** (2004), ***Gathering Blue*** (2000), and ***Son*** (2015).

Rex, Adam. ***Smek for President.*** Illus. Keeli McCarthy. Hyperion, 2016. Ages 11–15.

Sachar, Louis. ***Fuzzy Mud***. Delacorte, 2015. Ages 10–14.

Scieszka, Jon. ***Spaceheadz.*** Illus. Shane Prigmore. Simon & Schuster, 2010. Ages 7–12.

Scieszka, Jon. ***Frank Einstein and the Antimatter Motor.*** Illus. Brian Biggs. Amulet, 2014. Ages 8–12.

Yancey, Richard. ***The 5th Wave.*** Putnam, 2013. Ages 14–16.

Related Films, Videos, and DVDs

BFG (2016). Author: Roald Dahl (1982). 117 minutes.

The Chronicles of Narnia: The Lion, the Witch and the Wardrobe (2005). Author: C. S. Lewis (1955). 140 minutes.

City of Ember (2008). Author: Jeanne DuPrau (2003). 95 minutes.

Coraline (2009). Author: Neil Gaiman (2002). 100 minutes.

Ella Enchanted (2004). Author: Gail Carson Levine (1997). 96 minutes.

The Giver (2014). Author: Lois Lowry (1993). 97 minutes.

The Golden Compass (2007). Author: Philip Pullman (1996). 113 minutes.

Harry Potter and the Sorcerer's Stone (2001). Author: J. K. Rowling (1998). 152 minutes.

The Hobbit: An Unexpected Journey (2012). Author: J. R. R. Tolkien (1937). 169 minutes.

The Hunger Games (2011). Author: Suzanne Collins (2008). 144 minutes.

Inkheart (2008). Author: Cornelia Funke (2003). 106 minutes.

A Monster Calls (2016). Author: Patrick Ness (2011). 108 minutes.

Shrek (2001). Author: William Steig (1990). 90 minutes. Sequels.

The Water Horse (2007). Author: Dick King-Smith (1998). 112 minutes.

Chapter 9

Realistic Fiction

Grace

It's wiggling the hook out
of the fish's mouth
watching the flash and form
dissolve in dark waters.
It's bitter words swallowed
before they push past
the gates of angry lips.
It's a back turning
a head shaking
a refusal to hear
an ugly rumor,
a compromising joke,
lies.
It's sandbags
passed hand to hand
by a river
that's tipping over,
or a guest bedroom bulging with refugees.
It's oatmeal
on cracked, swollen fly-bitten lips.
A book
whose words
seem meant for the reader
or postcard scenery
sliding past a window.
It's the perfect silence
of an empty room
all one's own.
It's this hand,
reaching out to yours.

—Tracie Vaughn Zimmer

Children of all ages are drawn to stories about people who seem like them or who are involved in familiar activities. Realistic stories deal with the realities of children's lives, the sad and harsh situations as well as the happy and humorous. Realistic fiction stories continue to have strong appeal to children and serve important roles in helping them gain perspective on their lives and world.

Definition and Description

Realistic fiction refers to stories that could happen to people and animals. The protagonists of these stories are fictitious characters created by the author, but their actions and reactions are quite like those of real people. Sometimes events in these stories are exaggerated or outlandish; however, it is within the realm of possibility for such improbable events to occur. On the other hand, some realistic fiction incorporates actual people, places, or events, in which case these factual aspects of the story need to be recorded accurately.

Contemporary realism is a term used to describe stories that take place in the present time and portray attitudes and mores of the present culture. Unlike realistic books of several decades ago that depicted only happy families and were never controversial, today's contemporary realism often focuses on current societal issues, such as death, racism, poverty, and homelessness. Contemporary books still tell of the happy, funny times in children's lives, but they also include the harsh, unpleasant times that are a part of many children's lives.

Because of the difficult nature of the issues in some realistic fiction, these books are sometimes the target of censors who argue that children need to be protected from harsh realities. In their attempts to protect the perceived "innocence" of children, adults fail to face the reality of children's lives. Many children are dealing with complex life situations; they read to battle the real monsters in their lives or to deal with situations that seem to be outside their control. Literature provides a way to gain valuable perspectives on these issues, to realize that they are not alone, and to experience the strategies used by characters to respond to challenging situations. They read for entertainment, but they also read because books provide them with hope as they face everyday fears and epic dangers. In addition, reading about other children's challenging situations can help those who are not facing these problems develop empathy. Children need perspective, not protection.

Authors of contemporary realistic fiction set their stories in the present or recent past. But in time features of these stories, such as dialogue and allusions to popular culture, customs, and dress, become dated and the stories are therefore no longer contemporary, though they may still be realistic. Older stories that obviously no longer describe today's world, though they may have once been contemporary realistic fiction, are labeled simply as realistic fiction. Older realistic fiction stories that are considered modern classics are included in this chapter.

Excellent Realistic Fiction to Read Aloud

Alexander, Kwame. *The Crossover.* Ages 10–14.

Alvarez, Julia. *How Tia Lola Learned to Teach.* Ages 8–12.

Cummings, Priscilla. *Red Kayak.* Ages 11–15.

de la Peña, Matt. *Last Stop on Market Street.* Illustrated by Christian Robinson. Ages 6–9.

DiCamillo, Kate. *Francine Poulet Meets the Ghost Raccoon.* Illustrated by Chris Van Dusen. Ages 6–9.

Graff, Lisa. *Absolutely Almost.* Ages 8–12.

Henkes, Kevin. *The Year of Billy Miller.* Ages 7–10.

Levy, Dana. *The Misadventures of the Family Fletcher.* Ages 8–12.

Martin, Ann. *Rain Reign.* Ages 8–12.

Nicholls, Sally. *Ways to Live Forever.* Ages 9–12.

O'Connor, Barbara. *The Small Adventure of Popeye and Elvis.* Ages 9–12.

Urban, Linda. *Hound Dog True.* Ages 8–12.

Evaluation and Selection of Realistic Fiction

The criteria for evaluating realistic fiction are the same as those for any work of fiction. Well-developed characters who change as a result of significant life events, a well-structured plot with sufficient conflict and suspense to hold the reader's interest, a time and place suitable to the storyline, and a worthy theme are basic literary elements for fiction. Specific evaluation issues in realistic fiction include:

- **Does the story permit some cause for hope?** Children need to trust that adverse and discouraging social situations can be overcome or ameliorated and that they can take action to make the world a better place in which to live. Children need hope that is realistic to their life situations, not wishful thinking or an unlikely happy ending.
- **Is the story a thin disguise for a heavy-handed moral lesson?** Realistic fiction often conveys values, such as kindness and generosity, but children resist stories that preach. The moral should not overwhelm the story, but be a logical outcome.
- **Is the story believable?** Are the events possible, even though all aspects are not probable? Sometimes an author goes close to the edge of the believable range to produce a more exciting, suspense-filled story but still should avoid the overuse of coincidence to resolve the plot.

Children deserve books offering a richness of experiences. An aspect of writing style that children greatly appreciate is humor. Humorous stories feature characters caught up in silly situations or involved in funny escapades, such as *Bink and Gollie* by Kate DiCamillo and *The Misadventures of the Family Fletcher* by Dana Levy. Balance humorous stories with serious and controversial books so children gain perspective on these difficult realities in their lives and world. Intermediate grade children report on reading interest surveys that realistic fiction is their favorite genre, so a strong book collection always needs to include a wide selection of these books.

The Significance of Character in Realistic Fiction

Although all of the literary elements are significant within realistic fiction, character plays a particularly critical role and often determines whether a book stays with a reader over time. As adults, we frequently forget the plot of favorite childhood books, but remember characters to whom we had a strong connection. Children need to share their personal connections and discuss the issues they find significant within a particular book and then revisit that book to consider the ways in which the author has developed intriguing characters. If literature is to help children understand life, then the portrayal of characters needs to be carefully considered by asking:

- How does the author reveal the character? We can come to know a character by the character's actions, speech, or appearance; visual depictions in illustrations; others' comments or thoughts; and the author's comments.
- Do characters act and talk in ways that are consistent with their age, gender, and culture?
- Do the characters grow and change in a believable manner over the course of the book?
- Does the author portray a range of qualities for major and minor characters to avoid stereotypes and to reflect their complexity as human beings with strengths and faults?

Historical Overview of Realistic Fiction

The earliest realistic stories were didactic and intended to teach morality and manners to young readers. The characters of the 1700s were wooden, lifeless boys and girls whose lives were spent in good works; however, in 1719, *Robinson Crusoe* by Daniel Defoe, an exciting survival story, was published for adults but became a popular book among children. Then in 1744, John Newbery began to publish children's books of realistic fiction intended to entertain as well as to educate. These two events laid the groundwork for establishing children's literature as a separate branch of literature.

The first type of realistic fiction for children that avoided heavy didactic persuasion was the adventure story. Imitators of *Robinson Crusoe* were many, including *The Swiss Family Robinson* by Johann Wyss of Switzerland in 1812. Later adventure stories from England were *Treasure Island* (1883) and *Kidnapped*

MILESTONES in the Development of Realistic Fiction

Date	Event	Significance
1719	*Robinson Crusoe* by Daniel Defoe (England)	Early survival/adventure on a desert island. Imitators include *The Swiss Family Robinson* by Johann Wyss (1812, Switzerland)
1868	*Little Women* by Louisa May Alcott (U.S.)	Popular early family story
1876	*The Adventures of Tom Sawyer* by Mark Twain (U.S.)	Classic adventure story set along the Mississippi River
1877	*Black Beauty* by Anna Sewell (England)	Early animal story deploring inhumane treatment of horses
1880	*Heidi* by Johanna Spyri (Switzerland)	An early international story popular in the United States
1883	*Treasure Island* by Robert Louis Stevenson (England)	Classic adventure story with pirates
1908	*Anne of Green Gables* by Lucy Maud Montgomery (Canada)	Early family story about an orphan and her new family
1911	*The Secret Garden* by Frances Hodgson Burnett (U.S.)	A classic sentimental novel of two children adjusting to life
1938	*The Yearling* by Marjorie Kinnan Rawlings (U.S.)	Classic animal story and coming-of-age story
1964	*Harriet the Spy* by Louise Fitzhugh (U.S.)	The beginning of the new realism movement
1970	*Are You There, God? It's Me, Margaret* by Judy Blume (U.S.)	Early book with frank treatment of puberty and physical maturation

(1886) by Robert Louis Stevenson, and from the United States, *The Adventures of Tom Sawyer* (1876) and *The Adventures of Huckleberry Finn* (1884) by Mark Twain.

Realistic family stories came on the scene during the 1800s with *Little Women* (1868) by Louisa May Alcott. The family story remained a favorite with such memorable books as *Anne of Green Gables* (1908) by Canadian Lucy Maud Montgomery and *The Secret Garden* (1911) by Frances Hodgson Burnett. Because their characters were orphans, these latter two books can be considered precursors of stories that address the needs of children with problems. Stories of happy and often large families peaked in the 1940s and 1950s in stories about the Moffat family by Eleanor Estes and the Melendy family by Elizabeth Enright. These happy family stories seem lighthearted compared with today's contemporary realism.

Another theme in realistic stories was children from other lands. *Hans Brinker, or The Silver Skates* (1865) by Mary Mapes Dodge and *Heidi* (1880) by Johanna Spyri of Switzerland are set in Holland and Switzerland, respectively. At the same time, realistic animal stories for children appeared, such as *Black Beauty* (1877) by Anna Sewell, a plea for humane treatment of animals that is quite sentimental and gives the horse human emotions and thoughts. Animal stories showing the maturing of the young human protagonist who assists the animal remain popular today.

Regional stories and stories about children of color appeared with more frequency in the 1940s. *Strawberry Girl* (1945) by Lois Lenski featured rural Florida and was one of the first regional stories. It was only in the 1960s and 1970s that books written by authors of color began to achieve national recognition. Two early noteworthy examples that portray African American childhood experiences are *Zeely* (1967) by Virginia Hamilton and *Stevie* (1969) by John Steptoe.

A new era in realistic fiction was ushered in with *Harriet the Spy* by Louise Fitzhugh in 1964. This story of an unhappy and, at times, unpleasant girl depicted Harriet, her parents, and her classmates as anything but ideal or sympathetic human beings. This trend toward a more explicitly truthful portrayal of life and the inclusion of many topics that were previously considered taboo continued in children's books in the 1970s and 1980s and still prevails. Controversial topics such as death, divorce, drugs, bullying, and gender identity, which have always been a part of childhood, became permissible topics. Parents and other adults were portrayed as they truly are with faults and strengths instead of as idealized figureheads. This newer, franker brand of realism, sometimes referred to as the ***new realism,*** changed the world of children's books. These books may be less lighthearted than their predecessors, but they are also more honest in portraying the actual lives of children.

Topics in Realistic Fiction

Realistic fiction highlights the child's world of relationships with self and others: the joys, sorrows, challenges, adjustments, anxieties, and satisfactions of human life. Realistic books often address more than one aspect of human life; thus, some realistic fiction books can be categorized by more than one of the following topics.

Relationships within Families

Stories about children and their relationships with parents and siblings are a natural focus because most children spend their childhood in close contact with family members. Family stories for younger children often portray a happy child with loving parents. In these stories, everyday activities from brushing teeth to cooking dinner are shown, such as in *What Happens on Wednesdays* by Emily Jenkins. Easy chapter books appealing to newly independent readers often show a child at play and explore sibling relationships, such as in *Clementine and the Family Meeting* by Sara Pennypacker and *Ling & Ting: Not Exactly the Same!* by Grace Lin. Novels for middle grade readers take on more difficult family issues, as in Kwame Alexander's novel in verse, *The Crossover*, in which two basketball-playing twins deal with changes in their relationship as well as their father's health struggles, all within the context of strong, loving family bonds.

Families in today's world have complicated and complex memberships, and books need to reflect this diversity in kinds of families. All children have the right to find themselves and their families in books, including single-parent families, adoptive families, foster families, same-sex parents, extended families, separated families, and reconstructed families of stepparents and stepchildren. Dana Levy's *The Misadventures of the Family Fletcher* relates the humorous adventures and warm family bonds of a multiracial family with two fathers, four adopted brothers, and a variety of pets as they deal with the disorder of their daily lives. Edwidge Danticat's *Mama's Nightingale* depicts a contemporary issue of a family separated by detainment because of the mother's immigration status. The importance of aunts, uncles, grandparents, stepparents, and cousins in children's lives is evident in *Waiting for Normal* by Leslie Connor about a girl's close ties to her stepfather and in *The Hello, Goodbye Window* by Norton Juster and Chris Raschka about a child's warm relationship with grandparents.

The difficulty children encounter in adjusting to new family situations is often a key plot element, such as in Laurel Croza's *From There to Here* where a young girl struggles with her family's move to the city, and Cynthia Kadohata's *Half a World Away* in which an emotionally troubled adopted child struggles with his family's decision to fly half a world away to adopt a baby. Realistic fiction does not shy away from showing the struggles of families as they face financial hardship, abandonment, death, and other hard issues. Those hardships are offset by the love that unites and creates a family, no matter what form that family unit may take.

Peer Friendships and Bullies

Learning how to cope with peers outside the warm security of family is a major concern for children. Many realistic stories show children figuring out how to get along with peers and how to develop close friendships in school and neighborhood settings. In *The Year of Billie Miller* by Kevin Henkes, Billie begins second grade with a bump on his head and many worries, and in *The Small Adventure of Popeye and Elvis* by Barbara O'Connor, Popeye longs for grand adventures and learns that life can be better with imagination and a friend. Keeping secrets is part of friendship, an issue a young girl struggles with in *Maddi's Fridge* when she realizes her friend's fridge is empty and tries to figure out a way to help a family experiencing hunger.

Many recent books focus on bullying in schools and the ways in which emotional and physical abuse can endanger and isolate a child, with some portraying that abuse in vivid detail. An American boy living in Japan faces relentless bullying by a vicious group of bullies in Holly Thompson's *Falling into the Dragon's Mouth*, whereas Karen Rivers' *The Girl in the Well Is Me* shares the stream of consciousness of a girl who ends up wedged partway down an abandoned well shaft after a bullying incident. The perspective in the picturebook *Red* by Jan De Kinder shifts to a bystander, a young girl torn between her fear of a bully on the playground and her sympathy for a classmate. Literature provides an opportunity to develop awareness of the harmful effects of bullying on children and to encourage compassion toward those who are targeted for real or perceived differences.

Physical, Emotional, Mental, and Behavioral Challenges

Many children must deal with difficult challenges in their lives. Some children have disabilities; others have a family member or a friend with a disability. These disabilities may be physical, such as scoliosis; emotional, such as bipolar disorder; mental, such as intellectual or learning disabilities; behavioral, such as hyperactivity; or a combination of these. Authors of children's books are becoming increasingly sensitive to the need for positive portrayals of individuals with disabilities as dealing with a challenge, not a "deficit." Children with these challenges need to find their lives reflected in books, as in Lynda Hunt's *Fish in a Tree* about a girl who acts out to hide the fact that she cannot read.

Well-written, honest stories can help children gain an understanding of, and empathy with, people who have disabilities. With the inclusion of special education students in classrooms, this trend can be an important educational resource. Cynthia Lord's *Rules* includes an autistic brother and a paraplegic friend as minor characters, and in Sarah Week's *So B. It,* the central character lives with her developmentally disabled mother and is cared for by a neighbor who is agoraphobic. Recent books are written from the perspective of the character who is dealing with a disability, such as Ann Martin's *Rain Reign* in the voice of a girl with Asperger's who collect homonyms and always follows rules, and Sharon Draper's *Out of My Mind* in the voice of a girl with cerebral palsy who discovers a device that allows her to speak for the first time.

Another trend is books in global settings, such as Eric Walters' picturebook, *My Name Is Blessing,* about a boy with a physical disability in Kenya, and A. L. Sonnichsen's novel in verse, *Red Butterfly,* about a girl with a physical disability who is a victim of China's adoption system.

Life within Local and Global Communities

Growing up includes the discovery of one's membership in a community, a group extending beyond the family. In some books, the community occurs within a school setting, as in Helen Frost's *Spinning through the Universe: A Novel in Poems from Room 214,* where students, the teacher, and the custodian share their thoughts in different poetic forms and voices.

In other books, the community setting is a neighborhood, such as *Seedfolks* by Paul Fleischman, in which a community garden brings a neighborhood together in chapters narrated by each character. *What Happened on Fox Street* by Tricia Springstubb focuses on the relationships within a blue-collar neighborhood, where tensions arise because of changing relationships and threatened land development. In *Last Stop on Market Street*, Matt de la Peña and Christian Robinson celebrate the grit and beauty of life in a deteriorating urban neighborhood and the actions ordinary people can take to make a difference. Communities can also fail to take action, as portrayed in Susan Kreller's *You Can't See the Elephants*, where people pretend not to see the physical abuse of children by a prominent community member of a small town.

Living in a diverse community involves establishing significant relationships that go across gender and race, but this diversity can also be a source of racism and discrimination. The books that most frequently portray racism tend to be historical fiction, providing a false impression that racism is in the past. Books such as *The Absolutely True Diary of a Part-Time Indian* by Sherman Alexie and *The Cruisers* by Walter Dean Myers challenge this misconception with contemporary portrayals.

With increasing interdependence among countries, young people will likely be more connected to the global world than ever before. Books set in global cultures can help children develop an awareness and sense of connection with people from these communities and an appreciation for people whose lives differ from their own. They particularly need contemporary images of life around the world because the majority of global novels are historical fiction, leading to misconceptions of these cultures as set back in time. Examples of contemporary novels include *City Boy* by Jan Michael, set in urban and rural Malawi; *Min-ji's Salon* by Eun-hee Choung, set in South Korea; and *Wanting Mor* by Rukhsana Khan, set in Afghanistan.

Global mobility, both chosen and forced, is common in today's world, so books are needed that portray children in cross-cultural encounters as they move between countries. In Naomi Shihab Nye's *The Turtle of Oman*, Aref has serious misgivings about temporarily moving from Oman to Michigan and spends his final week gathering memories with his grandfather to cope with his fear of the unknown. In *A Piece of Home* by Jerri Watts and Hyewon Yum, a young Korean boy leaves the familiar and must adapt to a new culture after his family's move to West Virginia.

Interactions with Animals

Animal stories continue to be a top choice for children as readers. The animal protagonist in realistic animal fiction behaves like an animal and is not personified. Usually, a child is a protagonist, as in *Because of Winn-Dixie* by Kate DiCamillo, in which a lonely girl's life is transformed by an old stray dog. A more unusual friendship between a child and a cow is portrayed in *Moo* by Sharon Creech. A recent trend is books featuring a child's relationship with an endangered animal, such as Mitali Perkin's *Tiger Boy* about the rescue of a tiger cub on India's Sunderbans islands and Eliot Schrefer's *Endangered* about a girl who flees with a bonobo from a sanctuary in the Congo when a revolution breaks out.

Animals are frequently the main characters in picturebooks where the story is realistic, but family members are visually portrayed as animals. Although technically these books are classified as fantasy, they focus on realistic events without fantastic or magical elements. Anthony Browne uses gorillas for *My Mom* and *My Dad,* where the characters are not talking gorillas but parents who happen to be portrayed as animals. Kevin Henkes has characters who act as human beings but are visually portrayed as mice in *Lily's Purple Plastic Purse* and *Penny and Her Song*. Letting animals play out human roles provides intellectual and emotional distance and opens a safe space for young children to reflect on the issues and choices in their lives.

The Thrill of Sports, Mystery, and Adventure

Sports, mysteries, and adventures remain popular genres that have wide appeal, particularly for reluctant readers. Sports stories often present a story in which a child struggles to become accepted as a member of a team and eventually succeeds through determination and hard work. Good examples are *Fast Break* by Mike Lupica, in which a basketball star is placed with a foster family, and *New Kid* by Tim Green, about a baseball player who struggles with game-day stress and bullies. Although traditionally written with boys as the main characters, some sports stories feature girls as protagonists, such as the graphic novel *Roller Girl* by Victoria Jamieson about a girl's love of roller derby and her changing friendships.

Mysteries range from simple "whodunits" to complex character stories. The element of suspense is a strong part of the appeal of these stories. In *Book Scavenger* by Jennifer Bertman, two children race around dodging thugs and solving codes and ciphers left behind by the creator of an online game involving books hidden in various cities. Mysteries have won more state children's choice awards than any other type of story. The Edgar Allan Poe Award for Juvenile Mystery Novels, given to U.S. authors, can be helpful in selecting good mysteries (see Appendix A).

Recent series of interest to mystery readers are the Bloodwater Mysteries by Pete Hautman and Mary Logue, the 39 Clues by Rick Riordan and other authors, and the Hunter Morgan mysteries by Patricia Reilly Giff. An established series with a female protagonist, the Sammy Keyes series by Wendelin Van Draanen, remains popular.

Stories of adventure are ones in which the young protagonist must rely on will and ingenuity to pursue a quest or survive a life-threatening situation. Phyllis Reynolds Naylor's *Going Where It's Dark* combines survival in the wilderness with survival in the world of bullies and Buck's journey to combat his stuttering with his quest to explore a newly discovered cave. Survival adventure books have a strong appeal to children because these adventures occur outside the control of adults.

Gender and Sexuality

One recent trend is books in which children explore their gender identities and express themselves in ways that challenge expected gender behaviors. In *Morris Mickelwhite and the Tangerine Dress* by Christine Baldacchino and Isabelle Malenfant, Morris loves to wear a tangerine dress from the dress-up center, even though his classmates make fun of him until he uses his imagination to win them over. Alex Gino's *George* may be a boy outwardly but inside she is a girl who desperately wants to play Charlotte in her fourth-grade class production of *Charlotte's Web*. Although there are setbacks, George finds a way to persuade her family to see who she really is, particularly through the support of her best friend Kelly.

The emergence of romantic feelings and relationships are part of the preteen years, particularly in middle school as children gain awareness of their sexual orientation and attraction to opposite-sex or same-sex peers. Although romantic relationships are depicted along with growing sexuality in children's books, books depicting sexual activity are primarily for an older teen audience. Some books depict boy-girl relationships, such as *Under the Watsons' Porch* by Susan Shreve and *Deep Down Popular* by Phoebe

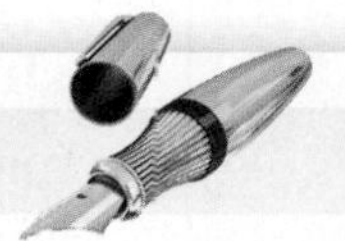

Notable Authors of Realistic Fiction

Kwame Alexander, author of sports-themed novels in verse set within middle-class African American families. *The Crossover* (Newbery award)*; Booked.* http://kwamealexander.com/

Julia Alvarez, author of novels about family and community, with a focus on bilingualism and immigration. *Return to Sender* and Tia Lola series. www.juliaalvarez.com

Sharon Creech, author of novels about girls seeking to find themselves. *Walk Two Moons; Ruby Holler; Moo.* www.sharoncreech.com

Jack Gantos, author of Joey Pigza novels about a boy with attention deficit disorder. *Joey Pigza Swallowed the Key; Joey Pigza Loses Control.* www.jackgantos.com

Lisa Graff, author of middle-grade novels with strong characterization. *Absolutely Almost*; *Lost in the Sun.* www.lisagraff.com

Polly Horvath, author of humorous family stories, set in Canada. *One Year in Coal Harbor; The Canning Season* (National Book Award); *My One Hundred Adventures.* www.pollyhorvath.com

Lenore Look, author of short chapter books on Chinese American family life and relationships. *Ruby Lu, Star of the Show; Alvin Ho: Allergic to Girls, School, and Other Scary Things.*

Barbara O'Connor, author of quiet stories about life in small towns. *How to Steal a Dog; The Small Adventure of Popeye and Elvis; On the Road to Mr. Mineo's.* www.barboconnor.com

Katherine Paterson, author of stories featuring relationships with peers and family and major life issues. *The Great Gilly Hopkins; Bridge to Terabithia.* www.terabithia.com

Raina Tegelmeier, author/illustrator of graphic novels about family and school based on her life. *Smile; Sisters; Drama.* http://goraina.com

Jacqueline Woodson, author of novels with African American characters on issues of sexuality, abuse, and race. *Locomotion; After Tupac and D Foster.* www.jacquelinewoodson.com

Stone. Books portraying same-sex attractions and the struggle to understand sexual orientation are a trend in young adult literature, but still infrequent in the middle grades. In *Totally Joe* by James Howe, Joe uses a school autobiography assignment to work up the courage to tell his family and friends he is gay.

Difficult Life Decisions and Coming of Age

Characters in many realistic fiction novels face moments of crisis, situations of great difficulty, or events in which a decision can change their life. Through these stories, children can understand the difficult decisions faced by the character and can discuss the consequences that may result from their choices. Using a book in which a character is faced with a difficult moral choice can stimulate lively discussions, such as Priscilla Cummings's *Red Kayak,* in which a 13-year-old boy faces a conflict between telling police the truth in a tragic accidental death or remaining silent and loyal to his friends.

A growing number of books are set in cities where gangs, drug wars, and abandonment are life threatening, such as *Nobody Knows* by Shelley Tamaka, a heartbreaking tale of four children who are abandoned in a nice Tokyo neighborhood where neighbors fail to notice their desperation, leading to tragic consequences. In *Small as an Elephant* by Jennifer Jacobson, a boy who has been abandoned in a campground by his bipolar mother attempts to make his way back to the city.

A recent set of books explores immigration, particularly where the characters lack legal status and live with the constant fear of deportation, as in *Ask Me No Questions* by Marina Budhos, in which a Muslim family struggles to survive after 9-11. In Julie Alvarez's *Return to Sender,* a farm family's survival depends on undocumented migrant Mexican workers who are also struggling to survive amid the threat of immigration raids.

Another recent trend is refugee and war stories, such as *A Long Walk to Water* by Linda Sue Park, based on the life of a boy separated from his family in the Sudan war. Andrea Pinkney's *The Red Pencil,* also set in the Sudan, uses verse to tell the story of a girl struggling to survive after an attack on her village forces her family to flee to an overcrowded refugee camp.

From birth to age 10, most children's lives revolve around family, friends, and classmates, but during the preteen and teen years, a shift toward self-discovery and independence occurs. Rapid growth and change are seen in the physical, emotional, moral, and intellectual domains of life. These changes and the struggles encountered as children move toward adulthood are referred to as ***coming-of-age stories.*** These books focus on a particular event in a child's life that signal a change from child to adult, such as a boy with recurrent cancer who runs away to fulfill his dream of climbing Mount Rainier in Dan Gemeinhart's

The Honest Truth or a girl's investigation of the rare jellyfish she is convinced took the life of her best friend in Ali Benjamin's *The Thing about Jellyfish*. Life situations force these characters to make difficult choices and so reach new understandings about themselves and their world.

Reader Connections: Paired Character Trait Books

Realistic stories in which characters are faced with difficult life choices can engage children in considering their core values. A powerful piece of literature can address the complexities of how these values play out in actual life situations, resisting simplistic doctrines of right and wrong. Moralizing is seldom appreciated by children. If the moral or lesson overpowers the story, children resist the obvious preaching and balk at reading such stories. They want powerful stories that excite, amuse, and inspire.

Paired sets of picturebooks for the six values identified by the Josephson Institute of Ethics as core values or character traits can provoke thought-provoking discussions. For each value, a picturebook that addresses the trait in a straightforward manner can be paired with a book that raises questions about the situational complexity of the value, questioning, for example, whether it's always wrong to tell a lie. Reading and responding to paired books can help children formulate their own understandings of the complexities of these values. They can engage in textual analysis by searching for evidence to support their interpretations on the ways in which these values are addressed within each book. A novel with diverse perspectives on a particular value is identified for each character trait and could be used as a whole class read-aloud or small group discussion book.

Trustworthiness: Build trust through integrity, honesty, loyalty, promise keeping.
- Bunting, Eve. *A Day's Work*. Illustrated by David Diaz.
- Amado, Elisa. *Tricycle*. Illustrated by Alfonso Ruano.
- Literature discussion novel: Gemeinhart, Dan. *The Honest Truth*.

Respect: Honor the dignity and worth of each person.
- O'Neill, Alexis. *The Recess Queen*. Illustrated by Laura Huliska-Beith.
- Coffelt, Nancy. *Fred Stays with Me*. Illustrated by Tricia Tusa.
- Literature discussion novel: Draper, Sharon. *Out of My Mind*.

Responsibility: Show accountability, self-control, self-reliance, persistence, hard-working traits.
- Wyeth, Sharon. *Something Beautiful*. Illustrated by Chris Soentpiet.
- Bang, Molly. *When Sophie Gets Angry—Really, Really Angry . . . .*
- Literature discussion novel: Cummings, Priscilla. *Red Kayak*.

Fairness: Demonstrate consistent, careful decision making, equitable treatment.
- Khan, Rukhsana. *Big Red Lollipop*. Illustrated by Sophie Blackall.
- Recorvits, Helen. *Yoon and the Jade Bracelet*. Illustrated by Gabi Swiatkowska.
- Literature discussion novel: Stead, Rebecca. *Goodbye, Stranger*.

Caring: Be kind, compassionate, empathetic, forgiving, grateful.
- Fleming, Virginia. *Be Good to Eddie Lee*. Illustrated by Floyd Cooper.
- Steptoe, John. *Stevie*.
- Literature discussion novel: Palacio, R. J. *Wonder*.

Citizenship: Obey laws, improve well-being of others, engage in active participation.
- Anzaldúa, Gloria. *Friends from the Other Side*. Illustrated by Consuelo Méndez.
- Brandt, Lois. *Maddi's Fridge*. Illustrated by Vinicius Vogel.
- Literature discussion novel: Kreller, Susan. *You Can't See The Elephants*.

Realistic fiction presents familiar situations with which children can readily identify and portrays settings not so different from the homes, schools, towns, and cities in which they live or hear about in the news. The protagonists of these stories are frequently testing themselves as they grow toward adulthood; young readers can therefore empathize and gain insight into their own situations. Keeping current with realistic stories is essential to providing a wide range of books that will entertain, encourage, and inspire students.

Invitations for Further Investigation

- In small groups, read and discuss a paired picturebook set for one of the character values. Create a web of words that describe the value and the complex issues in how that value plays out in different situations. Also read the novel associated with that value and add to the web.
- Create a list of favorite childhood books or stories that have stayed in your memory. Revisit one of those books to determine why that book had such a strong appeal for you as a child and to examine the portrayal of the characters in the book.
- Select a realistic fiction novel, and create a heart map that shows the ideas, values, and people that are important to one of the main characters and that also depicts how that character changes across the novel. Create a list of the literary strategies used by the author to help you get to know that character.
- Select and read several winners of the Edgar Allan Poe Award for Juvenile Mystery Novels (see Appendix A). Compare and contrast these novels, considering the source and type of mystery, the devices used to cause suspense, and the elements of realism and fantasy in each story.
- Select 10–15 realistic fiction novels suitable for a particular grade level. Booktalk and display these novels for a small group of students; then ask them to complete an interest survey. What did you discover about their reading preferences?
- Gather a set of picturebooks that use animals as main characters. Consider which are portrayed as real animals, which are based in realistic situations with animals taking the role of humans, and which are fantasy with talking animals. Consider the role of animals in books for children by reading Burke and Copenhaver (2004).

References

Burke, C., & Copenhaver, J. (2004). Animals as people in children's literature. *Language Arts 81*(3), 205–213.

Zimmer, T. V. (2012). Grace. In J. Corcoran (Ed.), *Dare to dream . . . change the world.* Tulsa, OK: Kane Miller.

Recommended Realistic Fiction Books

Ages indicated refer to content appropriateness and conceptual and interest levels. Formats other than novels will be coded as follows:

(**PB**) Picturebook
(**GR**) Graphic novel
(**COL**) Short story collection
(**NV**) Novel in verse

Relationships within Families

Alexander, Kwame. ***The Crossover.*** Houghton Mifflin Harcourt, 2014. (**NV**). Ages 10–14. Also ***Booked.*** (2016). (African American)

Arnaldo, Monica. ***Arto's Big Move.*** Owlkids, 2014. (**PB**). Ages 5–8. (Canada)

Baskin, Nora. ***Ruby on the Outside***. Simon & Schuster, 2015. Ages 10–14.

Bateson, Catherine. ***Being Bee.*** Holiday, 2007. Ages 8–12. (Australia)

Bauer, Joan. ***Soar.*** Viking, 2015. Ages 9–13.

Birdsall, Jeanne. ***The Penderwicks: A Summer Tale of Four Sisters, Two Rabbits, and a Very Interesting Boy.*** Knopf, 2005. Ages 9–12.

Browne, Anthony. ***My Dad.*** Grimm, 2001. (**PB**). Ages 5–9. Also ***My Mom.*** Grimm (2005). (**PB**). (U.K.)

Connor, Leslie. ***Waiting for Normal.*** Katherine Tegan Books, 2008. Ages 10–13.

Creech, Sharon. ***Ruby Holler.*** HarperCollins, 2002. Ages 8–11. Also ***Walk Two Moons*** (1994) and ***The Boy on the Porch*** (2013).

Crossan, Sarah. ***Apple and Rain: A Story to Fix a Broken Heart***. Bloomsbury, 2015. Ages 11–14. (U.K.)

Croza, Laurel. ***From There to Here***. Illus. Matt James. Groundwood, 2014. (**PB**). Ages 6–8. (Canada)

Danticat, Edwidge. ***Mama's Nightingale: A Story of Immigration and Separation***. Illus. Leslie Staub. Dial, 2015. (**PB**). Ages 5–8. (Haitian American)

Garden, Nancy. ***Molly's Family***. Illus. Sharon Wooding. Farrar, 2004. (**PB**). Ages 5–8.

Gephart, Donna. ***Death by Toilet Paper***. Delacorte, 2014. Ages 9–12.

Graff, Lisa. ***Absolutely Almost.*** Puffin, 2015. Ages 8–12.

Henkes, Kevin. ***Lilly's Purple Plastic Purse.*** Greenwillow, 1996. (**PB**). Ages 5–8. Also ***Penny and Her Song*** (2012) (**PB**).

Horvath, Polly. ***The Canning Season.*** Farrar, 2003. Ages 12–16. Also ***My One Hundred Adventures*** (2008) and ***One Year in Coal Harbor*** (2014). (Canada)

Jacobson, Jennifer. ***Paper Things***. Candlewick, 2015. Ages 10–14.

Jenkins, Emily. ***What Happens on Wednesdays***. Illus. Lauren Castillo. Frances Foster Books, 2007. (**PB**). Ages 3–6.

Juster, Norton. ***The Hello, Goodbye Window.*** Illus. Chris Raschka. Hyperion, 2005. (**PB**). Ages 4–7.

Kadohata, Cynthia. ***Half a World Away.*** Atheneum, 2014. Ages 10–14. (Kazakhstan)

Khan, Ruksana. ***Big Red Lollipop.*** Illus. Sophie Blackall. Viking, 2010. (**PB**). Ages 4–8. (Pakistani Canadian)

Levy, Dana. ***The Misadventures of the Family Fletcher.*** Yearling, 2015. Ages 8–12. (Multiracial)

Lin, Grace. ***Ling & Ting: Not Exactly the Same!*** Little Brown, 2010. (**COL**). Ages 6–9. (Chinese American)

Look, Lenore. ***Ruby Lu, Star of the Show***. Atheneum, 2011. Ages 8–11. (Chinese American)

Look, Lenore. ***Alvin Ho: Allergic to the Great Wall, the Forbidden Palace, and Other Tourist Attractions***. Schwartz & Wade, 2014. Ages 6–10. (Chinese American)

McKay, Hilary. ***Forever Rose.*** M. K. McElderry Books, 2008. Ages 10–14. Series. (U.K.)

O'Connor, Barbara. ***How to Steal a Dog***. Farrar, 2007. Ages 10–12.

Paterson, Katherine. ***The Great Gilly Hopkins.*** Crowell, 1978. Ages 9–12.

Pennypacker, Sara. ***Clementine and the Family Meeting.*** Disney/Hyperion Books, 2011. (**PB**). Ages 7–10.

Schiffer, Miriam B. ***Stella Brings the Family***. Illus. Holly Clifton-Brown. Chronicle, 2015. (**PB**). Ages 4–8.

Scieszka, Jon, editor. ***Guys Write for Guys Read: Boys' Favorite Authors Write about Being Boys.*** Viking, 2005. (**COL**). Ages 10–14.

Smith, Hope Anita. ***The Way a Door Closes.*** Illus. Shane W. Evans. Holt, 2003. (**NV**). Ages 10–13. Also ***Keeping the Night Watch*** (2008). (African American)

Sovern, Megan. ***The Meaning of Maggie***. Chronicle, 2014. Ages 9–12.

Suneby, Elizabeth. ***Razia's Ray of Hope: One Girl's Dream of an Education***. Illus. Suana Verelst. Kids Can, 2013. (**PB**). Ages 8-11. Afghanistan.

Telgemeier, Raina. ***Sisters.*** Graphix, 2014. (**GR**). Ages 7–13.

Tolan, Stephanie S. ***Surviving the Applewhites.*** HarperCollins, 2002. Ages 10–14.

Tupper Ling, Nancy. ***Double Happiness.*** Illus. Alina Chau. Chronicle, 2015. (**PB**). Ages 5–8. (Chinese American)

Underwood, Deborah. ***Bad Bye, Good Bye***. Illus. Jonathan Bean. Houghton Mifflin Harcourt, 2014. Ages 4–8.

Williams, Vera B. ***Amber Was Brave, Essie Was Smart: The Story of Amber and Essie Told Here in Poems and Pictures.*** Greenwillow, 2001. (**NV**). Ages 6–10.

Peer Friendships and Bullies

Bradt, Lois. ***Maddi's Fridge***. Illus. Vinicius Vogel. Flashlight Press, 2014. (**PB**). Ages 5–8.

Britt, Fanny. ***Jane, the Fox & Me***. Illus. Isabelle Arsenault. Translated from French. Groundwood, 2013. (**GR**). Ages 10–13. (Canada)

Brown, Gavin. ***Josh Baxter Levels Up***. Scholastic, 2016. Ages 10–14.

Castellucci, Cecil. ***The Plain Janes.*** Illus. Jim Rugg. DC Comics, 2007. (**GR**). Ages 12–18.

Creech, Sharon. ***Love That Dog.*** HarperCollins, 2001. (**NV**). Ages 9–14.

De Kinder, Jan. ***Red.*** Translated from Dutch. Eerdmans, 2015. (**PB**). Ages 5–8. (Netherlands)

DiCamillo, Kate, and McGhee, Alison. ***Bink & Gollie.*** Illus. Tony Fucile. Candlewick, 2010. (**PB**). Ages 6–9.

Harper, Charise. ***Just Grace.*** Houghton, 2007. Ages 7–9.

Henkes, Kevin. ***The Year of Billy Miller.*** Greenwillow, 2013. Ages 7–10. Also ***Bird Lake Moon*** (2008).

Howe, James. ***The Misfits.*** Simon & Schuster, 2001. Ages 10–13.

Kelly, Erin E. ***Blackbird Fly.*** Greenwillow, 2015. Ages 9–14. (Filipino American)

Kinney, Jeff. ***Diary of a Wimpy Kid***. Amulet, 2007. Ages 10–14. Series.

Lowry, Lois. ***Gooney Bird Greene.*** Houghton, 2002. Ages 7–9. Series.

Ludwig, Trudy. ***The Invisible Boy.*** Knopf, 2013. Illus. Patrice Barton. (**PB**). Ages 5–7.

Mann, Elizabeth. ***Little Man.*** Mikaya Press, 2014. Ages 10–14. (Caribbean)

Myers, Walter Dean. ***Scorpions.*** Harper, 1988. Ages 10–16. (African American)

O'Connor, Barbara. ***The Small Adventure of Popeye and Elvis.*** Farrar, 2009. Ages 8–12.

Paterson, Katherine. ***Bridge to Terabithia.*** Crowell, 1977. Ages 9–13.

Pennypacker, Sara. ***Clementine.*** Illus. Marla Frazee. Hyperion, 2006. Ages 7–10.

Rivers, Karen. ***The Girl in the Well Is Me.*** Algonquin, 2016. Ages 10–16.

Schusterman, Neal. ***Antsy Does Time.*** Dutton, 2008. Ages 11–15.

Scieszka, Jon, editor. ***Funny Business.*** Walden Pond, 2010. (**COL**). Ages 9–13.

Spinelli, Jerry. ***Eggs***. Little, Brown, 2007. Ages 9–12. Also ***Wringer*** (1997).

Springstubb, Tricia. ***Moonpenny Island.*** Illus. Gilbert Ford. Blazer + Bray, 2015. Ages 8–12.

Stead, Rebecca. ***Goodbye Stranger.*** Wendy Lamb Books, 2015. Ages 11–14.

Thompson, Holly. ***Falling into the Dragon's Mouth.*** Holt, 2016. (**NV**). Ages 10–13. (Japan)

Tarshis, Lauren. ***Emma-Jean Lazarus Fell out of a Tree.*** Dial, 2007. Ages 10–14.

Urban, Linda. ***Hound Dog True***. Harcourt, 2011. Ages 8–12.

Weeks, Sarah. ***Save Me a Seat***. Scholastic, 2016. Ages 8–12. (Indian American)

Physical, Emotional, Mental, and Behavioral Challenges

Baskin, Nora Raleigh. ***Anything but Typical.*** Simon & Schuster, 2009. Ages 10–14. (Autism)

Draper, Sharon. ***Out of My Mind.*** Atheneum, 2010. Ages 9–12. (Cerebral palsy)

Erskine, Kathryn. ***Mockingbird.*** Philomel, 2010. Ages 8–12. (Asperger's syndrome)

Gantos, Jack. ***I Am Not Joey Pigza.*** Farrar, 2007. Ages 10–13. (Attention deficit/hyperactivity)

Hunt, Lynda M. ***Fish in a Tree***. Nancy Paulsen, 2015. Ages 10–12. (Dyslexia)

Jonsberg, Barry. ***The Categorical Universe of Candice Phee***. Chronicle, 2014. Ages 10–14. (Australia, autism)

Kerz, Anna. ***Better Than Weird***. Orca, 2011. Ages 10–14. (Autism; Canada)

Lord, Cynthia. ***Rules.*** Scholastic, 2006. Ages 9–13. (Autism, paraplegia)

Martin, Ann M. ***Rain Reign***. Feiwel and Friends, 2014. Ages 8–12. (Asperger's)

Moulton, Erin. ***Chasing the Milky Way***. Philomel, 2014. Ages 9–12. (Bipolar)

Nicholls, Sally. ***Ways to Live Forever.*** Scholastic, 2008. Ages 9–12. (Leukemia; U.K.)

Palacio, R. J. ***Wonder***. Knopf, 2012. Ages 8–14. (Facial abnormalities)

Schumacher, Julie. ***Black Box.*** Delacorte, 2008. Ages 12–18. (Depression)

Sonnichsen, A. L. ***Red Butterfly***. Illus. Amy June Bates. Simon & Schuster, 2015. Ages 8–12. (Adoption, physical disability; China)

Walters, Eric. ***My Name Is Blessing***. Illus. Eugenie Fernandes Tundra, 2013. (**PB**). Ages 4–8. (Physical disability; Kenya)

Weeks, Sarah. ***So B. It.*** HarperCollins, 2004. Ages 10–14. (Intellectual disability, agoraphobia)

Life within Local and Global Communities

Alexi, Sherman. ***The Absolutely True Diary of a Part-Time Indian.*** Little, Brown, 2007. Ages 12–18. (Spokane Indian)

Alvarez, Julia. ***How Tia Lola Learned to Teach***. Knopf, 2010. Ages 9–12. (Dominican American)

Campoy, F. Isabel. ***Maybe Something Beautiful.*** Houghton Mifflin Harcourt, 2016. (**PB**). Ages 4–7. (Mexican American)

Choung, Eun-hee. ***Minji's Salon***. Kane/Miller, 2008. Ages 6–9. (Korea)

Craig, Colleen. ***Afrika.*** Tundra, 2008. Ages 12–15. (South Africa)

de la Pena, Matt. ***Last Stop on Market Street.*** Illus. Christian Robinson. Putnam, 2015. (**PB**). Ages 3–6. (African American)

Fleischman, Paul. ***Seedfolks.*** HarperCollins, 1997. Ages 10–14.

Frost, Helen. ***Spinning through the Universe: A Novel in Poems from Room 214.*** Farrar, 2004. (**NV**). Ages 11–14.

Graham, Bob. ***A Bus Called Heaven.*** Candlewick, 2011. (**PB**). Ages 3–8. (Australia)

Isabella, Jude. ***The Red Bicycle***. Illus. Simone Shin. (**PB**). 8–10. (Burkina Faso)

Khan, Rukhsana. ***Wanting Mor***. Groundwood, 2009. Ages 12–15. (Afghanistan)

Kreller, Susan. ***You Can't See the Elephants.*** Translated from German. Putnam, 2015. Ages 12–14.

Mateo, Jose Manuel. ***Migrant***. Illus. Javier Martinez Pedro. Abrams, 2014. Translated from Spanish. Bilingual. Ages 7–12. (Mexico)

Michael, Jan. ***City Boy***. Clarion, 2009. Ages 10–14. (Malawi)

Myers, Walter Dean. ***The Cruisers.*** Scholastic, 2010. Ages 9–13. (African American)

Na, An. ***A Step from Heaven.*** Front Street, 2001. Ages 13–18. (Korean American)

Naidoo, Beverley. ***The Other Side of Truth.*** Harper-Collins, 2001. Ages 11–14. (Nigeria, London)

Nye, Naomi. ***The Turtle of Oman.*** Greenwillow, 2014. Ages 8–12. (Oman)

O'Connor, Barbara. ***On the Road to Mr. Mineo's.*** Frances Foster, 2012. Ages 9–12.

Patron, Susan. ***The Higher Power of Lucky***. Atheneum, 2006. Ages 9–12.

Powers, J. L. ***Amina.*** Allen & Unwin, 2013. Ages 12-14. (Somalia)

Resau, Laura. ***What the Moon Saw.*** Delacorte, 2006. Ages 10–15. (Mexican American)

Resau, Laura. ***Red Glass.*** Delacorte, 2007. Ages 11–15. (Mexico)

Rocklin, Joanne. ***One Day and One Amazing Morning on Orange Street.*** Amulet, 2011. Ages 8–12.

Springstubb, Tricia. ***What Happened on Fox Street.*** Balzer and Bray, 2010. Ages 8–12.

Walters, Eric. ***Hope Springs.*** Illus. Eugenie Fernandes. Tundra, 2013. (**PB**). Ages 6–9. (Kenya)

Watts, Jeri H. ***A Piece of Home.*** Illus. Hyewon Yum. Candlewick, 2016. (**PB**). Ages 5–10. (Korea)

Williams-Garcia, Rita. ***No Laughter Here.*** HarperCollins, 2004. Ages 10–14. (Nigerian American)

Woodson, Jacqueline. ***Locomotion.*** Putnam, 2003. (**NV**). Ages 9–12. (African American)

Interactions with Animals

Adderson, Caroline. ***Norman, Speak!*** Groundwood, 2014. (**PB**). Ages 4–8.

Creech, Sharon. ***Moo.*** HarperCollins, 2016. Ages 8–12.

DiCamillo, Kate. ***Because of Winn-Dixie.*** Candlewick, 2000. Ages 8–11.

DiCamillo, Kate. ***Francine Poulet Meets the Ghost Raccoon.*** Candlewick, 2015. Ages 6–9.

Foreman, Jack. ***Say Hello.*** Illus. Michael Foreman. Candlewick, 2008. (PB) Ages 5–8. (U.K.)

Hiaasen, Carl. ***Hoot.*** Knopf, 2003. Ages 10–14.

Lewis, Gill. ***Moon Bear***. Atheneum, 2015. Ages 10-14. (Laos)

Mattick, Lindsay. ***Finding Winnie***. Illus. Sophie Blackall. Little, Brown, 2015. (**PB**). Ages 5–9.

O'Connor, Barbara. ***How to Steal a Dog.*** Farrar, Straus and Giroux, 2007. Ages 8–12.

Perkins, Mitali. ***Tiger Boy.*** Illus. Jamie Hogan. Charlesbridge, 2015. Ages 8–11. (India)

Schrefer, Eliot. ***Endangered.*** Scholastic, 2012. Ages 12–18. (Congo)

The Thrill of Sports, Mystery, and Adventure

Balliett, Blue. ***Chasing Vermeer.*** Illus. Brett Helquist. Scholastic, 2004. Ages 9–14.

Beil, Michael. ***The Red Blazer Girls: The Ring of Racamadour***. Knopf, 2009. Ages 10–14.

Broach, Elise. ***Missing on Superstition Mountain.*** Holt, 2011. Ages 8–12.

Brown, Monica. ***Lola Levine Is Not Mean.*** Illus. Angela N. Dominguez. Little, Brown, 2015. Ages 6–10. (Biracial)

Chambliss Bertman, Jennifer. ***Book Scavenger.*** Christy Ottaviano Books, 2015. Ages 8–12.

Cheshire, Simon. ***The Treasure of Dead Man's Lane and Other Case Files.*** Roaring Brook, 2009. Ages 8–12.

Curtis, Christopher Paul. ***Mr. Chickee's Funny Money.*** Random House, 2005. Ages 9–13. (African American)

DeFelice, Cynthia. ***Fort.*** Farrar, 2015. Ages 10–14.

Deuker, Carl. ***Gym Candy.*** Houghton, 2007. Ages 13–18.

Doyle, Roddy. ***Wilderness.*** Scholastic, 2007. Ages 11–16. (Iceland)

Feinstein, John. ***The Walk On.*** Knopf, 2014. Ages 11–15.

FitzGerald, Dawn. ***Soccer Chick Rules.*** Roaring Brook, 2006. Ages 10–14.

Gannon, Nicholas. ***The Doldrums.*** Greenwillow, 2015. Ages 7–11.

George, Jean. ***My Side of the Mountain.*** Dutton, 1959. Ages 9–12.

Giff, Patricia R. ***Hunter Moran Saves the Universe.*** Holiday House, 2012. Ages 9–12.

Grabenstein, Chris. ***Escape from Mr. Lemoncello's Library.*** Random House, 2013. Ages 9–13. Also ***Mr. Lemoncello's Olympics***. (2016).

Green, Tim. ***New Kid.*** Harper, 2014. Ages 10–14.

Hautman, Pete, and Logue, Mary. ***Doppelganger.*** Putnam, 2008. Ages 11–15. Bloodwater Mysteries.

Hiaasen, Carl. ***Chomp.*** Knopf, 2012. Ages 10–14.

Jamieson, Victoria. ***Roller Girl.*** Dial, 2015. Ages 9–13.

Koertge, Ron. ***Shakespeare Bats Cleanup.*** Candlewick, 2003. Ages 11–14.

Lupica, Mike. ***The Batboy.*** Philomel, 2010. Ages 10–14. Also ***Fast Break*** (2015).

Maddox, Jake. ***Running Rivals.*** Illus. Tuesday Mourning. Stone Arch, 2009. Ages 8–12.

Naylor, Phyllis R. ***Going Where It's Dark.*** Delacorte, 2016. Ages 8–12.

Paulsen, Gary. ***Hatchet.*** Bradbury, 1987. Ages 9–12.

Riordan, Rick. ***The Maze of Bones.*** Scholastic, 2008. Ages 9–13. 39 Clues series.

Ritter, John H. ***The Boy Who Saved Baseball.*** Philomel, 2003. Ages 10–13.

Roberts, Ken. ***Thumb and the Bad Guys.*** Illus. Leanne Franson. Groundwood, 2009. Ages 8–12.

Salisbury, Graham. ***Calvin Coconut: Hero of Hawaii.*** Wendy Lamb, 2011. Ages 7–10. (Hawaii)

Selfors, Suzanne. ***Smells like Treasure.*** Little, Brown, 2011. Ages 8–12.

Snicket, Lemony. ***The End: Book the Thirteenth.*** HarperCollins, 2006. Ages 10–14.

Snicket, Lemony. ***File Under: 13 Suspicious Incidents.*** Little, Brown, 2014. Ages 8–14.

Springer, Nancy. ***The Case of the Cryptic Crinoline: An Enola Holmes Mystery.*** Penguin, 2009. Ages 10–14.

Stewart, Trenton Lee. ***The Mysterious Benedict Society.*** Little, Brown, 2007. Ages 10–14.

Turnage, Sheila. ***Three Times Lucky.*** Dial, 2012. Ages 10–14. Also ***The Ghosts of Tupelo Landing.*** (2014).

Van Draanen, Wendelin. ***Sammy Keyes and the Kiss Goodbye.*** Knopf, 2014. Ages 10–13.

Gender and Sexuality

Baldacchino, Christine. ***Morris Micklewhite and the Tangerine Dress.*** Illus. Isabelle Malenfant. Groundwood, 2014. (**PB**). Ages 4–8. (Canada)

Baskin, Nora Raleigh. ***The Summer before Boys.*** Simon & Schuster, 2011. Ages 9–12.

Federle, Tim. ***Better Nate than Ever.*** Simon & Schuster, 2013. Ages 8–13.

Feinstein, John. ***The Sixth Man.*** Knopf, 2015. Ages 12–16.

Freitas, Donna. ***The Possibilities of Sainthood.*** Farrar, 2008. Ages 12–15.

Gino, Alex. ***George.*** Scholastic, 2015. Ages 9–12.

Howe, James. ***Totally Joe.*** Atheneum, 2005. Ages 10–14.

Moskowitz, Hannah. ***Marco Impossible.*** Roaring Brook Press, 2013. Ages 11–14.

Naylor, Phyllis Reynolds. ***Almost Alice***. Atheneum, 2008. Ages 10–15.

Polansky, Ami. ***Gracefully Grayson.*** Hyperion, 2014. Ages 10–14.

Shreve, Susan. ***Under the Watsons' Porch***. Knopf, 2004. Ages 10–14.

Spinelli, Jerry. ***Stargirl.*** Knopf, 2000. Ages 11–15. Also ***Love, Stargirl*** (2007).

Stone, Phoebe. ***Deep Down Popular.*** Scholastic, 2008. Ages 10–14.

Difficult Life Decisions and Coming of Age

Alvarez, Julia. ***Return to Sender***. Knopf, 2009. Ages 9–12. (Mexican American)

Amado, Elisa. ***Tricycle.*** Illus. Alfonso Ruano. Groundwood, 2007. (**PB**). Ages 5–9. (Guatemala)

Anderson, John D. ***Ms. Bixby's Last Day***. Walden Pond Press, 2016. Ages 8–12.

Anzaldúa, Gloria. ***Friends from the Other Side.*** Illus. Consuelo Méndez. Children's Book Press, 1993. (**PB**). Ages 8–12. (Mexican American)

Arnold, Elana K. ***The Question of Miracles***. Houghton Mifflin Harcourt, 2015. Ages 10–14.

Bang, Molly. ***When Sophie Gets Angry—Really, Really Angry . . . .*** Blue Sky, 1999. (**PB**). Ages 5–9.

Basssoff, Leah. ***Lost Girl Found***. Groundwood, 2014. Ages 12–14. (Sudan)

Benjamin, Ali. ***The Thing about Jellyfish***. Little, Brown, 2015. Ages 12–15.

Budhos, Marina. ***Ask Me No Questions***. Atheneum, 2006. (Bangladeshi American)

Bunting, Eve. ***A Day's Work.*** Illus. Ronald Himler. Clarion, 1994. (**PB**). Ages 5–9. (Mexican American)

Carter, Caela. ***My Life with the Liars***. Harper, 2016. Ages 9–14.

Coffelt, Nancy. ***Fred Stays with Me.*** Illus. Tricia Tusa. Little, Brown, 2007. (**PB**). Ages 5–9.

Cummings, Priscilla. ***Red Kayak.*** Dutton, 2004. Ages 11–15.

Fitzgerald, Sarah. ***The Apple Tart of Hope***. Holiday House, 2015. Ages 10–14. (Ireland)

Fitzmaurice, Kathryn. ***The Year the Swallows Came Early.*** Bowen, 2009. Ages 9–12.

Fleming, Virginia. ***Be Good to Eddie Lee.*** Illus. Floyd Cooper. Philomel, 1993. (**PB**). Ages 5–9.

Gemeinhart, Dan. ***The Honest Truth***. Scholastic, 2015. Ages 9–13.

Graff, Lisa. ***Lost in the Sun***. Philomel, 2015. Ages 9–12.

Griffin, Paul. ***When Friendship Followed Me Home***. Dial, 2016. Ages 10–14.

Harrington, Karen. ***Mayday***. Little, Brown, 2016. Ages 10–14.

Henkes, Kevin. ***Olive's Ocean.*** Greenwillow, 2003. Ages 10–13.

Jacobson, Jennifer. ***Small as an Elephant.*** Candlewick, 2011. Ages 10–14.

Jain, Mahak. ***Maya***. Illus. Elly MacKay. Owlkids, 2016. Ages 4–10. (India)

Myers, Walter Dean. ***Lockdown.*** Amistad, 2011. Ages 12–18. (African American)

O'Neill, Alexis. ***The Recess Queen.*** Illus. Laura Huliska-Beith. Scholastic, 2002. (**PB**). Ages 5–9.

Park, Linda Sue. ***A Long Walk to Water***. Clarion, 2010. Ages 10–14. (Sudan)

Pinkney, Andrea D. ***The Red Pencil***. Illus. Shane Evans. Little, Brown, 2014. Ages 8–12. (Sudan)

Recorvits, Helen. ***Yoon and the Jade Bracelet.*** Illus. Gabi Swiatkowska. Farrar, 2008. (**PB**) Ages 5–9. (Korean American)

Resau, Laura. ***Star in the Forest***. Delacorte, 2010. Ages 9–12. (Mexican American)

Senzai, N. H. ***Shooting Kabul***. Simon & Schuster, 2010. Ages 9–14. (Afghanistan)

Spinelli, Jerry. ***Maniac Magee.*** HarperCollins, 1990. Ages 9–12.

Steptoe, John. ***Stevie.*** HarperCollins, 1969. (**PB**). Ages 5–9. (African American)

Tanaka, Shelley. ***Nobody Knows***. Groundwood, 2012. Ages 11–14. (Tokyo)

Woodson, Jacqueline. ***After Tupac and D Foster.*** Putnams, 2010. Ages 12–18. (African American)

Wyeth, Sharon Dennis. ***Something Beautiful.*** Illus. Chris K. Soentpiet. Doubleday, 1998. (**PB**). Ages 5–9. (African American)

Related Films, Videos, and DVDs

Alexander and the Terrible, Horrible, No Good, Very Bad Day (2014). Author: Judith Viorst (1987). 91 minutes.

Because of Winn-Dixie (2005). Author: Kate DiCamillo (2000). 106 minutes.

Bridge to Terabithia (2007). Author: Katherine Paterson (1977). 96 minutes.

Diary of a Wimpy Kid (2010). Author: Jeff Kinney (2007). 92 minutes.

Finding Winnie (2016). Author: Linday Mattick (2015). 22 minutes.

The Great Gilly Hopkins (2016). Author: Katherine Paterson (1978). 98 minutes.

Holes (2003). Author: Louis Sachar (1998). 117 minutes.

Hoot (2006). Author: Carl Hiaasen (2002). 91 minutes.

Last Stop on Market Street (2016). Author: Matt de la Peña (2015). 10 minutes.

Lemony Snicket's A Series of Unfortunate Events (2004). Author: Daniel Handler, ***The Bad Beginning*** (1999). 107 minutes.

Shiloh (1997). Author: Phyllis Reynolds Naylor (1991). 93 minutes.

Chapter 10

Historical Fiction

Ancestors

On the wind-beaten plains
once lived my ancestors.
In the days of peaceful moods,
they wandered and hunted.
In days of need or greed,
they warred and loafed.
Beneath the lazy sun, kind winds above,
they laughed and feasted.
Through the starlit night, under the moon,
they dreamed and loved.
Now, from the wind-beaten plains,
only their dust rises.

—Grey Cohoe

Historical fiction makes the past come alive, inviting readers to immerse themselves into another time and place. Stories of the past provide us with a sense of humanity and memory. Milton Meltzer (1981) argues that we need history to compare our current experiences with the past to make sense of our lives. Without history, we are locked in the current moment, blinded from understanding that moment. We need stories of the past to locate ourselves in the larger continuum of life and to envision reasons for taking action to create change.

Definition and Description of Historical Fiction

Historical fiction is realistic fiction set in a time remote enough from the present to be considered history. Stories about events that occurred at least one generation (20 years or more) before the date of the original publication are included in this chapter. Authors write about time periods in which they did not live or that occurred more than 20 years before their books. This distance provides them with contextual perspectives from which to view the significance and interpretations of these events. Authors often blend historical facts with imaginary characters and an invented plot. The events in their plots must be within the realm of possibility, constructed around actual historical events, authentic period settings, and real historical figures.

In the most common form of historical fiction, the main characters are imaginary, but some secondary characters are actual historical figures. In the classic novel *Johnny Tremain* by Esther Forbes, Johnny, a fictitious character, is apprenticed to a silversmith during the U.S. Revolutionary War period and encounters Samuel Adams, John Hancock, and Paul Revere. *One Crazy Summer* by Rita Williams-Garcia is set in Oakland, California, in the summer of 1968. When three sisters visit the mother they barely know, they are sent to a Black Panther summer camp, where they encounter well-known Black Panthers, such as Huey Newton, and actual events, such as the death of Bobby Hutton.

In another form of historical fiction, the social traditions, customs, and values of the relevant period are described within an accurate physical place but with no mention of an actual historical event or actual historical figures as characters. In *The Witch of Blackbird Pond* by Elizabeth George Speare, the Puritan way of life in 1600s Connecticut is depicted in a story about Kit from Barbados, who becomes involved in a witchcraft trial. In *A Night Divided*, by Jennifer Nielsen, Gerta is separated from her father and brother, who are caught in the West by the building of the Berlin Wall in 1961. When Gerta receives a message from her father, her fierce desire for freedom leads her to a dangerous plan to dig a tunnel under the wall to bring her family back together.

There are historical stories in which elements of fantasy are found, and so are not considered historical fiction. For example, time warps and other supernatural features pop up in Rebecca Stead's *When You Reach Me* and Margaret Peterson Haddix's *Found*. These stories are ***historical fantasy*** and are included in the chapter on fantasy.

Evaluation and Selection of Historical Fiction

In evaluating historical fiction, the criteria for any well-written story are relevant, particularly whether the book tells an engaging story with rounded complex characters with whom children can identify. Also of significance is whether the book highlights universal themes that are thought-provoking without being didactic.

Award lists provide sources of recent books that offer readers the human side of history. The Scott O'Dell Award, established in 1982, honors the most outstanding work of children's historical fiction published in the previous year. The work must be written by a U.S. citizen and be set in the New World. The Scott O'Dell Award winners found in Appendix A are a source of outstanding historical fiction. The National Council for the Social Studies publishes an annual list of the most notable trade books in the field of social studies in the May/June issue of *Social Education*. This list includes many works of historical fiction as well as nonfiction works and is a useful source to locate recent books.

The Significance of Setting and Point of View in Historical Fiction

Two literary elements that are particularly significant for historical fiction are ***setting*** and ***point of view.*** The story must be told within an authentic time and place that come alive for readers and that acknowledge differing perspectives on those events and times. Unlike the general settings of folklore, historical fiction depends on integral settings that are essential to understanding the story and the actions and beliefs of the characters. The following criteria should be considered:

- ***Is the setting described in rich details that are accurate and authentic for that time and place?*** A setting must be described in enough detail to provide an authentic sense of time and place without overwhelming the story. Details such as hair and clothing styles, home architecture and furnishings, foods and food preparation, and modes of transportation must be subtly woven into the story to provide a convincing, authentic period setting.
- ***Do the characters act and think within the traditions and norms of their times?*** The connections between setting and actions must be evident so that readers understand the ways in which the characters are influenced by time and place. In most historical fiction, setting takes on the role of clarifying the conflict by showing how the time and place affect the action. Other roles include setting as antagonist, setting that illuminates character, setting that establishes mood, and setting as a symbol (Lukens, 2012).
- ***Is the dialogue authentic to the time period as well as understandable to children?*** Expressing the language or dialect of the period presents a challenge for authors, especially in creating dialogue. If the speech of the period differs greatly from that of today, the author must decide whether to remain true to the language of the time, which can cause difficulties in comprehending, or change the language to modern phrasing and risk losing the authenticity of the period. The language should not jar the reader by its obvious inappropriateness or lose the reader by its extreme difficulty. Most authors strive for a middle ground by retaining some flavor of language difference but making modifications to be understandable to the child reader. Authors need to be careful not to include terms or slang common in today's world but that would have been unknown in the time period of the story.
- ***Are multiple perspectives about the events and issues shared through the various characters? Or does the book highlight only one group's interpretation of an event?*** Many adults are unaware that the history they learned as children may have been biased or one-sided. Authors usually attempt to integrate more complex interpretations of historical events by including events and facts that are typically excluded from history textbooks and adding characters who reflect differing experiences and perspectives. The challenge is to do so but still have characters act in historically authentic ways.

Reading novels with differing perspectives on the same event invites readers to closely examine how setting and perspective impact characters' actions and beliefs. For example, reading the Little House series about pioneer life by Laura Ingalls Wilder alongside Louise Erdrich's series on the displacement of an Ojibwa family provides a powerful contrast in experiences and viewpoints between pioneers and American

Excellent Historical Fiction to Read Aloud

Bradley, Kimberly Brubaker. *The War That Saved My Life.* Ages 9–12.

Bruchac, Joseph. *Talking Leaves.* Ages 9–12.

DiCamillo, Kate. *Raymie Nightingale.* Ages 9–12.

Draper, Sharon. *Stella by Starlight.* Ages 9–12.

Engle, Margarita. *Drum Dream Girl: How One Girl's Courage Changed Music.* Illustrated by Rafael López. Ages 4–8.

Fleming, Candace. *Papa's Mechanical Fish.* Illustrated by Boris Kulikov. Ages 4–8.

Kadohata, Cynthia. *Weedflower.* Ages 11–18.

Levine, Ellen. *Henry's Freedom Box.* Illustrated by Kadir Nelson. Ages 7–12.

Park, Linda Sue. *When My Name Was Keoko.* Ages 10–14.

Ryan, Pam Muñoz. *Echo.* Ages 9–14.

Sheth, Kashmira. *Keeping Corner.* Ages 12–18.

Vanderpool, Clare. *Moon over Manifest.* Ages 11–15.

Indians. Reading *When My Name Was Keoko* by Linda Sue Park alongside *So Far from the Bamboo Grove* by Yoko Watkins offers contrasting views on the Japanese occupation of Korea—the first from the view of two Korean siblings who are forced to take on Japanese culture and language and the second from a child whose father is a Japanese soldier enforcing the occupation.

Historical Overview of Historical Fiction

Although historical stories were written for children as early as the 1800s, few titles of interest remain from those early years because of their emphasis on exciting events and idealized real-life characters—much in the style of heroic legends. Between World War I (WWI) and World War II (WWII), a few historical stories appeared in which well-developed characters were portrayed in authentic period settings. Between 1932 and 1943, the first eight books of the Little House series by Laura Ingalls Wilder were published. *Johnny Tremain* by Esther Forbes was awarded the Newbery Medal in 1944.

The period of 15 years right after WWII saw a flowering of historical fiction for children in both English and U.S. literature. Examples are *The Door in the Wall* by Marguerite de Angeli (1949); *Calico Captive* by Elizabeth George Speare (1957); the Newbery Medal book *The Witch of Blackbird Pond* by Elizabeth George Speare (1958); and *The Cabin Faced West* by Jean Fritz (1958). In 1954, the Laura Ingalls Wilder Award was established to honor an author or illustrator whose books, published in the United States, have made a substantial and lasting contribution to children's literature. By 1960, the genre of historical fiction was well established.

Historical fiction continues to flourish today. Some older historical fiction novels have been criticized for portraying specific cultural groups in a negative light. For example, two Newbery Medal winners, *Caddie Woodlawn* by Carol Ryrie Brink and *The Matchlock Gun* by Walter D. Edmonds, include negative portrayals of American Indians. Misrepresentations and omissions of American Indians and other people of color in history books and historical fiction have been challenged by authors who are insiders to these cultures. These authors have contributed excellent works on the early experiences of their cultural groups in North America, such as *The Birchbark House* and its sequels by Louise Erdrich and *Journey to Topaz* by Yoshiko Uchida.

MILESTONES in the Development of Historical Fiction

Date	Event	Significance
1888	*Otto of the Silver Hand* by Howard Pyle	Early recognized work of historical fiction
1929	*The Trumpeter of Krakow* by Eric Kelly awarded the Newbery Medal	National recognition for an early work of historical fiction
1932–1943	Publication of *Little House* series by Laura Ingalls Wilder	Classic historical fiction
1944	*Johnny Tremain* by Esther Forbes awarded the Newbery Medal	Classic historical adventure set in American Revolution era
1949–1960	Many historical novels published, including novels by Elizabeth George Speare and Rosemary Sutcliff	Dramatic increase in the quality and quantity of historical novels for children
1961	Scott O'Dell's *Island of the Blue Dolphins* awarded the Newbery Medal	Landmark book of historical fiction with a strong female protagonist from a marginalized culture
1971	*Journey to Topaz* by Yoshiko Uchida	Early historical work by an author of color (Japanese American)
1975	*The Song of the Trees* by Mildred Taylor	First in a series about an African American family, starting in the Depression era
1982	Establishment of Scott O'Dell Award	Award for outstanding historical novel set in North America
1997	*Out of the Dust* by Karen Hesse awarded the Newbery Medal	Recognition for a novel in verse, new trend in children's fiction

Themes in Historical Fiction

Historical fiction can be organized according to universal themes that occur over the course of history or chronologically by historical periods. This chapter is organized around themes that extend across time and place in history as an approach for sharing historical fiction with children. A theme, such as seeking freedom, can be explored through a text set of books set in different times and places. This chapter suggests a particular set of themes, but others can be developed through reading historical fiction and identifying themes that go across the books. Once the set is gathered, children can read across the books and construct a chart comparing the books based on time, place, actions, and beliefs related to that theme.

Another way to organize historical fiction is to build units of study around periods in world and U.S. history. Note that the recommended books listed at the end of the chapter indicate the time period and historical setting/event for each book so that you can identify books for a particular historical period.

Mystery and Adventure

Historical fiction that connects to children's interest in suspense and adventure provides an entry for readers, some of whom are reluctant to engage with this genre because they associate history with dry, boring facts instead of a compelling story. In particular, mystery stories where children solve crimes have strong appeal, such as Beth Fantaskey's *Isabel Feeney, Star Reporter*, in which a young girl who wants to be a news reporter investigates a murder in 1920s Chicago, and Laura Fitzgerald's *The Gallery*, which incorporates art, history, and literary classics to solve a mystery in 1920s New York City.

Some books focus on the everyday adventures of children, such as *Dead End in Norvelt* by Jack Gantos, about a boy's summer in 1952 Pennsylvania doing "stupid stuff" and getting into trouble. Matt Phelan's *Bluffton: My Summers with Buster* is a graphic novel set in a sleepy Michigan town in 1908 where nothing ever happens—until a troupe of vaudeville performers arrives at a nearby resort to spend the summer.

Although some mysteries are humorous adventures, others take a more serious tone, as in Amy Timberlake's *One Came Home*, set in 1871 Wisconsin. Georgie refuses to believe that her missing sister has been murdered and sets out on a perilous journey to track her steps. The mystery that Lizzie is trying to solve in Gennifer Choldenko's *Chasing Secrets* is the cause of the bubonic plague outbreak in 1900 San Francisco; an issue of particular urgency because of mobs threatening to burn down Chinatown. Adventure takes an even darker turn when one's survival is at risk. In Sara Joiner's *After the Ashes*, a volcanic eruption in 1883 on an island in the Dutch East Indies kills nearly everyone around Katrien, who must join forces with a former enemy to survive.

Historical mysteries and adventure stories require the main character to draw on inner strength and to reason through complex problems. One recent trend is the portrayal of girls as gutsy, resourceful thinkers who take action in difficult situations.

Notable Authors of Historical Fiction

Avi, author of historical fiction novels in many time periods. *Crispin: The Cross of Lead* (Newbery medal); *City of Orphans; Catch You Later, Traitor*. www.avi-writer.com

Christopher Paul Curtis, author of African American historical novels. *Bud, Not Buddy* (Newbery medal); *The Watsons Go to Birmingham—1963* (Newbery honor)*; Elijah of Buxton.* www.christopherpaulcurtis.com

Karen Cushman, author of Newbery acclaimed historical novels set in the Middle Ages. *Catherine, Called Birdy; The Midwife's Apprentice.* www.karencushman.com

Karen Hesse, author of Newbery Medal winner *Out of the Dust*, a novel in verse, and novels in different voices, *Witness.*

Linda Sue Park, author whose novels focus on historical eras in Korea. *A Single Shard* (Newbery Medal)*; When My Name Was Keoko*. www.lindasuepark.com

Margi Preus, author of historical fiction set in Norway and Japan. *Shadow on the Mountain; Heart of a Samurai; The Bamboo Sword.* www.margipreus.com/

Graham Salisbury, author of historical novels set in the Hawaiian Islands. *House of the Red Fish; Eyes of the Emperor*. www.grahamsalisbury.com

Gary Schmidt, author of historical fiction novels on difficult social issues and coming-of-age themes. *Lizzie Bright and the Buckminster Boy; Wednesday Wars; Okay for Now*. www.hmhco.com/bookstore/authors/Gary-Schmidt/2230485

Forced Journeys of Transformation

Characters in historical fiction are often forced into journeys that involve war, enslavement, or some other difficult situation that causes them to flee. These forced journeys involve more than a physical movement to a new place as characters undergo psychological and social changes that transform them as human beings. In Kimberly Brubaker Bradley's *The War That Saved My Life*, a young girl, Ada, with a physical disability is evacuated to the English countryside during WWII. This forced journey is a positive one that brings purpose and freedom into Ada's life as she escapes an abusive home. Another example of multiple journeys resulting from war is *The Great War*, a collection of 11 short stories about WWI, with each writer telling of a journey inspired by an object that evokes the conflict and human cost of war.

Sometimes the forced journey is one of enslavement, as in Monica Edinger's *Africa Is My Home*, which tells the story of the *Amistad* slave ship from a child's point of view, or of survival on the streets, as in Deborah Hopkinson's *A Bandit's Tale*, set in 1887 New York City. Confinement is another example of a forced journey in Lois Sepahban's Paper Wishes when Manami and her parents are forced to relocate from Bainbridge Island to a Japanese American internment camp in 1942. These books depict the resiliency of young people as they struggle to survive in dark times.

Fear and Intolerance

A theme that reoccurs across history is the fear and intolerance that humans inflict on each other because of perceived "differences." Sometimes that intolerance is evidenced in war, as in Skila Brown's *Caminar*, a novel in verse about the massacre of villagers during the1981 Guatemalan civil war. Other times, the intolerance is relevant to current issues, as in Firoozeh Dumas's *It Ain't So Awful, Falafel*, about prejudice toward Iranians in California during the Iranian hostage crisis in the late 1970s.

Intolerance can take many forms. In Kristin Levine's *The Paper Cowboy*, the fear of Communism in 1950s Illinois leads to unjust accusations, much as the fear of witchcraft led to the Salem Witch Trials in *The Witch of Blackbird Pond* by Elizabeth Speare. Pam Muñoz Ryan's *Echo* is set amidst the bigotry and violence of WWII as three children in different locations use the power of music to face discrimination and fear. Intolerance can also take the form of bullying as the result of social status. In Lauren Wolk's *Wolf Hollow*, set in the United States during WWII, a bully first targets Annabelle and then shifts her attention to a homeless WWI veteran. Historical fiction allows readers to experience the consequences of fear and intolerance through characters whom they have come to care about and feel connected to.

Resistance and Challenges to Injustice

The theme of fear and intolerance can lead to feelings of guilt or helplessness for readers, so it's important to balance these books with ones in which children have the courage to take a stand and resist injustice. These books bring a hope for change, even in dark, difficult situations, and refuse to accept injustice as "just the way the world works." In Sharon Draper's *Stella by Starlight*, Stella and her family face the threat of the Ku Klux Klan in 1932 North Carolina, but the small African American community bands together to act with courage, despite the threat of violence. In 1847, a new law denying African American children in St. Louis the right to an education is challenged with subversive ingenuity in Deborah Hopkinson's *Steamboat School*.

Resistance is often found in books about war, such as Jennifer Elvgren's picturebook *The Whispering Town*, about the Danish resistance movement during WWII that smuggled Jews out of Denmark. Some historical fiction portrays strikes by workers because of dangerous working conditions, such as in Katherine Paterson's *Bread and Roses, Too,* about the mill workers' strike in 1912 Massachusetts. Another form of resistance involves the portrayal of the women's suffrage movement and individual challenges by young girls whose dreams are limited because of gender. Margarita Engle and Rafael Lopez tell the story of one such girl in *Drum Dream Girl*, as a Chinese-African-Cuban girl finds a way to break Cuba's taboo against female drummers. These depictions of resistance provide children with hope for the possibility of change and strategies to advocate for those changes.

Facing Adversity through Relationships

Although humor and heartwarming stories are present in historical fiction, many books portray difficult situations in which children face problems that seem insurmountable. These situations of adversity are balanced with the strength and courage children gain from close loving relationships with families, friends, or animals. In Christopher Paul Curtis's *The Watsons Go to Birmingham—1963*, the prejudice faced by Kenny in the Deep South is made bearable by the close-knit African American family that surrounds him. The relationships that sustain in Kate DiCamillo's *Raymie Nightingale* are those of friendship between three girls as they prepare to compete in a talent pageant. Set in 1975 small town Florida, Raymie is determined to win to gain the attention of her father, who has run away with a dental hygienist.

Sometimes the friendships that are portrayed cut across culture and language as in Margi Preus's *The Bamboo Sword*, set in isolationist Japan in 1853. Yoshi, who dreams of becoming a samurai, develops an unlikely friendship with Jack, who has dangerously wandered away from the U.S. delegation. In alternating verse and perspectives, a Roanoke Indian girl and an English girl describe their developing friendship in *Blue Birds* by Caroline Rose, set in the "Lost Colony" of 1587 Roanoke Island.

Children have a special connection to animals, so it's no surprise that some historical fiction is based around a child's relationship with dogs and horses. In Dan Gemeinhart's *Some Kind of Courage*, an orphaned boy goes in search of his pony, sold off by a greedy guardian in the Wild West of 1890 Washington State. The unconditional love of an animal can sustain a child through difficult times.

Ingenuity and Innovation

One theme that often lends itself to more lighthearted historical stories is that of characters who use ingenuity to develop innovative solutions to their problems. Sometimes that ingenuity leads to an invention, as in *Queen Victoria's Bathing Machine* by Gloria Whelan and Nancy Carpenter, in which Prince Albert comes up with a creative solution to Queen Victoria's desire to swim without her devoted subjects glimpsing her bathing suit. Other times, the ingenuity is trickery, as in Christoph Niemann's *The Potato King,* in which the Prussian king uses reverse psychology, forbidding people to enter his potato fields, to make the potato popular as a food source.

Reader Connections: Understanding Historical Contexts

Children often have limited knowledge of history and historical context—the background and environment that surrounded past events, including how people lived and worked. Reading or listening to historical fiction can create an understanding of the past and an appreciation of the lives of people who lived in earlier times. Smith, Monson, and Dobson (1992) found that fifth grade students in classrooms where historical novels were used along with the social studies textbook recalled more historical facts and indicated greater enjoyment of social studies than students in classrooms with a similar curriculum but without the addition of historical novels.

Past events presented in a purely factual manner can seem irrelevant and sometimes unbelievable to children. By presenting these events in a story that shows how the events affected the lives of characters much like themselves, children better understand, and are more likely to remember, the events. Historical stories help them connect to the emotions engendered by past events—the fear of intolerance and the excitement of exploration. In addition, children can compare their lives with the lives of characters and better understand how context affects people's lives, including their own, as well as consider how their lives may change in the future.

Many children are not familiar with historical fiction and stay at a distance, assuming these books are boring. You will have an important role in displaying these books in the classroom and library, introducing them in booktalks, selecting them for read-alouds, and presenting them in text sets for independent reading.

A reader response engagement that builds interest, knowledge, and contextual understanding of the time and place is the *jackdaw,* a collection of artifacts or copies of realia from a particular historical period or event. The term *jackdaw* refers to a common European bird known to collect colorful objects for its nest. Educators use the term to refer to a collection of concrete artifacts that connect historical books with the real events of the times (Dodd, 1999). For example, as you read aloud *When My Name was Keoko,* children can research and gather maps of Korea and Asia, time lines of events, old newspaper clippings, examples of the two written languages, images of Korean cultural symbols, newspaper articles on recent negotiations between Korea and Japan related to atrocities toward Korean women during the occupation, and artifacts such as flags and dolls in traditional clothing.

Jackdaws are created by teachers, librarians, and children working together to collect a wide array of related materials in their original form or in reproductions, including maps, time lines, diary entries, recipes, newspaper clippings, music, clothing, artwork, letters, advertisements, old photographs, and books of the era. These informational materials and objects are placed in a decorated box or suitcase with labels and explanations or set up as a museum display. Given the increased emphasis on informational texts in the Common Core State Standards, jackdaws are an excellent means of engaging students in a wide range of information focused around a particular time period.

Commercial jackdaw kits of reproductions are available, and some museums loan out "heritage trunks" for regional history. The Library of Congress provides access to primary sources at www.loc.gov/teachers, as does Primary Source, http://www.primarysource.org/, which has online curriculum units with documents and photographs.

Historical fiction offers children the opportunity to live through the experiences of the past, not just gain knowledge about those events and people. They are able to explore the difficult choices and human contradictions that define our world, while still maintaining hope for making a change in their present and future worlds through imagining the past.

Invitations for Further Investigation

- Read a historical novel and examine the ways in which the setting influences the actions and beliefs of the main character—to clarify conflict, serve as antagonist, illuminate character, establish mood, or to act as symbol (Lukens, 2012).
- Select and read a historical fiction novel, then research the time period and location of its setting. Develop a time line to display and contrast the historical facts and the story events. Create a jackdaw of objects that explore the historical context of this novel.
- Choose a particular period or historical event, and locate several recommended works of historical fiction set in that era. Read them to analyze the perspectives presented in these books and the authors' backgrounds and methods of research to determine whether they reflect a range of viewpoints on the period.
- Select one of the themes found in historical fiction novels. Compare and contrast several books that exemplify the theme and that cut across different periods. Create a chart to compare the way the theme plays out in the set of books.

References

Cohoe, G. (1972). Ancestors. In T. Allen (Ed.), *The whispering wind: Poetry by young American Indians.* New York: Doubleday.

Dodd, E. (1999). Echoes of the past. *Childhood Education, 75*(3), 136–141.

Lukens, R. (2012). *A critical handbook of children's literature,* 9th ed. New York: Pearson.

Meltzer, M. (1981). Beyond the span of a single life. In B. Hearne (Ed.), *Celebrating children's books*. New York: Lothrop.

Smith, J. A., Monson, J. A., & Dobson, D. (1992). A case study on integrating history and reading instruction through literature. *Social Education, 56,* 370–375.

Recommended Historical Fiction Books

Ages refer to content appropriateness and conceptual and interest levels. Formats other than novels are coded:

(**PB**) Picturebook
(**COL**) Short story collection
(**GR**) Graphic novel
(**NV**) Novels in verse

Mystery and Adventure

Ahlberg, Allan. ***The Baby in the Hat.*** Illus. Andre Amstutz. Candlewick, 2008. (**PB**). Ages 4–8. (London, 1688–1697)

Blackwood, Gary. ***Curiosity.*** Puffin, 2015. Ages 11–14. (Philadelphia, 1835)

Choldenko, Gennifer. ***Al Capone Does My Homework.*** Puffin, 2014. Ages 10–14. Series. (Alcatraz, 1936)

Choldenko, Gennifer. ***Chasing Secrets.*** Wendy Lamb, 2015. Ages 8–14. (San Francisco, Chinatown, 1900)

Collins, Pat Lowery. ***Daughter of Winter.*** Candlewick, 2010. Ages 9–13. (Wampanoag Indians, Massachusetts, 1849)

Davis, Tony. ***Future Knight.*** Illus. Gregory Rogers Delacorte, 2007. Ages 9–12. Series. (England, Middle Ages)

DeFelice, Cynthia. ***Bringing Ezra Back.*** Farrar, 2006. Ages 9–13. (Ohio, 1830s). Sequel to ***Weasel*** (1990)

Edge, Christopher. ***Twelve Minutes to Midnight.*** Whitman, 2014. Ages 8–12. (London, 1899)

Fantaskey, Beth. ***Isabel Feeney, Star Reporter.*** Houghton Mifflin Harcourt, 2016. Ages 9–12. (Chicago, 1920s)

Fitzgerald, Laura. ***The Gallery.*** Dial, 2016. Ages 9–13. (New York, 1920s)

Gantos, Jack. ***Dead End in Norvelt***. Farrar, 2011. Ages 11–14. (Small-town Pennsylvania, 1960s)

Holm, Jennifer. ***Full of Beans.*** Random House, 2016. Ages 9–12. (Florida, Great Depression, 1934)

Hopkinson, Deborah. ***The Great Trouble: A Mystery of London, the Blue Death, and a Boy Called Eel***. Knopf, 2013. Ages 9–12. (Cholera epidemic, London, 1854)

Hull, N. L. ***On Rough Seas.*** Clarion, 2008. Ages 9–13. (England to Dunkirk, WWII, 1939)

Joiner, Sara. ***After the Ashes.*** Holiday House, 2015. Ages 10–15. (Dutch East Indies, 1883)

Lawrence, Caroline. ***The Man from Pomegranate Street.*** Orion, 2009. Ages 11–14. Roman mystery series. (A.D. 81)

Lawrence, Iain. ***The Wreckers.*** Delacorte, 1998. Ages 10–14. Trilogy. (Adventures on the high seas, 1800s; England, Caribbean)

MacColl, Michaela. ***Promise the Night.*** Chronicle, 2011. Ages 11–15. (British in Kenya, 1912)

Phelan, Matt. ***Bluffton: My Summers with Buster.*** Candlewick, 2013. Ages 9–12. (Michigan, 1908)

Platt, Richard. ***Egyptian Diary: The Journal of Nakht, Young Scribe.*** Illus. David Parkins. Candlewick, 2014. Ages 9–11. (Ancient Egypt, 1475 B.C.)

Timberlake, Amy. ***One Came Home.*** Knopf, 2013. Ages 9–12. (Wisconsin, 1981)

Voigt, Cynthia. ***The Book of Lost Things.*** Illus. Iacopo Bruno. Knopf, 2013. Ages 9–13. (Europe, early 1900s). Trilogy.

Zimmer, Tracie Vaughn. ***The Floating Circus.*** Bloomsbury, 2008. Ages 11–16. (Circus barge, New Orleans, 1850s)

Forced Journeys of Transformation

Almond, David, editor. ***The Great War: Stories Inspired by Items from the First World War.*** Illus. Jim Kay. Candlewick, 2015. (**COL**). Ages 8–12. (Effects of war, WWI)

Avi. ***Crispin: The End of Time.*** Balzer & Bray, 2010. Ages 10–15. (France, 14th century). Also ***Crispin: At the Edge of the World*** (2006) and ***Crispin: The Cross of Lead*** (2002).

Bradley, Kimberly Brubaker. ***The War That Saved My Life.*** Dial, 2015. Ages 8–12. (Evacuation, England, WWII)

Curtis, Christopher Paul. ***Elijah of Buxton.*** Scholastic, 2007. Ages 11–14. (Canada, freed slaves, 1849)

Cushman, Karen. ***Catherine, Called Birdy.*** Clarion, 1994. Ages 11–15. (England, manor life, 1290s). Also ***The Midwife's Apprentice*** (1995). Ages 12–16. (England, Middle Ages) and ***Matilda Bone*** (2000). Ages 11–15. (Medieval England, medical practitioner)

Edinger, Monica. ***Africa Is My Home: A Child of the Amistad.*** Illus. Robert Byrd. Candlewick, 2015. Ages 10–14. (Slave ship, Africa to New England, 1839)

Edwardson, Debby D. ***My Name Is Not Easy***. Cavendish, 2011. Ages 12–15. (Alaska, Inupiaq, Catholic boarding school, five narrators, 1960s)

Erdrich, Louise. ***The Porcupine Year.*** HarperCollins, 2008. Ages 9–14. (Displaced Ojibwe family, 1852). Also, ***The Birchbark House*** (1999), ***The Game of Silence*** (2005), and ***Chickadee*** (2012).

Erskine, Kathryn. ***The Badger Knight.*** Scholastic, 2014. Ages 10–13. (England, Middle Ages, 1346)

Forbes, Esther. ***Johnny Tremain.*** Houghton, 1943. Ages 10–13. (U.S. Revolutionary War, 1770s)

Frost, Helen. ***The Braid.*** Farrar, 2006. Ages 12–16. (**NV**). (Scotland to Canada, 1850s)

Giff, Patricia Reilly. ***Nory Ryan's Song.*** Delacorte, 2000. Ages 9–13. (Ireland, potato famine, 1845). Sequels are ***Maggie's Door*** (2003) and ***Water Street*** (2006).

Hopkinson, Deborah. ***A Bandit's Tale: The Muddled Misadventures of a Pickpocket.*** Knopf, 2016. Ages 8–12. (Italy to New York, 1887)

Johnson, Angela. ***All Different Now: Juneteenth, The First Day of Freedom.*** Simon & Schuster, 2014. (**PB**). Ages 5–9. (Emancipation of slaves, June 19, 1865)

Lai, Thanhha. ***Inside Out & Back Again.*** Harper, 2011. (**NV**). Ages 9–14. (Vietnamese immigrants, Alabama, 1975)

Lawrence, L. S. ***Escape by Sea***. Holiday, 2008. Ages 12–18. (Roman Empire, Punic War 218–201 B.C.)

Levine, Ellen. ***Henry's Freedom Box.*** Illus. Kadir Nelson. Scholastic, 2007. (**PB**). Ages 7–12. (Virginia, 1849)

Nelson, Marilyn. ***My Seneca Village.*** Namelos, 2015. (**NV**). Ages 10-14. (1825–1857)

Nelson, Theresa. ***The Year We Sailed the Sun.*** Illus. Iacopo Bruno. Knopf, 2013. Ages 9–12. (St. Louis, gangs, 1911)

Nielsen, Jennifer. ***A Night Divided.*** Scholastic, 2015. Ages 9–12. (East Germany, Berlin Wall, 1961)

Philbrick, W. R. ***The Mostly True Adventures of Homer P. Figg.*** Blue Sky, 2009. Ages 9–14. (U.S. Civil War)

Preus, Margi. ***Heart of a Samurai: Based on the True Story of Nakahama Manjiro.*** Amulet, 2010. Ages 9–14. (Japan, 1827–1898)

Ryan, Pam Muñoz. ***Esperanza Rising.*** Scholastic, 2000. Ages 9–13. (Mexico and U.S., Depression era)

Santiago, Chiori. ***Home to Medicine Mountain***. Children's Book Press, 1988. (**PB**). Ages 8–11. (Boarding school, 1930s, Maidu Indians)

Sepahban, Lois. ***Paper Wishes.*** Margaret Ferguson Books, 2016. Ages 8–12. (Japanese American, Manzanar, WWII)

Sepetys, Ruta. ***Between Shades of Gray.*** Philomel, 2011. Ages 13–18. (Lithuania, Stalin, 1925–1953)

Sheth, Kashmira. ***Keeping Corner.*** Hyperion, 2007. Ages 12–18. (India, child widow, 1918)

Shulevitz, Uri. ***How I Learned Geography.*** Farrar Straus Giroux, 2008 (**PB**). Ages 5–8. (Germany, Warsaw, Poland, WWII)

Simon, Richard. ***Oskar and the Eight Blessings.*** Illus. Mark Siegel. Roaring Brook, 2015. (**PB**). Ages 4–8. (New York, 1938)

Watkins, Yoko Kawashima. ***So Far from the Bamboo Grove.*** Beech Tree, 1986. Ages 10–15. (Japanese Occupation in Korea, 1939–1945)

Wolf, Joan. ***Someone Named Eva.*** Clarion, 2007. Ages 11–16. (Czechoslovakian survivor, WWII, 1942)

Yohalem, Eve. ***Cast Off: The Strange Adventures of Petra De Winter and Bram Broen.*** Dial, 2015. Ages 9–14. (Dutch East Indies, Amsterdam, 1663)

Fear and Intolerance

Avi. ***Catch You Later, Traitor.*** Algonquin, 2015. (**NV**). Ages 9–12. (Brooklyn, 1951, fear of Communists)

Brown, Skila. ***Caminar.*** Candlewick, 2014. (**NV**). Ages 10–14. (Guatemalan civil war, 1981)

Bruchac, Joseph. ***The Winter People.*** Dial, 2002. Ages 11–16. (French and Indian War, Abenaki, 1759)

Bryant, Jennifer. ***Ringside, 1925: Views from the Scopes Trial.*** Knopf, 2008. (**NV**). Ages 11–16. (Tennessee, 1925, multiple voices)

Carvell, Marlene. ***Sweetgrass Basket.*** Dutton, 2005. Ages 12–15. (American Indian boarding school, early 1900s, Mohawk)

Decker, Timothy. ***Run Far, Run Fast.*** Front Street, 2007. (**GR**). Ages 9–12. (Black Plague, 1348, Europe)

Dumas, Firoozeh. ***It Ain't So Awful, Falafel.*** Clarion, 2016. Ages 8–12. (Iranian American, San Francisco, 1970s)

Engle, Margarita. ***Silver People: Voices from the Panama Canal.*** Houghton Mifflin Harcourt, 2014. (**NV**). Ages 10–14. (Panama, 1906)

Hesse, Karen. ***Witness.*** Scholastic, 2001. (**NV**). Ages 10–18. (Vermont, Ku Klux Klan, 1924). Series of poems in five acts.

Hilton, Marilyn. ***Full Cicada Moon.*** Dial, 2015. (**NV**). Ages 8–12. (Vermont, 1969, biracial)

Levine, Kristin. ***The Paper Cowboy.*** Putnam, 2014. Ages 10–13. (Illinois, 1950s)

Morpurgo, Michael. ***Listen to the Moon.*** Feiwel & Friends, 2015. Ages 10–14. (England, WWI, 1915)

Ryan, Pam Munoz. ***Echo.*** Scholastic, 2015. Ages 9–14. (Germany, Pennsylvania, California, WWII)

Salisbury, Graham. ***House of the Red Fish.*** Random House, 2006. Ages 10–15. Sequel to ***Under the Blood-Red Sun.*** (Japanese Americans, Hawai'i, WWII)

Smith, Dan. ***My Brother's Secret***. Scholastic, 2015. Ages 9-12. (U.K., 1941, WWII)

Speare, Elizabeth George. ***The Witch of Blackbird Pond.*** Houghton, 1958. Ages 10–14. (U.S. Northeast, 1680s)

Uchida, Yoshiko. ***Journey to Topaz.*** Illus. Donald Carrick. Scribner's, 1971. Ages 10–14. (Internment of Japanese Americans, WWII)

Vawter, Vince. ***Paperboy.*** Delacorte, 2013. Ages 10–14. (Memphis, 1959)

Wiles, Deborah. ***Countdown.*** Scholastic, 2010. Ages 9–12. (U.S., 1960s)

Wolf, Lauren. ***Wolf Hollow.*** Dutton, 2016. Ages 9–13. (Pennsylvania, WWII)

Yelchin, Eugene. ***Breaking Stalin's Nose.*** Holt, 2011. Ages 9–12. (Russia, 1960s)

Resistance and Challenging Injustice

Anderson, Laurie Halse. ***Chains.*** Simon & Schuster, 2008. Ages 11–15. (New York City, enslaved sisters, 1776). Also ***Forge*** (2010). (Valley Forge, 1777)

Anderson, M. T. ***The Pox Party,*** Candlewick, 2006. Ages 12–16. (Slavery, U.S. Revolutionary War, 1775). Also ***The Kingdom of Waves*** (2008). Astonishing Life of Octavian Nothing series.

Bartoletti, Susan Campbell. ***The Boy Who Dared.*** Scholastic, 2008. Ages 12–18. (Germany, resistance movement, 1933–1945)

Brown, Don. ***Kid Blink Beats the World.*** Roaring Brook, 2004. (**PB**). Ages 7–11. (Labor strikes, 1899)

Cole, Henry. ***Unspoken: A Story from the Underground Railroad.*** Scholastic, 2012. (**PB**). Ages 7–10. (Virginia, 1860s, wordless)

Couloumbis, Audrey. ***War Games.*** Random House, 2009. Ages 9–13. (Greece, Nazi occupation, WWII)

Draper, Sharon. ***Stella by Starlight.*** Atheneum, 2015. Ages 9–13. (North Carolina, Ku Klux Klan, 1932)

Dublin, Anne. ***44 Hours or Strike!*** Second Story, 2015. Ages 12–15. (Toronto, Canada, 1931)

Elvgren, Jennifer. ***The Whispering Town.*** Illus. Fabio Santomauro. Kar-Ben, 2014. (**PB**). Ages 5–8. (Denmark, 1943, WWII resistance)

Engle, Margarita. ***The Surrender Tree: Poems from Cuba's Struggle for Freedom.*** Holt, 2008. Ages 12–18. (Cuba, 1810–1899)

Engle, Margarita. ***Drum Dream Girl: How One Girl's Courage Changed Music.*** Houghton Mifflin Harcourt, 2015. (**PB**). Ages 3–8. (Cuba, 1920s)

Grimes, Nikki. ***Chasing Freedom: The Life Journeys of Harriet Tubman and Susan B. Anthony.*** Illus. Michele Wood. Orchard Books, 2015. (**PB**). Ages 8–12. (1904, imagined conversation on human rights, three voices).

Hopkinson, Deborah. ***Steamboat School: Inspired by a True Story.*** Disney Hyperion, 2016. (**PI**). Ages 5–8. (St. Louis, equal rights in education, 1847)

Hughes, Shirley. ***Hero on a Bicycle.*** Candlewick, 2013. Ages 10–14. (Italy, Resistance, 1944, WWII)

Jacobson, Darlene Beck. ***Wheels of Change.*** Illus. Marissa Moss. Creston, 2014. Ages 8–11. (Washington, D.C., Suffrage, 1908)

Kidd, Ronald. ***Night on Fire.*** Whitman, 2015. Ages 9–13. (Alabama, Freedom Riders, 1961)

Mason, Margaret H. ***These Hands.*** Illus. Floyd Cooper. Houghton Mifflin, 2010. (**PB**). Ages 5–8. (African Americans, civil rights era)

McCully, Emily Arnold. ***The Escape of Oney Judge: Martha Washington's Slave Finds Freedom.*** Farrar, 2007. (**PB**). Ages 9–12. (Washington, DC, late 1800s)

Park, Linda Sue. ***When My Name Was Keoko.*** Clarion, 2002. Ages 10–14. (Japanese occupation of Korea, 1940s)

Paterson, Katherine. ***Bread and Roses, Too.*** Clarion, 2006. Ages 10–14. (Massachusetts, mill workers' strike, 1912)

Preus, Margi. ***Shadow on the Mountain.*** Amulet, 2012. Ages 10–14. (Norway, WWII, Resistance, 1940)

Raven, Margot. ***Night Boat to Freedom.*** Illus. E. B. Lewis. Farrar, 2006. (**PB**). Ages 7–10. (Slavery, Kentucky)

Russell, Ching Yeung. ***Tofu Quilt.*** Lee & Low, 2009. (**NV**). Ages 9–12. (Hong Kong, 1960s)

Schmidt, Gary. ***Lizzie Bright and the Buckminster Boy.*** Clarion, 2004. Ages 11–15. (Maine, race relations, 1912)

Wiles, Deborah. ***Revolution.*** Scholastic, 2014. Ages 11–15. (Mississippi, 1964)

Facing Adversity through Relationships

Abirached, Zeina. ***A Game for Swallows: To Die, to Leave, to Return.*** Graphic Universe, 2012. (**GR**). Ages 12–18. (Beirut, Lebanese Civil War, 1981)

Avi. ***City of Orphans.*** Anthem, 2011. Ages 10–14. (New York, immigrants, 1865–1898)

Bildner, Phil. ***The Soccer Fence: A Story of Friendship, Hope and Apartheid in South Africa.*** Illus. Jesse Joshua Watson. Putnam, 2014. (**PB**). Ages 5–9. (South Africa, 1990s)

Bolden, Tonya. ***Finding Family.*** Bloomsbury, 2010. Ages 9–12. (West Virginia, African Americans, early 1900s)

Burg, Ann E. ***All the Broken Pieces.*** Scholastic, 2009. (**NV**). Ages 11–15. (Vietnam War era, Amerasian, adoption)

Curtis, Christopher Paul. ***The Watsons Go to Birmingham—1963.*** Delacorte, 1995. Ages 8–12. (Flint, Michigan; Birmingham, Alabama; civil rights movement)

Curtis, Christopher Paul. ***Bud, Not Buddy.*** Delacorte, 1999. Ages 9–13. (Michigan, Depression era)

Curtis, Christopher Paul. ***The Madman of Piney Woods.*** Scholastic, 2014. Ages 9–13. (Canada, 1901)

Cushman, Karen. ***Alchemy and Meggy Swan.*** Clarion, 2010. Ages 11–14. (London, 1573)

DiCamillo, Kate. ***Raymie Nightingale.*** Candlewick, 2016. Ages 9–14. (Florida, 1975)

Ehrlich, Esther. ***Nest.*** Yearling, 2016. Ages 8–12. (Cape Cod, 1960s)

Flood, Nancy Bo. ***Warriors in Crossfire.*** Front Street, 2010. Ages 12–16. (WWII, South Pacific, 1944)

Gallagher, Brian. ***Friend or Foe: Which Side Are You On?*** O'Brien Press, 2015. Ages 8–14. (Ireland, 1916)

Gemeinhart, Dan. ***Some Kind of Courage.*** Scholastic, 2016. Ages 8–12. (Washington, 1890)

Hendrix, John. ***Shooting at the Stars: The Christmas Truce of 1914.*** Abrams, 2014. (**PB**). Ages 7–12. (WWII, 1912)

Hesse, Karen. ***Out of the Dust.*** Scholastic, 1997. (**NV**). Ages 11–18. (Oklahoma, 1930s)

Hill, Kirkpatrick. ***Bo at Ballard Creek.*** Illus. LeUyen Pham. Square Fish, 2014. Ages 8–12. (Alaska, Gold Rush, 1920s)

Holm, Jennifer. ***Sunny Side Up.*** Illus. Matthew Holm. Graphix, 2015. (**GR**). Ages 9–11. (Florida, 1970s)

Holm, Jennifer. ***Turtle in Paradise.*** Random House, 2010. Ages 9–12. (U.S., Key West, 1935, Depression)

Holt, Kimberly Willis. ***When Zachary Beaver Came to Town.*** Holt, 1999. Ages 10–14. (Small town, Texas, 1971)

Holt, Kimberly Willis. ***The Water Seeker.*** Holt, 2010. Ages 11–14. (U.S. frontier, 1833–1859)

Johnston, Tony. ***Bone by Bone by Bone.*** Roaring Brook, 2007. Ages 11–16. (Race relations in Tennessee, 1950s)

Kadohata, Cynthia. ***Weedflower.*** Simon & Schuster, 2006. Ages 10–14. (Japanese American internment, Arizona, WWII, Mohave Indians)

Kelly, Jacqueline. ***The Evolution of Calpurnia Tate.*** Henry Holt, 2009. Ages 10–14. (U.S., Texas, 1899)

Larson, Kirby. ***Dash.*** Scholastic, 2014. Ages 8–12. (Japanese American internment, WWII)

Park, Linda Sue. ***A Single Shard.*** Clarion, 2001. Ages 9–13. (Korean village, 1100s)

Park, Linda Sue. ***The Firekeeper's Son.*** Illus. Julie Downing. Clarion, 2003. (**PB**). Ages 8–12. (Korea, 1800s)

Peck, Richard. ***A Year Down Yonder.*** Dial, 2000. Ages 10–15. (Southern Illinois, Depression, 1937)

Preus, Margi. ***The Bamboo Sword.*** Amulet, 2015. Ages 9–13. (Japan, 1853)

Rose, Caroline Starr. ***Blue Birds.*** Putnam, 2015. Ages 10–13. (England to Virginia, 1587)

Schmidt, Gary D. ***Okay for Now.*** Clarion, 2011. Ages 11–14, (U.S., Vietnam War era, 1968)

Selznick, Brian. ***Wonderstruck***. Ages 9–14. (**PB**). Scholastic, 2011. (New York, 1977, deaf)

Vanderpool, Clare. ***Moon over Manifest.*** Delacorte, 2010. Ages 10–14. (Kansas, 1936, Depression)

Wein, Elizabeth. ***The Lion Hunter: The Mark of Solomon.*** Viking, 2007. Ages 12–16. (Ethiopia, sixth century)

White, Ruth. ***Little Audrey.*** Farrar, 2008. Ages 9–13. (Virginia coal mining, 1948)

Williams-Garcia, Rita. ***One Crazy Summer.*** *Amistad*, 2010. Ages 8–14. (Oakland, California, Black Panthers, 1968). Also ***P.S. Be Eleven*** (2013) and ***Gone Crazy in Alabama*** (2015).

Zusak, Markus. ***The Book Thief.*** Knopf, 2006. Ages 13–18. (Munich, Germany, WWII, foster child)

Ingenuity and Innovation

Addy, Sharon. ***Lucky Jake.*** Illus. Wade Zahares. Houghton Mifflin, 2007. (**PB**). Ages 5–8. (U.S. gold rush)

Beebe, Katy. ***Brother Hugo and the Bear.*** Illus. S. D. Schindler. Eerdmans, 2014. (**PB**). Ages 5–9. (Middle Ages, bookmaking)

Bruchac, Joseph. ***Talking Leaves.*** Dial, 2016. Ages 9–12. (Cherokee alphabet, Sequoyah)

Fern, Tracey. ***Pippo the Fool.*** Illus. Paul Estrada. Charlesbridge, 2009. (**PB**). Ages 5–9. (Renaissance, Italy 1400s)

Fleming, Candace. ***Papa's Mechanical Fish.*** Illus. Boris Kulikov. Farrar Strauss Giroux, 2013. (**PB**). Ages 4–8. (1851, invention, submarine)

Millen, C. M. ***The Ink Garden of Brother Thophane.*** Illus. Andrea Wisnewski. Charlesbridge, 2010. (**PB**). Ages 6–9. (Ireland, 1172)

Niemann, Chistoph. ***The Potato King.*** Owlkids, 2015. (**PB**). Ages 4–8. (Prussia/German).

Selznick, Brian. ***The Invention of Hugo Cabret.*** Scholastic, 2007. (**PB**). Ages 9–13. (Paris, 1930s)

Smucker, Anna Egan. ***Brother Giovanni's Little Reward: How the Pretzel Was Born.*** Eerdmans, 2015. (**PB**). Ages 5–9. (Italy, medieval)

Whelan, Gloria. ***Queen Victoria's Bathing Machine.*** Illus. Nancy Carpenter. Simon & Schuster, 2014. (**PB**). Ages 4–8. (Victorian Era, late 1800s)

Winter, Jonah. ***The Fabulous Feud of Gilbert and Sullivan.*** Illus. Richard Egielski. Scholastic, 2009. (**PB**). Ages 5–8. (England, late 1800s)

Related Films, Videos, and DVDs

Grandfather's Journey. (2008). Author: Allen Say (1993). 9 minutes.

Henry's Freedom Box. (2009). Author: Ellen Levin (2007). 12 minutes.

My Louisiana Sky. (2001). Author: Kimberly Willis Holt (1998). 98 minutes.

The Book Thief (2013). Author: Marcus Zuzak (2006). 131 minutes.

The Other Side (2012). Author: Jacqueline Woodson (2001). 8 minutes.

Sarah, Plain and Tall. (1991) and ***Skylark*** (1999). Author: Patricia MacLachlan (1985, 1994). 98 minutes.

Chapter 11

Nonfiction: Biography and Informational Books

I'd Like a Story

I'd like a story of
Ghosts on gusty nights,
Wild island ponies galloping
With manes that wave like kites,
A book that knows the lowdown
On what to feed giraffes,
A book of nutty nonsense
That's nothing much—just laughs—

A book to read to find out
How basketball stars shoot,
Why dinosaurs all died out,
What do computers compute,
Which sail a mizzen sail is,
Can Martians really be,
How heavy a blue whale is,
Weighed side by side with me—

A book to curl in bed with,
To browse in by a brook—
Anytime!
Anyplace!
I'd like a book!

—X. J. Kennedy

Children are naturally curious with an intense interest in the world and people around them. Nonfiction, which includes both informational books and biography, nourishes this curiosity with interesting facts and explanations along with provocative questions and critical issues that encourage a thirst for further inquiry. Dry, bland textbooks that fail to engage children as inquirers can be replaced by innovative and intriguing books that are excellent resources for children's interests as well as the school curriculum.

Definition and Description of Biography

Biography gives factual information about the lives of actual people, including their experiences, influences, accomplishments, and legacies, conveyed through an engaging narrative writing style. An ***autobiography*** is similar to biography, except that authors tell about their own lives. ***Memoirs,*** although related to autobiographies, are the authors' reflections on the meaning of a particular set of experiences in their lives rather than on the events themselves (Bomer, 2005).

Reading biographies allows children to find inspiration in the lives and accomplishments of people, many of whom overcame hardship in their early years to succeed and make their mark on history. They learn history from the contexts of the lives of historical figures and come to recognize the importance of childhood experiences in shaping who we become as adults.

Biographies can be classified by coverage of the person's life. In evaluating the following types of biographies, a balance is needed between adequately covering the person's life and overwhelming children with too much detail and complexity.

- The ***complete biography*** covers the entire life of a person from birth to death, as in Tonya Bolden's *George Washington Carver* and Candace Fleming's *Presenting Buffalo Bill.*
- The ***partial biography*** covers only part of the life of the subject. Biographies for young children are often this type, as are biographies of living persons. *Grandfather Gandhi* by Arun Gandhi and Evan Turk focuses on Gandhi as an old man through loving interactions with his grandson.
- The ***collected biography*** includes the life stories of several people in one book, organized into chapters, such as *Hand in Hand: Ten Black Men Who Changed America* by Andrea Davis Pinkney and Brian Pinkney.
- The ***biography series*** is a multivolume set of books with each book containing one separate biography, such as the First Biographies series by David A. Adler with books on Thomas Jefferson, Martin Luther King Jr., and Jackie Robinson, and Kathleen Krull's new series on Women Who Broke the Rules.
- **Autobiography** and **memoir** provide authors with an opportunity to tell their own life stories. A recent trend is memoirs in which children's authors and illustrators reflect on their life experiences through themes of significance to their identities and work. Jacqueline Woodson's *Brown Girl Dreaming* is a novel in verse around family and telling stories amidst racial discrimination, whereas Allen Say's *The Inker's Shadow* centers on his first three years in the United States from Japan and themes of isolation, discrimination, and persistence in his dream to be a cartoonist.

MILESTONES in the Development of Biographies

Date	Book	Significance
1939	***Abraham Lincoln*** by Ingri and Edgar Parin d'Aulaire	Early picturebook biography; first biography to win the Caldecott Medal
1940	***Daniel Boone*** by James H. Daugherty	First biography to win the Newbery Medal
1952	***Diary of a Young Girl*** by Anne Frank	Autobiography of the Jewish Holocaust
1988	***Lincoln: A Photobiography*** by Russell Freedman	First nonfictional photo essay to win a Newbery Medal
1990	First Orbis Pictus Award for ***The Great Little Madison*** by Jean Fritz	Nonfiction as a genre is recognized; first winner is a biography
2001	First Robert F. Sibert Informational Book Medal for ***Sir Walter Ralegh and the Quest for El Dorado*** by Marc Aronson	Nonfiction as a genre is recognized; first winner is a biography

Evaluation and Selection of Biography

Biographies tell an engaging story about complex real people, so the criteria for evaluation involve the need to tell a well-written story that is based in documented facts, events, people, and primary source materials and records. The criteria for historical fiction are relevant to biography, but additional questions include:

- **Is the person of interest to children?** Their lives or accomplishments should connect in some way to young readers' experiences and interests.
- **Is the person presented as a human being with strengths and faults?** The facts should be accurate, with no idealization of the person, but rather showing his or her faults as well as strengths and providing multiple perspectives on the person's actions and beliefs.
- **Is the depth of coverage appropriate for the intended audience?** Biographers need to select how much to tell of the person's life story and which aspects of his or her life will be of interest and meaningful to children.
- **Is the documentation of details unobtrusive and integrated into the narrative?** Documentation supporting the events and perspectives must be included, but extensive citation within the text is distracting for children as readers. Typically, citations are included at the end of the book.

In selecting biographies for a collection, another criterion to consider is whether the collection contains books that reflect people from a range of cultural experiences (e.g., female and male, ethnicities, abilities) as well as backgrounds. Political and entertainment figures along with athletes dominate the field, so you need to make careful selections to ensure that children have a wide range of biographies available that reflect the many people whose lives are of interest and value to them. There are no awards specific to biography; however, the Orbis Pictus Award for Nonfiction and the Robert F. Sibert Award for Nonfiction do name biographies as award winners.

As nonfiction, biography is evaluated on accuracy of information; however, more latitude is given to biographies for children, and biographers use varying degrees of invention in their narratives. This invention ranges from choosing what aspects of the person's life to emphasize as the theme of the book (e.g., challenging injustice or the valuing of story) to actually inventing fictional characters and conversation. Biographies can be classified and evaluated by degree of documentation.

In ***authentic biography,*** all factual information is documented through eyewitness accounts, written documents, letters, diaries, and audio and video recordings, as found in books such as *Painting the Wild Frontier: The Art and Adventures of George Catlin* by Susanna Reich. Details in the lives of people who lived long ago, such as conversations, are often difficult to document, so biographers use devices to make their writing lively, such as

- interior monologue (telling what someone probably thought or said to himself or herself based on known actions)
- indirect discourse (reporting the gist of what someone said without using quotation marks)
- attribution (interpretation of known actions to determine probable motives)
- inference (reasoning to derive one idea from another)

Fictionalized biography is based on careful research, but the author creates dramatic episodes from known facts using imagined conversation. The conversation is carefully structured around known pertinent facts, but the actual words are invented by the author. *The Dreamer* by Pam Muñoz Ryan fictionalizes the life of Chilean poet Pablo Neruda by creating his dreamy inner world, based on careful research and Neruda's poetry. In writing *No Crystal Stair*, Vaunda Micheaux Nelson did exhaustive research and interviews about her great-uncle, Lewis Michaux, a civil rights leader and bookstore owner, but filled in the gaps with informed speculation by writing in different voices of 36 historical figures.

Much artistic license is allowed in ***biographical fiction,*** including invented dialogue, fictional secondary characters, and some reconstructed action. The known achievements of the person are reported accurately, but in other respects these works are as much fiction as fact. An example is *My Uncle Emily* by Jane Yolen in which a young boy spends time with his aunt, the reclusive poet Emily Dickinson.

The Significance of Point of View in Biography

Point of view is an important literary element to explore within biography, particularly the point of view from which an author constructs the narrative of the person whose life is the focus. One way to evaluate

Notable Authors of Biographies

Andrea Davis Pinkney, author of biographies of African American leaders in art, music, and politics, illustrated by Brian Pinkney. *Martin & Mahalia; Hand in Hand; Ella Fitzgerald; Boycott Blues.* http://andreadavispinkney.com/

Monica Brown, author of bilingual picturebook biographies of Latinos across the Americas. *Pablo Neruda, a Poet of the People; Tito Puente, Mambo; Pelé, King of Soccer; My Name is Celia.* www.monicabrown.net/

Bryan Collier, illustrator of picturebook biographies of African Americans, using mixed-media collages. *Trombone Shorty; Dave the Potter; Rosa. Martin's Big Words.* www.bryancollier.com/

Raúl Colón, illustrator of picturebook biographies on women and people of color, using etched colored pencil and watercolor illustrations. *Fearless Flyer; Solving the Puzzle Under the Sea; Leontyne Price; Portraits of Hispanic American Heroes; Alicia Alonso.*

Candace Fleming, author of middle grade biographies, scrapbook format of photos, maps, and handwritten notes. *The Lincolns: A Scrapbook Look at Abraham and Mary; Amelia Lost: The Life and Disappearance of Amelia Earhart; The Family Romanov.* www.candacefleming.com

Carole Boston Weatherford, author of African American biographies and historical informational books. *Voice of Freedom: Fannie Lou Farmer; Gordon Parks; Freedom in Congo Square; Leontyne Price; Before John Was a Jazz Giant.* https://cbweatherford.com/

point of view is to read several biographies on the same person to compare perspectives and to provide alternative views to those of a particular author. For example, events in the life of Mark Twain can be compared through three perspectives: *The Trouble Begins at 8: A Life of Mark Twain in the Wild, Wild West* is told in a typical narrator voice by author Sid Fleischman; *The Extraordinary Mark Twain (According to Suzy)* by Barbara Kerley is based on a biography written by Twain's 13-year-old daughter; and *The Adventures of Mark Twain* by Robert Burleigh is told from the perspective of Twain's famous character, Huck Finn.

Another excellent set of biographies is five picturebooks on the life of Wangari Maathai, who started a movement of women to replant trees in Kenya. The books differ in their focus on her life story and in whether her actions are represented as individualistic or as part of a broader social movement. *Mama Miti* (Donna Jo Napoli), *Wangari's Trees of Peace* (Jeanette Winter), *Painting the Trees of Kenya* (Claire Nivola), *Seeds of Change* (Jen C. Johnson), and *Wangari Maathai* (Franck Prevot) can be compared to examine which aspects of her life and political issues are highlighted and to determine the author's point of view and interest in Wangari's work.

Historical Overview of Biography

Children's biographies reflect the moral, political, and social values of the times in which they are written. Early U.S. biographies were often didactic, providing life lessons for children. In the mid-1800s, Samuel G. Goodrich (Peter Parley) wrote idealized biographies of famous men and women, treating them as heroic figures rather than as human beings with flaws. In 1880, Reverend Mason Weems wrote *The Life and Memorable Acts of George Washington,* establishing a long-lasting trend of portraying national leaders as paragons of virtue. It was not until the 1920s that some biographers drew on the new fields of psychology and sociology to emphasize understanding people's motivations and examining their early years.

Award-winning biographies from 1930 to 1960 include *Abraham Lincoln* by Ingri and Edgar Parin d'Aulaire, *Daniel Boone* by James Daugherty, and *Carry On, Mr. Bowditch* by Jean Lee Latham. In the 1960s and 1970s, children's biographies were affected by the more liberal attitudes and open topics of the new realism that revolutionized children's fiction. Before this time, certain people (women, people of color) and topics (personal weaknesses, mistakes, tragedies) were seldom found in children's biographies. By the 1970s, this attitude changed, as Russell Freedman (1988) pointed out in his Newbery Medal speech: "The hero worship of the past has given way to a more realistic approach, which recognizes the warts and weaknesses that humanize the great" (p. 447).

Excellent Biographies to Read Aloud

Andrews, Tony. *Trombone Shorty.* Illustrated by Bryan Collier. Ages 5–7.

Brown, Monica. *Tito Puente, Mambo King/Rey del mambo.* Illustrated by Rafael López. Ages 5–8.

Bryant, Jennifer. *The Right Word: Roget and His Thesaurus.* Illustrated by Melissa Sweet. Ages 6–10.

Fleischman, Sid. *The Trouble Begins at 8: A Life of Mark Twain in the Wild, Wild West.* Ages 10–15.

Gandhi, Arun. *Grandfather Gandhi.* Illustrated by Evan Turk. Ages 6–9.

Nivola, Claire A. *Planting the Trees of Kenya: The Story of Wangari Maathi.* Ages 6–9.

Pinkney, Andrea Davis. *Hand in Hand: Ten Black Men Who Changed America.* Illustrated by Brian Pinkney. Ages 10–14.

Ryan, Pam Muñoz. *The Dreamer.* Illustrated by Peter Sís. Ages 10–14.

Tonatiuh, Duncan. *Separate Is Never Equal: Sylvia Mendez and Her Family's Fight for Desegregation.* Ages 6–10.

Weatherford, Carole Boston. *Voice of Freedom: Fannie Lou Hamer, Spirit of the Civil Rights Movement.* Illustrated by Ekua Holmes. Ages 9–14.

Definition and Description of Informational Books

Informational books give verifiable factual information or explain some aspect of the biological, social, or physical world. These books are literature, not textbooks, and differ in the quality of the writing and illustrations and in their intent. Although textbooks are written with the intention of teaching a large body of facts from the view of an expert imparting that knowledge to children, well-written informational literature focuses on a particular topic or issue to engage children's curiosity from the perspective of one enthusiast sharing with another.

Writing in informational books is often referred to as ***expository,*** writing that explains, whereas fiction writing is called ***narrative,*** writing that tells a story. This distinction is overly simplistic, as both fiction and nonfiction books use narrative and expository modes, and all well-written informational literature contains an underlying narrative arc that engages readers (Newkirk, 2014). A science information book such as *The Great White Shark Scientist* by Sy Montgomery includes the story of that scientist's life along with information on great white sharks, whereas Russell Freedman's *Angel Island* includes the stories of Asian immigrants as well as historical information about this early 1900s immigration station in California. These books introduce the community and processes of scientists and historians; they don't just give facts. The difference is that informational books are about reality, and the events, people, places, and ideas must exist, whereas anything can be made up in fiction writing (Colman, 2007).

The distinction between informational books and biography is often a very blurred line because many informational books include the stories of those involved in that history or scientific exploration. The distinction is one of focus, whether the main focus is to tell the story of a particular event or research project or to tell the story of an individual involved in that event. Susan Bartoletti's *Terrible Typhoid Mary* is a biography of the immigrant cook who was jailed and accused of spreading typhoid in 1906, whereas Gail Jarrow's *Fatal Fever* is an informational book highlighting the medical mystery and the medical team who identified Mary as a typhoid carrier.

Although school and public library records indicate that informational literature makes up 50 to 85 percent of book circulation for children, research studies and test scores indicate that U.S. elementary students score better on reading fiction than on reading information. One reason for this discrepancy is a lack of classroom experience with informational literature in the early grades, where fiction is the dominant choice for read-alouds. This gap is shifting because the Common Core Standards recommend a 50/50 split between informational and literary texts, starting in kindergarten.

Many recent research studies have focused on the reading of informational books in the elementary grades. Studies by Duke (2000) and Jeon, Gaffney, and Choi (2010) indicate the lack of time and availability of nonfiction in elementary classrooms. Maloch (2008) found that children need meaningful opportunities to interact with informational texts, support in understanding complex concepts, discussion of new terminology, and teaching of text structures. These studies reveal that only through repeated experience with informational books do children learn how to read and write that genre, which is significant because most day-to-day reading (textbooks, news reports, instructions, recipes, etc.) is expository from middle school through adulthood. A key factor in comprehending informational text is that readers connect new information in the text to their current understandings and experiences.

In the early grades particularly, teachers and librarians may have to take the lead in introducing informational literature to children, because parents and caregivers traditionally select fiction for read-alouds. Selecting excellent informational books for reading aloud and suggesting these books to parents for at-home reading is a good way to begin. Calling attention to children's existing knowledge on a topic and noting the various text structures, while reading helps them learn to read and appreciate this genre. In addition, informational books can be promoted as options in self-choice reading, added to classroom and school library collections, and used across the curriculum.

Types of Informational Books

The types of informational books are based on format and how information is presented on the page, rather than the information itself. The most common formats are:

- ***Informational chapter book.*** This format features a large amount of text organized into chapters, along with graphics and illustrations, such as *Bomb: The Race to Build and Steal the World's Most Dangerous Weapon* by Steve Sheinken and *Moonbird: A Year on the Wind with the Great Survivor B95* by Phillip Hoose.
- ***Informational picturebook*** This format features brief text and large, uncomplicated illustrations that are essential to conveying information, such as found in *Locomotive* by Brian Floca and *Parrots over Puerto Rico* by Susan Roth and Cindy Trumbore.
- ***Informational graphic novels.*** This graphic novel format has moved into informational books, with cartoon panels and speech bubbles providing information to engage readers. Don Brown won multiple awards for *Drowned City*, a graphic novel account of the Hurricane Katrina disaster, and Maris Wicks effectively uses this format in *Human Body Theater* about the systems of the body.
- ***Concept picturebook*** This type of picturebook presents one or two scientific or social concepts through brief, uncomplicated text accompanied by numerous large illustrations. Originally conceived for young children, these books are also written for older children, such as *Before After* by Anne-Margot Ramstein, which has before-and-after sequences depicting the passage of time that start out simple and become increasingly complex as well as philosophical.
- ***Photo essay.*** Presentation of information in the photo essay is equally balanced between text and illustration with excellent information-bearing photographs and a crisp, condensed writing style. Photo essays are generally written for children in the intermediate grades and up, such as Larry Dane Brimner's *Birmingham Sunday*, about the bombing of an African American church in 1963, and Catherine Thimmesh's *Team Moon*, about the Apollo 11 mission.
- ***Fact books.*** Presentation of information in these books is mainly through lists, charts, and tables in almanacs, books of world records, and sports trivia and statistics books, such as *Guinness World Records.*
- ***Informational book series.*** Series books consist of multiple books that share a general topic, format, writing style, and reading level. Some series books only convey facts and generalizations about the topic, while others, such as HarperCollins' Let's-Read-and-Find-Out Science series, are characterized by careful research and high-quality writing and illustration. A series can have a sole author–illustrator team, as in Scholastic's Magic School Bus series by Joanna Cole and Bruce Degen, or each book can be created by a different author–illustrator team, as in Houghton Mifflin's Scientists in the Field series. Informational series books are published for all age groups and on topics tailored to school curricula.
- ***Multigenre books.*** These books combine elements of both fiction and nonfiction and present accurate factual information alongside an entertaining ribbon of fiction or poetry, such as the well-known Magic School Bus books by Joanna Cole. *Where in the Wild?* by David M. Schwartz and Yael Schy, with fold-out illustrations by Dwight Kuhn, combines poetry with facts about animal camouflage in the wild.
- ***Activity books.*** This format is organized around directions for activities, such as crafts, recipes, or experiments, as in Vicki Cobb's *See for Yourself: More than 100 Amazing Experiments.*

• ***Reference books.*** Encyclopedias, dictionaries, and atlases serve as references and provide an overall coverage of a large topic with many facts, such as Thomas Holtz's high interest *Dinosaurs: The Most Complete, Up-To-Date Encyclopedia for Dinosaur Lovers of All Ages* and Steve Jenkins's compendium of fascinating animal facts, *The Animal Book.* A recent bestseller, *Maps* by Aleksandra Mizielinska and Daniel Mizielinski, provides 52 world maps with lavish illustrations that indicate historical sites, famous people, cultural events, and iconic plants and animals for each country.

Evaluation and Selection of Informational Books

Children should be offered a variety of books on a particular topic so they can compare information across books and consider a range of perspectives. No one book can cover a topic completely, and not every informational book needs to meet every criterion to be effective. The following selection criteria should be considered:

• **Is the book written in a clear, direct, easily understandable style?** A tight, compressed, but conversational, writing style that is clear, simple, and vivid has become frequent in nonfiction. The author's enthusiastic voice is featured, instead of an impersonal scholarly tone.

• **Is the information accurate, authoritative, and current?** Compare the information in a book with other recently published sources on the topic. In addition, look for information on the sources used by the author, the author's research processes, and acknowledgment of expert consultants. These sources need to be credible and involve multiple perspectives. They are usually found in reference lists, further reading suggestions, author's notes, or end notes.

• **Does the book avoid personification?** Personification involves attributing human qualities to animals, material objects, or natural forces and is considered factually inaccurate. Personification is effective in fantasy but not in an informational book.

• **Is the information presented as a means of supporting conceptual understanding, and does it encourage analytical thinking?** The book should include explanations of facts, not just facts, so that readers can build conceptual understandings. Presentation of information should go from known to unknown, general to specific, or simple to more complex. Generalizations must be supported by evidence, such as facts and examples.

• **Does the book introduce readers to strategies for inquiry?** Readers should come to an understanding about the ways in which scientists and historians work together and their inquiry strategies and tools. Sy Montgomery's *The Octopus Scientist* and Scott Nelson's *Ain't Nothing but a Man: My Quest to Find the Real John Henry* show how scientists and historians go about their work. Loree Griffin Burns provides examples of children engaged in backyard research in *Citizen Scientists*.

• **Is the book organized around a theme or idea that brings coherence to the information?** Although an informational book may communicate hundreds of facts about a topic, the theme answers the question "What's the point?" The information should lead to ideas that invite readers to invest themselves. Sometimes the theme will be a cognitive concept, such as the way cholera was spread; in other cases, it will be an understanding, such as an awareness of social injustices in U.S. history, as found in Larry Dane Brimner's *Strike* on the poor working conditions and pay of farm workers.

• **Does the book distinguish between fact, theory, and opinion?** Theories or opinions should be flagged by carefully placed phrases such as "maybe," "is believed to be," or "perhaps." Given the shift to narrative writing styles and the blending of fact and fiction, a clear distinction between fact and fiction is increasingly significant.

• **Are the depth and complexity of the topic or concept appropriate for the intended audience?** The experiences and understandings that children bring to the topic should be considered. Issues include underestimating children's abilities, providing explanations that are beyond children's current understandings or interests, or oversimplifying to the point of inaccuracy. A balance of child-friendly language and scientific rigor is needed.

• **Are the captions and labels clearly written and informative?** The captions should help readers easily access the information included in illustrations, graphs, charts, and maps.

• **Are the reference aids appropriate to the content and useful resources?** Reference aids such as tables of contents, indexes, pronunciation guides, glossaries, maps, charts, and tables make information easier to find and retrieve, more comprehensible, and more complete. The specific aids included for a particular book should be relevant to the content and useful for readers.

Excellent Informational Literature to Read Aloud

Coy, John. *Their Great Gift: Courage, Sacrifice and Hope in a New Land.* Photographs by Wing Young Huie. Ages 5–9.

Floca, Brian. *Locomotive.* Ages 6–9.

Hopkinson, Deborah. *Titanic: Voices from the Disaster.* Ages 8–14.

Jenkins, Steve, and Robin Page. *How to Swallow a Pig: A Step-by-Step Guide from the Animal Kingdom.* Ages 4–9.

Nelson, Kadir. *We Are the Ship: The Story of Negro League Baseball.* Ages 9–13.

Roth, Susan, and Cindy Trumbore. *The Mangrove Tree: Planting Trees to Feed Families.* Ages 7–10.

Schaefer, Lola. *Just One Bite: 11 Animals and Their Bites at Life Size!* Illustrated by Geoff Waring. Ages 5–8.

Schlitz, Laura. *Good Masters! Sweet Ladies! Voices from a Medieval Village.* Illustrated by Robert Byrd. Ages 9–13.

Weatherford, Carole Boston. *Freedom in Congo Square.* Illustrated by R. Gregory Christie. Ages 6–9.

- **Is the book visually attractive to the child?** An intriguing cover, impressive or humorous illustrations, and balance of text and illustrations make books look interesting to a child. Check for interesting visual features and an attractive design format.
- **Are the format and artistic medium appropriate to the content?** The illustrations should match the intent and level of detail of the text. Childlike illustrations, for example, can fail to provide the detail needed to support the text. Engineered pop-up illustrations are appropriate when three dimensions are required to give an accurate sense of placement of the parts of a whole, as in human anatomy.

The National Council of Teachers of English's Orbis Pictus Award for Outstanding Nonfiction for Children and the American Library Association's Robert F. Sibert Informational Book Medal spotlight the best works of nonfiction published in the preceding year (see Appendix A). In addition, the National Science Teacher Association publishes an annual list of Outstanding Science Trade Books for Students K–12 (www.nsta.org/publications/ostb) and the National Council for the Social Studies creates an annual list of Notable Social Studies Trade Books for Young People (www.socialstudies.org/resources/notable).

The Significance of Style in Informational Books

Understanding the parts, or elements, of informational books and how they work together can help you become more analytical in evaluating and selecting these books. Style is how authors and illustrators, with their readers in mind, express themselves in their respective media. Sentence length and complexity, word choice, and formal versus conversational tone are part of an expository style, as are use of technical vocabulary, captions, and graphic elements such as tables, charts, illustrations, photographs, diagrams, maps, and indexes. Shelley Tanaka's colorful language and use of large, richly colored photographs, maps, sidebars, and a time line in *Mummies: The Newest, Coolest, and Creepiest from Around the World* demonstrate how style can make informational literature more interesting.

The ***features*** used by authors have different purposes that readers need to be able to use as tools to understand informational books:

- The ***table of contents*** overviews the main ideas and organization of the book, whereas an ***index*** identifies the specific page where a reader can find a particular topic.
- ***Maps***, ***diagrams,*** and ***graphs*** provide visual displays of information that show relationships between the parts, whereas ***cutaways*** and ***cross-sections*** let the reader look inside something.
- ***Glossaries*** help readers understand the definitions of important words in comparison to ***pronunciation keys*** that help readers learn how to say a word.
- Pages often have words in a variety of ***fonts*** and ***type sizes,*** with bold and italic words signaling importance.

Each author uses different combinations of these tools, based on audience and purpose, in ways that affect the accessibility of a book for readers. Readers spend more time studying these features and the illustrations and less time reading text in informational books as compared to fiction.

Another aspect of style is the ***structure*** of how an author organizes the information to be presented. Many children are familiar and comfortable with the chronological structure of fiction, but not the wide range of structures found in informational texts. Some informational books use a single text structure; others, particularly longer works, use several. These structures include:

- ***Description.*** The author gives the characteristics of the topic, with the main topic organized around related subtopics (e.g., *Spiders* by Nic Bishop).
- ***Sequence.*** The author lists items in order, usually chronologically or numerically (e.g., *Titanic: Voices from the Disaster* by Deborah Hopkinson).
- ***Comparison.*** The author juxtaposes two or more components and lists their similarities and differences (e.g., *The Family Romanov* by Candace Fleming contrasts the lives of the Russian czar's family with the lives of common people).
- ***Cause and effect.*** The author states an action and shows the effect, or result, of this action (e.g., *The Mangrove Tree: Planting Trees to Feed Families* by Susan Roth and Cindy Trumbore).
- ***Problem and solution*** or ***question and answer.*** The author states a problem and its solution or solutions (e.g., *The Case of the Vanishing Golden Frogs: A Scientific Mystery* by Sandra Markle).

Historical Overview of Informational Literature

The history of children's informational literature is linked to the publication of John Amos Comenius's *Orbis Pictus (The World in Pictures)* in 1657. Not only was this the first picturebook, but it was also an informational book. This promising beginning was cut short, however, by the Puritan Movement. For nearly 200 years, the vast majority of books published for and read by children were intended for moralistic instruction rather than information.

Rapid development of informational literature as a genre began in the 1950s and 1960s in response to the launching of *Sputnik*, the first artificial space satellite, by the former Soviet Union. Competing in the race for space exploration and new technology, the U.S. Congress funneled money into science education, and publishers responded with new and improved science trade books. Informational picturebooks for primary grades were introduced, leading to a trend toward more illustrations and less text in informational books at all levels.

As the stature of informational literature rose and more top authors and illustrators were engaged in its production, the quality of research, writing, and art in these books improved. A lighter, yet factual, narrative tone balanced with high-quality, informative illustrations and graphics emerged as the preferred nonfiction style.

In 1990, the National Council of Teachers of English established the Orbis Pictus Award for Outstanding Nonfiction for Children and, in 2001, the American Library Association established the Robert F. Sibert Informational Book Medal, signaling the acceptance of informational literature as an equal player in the field of children's literature. The dull, pedantic fact books that many adults remember from childhood have been replaced with books that have an engaging writing style, an emphasis on visual design, and a focus on accuracy about topics that intrigue children.

MILESTONES in the Development of Informational Literature

Date	Book	Significance
1657	*Orbis Pictus* by John Amos Comenius	First known work of nonfiction for children
1683	New England Primer	First concept book for American children; reflected didacticism of the Puritan era
1922	*The Story of Mankind* by Hendrik Van Loon	Won the first Newbery Medal; greatly influenced children's books with its lively style and creative approach
1960	Let's-Read-and-Find-Out series by Franklyn Branley and Roma Gans	Introduced the science concept picturebook for young children
1990 and 2001	Orbis Pictus Award for Nonfiction (1990) and Robert F. Sibert Informational Book Medal (2001) established	Informational literature as a genre is recognized

Notable Authors and Illustrators of Informational Literature

Susan Campbell Bartoletti, author of books about historic periods of oppression. *Hitler Youth; Black Potatoes; Terrible Typhoid Mary.* www.scbartoletti.com

Nic Bishop, author/illustrator known for extreme close-up photographs of the natural world. *Spiders; Frogs; Red-Eyed Tree Frog* (with Joy Cowley). www.nicbishop.com

Tonya Bolden, author of books on African American history. *How to Build a Museum; Emancipation Proclamation; Searching for Sarah Rector.* www.tonyaboldenbooks.com/

Don Brown, author/illustrator of picturebooks and graphic novels on U.S. history. *Drowned City; The Great American Dust Bowl; Kid Blink Beats the World.* www.booksbybrown.com/

Brian Floca, author/illustrator of historical picturebooks, using pen-and-ink and watercolors. *Locomotive* (Caldecott medal); *Moonshot; Lightship; Ballet for Martha.* http://brianfloca.com/

Russell Freedman, author of informational books about U.S. and world history. *Who Was First? Discovering the Americas; Angel Island; Because They Marched; The War to End All Wars.*

Steve Jenkins, author/illustrator of picturebooks with textured cut-paper illustrations of animals. *Animals by Numbers; How to Swallow a Pig; Creature Features.* www.stevejenkinsbooks.com

David Macaulay, author/illustrator of books on the construction of buildings and explanations of how things work. *Built to Last; The Way Things Work Now.* http://hmhbooks.com/davidmacaulay/

Pamela Turner, author of photo essays on scientists in the field, many in global settings. *The Dolphins of Shark Bay; Crow Smarts; Life on Earth—And Beyond.* www.pamelasturner.com

Topics of Informational Books

Informational literature is one of the largest single genres in children's literature, in that everything known to humankind is a conceivable topic. Organizing such an enormous variety of topics can be done in a variety of ways, one of which is a scientific approach, dividing the world of information into the biological, the physical, the applied, and the social sciences, along with the humanities. These books are particularly important as resources for STEM (science, technology, engineering, and mathematics) as well as STEAM (adds the arts) education, with all areas receiving a great deal of emphasis and funding in schools.

Biological Science

Biological science deals with living organisms and their related laws and phenomena. The vast majority of science books fall into this category, with topics that interest children, such as dinosaurs, wild animals, ecology, and the environment. Children are especially fascinated by books on intriguing animals, such as *Neighborhood Sharks* by Katherine Roy and *How to Swallow a Pig: Step-by-Step Advice from the Animal Kingdom* by Steve Jenkins and Robin Page.

A subtopic of biological science that deserves special attention is human anatomy and sexuality. Young children are naturally interested in their bodies, and that interest grows with puberty. Experts in the field of sex education suggest honest, straightforward answers to children's questions about their bodies, bodily functions, sex, and sexual orientation. Books on these topics are not necessarily appropriate for elementary schools but are meant for parents as a resource to share with children. Teachers and librarians should be able to recommend age-appropriate books, such as Robie Harris's *It's So Amazing! A Book about Eggs, Sperm, Birth, Babies, and Families,* illustrated by Michael Emberley.

Physical Science

Physical science, also referred to as ***natural science,*** deals primarily with nonliving materials. Rocks, landforms, oceans, the stars, and the atmosphere and its weather and seasons are topics that children can explore within the fields of geology, geography, oceanography, astronomy, and meteorology. Children can satisfy their curiosity about extreme weather in *Seymour Simon's Extreme Earth Records* as well as locate books needed for class inquiries, such as Brian Floca's *Moonshot: The Flight of Apollo 11.*

Applied Science

Applied science deals with the practical applications of science devised by people. All machines—from simple levers to supercomputers, from bicycles to space rockets—are part of this field, and many children are interested in finding out how they work. Other aspects of applied science include the use of medicine to cure diseases; the processes by which food is produced, prepared, packaged, and marketed; and the design and manufacture of toys—topics of great interest to children. Children spend hours poring over the details in books, such as David Macaulay's *Built to Last* on architecture and *The Way Things Work Now* on machines.

A specific type of book—the ***experiment*** or ***how-to book***—capitalizes on children's desire for hands-on activities, as found in *Chemistry Science Fair Projects Using Inorganic Stuff* by Robert Gardner and Barbara G. Conklin. These books range from directions for scientific experiments to cookbooks, guides to hobbies, and directions for small construction projects, such as clubhouses.

Social Science

Social science deals with the institutions and functioning of society and the interpersonal relationships of individuals within a society, both in current events and historically. Children can learn about forms of government, religions, countries and cultures, money, and transportation, as well as life-changing historical events. Most children have a natural interest in books about careers, family relationships, and leisure activities. These books range from a focus on young children's interests in Maya Ajmera's *What We Wear: Dressing Up Around the World* to those of older readers in *What the World Eats* by Faith D'Aluisio and Peter Menzel and include depictions of current events, such as *Hands Around the Library: Protecting Egypt's Treasured Books* by Susan Roth and Karen Abouraya, as well as historical events, such as Kadir Nelson's *We Are the Ship: The Story of the Negro Baseball League.*

Current trends include books on the civil rights movement and World War II (WWII), providing a range of perspectives and foci on these events and reflecting an interest in both U.S. and world history. Recent WWII books highlight resistance movements, ranging from the Danish resistance in Deborah Hopkinson's *Courage & Defiance* to Jewish resistance efforts in Doreen Rappaport's *Beyond Courage* and the White Rose movement by German youth in Russell Freedman's *We Will Not Be Silent.* Immigration, an issue of current concern, receives both historical and contemporary treatment in books such as Ann Bausum's *Denied, Detained, Deported*; Russell Freedom's *Angel Island*; and John Coy's *Their Great Gift.*

Humanities

The ***humanities*** deal with fields that are cultural or artistic. Books of interest include those about the fine arts of drawing, painting, and sculpture; the performing arts of singing, dancing, making instrumental music, and acting; and handicrafts. Because many children are artistically creative and engage with dance, music, and drawing, they can read about the arts to learn new techniques or to draw inspiration from the experiences of others, as in *Ada's Violin* by Susan Hood and Sally Comport about children in Paraguay who built an orchestra from recycled trash found in the landfill on which their town is built. Books can make the arts more accessible to children by explaining what to look for in an art piece, such as Kimberley Lane's *Come Look with Me: Latin American Art.* Books can also reveal history as in *Freedom on Congo Square* by Carole Weatherford and Gregory Christie about the birthplace of jazz on Congo Square in New Orleans, where slaves gathered each Sunday.

Reader Connections: Pairing Fact and Fiction

One effective strategy for engaging children with informational books and addressing Common Core Standards is to pair an informational book with a related fiction book to encourage response and critical thinking. Pairing informational and literary texts immerses readers into a story world that takes them to another time and place, bringing alive their imaginations, and at the same time provides information that makes the story "real" and can help them analyze the fiction world.

Examples of possible pairs of fiction novels and informational books include:

- *Nory Ryan's Song* (Patricia Reilly Giff) with *Black Potatoes: The Story of the Great Irish Potato Famine* (Susan Bartoletti)
- *Out of the Dust* (Karen Hesse) with *Children of the Dust Bowl* (Jerry Stanley)
- *Weedflower* (Cynthia Kadahota) with *Imprisoned* (Martin Sandler)
- *Flush* (Carl Hiaasen) with *Tracking Trash* (Loree Griffin Burns)
- *Project Mulberry* (Linda Sue Park) with *The Story of Silk* (Richard Sobol)

For young children, pairing fiction with informational books helps sort out the characteristics of fiction and nonfiction texts and develop reading strategies. By listening to read-alouds of paired books, children are invited to discuss and compare the ideas and content as well as note the organizational structures and features that distinguish the two types of texts. Before analyzing the texts, however, children need time to first share their personal connections and what surprised or interested them in the books. In addition, although fiction is meant to be read aloud cover to cover, informational books often do not need to be read aloud in this way. Some shorter books can easily be read in one sitting, but others are designed to read aloud only the relevant portions.

Examples of paired picturebooks and informational books include:

- *Owl Moon* (Jane Yolen) with *All about Owls* (Jim Arnosky)
- *Stellaluna* (Janell Cannon) with *Outside and Inside Bats* (Sandra Markle)
- *A Color of My Own* (Leo Lionni) with *Chameleon, Chameleon* (Joy Cowley and Nic Bishop)
- *The Doorbell Rang* (Pat Hutchins) with *Fraction Fun* (David Adler)
- *John Henry* (Julius Lester) with *Ain't Nothing but a Man: My Quest to Find the Real John Henry* (Scott Nelson)

Many examples of paired picturebooks to teach life science can be found in *Perfect Pairs* by Melissa Stewart and Nancy Chesley (2014).

Today's nonfictional literature for children meets the needs and interests of young readers in quality, variety, and reader appeal. With these books, children's appetites for learning can be fed while fueling their curiosity for more information.

Invitations for Further Investigation

- In a small group, select four to six informational books on a social studies or science topic/theme. Read and discuss your responses to the books, webbing connections and issues. Identify differences across the books in their approaches and perspectives on the topic.
- Choose an informational book to analyze. Identify the type, features, and structure of these books using the information in this chapter. Also examine the book based on the selection criteria. List the strategies needed by readers to understand the features in the book.
- Locate and read several books for young people on a controversial topic such as evolution or sexuality. Examine how these books address the topic and consider in what contexts these books would be appropriate for children.
- Read one of the suggested paired book sets with a partner. Develop a comparison chart or Venn diagram to identify the similarities and differences in how that topic is explored in the two books. Discuss the ways in which the two books play off each other for you as readers in understanding the events.
- Create your own pairings of informational books with books from other genres. Choose a topic and grade level and generate several paired book sets that could be used to explore information or issues in the unit.

References

Bomer, K. (2005). *Writing a life: Teaching memoir.* Portsmouth, NH: Heinemann.

Freedman, R. (1988). Newbery Medal acceptance. *The Horn Book, 64*(4), 444–451.

Colman, P. (2007). A new way to look at literature: A visual model for analyzing fiction and nonfiction texts. *Language Arts, 84*(3), 257–268.

Duke, N. K. (2000). 3.6 minutes a day: The scarcity of informational texts in first grade. *Reading Research Quarterly, 35*(2), 202–225.

Jeong, J., Gaffney, J. & Choi, J. (2010). Availability and use of informational texts in second-, third-, and fourth-grade classrooms. *Research in the Teaching of English, 44*(4), 415–456.

Maloch, B. (2008). Beyond exposure: The uses of informational texts in a second grade classroom. *Research in the Teaching of English, 42*(3), 315–362.

Newkirk, T. (2014). *Minds made for stories: How we really read and write informational and persuasive text.* Portsmouth, ME: Stenhouse.

Stewart, M. & Chesley, N. (2014). *Perfect pairs: Using fiction and nonfiction picture books to teach life science, K-2.* Portsmouth, ME: Stenhouse.

Recommended Biography

Ages refer to content appropriateness and conceptual and interest levels. Formats other than informational chapter books are coded:

(PB) Picturebook
(COL) Short story collection
(GR) Graphic novel

Biographies—United States

Alcorn, Stephen. ***Odetta, The Queen of Folk.*** Scholastic, 2010. (**PB**). Ages 5–9. (African American folk singer, 1930–2008)

Andrews, Troy. ***Trombone Shorty.*** Illus. Bryan Collier. Abrams, 2015. (**PB**). Ages 4–8. (African American jazz musician, autobiography, contemporary)

Armand, Glenda. ***Ira's Shakespeare Dream.*** Illus. Floyd Cooper. Lee & Low, 2015. (**PB**). Ages 6–9. (African American actor, England, 1800s)

Atkins, Jeannine. ***Borrowed Names: Poems About Laura Ingalls Wilder, Madam C. J. Walker, Marie Curie, and their Daughters.*** Holt, 2010. (**NV**). Ages 13–18. (Successful women born in 1867, mother-daughter relationships)

Bartoletti, Susan. ***Terrible Typhoid Mary: A True Story of the Deadliest Cook in America.*** Houghton Mifflin Harcourt, 2015. Ages 10–14 (New York, early 1900s)

Barton, Chris. ***The Amazing Age of John Roy Lynch.*** Illus. Don Tate. Eerdmans, 2015. (**PB**). Ages 7–10. (African American politician, 1847–1939)

Bolden, Tonya. ***George Washington Carver.*** Abrams, 2008. (**PB**). Ages 8–12. (African American scientist and inventor, 1864–1943)

Bolden, Tonya. ***Searching for Sarah Rector.*** Abrams, 2014. Ages 10–14. (African American landowner, 1902–1967)

Bridges, Ruby, and Margo Lundell. ***Through My Eyes.*** Scholastic, 1999. Ages 9–16. (Civil rights, school integration, South, 1960)

Brimner, Larry Dane. ***The Rain Wizard: The Amazing, Mysterious, True Life of Charles Mallory Hatfield.*** Calkins Creek, 2015. Ages 9–12. (California, 1875–1958)

Brown, Don. ***A Wizard from the Start.*** Houghton Mifflin, 2010. (**PB**). Ages 6–9. (Thomas Edison, inventor, 1847–1931)

Bryant, Jennifer. ***A River of Words: The Story of William Carlos Williams.*** Illus. Melissa Sweet. Eerdmans, 2008. (**PB**). Ages 7–10. (African American poet, 1883–1963)

Bryant, Jennifer. ***A Splash of Red: The Life and Art of Horace Pippin.*** Illus. Melissa Sweet. Knopf, 2013. (**PB**). Ages 5–11. (African American artist, 1888–1946)

Burleigh, Robert. ***The Adventures of Mark Twain.*** Illus. Barry Blitt. Atheneum, 2011. (**PB**). Ages 7–9. (Author, 1872–1896)

Byrd, Robert. ***Electric Ben: The Amazing Life and Times of Benjamin Franklin.*** Dial, 2012. (**PB**). Ages 7–10. (Inventor, 1706–1790)

Capaldi, Gina. ***A Boy Named Beckoning: The True Story of Dr. Carlos Montezuma, A Native American Hero.*** Carolrhoda, 2008. (**PB**). Ages 7–10. (Yavapi Indian, Arizona, late 1800s)

Cline-Ransome, Lesa. ***Benny Goodman & Teddy Wilson: Taking the Stage as the First Black-and-White Jazz Band in History.*** Illus. James Ransome. Holiday House, 2014. (**PB**). Ages 6–9. (1935–1936, musicians, race relations)

Cline-Ransome, Lesa. ***My Story, My Dance: Robert Battle's Journey to Alvin Ailey.*** Illus. James Ransome. Simon & Schuster, 2015. (**PB**). Ages 6–9. (African American dancer, 1972 to present)

Cummins, Julie. ***Women Daredevils: Thrills, Chills, and Frills.*** Illus. Cheryl Harness. Dutton, 2007. (**COL**). Ages 8–12. (Stunt performers, 1880–1929)

Davis, Kathryn. ***Mr. Ferris and His Wheel.*** Illus. Gilbert Ford. Houghton Mifflin Harcourt, 2014. (**PI**). Ages 5–8. (Civil engineering, 1859–1896) de la Peña, Matt. ***A Nation's Hope: the True Story of Boxing Legend Joe Louis.*** Illus. Kadir Nelson. Dial, 2011. Ages 5–9. (African American boxer, WWII, 1938)

Denenberg, Barry. ***Lincoln Shot: A President's Life Remembered.*** Illus. Christopher Bing. Feiwel & Friends, 2008. Ages 10–15. (Oversize newspaper format; president, 1865)

Fern, Tracey E. ***W Is for Webster: Noah Webster and His American Dictionary.*** Illus. Boris Kulikov. Farrar, 2015. (**PI**). Ages 5–10. (1758–1843)

Fleischman, Sid. ***The Trouble Begins at 8: A Life of Mark Twain in the Wild, Wild West.*** HarperCollins, 2008. Ages 10–15. (Author, 1835–1910)

Fleming, Candace. ***The Lincolns: A Scrapbook Look at Abraham and Mary.*** Random House, 2008. Ages 11–15. (President and First Lady,1809–1882)

Fleming, Candace. ***Amelia Lost: The Life and Disappearance of Amelia Earhart.*** Schwartz & Wade, 2011. Ages 9–14. (Female pilot, 1897–1937)

Fleming, Candace. ***Presenting Buffalo Bill.*** Roaring Brook, 2016. Ages 10–14. (Chapters alternate between husband and wife; 1809–1882)

Fradin, Dennis. ***Duel! Burr and Hamilton's Deadly War of Words.*** Illus. Larry Day. Walker, 2008. (**PB**). Ages 8–11. (Weehawken, New Jersey, duel, 1804)

Fradin, Judith, and Dennis Fradin. ***Jane Addams: Champion of Democracy.*** Clarion, 2006. Ages 12–14. (Female social reformer, 1860–1935)

Freedman, Russell. ***Lincoln: A Photobiography.*** Clarion, 1987. Ages 9–12. (President, 1809–1865)

Freedman, Russell. ***Abraham Lincoln and Frederick Douglass: The Story Behind an American Friendship.*** Clarion, 2012. Ages 9–14. (U.S. president, African American abolitionist, 1863)

Fritz, Jean. ***And Then What Happened, Paul Revere?*** Coward, 1973. Ages 8–10. Also ***Can't You Make Them Behave, King George?*** (Revolutionary War, 1775–1783)

Giovanni, Nikki. ***Rosa.*** Illus. Bryan Collier. Holt, 2005. (**PB**). Ages 8–11. (Civil rights activist, 1955)

Golio, Gary. ***Jimi: Sounds like a Rainbow; A Story of the Young Jimi Hendrix.*** Illus. Javaka Steptoe. Clarion, 2010. Ages 8–11. (African American musician, 1960s/1970s)

Greenberg, Jan. ***The Mad Potter: George E. Ohr, Eccentric Genius.*** Roaring Brook, 2013. (**PB**). Ages 7–12. (Artist, 1857–1918)

Hale, Nathan. ***The Underground Abductor.*** Amulet, 2015. (**GR**). Ages 7–13. (Underground Railroad, Harriet Tubman 1820–1913)

Hoose, Phillip. ***We Were There, Too! Young People in U.S. History.*** Farrar, 2001. Ages 10–13. (A collective biography of 60 young people who influenced their times)

Hoose, Phillip. ***Claudette Colvin: Twice Toward Justice.*** Melanie Kroupa, 2009. Ages 12–18. (Civil Rights era, 1955)

Jarrow, Gail. ***The Amazing Harry Kellar: Great American Magician.*** Calkins Creek, 2012. Ages 10–14. (Magician, 1849–1922)

Kanefield, Teri. ***The Girl from the Tar Paper School: Barbara Rose Johns and the Advent of the Civil Rights Movement.*** Abrams, 2014. Ages 10–14. (Civil Rights, 1935–1991)

Kerley, Barbara. ***What to Do about Alice? How Alice Roosevelt Broke the Rules, Charmed the World, and Drove Her Father Crazy.*** Illus. Edwin Fotheringham. Scholastic, 2008. (**PB**). Ages 5–10. (President Theodore Roosevelt's daughter, White House, late 1800s)

Kerley, Barbara. ***The Extraordinary Mark Twain (according to Susy).*** Illus. Edwin Fotheringham. Scholastic, 2010. (**PB**). Ages 7–11. (Author, 1872–1896)

Kerley, Barbara. ***A Home for Mr. Emerson.*** Illus. Ed Fotheringham. Scholastic, 2013. (**PB**). Ages 8–12. (Philosopher, 1803–1882)

Krull, Kathleen. ***Women Who Broke the Rules: Sacajawea.*** Illus. Matt Collins. Bloomsbury, 2015. Ages 9–11. (Lewis and Clark Expedition, 1804–1806). Series

Lang, Heather. ***Fearless Flyer: Ruth Law and Her Flying Machine.*** Illus. Raúl Colón. Calkins Creek, 2016. (**PB**). Ages 5–8. (Aviation, cross-country flight, 1916)

Lutes, Jason, and Nick Bertozzi. ***Houdini: The Handcuff King.*** Hyperion, 2007. (**GR**). Ages 11–15. (Magician, 1908)

Markel, Michelle. ***Brave Girl: Clara and the Shirtwaist Markers' Strike of 1909.*** Balzer + Bray, 2013. (**PB**). Ages 5–9. (Labor movement, 1909)

McDonnell, Patrick. ***Me … Jane.*** Little, Brown, 2011. (**PB**). Ages 2–10. (Conservationist, 1934 to present)

Nelson, Marilyn. ***Carver: A Life in Poems.*** Front Street, 2000. Ages 12–16. (**NV**). (African American scientist, 1864–1943)

Nelson, S. D. ***Black Elk's Vision: A Lakota Story.*** Abrams, 2010. Ages 10–14. (Lakota, 1863–1950)

Nelson, Vaunda Micheaux. ***No Crystal Stair: A Documentary Novel of the Life and Work of Lewis Michaux, Harlem Bookseller.*** Illus. R. Gregory Christie. Carolrhoda, 2012. Ages 12–18. (African American activist, 1885–1976)

Nelson, Vaunda Micheaux. ***The Book Itch: Freedom, Truth, & Harlem's Greatest Bookstore.*** Illus. R. Gregory Christie. Carolrhoda, 2015. (**PB**). Ages 7–10. (African American bookseller, 1930s)

Nivola, Claire A. ***Life in the Ocean: The Story of Oceanographer Sylvia Earle.*** Farrar, 2012. (**PB**). Ages 5–9. (Oceanographer, 1935–present)

Nobleman, Marc Tyler. ***Boys of Steel: The Creators of Superman.*** Illus. Ross MacDonald. Knopf, 2008. (**PB**). Ages 6–8. (Inventors of the cartoon character, 1930s)

Parker, Robert Andrew. ***Piano Starts Here: The Young Art Tatum.*** Schwartz & Wade, 2008. (**PB**). Ages 6–10. (African American jazz musician, 1910–1956)

Phelan, Matt. ***Around the World: Three Remarkable Journeys.*** Candlewick, 2011. (**GR**). Ages 10–13. (Thomas Stevens, Nellie Bly, Joshua Slocum, world travel, 1900s)

Pinkney, Andrea Davis. ***Hand in Hand: Ten Black Men Who Changed America.*** Illus. J. Brian Pinkney. Disney/Jump at The Sun, 2012. (**COL**). Ages 10–15. (Social change)

Pinkney, Andrea Davis. ***Martin & Mahalia: His Words, Her Song.*** Illus. J. Brian Pinkney. Little Brown, 2013. (PB). Ages 6–12. (Civil rights, gospel, Martin Luther King Jr., 1929–1968, Mahalia Jackson, 1911–1972)

Powell, Patricia Hruby. ***Josephine: The Dazzling Life of Josephine Baker.*** Illus. Christian Robinson. Chronicle, 2014. (**PB**). Ages 6–12. (African American dancer, 1906–1975)

Rappaport, Doreen. ***Martin's Big Words: The Life of Dr. Martin Luther King, Jr.*** Illus. Bryan Collier. Hyperion, 2001. (**PI**). Ages 8–10. (Civil rights activist, 1929–1968)

Rappaport, Doreen. ***Abe's Honest Words: The Life of Abraham Lincoln.*** Illus. Gary Kelley. Hyperion, 2008. (**PB**). Ages 6–10. (Quotations from speeches and writings, 1809–1865)

Rappaport, Doreen. ***Eleanor, Quiet No More: The Life of Eleanor Roosevelt.*** Illus. Gary Kelley. Disney/Hyperion, 2009. (**PB**). Ages 7–10. (First lady, 1884–1962)

Ray, Deborah Kogan. ***Down the Colorado: John Wesley Powell, the One-Armed Explorer.*** Farrar, 2007. (**PB**). Ages 8–11. (Western exploration, 1869)

Reich, Susanna. ***Painting the Wild Frontier: The Art and Adventures of George Catlin.*** Clarion, 2008. Ages 12–18. (Painter of American Indian life, 1796–1872)

Richardson, Jael Ealey. ***The Stone Thrower.*** Illus. Matt James. Groundwood, 2016. (**PB**). Ages 6–8. (African American football player, 1950s/1960s)

Robertson, Robbie. ***Legends, Icons & Rebels: Music That Changed the World.*** Tundra, 2015. (**COL**). Ages 12–18. (Musicians, 1925–1968)

Rosenstock, Barbara. ***Thomas Jefferson Builds a Library.*** Illus. John O'Brien. Calkins Creek, 2013. (**PB**). Ages 6–9. (Library of Congress, U.S. president, 1743–1826)

Rumford, James. ***Sequoyah: The Man Who Gave His People Writing.*** Houghton, 2004. (**PB**). Ages 6–10. (Cherokee leader, language, 1770–1843)

Russell-Brown, Katheryn. ***Little Melba and Her Big Trombone.*** Illus. Frank Morrison. Lee & Low, 2014. (**PB**). Ages 4–8. (African American jazz musician, 1926–1999)

Ryan, Pam Muñoz. ***When Marian Sang: The True Recital of Marian Anderson.*** Illus. Brian Selznick. Scholastic, 2002. (**PB**). Ages 6–10. (African American singer, 1897–1993)

Sandler, Martin W. ***Lincoln through the Lens: How Photography Revealed and Shaped an Extraordinary Life.*** Walker, 2008. Ages 12–15. (President, 1809–1865)

Schanzer, Rosalyn. ***George vs. George: The American Revolution as Seen from Both Sides.*** National Geographic, 2004. Ages 9–12. (Revolutionary War, King George, George Washington, 1775–1783)

Sheinkin, Steve. ***The Notorious Benedict Arnold: A True Story of Adventure, Heroism & Treachery.*** Roaring Brook, 2010. Ages 10–18. (Revolutionary War, 1741–1801)

Silvey, Anita. ***Henry Knox: Bookseller, Soldier, Patriot.*** Illus. Wendell Minor. Clarion, 2010 (**PB**). Ages 6–9. (Boston, Revolutionary War, 1775–1783)

Sisson, Stephanie. ***Star Stuff: Carl Sagan and the Mysteries of the Cosmos.*** Roaring Brook, 2014. (**PB**). Ages 4–8. (Astronomer, 1934–1996)

Stanley, Diane. ***Ada Lovelace, Poet of Science: The First Computer Programmer.*** Illus. Jessie Hartland. Simon & Schuster, 2016. (**PB**). Ages 7–10. (British, 1815–1852)

Stone, Tanya Lee. ***Sandy's Circus: A Story about Alexander Calder.*** Illus. Boris Kulikov. Viking, 2008. (**PB**). Ages 5–9. (Calder's wire sculptures, Paris, 1920s)

Stone, Tanya Lee. ***Who Says Women Can't Be Doctors? The Story of Elizabeth Blackwell.*** Illus. Marjorie Priceman. Holt, 2013. (**PB**). Ages 5–9. (Physician, 1821–1910)

Stone, Tanya Lee. ***The House That Jane Built: A Story about Jane Addams.*** Illus. Kathryn Brown. Holt, 2015. (**PB**). Ages 5–9. (Social activist, Chicago, 1880s)

Sweet, Melissa. ***Balloons over Broadway: The True Story of the Puppeteer of Macy's Parade.*** Houghton Mifflin, 2012. (**PB**). Ages 5–9. (Tony Sarg, inventor, 1920s)

Tate, Don. ***It Jes' Happened: When Bill Traylor Started to Draw.*** Illus. R. Gregory Christie. Lee & Low, 2012. (**PB**). Ages 6–11. (African American artist, 1854–1949)

Tavares, Matt. ***Henry Aaron's Dream.*** Candlewick, 2010. (**PB**). Ages 5–9. (African American, baseball, 1947)

Tonatiuh, Duncan. ***Separate Is Never Equal: Sylvia Mendez & Her Family's Fight for Desegregation.*** Abrams, 2014. (**PB**). Ages 6–9. (Desegregation, California, Mexican American court case, 1946)

Weatherford, Carole. ***Moses: When Harriet Tubman Led Her People to Freedom.*** Illus. Kadir Nelson. Disney/Jump at the Sun, 2006. (**PB**). Ages 7–11. (Underground Railroad, 1820–1913)

Weatherford, Carole. ***Leontyne Price: Voice of a Century.*** Illus. Raúl Colón. Knopf, 2014. (**PB**). Ages 5–8. (African American opera singer, 1927 to present)

Weatherford, Carole. ***Gordon Parks: How the Photographer Captured Black and White America.*** Illus. James Christoph. Whitman, 2015. (**PB**). Ages 10–14. (African American photographer, 1912–2006)

Weatherford, Carole. ***Voice of Freedom: Fannie Lou Hamer, Spirit of the Civil Rights Movement.*** Illus. Ekua Holmes. Candlewick, 2015. (**PB**). Ages 10–14. (Civil Rights)

Wing, Natasha. ***An Eye for Color: The Story of Josef Albers.*** Illus. Julia Breckenreid. Holt, 2009. (**PB**). Ages 5–9. (German-born American artist, 1975)

Winter, Jeanette. ***The Watcher: Jane Goodall's Life with the Chimps.*** Schwartz & Wade, 2011. (**PB**). Ages 7–11. (Primatologist, 1934 to present)

Winter, Jonah. ***You Never Heard of Sandy Koufax?!*** Illus. Andre Carrilho. Schwartz & Wade, 2009. (**PB**). Ages 7–10. (Jewish baseball player, 1965)

Wise, Bill. ***Louis Sockalexis: Native American Baseball Pioneer.*** Illus. Bill Fransworth. Lee & Low, 2007. (**PB**). Ages 9–11. (Penobscot Indian, baseball, 1897)

Yolen, Jane. ***My Uncle Emily.*** Illus. Nancy Carpenter. Philomel, 2009. (**PB**). Ages 5–8. (Amherst, Massachusetts, Emily Dickinson, 1830–1886)

Yoo, Paula. ***Sixteen Years in Sixteen Seconds: The Sammy Lee Story.*** Illus. Dom Lee. Lee & Low, 2005. (**PB**). Ages 6–10. (Korean immigrant diver, 1932)

Biographies – Global

Abirached, Zeina. ***I Remember Beirut.*** Trans. Edward Gauvin. Graphic Universe, 2014. (**GR**). Ages 12–18. (Translated from French, Lebanese civil war, 1975–1990)

Barakat, Ibtisam. ***Tasting the Sky: A Palestinian Childhood.*** Farrar, 2007. Ages 12–16. (Memoir, Palestine, Six Day War, 1967)

Bernier-Grand, Carmen. ***Alicia Alonso: Prima Ballerina.*** Illus. Raúl Colón. Cavendish, 2011. (Dance, blindness, Cuba, 1921–2012)

Bernier-Grand, Carmen T. ***Frida: Viva la Vida! Long Live Life!*** Illus. David Diaz. Cavendish, 2007. (**PB, NV**). Ages 12–18. (Mexican artist, 1907–1954). Also ***Diego: Bigger than Life.*** Illus. David Diaz. (2009). (**PB, NV**). Ages 13–16. (Mexican painter, 1886–1957)

Brown, Monica. ***Pablo Neruda: Poet of the People.*** Illus. Julie Paschkis. Holt, 2011. (**PB**). Ages 4–11. (Chilean poet, 1904–1973)

Bryant, Jennifer. ***The Right Word: Roget and His Thesaurus.*** Illus. Melissa Sweet. Eerdmans, 2014. (**PB**). Ages 6–10. (England, 1779–1869)

Burleigh, Robert. ***Napoléon: The Story of the Little Corporal.*** Abrams, 2007. (**PB**). Ages 10–14. (General, French Revolution, 1769–1821)

Christensen, Bonnie. ***Django.*** Roaring Brook, 2009. (**PB**). Ages 6–12. (Gypsy jazz musician, disability, Paris, 1910–1953)

Cline-Ransome, Lesa. ***Young Pelé: Soccer's First Star.*** Illus. James E. Ransome. Random House, 2007. (**PB**). Ages 5–9. (Brazilian soccer star, 1950s–1970s)

Debon, Nicolas. ***The Strongest Man in the World: Louis Cyr.*** Groundwood, 2007. (**GR**). Ages 7–11. (Canada, 1863–1912)

Ellis, Deborah. ***Kids of Kabul.*** Groundwood, 2012. Ages 12–15. (Afghanistan, contemporary)

Engle, Margarita. ***Lion Island.*** Atheneum, 2016. (**NV**). Ages 11–16. (Cuba, civil rights, Antonio Chuffat, 1870s)

Fleischman, Sid. ***Sir Charlie Chaplin: The Funniest Man in the World.*** Greenwillow, 2010. Ages 12–16. (England, comedian 1889–1977)

Freedman, Russell. ***Confucius: The Golden Rule.*** Illus. Frédéric Clément. Scholastic, 2002. (**PB**). Ages 9–14. (China, philosopher, 551–479 BC)

Freedman, Russell. ***The Adventures of Marco Polo.*** Illus. Bagram Ibatoulline. Scholastic, 2006. Ages 12–15. (Vienna to Asia, 1254–1323)

Gandhi, Arun. ***Grandfather Gandhi.*** Illus. Evan Turk. Atheneum, 2014. (**PB**). Ages 4–8. (India, activist and pacifist, 1869–1948)

Heiligman, Deborah. ***The Boy Who Loved Math: The Improbable Life of Paul Erdos.*** Illus. LeUyen Pham. Roaring Brook, 2013. (**PB**). Ages 3–9. (Hungarian mathematician, 1913–1996)

Johnson, Jen C. ***Seeds of Change.*** Illus. Sonia Sadler, Lee and Low, 2010. (**PB**). Ages 7–10. (Kenyan conservationist, 1940–present)

Krull, Kathleen. ***Albert Einstein.*** Illus. Boris Kulikov. Viking, 2009. Ages 12–15. (German-born physicist, 1879–1955)

Krull, Kathleen. ***Kubla Khan: The Emperor of Everything.*** Illus. Robert Byrd. Viking, 2010. (**PB**). Ages 5–10. (China, Mongolian ruler, 1216–1294)

Landmann, Bimba. ***In Search of the Little Prince: The Story of Antoine de Saint-Exupery.*** Eerdmans, 2014. (**PB**). Ages 6–11. Translated from Italian. (French pilot, 1900–1944)

McGinty, Alice. ***Darwin.*** Illus. Mary Azarian. Houghton Mifflin, 2009. (**PB**). Ages 5–9. (England, naturalist, 1809–1882)

Morales, Yuyi. ***Viva Frida.*** Roaring Brook, 2014. (**PB**). Ages 3–6. (Mexican artist)

Napoli, Donna Jo. ***Mama Miti: Wangari Maathai and the Trees of Kenya.*** Illus. Kadir Nelson. Simon & Schuster, 2010. (**PB**). Ages 5–9. (Kenyan environmentalist, 1940 to present)

Nivola, Claire A. ***Planting the Trees of Kenya: The Story of Wangari Maathi.*** Farrar, 2008. (**PB**). Ages 6–9. (Kenyan environmentalist, 1940 to present)

Place, François. ***The Old Man Mad about Drawing: A Tale of Hokusai.*** Trans. William Rodarmor. Godine, 2003. Ages 10–14. Translated from French. (Japan, social life and customs, 1760–1849)

Prevol, Franck. ***Wangari Maathai: The Woman Who Planted Millions of Trees.*** Illus. Aurelia Fronty. Charlesbridge, 2015. (**PB**). Ages 7–12. Translated from French. (Kenya environmentalist, 1940 to present)

Rosenstock, Barb. ***The Noisy Paint Box: The Colors and Sounds of Kandinsky's Abstract Art.*** Illus. Mary GrandPre. Knopf, 2014. (**PB**). Ages 5–10. (Russian artist, 1866–1944)

Ryan, Pam Muñoz. ***The Dreamer.*** Illus. Peter Sís. Scholastic, 2010. (**PB**). Ages 9–14. (Chile, Pablo Neruda, 1904–1973)

Serrano, Francisco. ***The Poet King of Tezcoco: A Great Leader of Ancient Mexico.*** Trans. Trudy Balch and Jo Anne Engelbert. Illus. Pablo Serrano. Groundwood, 2007. (**PI**). Ages 10–14. Translated from Spanish. (Mexico, indigenous, King Nezahualc-yotl, 1400s)

Sís, Peter. ***The Wall: Growing Up behind the Iron Curtain.*** Farrar, 2007. (**PB/GR**). Ages 10–15. (Autobiography, Czech Republic, Communist era, 1960s)

Sís, Peter. ***The Pilot and the Little Prince: The Life of Antoine de Saint-Exupery.*** Frances Foster Books, 2014. (**PB**). Ages 6–12. (French pilot, 1900–1944)

Snyder, Laurel. ***Swan: The Life and Dance of Anna Pavlova.*** Illus. Julie Morstad. Chronicle, 2015. (**PB**). Ages 6–9. (Russian ballerina, 1881–1931)

Tavares, Matt. ***Growing Up Pedro.*** Candlewick, 2015. (**PB**). Ages 8–12. (Dominican baseball player, Pedro Martinez, 1971 to present)

Tonatiuh, Duncan. ***Funny Bones: Posada and His Day of the Dead Calaveras.*** Abrams, 2015. (**PB**). Ages 7–13. (Mexican artist, Jose Guadalupe Posada, 1852–1913)

Turner, Pamela. ***Samurai Rising: The Epic Life of Minamoto Yoshitsune.*** Illus. Gareth Hind. Charlesbridge, 2016. Ages 10–14. (Japanese, 1159–1189)

Warren, Andrea. ***Charles Dickens and the Street Children of London.*** Houghton, 2011. Ages 12–15. (England, 1812–1870)

Winter, Jeanette. ***Wangari's Tree of Peace.*** Harcourt, 2008 (**PB**). Ages 5–8. (Kenya, environmentalist, 1940 to present)

Winter, Jonah. ***The Secret World of Hildegard.*** Illus. Jeanette Winter. Scholastic, 2007. (**PB**). Ages 7–12. (Germany, composer, 1100s)

Yoo, Paula. ***Twenty-Two Cents: Muhammad Yunus and the Village Bank.*** Illus. Jamel Akib. Lee & Low, 2014. (**PB**). Ages 6–11. (Bangladesh, economist, 1940 to present)

Memoir

Bell, Cece. ***El Deafo.*** Amulet, 2014. (**GR**). Ages 8–12. (Deaf author/illustrator)

Chikwanine, Michael, and Humphreys, Jessica. ***Child Soldier.*** Illus. Claudia Davila. Kids Can Press, 2015. (**GR**). Ages 10–14. (Congo, 1990s)

Ehlert, Louis. ***The Scraps Book: Notes from a Colorful Life.*** Beach Lane, 2014. (**PB**). Ages 5–9. (Childhood, career as illustrator)

Engle, Margarita. ***Enchanted Air: Two Cultures, Two Wings: A Memoir.*** Atheneum, 2015. (**NV**). Ages 10–18. (Cuban American author)

Kamkwamba, William. ***The Boy Who Harnessed the Wind.*** Illus. Anna Hymas. Dial, 2015. (**PB**). Ages 10–14. (Malawi, environmentalist)

Lewis, John, and Aydin, Andrew. ***March, Book One.*** Illus. Nate Powell. Top Shelf, 2013. (**GR**). Ages 11–14. (Memoir, civil rights movement, 1950s and 1960s)

Liu, Na. ***Little White Duck: A Childhood in China.*** Illus. Andres Vera Martinez. Graphic Universe, 2012. (**GR**). Ages 9–12. (Memoir, China childhood, 1970s–1980s)

Nelson, Marilyn. ***How I Discovered Poetry.*** Illus. Hadley Hooper. Dial, 2014. (**NV**). Ages 10–18. (African American poet, 1950s Civil Rights movement)

Say, Allen. ***The Inker's Shadow.*** Scholastic, 2015. (**GR**). Ages 10–14. (Japanese student at an American military academy, 1953–1956)

Tolstikova, Dasha. ***A Year without Mom.*** Groundwood, 2015. (**GR**). Ages 10–14. (Russia, 1990s)

Woodson, Jacqueline. ***Brown Girl Dreaming.*** Penguin, 2014. Ages 8–12. (African American author, childhood, 1960s and 1970s)

Young, Ed. ***The House Baba Built: An Artist's Childhood in China.*** Little, Brown, 2011. (**PB**). Ages 7–12. (Chinese artist, 1934)

Recommended Informational Books

Biological Science

Arnosky, Jim. ***Wild Tracks! A Guide to Nature's Footprints.*** Sterling, 2008. (**PB**). Ages 7–11.

Aston, Dianna. ***An Egg Is Quiet***. Illus. Sylvia Long. Chronicle, 2006. (**PB**). Ages 5–9. Also ***A Seed is Sleepy*** (2007) and ***A Beetle is Shy*** (2014).

Bishop, Nic. ***Frogs.*** Scholastic, 2008. (**PB**). Ages 7–10. Also ***Spiders*** (2007).

Bonner, Hannah. ***When Fish Got Feet, Sharks Got Teeth, and Bugs Began to Swarm: A Cartoon Prehistory of Life Long before Dinosaurs.*** National Geographic, 2007. (**PB**). Ages 8–11.

Butterworth, Chris. ***Sea Horse: The Shyest Horse in the Sea.*** Illus. John Lawrence. Candlewick, 2006. (**PB**). Ages 4–8. (Australia)

Campbell, Sarah. ***Growing Patterns: Fibonacci Numbers in Nature.*** Photos. Boyds Mills, 2010. (**PI**). Ages 6–9. Also ***Mysterious Patterns: Finding Fractals in Nature*** (2014).

Carson, Mary Kay. ***Park Scientists: Gila Monsters, Geysers, and Grizzly Bears in American's Own Backyard.*** Houghton, 2014. Ages 10–15.

Cate, Annette. ***Look Up! Bird-Watching in Your Own Backyard.*** Candlewick, 2013. (**PB**). Ages 8–15.

Cole, Joanna. ***The Magic School Bus and the Climate Change.*** Illus. Bruce Degen. Scholastic, 2010. (**PB**). Ages 7–9.

Cowley, Joy. ***Chameleon, Chameleon.*** Photos Nic Bishop. Scholastic, 2005. (**PB**). Ages 4–7. Also ***Red-Eyed Tree Frog*** (1999). (New Zealand)

Davies, Nicola. ***Deadly! The Truth about the Most Dangerous Creatures on Earth.*** Illus. Neal Layton. Candlewick, 2015. (**PB**). Ages 8–12.

Doner, Kim. ***On a Road in Africa.*** Tricyle Press, 2008. (**PB**). Ages 5–8. (Kenya)

Farrell, Jeanette. ***Invisible Allies: Microbes That Shape Our Lives.*** Farrar, 2016. Ages 12–18.

Frost, Helen. ***Monarch and Milkweed.*** Illus. Leonid Gore. Atheneum, 2008. (**PB**). Ages 4–7.

Gibbons, Gail. ***Ladybugs.*** Holiday, 2012. (**PB**). Ages 5–9. Many books for young children.

Harris, Robie. ***It's Perfectly Normal: A Book about Changing Bodies, Growing Up, Sex, and Sexual Health.*** Illus. Michael Emberley. Candlewick, 2009. Ages 11–14.

Harris, Robie. ***Who Has What? All about Girls' Bodies and Boys' Bodies.*** Illus. Nadine Bernard Wescott. Candlewick, 2011. Ages 5–10.

Harris, Robie. ***It's So Amazing!: A Book About Eggs, Sperm, Birth, Babies, and Families.*** Illus. Michael Emberley. Candlewick, 2014. Ages 6–10.

Holtz, Thomas. ***Dinosaurs: The Most Complete, Up-to-Date Encyclopedia for Dinosaur Lovers of All Ages.*** Illus. Luis Rey. Random House, 2007. Ages 10–14.

Hoose, Phillip. ***Moonbird: A Year on the Wind with the Great Survivor B95.*** Farrar Straus Giroux, 2012. Ages 10–18.

Jenkins, Martin. ***Can We Save the Tiger?*** Illus. Vicky White. Candlewick, 2011. (**PB**). Ages 5–9.

Jenkins, Steve. ***The Animal Book: A Collection of the Fastest, Fiercest, Toughest, Cleverest, Shyest—and Most Surprising—Animals on Earth.*** Houghton, 2009. Ages 5–10.

Jenkins, Steve. ***Bones: Skeletons and How They Work.*** Scholastic, 2010. (**PB**). Ages 7–11.

Jenkins, Steve. ***Creature Features: 25 Animals Explain Why They Look the Way They Do.*** Houghton, 2014. (**PB**). Ages 4–8.

Jenkins, Steve. ***How to Swallow a Pig: Step-By-Step Advice from the Animal Kingdom.*** Houghton, 2015. (**PB**). Ages 4–9.

Jenkins, Steve. ***Animals by the Numbers.*** Houghton, 2016. (**PB**). Ages 6–9. (infographics)

Jenkins, Steve, and Robin Page. ***How Many Ways Can You Catch a Fly?*** Houghton, 2008. (**PB**). Ages 4–8.

Kyi, Tanya Lloyd. ***50 Body Questions: A Book That Spills Its Guts.*** Illus. Ross Kinnaird. Annick Press, 2014. Ages 10–14.

Macaulay, David. ***The Way We Work: Getting to Know the Amazing Human Body***. Houghton, 2008. Ages 10–15.

Markle, Sandra. ***The Case of the Vanishing Golden Frogs: A Scientific Mystery.*** Millbrook, 2012. Ages 9–13.

Montgomery, Sy. ***Chasing Cheetahs: The Race to Save Africa's Fastest Cats.*** Illus. Nic Bishop. Houghton, 2014. Ages 10–15. (Tanzania)

Montgomery, Sy. ***The Great White Shark Scientist.*** Houghton, 2016. Ages 10–15.

O'Connell, Caitlin, and Donna Jackson. ***The Elephant Scientist.*** Houghton Mifflin, 2011. Ages 11–14. (Namibia)

Pringle, Laurence. ***Billions of Years, Amazing Changes: The Story of Evolution.*** Illus. Steve Jenkins. Boyds Mills Press, 2011. Ages 9–15. (Geology).

Roth, Susan, and Trumbore, Cindy. ***Parrots over Puerto Rico.*** Lee & Low, 2013. (**PB**). Ages 8–14. (Environment)

Roy, Katherine. ***Neighborhood Sharks: Hunting With the Great Whites of California's Farallon Islands.*** David Macaulay Studio, 2014. (**PB**). Ages 7–10. (Food chain).

Schaefer, Lola. ***Just One Bite: 11 Animals and Their Bites at Life Size!*** Illus. Geoff Waring. Chronicle, 2010. (**PB**). Ages 5–9.

Schaefer, Lola. ***Lifetime: The Amazing Numbers in Animal Lives.*** Illus. Christopher Silas Neal. Chronicle, 2013. (**PB**). Ages 4–8.

Schwartz, David, and Yael Schy. ***Where in the Wild? Camouflaged Creatures Concealed—and Revealed.*** Illus. Dwight Kuhn. Tricycle, 2007. (**PB**). Ages 5–9. (poetry/information).

Siy, Alexandra. ***Sneeze!*** Photos Dennis Kunkel. Charlesbridge, 2007. Ages 9–18.

Turner, Pamela. ***Life on Earth—and Beyond.*** Charlesbridge, 2008. Ages 10–13.

Turner, Pamela. ***The Dolphins of Shark Bay.*** Photos Scott Tuason. Houghton, 2013. Ages 10–15. (Australia)

Turner, Pamela. ***Crow Smarts: Inside the Brain of the World's Brightest Bird.*** Houghton, 2016. Ages 10–15.

Wicks, Maris. ***Human Body Theater***. First Second, 2015. (**GR**). Ages 12–14. Also ***Coral Reefs: Cities of the Ocean*** (2016).

Physical Science

Arnosky, Jim. ***The Brook Book: Exploring the Smallest Streams.*** Dutton, 2008. (**PB**). Ages 5–9.

Burns, Loree. ***Tracking Trash: Flotsam, Jetsam, and the Science of Ocean Motion.*** Houghton, 2007. Ages 10–13.

Cherry, Lynne. ***How We Know What We Know about Our Changing Climate.*** Photo. Gary Braasch. Dawn, 2008.

Deem, James. ***Bodies from the Ice: Melting Glaciers and the Recovery of the Past.*** Houghton, 2008. Ages 10–14.

Floca, Brian. ***Moonshot: The Flight of Apollo 11.*** Atheneum, 2009. (**PB**). Ages 6–9.

Harbo, Christopher. ***The Explosive World of Volcanoes with Max Axiom, Super Scientist.*** Capstone, 2008. (**GR**). Ages 9–12.

Lyon, George Ella. ***All the Water in the World.*** Illus. Katherine Tillotson. Atheneum, 2011. (**PB**). Ages 5–9.

Ramstein, Anne-Margot, and Aregui, Matthias. ***Before After.*** Translated from French. Candlewick, 2014. (**PB**). Ages 6–10.

Rusch, Elizabeth. ***Eruption! Volcanoes and the Science of Saving Lives.*** Houghton, 2013. Ages 10–14. (Philippines, Indonesia)

Simon, Seymour. ***Seymour Simon's Extreme Earth Records.*** Chronicle, 2012. Ages 7–12.

Simon, Seymour. ***Destination: Mars.*** HarperCollins, 2016. (**PB**). Ages 6–10.

Strauss, Rochelle. ***One Well: The Story of Water on Earth.*** Illus. Rosemary Woods. Kids Can, 2007. (**PB**). Ages 9–14.

Thimmesh, Catherine. ***Team Moon: How 400,000 People Landed Apollo 11 on the Moon.*** Houghton Mifflin, 2015. Ages 10–14. (1969).

Webb, Sophie. ***Far from Shore: Chronicles of an Open Ocean Voyage.*** Houghton, 2011. Ages 10–14. (Eastern Pacific Ocean)

Applied Science

Burns, Loree Griffin. ***Citizen Scientists: Be a Part of Scientific Discovery from Your Own Backyard.*** Illus. Ellen Harasimowicz. Holt, 2012. Ages 8–14. (Field research).

Carson, Mary Kay. ***Exploring the Solar System: A History with 22 Activities.*** Chicago Review, 2006. Ages 10–14.

Cobb, Vicki. ***See for Yourself: More than 100 Amazing Experiments.*** Illus. Dave Klug. Skyhorse, 2010. Ages 9–12.

Curlee, Lynn. ***Capital.*** Atheneum, 2003. (**PB**). Ages 7–11. Also ***Parthenon*** (2004) and ***Skyscrapers*** (2007).

Farndon, John. ***Megafast Trucks.*** Illus. Mat Edwards. Hungry Tomato, 2016. Ages 8–12.

Flaherty, Michael, editor. ***See How They Work & Look Inside Diggers.*** Flowerpot Press, 2015. (**PB**). Ages 5–9.

Gardner, Robert. ***Chemistry Science Fair Projects Using Inorganic Stuff: Using the Scientific Method.*** Enslow, 2010. Ages 10–13.

Jenkins, Steve. ***Just a Second: A Different Way to Look at Time.*** Houghton, 2011. (**PB**). Ages 4–7.

Leedy, Loreen. ***The Great Graph Contest.*** Holiday, 2005. (**PB**). Ages 6–8.

Levine, Shar. ***The Ultimate Guide to Your Microscope.*** Sterling, 2008. Ages 9–12.

Macaulay, David. ***Built to Last.*** Houghton, 2010. Ages 10–15.

Macaulay, David. ***How Machines Work: Zoo Break!*** DK/Penguin, 2015. Ages 7–9.

Macaulay, David. ***The Way Things Work Now.*** Houghton, 2016. Ages 10–15.

Overdeck, Laura. ***Bedtime Math.*** Illus. Jim Paillot Holiday, 2013. Ages 3–7.

Paul, Miranda. ***One Plastic Bag: Isatou Ceesay and the Recycling Women of Gambia***. Illus. Elizabeth Zunon. Milbrook, 2015. Ages 5–9. (Gambia)

Rockliff, Mara. ***Mesmerized: How Ben Franklin Solved a Mystery That Baffled All of France.*** Illus. Iacopo Bruno. Candlewick, 2015. (**PB**). Ages 8–10. (Scientific process).

Roth, Susan L. ***The Mangrove Tree: Planting Trees to Feed Families.*** Lee & Low, 2011. (**PB**). Ages 6–9. (Eritrea)

Rusch, Elizabeth. ***The Mighty Mars Rovers: The Incredible Adventures of Spirit and Opportunity.*** Houghton, 2012. Ages 10–14.

Thimmesh, Catherine. ***Scaly Spotted Feathered Frilled: How Do We Know What Dinosaurs Really Looked Like?*** Houghton, 2013. Ages 11–13. (Process of paleontologists).

Walsh, Melanie. ***10 Things I Can Do To Help My World.*** Candlewick, 2008. (**PB**). Ages 5–8.

Social Science – United States

Bausum, Ann. ***Denied, Detained, Deported: Stories from the Dark Side of American Immigration.*** National Geographic, 2009. Ages 10–14.

Bolden, Tonya. ***Emancipation Proclamation: Lincoln and the Dawn of Liberty.*** Abrams, 2013. Ages 12–15. (1861–1865).

Brimner, Larry Dane. ***Birmingham Sunday.*** Calkins Creek, 2010. Ages 10–14. (Photo essay; church bombing, Alabama, 1963).

Brimner, Larry Dane. ***Strike! The Farm Workers' Fight for Their Rights.*** Calkins Creek, 2014. Ages 12–16. (1960s, Cesar Chavez).

Brown, Don. ***Drowned City: Hurricane Katrina & New Orleans.*** Houghton, 2015. (**GR**). Ages 12–18. (Hurricane, 2005).

Coy, John. ***Game Changer: John McLendon and the Secret Game.*** Illus. Randy DuBurke. Carolrhoda, 2015. (**PB**). Ages 7–11. (Basketball, race, 1944).

Coy, John. ***Their Great Gift: Courage, Sacrifice, and Hope in a New Land.*** Carolrhoda, 2016. (**PB**). Ages 5–9. (Contemporary immigration).

Floca, Brian. ***Lightship.*** Atheneum, 2007. (**PB**). Ages 5–7. (Early 1900s).

Floca, Brian. ***Locomotive.*** Atheneum, 2013. (**PB**). Ages 4–10. (1869, transcontinental railroad).

Fradin, Judith Bloom. ***The Price of Freedom: How One Town Stood Up to Slavery.*** Illus. Eric Velasquez. Walker, 2013. (**PB**). Ages 8–12. (Oberlin, Ohio, 1858)

Freedman, Russell. ***Kids at Work: Lewis Hine and the Crusade against Child Labor.*** Clarion, 1994. Ages 9–12. (Early 1900s).

Freedman, Russell. ***Who Was First? Discovering the Americas.*** Clarion, 2007. Ages 10–14. (Stone Age to 1492).

Freedman, Russell. ***Angel Island: Gateway to Gold Mountain.*** Clarion, 2013. Ages 9–14. (1892–1940).

Freedman, Russell. ***Because They Marched: The People's Campaign for Voting Rights That Changed America.*** Holiday House, 2014. Ages 12–17. (African American civil rights, Selma to Montgomery Rights March, 1965).

Hoose, Phillip. ***We Were There, Too! Young People in U.S. History.*** Farrar, 2001. Ages 10–13. (1492–1998).

Hopkinson, Deborah. ***Dive! World War II Stories of Sailors & Submarines in the Pacific.*** Scholastic, 2016. Ages 8–14. (WWII, 1941–1945)

Jarrow, Gail. ***Fatal Fever: Tracking Down Typhoid Mary.*** Calkins Creek, 2015. Ages 10–14. (1906, New York)

Levinson, Cynthia. ***We've Got a Job: The 1963 Birmingham Children's March.*** Peachtree, 2012. Ages 10–14. (1963, Alabama)

Macy, Sue. ***Wheels of Change: How Women Rode the Bicycle to Freedom.*** National Geographic, 2011. Ages 10–14. (Suffrage, late 1800s).

Murphy, Jim. ***An American Plague: The True and Terrifying Story of the Yellow Fever Epidemic of 1793.*** Clarion, 2003. Ages 9–14.

Murphy, Jim. ***The Giant and How He Humbugged America.*** Scholastic, 2012. Ages 10–14. (New York, 1869).

National Children's Book and Literary Alliance. ***Our White House: Looking In and Looking Out.*** Candlewick, 2008. (**COL**). Ages 9–13. (1792–2006).

Nelson, Kadir. ***We Are the Ship: The Story of the Negro League Baseball.*** Hyperion, 2008. (**PI**). Ages 9–13. (1920s–1940s).

Nelson, Scott. ***Ain't Nothing but a Man: My Quest to Find the Real John Henry.*** National Geographic, 2008. Ages 11–14.

Philip, Neil. ***The Great Circle: A History of the First Nations.*** Clarion, 2006. Ages 11–15. (1500–1900).

Rappaport, Doreen. ***Lady Liberty: A Biography.*** Illus. Matt Tavares. Candlewick, 2008. (**PB**). Ages 7–10. (1865–1886).

Rappaport, Doreen. ***Beyond Courage: The Untold Story of Jewish Resistance During the Holocaust.*** Candlewick, 2012. Ages 10–18. (1939–1945).

Sandler, Martin. ***Imprisoned: The Betrayal of Japanese Americans During World War II.*** Walker, 2013. (1939–1945).

St. George, Judith. ***So You Want to Be President?*** Illus. David Small. Philomel, 2012, updated. (**PB**). Ages 7–10. (1789-2010).

Stone, Tanya Lee. ***Courage Has No Color: The True Story of the Triple Nickles: America's First Black Paratroopers.*** Candlewick, 2013. Ages 10–18. (WWII, 1939–1945).

Walker, Sally. ***Written in Bone: Buried Lives of Jamestown and Colonial Maryland.*** Carolrhoda, 2009. Ages 12–15. (Colonial period)

Winters, Kay. ***Colonial Voices: Hear Them Speak.*** Illus. Larry Day. Dutton, 2008. Ages 9–12. (Boston, 1773)

Social Science – Global

Ajmera, Maya, Elise H. Derstine, and Cynthia Pon. ***What We Wear: Dressing Up Around the World.*** Photos. Charlesbridge, 2012. (**PB**). Ages 5–8.

Aleksandra, and Daniel Mizielinski. ***Maps.*** (**PB**). Candlewick, 2013. Ages 6–12. (Global)

Aronson, Marc, and Marina Budhos. ***Sugar Changed the World: A Story of Magic, Spice, Slavery, Freedom, and Science.*** Clarion, 2010. Ages 12–15. (10,000 years of history).

Barnard, Bryn. ***The Genius of Islam: How Muslims Made the Modern World.*** Knopf, 2011. (**PB**). Ages 10–14.

Bartoletti, Susan Campbell. ***Black Potatoes: The Story of the Great Irish Famine, 1845–1850.*** Houghton, 2001. Ages 12–16. (Ireland)

Bartoletti, Susan Campbell. ***Hitler Youth: Growing Up in Hitler's Shadow.*** Scholastic, 2005. Ages 11–14. (Nazis, Germany, 1939–1945).

Brown, Don. ***All Stations! Distress! April 15, 1912: The Day the Titanic Sank.*** Roaring Brook, 2008. (**PB**). Ages 6–12.

D'Aluisio, Faith, and Peter Menzel. ***What the World Eats.*** Tricycle, 2008. Ages 9–13.

Fleming, Candace. ***The Family Romanov: Murder, Rebellion, & the Fall of Imperial Russia.*** Schwartz & Wade, 2014. Ages 12–18. (Russia, early 1900s).

Freedman, Russell. ***The War to End All Wars: World War I.*** Clarion, 2010. Ages 12–18. (1914–1918).

Freedman, Russell. ***We Will Not Be Silent: The White Rose Student Resistance Movement That Defied Adolf Hitler.*** Clarion, 2016. Ages 10–14. (Germany, 1942–1943)

Hopkinson, Deborah. ***Titanic: Voices from the Disaster.*** Scholastic, 2012. Ages 8–16.

Hopkinson, Deborah. ***Courage & Defiance: Stories of Spies, Saboteurs, and Survivors in World War II Denmark.*** Scholastic, 2015. Ages 10–14. (WWII, Denmark).

Kennett, David. ***Pharaoh: Life and Afterlife of a God.*** Holtzbrinch, 2008. Ages 10–14. (Egypt, 1550–1070 BC).

Kerley, Barbara. ***One World, One Day.*** Photos. National Geographic, 2009. (**PB**). Ages 5–9.

Konrad, Marla. ***I Like to Play.*** Photos. Tundra, 2010. (**PB**). Ages 5–8. World Vision. (Global)

Mizielinska, Aleksandra, and Daniel Mizielinski ***Maps.*** (**PB**). Candlewick, 2013. Ages 6–12. (Global)

Murphy, Jim. ***Truce: The Day the Soldiers Stopped Fighting.*** Scholastic, 2009. Ages 10–14. (WWI, Europe, 1914).

O'Brien, Anne S. ***After Gandhi: One Hundred Years of Nonviolent Resistance.*** Charlesbridge, 2009. Ages 10–14. (1908–2003).

O'Brien, Tony, and Mike Sullivan. ***Afghan Dreams: Young Voices of Afghanistan.*** Bloomsbury, 2010. Ages 9–12. (Afghanistan, contemporary).

Robb, Don. ***Ox, House, Stick: The History of Our Alphabet.*** Illus. Anne Smith. Charlesbridge, 2007. (**PB**). Ages 9–12. (4,000 years to today).

Roth, Susan L. ***Hands around the Library: Protecting Egypt's Treasured Books.*** Dial, 2012. (**PB**). Ages 6–9. (Alexandria, Egypt, 2011).

Ruurs, Margriet. ***Families around the World.*** Illus. Jessica Rae Gordon. Kids Can Press, 2014. (**PB**). Ages 3–6. And ***School Days around the World*** (2015).

Schlitz, Laura. ***Good Masters! Sweet Ladies! Voices from a Medieval Village.*** Illus. Robert Byrd. Candlewick, 2007. Ages 9–13. (England, 1255)

Serres, Alain. ***I Have the Right to Be a Child.*** Illus. Aurélia Fronty. Trans. Helen Mixter. Groundwood, 2012. Ages 6-10. Translated from French. (Convention on the Rights of the Child).

Sheinkin, Steve. ***Bomb: The Race to Build and Steal the World's Most Dangerous Weapon.*** Roaring Brook, 2012. Ages 10–18. (WWII, nuclear bomb, spies, 1939–1945).

Shoveller, Herb. ***Ryan and Jimmy: And the Well in Africa that Brought Them Together.*** Kids Can, 2006. Ages 9–12. (Uganda).

Humanities

Ajmera, Maya. ***Music Everywhere!*** Charlesbridge, 2014. (**PB**). Ages 4–8.

Ancona, George. ***Ole! Flamenco.*** Lee & Low, 2010. Ages 9–12. (Photo essay).

Bryan, Ashley. ***Ashley Bryan's Puppets: Making Something from Everything.*** Atheneum, 2014. (**PB**). Ages 4–11.

Close, Chuck. ***Chuck Close: Face Book.*** Abrams, 2012. Ages 9–12.

Cummings, Pat, compiler–editor. ***Talking with Artists,*** Vols. 1, 2, 3. Bradbury, 1992, 1995, 1999. Ages 8–12.

Eric Carle Museum of Picture Book Art. ***Artist to Artist: 23 Major Illustrators Talk to Children about Their Art.*** Philomel, 2007. Ages 9–18.

Gerhard, Ana. ***Listen to the Birds: An Introduction to Classical Music.*** Illus. Cecilia Varela. The Secret Mountain, 2013. Ages 5–9. (Includes CD).

Greenberg, Jan, and Sandra Jordan. ***Ballet for Martha: Making Appalachian Spring.*** Illus. Brian Flores. Flash Point, 2010. (**PB**). Ages 9–12.

Helsby, Genevieve. ***Those Amazing Musical Instruments!*** Sourcebooks, 2007. Ages 9–14. (Includes CD).

Hill, Laban Carrick. ***When the Beat Was Born: DJ Kool Herc and the Creation of Hip Hop.*** Illus. Theodore Taylor. Roaring Brook, 2013. (**PB**). Ages 4–19. (1973–1986)

Hood, Susan. ***Ada's Violin: The Story of the Recycled Orchestra of Paraguay.*** Illus. Sally Wern Comport. Simon & Schuster, 2016. (**PB**). Ages 4–8. (Paraguay)

Lane, Kimberley. ***Come Look with Me: Latin American Art.*** Charlesbridge, 2007. Ages 10–14. Series includes African American, Asian, and American Indian art and women artists.

Levine, Gail Carson. ***Writing Magic: Creating Stories That Fly.*** HarperCollins, 2006. Ages 9–12.

National Gallery of Art. ***An Eye for Art: Focusing on Great Artists and Their Work.*** Chicago Review Press, 2013. Ages 7–12.

Pinkney, Andrea Davis. ***Rhythm Ride: A Road Trip through the Motown Sound.*** Roaring Brook, 2015. Ages 10–14. (Music, Detroit).

Salas, Laura Purdie. ***Catch Your Breath: Writing Poignant Poetry.*** Capstone Press, 2016. Ages 9–13.

Stringer, Lauren. ***When Stravinsky Met Nijinsky: Two Artists, Their Ballet, and One Extraordinary Riot.*** Harcourt, 2013. (**PB**). Ages 5–8. (Paris, 1913)

Sturm, James, Andrew Arnold, and Alexis Frederick-Frost. ***Adventures in Cartooning.*** First Second, 2009. Ages 9–12.

Sutcliffe, Jane. ***Will's Words: How William Shakespeare Changed the Way You Talk.*** Illus. John Shelley. Charlesbridge, 2016. (**PB**). Ages 7–10. (England, 1564–1616)

Thompson, Lauren. ***Ballerina Dreams.*** Photos James Estrin. Feiwel & Friends, 2007. (**PB**). Ages 5–8. (Cerebral palsy, dance).

Weatherford, Carole Boston. ***Freedom in Congo Square.*** Illus. R. Gregory Christie. Little Bee, 2016. (**PB**). Ages 6–9. (Music, dance, Louisiana, 1800s, slavery).

Related Films, Videos, and DVDs

Building Big. (2000, miniseries). Author: David Macaulay. 327 minutes.

Funny Bones: Posada and His Day of the Dead Calaveras. (2016). Author: Duncan Tonatiuh. 24 minutes.

Locomotive. (2014). Author: Brian Floca (2013). 23 minutes.

Magic School Bus. Author: Joanna Cole. 52 videos based on the book series, Scholastic videos online.

Voice of Freedom: Fannie Lee Hamer. (2016). Author: Carole Boston Weatherford (2015). 34 minutes.

What Do You Do with a Tail Like This? (2008). Authors: Robin Page and Steve Jenkins (2005). 8 minutes.

Chapter 12

Literature for a Diverse Society

All Mixed Up

What does multicultural mean?
Stuck in the middle
in between
all kinds of foods
and clothes
and talk?
Listening to bamboo flutes
play rock?
Turning tortillas
over the stove,
burning the tips
of chopsticks?

Why does my teacher love that word?
Is it something she ate—
or something she heard?
Loud drums
beating in the park?
Does she call me
multicultural
because my skin is
dark?

—Janet Wong

We live in a global society, filled with the richness of cultural diversity as well as the devastation of violence and racism. Literature can provide a pathway to understanding diverse ways of living, valuing our connections as human beings, and challenging inequities. The first part of this chapter, An Education That Is Multicultural and Intercultural, focuses on ways educators can make their curriculum relevant to children and to the interconnected world in which they live. The second part, Multicultural and International Literature, identifies literature that supports a culturally based curriculum.

Section One: An Education That Is Multicultural and Intercultural

A serious mismatch exists in U.S. schools today. School curricula and textbooks present predominantly mainstream European American perspectives. Moreover, the cadre of U.S. teachers is predominantly (83 percent) from European American suburban backgrounds (U.S. Department of Education, 2012). They have been taught to teach in ways that work best with people with similar backgrounds and often have not had close, sustained relationships with individuals from ethnic, cultural, and socioeconomic backgrounds that differ from their own. On the other hand, school populations in the United States are becoming increasingly diverse; 49 percent of the students in public schools during 2012 were children of color, indicating that the minority will soon become the majority (U.S. Department of Education, 2015).

The resulting mismatch has contributed to an education system that is not working for many students. The Office of National Assessment for Educational Progress reports a continuing reading achievement gap between whites and American Indians, Latinos, and African Americans. In 2015, 21 percent of white fourth-graders and 16 percent of Asian American fourth-graders scored below the basic level in reading, which stands in sharp contrast to the percentages for other ethnic groups—48 percent of African Americans, 45 percent of Latinos, and 48 percent of American Indians were below the basic level as fourth-graders and the numbers are much higher for those below proficiency (78–81 percent). Clearly, teachers need to become more familiar with the influence of culture on teaching and learning.

At the same time, U.S. classrooms are experiencing the largest influx of immigrants since the early 1900s, further increasing the diversity of students. More than 14 million immigrants settled in the United States between 2000 and 2010, coming from all parts of the world, with the majority from Mexico, China and Taiwan, India, Philippines, Vietnam, El Salvador, Cuba, and Korea (U.S. Census Bureau, 2010).

Educators in all parts of the country are increasingly likely to have students from diverse ethnic, racial, national, and language groups in their classrooms and libraries, whether in urban, suburban, or rural areas. This diversity is reflected in the global nature of our lives. Children will live and work in a world that is vastly different from the one in which we grew up. Rapid economic, technological, and social changes connect us across the globe. Knowledge of the world and of diverse cultures is no longer a luxury, but a necessity. Children need understandings of the diverse cultural groups within their own country and of global cultures outside of their borders.

An education that is multicultural and intercultural is one in which diverse cultural perspectives are woven throughout the curriculum and school life instead of being the focus of a special book or unit (Short, Day, & Schroeder, 2016). This orientation includes the following:

- Understanding one's own personal cultural identity
- Valuing the unique perspectives of cultural communities
- Connecting to the universal experiences that are shared across cultures
- Critiquing the inequities and injustices experienced by specific cultural groups
- Developing a commitment to taking action for a more just and equitable world

An education that is multicultural and intercultural is culturally responsive, culturally expansive, and culturally critical. Children's literature plays a crucial role by providing children with the opportunity to immerse themselves into story worlds and gain insights into how people feel, live, and think. They go beyond a tourist's perspective of simply gaining information about particular cultures to living *within* these cultures through their experiences with literature.

Culturally Responsive Curriculum

All children need to find their lives and cultural experiences reflected within classrooms and the books they read, but this is much more likely to occur for children from mainstream, European American families. Culturally responsive curriculum focuses on the need to develop teaching strategies and materials that are more consistent with the cultural orientations of ethnically and globally diverse students. Geneva Gay (2010) points out that using the cultural knowledge, experiences, frames of reference, and performance styles of ethnically diverse students makes learning more relevant and effective. You are culturally responsive when you:

- **Find reading materials that are relevant to children's lives.** To support all children as readers, you need to become personally acquainted with children and knowledgeable about books that are culturally relevant to their lives. For ethnically and globally diverse children this may be literature about young people whose lives and cultures are similar to their own. For second-language learners, this may be bilingual literature in the child's native tongue to make learning English easier and to signal the value of the child's first language. Children who rarely find their lives reflected in a book may dismiss literacy as irrelevant or even a threat to their identities.
- **Ensure that literature collections in libraries and classrooms reflect the cultural diversity of the community and world.** Even when local communities are culturally homogeneous, you should select books that reflect the diversity of the greater world. To do so, you need to access books from small presses that focus on specific ethnic groups and translated books originating from other countries.
- **Give children a choice in their reading material.** Giving children a choice in what they read acknowledges their lives and interests as significant and relevant within the classroom or library. Choice means providing access to less conventional formats, such as picturebooks for older readers, audiobooks, and graphic novels, as well as nonfiction materials such as manuals and magazines.
- **Conference with children about their reading as often as possible.** One-on-one discussions give you an opportunity to learn about children's reading interests and needs, express curiosity about their current reading, and suggest other books.

The search for culturally relevant literature recognizes that all children have multiple cultural identities, including gender, social class, family structure, age, religion, and language, as well as ethnicity and nationality. This broad understanding of culture as ways of living and being in the world that influence our actions, beliefs, and values is essential to understanding why culture matters in our lives. Culture influences how each of us thinks about ourselves and the world around us. Children from all cultures, including the mainstream, need to recognize that they have a particular perspective on the world before they can value, as well as critically examine, that perspective. This understanding, in turn, supports them in exploring other cultural perspectives.

Culturally Expansive Curriculum

A culturally expansive curriculum builds from awareness of children's own cultural identities to consider points of view that go beyond their own. Literature provides a window to ethnic and global cultures through in-depth inquiries into a particular culture and the integration of multiple cultural perspectives into units of inquiry.

An inquiry into a culture should include a range of books that reflects the diversity and complexity of that culture. In exploring Diné (Navajo) culture, for example, children can read historical fiction, such as *Little Woman Warrior Who Came Home* by Evangeline Parsons-Yazzie, along with traditional literature, such as *Ma'ii and Cousin Horned Toad* by Shonto Begay. They can examine contemporary life on the reservation in *Alice Yazzie's Year* by Ramona Maher and *Soldier Sister, Fly Home* by Nancy Bo Flood. One representation that is missing is contemporary books portraying Diné people living off the reservation. Engaging children with a range of representations challenges stereotypes and encourages them to examine the shared values and beliefs within a culture as well as the diversity of views and lives integral to every cultural community.

A culturally expansive curriculum becomes inclusive of multiple cultural perspectives across content areas through the integration of literature. The perspectives of those long neglected—American Indians,

Excellent International Literature to Read Aloud

Almond, David. *The Boy Who Climbed to the Moon.* Illustrated by Polly Dundar. Ages 8-11. (U.K.)

Brun-Cosme, Nadine. *Big Wolf and Little Wolf.* Ages 6–9. (France)

Chen, Zhiyuan. *Guji, Guji.* Ages 5–8. (Taiwan)

Das, Amrita. *Hope Is a Girl Selling Fruit.* Ages 10–14. (India)

Duman Tak, Bibi. *Soldier Bear.* Illustrated by Philip Hopman. Ages 9–12. (Poland)

Kobald, Irena. *My Two Blankets.* Illustrated by Freya Blackwood. Ages 6–9. (Australia)

Lagercrantz, Rose. *My Happy Life.* Illustrated by Eva Eriksson. Ages 6–10. (Sweden)

Lindelauf, Benny. *Nine Open Arms.* Ages 10–14. (Netherlands)

Skármeta, Antonio. *The Composition.* Illustrated by Alfonso Ruano. Ages 8–12. (Chile)

Yu, Li-Qiong. *A New Year's Reunion.* Illustrated by Zhu Cheng-Liang. Ages 6–9. (China)

African Americans, Latinos, and Asian Americans, to name a few—can be included in the social studies and history curriculum. Important contributions by scientists, such as Elijah McCoy, whose inventions revolutionized steam engines, and Gordon Soto, whose work with mangrove trees transformed an ecological system, can be included in the science curriculum. Works by authors who reflect a range of ethnic and global backgrounds can be included in the reading and literature curriculum. For example, a literature unit could focus on Francisco Jiménez, a Mexican American whose books describe the struggles of immigrants and their families who work in the California fields. One strategy is to read aloud one of the featured author's works while students discuss other books by that author in literature circles.

The goal of those who write, publish, and promote multicultural and global children's literature is to help young people learn about, understand, and ultimately accept those different from themselves, thus breaking the cycles of prejudice and oppression among peoples of different cultures. Progress toward this goal may well begin when young people read multicultural or global literature and realize how similar they are to children from cultures that differ from their own and how interesting those differences are. They are also challenged not to consider their own culture as the "norm" against which others are judged as strange or exotic. These books help build bridges and cross borders between people of different nationalities and cultures (Lehman, Freeman, & Scharer, 2010).

The books that are selected for read-alouds, booktalks, book displays, and text sets for independent reading or classroom studies should reflect the diversity of cultural experiences in the community as well as invite exploration of broader ethnic and global cultures. Booktalks, for example, might be used to connect children who read mainstream books with literature from a wider range of cultures that have a similar theme or genre. A collection of picturebooks on families, a common topic investigated in the primary grades, might include:

Families around the World by Margaret Ruirs, illustrated by Jessica Gordon (global)

I Love Saturdays y domingos by Alma Flor Ada, illustrated by Elivia Savadier (Mexican American, biracial)

Hot, Hot Roti for Dada-ji, F. Zia, illustrated by Ken Min (Indian American)

My Mei Mei by Ed Young (Chinese American, adoption)

Where's Jamela? by Niki Daly (South African)

A New Year's Reunion by Yu Li-Qiong, illustrated by Zhu Cheng-Liang (Chinese)

My Two Grannies by Floella Benjamin, illustrated by Margaret Chamberlain (British, biracial)

My Family Tree and Me by Dusan Petricic (Serbia)

Stella Brings the Family by Miriam Schiffer, illustrated by Holly Clifton-Brown (two fathers)

Culturally Critical Curriculum

Although multicultural education celebrates diversity and cross-cultural harmony, the more important goal has always been to transform society and ensure greater voice, equity, and social justice for marginalized groups (Gay, 2010). Raising issues of inequity, power, and discrimination is central to an education that is multicultural and intercultural. Paulo Freire (1970) believes that children can learn to critically read the world by questioning "what is" and "who benefits," instead of accepting inequity as the way things work in our society. Children use these questions to examine why these social problems exist and who benefits from keeping inequities in place. They also consider new possibilities by asking "what if" and taking action for social change. Through these questions, children develop a critical consciousness about their everyday world and the ways in which power plays out in their relationships and society.

Literature plays a significant role in social justice education by documenting the history and contemporary stories of marginalized peoples, presenting their perspectives, and providing a way for their voices to be heard. These perspectives are rarely included within textbooks and the standard curriculum. Literature supports children in considering multiple perspectives on complex social issues such as undocumented immigrants/refugees in *Friends from the Other Side* by Gloria Anzaldúa, *The Circuit* by Francisco Jiménez, *Two White Rabbits* by Jairo Buitrago and Rafael Yockteng, *Ask Me No Questions* by Maria Budhos, *A Time of Miracles* by Anne-Laure Bondoux, *The Bone Sparrow* by Zana Fraillion, and *The Arrival* by Shaun Tan.

A critical literacy or social justice curriculum has four dimensions (Lewison, Leland, & Harste, 2008), all of which can be supported by literature:

- Disrupting the commonplace by looking at the everyday through new lenses that challenge assumptions (e.g., *Stella Brings Her Family* by Miriam Schiffer, *Wringer* by Jerry Spinelli)
- Considering multiple perspectives that may be contradictory or offer alternative interpretations of history or current issues (e.g., *Voices in the Park* by Anthony Browne, *The London Jungle Book* by Bhajiu Shyam)
- Focusing on sociopolitical issues to examine societal systems and unequal power relationships and to get at the root causes of social problems (e.g., *The Good Garden* by Katie Smith Milway, *Looks like Daylight* by Deborah Ellis)
- Taking action and promoting social justice by taking a stand against oppression and acting to create change (e.g., *Maddi's Fridge* by Lois Brandt, *Moon Bear* by Gil Lewis)

Section Two: Multicultural and International Literature

Multicultural literature and international literature are not separate genres; rather, they cut across all genres. You will have noted many references to these books and authors throughout the previous genre chapters in discussions of trends and issues, notable author and illustrator lists, and recommended booklists. In an ideal, culturally integrated world, this integration of multicultural and international literature would be sufficient. But the groups and perspectives represented in multicultural literature have, until recently, been absent or misrepresented in books for children and remain underrepresented today. Furthermore, neither multicultural nor international literature is well known or fully recognized by teachers and librarians. These books are highlighted in this chapter so that they are not underrepresented in your classroom and library collections and engagements. Changing demographics in the United States and globalization of society mean that you will play a key role in preparing young people to live in a changing and ever more diverse world.

Definitions and Descriptions

Multicultural literature is sometimes defined broadly as all books about people and their individual or group experiences within a particular culture, including mainstream cultures. Usually it is defined more specifically as literature by and about groups that have been marginalized and disregarded by the dominant European American culture in the United States. This definition includes racial, ethnic, religious, and language minorities, those living with physical or mental disabilities, gays and lesbians, and people living in poverty. In this chapter, we highlight literature by and about the racial, religious, and language groups in the United States that have created a substantial body of children's literature. This includes literature by and about African Americans, Asian/Pacific Americans (including people of Chinese, Hmong, Japanese, Korean, and Vietnamese descent), Latinos (including Cuban Americans, Mexican Americans, Puerto Ricans, and others of Spanish descent), Americans of Arab and Persian heritage, religious cultures (including Buddhist, Hindu, Jewish, and Muslim), and American Indians (a general term referring to the many tribal nations in the United States).

Examples of books about other marginalized groups are found throughout the genre chapters, especially in the lists of recommended books. Books that highlight characters marginalized because of disability or sexual orientation are found in the chapter on realistic fiction.

- ***International literature*** in the United States refers to books that are set in countries outside of the United States. The focus of this chapter is on books originally written and published in other countries for children of those countries and then republished in this country. These books can be subdivided into three categories:
  - ***English language books.*** Books originally written in English in another country and then published or distributed in the United States. Examples include *How to Heal a Broken Wing* by Bob Graham (Australia) and the Harry Potter series (United Kingdom).
  - ***Translated books.*** Books written in a language other than English in another country, then translated into English and published in the United States. Examples include *Hope Is a Girl Selling Fruit* by Amrita Das (India) and *Inkheart* by Cornelia Funke (Germany).
  - ***Foreign language books.*** Books written and published in a language other than English in another country, then published or distributed in the United States in that language. One example is *Le Petit Prince* by Antoine de Saint-Exupéry (France).

Many authors and illustrators of books set in international contexts are from the United States. These books are written and published in the United States primarily for an audience of U.S. children rather than written for children of that specific culture. These books, often referred to as ***global literature,*** have been integrated into other chapters so are not highlighted in this chapter. Categories of global literature include:

- Books written by immigrants from another country who now reside in the United States and write about their country of origin; for example, *The Keeping Corner* by Kashmira Sheth (India).
- Books written by authors who move between global cultures on a regular basis, such as Baba Wagué Diakité who lives in the United States and regularly spends time in Mali, his culture of origin.
- Books written by American authors who draw from their family's heritage in their country of origin but whose own experiences have been in the United States; for example, *When My Name Was Keoko* by Linda Sue Park (Korea).
- Books written by an author who lived in another country for a significant amount of time; for example, *Colibrí* by Ann Cameron (Guatemala).
- Books written by authors who research a particular country and who may or may not have visited that country as part of their research; for example, *This Thing Called the Future* by J. L. Powers (South Africa).
- Books written by an author in collaboration with someone from that culture; for example, *Four Feet, Two Sandals* by Karen Lynn Williams and Khadra Mohammed (Pakistan).

The Value of Multicultural and International Literature

Multicultural and international literature builds bridges of understanding across countries and cultures, connecting children to their home cultures and to the world beyond their homes. This literature benefits children in the following ways:

- Gives young people who are members of marginalized groups or recent immigrants the opportunity to develop a better sense of who they are and of their agency.
- Develops an understanding of and appreciation for diverse cultures, bringing alive those histories, traditions, and people.
- Addresses contemporary issues of race, religion, poverty, exceptionalities, and sexual orientation from the perspectives of members of those groups to provide a more complete understanding of current issues and of the people who belong to these groups, thus challenging prejudice and discrimination.
- Adds the perspective of marginalized groups and global cultures to the study of history, thereby giving children a more complete understanding of past events.

- Helps young people realize the social injustices endured by particular peoples in the United States and around the world, both now and in the past, to build a determination to work for a more equitable future.
- Builds children's interest in the people and places they are reading about and paves the way to a deeper understanding and appreciation of the geographical and historical content encountered in textbooks and later content-area studies.
- Provides authenticity through literature written by insiders to a country, region, or ethnic group and allows members of that group to define themselves. These portrayals challenge the typical media coverage of violence and crises.
- Develops a bond of shared experience with children of other ethnicities and nations and enables them to acquire cultural literacy with a global perspective.

Although textbooks can provide children with information about a country, literature invites them into the world of children from that culture and provides rich details about daily life, human emotions, and relationships, answering the questions that are significant to children. The textbook may provide facts about the country, but novels about the country show the implications of the facts for children's lives and help readers "live in" the country for a time (Lehman, Freeman, & Scharer, 2010).

Evaluation and Selection of Multicultural and International Literature

In addition to the requirement that literature have high literary merit, multicultural and international books need to be examined for ***cultural authenticity:*** the extent to which a book reflects the core beliefs and values and depicts the details of everyday life and language for a specific cultural group. Given the diversity within all cultural groups, there is never one image of life within any culture, and so underlying world views are often more important to consider. Readers from the culture depicted in a book need to be able to identify and feel affirmed that what they are reading rings true in their lives; readers from another culture need to be able to identify and learn something of value about cultural similarities and differences (Fox & Short, 2003). The following criteria should be considered when evaluating and selecting multicultural and international books for libraries and classrooms:

- **Authenticity of cultural beliefs and values from the perspective of that group.** Research the background of the author and illustrator to determine their experiences or research related to this story (e.g., check their websites). Examine the values and beliefs of characters and whether they connect to the actual lives of people from that culture.
- **Accuracy of cultural details in text and illustrations.** Examine the details of everyday life, such as food, clothing, homes, and speech patterns, represented in the book and whether they fit within the range of experiences of that culture.
- **Integration of culturally authentic language.** Look for the natural integration of the language or dialect of a specific cultural group, especially within dialogue. Some terms or names in the original language of translated books, for example, should be retained. Check whether a glossary is included if needed.
- **Power relationships between characters.** Examine which characters are in roles of power or significance in a book, with a particular focus on how the story is resolved and who is in leadership and action roles.
- **Perspectives and audience.** Look at whose perspectives and experiences are portrayed and who tells the story. In particular, consider whether the story is told from a mainstream or European American perspective *about* ethnically or globally diverse characters. Also consider whether the intended audience is children from within that culture or if the book was written to inform a mainstream audience about a culture.
- **Balance between historic and contemporary views of groups.** The majority of literature about global and ethnic cultures is found in the genres of traditional literature and historical fiction, creating stereotypes of these cultures as dated and set in the past. Search for books that reflect contemporary images.
- **Adequate representation of any group within a collection.** No one book can definitively describe a culture or cultural experience. Look for a range of books that provide multiple representations of a

culture and be aware of particular images that are overrepresented—for example, almost all of the picturebooks on Korean Americans depict them as newly arrived immigrants to the United States and most books depict the Middle East as a rural landscape of sand and camels. These overrepresentations reflect and create stereotypes of a particular group and do not reflect the diversity of experiences within that group.

Book awards can guide teachers and librarians toward high-quality multicultural and international books. The best known of these is the Coretta Scott King Award, given annually to an African American author and illustrator whose books are judged to be the most outstanding inspirational and educational literature for children. The Américas Award and the Pura Belpré Award, which honor outstanding Latino authors and illustrators of children's books, are good resources for locating authentic literature across Latino contexts. Other awards include the Asian/Pacific American Award for Literature, honoring outstanding work of Asian American authors and illustrators, and the American Indian Youth Literature Award, honoring the best writing and illustrations by and about American Indians. Awards such as these encourage the publication of more and better quality literature highlighting the experiences of diverse cultures.

Awards for international literature are plentiful. The Mildred L. Batchelder Award is given to a U.S. publisher of the most distinguished translated children's book, thus encouraging the translation and publication of international books in the United States (see Appendix A). The Outstanding International Books List (www.usbby.org) and Notable Books for a Global Society (http://www.clrsig.org/nbgs.php) are annual award lists. Also, many countries have their own national awards, similar to the Newbery and Caldecott awards in the United States. The Hans Christian Andersen award winners and nominees are a good source of the most outstanding authors and illustrators from around the world (www.ibby.org). Worlds of Words (www.wowlit.org) has a searchable database of global and international literature available in the United States and several online journals with book reviews of cultural authenticity and vignettes on global literature in classrooms.

In addition, small presses have become a source of multicultural and international books that are particularly valuable for their cultural points of view.

Asian American Curriculum Project. Publishes and distributes Asian American books from small presses. www.asianamericanbooks.com. (Also see Asia for Kids at www.afk.com).

Cinco Puntos. Focuses on stories of the U.S.–Mexico border region, the Southwest, and Mexico. www.cincopuntos.com.

Piñata Books/Arte Público. Publishes children's books with a Latino perspective, including bilingual books. https://artepublicopress.com/about-pinata-books-2/.

Just Us Books. Produces Afrocentric books that enhance the self-esteem of African American children. www.justusbooks.com.

Lee & Low Books. Asian American–owned small press. Stresses authenticity in stories for Asian American, Latino, and African American children. Includes the Children's Book Press imprint. www.leeandlow.com.

Oyate. Evaluates books with Native themes and distributes books, particularly those written and illustrated by Native people. Native American evaluators and organization. www.oyate.org.

Salina Bookshelf. Small press with a focus on the Diné tribe. http://www.salinabookshelf.com.

Evaluating and selecting multicultural and international literature for your classroom or library, although essential, is not enough to ensure that children will actually read the books. Without adult guidance, children tend to choose books about children like themselves, so invite them to explore these books through reading the books aloud, giving booktalks, and encouraging discussion in literature circles.

Multicultural Literature

Historical Overview of Multicultural Literature

Many cultures living in the United States were ignored within children's books or portrayed as crudely stereotyped characters, objects of ridicule, or shadowy secondary characters. Books with blatant racism, such as Helen Bannerman's *The Story of Little Black Sambo* (1900) and Hugh Lofting's *The*

MILESTONES in the Development of Multicultural Literature

Date	Event	Significance
1932	*Waterless Mountain* by Laura Armer wins Newbery Medal	One of few books about people of color in early 1900s
1946	*The Moved-Outers* by Florence C. Means wins Newbery Honor	Challenges stereotyped depictions of people of color
1949	*Story of the Negro* by Arna Bontemps wins Newbery Honor	First author of color to win a Newbery Honor
1950	*Song of the Swallows* by Leo Politi wins Caldecott Medal	First picturebook with a Latino protagonist to win the Caldecott
1963	*The Snowy Day* by Ezra Jack Keats wins Caldecott Medal	First picturebook with an African American protagonist to win the Caldecott
1965	"The All-White World of Children's Books" by Nancy Larrick	Called attention to the lack of multicultural literature
1969	Coretta Scott King Award founded	Promotion of African American literature and authors
1975	*M. C. Higgins, the Great* by Virginia Hamilton wins Newbery Medal	First book by an author of color to win the Newbery
1976	*Why Mosquitoes Buzz in People's Ears* illustrated by Leo and Diane Dillon wins Caldecott	First picturebook by an African American illustrator to win the Caldecott
1990	*Lon Po Po: A Red-Riding Hood Story from China* by Ed Young wins Caldecott Medal	First picturebook by a Chinese American illustrator to win the Caldecott
1993	Américas Award founded	Encouraged publication of books portraying Latinos globally
1994	*Grandfather's Journey* written and illustrated by Allen Say wins Caldecott Medal	First picturebook by a Japanese American illustrator to win the Caldecott
1996	Pura Belpré Award founded	Promotes Latino literature, authors, and illustrators

Voyages of Dr. Dolittle (1922), have either been rewritten to eliminate the racism or have disappeared from libraries.

The first indication of change came in 1949 when an African American author, Arna Bontemps, became the first author of color to win a Newbery Honor Award, for *Story of the Negro.* A more sympathetic attitude toward diverse ethnic cultures emerged in the 1950s through the positive, yet still patronizing, treatment of multicultural characters in Newbery Medal books such as *Amos Fortune, Free Man* by Elizabeth Yates (1950) and *... And Now Miguel* by Joseph Krumgold (1953).

The civil rights movement of the 1960s focused attention on the social inequities and racial injustices that prevailed in the United States and resulted in two landmark publications. The first of these was *The Snowy Day* by Ezra Jack Keats (1962), the first Caldecott Medal book with an African American protagonist. The second publication was a powerful article in 1965 by Nancy Larrick, "The All-White World of Children's Books," which reported that African Americans were omitted entirely or scarcely mentioned in nearly all U.S. children's books. American trade book publishers, the education system, and the public library system were called on to fill this void.

The Coretta Scott King Award was established in 1969 to recognize African American authors, but it was not until 1975 that an author of color, Virginia Hamilton, won a Newbery Medal. The prevailing opinion among U.S. children's book publishers and professional reviewers shifted to focus on members of a group as the ones most able to write authentically about their own cultures and experiences. European American authors were no longer as likely to win major awards for writing about children of color as they were in the early 1970s.

The late 1990s saw the long overdue development of Latino literature. Bilingual books published in response to the demands of ESOL/ELL (English for speakers of other languages/English language learners) programs, and the founding of the Américas Award and the Pura Belpré Awards contributed to this growth.

Although the past several decades have seen positive changes in the status of multicultural literature in the United States, there is still a marked shortage of books and of authors and illustrators from within those cultures. The Cooperative Children's Book Center (Horning, Lindgren, & Schliesman, 2016) reported the following statistics based on their review of approximately 3,400 new children's and young adult books in 2015:

- 7.6 percent (259 books) had significant African or African American content (89 were by Black authors and/or illustrators)
- 3.3 percent (115 books) had significant Asian/Pacific or Asian/Pacific American content (41 were created by authors and/or illustrators of Asian/Pacific heritage)
- 2.4 percent (84 books) had significant Latino content (39 were created by Latino authors and/or illustrators)
- 1.2 percent (41 books) featured American Indian themes, topics, or characters (18 were created by American Indian authors and/or illustrators)

A broader indication of the shortage is that approximately 14 percent of the new books published for children in 2015 were by or about people of color, even though these groups represent 49 percent of the children currently in U.S. schools (U.S. Department of Education, 2015). Another problematic indicator is that the number of books depicting people of color steadily decreased from 2008 to 2013, with only 7 percent in 2013, leading to a huge outcry and many new initiatives that resulted in the current 14 percent. One of those initiatives, WeNeedDiverseBooks, is a grassroots organization that advocates for change in the publishing industry to produce and promote more books featuring diverse characters.

In addition to not enough books, subtle issues of racism and stereotypes continue to be problematic. All children have the right to see themselves within a book and to find the truth of their experiences, rather than misrepresentations. Many challenges remain in the writing and publication of multicultural literature.

Types of Multicultural Literature

Each ethnic group contains subgroups that differ from one another in country of origin, language, race, traditions, and present location. You will need to be conscious of and sensitive to these differences and guard against presenting these groups as uniform or selecting literature that does so. Gross overgeneralization is not only inaccurate but also a form of stereotyping.

African American Literature Of all marginalized groups living in the United States, African Americans have produced the largest and most rapidly growing body of children's literature (Bishop, 2007). Every genre is well represented, but none better than poetry, such as *The Blacker the Berry* by Joyce Carol Thomas and *Sweethearts of Rhythm* by Marilyn Nelson. Because it is so personal, poetry digs deep within a culture, as is evident in the sensitive yet powerful work of Nikki Giovanni, Nikki Grimes, Eloise Greenfield, Langston Hughes, Marilyn Nelson, and Joyce Carol Thomas. Jacqueline Woodson's moving childhood memoir, *Brown Girl Dreaming,* reflects a current trend toward writing novels in verse.

Tapping into rich oral traditions, African Americans have contributed Anansi the Spider, Brer Rabbit, and John Henry as favorite folklore characters. African Americans have reclaimed their tales by retelling (without racist elements) stories that were first written by European American authors, as in Julius Lester's retelling of Joel Chandler Harris's *The Tales of Uncle Remus*. Authors also create original folktales, combining history and legends in books like *Porch Lies* by Patricia McKissack.

African Americans have told the stories of their lives in the United States through both historical and realistic fiction. The stories for older readers often include painfully harsh accounts of racial oppression, as in *Elijah of Buxton* by Christopher Paul Curtis and Mildred Taylor's historical fiction saga of the close-knit Logan family, including *Roll of Thunder, Hear My Cry.* Contemporary novels, such as Jacqueline Woodson's *Locomotion* and Kwame Alexander's *The Crossover*, depict current issues and struggles of more subtle racism.

Many picturebooks focus on historical events, particularly slavery or civil rights, but the range of topics is expanding, as evidenced in books such as *Looking like Me* by Walter Dean Myers, illustrated by Christopher Myers, and Matt de la Peña's *Last Stop on Market Street*, illustrated by Christian Robinson. Outstanding illustrators include Leo and Diane Dillon, Jerry Pinkney, Brian Pinkney, E. B. Lewis, Bryan Collier, Kadir Nelson, Floyd Cooper, and Christian Robinson.

African American nonfiction consists of primarily informational books on the civil rights era, such as Elizabeth Partridge's *Marching for Freedom*, and biographies featuring a broader spectrum of achievement,

Notable Authors and Illustrators of Multicultural Literature

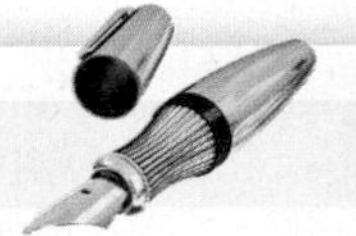

African American

Floyd Cooper, illustrator of picturebooks on African American history, oil erasure process. *The Blacker the Berry; A Dance like Starlight; These Hands; Brick by Brick.* http://www.floydcooper.com/

Leo and Diane Dillon, illustrators of two Caldecott Medal books. Leo was the first African American to win a Caldecott Medal. *Why Mosquitoes Buzz in People's Ears; Ashanti to Zulu.*

Patricia McKissack, author of modern African American folktales and historical books. *Goin' Someplace Special; Best Shot in the West: The Adventures of Nat Love; Porch Lies.*

Walter Dean Myers, author of realistic fiction about difficult issues in urban settings. Many of his picturebooks are illustrated by his son, Christopher Myers. *Scorpions; The Cruisers; Looking Like Me; We Are America.* www.walterdeanmyers.net

Kadir Nelson, illustrator/author of historical picturebooks with dramatic expressive paintings. *We Are the Ship; Henry's Freedom Box; Heart and Soul.* www.kadirnelson.com

Mildred Taylor, award-winning author of historical fiction about growing up black in the 1940/1950s South. *Roll of Thunder, Hear My Cry; Song of the Trees; The Gold Cadillac.*

Rita Williams-Garcia, author of award-winning historical fiction about three sisters, set in late 1960s. *One Crazy Summer; P.S. Be Eleven; Gone Crazy in Alabama.*

Jacqueline Woodson, author of introspective novels dealing with adversity and loss. *Brown Girl Dreaming; Locomotion; The Other Side; Show Way.* www.jacquelinewoodson.com

Asian/Pacific American

Cynthia Kadohata, author of realistic and historical fiction about Japanese American experiences. *Kira-Kira* (Newbery Medal); *Weedflower; The Thing About Luck* (National Book Award). http://cynthiakadohata.com/

Grace Lin, author/illustrator of picturebooks and novels on Taiwanese American experiences and Chinese traditional literature. *Where the Mountain Meets the Moon; The Year of the Dog*; *Ling & Ting.* http://www.gracelin.com

Linda Sue Park, author of historical and realistic fiction about Korean and Korean American experiences. *Keeping Score; When My Name Was Keoko; The Single Shard.* www.lindasuepark.com

Allen Say, illustrator/author of picturebooks on the cultural struggles of Japanese American and Japanese characters; uses evocative watercolors. *Grandfather's Journey; Drawing from Memory* (memoir); *The Favorite Daughter.*

Kashmira Sheth, author of historical and realistic fiction about India and Indian Americans. *Keeping Corner; Sona and the Wedding Game; My Dadima Wears a Sari.* http://kashmirasheth.com/

Latino

Francisco Jiménez, author of autobiographical stories on his experiences as an undocumented Mexican farm worker. *The Circuit; Breaking Through; Reaching Out.*

Rafael López, illustrator with a graphic style and visual symbols based in Mexican traditions. *Book Fiesta; Tito Puente; Maybe Something Beautiful.* www.rafaellopez.com

Yuyi Morales, illustrator/author of picturebooks combining storytelling and images from Mexican traditions. *Just in Case; Viva Frida; Niño Wrestles the World.* www.yuyimorales.com

Pam Muñoz Ryan, author of novels drawn from her Mexican American heritage and background in bilingual education. *Becoming Naomi Leon; Esperanza Rising.* www.pammunozryan.com

Duncan Tonatiuh, illustrator/author of picturebooks on Mexican and Mexican American experiences, digital collages with ancient Mexican art influences. *Pancho Rabbit and the Coyote; Separate Is Never Equal; Funny Bones.* http://www.duncantonatiuh.com/

American Indian

Sherman Alexie, Spokane/Coeur d'Alene author of realistic fiction of Native experiences. *The Absolutely True Diary of a Part-Time Indian; Thunder Boy, Jr.* http://fallsapart.com/

Joseph Bruchac, Abenaki author of historical novels and traditional literature. *Talking Leaves; The Hunter's Promise; Code Talker.* www.josephbruchac.com

Louise Erdrich, author of historical fiction about an Ojibwa tribe on Lake Superior. *The Birchbark House; The Game of Silence; The Porcupine Year.*

S. D. Nelson, illustrator/author of traditional and historical Lakota picturebooks. *Black Elk's Vision; Sitting Bull; Walking on Earth and Touching the Sky.* www.sdnelson.net

Religious Cultures

Eric Kimmel, author of traditional literature based in Jewish traditions and global cultures. *Wonders and Miracles: The Passover Companion; The Golem's Latkes.* www.ericakimmel.com

Asma Mobin-Uddin, Pakistani American author of picturebooks about Muslim American experiences and Islamic religious traditions. *My Name Is Bilal; A Party in Ramadan.* www.asmamobinuddin.com

such as *Best Shot in the West: The Adventures of Nat Love* by Pat McKissack. Kadir Nelson's *Heart and Soul* combines historical information and biography to create powerful narratives and dramatic images depicting the contributions of African Americans to the history of America. Charles Smith's *28 Days: Moments in Black History That Changed the World* grew out of his frustration at hearing the same Black History stories year after year.

American Indian Literature Almost from the moment that European explorers landed in North America some 500 years ago, American Indians suffered at the hands of European Americans. Consequently, books written from an American Indian perspective often focus on oppression and racism, ranging from historical novels, such as *Talking Leaves* by Joseph Bruchac, to contemporary novels, such as *The Absolutely True Diary of a Part-Time Indian* by Sherman Alexie, and picturebooks, such as the Canadian *Shin-Chi's Canoe* by Nicola I. Campbell, illustrated by Kim LaFave. Appreciation, celebration, and protection of nature are also recurrent themes in books such as *Walking on Earth and Touching the Sky,* a collection of writing by Lakota youth, edited by Timolthy McLaughlin and illustrated by S. D. Nelson.

Although much has been written about American Indians, relatively little has been written by members of these cultures, so this body of literature is dominated by outsider perspectives and issues of authenticity. Another imbalance is that the majority of books continue to be traditional literature and historical fiction, with few contemporary books to challenge stereotypes that American Indians lived "long ago." A further issue is that many tribal nations have few or no children's books available about their specific nation, while others, such as the Diné (Navajos), have a larger body of work. Small tribal presses are producing books for their own children, but many of these are difficult to access. Oyate (www.oyate.org) provides an online catalog of books from small tribal presses.

American Indians who are known for their children's books include Joseph Bruchac for his historical and realistic novels and retold stories, Tim Tingle for his retold stories, and S. D. Nelson and Shonto Begay for their illustrations.

Arab American and Persian American Literature Americans of Arabic or Persian heritage are often called Muslim Americans, a term that refers to people who follow the religion of Islam and includes people from every region of the world. More accurate terms are Persian Americans, who trace their heritage to Iran, and Arab Americans, who trace their heritage to the Arab world, including North Africa and the Middle East. This body of literature continues to be small, with contemporary books, such as the Pakistani Canadian picturebook *Big Red Lollipop* by Rukhsana Khan, the Afghan American novel *Saving Kabul Corner* by N. H. Senzai, and the Iranian American novel *It Ain't So Awful, Falafel* by Firoozeh Dumas. Not surprisingly many of the novels focus on the fear and intolerance encountered by the characters, who find themselves taunted as terrorists.

Because the Islamic faith is so integral to the lives of people from Arab and Persian heritage, some books focus on religious practices such as Ramadan, the wearing of the hijab, or prayer. Asma Mobin-Uddin's *My Name Is Bilal* is a picturebook for older readers, illustrated by Barbara Kiwak, which explores fitting into the mainstream while remaining true to Islamic beliefs. Maha Addasi's *Time to Pray,* a picturebook for younger readers, focuses on a young Muslim girl who visits her grandmother and learns the rituals for prayer.

Asian/Pacific American Literature Asian American and Pacific American children's literature consists primarily of stories about Chinese Americans, Japanese Americans, and Korean Americans, possibly because these groups have lived in the United States longer than others. A major theme in much of the fiction for older readers is the oppression that drove the people out of their homelands or the prejudice and adjustments that they faced as newcomers in this country. More recently, books have focused on bicultural identify, learning to appreciate one's cultural heritage, as well as developing a strong identity as an American, such as Thanhha Lai's *Inside Out and Back Again* and Wendy Wan Long Shang's *The Great Wall of Lucy Wu.*

Traditional stories from Asia retold in English have contributed many interesting folktales, such as Yumi Heo's *Lady Hahn and Her Seven Friends*. Characters who are generally thought of as European, such as Little Red Riding Hood and Cinderella, have their Asian counterparts, as exemplified in *Lon Po Po: A Red-Riding Hood Story from China,* translated and illustrated by Ed Young, and *Yeh-Shen: A Cinderella Story from China* by Ai-Ling Louie, illustrated by Ed Young.

Excellent Multicultural Literature to Read Aloud

Alexie, Sherman. *Thunder Boy Jr.* Illustrated by Yuyi Morales. Ages 4–6. (American Indian).

Brown, Monica. *Marisol McDonald Doesn't Match.* Illustrated by Sara Palacios. Ages 5–8. (Biracial)

Curtis, Christopher Paul. *The Watsons Go to Birmingham—1963.* Ages 9–12. (African American)

García, Christina. *I Wanna Be Your Shoebox.* Ages 8–11. (Jewish, Latina)

Kadahota, Cynthia. *Weedflower.* Ages 11–14. (Japanese American)

Look, Lenore. *Alvin Ho: Allergic to Girls, School, and Other Scary Things.* Ages 9–12. (Chinese American)

Morales, Yuyi. *Niño Wrestles the World.* Ages 5–8. (Mexican American)

Myers, Walter Dean. *Looking Like Me.* Illustrated by Christopher Myers. Ages 6–9. (African American)

Sheth, Kashmira. *Sona and the Wedding Game.* Illustrated by Yoshiko Jaeggi. Ages 6–9. (Indian American)

Williams-Garcia, Rita. *One Crazy Summer.* Ages 11–14. (African American).

Asian American artists have brought the sophisticated style and technical artistry of Asia to their illustrations. Ed Young's use of screenlike panels and exotic, textured paper and Allen Say's precision in his oil paintings are noteworthy in *My Mei Mei* by Ed Young and *Grandfather's Journey* by Allen Say. Both have also written picturebook autobiographies of their childhoods.

The body of Asian/Pacific American children's literature is rapidly expanding, particularly in realistic and historical fiction, through authors such as Linda Sue Park, Cynthia Kadohata, Lenore Look, Grace Lin, and Kashmira Sheth, and with a recent focus on books from India. The Asian/Pacific American Award for Literature, along with small presses and distributors, has also expanded this body of literature. The Pacific is still not represented well, although Hawai'i has a history of small presses and traditional literature. A notable recent Hawaiian title is *Surfer of the Century* by Ellie Crowe, illustrated by Richard Waldrep.

Latino Literature Few Latino children's books are published in the United States despite the fact that Latinos represent an estimated 13 percent of the population and are considered the fastest-growing segment of the population (U.S. Census Bureau, 2010). The books that are available mainly focus on the experiences of Mexican Americans and Puerto Ricans, with a few books based on Cuban American experiences. This body of literature continues to be filled with stereotyped portrayals of Latinos living in poverty and struggling to learn English. Many of the books focus on surface aspects of culture, such as festivals and food, rather than the everyday lives of Latino children. One positive trend is the integration of Spanish phrases and words into books written in English to reflect the cognitively complex code-switching of bilingual speakers.

One exciting development is the number of outstanding Latino authors and illustrators who are creating books for children, including Alma Flor Ada, Yuyi Morales, Francisco Jiménez, Juan Felipe Herrera, Maya Christina González, Monica Brown, Pam Muñoz Ryan, Duncan Tonatiuh, Raúl Colón, Rafael López, and Margarita Engle. Their books include *Niño Wrestles the World* by Yuyi Morales, *Becoming Naomi Leon* by Pam Muñoz Ryan, and *Marisol McDonald Doesn't Match* by Monica Brown.

The Américas Award (honoring a U.S. work that authentically presents Latino experiences in Latin America, the Caribbean, or the United States) and the Pura Belpré Award (honoring outstanding Latino authors and illustrators) promote high-quality Latino literature. A recent book on Latino literature by Clark, Flores, Smith, and Gonzalez (2015) references current issues and books as well as uses in the classroom.

Religious Cultures Literature Christianity dominates children's books as the mainstream religious culture in the United States. Books that portray other religious cultures, including Buddhist, Hindu, Jewish, and Muslim cultures, are difficult to find. Contemporary children's fiction set within the context of a religious culture and written from the perspective of a member of that religion is especially scarce. Nonfiction and folklore on religion are somewhat more plentiful. Demi is known for her picturebook biographies about Buddha and Muhammad.

The body of Jewish children's literature is by far the largest produced by any nonmainstream religious culture in the United States and mainly focuses on the Jewish Holocaust in Europe during the 1930s and 1940s. The racism that led to the Holocaust and the death camps are recurring themes in fiction and nonfiction for older readers. Because many Jewish people immigrated to the United States as the Nazi threat grew in Europe, much of the Holocaust literature is written by eyewitnesses or authors who base their stories on real people and events, such as *Black Radishes* by Susan Meyer and *Always Remember Me* by Marisabina Russo. A recent trend is Holocaust novels set in other parts of the world, such as *Tropical Secrets: Holocaust Refugees in Cuba* by Margarita Engle and *A Faraway Island* by Annika Thor about Jewish children sent to Sweden.

Illustrated Jewish folktales offer witty stories of high literary quality to complement the strong informational books about Jewish holidays and traditions. One concern is the lack of picturebooks and novels reflecting contemporary Jewish American experiences, although a few are emerging, such as *Gathering Sparks* by Howard Schwartz and *I Wanna Be Your Shoebox* by Cristina García. Barry Deutsch's *Hereville: How Mirka Got Her Sword* is particularly interesting as a graphic novel fantasy about a modern Orthodox Jewish girl who wants to fight dragons.

The Jewish community has promoted literary excellence through the National Jewish Book Awards and the Association of Jewish Libraries' Sydney Taylor Awards.

Bilingual Literature ***Bilingual books*** provide the text in two languages, frequently English/Spanish to reflect the rapid growth of the Latino population in the United States. Picturebooks and shorter chapter books predominate because longer books in two languages would be bulky and costly and are not useful for advanced readers. These books are helpful to children in ESOL/ELL and world language programs. They also provide a way to value and maintain literacy in a child's first language. However, not all bilingual books have artful or even accurate translations, so careful selection is advisable. The concept book *My Colors, My World/Mis colores, mi mundo* by Maya Christina González involves a child's search for the colors hidden in her desert environment through poetic text in English and Spanish. A few bilingual books reflecting Asian languages, such as *Cooper's Lesson* by Sun Yung Song, in Korean/English, are also being published.

MILESTONES in the Development of International Children's Literature

Date	Event	Significance
1697	*Tales of Mother Goose* by Charles Perrault	Earliest folktales from France
1719/ 1726	*Robinson Crusoe* by Daniel Defoe/ *Gulliver's Travels* by Jonathan Swift	Two early adult adventure books from England adopted by children
1812	*Nursery and Household Tales* by Jacob and Wilhelm Grimm	Traditional folktales from Germany
1836	*Fairy Tales* by Hans Christian Andersen	Early modern folktales from Denmark
1846	*Book of Nonsense* by Edward Lear	Early humorous poetry from England
1865	*Alice's Adventures in Wonderland* by Lewis Carroll	Classic English modern fantasy
1880	*Heidi* by Johanna Spyri	Early realistic story from Switzerland
1881	*The Adventures of Pinocchio* by Carlo Collodi	Modern fantasy from Italy
1883	*Treasure Island* by Robert Louis Stevenson	Adventure tale by a Scottish author
1894	*The Jungle Book* by Rudyard Kipling	Animal stories set in India by an English author
1901	*The Tale of Peter Rabbit* by Beatrix Potter	Classic English picturebook
1908	*The Wind in the Willows* by Kenneth Grahame	Animal fantasy from England
1908	*Anne of Green Gables* by Lucy Maud Montgomery	Realistic family story from Canada
1926	*Winnie-the-Pooh* by A. A. Milne	Personified toy story from England
1928	*Bambi* by Felix Salten	Personified deer story from Germany
1931	*The Story of Babar* by Jean de Brunhoff	Personified elephant story from France
1945	*Pippi Longstocking* by Astrid Lindgren	Classic fantasy from Sweden

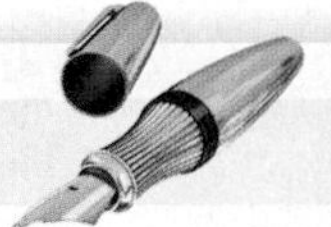

Notable Authors and Illustrators of International Literature

Zeina Abirached, Lebanese illustrator and graphic novelist who writes about her childhood during the Lebanese Civil War. *I Remember Beirut; A Game of Swallows.*

Anthony Browne, British author and illustrator whose stark surrealism comments on social issues. Children's Laureate. *Voices in the Park; Me and You; The Tunnel; Willy the Wimp.* www.anthonybrownebooks.com/

Jiang Hong Chen, Chinese author/illustrator living in France who explores Chinese legends, history, and traditional illustration styles. *Mao and Me; The Magic Horse of Han Gan; Little Eagle.*

Cornelia Funke, German author of award-winning fantasy novels, including the Inkheart trilogy. *The Dragon Rider; The Thief Lord; Inkheart; Reckless.* www.corneliafunke.de

Bob Graham, Australian author and illustrator of whimsical picturebooks. *How to Heal a Broken Wing; April and Esme: Tooth Fairies; A Bus Called Heaven.*

Emily Gravett, British author/illustrator of picturebooks with intricate details and dry humor. *Little Mouse's Big Book of Fears; Wolves; Orange Pear Apple Bear; The Rabbit Problem.* www.emilygravett.com

Ana Maria Machado, Brazilian author, winner of the Hans Christian Andersen Medal, known for her use of magical realism and writing across many genres. *Until the Day Arrives; What a Party!; From Another World.*

Michael Morpurgo, British author who is a master storyteller across many genres; many of his books have a focus on war and animals. *Half a Man; Sir Gawian and the Green Knight; An Elephant in the Garden.* www.michaelmorpurgo.com/

Beverley Naidoo, South African author and Carnegie Medalist whose novels deal with social justice issues. *The Other Side of Truth; Burn My Heart; Journey to Jo'burg.* www.beverleynaidoo.com

Shaun Tan, Malaysian-Australian author/illustrator who explores social and political issues through surreal imagery. *The Arrival; Tales from Outer Suburbia; Lost and Found.* www.shauntan.net

International Literature

Historical Overview of International Literature

Much of the children's literature that was available in the United States from the 1600s to the early 1900s came from Europe. These early children's books have become such an important part of our cultural heritage that we often fail to remember that they were originally published in other countries and languages. Books such as *Robinson Crusoe, Heidi, Pinocchio*, and *Alice in Wonderland* are actually international literature.

With the rapid growth in the U.S. children's book field in the 20th century, the flow of books from other countries became overshadowed by large numbers of U.S. books. In addition, during World War II (WWII), little cultural exchange occurred across international borders. The end of WWII saw a change in the international mood, leading to the establishment of the field of international children's literature and a global increase in children's books in translation. This movement was supported by the International Board on Books for Young People (IBBY; www.ibby.org), an organization involving people from many nations who are involved in all aspects of the children's book field. IBBY publishes *Bookbird: Journal of International Children's Literature*. The U.S. affiliate is the USBBY (www.usbby.org).

Specific awards include the Middle East Book Awards for a picturebook, novel, and nonfiction book by the Middle East Outreach Council (www.meoc.us/meoc/book-awards). The Children's Africana Book Awards are presented to authors and illustrators of children's books on Africa published in the United States (http://africaaccessreview.org/childrens-africana-book-awards/). *Anansesem* is an online journal that reviews and publishes children's books that feature the Caribbean.

We are all citizens of an ever-changing world. Our lives are going global, connected by the stories we share across cultures. International literature immerses children in stories to gain insights into how people live, think, and feel in other times and places. We need to promote more literary exchanges with countries whose bodies of literature are growing rapidly to bring more of the world's best literature to children's attention. We also must encourage the development of stronger literature from countries that have not had the resources to support the writing and publication of their own national literature.

International Literature by World Regions

The international books that are most often available in the United States have been and continue to be books from English-speaking countries, with the largest numbers from England, Australia, and Canada. Although the books do not require translation, they are often published in the United States with changes in spelling, character and place names, and sometimes titles and cover illustrations. The major awards and award winners from English-speaking countries are in Appendix A.

Translated books come to the United States from around the world, but the largest numbers are from Western Europe, particularly Sweden, Norway, Denmark, Switzerland, the Netherlands, Germany, France, and Belgium. A few books come from Italy and Spain, such as the 2016 Batchelder, *The Wonderful Fluffy Little Squishy*, by Beatrice Alemagna, a picturebook about a young girl searching for the perfect birthday gift.

Most translated children's books from the Middle East are novels for middle graders or young adults and come to the United States from Israel, such as *Adam & Thomas* by Aharon Apelfeld. Books from or set in other countries in this region—such as *A Game for Swallows* by Zeina Abirached, a graphic novel about the Lebanese Civil War—are significant because of their rarity.

Translated children's books from Asia were mostly from Japan, but books from Korea, China, Taiwan, and India are available. Japan and Korea have a sophisticated field of book illustrating, and many beautifully illustrated picturebooks are making their way to the United States, such as *New Clothes for New Year's Day* by Hyun-Joo Bae and *Pool* by JiHyeon Lee.

African nations, with the exception of the Republic of South Africa, have produced few examples of children's literature exported to the United States, primarily because of economics. Publishing books is expensive, especially in full color, so the publishing industry is not firmly established in these countries. Books of realistic fiction portraying contemporary life in an African country are rare, and those that are available are typically written by British authors, such as *City Boy* by Jan Michael. British authors are also writing historical fiction about English children growing up in African countries, such as Trilby Kent's *Stones for My Father,* set in South Africa.

One of the challenges for those who work with children is combating the ignorance at the root of racial, cultural, and religious prejudice and intolerance. Children's literature, particularly the rich multicultural and international selections that are currently available, is a powerful tool in this effort in depicting the connections that bring us together as human beings. We are connected by a shared humanity and by the uniqueness that each culture contributes to a richly diverse world, providing unity within difference. Children need to find their own lives reflected within a book as well as imagine cultural ways of living and thinking beyond their own. Integrating a literature that is multicultural and intercultural into classrooms and libraries builds bridges of understanding across cultures.

Invitations for Further Investigation

- Select a marginalized group whose perspectives have been omitted or inadequately covered in U.S. history. Examples include American Indians and their forced removal to reservations in the 1800s, Japanese Americans and their internment in prison camps during WWII, and Chinese Americans and their role in the construction of the transcontinental railroad in the 1860s. Read several pieces of historical fiction or nonfiction about that era written from the perspective of that group. Discuss the perspectives offered by these books as compared with a U.S. history textbook.
- Choose a global issue, such as war, conservation, child labor, or hunger, and pull together a text set of seven to ten books that explore this issue across multiple cultures. Compare the perspectives on this issue from these different cultures.
- Select a country or region outside the United States that you would like to explore. Compile an annotated bibliography of 10–15 children's books, both fiction and nonfiction, that could interest young people in exploring the country or region.

References

Bishop, R. S. (2007). *Free within ourselves: The development of African American children's literature.* Portsmouth, NH: Heinemann.

Clark, E., Flores, B., Smith, H., González, D. (2015). *Multicultural literature for Latino bilingual children.* New York: Rowman & Littlefield.

Fox, D., & Short, K. (2003). *Stories matter: The complexity of cultural authenticity in children's literature.* Urbana, IL: National Council of Teachers of English.

Freire, P. (1970). *Pedagogy of the oppressed.* New York: Continuum.

Gay, G. (2010). *Culturally responsive teaching* (2nd ed.). New York: Teachers College Press.

Horning, K. T., Lindgren, M. V., & Schliesman, M. (2016). *CCBC Choices, 2015.* Madison, WI: University Publications.

Larrick, N. (1965, September 11). The all-white world of children's books. *Saturday Review,* 63–65, 84–85.

Lehman, B., Freeman, E., & Scharer, P. (2010). *Reading globally, K–8.* Thousand Oaks, CA: Corwin.

Lewison, M., Leland, C., & Harste, J. (2008). *Creating critical classrooms.* New York: Erlbaum.

Short, K., Day, D., & Schroeder, J. eds. (2016). *Teaching globally: Reading the world through literature.* Portsmouth, ME: Stenhouse.

U.S. Census Bureau. (2010). www.census.gov.

U.S. Department of Education. (2015). *The Condition of Education 2015.* Washington, DC: NCES.

Wong, J. (1994). All mixed up. In J. Wong, *Good luck gold and other poems.* New York: Simon & Schuster.

Recommended Multicultural Books

Ages refer to content appropriateness and conceptual and interest levels. Formats other than chapter books are coded:

(**PB**) Picturebook
(**COL**) Short story collection
(**GR**) Graphic novel
(**NV**) Novel in verse

African American Literature

Alexander, Kwame. ***The Crossover.*** Houghton, 2014. (**NV**). Ages 9–12.

Aston, Dianna H. ***The Moon over Star.*** Illus. Jerry Pinkney. Dial, 2008. (**PB**). Ages 5–8.

Bolden, Tonya. ***How to Build a Museum: Smithsonian's National Museum of African American History and Culture.*** Viking, 2016. Ages 10–13.

Bryan, Ashley. ***Ashley Bryan: Words to My Life's Song.*** Atheneum, 2009. (**PB**). Ages 8–12.

Cline-Ransome, Lesa. ***Words Set Me Free: The Story of Young Frederick Douglass.*** Illus. James Ransome. Simon & Schuster, 2012. (**PB**). Ages 6–9. Also ***Light in the Darkness*** (2013).

Curtis, Christopher Paul. ***Elijah of Buxton.*** Scholastic, 2007. Ages 9–12.

Draper, Sharon. ***Stella by Starlight.*** Atheneum, 2015. Ages 9–13.

Evans, Shane. ***Underground.*** Roaring Brook, 2011. (**PB**). Ages 6–9.

Grimes, Nikki. ***Words with Wings.*** Boyds Mills, 2013. (**NV**). Ages 8–12.

Hamilton, Virginia. ***M. C. Higgins, The Great.*** Aladdin, 1974. Ages 9–12.

Johnson, Angela. ***Wind Flyers***. Illus. Loren Long. Simon & Schuster, 2007. (**PB**). Ages 6–9.

Johnson, Angela. ***All Different Now: Juneteenth, the First Day of Freedom.*** Illus. E. B. Lewis. Simon & Schuster, 2014. (**PB**). Ages 5–9.

Levine, Ellen. ***Henry's Freedom Box.*** Illus. Kadir Nelson. Scholastic, 2007. (**PB**). Ages 5–8.

McKissack, Patricia, and Fred McKissack. ***Porch Lies: Tales of Slicksters, Tricksters, and Other Wily Characters.*** Illus. André Carrilho. Schwartz & Wade, 2006. (**PB**). Ages 7–10.

McKissack, Patricia, and Fred McKissack. ***Best Shot in the West: The Adventures of Nat Love.*** Illus. Randy DuBurke. Chronicle, 2012. (**GR**). Ages 12–15.

Myers, Walter Dean. ***Looking Like Me.*** Illus. Christopher Myers. Egmont, 2009. (**PB**). Ages 6–9. Also ***We Are America*** (Collins, 2011).

Myers, Walter Dean. ***The Cruisers.*** Scholastic, 2010. Ages 10–14. Series.

Nelson, Kadir. ***We Are the Ship: The Story of Negro League Baseball.*** Hyperion, 2008. Ages 7–10.

Nelson, Kadir. ***Heart and Soul: The Story of America and African Americans.*** Balzer & Bray, 2011. Ages 9–12.

Nelson, Marilyn. ***Sweethearts of Rhythm: The Story of the Greatest All-Girl Swing Band in the World.*** Illus. Jerry Pinkney. Dial, 2009. (**PB**). Ages 10–14. (Poetry and biography).

Partridge, Elizabeth. ***Marching for Freedom.*** Viking, 2009. Ages 10–14.

Pinkney, Andrea. ***Boycott Blues: How Rosa Parks Inspired a Nation.*** Illus. Brian Pinkney. Greenwillow, 2008. (**PB**). Ages 5–8. Also ***Sit-In: How Four Friends Stood Up by Sitting Down*** (Little Brown, 2010)

Reynolds, Jason. ***As Brave As You.*** Atheneum, 2016. Ages 9–12.

Smith, Charles R. ***28 Days: Moments in Black History That Changed the World.*** Illus. Shane Evans. Roaring Brook, 2015. (**PB**). Ages 4–10.

Taylor, Mildred. ***Roll of Thunder, Hear My Cry.*** Dial, 1976. Ages 9–12.

Thomas, Joyce Carol. ***The Blacker the Berry.*** Illus. Floyd Cooper. Joanna Cotler, 2008. (**COL**). Ages 5–8.

Weatherford, Carole Boston. ***Voice of Freedom: Fannie Lou Hamer, Spirit of the Civil Rights Movement.*** Illus. Ekua Holmes. Candlewick, 2015. (**PB**). Ages 10–14.

Williams-Garcia, Rita. ***One Crazy Summer***. Amistad, 2010. Ages 11–14. Also, ***P.S. Be Eleven*** (2013) and ***Gone Crazy in Alabama*** (2015)

Woodson, Jacqueline. ***The Other Side.*** Illus. E. B. Lewis. Putnam, 2001. (**PB**). Ages 5–8.

Woodson, Jacqueline. ***Locomotion.*** Putnam, 2003. (**NV**). Ages 9–12.

Woodson, Jacqueline. ***Brown Girl Dreaming.*** Penguin, 2014. (**NV**). Ages 8–12.

American Indian Literature

Alexie, Sherman. ***The Absolutely True Diary of a Part-Time Indian.*** Little, Brown, 2007. Ages 14–16. (Spokane/Coeur d'Alene)

Alexie, Sherman. ***Thunder Boy Jr.*** Illus. Yuyi Morales. Little, Brown, 2016. (**PB**). Ages 4–7.

Begay, Shonto. ***Ma'ii and Cousin Horned Toad.*** Scholastic, 1992. (**PB**). Ages 6–9. (Diné/Navajo)

Bruchac, Joseph. ***Code Talker.*** Dial, 2005. Ages 12–15. (Diné/Navajo)

Bruchac, Joseph. ***The Hunter's Promise: An Abenaki Tale.*** Illus. Bill Farnsworth. Wisdom Tales, 2015. (**PB**). Ages 6–8. (Abenaki)

Bruchac, Joseph. ***Talking Leaves.*** Dial, 2016. Ages 9–12. (Sequoyah; Tsalagi/Cherokee)

Campbell, Nicola I. ***Shin-Chi's Canoe.*** Illus. Kim LaFave. Groundwood, 2008. (**PB**). Ages 5–8. (Interior Salish/Métis/Canada)

Carvell, Marlene. ***Sweetgrass Basket.*** Dutton, 2005. Ages 10–14. (Mohawk)

Charleyboy, Lisa and Mary Beth Leatherdal (editors). ***Dreaming in Indian: Contemporary Native American Voices.*** Annick Press, 2014. (**COL**). Ages 12–17.

Ellis, Deborah. ***Looks like Daylight: Voices of Indigenous Kids.*** Groundwood, 2013. (**COL**). Ages 12–16.

Erdrich, Louise. ***The Birchbark House.*** Hyperion, 1999. Ages 8–12. Also ***The Game of Silence*** (2005), ***The Porcupine Year*** (2008), ***Chickadee*** (2012). (Ojibwe)

Flood, Nancy Bo. ***Soldier Sister, Fly Home.*** Charlesbridge, 2016. Ages 10–14. (Diné/Navajo)

Maher, Ramona. ***Alice Yazzie's Year.*** Illus. Shonto Begay. Tricycle, 2003. (**PB**). (Diné/Navajo)

Marshall, Joseph. ***In the Footsteps of Crazy Horse.*** Illus. Jim Yellowhawk. Amulet, 2015. Ages 9–12. (Lakota)

McLaughlin, Timothy. ***Walking on Earth and Touching the Sky: Poetry and Prose by Lakota Youth at Red Cloud Indian School.*** Illus. S.D. Nelson. Abrams, 2012. Ages 9–12. (Lakota)

Medicine Crow, Joseph. ***Counting Coup: Becoming a Crow Chief on the Reservation and Beyond.*** National Geographic, 2006. Ages 10–14. (Absarokee)

Messinger, Carla, and Susan Katz. ***When the Shadbush Blooms.*** Illus. David K. Fadden. Tricycle, 2007. (**PB**). Ages 5–8. (Lenape)

Nelson, S. D. ***Black Elk's Vision: A Lakota Story.*** Abrams, 2010. (**PB**). Ages 9–12. (Lakota)

Nelson, S. D. ***Sitting Bull: Lakota Warrior and Defender of His People.*** Abrams, 2015. Ages 10–13. (Lakota)

Nicholson, Caitlin Dale, and Leona Morin-Neilson. ***Niwechihaw = I Help.*** Illus. Caitlin Dale Nicholson. Groundwood, 2008. (**PB**). Ages 5–8. (Cree)

Parsons-Yazzie, Evangeline. ***Dzani Yazhi Naazbaa': Little Woman Warrior Who Came Home; A Story of the Navajo Long Walk.*** Illus. Irving Toddy. Salina Bookshelf, 2005. (**PB**). Ages 8–11. (Diné/Navajo)

Tingle, Tim. ***Saltpie: A Choctaw Journey from Darkness into Light.*** Illus. Karen Clarkson. Cinco Puntos, 2010. (**PB**). Ages 6–10. (Choctaw)

Arab American and Persian American Literature

Addasi, Maha. ***Time to Pray.*** (Bilingual). Illus. Ned Gannon. Boyds Mills, 2010. (**PB**). Ages 6–9. (Pakistani American, Muslim)

Budhos, Marina Tamar. ***Ask Me No Questions.*** Simon Pulse, 2006. Ages 10–14. (Bangladeshi American)

Dumas, Firoozeh. ***It Ain't So Awful, Falafel.*** Clarion, 2016. Ages 8–12. (Iranian American)

Jalali, Reza. ***Moon Watchers: Shirin's Ramadan Miracle.*** Illus. Anne Sibley O'Brien. Tilbury House, 2010. (**PB**). Ages 6–9. (Iranian American, Muslim)

Khan, Hena. ***Night of the Moon.*** Illus. Julie Paschkis. Chronicle, 2008. (**PB**). Ages 4–8. (Pakistani American, Muslim)

Khan, Rukhsana. ***Big Red Lollipop.*** Illus. Sophie Blackall. Viking, 2010. (**PB**). Ages 3–5. (Pakistani Canadian)

Mobin-Uddin, Asma. ***My Name Is Bilal.*** Illus. Barbara Kiwak. Boyds Mills, 2005. (**PB**). Ages 9–12. (Pakistani American, Muslim)

Mobin-Uddin, Asma. ***A Party in Ramadan.*** Illus. Laura Jacobsen. Boyds Mills, 2009. (**PB**). Ages 5–8. (Pakistani American, Muslim). Also ***The Best Eid Ever*** (2007)

Senzai, N. H. ***Shooting Kabul.*** Simon & Schuster, 2010. Ages 9–14. (Afghan American). Also ***Saving Kabul Corner*** (2014)

Asian/Pacific American Literature

Bahk, Jane. ***Juna's Jar.*** Illus. Felicia Hoshino. Lee & Low, 2015. (**PB**). Ages 4–7. (Korean American)

Barasch, Lynne. ***Hiromi's Hands.*** Lee & Low, 2007. (**PB**). Ages 5–8. (Japanese American)

Crowe, Ellie. ***Surfer of the Century: The Life of Duke Kahanamoku.*** Illus. Richard Waldrep. Lee & Low, 2007. (**PB**). Ages 8–11. (Hawaiian)

Heo, Yumi. ***Ten Days and Nine Nights: An Adoption Story.*** Schwartz & Wade, 2009. (**PB**). Ages 5–8. (Korean American)

Heo, Yumi. ***Lady Hahn and Her Seven Friends.*** Holt, 2012. (**PB**). Ages 4–7. (Korean)

Kadohata, Cynthia. ***Weedflower.*** Atheneum, 2006. Ages 11–14. (Japanese American)

Kadohata, Cynthia. ***The Thing about Luck.*** Illus. Julia Kuo. Atheneum, 2013. Ages 10–14. (Japanese American)

Kelly, Erin Entrada. ***Blackbird Fly.*** New York: Greenwillow. Ages 9–14.

Krishnaswami, Uma. ***The Grand Plan to Fix Everything.*** Illus. Abigail Halpin. Atheneum, 2011. Ages 9–13. (East Indian American)

Krishnaswami, Uma. ***Book Uncle and Me.*** Groundwood, 2016. Ages 7–10. (East Indian American)

Lazo Gilmore, Dorina. ***Cora Cooks Pancit.*** Illus. Kristi Valiant. Shen's, 2009. (**PB**). Ages 5–9. (Filipino American)

Lin, Grace. ***The Year of the Dog.*** Little, Brown, 2006. Ages 8–11. (Taiwanese American)

Look, Lenore. ***Ruby Lu: Empress of Everything.*** Atheneum, 2006. Illus. Anne Wildsorf. Ages 6–9. (Chinese American)

Look, Lenore. ***Alvin Ho: Allergic to Girls, School, and Other Scary Things.*** Illus. LeUyen Pham. Schwartz & Wade, 2008. Ages 9–12. (Chinese American)

Ly, Many. ***Roots and Wings.*** Delacorte, 2008. Ages 12–16. (Cambodian American)

Moss, Marissa. ***Barbed Wire Baseball.*** Illus. Yuko Shimizu. Abrams, 2013. (**PB**). Ages 7–10. (Japanese American)

Park, Linda Sue. ***Keeping Score.*** Clarion, 2008. Ages 9–12. (Korean American)

Roth, Susan, and Cindy Trumbore. ***The Mangrove Tree; Planting Trees to Feed Families.*** Lee & Low, 2011. (**PB**). Ages 8–10. (Japanese American)

Salisbury, Graham. ***Night of the Howling Dogs.*** Wendy Lamb Books, 2007. Ages 8–11. (Hawaiian)

Say, Allen. ***The Favorite Daughter.*** Arthur A. Levine Books, 2013. (**PB**). Ages 5–8. (Japanese American)

Shang, Wendy. ***The Great Wall of Lucy Wu.*** Scholastic, 2011. Ages 9–12. (Chinese American)

Sheth, Kashmira. ***Sona and the Wedding Game.*** Illus. Yoshiko Jaeggi. Peachtree, 2015. (**PB**). Ages 6–9. (East Indian American)

Uegaki, Cheri. ***Hana Hashimoto, Sixth Violin.*** Illus. Qin Leng. Kids Can, 2014. (**PB**). Ages 5-8. (Japanese American)

Yep, Laurence. ***The Dragon's Child: A Story of Angel Island.*** HarperCollins, 2008. Ages 9–12. (Chinese American)

Young, Ed. ***My Mei Mei.*** Philomel, 2006. (**PB**). Ages 4–7. (Chinese American)

Zia, F. ***Hot, Hot, Roti for Dada-ji.*** Illus. Ken Min. (**PB**). Ages 5–8. (East Indian American)

Latino Literature

Ada, Alma Flor. ***I Love Saturdays y domingos.*** Illus. Elivia Savadier. Atheneum, 2002. (**PB**). Ages 4–8. (Mexican American, biracial)

Ada, Alma Flor. ***Yes! We Are Latinos: Poems and Prose About the Latino Experience.*** Illus. David Diaz. Charlesbridge, 2016. (**COL**). Ages 10–14. (Latino American)

Alvarez, Julia. ***How Tia Lola Ended Up Starting Over.*** Knopf, 2011. Ages 9–12. (Dominican American). Series.

Ancona, George. ***Capoeira: Game! Dance! Martial Art!*** Lee & Low, 2007. Ages 10–14. (Brazilian American)

Brown, Monica. ***Marisol McDonald Doesn't Match.*** Illus. Sara Palacios. Children's Book Press, 2008. (**PB**). Ages 5–8. (Peruvian/Scottish/American)

Buitrago, Jairo. ***Two White Rabbits.*** Illus. Rafael Yockteng. Groundwood, 2015. (**PB**). Ages 4–10. (Mexican American)

Campoy, F. Isabel. ***Maybe Something Beautiful.*** Illus. Rafael López. Houghton, 2016. (**PB**). Ages 4–7. (Mexican American)

Colon, Edie. ***Goodbye, Havana! Hola, New York!*** Illus. Raul Colon. Simon & Schuster, 2011. (**PB**). Ages 4–8. (Cuban American)

Engle, Margarita. ***Enchanted Air: Two Cultures, Two Wings: A Memoir.*** Atheneum, 2015. (**NV**). Ages 10–18. (Cuban American)

González, Lucia M. ***The Storyteller's Candle.*** Illus. Lulu Delacre. Children's Books Press, 2008. (**PB**). Ages 5–8. (Puerto Rican American)

Herrera, Juan Felipe. ***Portraits of Hispanic American Heroes.*** Illus. Raul Colon. Dial, 2014. (**COL**). Ages 8–12. (Latino American)

Jiménez, Francisco. ***The Circuit: Stories from the Life of a Migrant Child.*** Houghton, 1999. Ages 10–14. Also ***Breaking Through*** (2001) and ***Reaching Out*** (2008). (Mexican American)

Medina, Meg. ***Mango, Abuela, and Me.*** Illus. Angel Dominguez. Candlewick, 2015. (**PB**). Ages 4–7. (Cuban American).

Mora, Pat. ***Book Fiesta! Celebrate Children's Day, Book Day/ Celebremos el día de los niños, el día de los libros.*** Illus. Rafael López. Rayo, 2009. (**PB**). Ages 5–8. (Mexican American)

Morales, Yuyi. ***Just in Case.*** Chronicle, 2008. (**PB**). Ages 5–8. (Mexican American)

Morales, Yuyi. ***Niño Wrestles the World.*** Roaring Brook, 2013. (**PB**). Ages 4–8. (Mexican American)

Ryan, Pam Muñoz. ***Becoming Naomi León.*** Scholastic, 2004. Ages 11–15. (Mexican American)

Soto, Gary. ***Chato and the Party Animals.*** Illus. Susan Guevara. Putnam, 2000. (**PB**). Ages 5–8. (Mexican American)

Tafolla, Carmen. ***What Can You Do with a Rebozo?*** Illus. Amy Cordova. Tricycle, 2008. (**PB**). Ages 5–8. (Mexican American)

Tonatiuh, Duncan. ***Pancho Rabbit and the Coyote: A Migrant's Tale.*** Abrams, 2013. (**PB**). Ages 5–9. (Mexican American)

Velasquez, Eric. ***Looking for Bongo.*** Holiday House, 2016. (**PB**). Ages 2–5. (Puerto Rican)

Religious Cultures Literature

Ajmera, Marya. ***Faith.*** Charlesbridge, 2009. (**PB**). Ages 3–10. (Multiple religions)

Cooper, Helen. ***The Golden Rule.*** Illus. Gabi Swiatkowska. Abrams, 2007. (**PB**). Ages 5–8. (Multiple religions)

Cunnane, Kelly. ***Deep in the Sahara.*** Illus. Hoda Hadadi. Schwartz & Wade, 2013. (**PB**). Ages 5–7. (Muslim, Mauritania)

Dauvillier, Loic. ***Hidden: A Child's Story of the Holocaust.*** Illus. Marc Lizano. First Second, 2014. (**GR**). Ages 6–13. Translated from French. (Jewish, Paris)

Demi. ***Buddha.*** Holt, 1996. (**PB**). Ages 5–8. (Buddhist). Also ***Muhammad*** (2003). (Muslim)

Deutsch, Barry. ***Hereville: How Mirka Got Her Sword.*** Illus. J. Richmond. Amulet, 2010. (**GR**). Ages 9–12. (Jewish)

Engle, Margarita. ***Tropical Secrets: Holocaust Refugees in Cuba.*** Holt, 2009. (**NV**). Ages 12–15. (Jewish)

García, Cristina. ***I Wanna Be Your Shoebox.*** Simon & Schuster, 2008. Ages 8–11. (Jewish)

Gershator, Phillis. ***Sky Sweeper.*** Illus. Holly Meade (**PB**). Farrar, 2007. (Buddhist)

Goldblatt, Mark. ***Finding the Worm.*** Random House, 2015. Ages 11–14. (Jewish)

Haynes, Emily. ***Ganesha's Sweet Tooth.*** Chronicle, 2012. (**PB**). Ages 5–8. (Hindu)

Khan, Hena. ***Golden Domes and Silver Lanterns: A Muslim Book of Colors.*** Illus. Mehrdokht Amini. Chronicle, 2012. (**PB**). Ages 4–7. (Muslim)

Kimmel, Eric. ***The Golem's Latkes.*** Illus. Aaron Jasinski. Cavendish, 2011. (**PB**). Ages 6–9. (Jewish)

Meyer, Susan. ***Black Radishes.*** Delacorte, 2010. Ages 9–12. (Jewish). Also ***Skating with the Statue of Liberty*** (2016)

Prins, Marcel. ***Hidden Like Anne Frank: Fourteen True Stories of Survival.*** Arthur A. Levine Books, 2014. (**COL**). Ages 12–18. (Jewish)

Russo, Marisabina. ***Always Remember Me: How One Family Survived World War II.*** Atheneum, 2005. (**PB**). Ages 8–11. (Jewish)

Schwartz, Howard. ***Gathering Sparks.*** Ill. Kristina Swarner. Roaring Brook, 2010. (**PB**). Ages 5–9. (Jewish)

Sinykin, Sheri. ***Zayde Comes to Live.*** Illus. Kristina Swarner. Peachtree, 2012. (**PB**). Ages 5–8. (Jewish)

Vernick, Shirley. ***The Blood Lie.*** Cinco Puntos, 2011. Ages 11–14. (Jewish)

Wayland, April Halprin. ***New Year at the Pier: A Rosh Hashanah Story.*** Illus. Stephane Jorisch. Dial, 2010. (**PB**). Ages 5–9. (Jewish)

Zia, F. ***The Garden of My Imaan.*** Peachtree, 2016. Ages 8–12. (Muslim, East Indian American)

Bilingual Literature

Alarcón, Francisco X. ***Poems to Dream Together/Poemas para soñar juntos.*** Illus. Paula Barragán. Lee & Low, 2005. (**COL**). Ages 8–12. (English/Spanish)

Ancona, George. ***Mi barrio/My Neighborhood.*** Children's Press, 2004. (**PB**). Ages 5–8. We Are Latinos series.

Argueta, Jorge. ***Arro con leche: Un poema para cocinar.*** Illus. Fernando Vilela. Groundwood, 2010. (**PB**). Ages 6–9. (English/Spanish)

Brown, Mónica. ***Pelé, King of Soccer/Pelé, el rey del fútbol.*** Trans. Fernando Gayesky. Illus. Rudy Gutierrez. Rayo, 2009. (**PB**). Ages 5–8. (English/Spanish)

Brown, Mónica. ***Tito Puente, Mambo King/Tito Puente, Rey del Mambo.*** Illus. Rafael López. Rayo, 2013. (**PB**). Ages 4–8. (English/Spanish)

Brown, Mónica. ***Maya's Blanket/La manta de Maya.*** Illus. David Diaz. Children's Book Press, 2015. (**PB**). Ages 5–9. (English/Spanish)

Colato Laínez, René. ***Playing Lotería/El juego de la lotería.*** Illus. Hill Arena. Luna Rising, 2005. (**PB**). Ages 5–8. (English/Spanish)

Colato Laínez, René. ***René Has Two Last Names: René tiene dos apellidos.*** Trans. Gabriela Baeza Ventura. Illus. Fabiola Grauller. Piñata, 2009. (**PB**). Ages 5–8.

Cumpiano, Ina. ***Quinito, Day and Night/Quinito, día y noche.*** Illus. José Ramírez. Children's Book Press, 2008. (**PB**). Ages 5–8. (English/Spanish)

Dumas Lachtman, Ofelia. ***Pepita and the Bully/Pepita y la peleonera.*** Trans. Gabriela Baeza Ventura. Illus. Alex Pardo DeLange. Piñata, 2011. (**PB**). Ages 5–8. (English/Spanish)

Garza, Carmen Lomas, with Harriet Rohmer. ***In My Family/En mi familia.*** Trans. Francisco X. Alarcón. Children's Book Press, 1996. (**PB**). Ages 5–12. (English/Spanish)

Garza, Xavier. ***Lucha Libre: The Man in the Silver Mask.*** Trans. Luis Humberto Cristhwaite. Cinco Puntos, 2005. (**PB**). Ages 8–11. Also ***Maximillian and the Lucha Libre Club*** (2016). (English/Spanish).

Gonzales Bertrand, Diane. ***The Party for Papa Luis/La fiesta para Papa Luis.*** Trans. Gabriela Baeza Ventura. Illus. Alejandro Galindo. Piñata, 2010. (**PB**). Ages 5–8. (English/Spanish).

González, Maya Christina. ***My Colors, My World/Mis colores, mi mundo.*** Children's Book Press, 2007. (**PB**). Ages 5–8. (English/Spanish)

González, Maya Christina. ***Call Me Tree/Llamame arbol.*** Children's Book Press, 2014. (**PB**). Ages 3–8. (English/Spanish)

Hayes, Joe. ***Don't Say a Word, Mama/No digas nada, mama.*** Illus. Esau Andrade Valencia. Cinco Puntos, 2012. (**PB**). Ages 6–9. (English/Spanish)

Lee-Tai, Amy. ***A Place Where Sunflowers Grow.*** Trans. Marc Akio Lee. Illus. Felicia Hoshino. Children's Book Press, 2006. (**PB**). Ages 5–8. (English/Japanese)

Mora, Pat. ***Let's Eat!/¡A comer!*** Illus. Maribel Suarez. Rayo, 2008. (**PB**). Ages 3–6. (English/Spanish)

Mora, Pat. ***The Remembering Day.*** Illus. Robert Casilla. Pinata Books, 2015. (**PB**). Ages 5–8. (English/Spanish)

Rivera-Ashford, Roni Capin. ***My Tata's Remedies/Los remedios de mi tata.*** Illus. Antonio Castro. Cinco Puntos, 2015. (**PB**). Ages 6–11. (English/Spanish)

Robles, Anthony. ***Lakas and the Makibaka Hotel/Si Lakas at ang Makibaka Hotel.*** Trans. Eloisa D. de Jesús. Illus. Carl Angel. Children's Book Press, 2006. (**PB**) Ages 7–9. (English/Tagalog)

Shin, Sun Yung. ***Cooper's Lesson.*** Trans. Min Paek. Illus. Kim Cogan. Children's Book Press, 2004. (**PB**). Ages 5–8. (English/Korean)

Tran, Truong. ***Going Home, Coming Home/Ve Nha, Tham Que Huong.*** Illus. Ann Phong. Children's Book Press, 2003. (**PB**). Ages 5–8. (English/Vietnamese)

Wu, Faye-Lynn. ***Chinese and English Nursery Rhymes.*** Illus. Kieren Dutcher. Tuttle, 2010. (**PB**). Ages 4–7. (Chinese/English)

Recommended International Books

Ages refer to content appropriateness and conceptual and interest levels. Country of original publication is noted. Formats other than chapter books are coded:

(**PB**) Picturebooks
(**COL**) Short story collection

English-Language Books

Almond, David. ***The Boy Who Climbed into the Moon.*** Illus. Polly Dunbar. Candlewick, 2010. Ages 8–11. (U.K.)

Baker, Jeannie. ***Circle.*** Candlewick, 2016. (**PB**). Ages 4–9. (Australia)

Baker-Smith, Grahame. ***Farther.*** Templar Books, 2010. (**PB**). Ages 5–8. (U.K.)

Bateson, Catherine. ***Being Bee.*** Holiday House, 2007. Ages 9–12. (Australia)

Benjamin, Floella. ***My Two Grannies.*** Illus. Margaret Chamberlain. Francis Lincoln, 2008. (**PB**). Ages 6–9. (U.K.)

Brahmachari, Sita. ***Mira in the Present Tense.*** Whitman, 2013. Ages 9–12. (U.K., Jewish, East Indian)

Browne, Anthony. ***Voices in the Park.*** DK, 2001. (**PB**). Ages 8–11. Also ***Me and You*** (Farrar, 2009). (U.K.)

Browne, Anthony. ***What If…?*** Candlewick, 2014. (**PB**). Ages 4–8. (U.K.)

Child, Lauren. ***Ruby Redfort Look into My Eyes.*** Candlewick, 2012. Ages 9–14. (U.K.)

Colfer, Eoin. ***Artemis Fowl.*** Hyperion, 2001. Ages 10–12. (Ireland). Series.

Cottrell Boyce, Frank. ***The Astounding Broccoli Boy.*** Walden Pond, 2015. Ages 9–14. (U.K.)

Crossley-Holland, Kevin. ***Crossing to Paradise.*** Scholastic, 2008. Ages 10–15. (U.K.)

Croza, Laurel. ***I Know Here.*** Illus. Matt James. Groundwood, 2010. (**PB**). Ages 5–8. (Canada)

Daly, Niki. ***Where's Jamela?*** Farrar, 2004. (**PB**). Ages 5–8. (South Africa)

Daly, Niki. ***The Herd Boy.*** Eerdmans, 2012. (**PB**). Ages 6–10. (South Africa)

Diakité, Baba Wagué. ***A Gift from Childhood: Memories of an African Boyhood.*** Groundwood, 2010. Ages 9–12. (Mali)

Dowd, Siobhan. ***The London Eye Mystery.*** David Fickling, 2008. Ages 8–11. (U.K.)

Fan, Terry. ***The Night Gardener.*** Illus. Eric Fan. Simon & Schuster, 2016. (**PB**). Ages 5–8. (Canada)

Foreman, Michael. ***The Tortoise and the Soldier.*** Holt, 2015. Ages 8–12. (U.K.)

Fox, Mem. ***Wilfrid Gordon McDonald Partridge.*** Illus. Julie Vivas. Kane/Miller, 1985. (**PB**). Ages 5–8. (Australia)

Fox, Mem. ***Koala Lou.*** Illus. Pamela Lofts. Harcourt Brace, 1988. (**PB**). Ages 4–7. (Australia)

Fraillon, Zana. ***The Bone Sparrow.*** Hyperion, 2016. Ages 10–14. (Australia)

French, Jackie. ***Diary of a Wombat.*** Illus. Bruce Whatley. Clarion, 2003. (**PB**). Ages 5–7. (Australia)

French, Simon. ***My Cousin's Keeper.*** Candlewick, 2014. Ages 9–12. (Australia)

Gardner, Lyn. ***Into the Woods.*** Illus. Mini Grey. Random House, 2007. Ages 8–11. (U.K.)

Garland, Sarah. ***Azzi in Between.*** Frances Lincoln Children's Books, 2012. (**GR**). Ages 7–9. (U.K., refugee).

Gay, Marie-Louise. ***Read Me a Story, Stella.*** Groundwood, 2013. (**PB**). Ages 3–5. (Canada)

Gleeson, Libby. ***Half a World Away.*** Illus. Freya Blackwood. Scholastic, 2007. (**PB**). Ages 5–8. (Australia)

Graham, Bob. ***How to Heal a Broken Wing.*** Candlewick, 2008. (**PB**). Ages 5–8. (Australia)

Gravett, Emily. ***Wolves.*** Simon & Schuster, 2006. (**PB**). Ages 5–8. Also ***Little Mouse's Big Book of Fears*** (2008). (U.K.)

Grey, Mini. ***Traction Man Meets Turbodog.*** Knopf, 2008. (**PB**). Ages 5–8. (U.K.)

Grill, William. ***Shackleton's Journey.*** Flying Eye Books, 2014. (**PB**). Ages 9–12. (U.K.)

Hartnett, Sonya. ***The Midnight Zoo.*** Candlewick, 2010. Ages 10–14. (Australia)

Hartnett, Sonya. ***The Children of the King.*** Candlewick, 2014. Ages 11–14. (Australia)

Haughton, Chris. ***Shh! We Have a Plan.*** Candlewick, 2014. (**PB**). Ages 5–7. (U.K.)

Ibbotson, Eva. ***One Dog and His Boy.*** Scholastic, 2011. Ages 9–14. (U.K.).

Ihimaera, Witi. ***Whale Rider.*** Harcourt, 2003. Ages 12–15. (New Zealand)

Jordan-Fenton, Christy. ***Not My Girl.*** Illus. Gabrielle Grimard. Annick, 2014. (**PB**). Ages 5–9. (Canada, Inuit)

Jordan-Fenton, Christy, and Margaret Pokiak-Fenton. ***Fatty Legs.*** Annick, 2011. Ages 9–12. (Canada, Inuit)

Kalluk, Celina. ***Sweetest Kulu.*** Illus. Alexandria Neonakis. Inhabit Media, 2014. (**PB**). Ages 5–9. (Canada, Inuit).

Kent, Trilby. ***Stones for My Father.*** Tundra, 2011. Ages 10–14. (South Africa)

Kobald, Irena. ***My Two Blankets.*** Illus. Freya Blackwood. Houghton, 2014. (**PB**). Ages 4–10. (Australia)

Lester, Alison. ***Are We There Yet? A Journey around Australia.*** Kane/Miller, 2005. (**PB**). Ages 5–8. (Australia)

Lightfoot, Gordon. ***Canadian Railroad Trilogy.*** Illus. Ian Wallace. Groundwood, 2010. (**PB**). Ages 9–12. (Canada)

Little, Jean. ***Willow and Twig.*** Viking, 2003. Ages 11–14. (Canada)

Lofthouse, Liz. ***Ziba Came on a Boat.*** Illus. Robert Ingpen. Kane/Miller, 2007. Ages 8–12. (**PB**). (Australia)

Maclear, Kyo. ***Virginia Wolf.*** Illus. Isabelle Arsenault. Kids Can, 2012. (PB). Ages 5-9. (Canada)

McCaughrean, Geraldine. ***The Death-Defying Pepper Roux.*** Harper, 2009. Ages 10–14. (U.K.)

McKay, Hilary. ***Binny for Short.*** Margaret K. McElderry Books, 2013. Ages 8–14. (U.K.)

Michael, Jan. ***City Boy.*** Clarion, 2009. Ages 10–14. (U.K., set in Malawi).

Milway, Katie Smith. ***The Good Garden: How One Family Went from Hunger to Having Enough.*** Illus. Sylvie Daigneault. Kids Can Press, 2010. (**PB**). Ages 9–12. (Honduras). Also ***One Hen*** (2008). (Ghana). ***Mimi's Village: How Basic Health Care Transformed It*** (2012). (Kenya). (published in Canada)

Morpurgo, Michael. ***Half a Man.*** Illus. Gemma O'Callaghan. Candlewick, 2015. Ages 12–16. (U.K.)

Naidoo, Beverley. ***Burn My Heart.*** Amistad, 2009. Ages 10–14. (Kenya)

Newman, John. ***Mimi.*** Candlewick, 2010. Ages 9–12. (Ireland)

Nicholls, Sally. ***Ways to Live Forever.*** Scholastic, 2008. Ages 8–11. (U.K.)

Parkinson, Siobhan (editor). ***Magic!: New Fairy Tales by Irish Writers.*** Illus. Olwyn Whelan. Frances Lincoln, 2015. Ages 8–12. (Ireland)

Pendziwol, Jean. ***Marja's Skis.*** Illus. Jirina Marton. Groundwood, 2007. (**PB**). Ages 5–8. (Canada)

Petricic, Dusan. ***My Family Tree and Me.*** Kids Can Press, 2015. (**PB**). Ages 4–9. (Asia, Europe)

Pinfold, Levi. ***Black Dog.*** Templar, 2011. (**PB**). Ages 4–8. (U.K.)

Pratchett, Terry. ***Nation.*** HarperCollins, 2008. Ages 12–15. (U.K.)

Pullman, Philip. ***The Golden Compass.*** Knopf, 1996. Ages 12–15. Dark Materials trilogy. (U.K.)

Ravishankar, Anushka. ***Elephants Never Forget.*** Illus. Christiane Pleper. Houghton, 2010. (**PB**). Ages 5–8. (India)

Reeve, Philip. ***Fever Crumb.*** Scholastic, 2009. Ages 12–15. Series. (U.K.)

Rodda, Emily. ***The Key to Rondo.*** Scholastic, 2008. Ages 8–11. (Australia)

Rogers, Stan. ***Northwest Passage.*** Illus. Matt James. Groundwood, 2013. (**PB**). Ages 8–12. (Canada)

Rosen, Michael. ***Michael Rosen's Sad Book.*** Illus. Quentin Blake. Candlewick, 2005. (**PB**). Ages 8–11. (U.K.)

Rosoff, Meg. ***Meet Wild Boars.*** Illus. Sophie Blackall. Holt, 2005. (**PB**). Ages 4–8. (U.K.)

Rowling, J. K. ***Harry Potter and the Sorcerer's Stone.*** Scholastic, 1998. Ages 9–13. (U.K.)

Tan, Shaun. ***The Arrival.*** Scholastic, 2007. (**PB**). Ages 10–14. (Australia)

Trottier, Maxine. ***Migrant.*** Illus. Isabelle Arsenault. Groundwood, 2011. (**PB**). Ages 5–9 (Canada)

Waddell, Martin. ***Captain Small Pig.*** Illus. Susan Varley. Peachtree, 2009. (**PB**). Ages 5–8. (Canada)

Wallace, Ian. ***The Slippers' Keeper.*** Groundwood, 2015. (**PB**). Ages 5–8. (U.K.)

Wild, Margaret. ***Fox.*** Illus. Ron Brooks. Kane/Miller, 2001. (**PB**). Ages 6–8. (Australia)

Wild, Margaret. ***Woolvs in the Sitee.*** Illus. Anne Spudvilas. Front Street, 2007. (**PB**). Ages 10–14. (Australia)

Williams, Michael. ***Now Is the Time for Running.*** Little, Brown, 2011. Ages 12–15. (South Africa)

Wilson, Jacqueline. ***Candyfloss.*** Illus. Nick Sharratt. Roaring Book Press, 2007. Ages 10–14. (U.K.)

Wynne-Jones, Tim. ***Rex Zero and the End of the World.*** Farrar, 2007. Ages 8–11. (Canada)

Translated Books

Abirached, Zeina. ***A Game for Swallows: To Die, to Leave, to Return.*** Trans. from French by Edward Gauvin. Graphic Universe, 2012. (**GR**). Ages 12–18. (Memoir, Beirut)

Akbarpur, Ahmad. ***Good Night, Commander.*** Trans. from Farsi by Shadi Eskandani. Illus. Morteza Zahedi. Groundwood, 2010. (**PB**). Ages 6–9. (Iran)

Alemagna, Beatrice. ***The Wonderful Fluffy Little Squishy.*** Trans. from Italian. Enchanted Lion, 2015. (**PB**). Ages 4–8. (Italy)

Apelfeld, Aharon. ***Adam & Thomas.*** Trans. from Hebrew by Yaacov Jeffery Green. Illus. Philippe Dumas. Seven Stories, 2015. Ages 10–18.

Baasansuren, Bolormaa. ***My Little Round House.*** Trans. from Japanese by Helen Mixter. Groundwood, 2010. (**PB**). Ages 5–8. (Mongolia)

Bae, Hyun-Joo. ***New Clothes for New Year's Day.*** Trans. from Korean. Kane/Miller, 2007. (**PB**). Ages 5–8. (South Korea)

Bondoux, Anne-Laure. ***A Time of Miracles.*** Trans. from French by Y. Maudet. Delacorte, 2011. Ages 10–14. (France). Also ***The Killer's Tears*** (2006). (Chile)

Bredsdorff, Bodil. ***The Crow-Girl: The Children of Crow Cove.*** Trans. from Danish by Faith Ingwersen. Farrar, 2004. Ages 11–12. (Denmark). Also ***Eidi*** (2010).

Brun-Cosme, Nadine. ***Big Wolf & Little Wolf.*** Trans. from French by Claudia Bedrick. Illus. Olivier Tallee. Enchanted Lion, 2009. (**PB**). Ages 6–9. (France)

Chen, Jiang Hong. ***Mao and Me: The Little Red Guard.*** Trans. from French by Claudia Bedrick. Enchanted Lion, 2008. (**PB**). Ages 9–12. (Memoir, China).

Chen, Zhiyuan. ***Guji, Guji.*** Trans. from Chinese. Kane/Miller, 2004. (**PB**). Ages 5–8. (Taiwan)

Choung, Eun-Hee. ***Minji's Salon.*** Trans. from Korean. Kane/Miller, 2007. (**PB**). Ages 5–8. (South Korea)

Cohen-Janca, Irene. ***Mister Doctor: Janusz Korczak & the Orphans of the Warsaw Ghetto.*** Trans. from Italian by

Paula Ayer. Illus. Maurizio Quarello. Annick, 2015. Ages 11–15. (Poland)

Combres, Elizabeth. ***Broken Memory: A Novel of Rwanda.*** Trans. from French by Shelley Tanaka. Groundwood, 2009. Ages 12–15. (Rwanda)

D'Adamo, Francesco. ***Iqbal: A Novel.*** Trans. from French by Ann Leonori. Atheneum, 2003. Ages 9–12. (Pakistan)

Das, Amrita. ***Hope Is a Girl Selling Fruit.*** Trans. from Hindi. Tara, 2013. (**PB**). Ages 11–16. (India)

De Graaf, Anne. ***Son of a Gun.*** Trans. from Dutch. Eerdmans, 2012. Ages 11–13. (Liberia)

Dubuc, Marianne. ***The Lion and the Bird.*** Trans. from French by Claudia Bedrick. Enchanted Lion, 2014. (**PB**). Ages 4–7. (Canada)

Duman Tak, Bibi. ***Soldier Bear.*** Illus. Philip Hopman. Trans. from Dutch by Laura Watkinson. Eerdmans, 2011. Ages 9–12. (Poland/Europe). Also ***Mikis and the Donkey*** (2014).

Dumont, Jean-Francois. ***The Chickens Build a Wall.*** Trans. from French. Eerdmans, 2013. (**PB**). Ages 4–8. (France)

Dumont, Jean-Francois. ***I Am a Bear.*** Trans. from French. Eerdmans, 2015. (**PB**). Ages 6–8. (France).

Elschner, Geraldine. ***Like a Wolf.*** Trans. from French. Illus. Antoine Guilloppe. Minedition, 2015. (**PB**). Ages 4–8. (France)

Fang, Suzhen. ***Grandma Lives in a Perfume Village.*** Trans. from Chinese. Illus. Sonja Danowski. NorthSouth, 2015. (**PB**). Ages 5–8. (China)

Funke, Cornelia. ***The Thief Lord.*** Trans. from German by Oliver Latsch. Scholastic, 2002. Ages 10–14. (Germany). Also ***Inkheart*** (2003), ***Dragon Rider*** (2004), and ***Reckless*** (2011).

Hole, Stian. ***Garmann's Summer.*** Trans. from Norwegian by Don Bartlett. Eerdmans, 2008. (**PB**). Ages 5–8. (Norway)

Hole, Stian. ***Anna's Heaven.*** Trans. from Norwegian by Don Bartlett. Eerdmans, 2014. (**PB**). Ages 8–11. (Norway)

Konnecke, Ole. ***Anton Can Do Magic.*** Trans. from German by Catherine Chidgey. Lerner, 2011. (**PB**). Ages 5–8. (Germany)

Kris. ***A Bag of Marbles.*** Trans. from French by Edward Gauvin. Illus. Vincent Bailly. Based on the memoir of Joseph Joffo. Graphic Universe, 2013. (**GR**). Ages 11–18. (Jewish).

Kruusval, Catarina. ***Ellen's Apple Tree.*** Trans. from Swedish by Joan Sandin. R & S Books, 2008. (**PB**). Ages 5–8. (Sweden)

Lagercrantz, Rose. ***My Happy Life.*** Trans. from Swedish by Julia Marshall. Illus. Eva Eriksson. Gecko, 2012. Ages 6–10. (Sweden). Also ***My Heart is Laughing*** (2014).

Lat. ***Kampung Boy.*** First Second, 2006. Ages 10–12. Trans. from Malaysian. Also ***Town Boy*** (2007). (Malaysia)

Lee, JiHyeon. ***Pool.*** Trans. from Korean. Chronicle, 2015. (**PB**). Ages 4–8. (South Korea)

Lee, Suzy. ***The Zoo.*** Kane/Miller, 2007. (**PB**). Ages 5–8. Also ***Mirror*** (2003), ***Wave*** (2008), ***Shadow*** (2010). (Korea)

Lindelauf, Benny. ***Nine Open Arms.*** Trans. from Dutch by John Nieuwenhuizen. Illus. Dasha Tolstikova. Enchanted Lion, 2014. Ages 11–14. (Netherlands)

Lunde, Stein Erik. ***My Father's Arms Are a Boat.*** Trans. from Norwegian. Illus. Oyvind Torseter Enchanted Lion, 2012. (**PB**). Ages 4–8. (Norway)

Machado, Ana Maria. ***What a Party!*** Trans. from Portuguese. Groundwood, 2013. (**PB**). Ages 4–7.

Machado, Ana Maria. ***Until the Day Arrives.*** Trans. from Portuguese by Jane Springer. Groundwood, 2014. Ages 10–13. (Portugal to Brazil)

Mahe, Vincent. ***750 Years in Paris.*** Trans. from French. Nobrow, 2015. (**GR**). Ages 13–18. (France)

Matti, Truus. ***Departure Time.*** Trans. from Dutch by Nancy Florest-Flier. Namelos, 2011. Ages 10–14. (Netherlands)

Matti, Truus. ***Mister Orange.*** Trans. from Dutch by Laura Watkinson. Illus. Jenni Desmond. Enchanted Lion, 2012. Ages 10–14. (Netherlands)

Metselaar, Menno, and Ruud van der Rol. ***Anne Frank: Her Life in Words and Pictures.*** Trans. from Dutch by Arnold Pomerans. Roaring Brook, 2009. Ages 10–14. (Netherlands)

Moundlic, Charlotte. ***The Bathing Costume, or, The Worst Vacation of My Life.*** Trans. from French by Claudia Bedrick. Illus. Olivier Tallec. Enchanted Lion, 2013. (**PB**). Ages 6–9. (France)

Nakagawa, Chihiro. ***Who Made This Cake?*** Illus. Junji Koyose. Trans. from Japanese. Front Street, 2008. (**PB**). Ages 5–8. (Japan)

Nayar, Nandini. ***What Should I Make?*** Illus. Proiti Roy. Trans. from Hindi. Tricycle, 2009. (**PB**). Ages 5–8. (India)

Orlev, Uri. ***Run, Boy, Run.*** Trans. from Hebrew by Hillel Halkin. Houghton, 2003. Ages 10–13. (Israel)

Rasmussen, Halfdan. ***A Little Bitty Man and Other Poems for the Very Young.*** Trans. from Danish by Marilyn Nelson and Pamela Espeland. Illus. Kevin Hawkes. Candlewick, 2011. (**PI**). Ages 5–8. (Denmark)

Satrapi, Marjane. ***Persepolis.*** Trans. from French. Pantheon, 2003. (**GR**). Ages 10–14. (Iran)

Sellier, Marie. ***Legend of the Chinese Dragon.*** Trans. from French by Sibylle Kazeroid. Illus. Catherine Louis. NorthSouth, 2007. (**PB**). Ages 5–8. (Set in China)

Shyam, Bhajju. ***The London Jungle Book.*** Trans. from Hindi. Tara Books, 2013. (**PB**). Ages 8–12. (India)

Skármeta, Antonio. ***The Composition.*** Trans. from Spanish by Elisa Amado. Illus. Alfonso Ruano. Groundwood, 2000. (**PB**). Ages 8–12. (Chile)

Stolz, Joelle. ***The Shadows of Ghadames.*** Trans. from French by Catherine Temerson. Delacorte, 2004. Ages 11–14. (Libya)

Thor, Annika. ***A Faraway Island.*** Trans. from Swedish by Linda Schenck. Delcorte, 2009. Ages 9–12. Also ***The Lily Pond*** (2011) and ***Deep Sea*** (2015). (Sweden)

Uehashi, Nahoko. ***Morbito: Guardian of the Spirit.*** Trans. from Japanese by Cathy Hirano. Illus. Yuko Shimizu. Scholastic, 2008. Ages 10–14. (Japan)

Van Leeuwen, Joke. ***The Day My Father Became a Bush.*** Trans. from Dutch by Bill Nagelkerke. Gecko, 2014. Ages 9–12. (Netherlands)

Van Mol, Sine. ***Meena.*** Trans. from Dutch. Illus. Carianne Wijffels. Eerdmans, 2011. Ages 5–8. (Belgium)

Voorhoeve, Anne C. ***My Family for the War.*** Trans. from German by Tammi Reichel. Dials, 2012. Ages 12–18. (Germany)

Yan, Ma. ***The Diary of Ma Yan: The Struggles and Hopes of a Chinese Schoolgirl.*** Trans. from Mandarin by He Yanping. HarperCollins, 2005. Ages 10–14. (China)

Yu, Li-Qiong. ***A New Year's Reunion.*** Trans. from Chinese. Illus. Zhu Cheng-Liang. Candlewick, 2011. (**PB**). Ages 6–9. (China)

Yumoto, Kazumi. ***The Friends.*** Trans. from Japanese by Cathy Hirano. Farrar, 1996. Ages 10–14. (Japan)

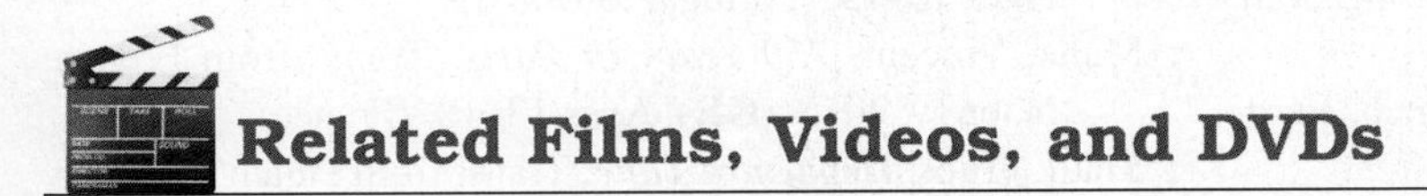

Related Films, Videos, and DVDs

I Hate English! (2006). Author: Ellen Levine (1989). 14 minutes. (Asian American)

I Love Saturdays y Domingos (2002). Author: Alma Flor Ada. Illustrated by Elvivia Savadier (2002). 18 minutes. (Bilingual).

Inkheart (2009). Author: Cornelia Funke (2003). 106 minutes. (Germany)

The Thief Lord (2006). Author: Cornelia Funke (2002). 99 minutes. (Germany/Australia)

War Horse (2011). Author: Michael Morpugo (2007/1982). 146 minutes. (England)

Part 3

Bringing Children and Books Together

Finding compelling books for children is only a first step. The ways in which we bring children and books together can either invite children to enthusiastically immerse themselves as readers or lead them to dread the worksheets they will have to complete once they finish reading a book.

Chapters 13 and 14 focus on curriculum and teaching strategies. Chapter 13 is framed by the political context that influences the use of literature in schools, particularly highlighting the Common Core State Standards. The two main approaches to teaching reading—basal reading programs and literature-based reading—are discussed in terms of strategies for incorporating literature into the teaching of reading. Features such as sample planning webs, evaluation checklists, and literature-related activities provide practical suggestions and advice to help you gain experience with literature. In addition, suggestions related to dealing with book challenges and censorship are addressed.

Chapter 14 presents strategies for engaging children with literature and eliciting their responses. The chapter and strategies are organized around three types of experiences with literature that have different purposes for readers. Reading Widely for Personal Purposes includes strategies for read-alouds, independent reading, booktalks, readers' theatre, and experiencing literature as multimodal texts. Reading Critically to Inquire about the World includes literature discussions, a variety of literature response engagements, using drama as response, and literature across the curriculum. Reading Strategically to Learn about Literacy focuses on using literature to learn about writing.

Chapter 13

Literature in the Curriculum

Reading

We get no good
By being ungenerous even to a book,
And calculating profits … so much help
By so much reading. It is rather when
We gloriously forget ourselves and plunge
Soul-forward, headlong, into a book's profound,
Impassioned for its beauty and salt of truth—
'Tis then we get the right good from a book.

—*Elizabeth Browning*

This chapter highlights the political context that surrounds the use of literature in classrooms and libraries, as well as broader issues of planning for engagements with literature, including dealing with book challenges. This chapter begins with a discussion of the Common Core State Standards and their impact on the ways in which schools are planning for literature and literacy. Different organizational structures for organizing a literature curriculum with children, such as genres, themes or topics, authors or illustrators, literary and visual elements, and notable books are overviewed, along with strategies for planning literature units. In addition, literature plays an important role in the teaching of reading and writing, either as a supplement to a basal reader program or through literature-based approaches. The latter part of the chapter includes sections on responding to book challenges, evaluating a literature program, and gaining experience with observing the use of literature in classrooms or libraries.

The Politics of Literacy and Literature

The teaching of reading has been a controversial and contested area of debate among educators and politicians. Calls for higher literacy standards are the focus of intense national and international interest and have led to the imposition of "one-size-fits-all" models of national literacy standards and high stakes testing through legislation and policy initiatives. Although initiatives on the teaching of reading have long evolved from public pressure, the increasing involvement of federal and state governments in specific decisions about literacy instruction to raise standards is a recent development. These public debates and government initiatives have often resulted in punitive legislation aimed at controlling educators (Shannon, 2013).

Congress created the ***National Reading Panel*** (NRP) in 1997 to assess the status of research-based knowledge about reading. The *Report of the National Reading Panel* (2000) was met with great skepticism because the panel's narrow definition of scientific research excluded the majority of research studies conducted over a 30-year period and resulted in a highly skewed set of recommendations. This report narrowed the teaching of reading to instruction in phonemic awareness, phonics, reading comprehension, fluency, and vocabulary. A large body of research studies on reading aloud and independent silent reading were not included because they did not meet the NRP's narrow definition of scientific research.

The ***No Child Left Behind*** (NCLB) Act was passed in 2001 and ***Reading First*** programs were established to implement the NRP components of reading instruction. By 2008, reading comprehension tests indicated that Reading First did *not* have statistically significant impacts on reading comprehension test scores in grades 1–3, and other national testing indicated that reading achievement scores for intermediate students either had not increased or were decreasing. These findings called into question the assumption that a phonics-based approach to reading instruction would produce better readers than other approaches.

Many schools adopted basal reader programs with highly controlled and stilted stories for young children, not recognizing that carefully selected literature can support children in developing reading skills. Nursery rhymes, predictable books, and poems help children develop phonemic awareness. Read-alouds, paired reading, readers' theatre, and choral reading increase fluency. Shared reading and repeated oral reading teach children sound–symbol relationships and increase their fluency. Independent silent reading of good literature, especially if followed by reflection, increases children's vocabulary and conceptual knowledge, as well as develops their reading comprehension.

Overemphasis of any one component of reading instruction, such as phonics, to the exclusion of all others in initial reading instruction is detrimental to students (Weaver, 2009). Programs advocating heavy emphasis on phonics without daily read-alouds or independent self-selected reading of excellent books often produce resistant readers. Daily read-alouds and independent silent reading demonstrate fluency, build meaningful vocabulary and conceptual knowledge, offer reading practice, and improve attitudes toward reading.

Accountability is a demand by government agencies for school systems and teachers to improve children's school achievement as demonstrated by test scores. The NCLB Act expanded accountability by requiring annual testing of reading and mathematics achievement for all students in grades 3–8 that were tied to student retention decisions, grading of schools, and news articles ranking schools according to test scores. Critics point out that the focus on multiple choice tests has dumbed down the curriculum and led to "drill and kill" approaches to teaching isolated skills as well as to pushing low-scoring students out of public schools to boost scores. The National Association of Educational Progress tracks trends in reading achievement and issues a report called the "Nation's Report Card." Data show that reading comprehension scores for 2015 remained unchanged at grade 4, with a slight decrease at grade 8, after several years of decline associated with NCLB. Many educators believe that the major reason for this decline was a decrease in voluntary reading among students (Krashen, 2011). As a result of NCLB, class time was spent on basic reading skills, diminishing curricular efforts in other subjects, including the enjoyment and appreciation of literature. As is often the case with policy initiatives, the shortcomings of NCLB and Reading First led to new initiatives based on a new set of standards and assessments.

Common Core State Standards

The current focus of national and state efforts is the Common Core State Standards (CCSS), with many states developing their own modified versions of these standards. These K–12 standards were developed by a group appointed by the National Governor's Association and the Council of Chief State School Officers. They examined research on the levels of literacy needed for success in college and careers and worked backward to determine the literacy knowledge they believed students needed at each grade level to be college and career ready by the end of high school. These grade-specific standards in reading, writing, speaking, listening, and language also set requirements for literacy in history/social studies, science, and technical content areas. These standards have had a significant impact on instruction because of state mandates that put schools under tremendous pressure to make changes in their instruction. Each state is developing performance-based assessments to measure student achievement and to evaluate teachers and schools on the standards.

Aspects of the CCSS impacting literature include:

- An increase in informational texts in classroom instruction and libraries, with a recommended 50/50 split between literary and informational texts starting in kindergarten and gradually increasing to 70/30 in high school. Because informational text previously was 10–15 percent of the texts in most primary classrooms, schools have greatly increased the availability and use of these texts.
- An emphasis on gradual increases across grade levels in the complexity of texts that children are reading. CCSS provides a list of text exemplars for each grade level along with excerpts from these texts to demonstrate expectations for text complexity to teachers and librarians as they select books with children.
- A focus on the close reading of texts and text analysis that require children to find and cite evidence in the text as they discuss key ideas and details, craft and structure, and knowledge and ideas from these texts. Text analysis is viewed as bringing rigor to reading with an emphasis on higher level critical reading skills.

As is often the case, some of these changes have led to imbalances and misunderstandings. Some schools now overemphasize informational reading, viewing fiction as only for enjoyment, not learning. Some administrators mistook the exemplar book lists of text complexity as core reading lists for all students, which is highly problematic because many of the books are dated and not culturally diverse. The lists are only intended as examples of increasing text complexity, not core reading. Another issue is that many schools only use quantitative lexile levels to determine the difficulty of a text, restricting children to books within a particular range. Lexile level is one aspect of text complexity in CCSS alongside teacher and librarian judgment about the difficulty of the text for a specific group of children engaged in a particular task.

The emphasis on close reading is a return to narrow definitions of what and how children read. Close reading is interpreted by policy makers as in-depth, step-by-step analysis of each part of the text to determine literal and inferential meanings. History indicates that this type of textual criticism turned off generations of readers because of the lack of purpose, meaning, and connections of ideas and issues significant to children (Langer, 2010). In addition, this emphasis is a misunderstanding of reader response as only the making of personal connections. Reader response begins with personal connection and interpretation, but readers then analyze their responses through dialogue based on evidence from their lives and the text (Rosenblatt, 1978).

Resources to support you in meeting the CCSS are integrated throughout this text—titles of books across themes and genres, discussions of the structures and types of informational texts, information about literary elements and text structures, methods for measuring text complexity, and ways to integrate

Table 13.1 Important Studies on Literature and Reading

Researchers	Participants	Findings
Ivey & Johnston, 2015	Four-year study of four eighth grade classrooms where teachers abandoned assigned readings for self-selected reading	Results indicated increased reading volume, fewer students failing the state test, and changes in peer relationships, self-regulation, and conceptions of self.
Aukerman & Schuldt (2016); Pantaleo (2014); Feathers & Arya (2012)	Second grade classroom; seventh grade classroom; six third grade students	Three studies used a range of methodologies to examine the role of illustrations in meaning-making from picturebooks and the multiple ways children engaged with illustrations.
Campano, Ghiso, & Sánchez (2013); Móller (2012)	Fourth grade African-American boys; fourth grade literature discussion group	Two long-term qualitative studies of children's responses to literature and the ways they considered issues of social justice and critical literacy
Fullerton & Colwell (2010)	Content analysis of multiple studies	Ethnographic content analysis of research from 1989 through 2009 to identify the benefits of small group literature discussions, the teacher's role, and the influence of gender and status
Maloch (2008)	Second grade classroom	Documented teacher support to build knowledge about informational texts through multiple opportunities with texts and learning text features
Santoro, Chard, Howard, & Baker (2008)	First grade students across multiple classrooms	Read-alouds when combined with comprehension instruction and discussion promoted growth in comprehension and vocabulary
Wilson, Martens, Arya, & Altwerger (2004)	84 urban, low SES second graders with different reading programs: scripted phonics-based programs and a literature-based reading program	No significant difference was found in phonics use; guided-reading students could describe settings and characters, retell stories cohesively, form inferences, and make connections. Findings contradict the National Reading Panel recommendations on phonics.
Worthy, Patterson, Salas, Prater, & Turner (2002)	24 struggling, resistant readers in grades three through five	Teachers who tailored instruction to children's needs, found materials that fit interests, and took time to inspire children to read were most effective in increasing motivation to read.
Anderson (1996)	Elementary grade students	Even slight increases (10 minutes a day) in time spent reading independently lead to gains in reading achievement. Amount of free reading in early grades helps determine reading ability in grades five and six.

text analysis with reader response. One emphasis within CCSS is reading across multiple texts to compare ideas and information. Examples of reader connections to facilitate this reading across texts and perspectives are included in the genre chapters.

You should also be aware of research findings about the value of literature for children in relation to literacy to counter these misunderstandings. Research studies summarized in Table 13.1 indicate that two engagements are especially important in teaching children to read: regularly reading aloud excellent literature and time for silent independent reading of free-choice material. Research studies in Table 13.2 show that reading and writing strategies and skills go hand in hand—a strong focus with CCSS as well.

Given the political context surrounding literacy and literature and the research on literature in the curriculum, literature can become a planned component in classrooms and libraries through two types of curricular frameworks. The first framework is a literature curriculum in which instruction is planned around literature as a discipline with a particular content of literary knowledge. The second framework involves the integration of literature into the literacy curriculum as reading materials to support the teaching of reading and writing in a basal reader program.

Table 13.2 Important Studies on Literature and Writing

Researchers	Participants	Findings
Kesler, Gibson, & Turansky (2016)	Fifth grade classroom	Results show the value of digital storytelling as a form of written response to historical fiction.
Journal of Children's Literature, Fall 2008	Series of case studies by researchers on the use of literature to support writing	Each research group presents a case study of the text structures found in literature and strategies for learning from these mentor texts to support comprehension and writing.
Jarvey, McKeough, & Pyryt (2008)	Two classes of fourth grade students	Comparison of two approaches to teaching children to write trickster tales. Documents the strategies within an approach that supported children in writing that genre.
Barrs (2000)	Eighteen fourth graders in five elementary schools in London whose reading and writing were analyzed during one school year	Children use the language and writing styles of books they read in their writing. Writing development was closely linked to reading development and vice versa.
Cantrell (1999)	Children in four third grade classrooms where teachers used recommended literacy practices to a high degree were compared with children in four classrooms where teachers used these practices to a low degree.	When teachers frequently used literature, integrated reading and writing, and taught reading and writing skills in context, children developed reading and writing skills at higher levels than in classrooms with isolated skill instruction.
Dressel (1990)	Fifth graders	Student writing was directly affected by the characteristics of read-alouds, regardless of reading ability. The better the quality of a read-aloud, the better the quality of student writing.

Planning a Literature Curriculum

Literature is more than a collection of well-written stories and poems. Literature is also a discipline with a body of knowledge, a course of study to teach children *about* literature—the terms used to define it, its components or elements and genres, and the craft of creating literature. The terms and elements of fiction are presented in Chapter 3; the terms and visual elements of illustrations are presented in Chapter 4; the terms and elements of nonfiction are presented in Chapter 12; and the genres and their characteristics are presented in Chapters 5 through 12.

A ***traditional approach*** to literature focuses on mastery of content. This approach places the teacher at the center, in that the teacher decides the agenda, dispenses the information, asks the questions, and often supplies the answers. The goal of this approach is for children to learn what the teacher tells them about the literature under study. The same approach occurs in libraries with the teaching of specific research skills that involve librarian-directed instruction.

Our focus is on an ***inquiry approach,*** which is grounded in problem-based learning and constructivist learning and focuses on how one learns. Children actively engage in posing questions that are significant to them as they explore the power of literature to examine the human condition. In an inquiry approach:

- Children's inquiry is guided by their *own* questions related to literature—questions they find compelling and honestly care about. During the inquiry process, children revise their questions as they learn, discuss, and share information with others. Collaborative learning, team projects, and small group discussions are emphasized.
- The process of how to search for and make sense of information about literature is emphasized so that the knowledge gained is conceptual and has wide application.

- Educators are facilitators rather than dispensers of knowledge who think collaboratively with students instead of providing answers.

An inquiry-based literature curriculum can be organized around genre, theme/topic, author/illustrator, literary elements, or notable books. An alternative is to create a hybrid literature curriculum by including aspects of several of these approaches.

Genres

By organizing a literature curriculum around literary genres, you provide a context for children to learn about the types of literature and the characteristics of each. An inquiry approach to genre typically begins by immersing children in exploring a wide range of books from that genre to develop a list of characteristics for that genre; for example, that works of historical fiction are always set in the past or that characters in folktales are two-dimensional. Children move to in-depth explorations of specific books within the genre and of the different ways these characteristics play out across the genre.

Cruz and Pollock (2004) share their experiences of immersing children in inquiry around fantasy as a genre. Their approach reflects an effective structure for engaging children in exploring literary elements and genre within a meaningful context by:

- Gathering and sorting a range of texts to determine which belong to the genre
- Reading aloud picturebooks and novels to discuss excellent examples of the genre
- Independently reading many books in the genre
- Charting their observations about the genre in various ways
- Discussing selected books from the genre in small group literature circles
- Writing their own stories based on their knowledge of the genre

One advantage of this plan is that children are exposed to a wide variety of literature across the school year. Knowledge of different genres gives children useful frameworks for understanding story types that support their comprehension as readers and their use of genre structures as writers. Planning involves choosing a genre, gathering a wide range of books, and selecting several representative books. Most educators choose to do one or two genre studies a year, selecting genres that will expand children's reading or that relate to state standards for a particular grade level.

Themes or Topics

Organizing a study of literature by theme or topic is the most frequent and effective way to engage children with literature. Focusing on the multiple connections and interpretations of issues and themes in a book gives children an opportunity to relate what they learn to their own lives. Themes and topics will vary according to their ages and experiences. Often, primary children are most interested in themes having to do with school and family life, while middle-grade children are intrigued by themes related to difficult social and global issues and to their own need for inner resources as they transition into adulthood. Examples of themes include:

- Taking action can make a difference in the world
- Force creates movement
- Systems organize our lives and world
- Belonging creates relationships as well as conformity
- Difference is a resource, not a problem
- Life is a journey across many kinds of pathways

Children often read or listen to a particular book or set of books and explore the theme through questioning, journaling, reflecting, discussing, writing, responding through drama and art, or further reading. Strategies to support discussion and response are in Chapter 14.

Books can also be organized around topics such as animals, friendship, family, transportation, and careers as a way to support children in locating books for independent reading. Organizing by topic, however, does not facilitate discussion and thoughtful connections across books because topics stay on the surface of the book, and do not facilitate digging into issues around which children can dialogue.

Authors or Illustrators

The goal of a curriculum organized by author or illustrator is to acquaint children with the books and styles of authors and illustrators. Children also gain knowledge of the lives of authors and illustrators and how these life experiences influenced their books as well as how they use particular literary or visual elements to tell their stories. This type of inquiry influences children's choices as readers, their comprehension and reading strategies, and their writing processes and strategies. Many times, these authors and their books become mentors for children as writers, a focus of the anchor standards for writing in the Common Core State Standards.

The choice of which authors and illustrators to highlight is guided by children's reading interests and as a means of introducing notable authors and illustrators. As children experience a sampling of the chosen author's or illustrator's work, attention is focused on trademark stylistic elements such as unusual use of words, color, or media, as well as themes, characters, or settings common to these works. Information about the person's life can be introduced through published or online interviews and even guest appearances by the author or illustrator. Websites, biographies, and biographical reference sources, such as *Something about the Author* (Gale, 2016) and *Children's Literature Review* (Gale, 2016), provide information about authors and illustrators. Many biographies and autobiographies of children's book authors and illustrators are available, as individual books, such as *The House That Baba Built: An Author's Childhood in China* by Ed Young and *Drawing from Memory* by Allen Say, or as books within a series, such as Richard Owen's Meet the Author series.

Literary and Visual Elements

Literary elements refer to character, plot, theme, style, and setting, whereas ***visual elements*** refer to artistic styles, media, and book format. A ***literary device*** is a style technique used to achieve a specific effect, such as using irony, symbolism, parody, and foreshadowing to add richness to stories. Parodies involve an allusion to a well-known text, such as the classic *Goodnight Moon* by Margaret Wise Brown (1947), a long-time favorite of young children who demand that it be read over and over. *Goodnight Goon* by Michael Rex (2008) and *Goodnight iPad* by Anne Droyd (2011) are parodies for older readers who recognize the way that an author has played on a classic text from their childhoods. Chapters 3 and 4 discuss these elements, and Chapters 5–12 include information on the elements as they relate to different genres of children's literature

The goal of a literature curriculum organized by literary and visual elements is to give children a better understanding of the craft of writing and illustrating so they can read more perceptively and appreciatively and apply this knowledge to their writing and artwork. Because this approach is analytical and somewhat abstract, it is often integrated into mini-lessons within a writing workshop rather than as a separate unit of study.

Careful selection of children's books to facilitate the investigation of a literary or visual element is crucial. The featured element must be prominent and be used by the author or illustrator with extraordinary skill to captivate readers. Books can be grouped across genres to demonstrate the same element. Picturebooks are particularly effective for presenting literary elements clearly and in relatively simple contexts to facilitate understanding. One resource for selecting picturebooks is Susan Hall's *Using Picture Storybooks to Teach Literary Devices,* Vols. 1–4 (1990, 1994, 2001, 2007).

Children's acquaintance with literary and visual elements should go beyond mere definition and include close reading of key passages or illustrations. These passages can be used to examine the author's or illustrator's craft at developing character, establishing mood, authenticating setting, or using such devices as inference, symbolism, or foreshadowing. Children can then explore these elements and devices in their own art, drama, and writing to give a personal and more complete understanding of these concepts, providing an evaluation of their grasp of these concepts.

Notable Books

Notable books are exemplary classic or contemporary books on award-winning lists. These books are read and analyzed for the features that contribute to their excellence, such as their relevance to readers, unique perspectives or insights, treatment of topics, memorable characters, or illustrations.

In the primary grades, you will most likely read notable books aloud, because most will be too difficult for independent reading. Reading aloud to children is important in the intermediate and middle grades as well, but children can also read these books independently. Analysis of notable books can occur through discussion (whole class or small group), dialogue journal writing (with you or a peer), or reading logs.

Regardless of the method children use to respond, they should be encouraged to relate the books to their own lives and to compare them to other books. Even if they are responding in more independent ways, such as journal writing, it is a good idea to invite them to share their thoughts with one another.

If you organize your literature curriculum by notable books, be careful to remain flexible in book selections from year to year so that the list of notable books reflects children's current interests and reading preferences. A list of notable books that never varies can result in disinterest and stale teaching.

Developing Literature Units

Initial planning for literature units includes establishing your goals for what children will explore or learn through the unit, selecting several books to receive in-depth focus (often called touchstone books), and gathering a collection of many books related to the unit focus. For example, initial planning for a science fiction unit on future worlds could involve identifying these core books:

- Independent reading—*The City of Ember* by Jeanne DuPrau (2003), *Under Their Skin* by Margaret Peterson Haddix (2016), *The House of the Scorpion* by Nancy Farmer (2002), *The Trap* by Steven Arntson (2015), *Cosmic* by Frank Boyce (2008), *The Green Book* by Jill Paton Walsh (1986)
- Read-aloud touchstone text—*The Giver* by Lois Lowry (1993)
- Small group literature circle books—*Gathering Blue* (2000), *Messenger* (2004), *Son* (2012) by Lois Lowry
- Featured author—*Looking Back: A Book of Memories* by Lois Lowry (2016)

Collecting, brainstorming, and organizing the activities are the final steps in planning for a literature curriculum. Two helpful tools in organizing the details of literature units are webs and lesson plans.

Webs A ***web*** is a graphic planning tool that reveals relationships between ideas and creates a visual overview of a literature unit, including focus, concepts, book titles, and activities. A web is a map that helps you focus on your goals and be able to adjust your teaching to encompass new ideas or to meet special needs and circumstances. You can use the web as a source for lesson plans as the unit unfolds.

Ideas for a web are generated through brainstorming. The main advantage of webbing is that the process clarifies and creates ideas for connections between concepts, books, and activities. Activities can be drawn across content areas—writing, reading, listening, thinking, speaking, art, crafts, drama, and music. Involving children in creating webs gives them a voice in planning and can provide original ideas and relationships that you had not considered. The web in Figure 13.1 shows ideas for a unit of study on the literary element of character. The web in Figure 13.2 is built around concepts relating to forced journeys and refugees. This web begins with literature to develop a conceptual understanding of journeys as movement along a pathway (physical, emotional, cultural, psychological, etc.) as a frame for an exploration of the topic of refugees.

Lesson Plans Lesson plans vary according to your needs and experiences, but lesson plans usually include the following components:

- ***Goals*** are the conceptual ideas/issues that are the purpose of the unit, essentially the "why" behind activities and lessons. These goals give a focus for your planning of activities but also leave space for children to pursue their inquiries. The goal for a literature unit on refugees might be that children understand the complex reasons for why people become refugees and how that affects their lives.
- ***Activities and materials*** indicate the preparation that you need to do for the experience, the materials needed, and the tasks or engagements for students. If you want students to understand the complex issues of refugees, you could read aloud the informational book *Denied, Detained, Deported* by Ann Bausum, and have children select from novels to read in small groups, such as *La Linea* by Ann Jamarillo, *Shooting Kabul* by N. H. Senzai, *Ask Me No Questions* by Marina Budhos, *Bone Sparrow* by Zana Fraillon, and *A Time of Miracles* by Anne-Laure Bondoux.
- ***Evaluation and reflection*** are your plans for evaluating children's understandings around the goals and your self-reflections on the effectiveness of the activities. ***Student evaluation*** can take the form of written reflections, oral questions, whole class or small group discussions, entries in student journals, and written, oral, artistic, and dramatic responses to literature. ***Self-evaluation*** is your reflections on children's interest in the activities, their understandings related to the goals, the plan's success in predicting time and materials needed, and the effectiveness of the activities and materials. During the literature unit, you will want to regularly evaluate children's understandings and questions and make adjustments in the plans.

Figure 13.1 Web Demonstrating Investigation of a Literary Element, Grades 2–4

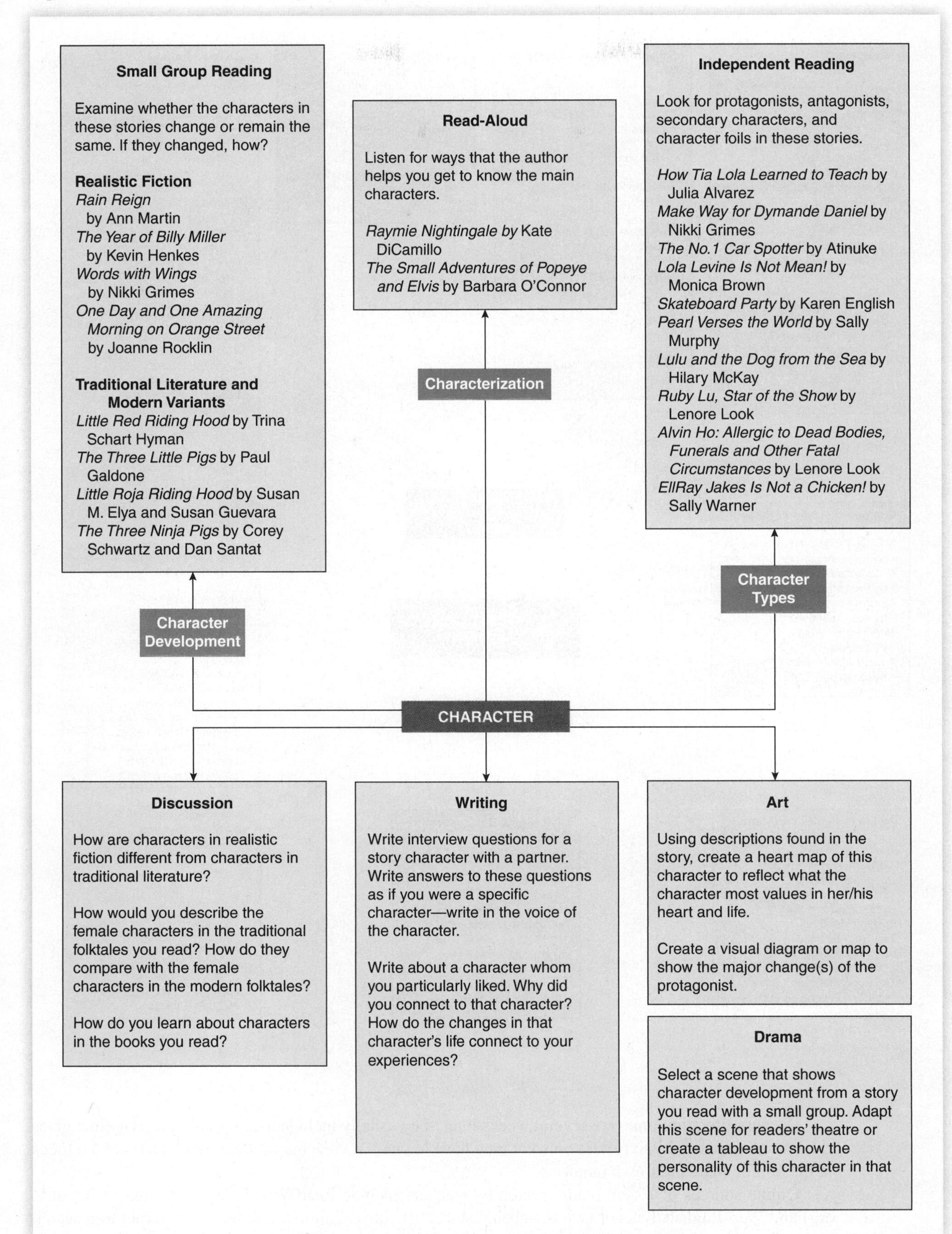

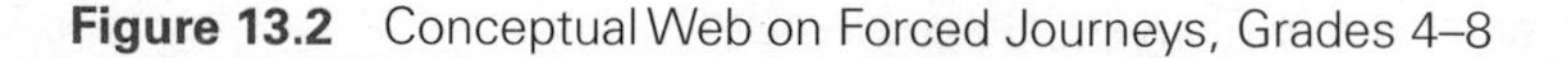

Figure 13.2 Conceptual Web on Forced Journeys, Grades 4–8

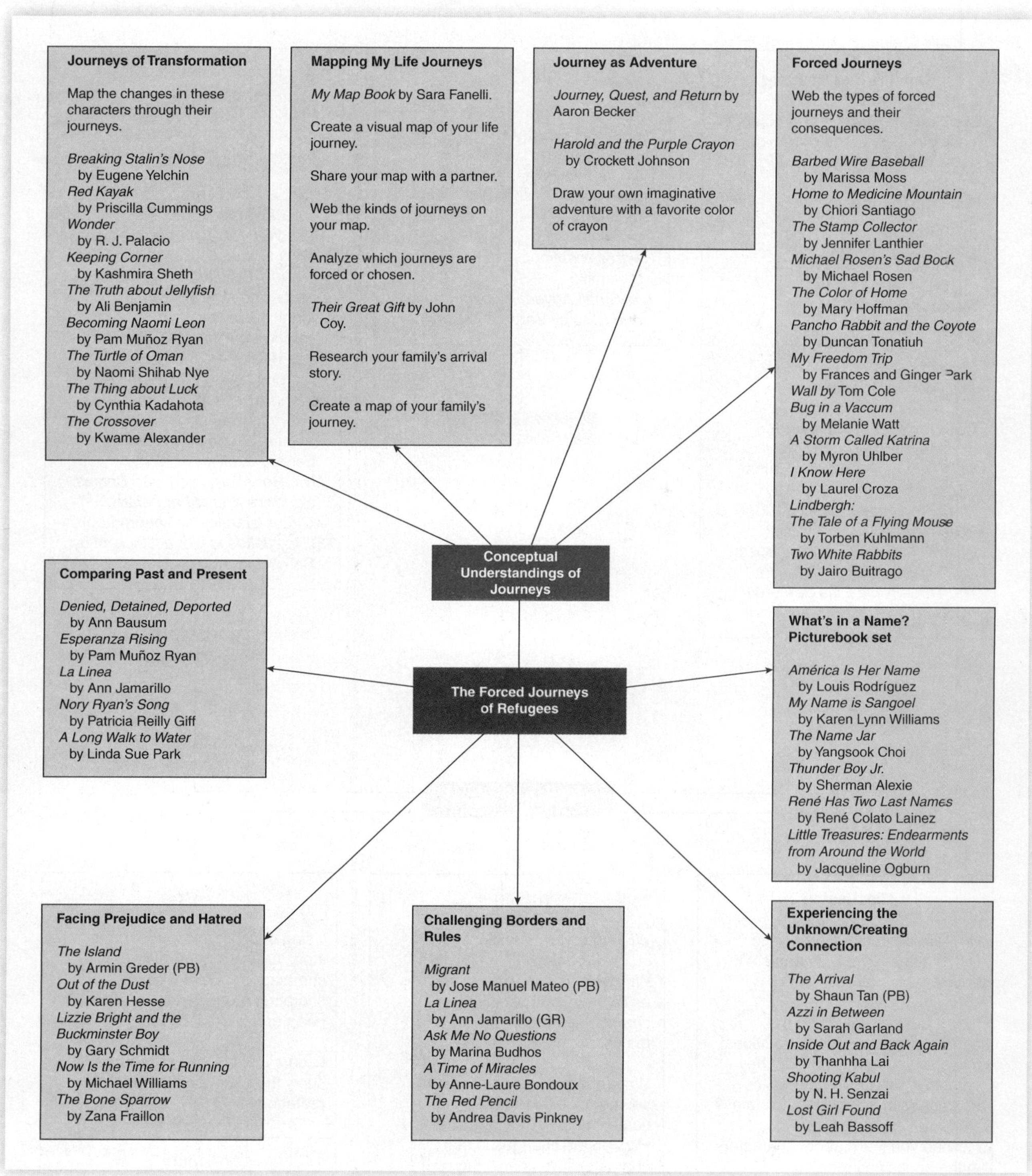

Because literature units are several weeks long, they usually include a culminating activity that gives children an opportunity to reflect on what they have learned, review major ideas, and celebrate the focus of the unit or share their own inquiries.

Online sources of lesson plans created by teachers include ReadWriteThink (www.readwritethink.org) and Web English Teacher (www.webenglishteacher.com). Children can use the Internet to research topics for literature units of study, locate websites for author studies, or identify sources for further research on a theme. Links to sites where children can find books on topics of interest and read others' comments on these books are found on the American Library Association's Great Websites for Kids (http://gws.ala.org/) in the Literature and Languages category.

Integrating Literature into a Literacy Curriculum

Literature is instrumental in helping children learn to read as well as keeping children's interest in reading alive, supporting struggling readers in strengthening their reading strategies, and encouraging all children to become lifelong readers. Two common approaches to teaching reading involve different roles for literature.

Basal Reading Program Supplemented by Children's Literature

The most common approach to the teaching of reading in schools is the ***basal reader*** or ***anthology*** supplemented by children's literature. Basal reading programs have been the traditional approach to teaching reading in U.S. elementary schools for decades. These programs consist of a series of readers that are written at successively more difficult levels. The core materials include a student reader, a teacher's manual, student workbooks, and tests. A basal program provides teachers with an instructional framework on which to build along with reading selections and related activities.

Guided reading consists of small group instruction, assessment of children's reading levels, books "leveled" by reading difficulty, explicit instruction on reading strategies to improve comprehension, and short-term intervention for children who struggle. A widely used guided reading program is the Fountas and Pinnell Leveled Books Program, published by Heinemann.

The learning theory on which basal reading materials are based holds that learning complex skills begins with mastering the simplest components of that skill before attempting the next larger components, and so on until the whole skill is learned. In terms of learning to read, letters of the alphabet are learned first, followed by letter-sound patterns, words, and then sentences. Finally, when the components of reading are learned, whole works of literature, such as stories, plays, and poems, are read. This theory is challenged by those who believe that reading is a meaning-based process rather than a skill that is mechanical and additive (Weaver, 2009).

In the 1980s, U.S. publishers of basal readers made an effort to improve the quality of stories in basal readers and integrated more multicultural stories and excerpts from high-quality literature, such as a chapter or episode from a longer children's book. These changes were incorporated while retaining the skill-based instruction and the belief that reading is learned from part to whole.

Basal readers are not a substitute for real books. Even though some basal stories are good literature, instead of excerpts or adaptations, the brevity of these selections is a problem for middle-grade children who are capable of reading novel-length chapter books and should be doing so regularly. Children in classes where anthologies and basal readers are used exclusively are denied the all-important self-selection of reading materials from a wide variety of books and the challenge of longer chapter books.

Another issue is that in-depth text analysis, which is at the heart of the Common Core State Standards, requires complex texts and novels for characters and issues to develop and change over time. Children need whole texts with multiple layers of meaning, not simplified stories and excerpts, if they are to engage in critical reading and search for intertextual connections across and within texts.

Ideally, each teacher should be able to choose the approach to teaching reading that best suits his or her philosophy of learning and teaching. In many school districts across the U.S., however, the basal approach to teach reading is mandated. Even more restrictive is the lockstep methods of teaching reading that rely on highly scripted, prescribed lesson plans that must be followed with no accommodation. In a three-year study on methods of teaching reading, Ryder, Sekulski, and Silberg (2003) found that this type of direct instruction has limited applicability, should not be used as the main method of reading instruction, and is not as effective as methods that allow teachers to engage in a more flexible approach that adapts to children's needs.

Many teachers, despite mandates, have moved away from a "read-every-page-or-bust" attitude toward these programs. They have found ways to improve their teaching of reading by using the basal in innovative ways that eliminate some of the skill exercises and provide time for reading real books. Guidelines drawn from the work of these teachers are:

- Use only the best literary selections in the basal, and substitute good literature for the rest.
- Have children read the better-written basal selections for enjoyment or discussion, and eliminate some of the skill lessons that take the focus away from meaning.
- Eliminate worksheets used to keep children busy while the teacher meets with small groups. Children can read self-choice books until their group meets.
- Eliminate the stigma of ability grouping through whole-class studies of a particular book and heterogeneous small groups that meet to discuss a book. Use the time saved for one-on-one conferences with children about what they are reading.
- Use phonics and skills lessons from the basal reader only when a particular student or group of students needs those skills. Children do not learn according to an imposed schedule, but only when they need that skill and are ready to learn. Use the time saved from ineffective exercises to read aloud or for children to read self-choice books.
- Avoid the literal-level comprehension questions at the end of basal lessons that trivialize the stories and demean children. Use the time saved to invite children to share personal connections or to respond to the story in writing, drama, or art.
- Make phonics instruction or word study a regular but brief (10–15 minutes) part of primary grade reading instruction instead of taking the majority of time. Use that time to read and talk about good books.
- Basal readers for older students contain individual chapters excerpted from novels. Have children read these chapters as a preview to decide which novel to read.
- Create a text set of picturebooks that build from the themes, topics, and authors in the basal and that extends the basal units into real books.

Basal readers are most effective when used alongside a wide variety of literature that reflects children's interests and reading abilities. The basal reader provides guidance and structure, whereas literature provides the variety, self-selection, and interest that motivate children to want to read. The role of literature as supplemental materials is increasingly important for classrooms in order to encourage the level of thinking and text complexity required by the Common Core State Standards.

Reading Incentive Programs Some schools have purchased commercially produced ***reading incentive programs*** to motivate children to read more widely as a supplement to a basal reader. These programs have computerized management components to track progress. Many, such as *Accelerated Reader,* include a pretest for assigning a reading level to each child for a certain level of books that have a predetermined number of points according to difficulty as determined by the program developers. After children finish reading a book, they complete a multiple-choice test to assess literal comprehension and earn points and prizes based on their scores.

Reports on the success of such programs are mixed. Many schools report disappointment and concerns about whether such programs are having a positive impact on children's interest in reading because:

- Children's free choices for reading are limited, and children only value books in the program's database due to the reward system.
- Extrinsic rewards can diminish the desire of children to read for pleasure and personal enjoyment of literature, and reading is often deemphasized.
- Testing children's literal comprehension can interfere with reading books to experience the world of that story and often emphasize inconsequential material to the detriment of the development of critical thinking.
- Many children find ways to gain the rewards without reading the books, such as asking others for answers, skimming for frequently tested details, or seeing the movie.
- These programs are costly and take away from funds for purchasing literature for classrooms and school libraries. The program selections soon become dated.

You can design your own reading incentive programs in which children keep a record of their free-choice reading, have opportunities to respond to books in a variety of ways, and work toward individual reading goals. Rewards, such as a special celebration party, are aimed at the entire class, not individuals, for reaching goals.

Literature-Based Reading

Literature-based reading is an approach to teaching reading through real books. The learning theory on which literature-based reading is grounded holds that children learn by searching for meaning in the world around them, engaging in inquiry into issues from their reading, and examining their strategies as readers.

Teachers and librarians using a literature-based approach structure their classroom and library environments to immerse children in good literature. Children hear literature read aloud several times a day, see good readers reading voluntarily, and discover that good books can entertain and tell them things they want to know. They read books they have chosen because they are interested in the topics. Frequent one-to-one conferences allow teachers to check comprehension, assess reading strategies, and form small groups or create lessons around strategies that need explicit attention and teaching to support reading development.

As in basal reading programs, explicit reading instruction is an important feature of literature-based reading, particularly in the primary grades. Phonics, concepts of print, vocabulary, and comprehension strategies are taught in literature-based reading, but within the context of interesting books. Unlike basal reading programs, these skills are never taught in isolation, where they have no real meaning, are never the focus of the entire reading period, and are taught only when needed.

Literature-based reading instruction addresses the components of instruction considered essential to the teaching of reading by the Common Core State Standards: engaging with text to analyze key ideas and details, craft and structure, and the integration of knowledge and ideas. By including daily read-alouds and self-choice independent reading, children are more likely to also develop positive attitudes toward reading, self-motivation to read, and a lifelong reading habit.

Key elements of the literature-based reading classroom or library include:

- Daily reading aloud of good literature
- Reading and research skills taught when needed within meaningful contexts, never in isolation
- Quantities of good books in the classroom (five or more books per child), selected to match specific interests and reading abilities of children, as well as regular opportunities to self-select books from the school library
- Daily silent reading by children of self-selected books
- Daily opportunities for children to orally share their responses to books with others
- Regular opportunities for children to respond to literature in a variety of ways, including writing, drama, and art
- Frequent individual student–teacher reading conferences

Decisions about what to teach, when to teach it, and what materials to use are based on the specific children in a classroom. These decisions and the responsibility for materials selection and acquisition may make literature-based reading more demanding of the professional judgment of teachers and librarians than other reading methods; however, this approach has proven to be effective not only in teaching children to read but also in creating a positive attitude toward reading and lifelong reading habits. Moreover, the focus on provocative materials and children's personal responses makes teaching more exciting and enjoyable.

The absence of a prescribed, lockstep program is one of the greatest strengths of literature-based reading, but it also makes this approach vulnerable. The following practices have no place in literature-based reading approaches:

- Using mediocre literature in the reading program solely on the basis of what is on hand with no regard to its appeal to children or its suitability to curricular goals
- Regularly using class sets of a book with a predetermined reading schedule and fill-in-the-blank worksheets (a practice referred to as "basalization of literature")
- Round-robin reading where each child takes a turn reading a section aloud to the group (while no one else pays attention)

- Selecting and assigning every book read by children
- Assigning book reports under the guise of a book response to check comprehension

There is no one right way to teach literature-based reading. The method cannot be packaged, so you need to understand the theory behind the practices as well as create an effective set of engagements and structures. Practical resources include *Story: Still the Heart of Literacy Learning* by Katie Egan Cunningham (2015), *Reading in the Wild: Cultivating Lifelong Reading Habits* by Donalyn Miller (2013); *Igniting a Passion for Reading* by Steven Layne (2009), and *Reading for Real* by Kathy Collins (2008).

Resources for a Literature-Based Curriculum

An effective literature-based curriculum is based on resources that include the school library media center, bookfairs, parents, guest authors and illustrators, and local public libraries as well as a strong classroom library collection.

- **School library media center.** A well-stocked, efficiently run library media center is the heart of a school. Ideally, library media specialists and teachers work collaboratively, with teachers informing librarians of their resource needs and librarians identifying and locating appropriate resources, keeping teachers updated with the newest literature, and suggesting ways to present books to students.
- **Bookfairs.** A bookfair is a book sale organized by a book vendor and held in the school building for several days. Bookfairs call attention to reading and send strong messages to children and parents about the importance of quality literature.
- **Parent partnerships.** Partnerships honor the resources and expertise of the home. Instead of teachers sending home worksheets and homework that interferes with family life, parents can read to their children, listen to their children read aloud, and take them to the library to select books. Some parents may be able to come to the classroom to listen to or read with children or to read aloud to small groups or individuals. Teachers can honor home cultures by inviting children and families to share oral stories, such as the origin of a child's name, birthday traditions, and favorite family games.
- **Guest authors and illustrators.** Authors and illustrators often visit schools to share about their creative processes and books. Such visits are powerful experiences that influence children as readers. Publisher websites and marketing departments have information on arranging author visits in person or through electronic media.
- **Local public library.** Public libraries provide many services in addition to loaning books, including interlibrary loan, summertime reading programs, and story hours for young children.

Classroom libraries usually have a permanent collection as well as a rotating collection that is checked out from the school or public library and changes regularly to provide depth and breadth to units of study and appeal to children's interests. A classroom library collection can be built inexpensively by:

- Requesting an allocation from your principal or the school parent/teacher organization for the purchase of books
- Submitting a small grant proposal to your school district, professional organization, or local foundations (banks, local businesses, etc)
- Involving children in paperback book clubs and taking advantage of bonus books
- Asking parents for donations of children's books that they plan to discard
- Establishing a "give a book to the classroom" policy for parents who want to celebrate a child's birthday or a holiday at school in some way
- Frequenting garage sales and library book sales, where good books are often quite cheap
- Taking advantage of discounts offered by some bookstores to educators. You might also check if there is a book jobber or wholesale dealer for a publisher in your area.

Classrooms collections need a coding system to streamline shelving and record keeping, such as color coding books by genre with colored tape on the spines. If possible, children should have responsibility for color coding, checking in/out, repairing, and reshelving books. Children can create book bins or baskets in the classroom library to sort books by topics that fit their interests and ways of thinking about books. A collection that provides easy access to great books is essential to creating a culture of reading in a classroom.

Responding to Censorship Challenges

The First Amendment to the U.S. Constitution guarantees all citizens the right to free speech and freedom of the press. Teaching children about their First Amendment rights is important because there are those who would take these rights away through censorship. ***Censorship*** is the removal, suppression, or restricted use of reading materials on the grounds that they are objectionable, often for moral reasons (Reichman, 2001). When someone attempts to remove material from the classroom or library, thereby restricting the access of others, it is called a ***challenge.*** Most book challenges occur locally, and most fail. When a challenge is successful and materials are removed from the curriculum or library, it is called a ***banning***.

These issues are important to consider when you face a censorship challenge:

- Teachers and librarians have the right and the obligation to select reading materials suitable for the education of children in schools. With this right comes the professional responsibility to select good-quality literature that furthers educational goals while remaining appropriate for the age and maturity level of children.
- Parents have the right to protect their children from materials or influences they see as potentially damaging. If a parent believes that material selected by a librarian or teacher is potentially harmful to his/her child, that parent has the right to bring this to the attention of the school and request that his/her child not be subjected to this material. Parents must indicate the reason for their concern.
- The school must take the parent's objection seriously and provide a reasonable substitute for the material. If an alternative procedure is necessary in the situation (e.g., the child will listen to a different book in another location), the alternative should respect the child and be sensitive to his/her feelings.
- The parent does *not* have the right to demand that the material in question be withheld from other children. This would interfere with the rights and professional duty of the teacher and school to educate students. Once a child is given a reasonable alternative, the school has fulfilled its obligation and should not interfere with the First Amendment rights of other children.

As adults, we cherish our right to choose our reading material and use this right nearly every day of our lives. Social studies and civics textbooks proudly proclaim the freedom of choice in the lives of citizens of the U.S. We need to teach children, by our actions as well as by our words, about their First Amendment rights. But do we, as parents, teachers, and librarians, actually extend these rights to children? Specifically,

- Do we allow outspoken special interest groups to influence the removal of good, but controversial, books from the library or classroom shelves, or do we stand by our convictions and book selections?
- Do we self-censor by only selecting books on "safe" topics, or do we select books on the basis of quality and age appropriateness?
- Do we listen to young readers' ideas and responses to books, or do we only ask them comprehension questions?
- Do we allow children to reject books that they do not like, or do we force them to read our selections?
- Do we engage children in critically analyzing books for authenticity and stereotyped representations?

The censorship database of the American Library Association's Office of Intellectual Freedom (OIF) indicates that the most censorship attempts from 1990–2010 came from parents (57%), library patrons (14%), and school administrators (10%). Of the 10,676 challenges reported to the OIF in these 20 years, 30 percent were based on material perceived to be "sexually explicit"; 25 percent were based on material perceived to have "offensive language"; and 21 percent were based on material perceived to be "unsuited to the age group." The OIF estimates that 75–80 percent of censorship attempts are not reported, so these figures are approximate.

Another significant source of censorship is teachers themselves. Wollman-Bonilla (1998) found that teachers often object to texts reflecting gender, ethnic, race, or class experiences that differ from their own. This subtle form of censorship is made worse by the fact that most teachers are unaware of their biases in text selection (Jipson & Paley, 1991). Wollman-Bonilla argued for the First Amendment rights of children, stating that we need to hear children's voices and understand their experiences if we are to know how books actually affect them, instead of assuming we already know the impact of books on children.

Teaching the First Amendment

Teaching children about their First Amendment rights can begin by posting a copy of the First Amendment, having them read it, and discussing what this amendment means to them and the consequences of its loss in their lives. If you post lists of children's books that some have declared "objectionable," children who have read these books can discuss why these books might be considered objectionable and why banning them violates their First Amendment rights. Children's fiction in which censorship plays a role is another resource for reading and discussion. Good examples for younger readers are *Arthur and the Scare-Your-Pants-Off Club* by Marc Brown and Stephen Krensky (1998), *Mr. Lemoncello's Library Olympics* by Chris Grabenstein (2016), and *The Landry News* by Andrew Clements (1999); for older readers, see *Americus* by M. K. Reed (2011) and *The Sledding Hill* by Chris Crutcher (2005). As teachers and librarians, we should promote the kinds of books that encourage critical thinking, inquiry, and self-expression, while maintaining respect for the views of others.

Dealing with Censorship Attempts

The American Library Association's (ALA) Office of Intellectual Freedom monitors the challenges made against children's books in the U.S. Most adults and children who have read the highly regarded books that often appear on "most challenged books" lists find the reasons given for the challenges perplexing, if not incredible. The following titles, for example, appeared on one or more of the ALA's "Top 10 Most Frequently Challenged Books of the Year" lists from 2010 to 2015:

- *And Tango Makes Three* by Justin Richardson and Peter Parnell for antiethnic and antifamily content, homosexuality, and religious viewpoint.
- IM Series (e.g., *Ttyl; ttfn; l8r; g8r)* by Lauren Myracle for offensive language, religious views, and sexually explicit content.
- The Hunger Games trilogy by Suzanne Collins for antiethnic and antifamily content, insensitivity, offensive language, occult/satanic content, and violence.
- *The Absolutely True Diary of a Part-Time Indian* by Sherman Alexie for offensive language, racism, religious viewpoint, and sexually explicit content.
- Alice (series) by Phyllis Reynolds Naylor for offensive language, sexually explicit content, and religious viewpoint.
- Captain Underpants series by Dav Pilkey for antifamily content, offensive language, and violence.
- *Nasreen's Secret School* by Jeanette Winter for religious viewpoint and violence.
- *It's Perfectly Normal* by Robie H. Harris for nudity, sex education, and sexually explicit content.
- Scary Stories series by Alvin Schwartz for occult/satanic content, religious viewpoint, and violence.
- Bone graphic novel series by Jeff Smith for political viewpoint, racism, and violence.

Often, individuals challenge books on the basis of a single word or phrase, or on hearsay, and have not read the book. Teachers and library media specialists have found that a written procedure is helpful for bringing reason into discussions with parents who want to censor school materials. Most procedures call for teachers and librarians to give would-be censors a complaint form and ask them to specify their concerns in writing. The advantages to this system is that everyone involved has time to reflect on the issue and to control their emotions, and the would-be censor is given time to read the book in its entirety, if he or she has not done so already. Developing written procedures and complaint forms are important tasks for a school curriculum committee. Figure 13.3 presents a form produced by the National Council of Teachers of English for reconsideration of a work of literature.

Figure 13.3 Citizen's Request for Reconsideration of a Work

Author_________ Paperback __________ Hardcover __________
Title ____
Publisher (if known) _____________________________________
Request initiated by ______________________________________
Telephone __________ Address __________ City __________ Zip Code __________
Complainant represents:

______ Himself/Herself

______ Name of Organization __________

(Identify other group)

1. Have you been able to discuss this work with the teacher or librarian who ordered it or used it?
_____ Yes _____ No

2. What do you understand to be the general purpose for using this work?
a. Provide support for a unit in the curriculum? _____ Yes _____ No
b. Provide a learning experience for the reader in one kind of literature? _____ Yes _____ No
c. Other ____

____

3. Did the general purpose for the use of the work, as described by the teacher or librarian, seem suitable to you? _____ Yes _____ No
If not, please explain. _______________________________________

4. What do you think is the general purpose of the author in this book? _____________

5. In what ways do you think a work of this nature is not suitable for the use the teacher or librarian wishes to carry out? ____

____

6. Have you been able to learn what the students' response to this work is? _____ Yes _____ No

7. What response did the students make?

____

8. Have you been able to learn from your school library what book reviewers or other students of literature have written about this work? _____ Yes _____ No

9. Would you like the teacher or librarian to give you a written summary of what book reviewers and other students have written about this book or film? _____ Yes _____ No

10. Do you have negative reviews of the book? _____ Yes _____ No

11. Where were they published?

12. Would you be willing to provide summaries of the reviews you have collected? _____ Yes _____ No

13. What would you like your library/school to do about this work?

_____ Do not assign/lend it to my child.

_____ Return it to the staff selection committee/department for reevaluation.

_____ Other—Please explain.

____

14. What work would you recommend that would convey as valuable a picture and perspective of the subject treated in place of this book? __________________________

Signature _________________ Date ___________

Source: Committee on the Right to Read (1982). *The students' right to read.* Urbana, IL: National Council of Teachers of English.

The American Library Association's Office for Intellectual Freedom has several publications about censorship, such as Reichman's *Censorship and Selection: Issues and Answers for Schools* (2001), which provide important information to schools (www.ala.org.). ALA and other organizations have collaboratively established a website of resources for Banned Books Week (www.bannedbooksweek.org/).

The National Council of Teachers of English has an Intellectual Freedom Center (www.ncte.org/action/anti-censorship) and offers a valuable document about censorship, *The Students' Right to Read* that explains the nature of censorship, the stand of those opposed to it, and ways to combat it. This document and the *Citizen's Request for Reconsideration of a Work* are available free of charge at www.ncte.org/positions/statements/righttoreadguideline.

Evaluating the Literature Program

Ongoing evaluation is part of responsible teaching because it reveals the strengths and needs of children and indicates where to focus instruction. Reading and mathematics dominate standardized tests in schools, and little or no attention is paid to children's growth in literary understanding. Portfolio assessment, conferencing, and observation can evaluate how well a literature program is meeting children's needs. Observation, when carefully directed, can provide a full description of children's progress and their strengths and needs, as well as of your literature program. It is also the most efficient method of assessment, since it can be done while one is engaged in other tasks.

Observation and Assessment of Learning

Evaluation of children in a literature curriculum focuses mainly on the curriculum's effect on children as readers, particularly through checklists for observation and assessment of various aspects of a literature program. Checklists should reflect differences in children's interactions with literature by grade level and experience. For example, preschool or first-grade teachers are likely to look for evidence that children use the terms *author* and *illustrator* in their discussions of books and recognize the work of specific authors and illustrators. Middle grade teachers would be more likely to look for evidence that children have developed an understanding of why specific authors and illustrators appeal to them and can use their literary structures as mentors for their writing. Teachers and librarians at all grade levels will look for evidence that children are enjoying reading and voluntarily choosing to read. Figure 13.4 gives an example of a possible evaluation instrument.

Figure 13.4 Checklist for Children's Involvement with Literature

Evaluator: ______________________ Date: ______________

Actions	Yes	No	Comment
Reading and Listening			
Child reads voluntarily and willingly	___	___	____________
Child enjoys reading and listening to literature	___	___	____________
Child reads for information	___	___	____________
Child reads and listens to a variety of fiction, nonfiction, and poems	___	___	____________
Response to Literature			
Child talks thoughtfully about books	___	___	____________
Child shares responses to books with peers	___	___	____________
Child is attentive during read-aloud sessions	___	___	____________

Actions	Yes	No	Comment
Child can discuss a fiction book in terms of	___	___	___
Character	___	___	___
Plot	___	___	___
Setting	___	___	___
Theme	___	___	___
Style	___	___	___
Child can discuss an informational book in terms of	___	___	___
Structure	___	___	___
Theme	___	___	___
Style	___	___	___
Child recognizes that different people have different responses to the same story	___	___	___
Child relates stories to personal experiences	___	___	___
Child compares and contrasts stories, author writing styles, and illustrator artistic styles	___	___	___
Selection of Literature			
Child knows how to select appropriate books for independent reading	___	___	___
Child knows how to use a computer to find, read about, and select books from the library	___	___	___
Child keeps a log of books read independently	___	___	___
Child develops personal preferences in books	___	___	___
Child tries new book genres	___	___	___

Observation and Assessment of Teacher Effectiveness

Regular self-assessment is an important part of professional development. The following checklists were conceived with preservice teachers and librarians in mind, mainly for the purposes of self-evaluation and guiding observation of the classrooms and libraries they visit as part of their coursework.

Checklist for Classroom and Library Environments The environment of a classroom or library is determined mainly by what the classroom teacher or librarian values in learning and teaching. These values determine how the space is arranged, which materials are available, and what sorts of events and activities are regularly scheduled, as noted in Figure 13.5.

Checklist for Teaching Activities Success in engaging children as lifelong readers does not depend on generous supplies of equipment or a certain physical layout, although these can be useful. It is what you do with literature that makes the biggest impression on children. Activities that create a positive and nonthreatening learning environment are the most successful with children, as evaluated in Figure 13.6.

Figure 13.5 Checklist for Promoting Literature through Classroom and Library Environments

Evaluator: ______________________ Date: ______________

Observations	Yes	No	Comment
Physical Layout			
Desks/tables are arranged to promote discussion	___	___	___________
Computers are easy to access	___	___	___________
Room has quiet areas for reading and thinking	___	___	___________
Reading area is well lit with comfortable seating	___	___	___________
Displays of children's response projects are evident	___	___	___________
Library materials are easy for children to reach and reshelve and are coded and organized logically	___	___	___________
Materials			
Trade books and audio books are available.	___	___	___________
Classroom/school library is adequate in	___	___	___________
Scope (variety of genres—fiction, nonfiction, poetry)	___	___	___________
Depth (variety of books within a genre)	___	___	___________
Quality (light reading for entertainment to excellent quality for study)	___	___	___________
Varying difficulty and reading abilities	___	___	___________
Recent books, along with old favorites	___	___	___________
Multicultural and international books	___	___	___________
Displays of books reflect the varying interests of children, as well as support classroom studies	___	___	___________
Scheduling			
Time is provided for regular self-choice reading	___	___	___________
Time is provided for browsing and selecting books regularly	___	___	___________
Time is provided for response to literature	___	___	___________

Figure 13.6 Checklist for Promoting Literature through Teaching Activities

Evaluator: ______________________ Date: ______________

Actions/Activities	Yes	No	Comment
Making Literature Enjoyable			
Read aloud daily from high-quality literature	___	___	___
Select books for read-aloud that	___	___	___
Reflect children's interests	___	___	___
Represent a wide variety of genres	___	___	___
Represent outstanding examples of each genre	___	___	___
Share poetry orally on a regular basis from a range of poets	___	___	___
Share stories through storytelling	___	___	___
Motivating Children to Read			
Introduce books regularly through booktalks	___	___	___
Introduce digital books and audiobooks	___	___	___
Encourage listening to audiobooks and reading along in print versions	___	___	___
Encourage children's responses to literature	___	___	___
By asking open-ended or divergent questions	___	___	___
By encouraging varied responses (oral, written, art, drama)	___	___	___
Invite children to choose books for independent reading, including both fiction and nonfiction options	___	___	___
Collaborate as teachers and librarians to encourage children as readers	___	___	___
Demonstrating Reading Behaviors			
Read your own books during silent reading time	___	___	___
Talk enthusiastically about books you read	___	___	___
Show children how to select books	___	___	___
Showing the Relevance of Literature			
Include literature that is culturally relevant to children in read-alouds, booktalks, and text sets	___	___	___
Integrate literature across the curriculum in science, social studies, language arts, and mathematics	___	___	___
Encouraging Literature Appreciation			
Create literature units	___	___	___
Reaching beyond the Classroom and Library			
Send read-aloud suggestions to parents	___	___	___
Encourage parents to visit the public library with their children	___	___	___
Invite parents and community leaders to read aloud to children at the school	___	___	___
Evaluation			
Record children's growth	___	___	___
In understanding literary concepts	___	___	___
In choices of books to read	___	___	___
In attitude toward reading	___	___	___
In quality of responses (verbal, written, artistic)	___	___	___

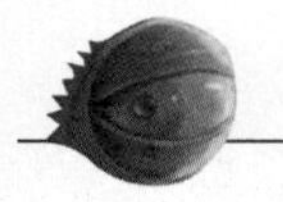

Invitations for Further Investigation

Many elementary and early childhood education and school librarian programs in universities include practicum experiences. These experiences provide opportunities to observe teaching strategies, acquire firsthand experiences with children, and explore theories and ideas from their courses. The following invitations can be explored in school-based practicums, particularly when shared with other preservice teachers or librarians to note similarities and differences in experiences.

Learning about Children as Readers

1. Interview three children, preferably at different levels of reading ability, to find their exposure to literature, attitudes toward reading, purposes for reading, and sources of reading material.
2. Interview several children about their reading interests, and then suggest appropriate titles for independent reading from books available in the school.
3. Conduct a class survey of reading interests, using the ideas described in Chapter 2. Compile and analyze findings to suggest titles for independent reading.

Learning to Engage Children with Literature

1. Booktalk a set of four or five books appropriate for a particular group of children, including informational, global, and multicultural literature. After the booktalk, display the books and observe children's interest in reading them.
2. Read aloud one or two picturebooks and a chapter book. After each read-aloud session, invite children to respond with connections and thoughts. Compare your experiences of reading aloud from the two types of books and children's responses to these books.
3. Select a poem, and work with children in arranging it for choral reading, rehearsing, and presenting the choral reading to an available audience.
4. Introduce children to a specific author or illustrator by demonstrating how to give an author or illustrator profile. ***Author and illustrator profiles*** usually include interesting facts about the author, a recent picture, one or two distinguishing characteristics of the author's work (such as favorite topics, themes, style of illustration or writing), your interests in the author's work, and other books written by the author. A one-page handout summarizing this information and listing major books is useful. Children presenting author or illustrator profiles can post their summary sheets on the class bulletin board or website. Variations to presenting author and illustrator reports orally to the class include:
   - Presenting the profile in first person as the author or illustrator (costumes or props)
   - Presenting the profile as a biographical skit about the author
   - Creating a poster or bulletin board display about the author or illustrator
   - Presenting the profile as an interview, with one child as the interviewer and the other taking the role of the author

Learning about Children's Responses to Literature

1. Select a picturebook or a chapter from a novel that involves four to six characters. Read it aloud to a group of children and engage them in a creative drama, readers' theatre, or graphic arts response to the book (see Chapter 14). Note children's insights into the book through their responses.
2. Help children design a literature-related display, such as a mural based on a whole-class read-aloud selection or a response to books read independently by children. This display can be mounted in the school hallway or library for observation by children in other classrooms.

References

Alexander, K. (2015). *The crossover*. New York: Macmillan.

Alexie, S. (2007). *The absolutely true diary of a part-time Indian*. New York: Little, Brown.

Alexie, S. (2016). *Thunder Boy Jr*. Morales, Y. (Illus.). New York: Little Brown.

Alvarez, J. (2010). *How Tia Lola learned to teach*. New York: Knopf.

American Library Association. (2016). *Frequently challenged books*. Retrieved from http://www.ala.org/bbooks/frequentlychallengedbooks/

Anderson, R. C. (1996). Research foundations to support wide reading. In V. Greaney (Ed.), *Promoting reading: Views on making reading materials accessible to increase literacy levels* (pp. 55–77). Newark, DE: International Reading Association.

Anderson, R. C., Hiebert, E. H., Scott, J. A., & Wilkinson, I. A. (1985). *Becoming a nation of readers: The report of the commission on reading*. Champaign, IL: Center for the Study of Reading.

Atinuke. (2011). *The no. 1 car spotter*. LaJolla, CA: Kane/Miller.

Aukerman, M. & Schuldt, L.C. (2016). The pictures can say more things: Change across time in young children's references to images and words during text discussion. *Reading Research Quarterly*, *51*(3), 267–287.

Barrs, M. (2000). The reader in the writer. *Reading, 34*(2), 54–60.

Bassoff, L. (2014). *Lost girl found*. Toronto: Groundwood.

Bausum, A. (2009). *Denied, detained, deported*. New York: National Geographic.

Becker, A. (2013). *Journey*. Somerville, MA: Candlewick. Also *Quest* (2014) and *Return* (2016).

Benjamin, A. (2015). *The thing about jellyfish*. New York: Little, Brown.

Bondoux, A. (2009). *A time of miracles*. New York: Delacorte.

Brown, M. (2015). *Lola Levine is not mean!* Dominguez, A. (Illus.). New York: Little, Brown.

Brown, M., & Krensky, S. (1998). *Arthur and the scare-your-pants-off club*. Brown, M. (Illus.). New York: Little, Brown.

Brown, M. W. (1947). *Goodnight moon*. Hurd, C. (Illus.). New York: HarperCollins.

Browning, E. B. (1902). Reading. In K. D. Wiggins & N. A. Smith (Eds.). *Golden numbers*. New York: Doubleday.

Budhos, M. (2006). *Ask me no questions*. New York: Atheneum.

Buitrago, J. (2015). *Two white rabbits*. Yockteng, R. (Illus.). Toronto: Groundwood.

Campano, G., Ghiso, M., & Sánchez, L. (2013). "Nobody knows the . . . amount of a person." Elementary students critiquing dehumanization through organic critical literacies. *Research in the Teaching of English*, *48*(1), 98–125.

Cantrell, S. C. (1999). The effects of literacy instruction on primary students' reading and writing achievement. *Reading Research and Instruction, 39*(1), 3–26.

Children's literature review: Excerpts from reviews, criticism, and commentary on books for children and young people, Vols. 1–208. (1976–2016). Farmington Hills, MI: Thomson Gale.

Choi, Y. (2001). *The name jar*. New York: Dell.

Clements, A. (1999). *The Landry News*. New York: Simon & Schuster.

Cole, T. (2014). *Wall*. Somerville, MA: Candlewick.

Collins, K. (2008). *Reading for real*. Portland, ME: Stenhouse.

Collins, S. (2008). *The hunger games*. New York: Scholastic.

Committee on the Right to Read. (1982). *The students' right to read*. Urbana, IL: National Council of Teachers of English.

Coy, J. (2016). *Their great gift: Courage, sacrifice and hope in a new land*. Minneapolis, MN: Carolrhoda.

Croza, L. (2010). *I know here*. James, M. (Illus.). Toronto, ON: Groundwood.

Crutcher, C. (2005). *The sledding hill*. New York: Harper-Collins.

Cruz, M., & Pollock, K. (2004). Stepping into the wardrobe: A fantasy genre study. *Language Arts, 81*(3), 184–195.

Cummings, P. (2004). *Red kayak*. New York: Dutton.

Cunningham, K. E. (2015). *Story: Still the heart of literacy learning*. Portsmouth, ME: Stenhouse.

DiCamillo, K. (2016). *Raymie Nightingale*. Somerville, MA: Candlewick.

Dressel, J. H. (1990). The effects of listening to and discussing different qualities of children's literature on the narrative writing of fifth graders. *Research in the Teaching of English, 24*(4), 397–414.

Droyd, A. (2011). *Goodnight iPad: A parody for the next generation*. New York: Blue Rider.

Duprau, J. (2003). *The city of Ember.* New York: Random House.

Elya, S. M. (2014). *Little Roja Riding Hood*. Guevara, S. (Illus.). New York: Penguin.

English, K. (2014). *Skateboard party*. Freeman-Hines, L. (Illus.). New York: Houghton Mifflin Harcourt.

Fanelli, S. (1995). *My map book*. New York: HarperCollins.

Farmer, N. (2002). *The house of the scorpion*. New York: Simon & Schuster.

Feathers, K. & Arya, P. (2012). The role of illustrations during children's reading. *Journal of Children's Literature, 38*(1), 36–42.

Fraillon, Z. (2016). *The bone sparrow*. New York: Disney.

Fullerton, S. K., & Colwell, J. (2010). Research on small-group discussions of literature: An analysis of three decades. In Jimenez, R., Risko, V., Hundley, M., & Rowe, D., *59th Yearbook of the National Reading Conference* (pp. 57–74). Oak Creek, WI: NRC.

Galdone, P. (1998). *The three little pigs*. New York: Houghton Mifflin Harcourt.
Garland, S. (2013). *Azzi in between*. London: Frances Lincoln.
Giff, P. R. (2000). *Nory Ryan's song*. New York: Delacorte.
Grabenstein, Chris (2016). *Mr. Lemoncello's Library Olympics*. New York: Random House.
Greder, A. (2008). *The island*. Chicago, IL: Allen & Unwin.
Grimes, N. (2009). *Make way for Dyamonde Daniel*. Christie, R. G. (Illus.). New York: Putnam.
Grimes, N. (2013). *Words with wings*. Honesdale, PA: Boyds Mills.
Hall, S. (1990). *Using picture storybooks to teach literary devices: Recommended books for children and young adults* (Vol. 1). Phoenix, AZ: Oryx. (Vol. 2, 1994; Vol. 3, 2001; Vol. 4, 2007; Santa Barbara, CA: Libraries Unlimited.)
Harris, R. H. (1994). *It's perfectly normal: A book about changing bodies, growing up, sex, and sexual health*. Emberley, N. (Illus.). New York: Candlewick.
Henkes, K. (2013). *The year of Billy Miller*. New York: Greenwillow.
Hesse, K. (1997). *Out of the dust*. New York: Scholastic.
Hoffman, M. (2002). *The color of home*. Littlewood, K. (Illus.). New York: Dial.
Hyman, T. S. (1983). *Little Red Riding Hood*. New York: Holiday House.
Isaacs, A. (1994). *Swamp Angel*. Zelinksy, P. (Illus.). New York: Schwartz & Wade.
Ivey, G. & Johnston, P. (2015). Engaged reading as a collaborative transformative practice. *Journal of Literacy Research, 47*(3), 297–327.
Jaramillo, A. (2006). *La línea*. New York: Roaring Brook.
Jarvey, M., McKeough, M., & Pyryt, M. (2008). Teaching trickster tales: A comparison of instructional approaches. *Research in the Teaching of English, 43*(1), 42–73.
Jipson, J., & Paley, N. (1991). The selective tradition in children's literature: Does it exist in the elementary classroom? *English Education, 23,* 148–159.
Johnson, C. (1983). *Harold and the purple crayon*. New York: HarperCollins.
Journal of Children's Literature. (2008). Special Issue: Children's books as mentor texts. *34*(2), 31–67.
Kadohata, C. (2013). *The thing about luck*. New York: Atheneum.
Kesler, T., Gibson, L., Turansky, C. (2016). Bringing the book to life: Responding to historical fiction using digital storytelling. *Journal of Literacy Research, 48*(3), 1–41.
Krashen, S. (2011). *Free voluntary reading*. Santa Barbara, CA: Libraries Unlimited.
Kuhlmann, T. (2014). *Lindbergh: The tale of a flying mouse*. New York: North-South.
Lai, T. (2011). *Inside out and back again*. New York: Harper.
Lainez, R. C. (2009). *René has two last names*. El Paso, TX: Piñata Books.
Langer, J. (2010). *Envisioning literature: Literary understanding and literature instruction*. New York: Teachers College.
Lanthier, J. (2013). *The stamp collector*. Thisdale, F. (Illus.). Toronto: Fitzhenry.
Layne, S. (2009). *Igniting a passion for reading*. Portland, ME: Stenhouse.
Look, L. (2011). *Alvin Ho: Allergic to dead bodies, funerals, and other fatal circumstances*. Pham, L. (Illus.). New York: Atheneum.
Look, L. (2011). *Ruby Lu, star of the show*. S. Choi (Illus.). New York: Atheneum.
Lowry, L. (1994). *The giver*. Boston, MA: Houghton. Also *Gathering blue* (2000), *Messenger* (2004), and *Son* (2012).
Lowry, L. (2000). *Looking back: A book of memories*. Boston, MA: Houghton.
Maloch, B. (2008). Beyond exposure: The uses of informational texts in a second grade classroom. *Research in the Teaching of English, 42*(3), 315–362.
Martin, A. (2014). *Rain reign*. New York: Feiwel & Friends.
Mateo, J. M. (2014). *Migrant*. Martinez, J. P. (Illus.). New York: Abrams.
McEwan, J. (2007). *Rufus the scrub does not wear a tutu*. Margeson, J. (Illus.). Plain City, OH: Darby Creek.
McKay, H. (2011). *Lulu and the dog from the sea*. Lamont, P. (Illus.). Park Ridge, IL: Whitman.
Miller, D. (2013). *Reading in the wild: Cultivating lifelong reading habits*. New York: Jossey-Bass.
Móller, K. (2012). Developing understandings of social justice: Critical thinking in action in a literature discussion group. *Journal of Children's Literature, 38*(2), 23–36.
Moss, M. (2013). *Barbed wire baseball*. Shimizu, Y. (Illus.). New York: Abrams.
Murphy, S. (2011). *Pearl verses the world*. Potter, H. (Illus.). Somerville, MA: Candlewick.
National Association of Educational Progress. (2015). *The Nation's Report Card: Reading 2015*. Washington, DC: National Center for Education Statistics, Institute of Education Sciences, U.S. Department of Education.
Nicholls, S. (2008). *Ways to live forever*. New York: Scholastic.
Nye, N. S. (2014). *The turtle of Oman*. New York: HarperCollins.
O'Connor, B. (2009). *The small adventure of Popeye and Elvis*. New York: Farrar.
Ogburn, J. *Little treasures: Endearments around the world*. Raschka, C. (Illus.). New York: Houghton Mifflin.
Palacio, R. J. (2012). *Wonder*. New York: Knopf.
Pantaleo, S. (2014). Exploring the artwork in picturebooks with middle years students. *Journal of Children's Literature, 40*(1), 15–26.
Park, F., & Park, G. (19998). *My freedom trip*. Jenkins, D. (Illus.). Honesdale, PA: Boyds Mills.
Park, L. S. (2010). *A long walk to water*. New York: Clarion.
Pinkney, A. D. (2014). *The red pencil*. New York: Little Brown.
Reed, M. K. (2011). *Americus*. New York: First Second/ Roaring Brook.

Reichman, H. (2001). *Censorship and selection: Issues and answers for schools.* Chicago, IL: American Library Association.

Rex, M. (2008). *Goodnight goon: A parody*. New York: Putnam.

Richardson, J., & Parnell, P. (2005). *And Tango makes three.* Cole, H. (Illus.). New York: Simon & Schuster.

Rocklin, J. (2011). *One day and one amazing morning on Orange Street*. New York: Amulet.

Rodriquez, L. (1997). *América is her name*. Willimantic, CT: Curbstone.

Rosen, M. (2008). *Michael Rosen's sad book*. Blake, Q. (Illus.). Somerville, MA: Candlewick.

Rosenblatt, L. M. (1978). *The reader, the text, the poem: The transactional theory of the literary work.* Carbondale, IL: Southern Illinois University Press.

Russo, M. (2011). *I will come back for you: A family in hiding during World War II*. New York: Schwartz & Wade.

Ryan, P. M. (2000). *Esperanza rising*. New York: Scholastic.

Ryan, P. M. (2004). *Becoming Naomi Leon*. New York: Scholastic.

Ryder, R. J., Sekulski, J. L., & Silberg, A. (2003). Results of direct instruction reading program evaluation longitudinal results: First through third grade, 2000–2003. Madison, WI: Wisconsin Department of Public Instruction.

Santiago, C. (2002). *Home to Medicine Mountain*. Lowery, J. (Illus.). San Francisco, CA: Children's Book Press.

Santoro, L., Chard, D., Howard, L., & Baker, S. (2008). Making the very most of classroom read-alouds to promote comprehension and vocabulary. *The Reading Teacher, 61*(5), 396–408.

Say, A. (2011). *Drawing from memory*. New York: Scholastic.

Schmidt, G. (2004). *Lizzie Bright and the Buckminster boy*. New York: Clarion.

Schwartz, C. R. (2013). *The three ninja pigs*. Santat, D. (Illus.). New York: Putnam.

Senzai, N. H. (2010). *Shooting Kabul*. New York: Simon & Schuster.

Shannon, P. (2013). *Closer readings of the Common Core*. Portsmouth, NH: Heinemann.

Sheth, K. (2007). *Keeping corner*. New York: Hyperion.

Something about the author: Facts and pictures about authors and illustrators of books for young people, Vols. 1–299 (1971–2016). Detroit: Gale.

Tan, S. (2006). *The arrival*. New York: Scholastic.

Tonatiuh, D. (2013). *Pancho Rabbit and the Coyote*. New York: Abrahms.

Uhlberg, M. (2011). *A storm called Katrina*. Bootman, C. (Illus.). Atlanta, GA: Peachtree.

Urban, L. (2011). *Hound dog true*. New York: Harcourt.

Walsh, J. P. (1986). *The green book*. New York: Farrar.

Warner, S. (2011). *EllRay Jakes is not a chicken!* Harper, J. (Illus.). New York: Penguin.

Watt, M. (2015). *Bug in a vacuum.* Toronto: Tundra.

Weaver, C. (2009). *Reading process.* Portsmouth, NH: Heinemann.

Williams, K. L. (2009). *My name is Sangoel*. Stock, C. (Illus.). New York: Erdmans.

Williams, M. (2011). *Now is the time for running*. New York: Little, Brown.

Wilson, G. P., Martens, P., Arya, P., & Altwerger, B. (2004). Readers, instruction, and the NRP. *Phi Delta Kappan, 86* (3), 242–246.

Wollman-Bonilla, J. E. (1998). Outrageous viewpoints: Teachers' criteria for rejecting works of children's literature. *Language Arts, 75*(4), 287–295.

Worthy, J., Patterson, E., Salas, R., Prater, S., & Turner, M. (2002). "More than just reading": The human factor in reaching resistant readers. *Reading Research and Instruction, 41*(2), 177–202.

Yelchin, E. (2011). *Breaking Stalin's nose*. New York: Holt.

Young, E. (2011). *The house that Baba built: An artist's childhood in China*. New York: Little, Brown.

Youngs, S. (2012). Injustice and irony: Students respond to Japanese American internment picturebooks. *Journal of Children's Literature, 38*(2), 37–49.

Chapter 14

Engaging Children with Literature

Oh, the Places You'll Go

Uh-huh, I've travelled
By car, train, boat, plane
To Kenya, Uganda
France, Italy, Spain.
Still many a country
I plan to explore
Here's how you do it
I've done it before.
Weather won't stop you
Nor cost of the flight
You'll fly the world over
By day and by night.
The means are at hand
You've not far to look
Oh, the places you'll go
When you travel by book.

—Ashley Bryan

Engagement with literature highlights the potential of a book to capture children's attention and invite their participation in fictional and informational story worlds. Authentic, well-written books are the first step, but they must be supported by significant experiences that bring children and books together for a variety of purposes. These experiences include reading widely for personal purposes, reading critically to inquire about the world, and reading strategically to learn about literacy.

These three types of experiences with literature can occur at different points throughout the school day. Gabriela, a 9-year-old, begins her day by pulling *To Dance: A Ballerina's Graphic Novel* (Siegel, 2006) out of her desk to pursue her personal inquiry on becoming a ballerina. After independent reading, the class moves into reading instruction and guided reading. The teacher works with Gabriela's group in a guided inquiry to analyze how authors use dialogue for character development in *Bink and Gollie* (DiCamillo, 2010). After lunch, the teacher reads aloud *Iqbal* (D'Adamo, 2001), the fictionalized story of a boy who led an influential movement against child labor in Pakistani carpet factories, as part of a collaborative inquiry on human rights. Students discuss the protagonist's anger and fear and his willingness to take action for freedom, despite the risks. They explore his strategies for taking action and their concerns about whether kids can make a difference in a world controlled by adults.

Balancing these experiences supports children's development as readers and as human beings. The emphasis across these three dimensions may shift as children become proficient readers and gain life experiences. Older readers may primarily focus on using reading to inquire, whereas young children focus more on reading for personal purposes and to learn about literacy. This shift in emphasis does not exclude the other types; all three should be integrated into the experiences offered to children, no matter what their age. Each serves a different purpose and highlights different books and roles for adults and children.

Reading Widely for Personal Purposes

Reading literature widely for personal purposes highlights choice and extensive reading for purposes that are significant to children's lives, ranging from enjoyment to personal inquiries on topics of interest. Reading widely involves engagement and demonstration; children are not focused on writing or talking about the book or using it for an activity. They just immerse themselves in reading alongside other readers. The goal is to create a lifelong habit of reading for purposes that matter to the reader—not because the teacher said so.

Children should have the opportunity to choose from a wide range of reading materials. Wide reading provides children with a broad background from which to develop comprehension and interpretation strategies, promotes positive attitudes about reading, and encourages the development of lifelong reading habits. Many adults stop engaging with books once they leave school and view reading as boring because of the lack of choice in schools. In addition, reading many materials with ease increases children's fluency and the integration of reading strategies.

The experiences that encourage reading widely for personal purposes include reading aloud, independent reading, shared reading, and experiencing literature through multimodal texts. The role of teachers and librarians is to provide a regularly scheduled time for reading and a variety of reading materials.

Reading Aloud by Teachers and Librarians

Reading aloud to children by family members, teachers, and librarians is essential for children's acquisition of reading strategies and positive attitudes toward reading. Read-alouds are the centerpiece of a literature curriculum. Beginning in their infancy and throughout the elementary and middle-school years, children should hear books and poems read aloud on a daily basis. Reading aloud to children is just as important in the intermediate grades as it is in primary grades. Important reasons to read aloud include:

- To encourage children to love reading and literature
- To share exciting and thought-provoking books that are beyond children's reading ability, but well within their listening ability
- To share books that will expand children's reading interests and expose them to new genres
- To increase children's abilities to think critically and understand connected discourse
- To help children understand literary devices and the conventions of story, such as genres, characters, settings, themes, and plot

- To expand and enrich vocabulary
- To provide a model of expressive, fluent reading
- To build knowledge and interest in ideas related to classroom inquiries and units
- To develop a sense of community and relationship

Three distinct aspects are essential to making read-aloud experiences effective: (1) selecting the literature to read, (2) preparing children for read-aloud time, and (3) reading the book aloud.

Book Selection No matter which book you choose to read aloud, first read the book to determine whether the story is enjoyable and worthy of children's time and appropriate for a particular group of children. You also can note ideas for how the story might lend itself to response.

Over a school year, you will want to read aloud a variety of poems, short stories, picturebooks, and chapter books of different genres and moods. You will also want to ensure that there is a balance of males and females as main characters in the books and that the main characters come from different backgrounds and cultural settings.

Lists of Excellent Books to Read Aloud are provided in Chapters 5 through 12. You may also want to look at Jim Trelease's *The Read-Aloud Handbook* (2013) and online sites, including Trelease's website and Goodreads' read-aloud book lists.

The most recognized books for children, though sometimes complex, deserve to be shared, including books that are challenging and need your support in interactions with children. Without this help, many children would never experience and enjoy some of the more difficult but worthwhile pieces of literature. Conversely, you will want to avoid books for reading aloud that children can consume eagerly on their own, reserving those books for booktalks and independent reading.

When first reading aloud to a new class, however, you may need to start with shorter and easier books that are popular with children. You can gradually build to longer, more challenging books as you become acquainted with children's interests and abilities.

Preparation You can prepare children for reading aloud by having them remove distractions, from their immediate vicinity, asking them to sit quietly in the designated place for read-aloud times, and ensuring they are ready to listen. If the book has concepts that you believe will baffle them, you may want to quickly establish a context for the book before beginning to read.

Introduce the book by stating the title, author, and illustrator, even with the smallest children. This teaches children that books are written and illustrated by real people called authors and illustrators. For global and multicultural literature use the book jacket to briefly tell how the author's and illustrator's backgrounds relate to the book's focus—for example, "This author lives in the U.S., but her parents came from Korea as adults, so she talked with them about their experiences and did research in libraries." You may need to look at the author's website to get this information, but first check the book jacket and look for an author's note or acknowledgment.

Sometimes you might ask children to predict what they believe the story will be about from looking at the cover and title or you might explain briefly why you chose this book to read. For example, you could say that you are reading this book because "it's another story by one of our favorite authors" or "this book will tell us more about what it was like to live in Korea right after World War II." You might decide to read aloud several picturebooks by the same author over the course of a week so children are aware of a notable author. Book introductions should be short and serve the purpose of inviting children to enter into the world of the story with you.

Reading Picturebooks Aloud Effectively Consider the following in reading aloud:

- Position yourself close to the class so that everyone can see the pictures.
- Show the pictures as you read. Remember that the text and pictures are carefully integrated in a picturebook to convey the story as a whole so children need to both hear and see the book.
- After the introduction, read the book aloud, placing emphasis on the meaning of the story. Think of reading aloud as a type of dramatic performance.
- Your body movements and facial expressions can enhance the drama of the read-aloud experience. Leaning forward during a scary, suspenseful part of a story and smiling or chuckling during a funny part can convey your involvement in the story.

• Maintain eye contact with children. Be sure you are aware of their nonverbal responses to this reading experience to determine if a word of explanation is needed.

• Read fiction from beginning to end without interruption except on an as-needed basis. Some books, such as concept books, informational books, and interactive books, do call for interactions during the read-aloud process. Young children, in particular, make connections throughout the reading of a book, rather than at the end.

Reading Chapter Books Aloud Effectively Many of the same considerations hold true with chapter book read-alouds. Of course, chapter books have few illustrations, so holding the book for children to see the pictures is not necessary. Some children may therefore enjoy sketching the images in their heads as they listen. In addition, chapter books are usually read aloud over a relatively long period, from a few days to many weeks.

Practices used successfully during chapter book read-alouds to hook children and keep them tuned into the book include:

• Keeping a chart of the characters—their names, relationships, and roles in the story—as the characters appear. This strategy is especially helpful for keeping track of key characters or plot elements as in *Where the Mountain Meets the Moon* by Grace Lin (2009), where Minli goes on a journey, encountering characters along the way whose relationship to each other is not clear until the end of the book.

• Designing and displaying a map of the story setting to track the events of the story as they occur. This visual aid can assist in following the characters' journey in quest fantasies.

• Developing a timeline on which the dates are set at intervals above the line and the story events placed below the line at the appropriate date. For historical fiction and biographies, a timeline can also include a third tier of historic events.

Several excellent resources for developing your strategies in reading aloud to children are Mem Fox's *Reading Magic* (2008) and Lester Laminack's *Unwrapping the Read Aloud* (2009).

Sharing Literature from Oral Traditions through Storytelling

Telling stories to children is particularly important for sharing literature from oral traditions. Many American Indian tribal nations, for example, have long traditions of oral literature. Some traditional stories are meant to be told only at certain times of the year or to particular audiences, and so are not appropriate to be published as a book that could be read at the wrong time or place. Instead, they need to be shared orally.

You can bring oral stories to life through personal expression and interpretation and use them to establish a close connection with children. Oral storytelling should be a regular part of classroom and library read-aloud experiences. Suggestions and resources for storytelling are in the chapter on traditional literature. Judy Freeman's *The Handbook for Storytime Programs* (2015) provides suggestions for how you can bring together a set of related oral stories, books, poems, and songs to engage children.

Independent Reading by Children

Another way for children to experience good literature is to read it themselves. Indeed, the ultimate goal of a literature program is to turn children into readers who, of their own free will, read self-selected literature with enjoyment, understanding, and appreciation. To assist children in becoming lifelong readers, you should set aside time each day for children to read independently. Kindergarteners and first-graders may spend only 10 minutes reading independently, and often a quiet hum occurs as they say the words aloud as they read or tell their own stories based on the illustrations. Older children often read silently for up to an hour.

Some schools have instituted ***sustained silent reading (SSR)*** programs on a schoolwide basis to promote the reading habit in children. A certain time each day is set aside for all students, teachers, librarians, coaches, principals, custodians, and office and kitchen staff to take a "reading break." The philosophy behind SSR programs is that children need to see adults who read and who place a high priority on reading. Children read materials of their own choosing and are not required to write book reports or give oral reports on these materials.

If your school uses a commercial reading incentive program, you may take advantage of the availability of the literature that is provided as part of the program. Use the program flexibly in ways that develop intrinsic motivation for reading, avoid the negative competitive aspects of the program, and help children achieve individual goals set for their independent reading.

Whether or not your school has an SSR program, you can provide children with an independent reading time each day. Remember that the goal is to have children read as many books and materials as possible, so they should not be required to write long responses. At most, they might be asked to keep a simple record sheet of their reading. Tips for establishing a successful independent reading time include:

- Have a well-stocked classroom collection of books—poetry, plays, picturebooks, novels, and information books, along with graphic novels and magazines.
- Regularly visit the school media center so that children can gather books that relate to their interests for independent reading.
- Conduct booktalks regularly so children are aware of books they want to read.
- Display new books attractively and show videos of notable authors talking about their books and craft. These techniques are effective in "selling" books to children.
- Schedule the same time each day for independent reading. Allow enough time for children to get well into their books and achieve satisfaction from the reading.
- Insist on attentiveness to books during this time. Primary-grade children often talk quietly in pairs about books or lip-read aloud individually. Children in intermediate grades can read silently and usually prefer to do so, although some boys prefer social interaction while reading.
- Spend the independent reading period engrossed in books, setting yourself as an example of a reader. Be knowledgeable and interested in what children are reading.

Retellings and dramatic play are another way that children engage in independent exploration of literature to make stories their own. As young children tell and retell stories, they develop their concept of story and expand their oral language. You can encourage retellings by creating a conducive environment in one area of the classroom or library with props, such as story puppets, feltboards with cut-out story figures, toys that can be used as characters (stuffed animals, dolls, plastic figures), wordless books, and favorite picturebooks. Some children take a book shared during a read-aloud and page through it, retelling the story from the pictures; others take puppets and recreate the story or make up an entirely new adventure with the same characters.

Audio or video recorders can inspire younger students to record and listen to their favorite stories, and older students can develop radio or television shows based on favorite books or record their readers' theatre performances.

Booktalks

A ***booktalk*** is an oral presentation by a teacher, librarian, or child who tells about a book to interest other children in reading it. Booktalks are not book reports, analyses of the author's style, or old-fashioned discussions of characters, setting, theme, and plot. Booktalks have been used effectively for years by librarians who developed this strategy into an art for the purpose of encouraging children to check out books. By giving booktalks on five to ten books each week from classroom and school library collections, you can invite children to read and experience good literature. Children can also give booktalks to induce others to read their favorite books. For more tips on booktalks, see www.nancykeane.com/booktalks and online YouTube videos. Tips for conducting booktalks include:

- Choose books that you like or that you think children will enjoy. Enthusiasm for a book is stimulating and infectious.
- Have the book available to show children as you give the booktalk. Book format elements—such as cover illustrations and the length, size, and shape of the book—influence book choices and can be considered only if children can see the book.
- Keep the booktalk brief, no more than two or three minutes (four to six sentences). Do not tell too much about the book or children will see no reason to read it.
- Tell the topic and something about the action in the story, but *do not tell the plot*. Feature a scene or character that the story revolves around, but do not discuss a scene that gives away the ending.
- Booktalk a group of books that share the same theme; talk briefly about each book and how it fits with the others.

The following is an example of a booktalk on *The House of the Scorpion* (2002) by Nancy Farmer:

> If you wonder what life will be like in the future, 100 years from now, you will enjoy reading *The House of the Scorpion,* a novel about Matt, a boy who has spent his life locked away in a hut because he is a clone and is an outcast hated by others. Matt discovers that he is the clone of El Patrón, the cruel ruler of Opium, a drug kingdom farmed by "eejits," brain-dead clones. Opium is located between the U.S. and Aztlán, once called Mexico. In El Patrón's household, Matt finds support from a cook and a bodyguard, and eventually Maria, who begins to care about Matt. When Matt realizes that his life is at risk, he makes a break for freedom and escapes to Aztlán, only to face more hardships and adventures. Matt wonders who he is, why he exists, and whether, as a clone, he has free will. *The House of the Scorpion* by Nancy Farmer has received many honors, including winning the National Book Award for young people's literature.

After a booktalk, place the book on a table for children to peruse and consider. Over time, give booktalks on a variety of books at different levels of reading difficulty, on different topics, and with male and female protagonists from many cultures. In this way, you can appeal to the wide range of interests and abilities within a group of children.

Shared Reading

Shared reading is a term used to describe teaching strategies that draw on the natural processes of literacy learning occurring in book-loving homes. These various strategies—***shared-book experience, choral reading,*** and ***paired reading***—provide children with opportunities to experience good literature as they are learning to read. The strategies are a modification of parent–child interactions with repeated readings of favorite books as the child gradually acquires an understanding of print and its relationship to our sound system and to the words we speak. A list of predictable books in shared reading activities can be found in Chapter 5.

The ***shared-book experience*** is used with groups of beginning readers. Enlarged-text books of 24" × 30" or larger, called ***Big Books,*** usually well-loved and predictable books such as Eric Carle's *The Very Hungry Caterpillar* (1968), are presented to groups of beginning readers in a sequence proposed by Holdaway (1982). First, favorite, well-known poems and songs are repeated in unison by children and adult, who points to the text of the Big Book. A review of the story is then used to teach skills in context. Following this activity, children engage in language play, such as alphabet games, rhymes, and songs that use letter names. Then a new story in Big Book format is read aloud and children are invited to join in on the predictable parts of the book. Later, children read independently from a wide selection of favorite books and compose original stories, often modeled after the new story.

Choral reading is reading aloud in unison or parts with a whole class, small group, or individuals so that children hear the text at the same time they read it. Choral reading can involve arranging a poem into speaking parts as a way to enjoy and interpret the poem (see Chapter 6). Choral reading can provide support for children who struggle as readers, typically by having less proficient children read in unison with more fluent readers or having a struggling child read chorally with a recorded version of the text. You can also read one-on-one with a child, so that you initially take the lead in the choral reading and then gradually quiet your voice as the child gains confidence and takes over the lead.

Paired reading, also known as partner reading or buddy reading, involves two people sharing the reading of a text in some way. Two children can share a text by reading back and forth to each other, changing off every other page or section of the book or taking different voices or parts of the text. Another variation, often used with struggling readers, involves you and a child reading side by side. The child reads aloud until she or he has difficulty, at which point you supply the word so that the reading can continue fluently.

In all of these strategies, well-chosen literature is important; the nature of the experience is companionable, not authoritative; and the child must see the text and hear the words simultaneously. Sometimes, you place a finger under each word as it is being read to draw the child's attention to the print. Selecting favorite, loved stories as well as meaningful, predictable stories is essential because the success of these strategies is contingent on frequent rereadings of the same book.

These variations of shared reading focus on the role of fluent reading experiences and multiple rereadings in learning to read. As children read stories over and over, they are able to attend to different aspects of the print and the story, learning something different about the text each time. They also develop a feeling of competence in themselves as readers, which is especially important for struggling readers who may not have experienced fluent reading.

Readers' Theatre

Readers' theatre is the oral presentation of literature by two or more actors and a narrator reading from a script. Unlike plays, there is little or no costuming or movement, no stage sets, and no memorized lines. Literature becomes a living experience for readers through the use of facial expressions, voice, and a few gestures. Children engage in multiple rereadings of the script to develop a fluent, expressive interpretation of the story to share with an audience. Features typically associated with readers' theatre include:

- The readers and narrator typically remain on the "stage" throughout the production.
- Readers use little movement; instead, they suggest action with gestures and facial expressions.
- Readers and narrator sit on chairs or stools, and performers usually remain seated throughout the performance. Sometimes, readers sit with their backs to the audience to suggest that they are not in a particular scene.
- No costumes or stage settings are necessary and, at most, should be suggestive to encourage the imaginations of the audience. The use of sound effects may enhance the performance and give the impression of a radio play.

You can develop scripts to adapt a work of literature enjoyed by children. Picturebooks readily lend themselves to adaptation, as do short stories and well-selected scenes from a favorite chapter book (see Figure 14.1). Roald Dahl's ***The BFG*** (1982) combines an exciting adventure to stop the evil people-eating giants with interesting dialogue between Sophie and the BFG (Big Friendly Giant), who uses words in unusual ways.

Stories that work well for a readers' theatre are natural-sounding dialogue, strong characterization, drama or humor, and a satisfactory ending. If the original work has extensive dialogue, the script writing is easy. The script usually begins with the title of the book, the name of the author, a list of characters, and an opening statement by the narrator. Following the introduction, the dialogue is written into script form, with the narrator(s) scripted for the remaining nondialogue, narrative parts.

Scripts can also be purchased, but finding scripts that are both well written and adapted from the literature you are using may prove difficult. If you decide to develop your own readers' theatre scripts from books, remember that the first script is the most difficult. Once you have created the first one, you will find out how easy the process is. Intermediate-grade students take readily to script development once they have experienced several scripts. Aaron Shepard's RT Page (www.aaronshep.com/rt) is a website guide to readers' theatre with tips on scripting, staging, and performing.

Figure 14.1 Sample Page of a Script Developed for Readers' Theatre

Adapted from *The BFG* by Roald Dahl

NARRATOR 1:	Imagine late one night you can't sleep, so you get out of bed, look out the window—and get the surprise of your life!
NARRATOR 2:	That's what happened to Sophie, because across the street she saw a giant, with a long, thin trumpet and a large suitcase.
NARRATOR 3:	When the giant saw Sophie, he reached through the window and grabbed her! Then he ran all night, until they reached his enormous cave.
BFG:	Now, what has us got here?
NARRATOR 1:	The Giant put the trembling Sophie on the table.
SOPHIE:	P-please don't eat me!
BFG:	Just because I is a giant, you think I is a man-gobbling cannybull! Me gobbling up human beans! This I never! All the other giants is gobbling them up every night, but not me! I is the Big Friendly Giant! I is the BFG!
SOPHIE:	But if you are so nice and friendly, why did you snatch me from my bed and run away with me?
BFG:	Because you saw me. The first thing you would be doing is scuddling around yodeling the news that you saw a giant, and then people would be coming rushing and bushing after me and they would be putting me into the zoo with all those squiggling hippodumplings and crocadowndillies!

Figure 14.2 Picturebooks Adaptable for Readers' Theatre Scripts

Bink and Gollie by Kate DiCamillo
The Cat, the Dog, Little Red, the Exploding Eggs, the Wolf, and Grandma by Diane Fox
Dog and Bear: Two Friends, Three Stories by Laura Vaccaro Seeger
Duck on a Tractor by David Shannon
Frog and Toad Are Friends by Arnold Lobel
I Am the Dog, I Am the Cat by Donald Hall
"I Have a Little Problem," Said the Bear by Heinz Janisch
Last Stop on Market Street by Matt de la Peña
Red: A Crayon's Story by Michael Hall

Figure 14.3 Novels Adaptable for Readers' Theatre Scripts

Because of Mr. Terupt by Rob Buyea
Bird in a Box, by Andrea Davis Pinkney
The Giver by Lois Lowry
One Day and One Amazing Morning on Orange Street by Joanne Rocklin
Seedfolks and ***Bull Run*** by Paul Fleischman
The BFG by Roald Dahl
The Small Adventure of Popeye and Elvis by Barbara O'Connor
A Tangle of Knots by Lisa Graff
Witness by Karen Hesse

Choice of literature can include virtually any literary genre—picturebooks, novels, biographies, long poems, letters, diaries, and journals. See Figure 14.2 and Figure 14.3 for books suitable for script development. Books written from multiple viewpoints are easy to adapt into a script, such as Karen Hesse's *Witness* (2001), a historical novel written as a series of poems in the first-person voices of eleven characters who tell the story of the Ku Klux Klan's activities in a small Vermont town in 1924. Lisa Graff's *A Tangle of Knots* (2013) requires adaptation, as the multiple perspectives are written in third person, but this mysterious and interconnected tale of events and circumstances makes an excellent readers' theatre. Variations on readers' theatre can be accomplished through the addition of background music, choral poems, and brief scenes from different stories tied together by a common theme.

Preparation for a readers' theatre presentation gives children an opportunity to strengthen their oral reading abilities and develop expressive skills. The group typically reads through the script once or twice and then works on refining the interpretive aspects of each performer. Decisions need to be made on the arrangement of chairs and speakers for greatest visual effect. Following each presentation, an evaluation is made by the group with the goal of improving future performances.

Readers' theatre is well suited to enactments of literary experiences. Children have the opportunity to construct meaning for a literary work in the medium of drama with considerable ease and pleasure.

Experiencing Literature as Multimodal Texts

In today's world, children are immersed in many multimedia experiences, including video games, tablets, and the Internet, that provide them with interactive digital, visual, auditory, and dramatic texts. Children's literature is increasingly available in a range of media, providing important points of access for many children. These multimodal texts include audiobooks, films, and digital books.

Audiobooks of children's literature in downloadable formats provide readings by well-known actors and professional readers. The American Library Association provides an annual list of Notable Children's

Recordings that are high quality recordings that are interesting and creative. Using audiobooks as a teaching tool includes:

- Listening to an audiobook as a class in place of the regular read-aloud. The novelty of the performance can add interest.
- Using audiobooks at a center where a group of children work independently. Provide each child with a copy of the book to follow the narration.
- Offering children who struggle with reading the option of listening to the audiobook while following the narration in a copy of the book as a homework option. Children who otherwise would be unable to participate in class discussions of the book with their peers will be able to contribute.
- Accessing free audiobooks through public libraries or websites such as www.librivox.org and www.gutenberg.org.

Films based on children's books provide a multimedia experience of a story. Children can compare how film is similar to and different from text. Both have plots, characters, settings, themes, styles, and points of view and have dialogue and narration. However, film adds the dimensions of sound (spoken words, music, and sound effects), photography or animation (color or black and white, angles, close-ups, and panoramas), and movement. Additionally, films have actual people or animated characters inhabiting the character roles and actual settings, whereas books ask readers to form their own images of characters and settings.

With a quick background in the elements of cinema, children can become better "readers" of film, equipped to discuss their personal responses to films based on literature. Usually, a film based on a book is viewed after the book has been read and discussed. The film then provides an opportunity to compare and contrast with the book while considering the differences between the two media and their potentials and limitations for storytelling. For some children the movie experience may be motivation to read the book or others in the same series or by the same author.

At the end of Chapters 5 through 12, lists of films related to each genre are provided. The American Library Association has an annual award, the Andrew Carnegie Medal for Excellence in Children's Video, given to the producer of a video. You can use these lists to select films based on books that are appropriate to the age level and connected to classroom inquiries. Sources for films and videos include:

- *The Video Source Book*, published by Cengage Gale, Detroit, MI. This annual reference lists media and provides sources for purchase and rental.
- High quality audio and video recordings of children's books are produced by Dreamscapes Media and Weston Woods.
- The Internet Movie Database (www.imdb.com) is a large film database with production, ratings, and other movie details with links to external reviews. A video distributor to consult is www.libraryvideocompany.com/.

Digital books and ***book apps*** are increasingly popular formats for accessing literature. Global digital books are available from the International Children's Digital Library (en.childrenslibrary.org) in different languages. Digital books are produced by a range of children's publishers and software suppliers. Many of these books provide interactive components, allowing children to click on a character or part of the setting to get additional information, dialogue, or sound effects, as well as narration to read along with. Scholastic produces Storia, interactive applications for e-books, a trend by other publishers as well.

Book apps can make words and stories come to life, engaging a child in a different experience with a story. Apps can be used as a reading experience, entertainment, reading extension, or educational tool (Koss, 2012). Features of apps include:

- Multiple narration options, including Read to Me, Read by Myself, Read and Do, Read and Record.
- Animation, particularly active animation, in which the user activates the animation by tapping or tilting the screen.
- Enhancements include a linked glossary, additional scenes, interactive elements in pictures to cause images to move, or linked sources of information related to elements of the story.
- Educational features, such as highlighting words as they are read, objects that narrate when touched, comprehension activities, or vocabulary support.

Although these apps can be entertaining, they can also distract children from the actual story. A recent study by the Cooney Center (2012) found that parents and their 3- to 6-year-old children engaged *less* with the content of the story when reading a book app and the children recalled fewer narrative details than when reading the print book. Just as with a book, interacting with children around a book app deepens understanding and encourages connections. Reviews and information on apps can be found on websites, including Kirkus Reviews, Digital Storytime, Digital Book World, and the Kapi award.

Electronic book (e-book) readers are not yet widely used in schools but are growing in popularity and are being integrated into classrooms and libraries as the technology develops and becomes more affordable. E-books are generally cheaper than paper books, take up less space, are environmentally less wasteful to produce, and are more easily distributed. They can make out-of-print books available and can make virtually any book available to readers who have access to the Internet. Access to full-text books is also available on smartphones. Publishing data, however, indicates that the majority of children and teens still prefer to own a physical copy of the book. Publisher statistics indicate that e-books are holding steady at 25 percent of the market instead of taking over the market as earlier predicted.

E-book readers provide access not only to books but also to newspapers, magazines, and blogs and are an important source of informational materials as required by the Common Core State Standards. As a result, greatly expanded choices of reading materials are available for children and literature for text sets and in-class reading. A disadvantage of some e-book readers is the lack of color graphic capability, making picturebooks, illustrated informational books, and graphic novels using color ineffective as e-books. Capabilities of e-book readers that facilitate reading include:

- A built-in dictionary so that readers can get a definition of a word by clicking on it
- Automatic searching and cross-referencing of text for finding earlier references to characters or events
- Nonpermanent highlighting
- Text-to-speech software that can automatically convert e-books to audiobooks

Plays, as a literary genre, are written, dramatic compositions or scripts intended to be acted. A play may be divided into parts called ***acts;*** in turn, each act may be divided into ***scenes.*** The script usually has set design, costumes, and stage directions, as well as dialogue provided for each actor. Plays are usually published in ***playbooks*** that can be purchased as a set for use in group reading situations.

A good play has a subject that appeals to children, interesting characters, and a problem that worsens before being resolved satisfactorily. Humor always appeals to children, and conflict between characters is needed for interest and drama. Some children's plays are adaptations of children's books, while others are ***original plays***—stories originating in play form. The following resources can be used to locate plays:

- *Children's Book and Play Review,* an online journal of play reviews (http://byucbmr.com/)
- International Association of Theatre for Children and Young People (U.S. national section is Theatre for Young Audiences, www.assitej-usa.org) and the American Alliance for Theatre and Education (www.aate.com)
- Smith and Kraus, publisher of plays and play anthologies (www.smithandkraus.com), and Eldridge Publishing, one of the oldest children's play publishers (www.histage.com)

Several children's authors have written play scripts. Examples include *Skellig: The Play* by David Almond (2005), *Zap* by Paul Fleischman (2005), *Monster* by Walter Dean Myers (1999), *Novio Boy: A Play* by Gary Soto (2006), and *Pushing Up the Sky* by Joseph Bruchac (2000). Sharon Creech's *Replay* (2005) has a play included at the end of the novel.

Children create a unique literary experience by performing a drama, one that immerses them in creating a story while building on their natural enjoyment of play. Plays can be read independently or in small groups, performed as readers' theatre, or performed as a drama for an audience.

Reading Critically to Inquire about the World

Reading literature critically to inquire about the world involves reading to consider serious issues in children's lives, society, and the content areas. These experiences support children in becoming critical and knowledgeable readers and thinkers. Readers are encouraged to engage deeply with the text and then to step back to share their connections and reflect critically with others about the text and their responses.

This intensive reading of a few books to think deeply and critically balances the extensive reading of many books. The books chosen for intensive reading have multiple layers of meaning and invite readers to linger longer. These books invite social interaction and discussion, as children need others to think about what they have read as they struggle with interpretation and understanding. Because the focus is on dialogue and thinking, the literature may be beyond their reading ability, with the text read aloud to them, particularly in the case of young children and struggling readers.

When children experience a story, they often want to respond or express their reactions to the experience in some way. Sharing their responses can involve thinking about the experience through a new form or medium. They develop a better understanding of what they experienced by organizing and deepening their feelings and thoughts, and discover that other readers' experiences with the same book may differ from theirs. Although it is important to give children opportunities to respond to books, not every book needs or merits a lengthy response. Rosenblatt (1978) points out that no two people have the same life experiences and that the transaction between the text, the reader, and the context is what provokes a particular response. Children can respond to their literary experiences in many different ways.

Children can also engage with literature as part of thematic studies or inquiries within content areas, such as math, science, and social studies. They read critically to compare information and issues across these books, learn facts about the topic, and consider conceptual issues. Literature becomes a tool for understanding the world and considering broader social and scientific issues, as well as a means of facilitating children's interest in a topic.

Literature Discussion

Whole-class discussion usually accompanies a read-aloud. In these discussions, the talk centers on how children feel and think about the book, characters, events, themes, and outcome. You can invite children to share their connections by asking, "What are you thinking?" instead of asking literal detail questions to check comprehension. In a class discussion, you often have a pivotal role as discussion leader. The problem is only a few children have an opportunity to express their viewpoints because of group size, so small groups are essential to engaging all children in talk.

Children can discuss their responses in a ***literature circle,*** where they meet in small groups to share their responses about a book they have read as a group or a book read aloud to the class. One of the goals of literature circles is for children to learn to work and think with one another and to value the opinions and views of others. The small group format is student led and provides more opportunities for dialogue. You do not need to be a member of the group, but if you do join a group, participate as a reader in sharing your responses and thoughts, rather than only asking questions.

The books for literature circles are organized around a particular theme as either ***shared book sets*** (multiple copies of the same text) or ***text sets*** (ten to twelve conceptually related picturebooks). Each small group reads a different shared book or text set related to the same broad theme (see Figures 14.4 and Figures 14.5).

Children are introduced to the selections through short booktalks and given time to browse the books. They list their first and second choices on ballots that are used to organize children into heterogeneous groups of four to six. Children reading chapter books determine how many pages to read a day to finish the book in one or two weeks. Reading goals that are not completed at school are considered homework. Children meet in a mini-circle for 10–15 minutes daily to check in with each other on their reading goals and share connections and confusions. Those who are struggling with the book can partner with someone or listen to a recording of the book.

Young children may not be able to independently read the more complex picturebooks that support literature discussion. The books can be read aloud to them by an adult, older buddy reader, or family member, or they can listen to a recording. Young children benefit from hearing the book read aloud several times. One option is to have the books read aloud at home for several days before the school discussion.

As children read, they respond by writing or sketching their connections, questions, and concerns. The responses may be in a literature log, on sticky notes placed in the book, on a graffiti board, or on a closed Internet network. Once children complete the book, they meet in literature circles for extended discussions, although some children may need to meet as they read if they are struggling readers or English language learners. Literature circles can last anywhere from two days to two weeks, depending on the length of the book and the depth of discussion. The discussions are open ended and provide time for readers to share their initial responses and then move to dialogue about issues in more depth using these procedures:

- Creating a web or consensus board to brainstorm the issues to explore further, based on initial sharing.
- Identifying an anomaly or concern to inquire about together as a group.

Figure 14.4 Shared Book Sets on Journeys for Literature Circles

Picturebooks

Each literature circle has multiple copies of one of these titles.

Amelia's Road by Linda Altman

Fox by Margaret Wild

Goin' Someplace Special by Patricia McKissack

Going Home by Eve Bunting

John Patrick Norman McHennessy: The Boy Who Was Always Late by John Burningham

Last Stop on Market Street by Matt de la Peña

The Pink Refrigerator by Tim Egan

Something Beautiful by Sharon Wyeth

Chapter Books

Each literature circle has multiple copies of one of these titles.

Becoming Naomi León by Pam Muñoz Ryan

Elijah of Buxton by Christopher Paul Curtis

The Golden Compass by Philip Pullman

Inside Out and Back Again by Thanhha Lai

Journey by Patricia MacLachlan

Lizzie Bright and the Buckminster Boy by Gary Schmidt

When My Name Was Keoko by Linda Sue Park

Where the Mountain Meets the Moon by Grace Lin

Figure 14.5 Text Sets on War and Conflict for Literature Circles

Conditions That Lead to War

The Butter Battle Book by Dr. Seuss

The Chickens Build a Wall by Jean-Francois Dumont

First Come the Zebras by Lynne Barasch

The Island by Amin Greder

The Island of the Skog by Steven Kellogg

The Rabbits by John Marsden, illustrated by Shaun Tan

The Tiger Who Would Be King by James Thurber, illustrated by JooHee Yoon

Tusk Tusk by David McKee

When I Grow Up, I Will Win the Nobel Peace Prize by Isabel Pin

The Wild Wombat by Udo Weigelt

War as an Institution

The Conquerors by David McKee

The End of War by Irmela Wendt

The Enemy by David Cali, illustrated by Serge Bloch

The Monkey Bridge by Rafe Martin

Patrol: An American Solider in Vietnam, by Walter Dean Myers, illustrated by Ann Grifalconi

The Roses in My Carpets by Rukhsana Khan

Sami and the Time of the Troubles by Florence P. Heide and Judith Heide Gilliland

The War by Anais Vaugelade

War and Peas by Michael Foreman

Waterloo & Trafalgar by Olivier Tallec

Consequences of War

Beyond Bullets: A Photo Journal of Afghanistan by Rafal Gerszak

The Bracelet by Yoshiko Uchida

Faithful Elephants by Yukio Tsuchiya

Fish for Jimmy by Katie Yamasaki

Good Night, Commander by Ahmad Akbarpour

Half Spoon of Rice by Icy Smith, illustrated by Sopaul Nhem

My Secret Camera by Mendel Grossman

The Orphans of Normandy by Nancy Amis

Rose Blanche by Roberto Innocenti

Sadako by Eleanor Coerr

Overcoming War

The Brave Little Parrot by Rafe Martin

The Cello of Mr. O by Jane Cutler

A Child's Garden: A Story of Hope, Michael Foreman

The Composition, by Antonio Skarmeta, illustrated by Alfonso Ruano

Gandhi by Demi

Hiroshima No Pika by Toshi Maruki

Let the Celebrations Begin! by Margaret Wild

A Place Where Sunflowers Grow by Amy Lee-Tai

Wall by Tom C. Cole

The Whispering Town by Jennifer Elvgren, illustrated by Fabio Santomauro

- Preparing for discussion of an issue by rereading sections of the book, writing or sketching in logs, marking relevant quotations with sticky notes, engaging in further research, or using a particular response engagement.
- Sharing ideas and connections related to the identified issue and engaging in dialogue around differing interpretations and perspectives.
- Returning to the web multiple times to identify another issue for discussion.

Text set discussions begin with each child reading one or two books from the set and meeting to share their books. Children often move between reading and sharing books with each other for a week before webbing connections and differences across the books in their set. They choose one of these issues to discuss in greater depth through inquiry and critique.

When children complete their literature circles, they present key ideas from their discussions to pull together their thinking about the book or text set. They either informally talk about their books and share their webs with classmates or create a formal presentation. To plan a formal presentation, they first list the most important ideas they want to share about their book and then brainstorm different ways to present these ideas (murals, skits, posters, dioramas, etc.), choosing one that best fits the ideas. A third option is to create a classroom newsletter in which each literature group writes about the books they read using visual sketches, webs, or charts.

The discussions in literature circles are more complex and generative if they are integrated into a broad class theme, such as identity or journeys, around which children are experiencing a range of engagements, including class read-alouds and browsing of other books on that theme. This theme may be connected to a unit of inquiry within the curriculum or to issues children are exploring in their lives.

When children have the opportunity to converse and dialogue about what they are reading, they explore their "in-process" understandings, consider alternative interpretations, and become critical inquirers. Literature circles support reading as a transactional process in which readers actively construct understandings of a text by bringing meaning to, as well as from, that text. They come to understand that there is no one meaning to be determined, but many possible interpretations to explore and critique. The primary intent of these discussions is to provide a space for readers to think about life from multiple perspectives, not to learn about literary elements or comprehension strategies.

Literature Response Engagements

Requiring children to list the author, title, date, genre, setting, main characters, and summary of the plot seldom leads them to delve more deeply into a book. Children usually view traditional book reports as tedious busywork and as a punishment for reading a book. Although teachers assign book reports to get children to read, children often report that they never read the book, but instead look at the bookflap, a page or two at the beginning and end, or an online book summary.

Literature response forms and worksheets are available online for use in literature-based reading approaches. These worksheets are often little more than disguised book report forms. Such comprehension assessment may be occasionally useful for reading instruction but is of no use if your interest is children's thinking about a book.

Readers deepen and extend their interpretations of literature when they respond in a variety of ways. When readers move from reading to writing, art, or drama, they take a new perspective on the piece of literature. In the process of exploring their thinking about a book through multiple literacies, they discover new meanings and expand their understandings of that book.

The following response engagements provide structures to encourage children to push their thinking about a book. These engagements stand in contrast to activities where they write a summary, retell a book, answer comprehension questions, or make a "cute" art project. Response engagements challenge children to find and explore the issues they find significant within a book, rather than answer the teacher's questions about the book. (See *Creating Classrooms for Authors and Inquirers by* Kathy G. Short and Jerome Harste, 1996, for more information about these engagements.)

- ***Freewrites.*** At the beginning of a group meeting, set a timer for five minutes and ask children to write continuously about their thoughts on a book; then turn and talk in the group. If the group is still not sure how to begin, one person can read aloud part of his/her freewrite. The group discusses the ideas and then moves to the next person.

- ***Post-ful thinking.*** Children put sticky notes on pages where they have a significant connection while reading and jot a quick comment. These connections are shared when the group meets to identify issues for discussion. The sticky notes can also be used to revisit the book around a particular issue by marking pages relevant to the issue as a way to prepare for the discussion.
- ***Literature logs.*** Children stop periodically while reading and respond to what they are thinking about, including questions and connections. These entries can take the form of a written response, sketch, web, chart, or quotes. Children reread the logs immediately before the group discussion to remind themselves of the issues.
- ***Collage reading/text rendering.*** Children mark quotes they see as significant as they read. In collage reading, group members read aloud quotes to each other. One person reads a quote, then someone else reads another quote, and the reading continues in no particular order. Readers choose when to read a quote in order to build on what someone else has read, but no comments are made about the quotes. Text rendering is similar, except the reader states why he/she chose the quote. There is no discussion until after the text rendering is finished.
- ***Graffiti boards.*** A large sheet of paper is placed on the table. Each group member takes a corner of the paper to write, web, and sketch thoughts about the book or text set. The comments, sketches, quotes, and connections are not organized; the major focus is on recording initial responses during or immediately after reading a book. Group members share from their graffiti entries to start the discussion. Webbing or charting can then be used to organize the connections that are shared.
- ***Save the last word for me.*** Readers note passages or quotes that catch their attention because they are interesting, powerful, confusing, or contradictory and put the quote on a 3" × 5" card. On the back of the card, they write why they found that particular passage noteworthy. In the group, one person shares a quote and the group briefly discusses their thinking while the initial person remains silent. When the discussion dies down, the person who chose the quote tells why he/she chose it. That person has the last word, then the group moves on to the next person. Young children can show a selected illustration from a picturebook instead of reading a quote.
- ***Sketch to stretch.*** After reading a book, children make a sketch (a quick graphic/symbolic drawing) of what the story meant to them, their connections to the book (not an illustration of the story). In the group, they show their sketch and discuss their symbols and ideas. After sharing sketches, the group chooses issues to explore in more depth.
- ***Webbing what's on my mind.*** After sharing initial responses, a group brainstorms a web of issues, themes, and questions that could be discussed from the book or text set. Using the web, the group decides on the one issue that is most interesting or causes the most tension to begin discussion. They can return to the web later to choose other ideas on the web. New ideas are added as they develop from the discussion.
- ***Consensus board.*** A large board is divided into four sections with a circle in the center. The circle contains the book's title or key theme. In the individual sections, each person writes or sketches personal connections to the book or theme. The group discusses these connections and comes to consensus on the issues or big ideas to explore further. These are written in the middle of the board for further discussion.
- ***Comparison charts/Venn diagrams.*** After reading a text set and discussing similarities and differences across the books, the group develops broad categories for close comparisons. A chart can be made with the books listed on the side and the categories across the top, using both pictures and words to make the comparisons in the boxes. A Venn diagram (two circles that overlap in the center) can be used to record overlaps and differences in particular issues from the books.
- ***Story ray.*** Each reader receives a three-foot narrow strip of paper (a ray) on which to create a visual essence of a selected chapter using colors, images, and a few words, with various art media and little or no white space. The rays are shared in the groups for each person to explain symbolism. The rays are then assembled on a large mural or wall in the shape of sun rays to reflect the unfolding of the novel.
- ***Mapping.*** Maps provide a way to organize thinking and explore relationships among ideas, people, and events. They can take a range of forms to show visual relationships, explore processes and change, and record movement of people or ideas, such as:
    - The journey of change for a character within a book or of an issue over the course of the book
    - Symbols that show the heart (the values and beliefs) or the mind (the thoughts and ideas) of a particular character

- A cultural x-ray in the shape of a person that shows a character's inner values and beliefs on a large heart inside the body and outer actions and qualities around the outside of the body
- A flowchart that explores how certain decisions made by a character create particular consequences

• ***Timelines and diagrams.*** Timelines can provide a way to consider how particular historical events influenced the characters in the story. After drawing a line on a long strip of paper, placing the dates below the line on scaled intervals, note the story events above the line and the events from history below the line. Timelines are also useful with text sets of historical sources.

Children who are new to working in groups often find that working in pairs is an easier way to become comfortable with discussion. Any of these response engagements may be used with partners rather than in a small group. There are also several response engagements that are particularly designed for partners. Here are two possibilities:

• ***Say something.*** Two people share the reading of a short story. The first person reads aloud a chunk of text (several paragraphs or a page) to the other person. When the reader stops, both of them "say something" by making a prediction, sharing personal connections, asking questions, or commenting on the story. The second person then reads aloud a chunk of text and again both "say something." The two readers continue alternating the reading of the story, commenting after each reading, until the story is completed.

• ***Written conversation.*** Have a silent conversation by talking on paper. Two people share a piece of paper and a pencil, talking about a book by writing back and forth to each other. No talking is allowed, except with young children, who often need to write and then read what they have written aloud in order for the other child to write back.

Drama as Response

Creative drama is informal drama that involves the reenactment of story experiences (McCaslin, 1990). It is improvisational and involves the actors creating dialogue and movement as they engage in the drama. Props may be used, but not scenery or costumes. Because of its improvisational nature and simplicity, creative drama places importance on the experience of the participants, not on performance for an audience. The Child Drama website (www.childdrama.com) has useful ideas and lesson plans for creative drama.

A picturebook, short story, or single scene from a chapter book may be dramatized. The most suitable stories to start with are relatively simple, involving two to six characters and high action, such as found in folktales. The steps in guiding creative drama are these:

• Children select a story to act out and listen to or read independently several times, paying attention to the characters and story scenes.

• Children list the characters and the scenes on the board or on chart paper.

• Children assign parts to actors. If enough are interested in dramatizing the same story, two or more casts of actors can be created. Each cast of characters can observe the performances of the others and learn from them.

• Each cast uses the list of scenes to review the plot, ensuring that all actors recall the events. Discuss the characters by describing their actions, dialogue, and appearance.

• Give the cast of characters a few minutes to decide how to handle the performance. Then run through it several times to work out the bumpy parts. Lines are improvised, not memorized.

Dramatic inquiry, also known as ***Drama in Education,*** involves using drama to create an imaginative space or drama world around critical moments in a story, rather than acting out a story (Heathcote, 1984). Children develop characters and situations and take on diverse perspectives that go beyond the book. Discussion supports readers in standing back and talking about events that happened to people in a different world. Dramatic inquiry puts children in the middle of events and within the world of the story as they explore their tensions and issues. Children explore multiple perspectives within and beyond the story boundaries through strategies such as the following:

- ***Tableaus.*** Each small group creates a frozen image without talk or movement to represent an idea or moment related to the story.
- ***Writing-in-role.*** Children assume the identity of a character and write a text from that perspective, such as a reflection on events or a journal entry.

- ***Hot seat.*** Children take on the roles of different characters and sit on the hot seat to respond to questions about their perspective on an issue from the story.
- ***News program.*** Children take on the role of television or newspaper reporters and interview characters from the book to retell an event from a range of perspectives.
- ***Perspective switch.*** Each child shifts perspectives and character roles, trying out the perspectives of characters opposed, supportive, or ambivalent to an issue.

These drama strategies take readers beyond reenactments of a story to their own drama worlds, giving them a lens for critically examining the events and margins of a story. *Action Strategies for Deepening Comprehension* (Wilhelm, 2002) offers examples of these drama strategies in responding to literature.

Literature across the Curriculum

Literature across the curriculum refers to the use of literature to replace or supplement textbooks in social studies, science, health, and mathematics. Literature provides more interesting and well-written accounts and perspectives on historical events and scientific information. In addition, textbooks often superficially cover large amounts of information, whereas nonfiction literature focuses on a particular topic in more depth, providing a context for inquiry into broader social and scientific issues. Children who struggle as readers can benefit from attractively illustrated and more accessible nonfiction literature. A collection of nonfiction literature of varying lengths and difficulties can meet the needs of children at different reading levels, unlike textbooks written on a single readability level.

Literature makes social studies content more memorable because the stories are presented from a child's point of view, allowing children to see the world through a narrative framework. Children are more likely to understand and remember history when presented as a story with characters, settings, and events. They can then move from an interest in the narrative to an interest in the historical information.

Literature also permits children to examine multiple perspectives on a topic, which facilitates critical thinking. By comparing historical information from various sources, children encounter differing perspectives on a particular era of history. In addition, literature often relates political and social events to relevant moral issues. Children can see how these events affected the lives of real people and understand the morality underlying their choices. Unlike textbook authors, who must write to satisfy all viewpoints, authors of children's literature are more likely to face controversial issues head-on. For ideas on planning a unit around the forced journeys of refugees see the web in Figure 13.2. Examples of literature offering a range of perspectives for a social studies inquiry on Japanese American internment camps and for a science unit about the moon can be found in Figure 14.6.

Informational literature in science and health presents different sources of information as a means to verify facts and provides a conceptual frame for raising awareness of the larger social issues. The increasing focus in schools on STEM (science, technology, engineering, and mathematics) highlights the important role that informational books can play in these fields. Children can compare the facts presented in the textbook with those found in various books on the same topic. Global warming, a topic frequently in the news, is addressed in a number of books. David Laurie and Cambria Gordon's *The Down-to-Earth Guide to Global Warming* (2007) and *How We Know What We Know about Our Changing Climate* by Lynne Cherry and Gary Braasch (2008) are two short, well-written informational books, whereas Marcus Sedgwick's science fiction novel *Floodland* (2001) features a girl who searches for her parents after the sea has risen as a result of global warming, causing cities to become islands. Young children can explore global warming through Jeanette Winter's *Nanuk, the Ice Bear* (2016) and Masako Yamashita's *Snow Children* (2012).

Many nonfiction books on health and science present information in interesting ways through graphs, tables, figures, photographs, and other visual presentations, coupled with a lively writing style. Steve Jenkins's *Animals by Numbers* (2016) introduces children to infographics in answering common questions about animals. Comparison of information from different sources can be readily provided when children are not limited to a single source for information. As children draw on various types of texts, they discover that literature has the power to educate the mind while enlightening the spirit.

Content-area reading is the ability to read to acquire, understand, and connect to new content in a particular discipline. In content-area classes children are often assigned textbooks, a type of expository text, which they frequently have more difficulty reading and understanding than narrative texts. You can make reading textbooks easier by teaching children how such texts are structured and explaining their specialized features. In Chapter 11, the elements and structures of informational texts are explained with examples. Heard and McDonough (2009), Duke (2014), and Beers and Probst (2016) provide many practical ideas on teaching reading and interpretation strategies for informational texts.

Figure 14.6 Text Sets for Multiple Perspectives in Science and Social Studies Units

The Moon

Come Back, Moon by David Kherdian, illustrated by Nonny Hogrogian (Pourquoi tale)

Comets, Stars, the Moon, and Mars: Space Poems and Paintings by Douglas Florian (Poetry)

The Dog Who Loved the Moon by Cristina Gárcia, illustrated by Sebastia Serra (Fantasy, Cuba)

A Full Moon Is Rising: Poems by Marilyn Singer, illustrated by Julia Cairns (Poetry, global)

If You Decide to Go to the Moon by Faith McNulty, illustrated by Steven Kellogg (Fantasy/science)

The Moon by Seymour Simon (Science)

Moon Man by Tomi Ungerer (Fantasy, France)

The Moon over Star by Dianna H. Aston, illustrated by Jerry Pinkney (Historical fiction)

Moonday by Adam Rex (Fantasy)

Moonshot: The Flight of Apollo 11 by Brian Floca (History)

Moontellers: Myths of the Moon from Around the World by Lynn Moroney, illustrated by Greg Shed (Myths, world)

Team Moon: How 400,000 People Landed Apollo 11 on the Moon by Catherine Thimmesh (History, aeronautics)

Thanking the Moon: Celebrating the Mid-Autumn Moon Festival by Grace Lin (Festival, Chinese American)

Japanese American Internment Camps/ World War II

Barbed Wire Baseball by Marissa Moss, illustrated by Yuko Shimizu (Historical fiction picturebook)

Baseball Saved Us by Ken Mochizuki, illustrated by Dom Lee (Historical fiction picturebook)

Dash by Kirby Larson (Historical fiction novel)

Dear Miss Breed: True Stories of the Japanese American Incarceration during World War II and a Librarian Who Made a Difference by Joanne Oppenheim (History)

A Diamond in the Desert by Kathryn Fitzmaurice (Historical fiction novel)

Fish for Jimmy by Katie Yamasaki (Historical fiction picturebook, autobiographical)

Flowers from Mariko by Rick Noguchi, illustrated by Michelle R. Kumata (Historical fiction picturebook)

Home of the Brave by Allen Say (Modern fable, picturebook)

Imprisoned: The Betrayal of Japanese Americans during World War II by Martin Sandler (History)

A Place Where Sunflowers Grow by Amy Lee-Tai, illustrated by Felicia Hoshino (Historical fiction picturebook)

Under the Blood-Red Sun by Graham Salisbury (Historical fiction novel, Hawai'i)

Weedflower by Cynthia Kadohata (Historical fiction novel)

Reading Strategically to Learn about Literacy

Reading literature to learn about literacy creates strategic readers who reflect on their reading processes and text knowledge. You can use these engagements to help children develop a repertoire of strategies for when they encounter difficulty, either in figuring out words or in comprehending, and to gain knowledge of text structures and literary elements. You can guide children's reflections on their reading processes by teaching lessons on strategies, literary elements, and text structures and by having children read literature that highlights particular reading strategies based on your knowledge of their needs. Children who have a range of effective reading strategies and text knowledge can problem solve when encountering difficulty so as to develop reading proficiency.

Many schools use commercial materials for reading instruction rather than literature. Although children are taught how to read through these materials, they do not necessarily develop the desire or habit of reading. They are capable of reading but are not engaged readers who are motivated, knowledgeable, and strategic.

Engagements with literature that focus on learning about literacy include guided reading, guided comprehension, conferencing, and mini-lessons in which children read books to examine their current reading strategies and develop new strategies. You need to carefully assess which readers are on the "edge of knowing" a particular strategy and form small groups who share similar needs for guided reading. Reading strategies are taught within the context of reading a book for meaning and then pulling back to talk about the strategies children used to make sense of that book or to figure out unfamiliar words.

Often literary instruction takes the form of worksheets where children list story elements, such as character, plot, and conflict, rather than thoughtfully considering how these elements influence meaning. Recently there has been a strong emphasis on genre studies. Some of these genre studies are formulaic, whereas others involve children in an inquiry approach to construct their understandings of the genre. These genre studies provide a way for children to explore literary elements and genres within a meaningful context. Author studies, in which children immerse themselves in reading and examining an author's whole body of work, are another meaningful context in which to examine particular literary elements and genres to learn about literature.

Writing provides an effective way to explore language and text structure, particularly if children use literary works as writing mentors. When children read and listen to stories, they gather vocabulary, sentence structures, stylistic devices, and story ideas and structures. Well-written stories and poems, such as those in Tables 14.1 and Tables 14.2, serve as mentors for children in their own writing. Children who have a rich literary background have a well-stocked storehouse of ideas and structures to use in their storytelling and writing.

Writing a story modeled after another story can be an enjoyable way to explore constructing meaning through particular text structures. Children can adapt a story form or idea into a new creation by creating another episode using the same characters, writing a different ending or a prequel to the story, or recasting the story from the perspective of another character. Examples of a change in point of view can be found in Jon Scieszka and Lane Smith's *The True Story of the 3 Little Pigs by A. Wolf* (1989), which gives the Big Bad Wolf's version. Children can also take a story set in the past and rewrite it with a modern-day setting, as in *Little Roja Riding Hood* by Susan Elya and Susan Guevara (2014), or have a character from the historical narrative become a visitor to modern times.

Many cultures view reading as necessary to a well-ordered society and to the moral well-being of the individual. Engagement with literature invites children to make meaning of texts in personally significant ways to facilitate learning of content and to develop positive lifelong reading attitudes and habits. In addition, children gain a sense of possibility for their lives and for society, along with the ability to consider others' perspectives and needs. Engagement with literature allows them to develop their own voices and, at the same time, go beyond self-interest to an awareness of broader human consequences.

Table 14.1 Using Literary Works as Writing Models in Grades 1–3

Literary Device/Element	Suggested Books
Characterization	***Marisol McDonald Doesn't Match*** by Monica Brown & Sara Palacios ***Penny and Her Marble*** by Kevin Henkes ***Big Wolf and Little Wolf*** by Nadine Brun-Cosme & Olivier Tallee ***Little Roja Riding Hood*** by Susan M. Elya & Susan Guevara
Dialogue	***I Want My Hat Back*** by Jon Klassen ***"I Have a Little Problem," Said the Bear*** by Heinz Zanisch ***Red: A Crayon Story*** by Michael Hall
Episodic Plot	***Bink and Gollie*** by Kate DiCamillo ***Dog and Bear: Two Friends, Three Stories*** by Laura V. Seeger ***Tales for Very Picky Eaters*** by Josh Schneider
Journal Writing	***Pictures from Our Vacation*** by Lynne Rae Perkins ***Diary of a Fly*** by Doreen Cronin ***The Day the Crayons Quit*** by Drew Daywalt & Oliver Jeffers
Setting	***Last Stop on Market Street*** by Matt de la Peña & Christian Robinson ***A New Year's Reunion*** by Yu Li-Qiong ***Goin' Someplace Special*** by Patricia McKissack

Table 14.2 Using Literary Works as Writing Models in Grades 4–7

Literary Device or Element	Suggested Books
Characterization	***The Watsons Go to Birmingham*** by Christopher Paul Curtis ***Raymie Nightingale*** by Kate DiCamillo ***The Thing about Luck*** by Cynthia Kadohata
Dialogue	***The Small Adventure of Popeye and Elvis*** by Barbara O'Connor ***My Name Is Not Easy*** by Debby Dahl Edwardson ***Sisters*** by Raina Telgemeier
Mood	***The Misadventures of the Family Fletcher*** by Dana Levy ***A Monster Calls*** by Patrick Ness ***Breaking Stalin's Nose*** by Eugene Yelchin
Journal Writing	***Diary of a Wimpy Kid*** by Jeff Kinney ***Ways to Live Forever*** by Sally Nicholls ***Hound Dog True*** by Linda Urban
Point of View	***A Tangle of Knots*** by Lisa Graff ***When My Name Was Keoko*** by Linda Sue Park ***The One and Only Ivan*** by Katherine Applegate
Flashbacks	***The Thing about Jellyfish*** by Ali Benjamin ***Hush*** by Jacqueline Woodson ***The Doldrums*** by Nicholas Gannon

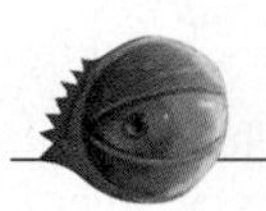

Invitations for Further Investigation

- Select a picturebook or scene from a novel to rewrite as a script for readers' theatre. If possible, try the piece with a group of children and reflect on their engagement.
- Read aloud a picturebook to a group of children, and engage them in a discussion using one of the literature response engagements. Reflect on this experience and what you learned from the students' responses. Read teacher vignettes from *WOW Stories* (www.wowlit.org/on-line-publications/stories) in which teachers reflect on their use of these engagements with children.
- Put together a group of text sets around a theme, such as power, conflict, change, journeys, identity, or relationships. Include a range of perspectives, genres, and cultures within your set of books. Include multimodal texts and oral literature as well as written literature.

References

Akbarpour, A. (2010*). Good night, Commander*. Zahedi, M. (Illus.). Toronto, ON: Groundwood.

Almond, D. (2005). *Skellig: The play*. New York: Delacorte.

Altman, L. J. (1995). *Amelia's road*. Sanchez, E. (Illus.). New York: Lee & Low.

Amis, N. (2003). *The orphans of Normandy*. New York: Atheneum.

Applegate, K. (2015). *The one and only Ivan*. New York: HarperCollins.

Aston, D. (2008). *The moon over star*. Pinkney, J. (Illus.). New York: Dial.

Barasch, L. (2009). *First come the zebras*. New York: Lee & Low.

Beers, K. & Probst, B. (2016). *Reading nonfiction*. Portsmouth, NH: Heinemann.

Benjamin, A. (2015). *The thing about jellyfish*. New York: Little, Brown.

Brown, M. (2012). *Marisol McDonald doesn't match*. Palacios, S. (Illus.). San Francisco, CA: Children's Book Press.

Bruchac, J. (2000). *Pushing up the sky: Seven Native American plays for children*. New York: Dial.

Brun-Cosme, N. (2009). *Big wolf & little wolf.* Tallee, O. (Illus.). New York: Enchanted Lion.
Bryan, A. (1988). Oh, the places you'll go. In *Book poems.* New York: Children's Book Council.
Bunting, E. (1998). *Going home.* Diaz, D. (Illus.). New York: HarperCollins.
Buyea, R. (2010). *Because of Mr. Terupt.* New York: Delacorte.
Cali, D. (2007). *The enemy.* Bloch, S. (Illus.). Albert Park, Victoria, Australia: Wilkins Farago.
Carle, E. (1968). *The very hungry caterpillar.* New York: Philomel.
Cherry, L. (2008). *How we know what we know about our changing climate.* Barusch, G. (Photos). New York: Dawn.
Coerr, E. (1993). *Sadako.* Young, E. (Illus.). New York: Putnam.
Cole, T. C. (2014). *Wall.* New York: Candlewick.
Cooney Center. (2012). *Print books vs. E-books.* Joanganzcooneycenter.org/Reports-35.htmloutlines
Creech, S. (2005). *Replay: A new book.* New York: Joanna Cotler Books.
Cronin, D. (2007). *The diary of a fly.* Bliss, H. (Illus.). New York: Joanna Cotler Books.
Curtis, C. P. (1995) *The Watsons go to Birmingham—1963.* New York: Delacorte.
Curtis, C. P. (2007). *Elijah of Buxton.* New York: Scholastic.
Cutler, J. (1999). *The cello of Mr. O.* Couch, G. (Illus.). New York: Puffin.
D'Adamo, F. (2001). *Iqbal.* New York: Aladdin.
Dahl, R. (1982). *The BFG.* New York: Farrar Straus Giroux.
David, L., & Gordon, C. (2007). *The down-to-earth guide to global warming.* New York: Orchard.
Daywalt, D. (2013*). The day the crayons quit.* Jeffers, O. (Illus.). New York: Penguin.
de Déu Prats, J. (2005). *Sebastian's roller skates.* Rovira, F. (Illus.). LaJolla, CA: Kane/Miller.
de la Peña, Matt. (2015). *Last stop on Market Street.* Robinson, C. (Illus.) New York: Putnam.
de Mari, S. (2006). *The last dragon.* New York: Hyperion.
Demi. (2001). *Gandhi.* New York: M. K. McElderry.
DiCamillo, K. (2010). *Bink and Gollie.* Fucile, T. (Illus.). Somerville, MA: Candlewick.
DiCamillo, K. (2016). *Raymie Nightingale*. Somerville, MA: Candlewick.
Dr. Seuss. (1984). *The butter battle book.* New York: Random House.
Duke, N. (2014). *Inside information: Developing powerful readers and writers of informational text through project-based instruction.* New York: Scholastic.
Dumont, J.F. (2013). *The chickens build a wall.* Grand Rapids, MI: Eerdmans.
Edwardson, D. (2011). *My name is not easy*. Tarrytown, NY: Cavendish.
Elvgren, J. (2014). *The whispering town.* Santomauro, R. (Illus.). Minneapolis, MN: Kar-Ben.
Elya, S.M. (2014). *Little Roja Riding Hood.* Guevara, S. (Illus.). New York: Putnam.
Farmer, N. (2002). *The house of the scorpion.* New York: Atheneum.
Fitzmaurice, K. (2012). *A diamond in the desert.* New York: Viking.
Fleischman, P. (1993). *Bull Run.* New York: HarperCollins.
Fleischman, P. (1997). *Seedfolks.* New York: HarperCollins.
Fleischman, P. (2005). *Zap.* New York: Candlewick.
Floca, B. (2009). *Moonshot: The flight of Apollo 11.* New York: Atheneum.
Florian, D. (2007). *Comets, stars, the moon, and Mars: Space poems and paintings.* New York: Harcourt.
Foreman, M. (2009). *A child's garden*. Somerville, MA: Candlewick.
Foreman, M. (2002). *War and peas.* Atlanta, GA: Andersen Press.
Fox, D. (2014). *The cat, the dog, Little Red, the exploding eggs, the wolf, and Grandma.* Fox, C. (Illus.). New York: Scholastic.
Fox, M. (2008). *Reading magic: Why reading aloud to children will change their lives forever.* New York: Mariner.
Freeman, J. (2015). *The handbook for storytime programs.* Chicago: American Library Association.
Gaiman, N. (2003). *The wolves in the walls.* New York: HarperCollins.
Gannon, N. (2015). *The doldrums*. New York: HarperCollins.
Garcia, C. (2008). *The dog who loved the moon.* Serra, S. (Illus.). New York: Atheneum.
Gerszak, R. (2011). *Beyond bullets: A photo journal of Afghanistan*. Toronto: Annick.
Graff, L. (2013). *A tangle of knots*. New York: Philomel.
Greder, A. (2007). *The island.* Melbourne, Australia: Allen & Unwin.
Grossman, B. (1989). *Tommy at the grocery store.* Chess, V. (Illus.). New York: Harper.
Grossman, M. (2000). *My secret camera.* San Diego, CA: Gulliver.
Hall, D. (1994). *I am the dog, I am the cat.* Moser, B. (Illus.). New York: Dial.
Hall, M. (2015). *Red: A crayon's story*. New York: HarperCollins.
Heard, G., & McDonough, J. (2009). A *place for wonder: Reading and writing nonfiction in primary grades.* Portland, ME: Stenhouse.
Heathcote, D. (1984). *Dorothy Heathcote: Collected writings on education and drama.* London: Hutchinson.
Heide, F. P., & Gilliland, J. H. (1992). *Sami and the time of the troubles.* Lewin, T. (Illus.). New York: Clarion.
Henkes, K. (2013). *Penny and her marble.* New York: Greenwillow.
Hesse, K. (2001). *Witness.* New York: Scholastic.
Holdaway, D. (1982). Shared book experience: Teaching reading using favorite books. *Theory into Practice, 21,* 293–300.
Innocenti, R. (1985). *Rose Blanche.* Minneapolis, MN: Creative Education.

Janisch, H. (2007). *"I have a little problem," said the bear.* Leffler, S. (Illus.). New York: North-South.
Jenkins, S. (2016). *Animals by numbers*. New York: Houghton Mifflin Harcourt.
Kadohata, C. (2006). *Weedflower.* New York: Atheneum.
Kadohata, C. (2014). *The thing about luck*. New York: Atheneum.
Kellogg, S. (1973). *The island of the Skog*. New York: Dial.
Khan, R. (1998). *The roses in my carpets*. Himler, R. (Illus.). New York: Holiday.
Kherdian, D. (2013). *Come back, moon*. Hogrogian, N. (Illus.). New York: Beach Lane.
Kinney, J. (2007). *Diary of a wimpy kid*. New York: Amulet.
Klassen, J. (2011). *I want my hat back*. Somerville, MA: Candlewick.
Koss, M. (2012). What to look for in children's book apps. *Literacy Daily*. Newark, DE: International Literacy Association.
Lai, T. (2011). *Inside out & back again*. New York: Harper.
Laminack, L. (2009). *Unwrapping the read aloud.* New York: Scholastic.
Larson, K. (2014). *Dash*. New York: Scholastic.
Laurie, D., & Gordon, C. (2007). *The down-to-earth guide to global warming*. New York: Orchard.
Lee-Tai, A. (2006). *A place where sunflowers grow.* Hoshino, F. (Illus.). San Francisco: Children's Book Press.
Levy, D. (2015). *The misadventures of the Family Fletcher*. New York: Yearling.
Lin, G. (2009). *Where the mountain meets the moon*. New York: Little Brown.
Lin, G. (2010). *Thanking the moon: Celebrating the Mid-Autumn Moon Festival.* New York: Knopf.
Li-Quiong, Yu. *A New Year's reunion*. Cheng-Liang, Z. (Illus.). Somerville, MA: Candlewick.
Lobel, A. (1970). *Frog and Toad are friends*. New York: Harper.
Lowry, L. (1993). *The giver.* New York: Houghton.
MacLachlan, P. (1993). *Journey*. New York: Yearling.
Marsden, J. (2003). *The rabbits*. Tan, S. (Illus.). Vancouver, BC: Simply Read Books.
Martin, R. (1997). *The monkey bridge*. Amiri, F. (Illus.). New York: Knopf.
Martin, R. (1998). *The brave little parrot*. Gaber, S. (Illus.). New York: Putnam.
Maruki, T. (1980). *Hiroshima no pika*. New York: Lothrop, Lee & Shepard.
McCaslin, N. (1990). *Creative drama in the classroom* (5th ed.). New York: Longman.
McKee, D. (1990). *Tusk tusk*. LaJolla, CA: Kane/Miller.
McKee, D. (2004). *The conquerors*. New York: Handprint.
McKissack, P. (2001). *Goin' someplace special.* Pinkney, J. (Illus.). New York: Atheneum.
McNulty, F. (2005). *If you decide to go to the moon*. Kellogg, S. (Illus.). New York: Scholastic.
Mochizuki, K. (1993). *Baseball saved us*. Lee, D. (Illus.). New York: Lee & Low.
Moroney, L. (1995). *Moontellers: Myths of the moon from around the world*. Shed, G. (Illus.). Flagstaff, AZ: Northland.
Moss, M. (2013). *Barbed wire baseball*. Shimizu, U. (Illus.). New York: Abrams.
Myers, W. D. (1999). *Monster.* New York: Harper Collins.
Myers, W. D. (2002). *Patrol: An American soldier in Vietnam*. Grifalconi, A. (Illus.). New York: HarperCollins.
Ness, P. (2011). *A monster calls*. Kay, J. (Illus.). Somerville, MA: Candlewick.
Nicholls, S. (2008). *Ways to live forever.* New York: Scholastic.
Noguchi, R. (2001). *Flowers from Mariko*. Kumata, K. R. (Illus.). New York: Lee & Low.
O'Connor, B. (2009). *The small adventure of Popeye and Elvis*. New York: Farrar.
Oppenheim, J. (2006). *Dear Miss Breed: True stories of the Japanese American incarceration during World War II and the librarian who made a difference*. New York: Scholastic.
Park, L. S. (2002). *When my name was Keoko*. New York: Clarion.
Perkins, L. R. (2007). *Pictures from our vacation*. New York: Greenwillow.
Pin, I. (2005). *When I grow up, I will win the Nobel Peace Prize*. New York: Farrar.
Pinkney, A. D. (2011). *Bird in a box*. New York: Little, Brown.
Pullman, P. (1996). *The golden compass*. New York: Knopf.
Rex, A. (2013). *Moonday*. New York: Disney.
Rocklin, J. *One day and one amazing morning on Orange Street*. New York: Amulet.
Rosenblatt, L. M. (1978). *The reader, the text, the poem: The transactional theory of the literary work*. Carbondale: Southern Illinois University Press.
Salisbury, G. (1994). *Under the blood-red sun*. New York: Delacorte.
Say, A. (2002). *Home of the brave*. New York: Houghton Mifflin.
Schmidt, G. (2004). *Lizzie Bright and the Buckminster boy*. New York: Clarion.
Schneider, J. (2011). *Tales for very picky eaters*. New York: Clarion.
Scieszka, J. (1989). *The true story of the 3 little pigs by A. Wolf.* Smith, L. (Illus.). New York: Viking.
Sedgwick, M. (2001). *Floodland*. New York: Delacorte.
Seeger, L. V. (2007). *Dog and bear: Two friends, three stories*. New York: Roaring Brook.
Shannon, D. (2016). *Duck on a tractor.* New York: Scholastic.
Short, K., & Harste, J. (1996). *Creating classrooms for authors and inquirers*. Portsmouth, NH: Heinemann.
Siegel, S. (2006). *To dance: A ballerina's graphic novel.* Siegel, M. (Illus.). New York: Simon & Schuster.
Simon, S. (2003). *The moon*. New York: Simon & Schuster.
Singer, M. (2011). *A full moon is rising: Poems*. Cairns, J. (Illus.). New York: Lee & Low.

Skarmeta, A. (2000). *The composition*. Ruano, A. (Illus.). Toronto: Groundwood.
Smith, C. (2010). *Half a spoon of rice*. Huem, S. (Illus.). Manhattan Beach, CA: East West.
Soto, G. (1997). *Novio boy: A play*. New York: Harcourt.
Spinelli, J. (2004). *Wringer.* New York: Harper.
Tallec, O. (2012). *Waterloo & Trafalgar*. New York: Enchanted Lion.
Telgemeier, R. (2012). *Sisters*. New York: Scholastic.
Thimmesh, C. (2006). *Team moon*. New York: Houghton Mifflin.
Thurber, J. (2015). *The tiger who would be king*. Yoon, J. (Illus.). New York: Enchanted Lion.
Trelease, J. (2013). *The read-aloud handbook* (7th ed.). New York: Penguin.
Tsuchiya, Y. (1988). *Faithful elephants.* Lewin, T. (Illus.). Boston: Houghton Mifflin.
Uchida, Y. (1993). *The bracelet.* Yardley, J. (Illus.). New York: Philomel.
Ungerer, T. (2009). *Moon man.* London: Phaidon.
Urban, L. (2011). *Hound dog true*. New York: Harcourt.
Vaugelade, A. (2001). *The war.* Minneapolis, MN: Carolrhoda.
Wendt, I. (1991). *The end of war.* Boratynski, A. (Illus.). New York: Pitspopany.
Wild, M. (1991). *Let the celebrations begin!* Vivas, J. (Illus.). New York: Orchard.
Wild, M. (2006). *Fox.* Brooks, R. (Illus.). LaJolla, CA: Kane/Miller.
Wilhelm, J. (2002). *Action strategies for deepening comprehension.* New York: Scholastic.
Willems, M. (2013). *That is NOT a good idea!* New York: Balzer + Bray.
Winter, J. (2016). *Nanuk the ice bear*. New York: Beach Lane.
Wolff, V. (1998). *Bat 6: A novel.* New York: Scholastic.
Yamasaki, K. (2013). *Fish for Jimmy*. New York: Holiday House.
Yamashita, M. (2012). *Snow children*. Toronto: Groundwood.
Yan, M. (2005). *The diary of Ma Yan.* New York: HarperCollins.
Yelchin, E. (2011). *Breaking Stalin's nose*. New York: Holt.

Appendix A

Children's Book Awards

Some of the following awards were established before 1995. For access to the complete lists of winners and honor books for these awards, go to the websites as indicated.

National, General Awards

The United States

Caldecott Medal

This award, established in 1938 by the Association for Library Service to Children division of the American Library Association, is given to the illustrator of the most distinguished picturebook for children published in the U.S. during the preceding year. Only U.S. residents or citizens are eligible. Award winners and honor books since 2000 are listed here. For the complete list of winners and honor books, go to http://www.ala.org/alsc/awardsgrants/bookmedia/caldecottmedal/caldecotthonors/caldecottmedal.

2016 ***Finding Winnie: The True Story of the World's Most Famous Bear*** by Lindsay Mattick. Illustrated by Sophie Blackall. Little, Brown. Ages 5–8. (Historical fiction, Canada/U.K.).

HONOR BOOKS

Trombone Shorty by Troy Andrews. Illustrated by Bryan Collier. Abrams. Ages 4–8. (Bio, African American).

Waiting by Kevin Henkes. Greenwillow. Ages 3–6. (Toy fantasy).

Voices of Freedom: Fannie Lou Hamer, Spirit of the Civil Rights Movement by Carole Boston Weatherford. Illustrated by Ekua Holmes. Candlewick. Ages 10–14. (Bio, African American).

Last Stop on Market Street by Matt de la Peña. Illustrated by Christian Robinson. Putnam's. Ages 3–6. (Realism, African American).

2015 ***The Adventures of Beekle: The Unimaginary Friend*** by Dan Santat. Little, Brown. Ages 3–7. (Fantasy).

HONOR BOOKS

Nana in the City by Lauren Castillo. Clarion. Ages 3–6. (Realism).

The Noisy Paint Box: The Colors and Sound of Kandinsky's Abstract Art by Barb Rosenstock. Illustrated by Mary GrandPré. Knopf. Ages 5–10. (Bio).

Sam & Dave Dig a Hole by Mac Barnett. Illustrated by Jon Klassen. Candlewick. Ages 4–8. (Fantasy).

Viva Frida by Yuyi Morales. Roaring Brook. Ages 3–6. (Bio, Mexico).

The Right Word: Roget and His Thesaurus by Jen Bryant. Illustrated by Melissa Sweet. Eerdmans. Ages 6–10. (Bio, U.K.).

This One Summer by Mariko Tamaki. Illustrated by Jillian Tamaki. First Second. Ages 13–18. (Realism).

2014 ***Locomotive*** by Brian Floca. Atheneum. Ages 4–10. (Informational).

HONOR BOOKS

Journey by Aaron Becker. Candlewick. Ages 2–6. (Fantasy, wordless).

Flora and the Flamingo by Molly Idle. Chronicle. Ages 4–7. (Realism, wordless).

Mr. Wuffles! by David Wiesner. Clarion. Ages 4–8. (Fantasy, wordless).

2013 ***This Is Not My Hat*** by Jon Klassen. Candlewick. Ages 4–8. (Fantasy).

HONOR BOOKS

Creepy Carrots! by Aaron Reynolds. Illustrated by Peter Brown. Simon & Schuster. Ages 4–7. (Fantasy).

Extra Yarn by Mac Barnett. Illustrated by Jon Klassen. Balzer + Bray. Ages 4–7. (Fantasy).

Green by Laura Vaccaro Seeger. Neal Porter. Ages 2–6. (Concept).

One Cool Friend by Toni Buzzeo. Illustrated by David Small. Dial. Ages 6–8. (Fantasy).

Sleep Like a Tiger by Mary Logue. Illustrated by Pamela Zagarenski. Houghton Mifflin. Ages 3–6. (Fantasy).

2012 ***A Ball for Daisy*** by Chris Raschka. Schwartz & Wade. Ages 3–7. (Realism/wordless).

HONOR BOOKS

Blackout by John Rocco. Disney-Hyperion. Ages 4–8. (Realism).

Grandpa Green by Lane Smith. Roaring Brook. Ages 5–11. (Realism).

Me . . . Jane by Patrick McDonnell. Little, Brown. Ages 5–8. (Bio).

2011 ***A Sick Day for Amos McGee*** by Philip C. Stead. Illustrated by Erin E. Stead. Roaring Brook. Ages 3–8. (Animal fantasy).

HONOR BOOKS

Dave the Potter: Artist, Poet, Slave by Laban Carrick Hill. Illustrated by Bryan Collier. Little, Brown. Ages 6–10. (Bio, African American).

Interrupting Chicken by David Ezra Stein. Candlewick Press. Ages 4–6. (Animal fantasy).

2010 ***The Lion & the Mouse*** by Jerry Pinkney. Little, Brown. Ages 3–8. (Folklore).

HONOR BOOKS

All the World, by Liz Garton Scanlon. Illustrated by Marla Frazee. Beach Lane Books. Ages 3–7. (Poetry).

Red Sings from Treetops: A Year in Colors, by Joyce Sidman. Illustrated by Pamela Zagarenski. Houghton Mifflin. Ages 4–8. (Poetry).

2009 ***The House in the Night*** by Susan Marie Swanson. Illustrated by Beth Krommes. Houghton Mifflin. Ages 3–5. (Fantasy).

HONOR BOOKS

A Couple of Boys Have the Best Week Ever by Marla Frazee. Harcourt. Ages 5–8. (Realism).

How I Learned Geography by Uri Shulevitz. Farrar. Ages 5–8. (Mixed genre).

A River of Words: The Story of William Carlos Williams by Jen Bryant. Illustrated by Melissa Sweet. Eerdmans. Ages 3–5. (Bio).

2008 ***The Invention of Hugo Cabret*** by Brian Selznick. Scholastic. Ages 8–12. (Fantasy).

HONOR BOOKS

Henry's Freedom Box: A True Story from the Underground Railroad by Ellen Levine. Illustrated by Kadir Nelson. Scholastic. Ages 7–10. (Bio, African American).

First the Egg by Laura Vaccaro Seeger. Roaring Brook. Ages 3–5. (Concept, toy book).

The Wall: Growing Up Behind the Iron Curtain by Peter Sís. Farrar. Ages 8–14. (Autobiography, Czech Republic).

Knuffle Bunny Too: A Case of Mistaken Identity by Mo Willems. Hyperion. Ages 3–6. (Realism).

2007 ***Flotsam*** by David Wiesner. Clarion. Ages 5–9. (Fantasy, wordless).

HONOR BOOKS

Gone Wild: An Endangered Animal Alphabet by David McLimans. Walker. Ages 8–14. (ABC, nonfiction).

Moses: When Harriet Tubman Led Her People to Freedom by Carole Boston Weatherford. Illustrated by Kadir Nelson. Hyperion/Jump at the Sun. Ages 7–11. (Bio, African American).

2006 ***The Hello, Goodbye Window*** by Norton Juster. Illustrated by Chris Raschka. Hyperion. Ages 4–7. (Realism).

HONOR BOOKS

Rosa by Nikki Giovanni. Illustrated by Bryan Collier. Holt. Ages 8–11. (Bio, African American).

Zen Shorts by Jon J. Muth. Scholastic. Ages 5–9. (Traditional, religious).

Hot Air: The (Mostly) True Story of the First Hot-Air Balloon Ride by Marjorie Priceman. Atheneum. Ages 4–8. (Historical fiction).

Song of the Water Boatman and Other Pond Poems by Joyce Sidman. Illustrated by Beckie Prange. Houghton. Ages 7–12. (Poetry).

2005 ***Kitten's First Full Moon*** by Kevin Henkes. Greenwillow. Ages 3–5. (Animal fantasy).

HONOR BOOKS

The Red Book by Barbara Lehman. Houghton. Ages 4–9. (Fantasy, wordless).

Coming on Home Soon by Jacqueline Woodson. Illustrated by E. B. Lewis. Putnam. Ages 5–8. (Historical fiction, African American).

Knuffle Bunny: A Cautionary Tale by Mo Willems. Hyperion. Ages 3–6. (Realism).

2004 ***The Man Who Walked between the Towers*** by Mordecai Gerstein. Roaring Brook. Ages 5–9. (Historical fiction).

HONOR BOOKS

Ella Sarah Gets Dressed by Margaret Chodos-Irvine. Harcourt. Ages 3–5. (Realism).

What Do You Do with a Tail Like This? by Steve Jenkins and Robin Page. Houghton Mifflin. Ages 4–7. (Informational).

Don't Let the Pigeon Drive the Bus! by Mo Willems. Hyperion. Ages 4–7. (Fantasy).

2003 ***My Friend Rabbit*** by Eric Rohmann. Roaring Brook. Ages 4–8. (Animal fantasy).

HONOR BOOKS

The Spider and the Fly by Mary Howitt. Illustrated by Tony DiTerlizzi. Simon & Schuster. Ages 6–12. (Poetry).

Hondo and Fabian by Peter McCarty. Holt. Ages 3–6. (Realism).

Noah's Ark by Jerry Pinkney. North-South. Ages 6–10. (Traditional).

2002 ***The Three Pigs*** by David Wiesner. Houghton Mifflin. Ages 5–7. (Traditional).

HONOR BOOKS

The Dinosaurs of Waterhouse Hawkins by Barbara Kerley. Illustrated by Brian Selznick. Scholastic. Ages 7–10. (Informational).

Martin's Big Words: The Life of Dr. Martin Luther King, Jr. by Doreen Rappaport. Illustrated by Bryan Collier. Hyperion. Ages 5–9. (Bio, African American).

The Stray Dog by Marc Simont. HarperCollins. Ages 4–7. (Realism).

2001 ***So You Want to Be President?*** by Judith St. George. Illustrated by David Small. Philomel. Ages 7–10. (Bio).

HONOR BOOKS

Casey at the Bat: A Ballad of the Republic Sung in the Year 1888 by Ernest L. Thayer. Illustrated by Christopher Bing. Handprint. Ages 7–12. (Poetry).

Click, Clack, Moo: Cows That Type by Doreen Cronin. Illustrated by Betsy Lewin. Simon & Schuster. Ages 6–9. (Animal fantasy).

Olivia by Ian Falconer. Atheneum. Ages 4–8. (Animal fantasy).

2000 ***Joseph Had a Little Overcoat*** by Simms Taback. Viking. Ages 4–7. (Traditional, pattern).

HONOR BOOKS

When Sophie Gets Angry—Really, Really Angry . . . by Molly Bang. Scholastic. Ages 4–6. (Realism).

A Child's Calendar by John Updike. Illustrated by Trina Schart Hyman. Holiday. Ages 5–9. (Poetry).

The Ugly Duckling adapted and illustrated by Jerry Pinkney. Morrow. Ages 4–7. (Modern folktale).

Sector 7 by David Wiesner. Clarion. Ages 5–9. (Fantasy, wordless).

Newbery Medal

This award, established in 1922 and sponsored by the Association for Library Service to Children division of the American Library Association, is given to the author of the most distinguished contribution to children's literature published during the preceding year. Only U.S. citizens or residents are eligible for this award. Award winners and honor books since 2000 are listed here. For the complete list of winners and honor books, go to http://www.ala.org/alsc/awardsgrants/bookmedia/newberymedal/newberyhonors/newberymedal.

2016 ***Last Stop on Market Street*** by Matt de la Peña. Putnam. Ages 3–6. (Realism, African American).

HONOR BOOKS

The War That Saved My Life by Kimberly Brubaker Bradley. Dial. Ages 8–12. (Historical fiction, World War II, U.K.).

Roller Girl by Victoria Jamieson. Dial. Ages 9–13. (Realism, graphic novel).

Echo by Pam Muñoz Ryan. Scholastic. Ages 9–14. (Historical fiction, WWII).

2015 ***The Crossover*** by Kwame Alexander. Houghton Mifflin Harcourt. Ages 9–12. (Realism, African American).

HONOR BOOKS

El Deafo by Cece Bell. Amulet. Ages 8 & up. (Autobiography, graphic novel).

Brown Girl Dreaming by Jacqueline Woodson. Penguin. Ages 10–14. (Memoir, African American).

2014 ***Flora & Ulysses: The Illuminated Adventures*** by Kate DiCamillo. Candlewick. Ages 8–12. (Fantasy).

HONOR BOOKS

Doll Bones by Holly Black. Margaret K. McElderry Books. Ages 10–14. (Fantasy).

The Year of Billy Miller by Kevin Henkes. Greenwillow. Ages 7–10. (Realism).

One Came Home by Amy Timberlake. Knopf. Ages 9–12. (Historical fiction).

Paperboy by Vince Vawter. Delacorte. Ages 10–14. (Historical fiction).

2013 ***The One and Only Ivan*** by Katherine Applegate. HarperCollins. Ages 8–12. (Fantasy).

HONOR BOOKS

Splendors and Glooms by Laura Amy Schlitz. Candlewick. Ages 9–13. (Historical fantasy).

Bomb: The Race to Build–and Steal–the World's Most Dangerous Weapon by Steve Sheinkin. Flash Point. Ages 10–15. (Informational).

Three Times Lucky by Sheila Turnage. Dial. Ages 10–14. (Realism).

2012 ***Dead End in Norvelt*** by Jack Gantos. Farrar Straus Giroux. Ages 8–14. (Historical fiction).

HONOR BOOKS

Inside Out & Back Again by Thanhha Lai. HarperCollins. Ages 8–12. (Historical fiction, Vietnamese-American).

Breaking Stalin's Nose by Eugene Yelchin. Holt. Ages 9–12. (Historical fiction, Russia).

2011 ***Moon over Manifest*** by Clare Vanderpool. Delacorte. Ages 11–16. (Historical fiction).

HONOR BOOKS

Turtle in Paradise by Jennifer L. Holm. Random House. Ages 11–14. (Historical fiction).

Heart of a Samurai by Margi Preus. Amulet. Ages 10–14. (Historical fiction, Japan).

Dark Emperor and Other Poems of the Night by Joyce Sidman. Illustrated by Rick Allen. Houghton Mifflin. Ages 6–10. (Poetry).

One Crazy Summer by Rita Williams-Garcia. Amistad. Ages 9–12. (Historical fiction, African American).

2010 ***When You Reach Me*** by Rebecca Stead. Wendy Lamb Books. Ages 9–14. (Fantasy).

HONOR BOOKS

Claudette Colvin: Twice Toward Justice by Phillip Hoose. Melanie Kroupa. Ages 11–15. (Bio).

The Evolution of Calpurnia Tate by Jacqueline Kelly. Holt. Ages 9–12. (Historical fiction).

Where the Mountain Meets the Moon by Grace Lin. Little, Brown. Ages 8–11. (Fantasy, China).

The Mostly True Adventures of Homer P. Figg by Rodman Philbrick. Blue Sky Press. Ages 9–12. (Historical fiction).

2009 ***The Graveyard Book*** by Neil Gaiman. Illustrated by Dave McKean. HarperCollins. Ages 10–14. (Fantasy).

HONOR BOOKS

The Underneath by Kathi Appelt. Illustrated by David Small. Atheneum. Ages 9–13. (Animal fantasy).

The Surrender Tree: Poems of Cuba's Struggle for Freedom by Margarita Engle. Holt. Ages 11–18. (Poetry, Cuba).

Savvy by Ingrid Law. Dial. Ages 10–12. (Fantasy).

After Tupac & D Foster by Jacqueline Woodson. Putnam. Ages 11–14. (Realism, African American).

2008 ***Good Masters! Sweet Ladies! Voices from a Medieval Village*** by Laura Amy Schlitz. Candlewick. Ages 9–13. (Informational, Europe).

HONOR BOOKS

Elijah of Buxton by Christopher Paul Curtis. Scholastic. Ages 9–13. (Historical fiction, African American).

The Wednesday Wars by Gary D. Schmidt. Clarion. Ages 10–13. (Historical fiction).

Feathers by Jacqueline Woodson. Putnam. Ages 9–12. (Realism).

2007 ***The Higher Power of Lucky*** by Susan Patron. Illustrated by Matt Phelan. Simon & Schuster. Ages 9–12. (Realism).

HONOR BOOKS

Penny from Heaven by Jennifer L. Holm. Random House. Ages 11–14. (Mixed genre: realism/historical fiction).

Hattie Big Sky by Kirby Larson. Delacorte. Ages 12–16. (Historical fiction).

Rules by Cynthia Lord. Scholastic. Ages 9–13. (Realism, autism).

2006 ***Criss Cross*** by Lynne Rae Perkins. Greenwillow. Ages 12–15. (Realism).

HONOR BOOKS

Whittington by Alan Armstrong. Illustrated by S. D. Schindler. Random House. Ages 9–14. (Traditional, animal fantasy, dyslexia).

Hitler Youth: Growing Up in Hitler's Shadow by Susan Campbell Bartoletti. Scholastic. Ages 11–15. (Collected biography, Germany).

Princess Academy by Shannon Hale. Bloomsbury. Ages 12–14. (Modern folklore).

Show Way by Jacqueline Woodson. Illustrated by Hudson Talbott. Putnam. Ages 7–12. (African American).

2005 ***Kira-Kira*** by Cynthia Kadohata. Atheneum. Ages 11–14. (Historical fiction, Japanese American).

HONOR BOOKS

Al Capone Does My Shirts by Gennifer Choldenko. Putnam. Ages 11–14. (Realism, autism).

The Voice That Challenged a Nation: Marian Anderson and the Struggle for Equal Rights by Russell Freedman. Clarion. Ages 11–14. (Photobiography, African American).

Lizzie Bright and the Buckminster Boy by Gary D. Schmidt. Clarion. Ages 13–16. (Historical fiction).

2004 ***The Tale of Despereaux: Being the Story of a Mouse, a Princess, Some Soup, and a Spool of Thread*** by Kate DiCamillo. Illustrated by Timothy Basil Ering. Candlewick. Ages 5–8. (Animal fantasy).

HONOR BOOKS

Olive's Ocean by Kevin Henkes. Greenwillow. Ages 9–12. (Realism).

An American Plague: The True and Terrifying Story of the Yellow Fever Epidemic of 1793 by Jim Murphy. Clarion. Ages 9–14. (Informational).

2003 ***Crispin: The Cross of Lead*** by Avi. Hyperion. Ages 8–12. (Historical fiction).

HONOR BOOKS

The House of the Scorpion by Nancy Farmer. Atheneum. Ages 11–14. (Science fiction).

Pictures of Hollis Woods by Patricia Reilly Giff. Random House. Ages 10–13. (Realism).

Hoot by Carl Hiaasen. Knopf. Ages 9–12. (Realism).

A Corner of the Universe by Ann M. Martin. Scholastic. Ages 11–14. (Realism).

Surviving the Applewhites by Stephanie S. Tolan. HarperCollins. Ages 12–16. (Realism).

2002 ***A Single Shard*** by Linda Sue Park. Clarion/Houghton. Ages 10–14. (Historical fiction, Korea).

HONOR BOOKS

Everything on a Waffle by Polly Horvath. Farrar. Ages 12–14. (Realism).

Carver: A Life in Poems by Marilyn Nelson. Front Street. Ages 12–14. (Poetry, bio).

2001 ***A Year Down Yonder*** by Richard Peck. Dial. Ages 10–14. (Historical fiction).

HONOR BOOKS

Because of Winn-Dixie by Kate DiCamillo. Candlewick. Ages 8–12. (Animal realism).

Hope Was Here by Joan Bauer. Putnam. Ages 12–14. (Realism).

Joey Pigza Loses Control by Jack Gantos. Farrar. Ages 9–12. (Realism, ADHD).

The Wanderer by Sharon Creech. HarperCollins. Ages 12–14. (Realism).

2000 ***Bud, Not Buddy*** by Christopher Paul Curtis. Delacorte. Ages 9–12. (Historical fiction, African American).

HONOR BOOKS

Getting Near to Baby by Audrey Couloumbis. Putnam. Ages 10–12. (Realism).

26 Fairmount Avenue by Tomie dePaola. Putnam. Ages 7–9. (Biography).

Our Only May Amelia by Jennifer L. Holm. HarperCollins. Ages 10–14. (Historical fiction).

Boston Globe–Horn Book Awards

These awards, established in 1967 and sponsored by the *Boston Globe* and *Horn Book Magazine,* are given to an author for outstanding fiction or poetry for children, to an illustrator for outstanding illustration in a children's book, and since 1976 to an author for outstanding nonfiction for children. Award winners and honor books since 2000 are listed here. For the complete list of award winners, go to http://www.hbook.com/boston-globe-horn-book-awards/#_.

2016 FICTION: ***The Lie Tree*** by Frances Hardinge. Amulet.

NONFICTION: ***Most Dangerous: Daniel Ellsberg and the Secret History of the Vietnam War*** by Steve Sheinkin. Roaring Brook Press.

ILLUSTRATION: ***Jazz Day: The Making of a Famous Photograph*** by Roxane Orgill. Illustrated by Francis Vallejo. Candlewick.

2015 FICTION: ***Cartwheeling in Thunderstorms*** by Katherine Rundell. Simon & Schuster.

NONFICTION: ***The Family Romanov: Murder, Rebellion, and the Fall of Imperial Russia*** by Candace Fleming. Schwartz & Wade.

ILLUSTRATION: ***The Farmer and the Clown*** by Marla Frazee. Beach Lane Books.

2014 FICTION: ***Grasshopper Jungle*** by Andrew Smith. Dutton.

NONFICTION: ***The Port Chicago 50: Disaster, Mutiny, and the Fight for Civil Rights*** by Steve Sheinkin. Roaring Book.

ILLUSTRATION: ***Mr. Tiger Goes Wild*** by Peter Brown. Little, Brown.

2013 FICTION: ***Eleanor & Park*** by Rainbow Rowell. St. Martin's Griffin.

NONFICTION: ***Electric Ben: The Amazing Life and Times of Benjamin Franklin*** by Robert Byrd. Dial.

ILLUSTRATION: ***Building Our House*** by Jonathan Bean. Farrar Straus and Giroux.

2012 FICTION: ***No Crystal Stair: A Documentary Novel of the Life and Work of Lewis Michaux, Harlem Bookseller*** by Vaunda Micheaux Nelson. Illustrated by R. Gregory Christie. Carolrhoda.

NONFICTION: ***Chuck Close: Face Book,*** by Chuck Close. Abrams.

ILLUSTRATION: ***Extra Yarn*** by Mac Barnett. Illustrated by Jon Klassen. Balzer + Bray.

2011 FICTION: ***Blink & Caution*** by Tim Wynne-Jones. Candlewick.

NONFICTION: ***The Notorious Benedict Arnold: A True Story of Adventure, Heroism, & Treachery*** by Steve Sheinkin. Flash Point/Roaring Brook.

ILLUSTRATION: ***Pocketful of Posies: A Treasury of Nursery Rhymes*** by Salley Mavor. Houghton.

2010 FICTION: ***When You Reach Me*** by Rebecca Stead. Random House.

NONFICTION: ***Marching for Freedom*** by Elizabeth Partridge. Viking.

ILLUSTRATION: ***I Know Here*** by Laurel Croza. Illustrated by Matt James. Groundwood.

2009 FICTION: ***Nation*** by Terry Pratchett. HarperCollins.

NONFICTION: ***The Lincolns: A Scrapbook Look at Abraham and Mary*** by Candace Fleming. Random House.

ILLUSTRATION: ***Bubble Trouble*** by Margaret Mahy. Illustrated by Polly Dunbar. Clarion.

2008 FICTION AND POETRY: ***The Absolutely True Diary of a Part-Time Indian*** by Sherman Alexie. Little, Brown.

NONFICTION: ***The Wall: Growing Up Behind the Iron Curtain*** by Peter Sís. Farrar.

ILLUSTRATION: ***At Night*** by Jonathan Bean. Farrar.

2007 FICTION AND POETRY: ***The Astonishing Life of Octavian Nothing, Traitor to the Nation, Volume I: The Pox Party*** by M. T. Anderson. Candlewick.

NONFICTION: ***The Strongest Man in the World: Louis Cyr*** by Nicolas Debon. Groundwood.

ILLUSTRATION: ***Dog and Bear: Two Friends, Three Stories*** by Laura Vaccaro Seeger. Roaring Brook.

2006 FICTION AND POETRY: ***The Miraculous Journey of Edward Tulane*** by Kate DiCamillo. Illustrated by Bagram Ibatoulline. Candlewick.

NONFICTION: ***If You Decide to Go to the Moon*** by Faith McNulty. Illustrated by Steven Kellogg. Scholastic.

ILLUSTRATION: ***Leaf Man*** by Lois Ehlert. Harcourt.

2005 FICTION AND POETRY: ***The Schwa Was Here*** by Neal Schusterman. Dutton.

NONFICTION: ***The Race to Save the Lord God Bird*** by Phillip Hoose. Farrar.

ILLUSTRATION: ***Traction Man Is Here!*** by Mini Grey. Knopf.

2004 FICTION AND POETRY: ***The Fire-Eaters*** by David Almond. Delacorte.

NONFICTION: ***An American Plague: The True and Terrifying Story of the Yellow Fever Epidemic of 1793*** by Jim Murphy. Clarion.

ILLUSTRATION: ***The Man Who Walked between the Towers*** by Mordicai Gerstein. Roaring Brook.

2003 FICTION AND POETRY: ***The Jamie and Angus Stories*** by Anne Fine. Illustrated by Penny Dale. Candlewick.

NONFICTION: ***Fireboat: The Heroic Adventures of the John J. Harvey*** by Maira Kalman. Putnam.

ILLUSTRATION: ***Big Momma Makes the World*** by Phyllis Root. Illustrated by Helen Oxenbury. Candlewick.

2002 FICTION AND POETRY: ***Lord of the Deep*** by Graham Salisbury. Delacorte.

NONFICTION: ***This Land Was Made for You and Me: The Life and Songs of Woody Guthrie*** by Elizabeth Partridge. Viking.

ILLUSTRATION: ***"Let's Get a Pup!" Said Kate*** by Bob Graham. Candlewick.

2001 FICTION AND POETRY: ***Carver: A Life in Poems*** by Marilyn Nelson. Front Street.

NONFICTION: ***The Longitude Prize*** by Joan Dash. Illustrated by Dušan Petricic. Farrar.

ILLUSTRATION: ***Cold Feet*** by Cynthia DeFelice. Illustrated by Robert Andrew Parker. DK Ink.

2000 FICTION: ***The Folk Keeper*** by Franny Billingsley. Atheneum.

NONFICTION: ***Sir Walter Ralegh and the Quest for El Dorado*** by Marc Aronson. Clarion.

ILLUSTRATION: ***Henry Hikes to Fitchburg*** by D. B. Johnson. Houghton.

National Book Award for Young People's Literature

This award, sponsored by the National Book Foundation, is presented annually to recognize the outstanding contribution to children's literature, in terms of literary merit, published during the previous year. The award committee considers books of all genres written for children and young adults by U.S. writers. The award carries a $10,000 cash prize.

2015 ***Challenger Deep*** by Neil Schusterman. HarperCollins.

2014 ***Brown Girl Dreaming*** by Jacqueline Woodson. Penguin.

2013 ***The Thing about Luck*** by Cynthia Kadohata. Atheneum.

2012 ***Goblin Secrets*** by William Alexander. Simon & Schuster.

2011 ***Inside Out & Back Again*** by Thanhha Lai. Harper.

2010 ***Mockingbird*** by Kathryn Erskine. Philomel Books.

2009 ***Claudette Colvin: Twice Toward Justice*** by Phillip Hoose. Farrar, Straus and Giroux.

2008 ***What I Saw and How I Lied*** by Judy Blundell. Scholastic.

2007 ***The Absolutely True Diary of a Part-Time Indian*** by Sherman Alexie. Little, Brown.

2006 ***The Astonishing Life of Octavian Nothing, Traitor to the Nation, Vol. 1: The Pox Party*** by M. T. Anderson. Candlewick.

2005 ***The Penderwicks*** by Jeanne Birdsall. Knopf.

2004 ***Godless*** by Pete Hautman. Simon & Schuster.

2003 ***The Canning Season*** by Polly Horvath. Farrar.

2002 ***The House of the Scorpion*** by Nancy Farmer. Atheneum.

2001 ***True Believer*** by Virginia Euwer Wolff. Atheneum.

2000 ***Homeless Bird*** by Gloria Whelan. HarperCollins.

Great Britain

Kate Greenaway Medal

This award, established in 1955 by the Chartered Institute of Library and Information Professionals, is given to the illustrator of the most distinguished work in illustration in a children's book first published in the U.K. during the preceding year. Award winners since 2000 are listed here. The complete list is at www.carnegiegreenaway.org.uk/greenaway/full_list_of_winners.php.

2015 ***Shackleton's Journey*** by William Grill. Flying Eye.

2014 ***This Is Not My Hat*** by Jon Klassen. Walker Books.

2013 ***Black Dog*** by Levi Pinfold. Templar.

2012 ***A Monster Calls*** by Jim Kay. Walker Books.

2011 ***FArTHER*** by Grahame Baker-Smith. Templar.

2010 ***Harry & Hopper*** by Freya Blackwood. Scholastic.

2009 ***Harris Finds His Feet*** by Catherine Rayner. Little Tiger Press.

2008 ***Little Mouse's Big Book of Fears*** by Emily Gravett. Macmillan.

2007 ***The Adventures of the Dish and the Spoon*** by Mini Grey. Jonathan Cape.

2006 ***Wolves*** by Emily Gravett. Macmillan.

2005 ***Jonathan Swift's "Gulliver"*** by Martin Jenkins. Illustrated by Chris Riddell. Walker.

2004 ***Ella's Big Chance*** by Shirley Hughes. Bodley Head.

2003 ***Jethro Byrd—Fairy Child*** by Bob Graham. Walker.

2002 ***Pirate Diary*** by Chris Riddell. Walker.

2001 ***I Will Never Not Ever Eat a Tomato*** by Lauren Child. Orchard.

2000 ***Alice's Adventures in Wonderland*** by Lewis Carroll. Illustrated by Helen Oxenbury. Walker.

Carnegie Medal

This award, established in 1936 by the Chartered Institute of Library and Information Professionals, is given to the author of the most outstanding children's book first published in English in the U.K. during the preceding year. Award winners since 2000 are listed here. The complete list of winners is at www.carnegiegreenaway.org.uk/carnegie/full_list_of_winners.php.

2015 ***Buffalo Soldier*** by Tanya Landman. Walker Books.

2014 ***The Bunker Diary*** by Kevin Brooks. Penguin Books.

2013 ***Maggot Moon*** by Sally Gardner. Hot Key Books.

2012 ***A Monster Calls*** by Patrick Ness. Walker Books.

2011 ***Monsters of Men*** by Patrick Ness. Walker Books.

2010 ***The Graveyard Book*** by Neil Gaiman. Bloomsbury.

2009 ***Bog Child*** by Siobhan Dowd. David Fickling.

2008 ***Here Lies Arthur*** by Philip Reeve. Scholastic.

2007 ***Just in Case*** by Meg Rosoff. Penguin.

2006 ***Tamar*** by Mal Peet. Walker.

2005 ***Millions*** by Frank Cottrell Boyce. Macmillan.

2004 ***A Gathering Light*** by Jennifer Donnelly. Bloomsbury.

2003 ***Ruby Holler*** by Sharon Creech. Bloomsbury/HarperCollins.

2002 ***The Amazing Maurice and His Educated Rodents*** by Terry Pratchett. Doubleday/HarperCollins.

2001 ***The Other Side of Truth*** by Beverly Naidoo. Puffin/HarperCollins.

2000 ***Postcards from No Man's Land*** by Aidan Chambers. Bodley Head.

Canada

The Governor General's Literary Awards

The Governor General's Literary Awards were inaugurated in 1937, with prizes for children's literature (text and illustration) added in 1987. The Canada Council for the Arts administers the awards and added prizes for books written in French. The current prize to winners in each category—$15,000—dates from 2000. In addition, publishers of the winning books receive $3,000 to assist with promotion.

2015 ILLUSTRATION: ***Sidewalk Flowers*** by JonArno Lawson. Illustrated by Sydney Smith. Groundwood Books.
TEXT: ***The Gospel Truth*** by Caroline Pignat. Red Deer Press.

2014 ILLUSTRATION: ***This One Summer*** by Mariko Tamaki. Illustrated by Jillian Tamaki. Groundwood Books.
TEXT: ***When Everything Feels Like the Movies*** by Raziel Reid. Arsenal Pulp Press.

2013 ILLUSTRATION: ***Northwest Passage*** by Stan Rogers. Illustrated by Matt James. Groundwood Books.
TEXT: ***The Unlikely Hero of Room 13B*** by Teresa Toten. Doubleday Canada.

2012 ILLUSTRATION: ***Virginia Wolf*** by Kyo Maclear. Illustrated by Isabelle Arsenault. Kids Can.
TEXT: ***The Reluctant Journal of Henry K. Larsen*** by Susin Nielsen. Tundra Books.

2011 ILLUSTRATION: ***Ten Birds*** by Cybèle Young. Kids Can.
TEXT: ***From Then to Now: A Short History of the World*** by Christopher Moore. Illustrated by Andrej Krystoforski. Tundra Books.

2010 ILLUSTRATION: ***Cats' Night Out*** by Caroline Stutson. Illustrated by Jon Klassen. Simon & Schuster.
TEXT: ***Fishtailing*** by Wendy Phillips. Coteau Books.

2009 ILLUSTRATION: ***Bella's Tree*** by Janet Russell. Illustrated by Jirina Marton. Groundwood Books.
TEXT: ***Greener Grass: The Famine Years*** by Caroline Pignat. Red Deer Press.

2008 ILLUSTRATION: ***The Owl and the Pussycat*** by Edward Lear. Illustrated by Stéphane Jorisch. Kids Can.
TEXT: ***The Landing*** by John Ibbitson. Kids Can.

2007 ILLUSTRATION: ***The Painted Circus*** by Wallace Edwards. Kids Can.
TEXT: ***Carnation, Lily, Lily, Rose: The Story of a Painting*** by Hugh Brewster. Kids Can.

2006 ILLUSTRATION: ***Ancient Thunder*** by Leo Yerxa. Groundwood.
TEXT: ***Pirate's Passage*** by William Gilkerson. Trumpeter.

2005 ILLUSTRATION: ***Imagine a Day*** by Sarah L. Thomson. Illustrated by Rob Gonsalves. Atheneum.
TEXT: ***The Crazy Man*** by Pamela Porter. Groundwood.

2004 ILLUSTRATION: ***Jabberwocky*** by Lewis Carroll. Illustrated by Stéphane Jorisch. Kids Can.
TEXT: ***Airborn*** by Kenneth Oppel. HarperCollins.

2003 ILLUSTRATION: ***The Song within My Heart*** by Dave Bouchard. Illustrated by Allen Sapp. Raincoast.
TEXT: ***Stitches*** by Glen Huser. Groundwood.

2002 ILLUSTRATION: ***Alphabeasts*** by Wallace Edwards. Kids Can.
TEXT: ***True Confessions of a Heartless Girl*** by Martha Brooks. Groundwood.

2001 ILLUSTRATION: ***An Island in the Soup*** by Mireille Levert. Groundwood.
TEXT: ***Dust*** by Arthur Slade. HarperCollins Canada.

2000 ILLUSTRATION: ***Yuck, a Love Story*** by Don Gillmore. Illustrated by Marie-Louise Gay. Stoddart Kids.
TEXT: ***Looking for X*** by Deborah Ellis. Groundwood.

Australia

Australian Children's Books of the Year Awards

The Children's Book Council of Australia sponsors five awards for excellence in children's books: the Picture Book of the Year Award (established in 1956); the Book of the Year for Early Childhood Award (established in 2001); the Book of the Year for Younger Readers Award (established in 1982); the Book of the Year for Older Readers Award (established in 1946); and the Eve Pownall Award for Information Books. Award winners since 2002 for Picturebook of the Year and 2000 for Book of the Year are listed here. For the complete list of winners, go to http://www.cbca.org.au/previous-winners.

Australian Picture Book of the Year Award (may be for mature readers.)

2015 ***My Two Blankets*** by Irena Cobald. Illustrated by Freya Blackwood. Little Hare Books.

2014 ***Rules of Summer*** by Shaun Tan. Hachette.

2013 ***The Coat*** by Julie Hunt. Illustrated Ron Brooks. Allen & Unwin.

2012 ***A Bus Called Heaven*** by Bob Graham. Walker Books.

2011 ***Mirror*** by Jeannie Baker, Walker Books, and ***Hamlet*** by Nicki Greenberg. Allen & Unwin.

2010 ***The Hero of Little Street*** by Gregory Rogers. Allen & Unwin.

2009 ***Collecting Colour*** by Kylie Dunstan. Lothian.

2008 ***Requiem for a Beast*** by Matt Ottley. Lothian.

2007 ***The Arrival*** by Shaun Tan. Lothian.

2006 ***The Short and Incredibly Happy Life of Riley*** by Colin Thompson. Lothian.

2005 ***Are We There Yet? A Journey Around Australia*** by Alison Lester. Viking.

2004 ***Cat and Fish*** by Joan Grant. Illustrated by Neal Curtis. Lothian.

2003 ***In Flanders Fields*** by Norman Jorgensen. Illustrated by Brian Harrison-Lever. Sandcastle.

2002 ***An Ordinary Day*** by Libby Gleeson. Illustrated by Armin Greder. Scholastic.

2001 ***Fox*** by Margaret Wild. Illustrated by Ron Brooks. Allen & Unwin.

2000 ***Jenny Angel*** by Margaret Wild. Illustrated by Anne Spudvilas. Penguin.

Australian Book of the Year for Early Childhood Award

2015 ***Go to Sleep, Jessie!*** by Libby Gleeson. Illustrated by Freya Blackwood. Little Hare.

2014 ***The Swap*** by Jan Ormerod. Illustrated by Andrew Joyner. Little Hare.

2013 ***The Terrible Suitcase*** by Emma Allen. Illustrated by Freya Blackwood. Omnibus Books.

2012 ***The Runaway Hug*** by Nick Bland. Illustrated by Freya Blackwood. Scholastic.

2011 ***Maudie and Bear*** by Jan Ormerod. Illustrated by Freya Blackwood. Little Hare Books.

2010 ***Bear & Chook by the Sea*** by Lisa Shanahan. Illustrated by Emma Quay. Lothian.

2009 ***How to Heal a Broken Wing*** by Bob Graham. Walker Books.

2008 ***Pearl Barley and Charlie Parsley*** by Aaron Blabey. Viking.

2007 ***Amy & Louis*** by Libby Gleeson. Illustrated by Freya Blackwood. Scholastic.

2006 ***Annie's Chair*** by Deborah Niland. Viking.

2005 ***Where Is the Green Sheep?*** by Mem Fox. Illustrated by Judy Horacek. Viking.

2004 ***Grandpa and Thomas*** by Pamela Allen. Viking.

2003 ***A Year on Our Farm*** by Penny Matthews. Omnibus/Scholastic Australia.

2002 ***"Let's Get a Pup!" Said Kate*** by Bob Graham. Walker/Candlewick.

Australian Children's Book of the Year for Younger Readers Award

2015 ***The Cleo Stories: The Necklace and the Present*** by Libby Gleeson. Illustrated by Freya Blackwood. Allen & Unwin.

2014 ***City of Orphans: A Very Unusual Pursuit*** by Catherine Jinks. Allen & Unwin.

2013 ***The Children of the King*** by Sonya Hartnett. Viking.

2012 ***Crow Country*** by Kate Constable. Allen & Unwin.

2011 ***The Red Wind*** by Isobelle Carmody. Viking.

2010 ***Darius Bell and the Glitter Pool*** by Odo Hirsch. Allen & Unwin.

2009 ***Perry Angel's Suitcase*** by Glenda Millard. Illustrated by Stephen Michael King. ABC Books.

2008 ***Dragon Moon*** by Carole Wilkinson. Black Dog.

2007 ***Being Bee*** by Catherine Bateson. University of Queensland Press.

2006 ***Helicopter Man*** by Elizabeth Fensham. Bloomsbury.

2005 ***The Silver Donkey*** by Sonya Hartnett. Viking.

2004 ***Dragonkeeper*** by Carole Wilkinson. Black Dog.

2003 ***Rain May and Captain Daniel*** by Catherine Bateson. University of Queensland Press.

2002 ***My Dog*** by John Heffernan. Illustrated by Andrew McLean. Scholastic Australia.

2001 ***Two Hands Together*** by Diana Kidd. Penguin.

2000 ***Hitler's Daughter*** by Jackie French. HarperCollins.

Awards for a Body of Work

Hans Christian Andersen Award

This international award, sponsored by the International Board on Books for Young People, is given every two years to a living author and to a living illustrator whose complete works have made important international contributions to children's literature. Awards before 2000 can be found at www.ibby.org.

2016 AUTHOR: Cao Wenxuan (China)
ILLUSTRATOR: Rotraut Susanne Berner (Germany)

2014 AUTHOR: Nahoko Uehashi (Japan)
ILLUSTRATOR: Roger Mello (Brazil)

2012 AUTHOR: Maria Teresa Andruetto (Argentina)
ILLUSTRATOR: Peter Sís (Czech Republic)

2010 AUTHOR: David Almond (U.K.)
ILLUSTRATOR: Jutta Bauer (Germany)

2008 AUTHOR: Jürg Schubiger (Switzerland)
ILLUSTRATOR: Roberto Innocenti (Italy)

2006 AUTHOR: Margaret Mahy (New Zealand)
ILLUSTRATOR: Wolf Erlbruch (Germany)

2004 AUTHOR: Martin Waddell (Ireland)
ILLUSTRATOR: Max Velthuijs (Netherlands)

2002 AUTHOR: Aidan Chambers (U.K.)
ILLUSTRATOR: Quentin Blake (U.K.)

2000 AUTHOR: Ana Maria Machado (Brazil)
ILLUSTRATOR: Anthony Browne (U.K.)

Laura Ingalls Wilder Award

This award, sponsored by the Association for Library Service to Children of the American Library Association, is given to a U.S. author or illustrator whose body of work has made a lasting contribution to children's literature. Between 1960 and 1980, the Wilder Award was given every five years. From 1980 to 2001, it was given every three years and from 2001 to 2015, every two years, and from 2016, every year.

2016 Jerry Pinkney

2015 Donald Crews

2013 Katherine Paterson

2011 Tomie dePaola

2009 Ashley Bryan

2007 James Marshall

2005 Laurence Yep

2003 Eric Carle

2001 Milton Meltzer

1998 Russell Freedman

1995 Virginia Hamilton

1992 Marcia Brown

1989 Elizabeth George Speare

1986 Jean Fritz

1983 Maurice Sendak

1980 Theodor S. Geisel (Dr. Seuss)

1975 Beverly Cleary

1970 E. B. White

1965 Ruth Sawyer

1960 Clara Ingram Judson

NCTE Excellence in Poetry for Children Award

For the list of award winners, see Chapter 6.

Awards for Specific Genres or Groups

Mildred L. Batchelder Award

This award, established in 1968 by the Association for Library Service to Children of the American Library Association, is given to the American publisher of a children's book considered to be the most outstanding of those books originally published in a country other than the U.S. in a language other than English and subsequently translated and published in the U.S. during the previous year. Award winners since 2000 are listed here. The complete list of winners is at www.ala.org/alsc/awardsgrants/bookmedia/batchelderaward/batchelderpast.

2016 ***The Wonderful Fluffy Little Squishy*** by Beatrice Alemagna. Enchanted Lion.

2015 ***Mikis and the Donkey*** by Bibi Dumon Tak. Translated from Dutch by Laura Watkinson. Illustrated by Philip Hopman. Eerdmans.

2014 ***Mister Orange*** by Truus Matti. Translated from Dutch by Laura Watkinson. Enchanted Lion.

2013 ***My Family for the War*** by Anne C. Voorhoeve. Translated from German by Tammi Reichel. Dial.

2012 ***Soldier Bear*** by Bibi Dumon Tak. Translated from Dutch by Laura Watkinson. Illustrated by Philip Hopman. Eerdmans.

2011 ***A Time of Miracles*** by Anne-Laure Bondoux. Translated from French by Y. Maudet. Delacorte.

2010 ***A Faraway Island*** by Annika Thor. Translated from Swedish by Linda Schenck. Delacorte.

2009 ***Moribito: Guardian of the Spirit*** by Nahoko Uehashi. Translated from Japanese by Cathy Hirano. Scholastic.

2008 ***Brave Story*** by Miyuki Miyabe. Translated from Japanese by Alexander O. Smith. VIZ Media.

2007 ***The Pull of the Ocean*** by Jean-Claude Mourlevat. Translated from French by Y. Maudet. Delacorte.

2006 ***An Innocent Soldier*** by Josef Holub. Translated from German by Michael Hofmann. Arthur A. Levine.

2005 ***The Shadows of Ghadames*** by Joëlle Stolz. Translated from French by Catherine Temerson. Delacorte.

2004 ***Run, Boy, Run*** by Uri Orlev. Translated from Hebrew by Hillel Halkin. Houghton Mifflin.

2003 ***The Thief Lord*** by Cornelia Funke. Translated from German by Oliver Latsch. Scholastic.

2002 ***How I Became an American*** by Karin Gündisch. Translated from German by James Skofield. Cricket.

2001 ***Samir and Yonatan*** by Daniella Carmi. Translated from Hebrew by Yael Lotan. Levine/Scholastic.

2000 ***The Baboon King*** by Anton Quintana. Translated from Dutch by John Nieuwenhuizen. Walker.

Coretta Scott King Awards

These awards, founded in 1970, are given to an African American author and an African American illustrator whose children's books, published during the preceding year, made outstanding inspirational and educational contributions to literature for children and young people. The awards are sponsored by the Ethnic and Multicultural Information Exchange Round Table of the American Library Association. Award winners since 2000 are listed here. For the complete list of winners, go to http://www.ala.org/emiert/coretta-scott-king-book-awards-all-recipients-1970-present.

2016 AUTHOR: ***Gone Crazy in Alabama*** by Rita Williams-Garcia. Amistad.
ILLUSTRATOR: ***Trombone Shorty*** by Troy Andrews and Bill Taylor. Illustrated by Bryan Collier. Abrams.

2015 AUTHOR: ***Brown Girl Dreaming*** by Jacqueline Woodson. Nancy Paulson Books.
ILLUSTRATOR: ***Firebird*** by Misty Copeland. Illustrated by Christopher Myers. Putnam.

2014 AUTHOR: ***P.S. Be Eleven*** by Rita Williams-Garcia. Amistad.
ILLUSTRATOR: ***Knock Knock: My Dad's Dream for Me*** by Daniel Beaty. Illustrated by Bryan Collier. Little, Brown.

2013 AUTHOR: ***Hand in Hand: Ten Black Men Who Changed America*** by Andrea Davis Pinkney. Disney/Jump at the Sun.
ILLUSTRATOR: ***I, Too, Am America*** by Langston Hughes. Illustrated by Bryan Collier. Simon & Schuster.

2012 AUTHOR: ***Heart and Soul: The Story of America and African Americans*** by Kadir Nelson. Balzer + Bray.
ILLUSTRATOR: ***Underground: Finding the Light to Freedom*** by Shane W. Evans. Roaring Brook Press.

2011 AUTHOR: ***One Crazy Summer*** by Rita Williams-Garcia. Amistad.
ILLUSTRATOR: ***Dave the Potter: Artist, Poet, Slave*** by Laban Carrick Hill. Illustrated by Bryan Collier. Little, Brown.

2010 AUTHOR: ***Bad News for Outlaws: The Remarkable Life of Bass Reeves, Deputy U.S. Marshal*** by Vaunda Micheaux Nelson. Illustrated by R. Gregory Christie. Carolrhoda.
ILLUSTRATOR: ***My People*** by Langston Hughes. Illustrated by Charles R. Smith, Jr. Atheneum.

2009 AUTHOR: ***We Are the Ship: The Story of Negro League Baseball*** by Kadir Nelson. Jump at the Sun.
ILLUSTRATOR: ***The Blacker the Berry*** by Joyce Carol Thomas. Illustrated by Floyd Cooper. HarperCollins.

2008 AUTHOR: ***Elijah of Buxton*** by Christopher Paul Curtis. Scholastic.
ILLUSTRATOR: ***Let It Shine*** by Ashley Bryan. Atheneum.

2007 AUTHOR: ***Copper Sun*** by Sharon Draper. Simon & Schuster/Atheneum.
ILLUSTRATOR: ***Moses: When Harriet Tubman Led Her People to Freedom*** by Carole Boston Weatherford. Illustrated by Kadir A. Nelson. Jump at the Sun/Hyperion.

2006 AUTHOR: ***Day of Tears: A Novel in Dialogue*** by Julius Lester. Jump at the Sun/Hyperion.
ILLUSTRATOR: ***Rosa*** by Nikki Giovanni. Illustrated by Bryan Collier. Holt.

2005 AUTHOR: ***Remember: The Journey to School Integration*** by Toni Morrison. Houghton.
ILLUSTRATOR: ***Ellington Was Not a Street*** by Ntozake Shange. Illustrated by Kadir Nelson. Simon & Schuster.

2004 AUTHOR: ***The First Part Last*** by Angela Johnson. Simon & Schuster.
ILLUSTRATOR: ***Beautiful Blackbird*** by Ashley Bryan. Atheneum.

2003 AUTHOR: ***Bronx Masquerade*** by Nikki Grimes. Dial.
ILLUSTRATOR: ***Talkin' about Bessie: The Story of Aviator Elizabeth Coleman*** by Nikki Grimes. Illustrated by E. B. Lewis. Orchard/Scholastic.

2002 AUTHOR: ***The Land*** by Mildred D. Taylor. Fogelman/Penguin Putnam.
ILLUSTRATOR: ***Goin' Someplace Special*** by Patricia McKissack. Illustrated by Jerry Pinkney. Atheneum.

2001 AUTHOR: ***Miracle's Boys*** by Jacqueline Woodson. Putnam.
ILLUSTRATOR: ***Uptown*** by Bryan Collier. Holt.

2000 AUTHOR: ***Bud, Not Buddy*** by Christopher Paul Curtis. Delacorte.
ILLUSTRATOR: ***In the Time of the Drums*** retold by Kim L. Siegelson. Illustrated by Brian Pinkney. Hyperion.

Gryphon Award for Transitional Books

The Gryphon Award is given annually to a book published in the preceding year in recognition of an English-language work of fiction or nonfiction for which the primary audience is children in kindergarten through grade 4. The title exemplifies those qualities that successfully bridge the gap in difficulty between books for reading aloud to children and books for practiced readers. The award, established in 2004, is sponsored by the Center for Children's Books at the Graduate School of Library and Information Science at the University of Illinois in Urbana–Champaign.

2016 ***Little Robot*** by Ben Hatke. First Second.

2015 ***Skateboard Party*** by Karen English. Illustrated by Laura Freeman. Clarion.

2014 ***Battle Bunny*** by Jon Scieszka, Mac Barnett, and Alex. Illustrated by Matthew Myers. Simon & Schuster.

2013 ***Island: A Story of the Galápagos*** by Jason Chin. Porter/Roaring Brook.

2012 ***Like Pickle Juice on a Cookie*** by Julie Sternberg. Illustrated by Matthew Cordell. Amulet/Adams.

2011 ***We Are in a Book!*** by Mo Willems. Hyperion.

2010 ***Adventures in Cartooning*** by James Sturm, Andrew Arnold, and Alexis Frederick-Frost. First Second.

2009 ***Frogs*** by Nic Bishop. Scholastic.

2008 ***Billy Tartle in Say Cheese!*** by Michael Townsend. Knopf.

2007 ***The True Story of Stellina*** by Matteo Pericoli. Knopf.

2006 ***Stinky Stern Forever*** by Michelle Edwards. Harcourt.

2005 ***Little Rat Rides*** by Monika Bang-Campbell. Harcourt.

2004 ***Bow Wow Meow Meow: It's Rhyming Cats and Dogs*** by Douglas Florian. Harcourt.

Pura Belpré Award

The Pura Belpré Award honors Latino writers and illustrators whose work best portrays, affirms, and celebrates the Latino cultural experience in a work of literature for youth. This award is sponsored by the Association for Library Service to Children and REFORMA, the National Association to Promote Library Service to the Spanish Speaking.

2016 AUTHOR: ***Enchanted Air: Two Cultures, Two Wings: A Memoir*** by Margarita Engle. Atheneum.
ILLUSTRATOR: ***Drum Dream Girl*** by Margarita Engle. Illustrated by Rafael López. Houghton Mifflin Harcourt.

2015 AUTHOR: ***I Lived on Butterfly Hill*** by Marjorie Agosín. Illustrated by Lee White. Atheneum.
ILLUSTRATOR: ***Viva Frida*** by Yuyi Morales. Roaring Brook.

2014 AUTHOR: ***Yaqui Delgado Wants to Kick Your Ass*** by Meg Medina. Candlewick.
ILLUSTRATOR: ***Niño Wrestles the World*** by Yuyi Morales. Roaring Brook.

2013 AUTHOR: ***Aristotle and Dante Discover the Secrets of the Universe*** by Benjamin Alire Sáenz. Simon & Schuster.
ILLUSTRATOR: ***Martín de Porres: The Rose in the Desert*** by Gary D. Schmidt. Illustrated by David Diaz. Clarion.

2012 AUTHOR: ***Under the Mesquite*** by Guadalupe Garcia McCall. Lee and Low.
ILLUSTRATOR: ***Diego Rivera: His World and Ours*** by Duncan Tonatiuh. Abrams.

2011 AUTHOR: ***The Dreamer*** by Pam Muñoz Ryan. Illustrated by Peter Sís. Scholastic.
ILLUSTRATOR: ***Grandma's Gift*** by Eric Velasquez. Walker.

2010 AUTHOR: ***Return to Sender*** by Julia Alvarez. Alfred A. Knopf.
ILLUSTRATOR: ***Book Fiesta! Celebrate Children's Day/Book Day; Celebremos El día de los niños/El día de los libros*** by Pat Mora. Illustrated by Rafael López. Rayo.

2009 AUTHOR: ***The Surrender Tree: Poems of Cuba's Struggle for Freedom*** by Margarita Engle. Henry Holt.
ILLUSTRATOR: ***Just In Case*** by Yuyi Morales. Roaring Brook Press.

2008 AUTHOR: ***The Poet Slave of Cuba: A Biography of Juan Francisco Manzano*** by Margarita Engle. Illustrated by Sean Qualls. Holt.
ILLUSTRATOR: ***Los Gatos Black on Halloween*** by Marisa Montes. Illustrated by Yuyi Morales. Holt.

2006 AUTHOR: ***The Tequila Worm*** by Viola Canales. Random House.
ILLUSTRATOR: ***Doña Flor: A Tall Tale about a Giant Woman with a Great Big Heart*** by Pat Mora. Knopf.

2004 AUTHOR: ***Before We Were Free*** by Julia Alvarez. Knopf.

ILLUSTRATOR: ***Just a Minute: A Trickster Tale and Counting Book*** by Yuyi Morales. Chronicle.

2002 AUTHOR: ***Esperanza Rising*** by Pam Muñoz Ryan. Scholastic.

ILLUSTRATOR: ***Chato and the Party Animals*** by Gary Soto. Illustrated by Susan Guevara. Putnam.

Distinguished Play Award

This award, sponsored by the American Alliance for Theatre and Education, honors the playwright(s) and the publisher of the work voted as the best play for young people published during the past calendar year (January to December). Three categories are included here: category B (plays primarily for elementary and middle school age audiences), category C for adaptations from existing children's literature for middle and secondary age audiences, and category D for adaptations from existing children's literature primarily for pre-K and elementary age audiences. Award winners since 2000 are listed here. The complete list is at http://www.aate.com/award-winners#Dist_Play.

2015 Category B: ***Super Cowgirl and Mighty Miracle*** by José Cruz González. Dramatic Publishing.

Category C: ***The Book of Everything*** by Richard Tulloch, from the novel by Guus Kuijer. Plays for Young Audiences.

Category D: ***Wiley and the Hairy Man: Musical Version,*** book by Suzan Zeder, music by Harry Pickens, lyrics by Suzan Zeder and Harry Pickens, adapted from the play by Suzan Zeder. Dramatic Publishing.

2014 Category B: ***With Two Wings*** by Anne Negri. Dramatic Publishing.

Category C: ***Walk Two Moons*** by Tom Arvetis, based on Sharon Cheech's novel. Dramatic Publishing.

Category D: ***Jackie & Me*** by Steven Dietz, based on the book by Dan Gutman. Dramatic Publishing.

2013 Category B: ***Don't Tell Me I Can't Fly*** by Y York. Dramatic Publishing.

Category C: ***Lizzie Bright and the Buckminster Boy*** by Cheryl West. Plays for Young Audiences.

Category D: ***Getting Near to Baby*** by Y York. Dramatic Publishing.

2012 Category B: ***Balloonacy*** by Barry Komhauser. Plays for Young Audiences.

Pirates! by Charles Way. Plays for Young Audiences.

Category C: ***A Boy Called Lizard*** by James J. Mellon, music and lyrics by James J. Mellon and Scott De Turk, based on the novel *Lizard* by Dennise Covington. Samuel French.

Category D: ***Eggs*** by Y York, based on the novel by Jerry Spinelli. Dramatic Publishing.

2011 Category B: ***A Best Friends Story*** by Sandra Fenichel Asher. Dramatic Publishing.

Category C: ***The Giver*** adapted by Eric Coble from the novel by Lois Lowry. Dramatic Publishing.

2010 Category B: ***Three*** by Colleen Neuman. Baker's Plays.

Category C: ***Bud, Not Buddy*** adapted by Reginald Andre Jackson from the novel by Christopher Paul Curtis. Dramatic Publishing.

Iqbal adapted for the stage by Jerome Hairston, story by Francesco D' Adamo, with translation by Ann Leonori. Plays for Young Audiences, a partnership of Seattle Children's Theatre and Children's Theatre Company–Minneapolis.

2009 Category B: ***Kindness*** by Dennis Foon. Dramatic Publishing.

Category C: ***Treasure Island*** adapted by Ken Ludwig from the novel by Robert Louis Stevenson. Samuel French.

2008 Category C: ***The Bluest Eye*** adapted by Lydia R. Diamond from the novel by Toni Morrison. Dramatic Publishing.

2007 Category B: ***La ofrenda*** by Jose Casas. Dramatic Publishing.

Category C: ***Roald Dahl's Danny the Champion of the World*** adapted by David Wood. Samuel French.

2006 Category B: ***The Forgiving Harvest*** by Y York. Dramatic Publishing.

2005 Category B: ***In the Garden of the Selfish Giant*** by Sandra Fenichel Asher. Dramatic Publishing.

Category C: ***The Rememberer*** by Steven Dietz, based on ***As My Sun Now Sets*** by Joyce Simmons Cheeka as told to Werdna Phillips Finley. Dramatic Publishing.

2004 Category C: ***Sarah, Plain and Tall*** adapted by Joseph Robinette from the book by Patricia MacLachlan. Dramatic Publishing.

2003 Category B: ***Salt and Pepper*** by Jose Cruz Gonzalez. Dramatic Publishing.

Category C: ***Spot's Birthday Party*** adapted for the stage by David Wood, based on the book by Eric Hill. Samuel French.

2002 Category C: ***Ezigbo, the Spirit Child*** dramatized by Max Bush. Anchorage Press Plays.

Category C: ***A Village Fable*** by James Still, music by Michael Keck. Dramatic Publishing.

2001 Category C: ***Afternoon of the Elves*** by Y York. Dramatic Publishing.

2000 Category B: ***The Wolf Child*** by Edward Mast. Anchorage Press.

Edgar Allan Poe Award (Mystery)—Best Juvenile Novel Category

This award, established in 1961 and sponsored by the Mystery Writers of America, is given to the author of the best mystery of the year written for young readers. Award winners since 2000 are listed here. For the complete list of winners, go to www.theedgars.com/edgarsDB/index.php and select "Best Juvenile" from the award category.

2016 ***Footer Davis Probably Is Crazy*** by Susan Vaught. Simon & Schuster.

2015 ***Greenglass House*** by Kate Milford. Clarion.

2014 ***One Came Home*** by Amy Timberlake. Random House.

2013 ***The Quick Fix*** by Jack D. Ferraiolo. Abrams.

2012 ***Icefall*** by Matthew J. Kirby. Scholastic.

2011 ***The Buddy Files: The Case of the Lost Boy*** by Dori Hillestad Butler. Albert Whitman.

2010 ***Closed for the Season*** by Mary Downing Hahn. Houghton Mifflin.

2009 ***The Postcard*** by Tony Abbott. Little, Brown.

2008 ***The Night Tourist*** by Katherine Marsh. Hyperion.

2007 ***Room One: A Mystery or Two*** by Andrew Clements. Simon & Schuster.

2006 ***The Boys of San Joaquin*** by D. James Smith. Simon & Schuster.

2005 ***Chasing Vermeer*** by Blue Balliett. Scholastic.

2004 ***Bernie Magruder & the Bats in the Belfry*** by Phyllis Reynolds Naylor. Atheneum.

2003 ***Harriet Spies Again*** by Helen Ericson. Random House/Delacorte.

2002 ***Dangling*** by Lillian Eige. Atheneum.

2001 ***Dovey Coe*** by Frances O'Roark Dowell. Simon & Schuster.

2000 ***The Night Flyers*** by Elizabeth McDavid Jones. Pleasant Company.

Scott O'Dell Award for Historical Fiction

This award, donated by the author Scott O'Dell and established in 1984, is given to the author of a distinguished work of historical fiction for children or young adults set in the New World and published in English by a U.S. publisher. The author must be a citizen of the U.S. Award winners since 2000 are listed here. For the complete list of winners, go to www.scottodell.com/pages/scotto'dellawardforhistoricalfiction.aspx.

2015 ***Dash*** by Kirby Lawson. Scholastic.

2014 ***Bo at Ballard Creek*** by Kirkpatrick Hill. Holt.

2013 ***Chickadee*** by Louise Erdich. HarperCollins.

2012 ***Dead End in Norvelt*** by Jack Gantos. Farrar, Straus & Giroux.

2011 ***One Crazy Summer*** by Rita Williams Garcia. Amistad.

2010 ***The Storm in the Barn*** by Matt Phelan. Candlewick.

2009 ***Chains*** by Laurie Halse Anderson. Simon & Schuster.

2008 ***Elijah of Buxton*** by Christopher Paul Curtis. Scholastic.

2007 ***The Green Glass Sea*** by Ellen Klages. Viking.

2006 ***The Game of Silence*** by Louise Erdrich. HarperCollins.

2005 ***Worth*** by A. LaFaye. Simon & Schuster.

2004 ***The River between Us*** by Richard Peck. Dial.

2003 ***Trouble Don't Last*** by Shelley Pearsall. Knopf.

2002 ***The Land*** by Mildred D. Taylor. Fogelman/Penguin.

2001 ***The Art of Keeping Cool*** by Janet Taylor Lisle. Atheneum.

2000 ***Two Suns in the Sky*** by Miriam Bat-Ami. Front Street/Cricket.

Orbis Pictus Award

This award, established in 1990 and sponsored by NCTE's Committee on Using Nonfiction in the Elementary Language Arts Classroom, is given to an author in recognition of excellence in writing of nonfiction for children published in the U.S. in the preceding year.

2016 ***Drowned City: Hurricane Katrina & New Orleans*** by Don Brown. Houghton Mifflin Harcourt.

2015 ***The Family Romanov: Murder, Rebellion & the Fall*** by Candace Fleming. Schwartz & Wade.

2014 ***A Splash of Red: The Life and Art of Horace Pippin*** by Jen Bryant. Illustrated by Melissa Sweet. Knopf.

2013 ***Monsieur Marceau: Actor Without Words*** by Leda Schubert. Illustrated by Gérard DuBois. Roaring Brook.

2012 ***Balloons over Broadway: The True Story of the Puppeteer of Macy's Parade*** by Melissa Sweet. Houghton Mifflin.

2011 ***Ballet for Martha: Making Appalachian Spring*** by Jan Greenberg and Sandra Jordan. Illustrated by Brian Floca. Roaring Brook.

2010 ***The Secret World of Walter Anderson*** by Hester Bass. Illustrated by E. B. Lewis. Candlewick.

2009 ***Amelia Earhart: The Legend of the Lost Aviator*** by Shelley Tanaka. Illustrated by David Craig. Abrams.

2008 ***M. L. K.: Journey of a King*** by Tonya Bolden. Abrams.

2007 ***Quest for the Tree Kangaroo: An Expedition to the Cloud Forest of New Guinea*** by Sy Montgomery. Photos by Nic Bishop. Houghton.

2006 ***Children of the Great Depression*** by Russell Freedman. Clarion.

2005 ***York's Adventures with Lewis and Clark: An African-American's Part in the Great Expedition*** by Rhoda Blumberg. HarperCollins.

2004 ***An American Plague: The True and Terrifying Story of the Yellow Fever Epidemic of 1793*** by Jim Murphy. Clarion.

2003 ***When Marian Sang*** by Pam Muñoz Ryan. Illustrated by Brian Selznick. Scholastic.

2002 ***Black Potatoes: The Story of the Great Irish Famine, 1845–1850*** by Susan Campbell Bartoletti. Houghton.

2001 ***Hurry Freedom: African Americans in Gold Rush California*** by Jerry Stanley. Crown.

2000 ***Through My Eyes*** by Ruby Bridges and Margo Lundell. Scholastic.

Robert F. Sibert Informational Book Medal

This award, established by the Association for Library Service to Children of the American Library Association in 2001, is awarded annually to the author of the most distinguished informational book published during the preceding year.

2016 ***Funny Bones: Posada and His Day of the Dead Calaveras*** by Duncan Tonatiuh. Abrams.

2015 ***The Right Word: Roget and His Thesaurus*** by Jen Bryant. Illustrated by Melissa Sweet. Eerdmans Books.

2014 ***Parrots over Puerto Rico*** by Susan L. Roth and Cindy Trumbore. Illustrated by Susan L. Roth. Lee & Low.

2013 ***Bomb: The Race to Build—and Steal—the World's Most Dangerous Weapon*** by Steve Sheinkin. Flash Point.

2012 ***Balloons over Broadway: The True Story of the Puppeteer of Macy's Parade*** by Melissa Sweet. Houghton Mifflin.

2011 ***Kakapo Rescue: Saving the World's Strangest Parrot*** by Sy Montgomery. Photographs by Nic Bishop. Houghton Mifflin.

2010 ***Almost Astronauts: 13 Women Who Dared to Dream*** by Tanya Lee Stone. Candlewick.

2009 ***We Are the Ship: The Story of Negro League Baseball*** by Kadir Nelson. Jump at the Sun.

2008 ***The Wall: Growing Up behind the Iron Curtain*** by Peter Sís. Farrar.

2007 ***Team Moon: How 400,000 People Landed Apollo 11 on the Moon*** by Catherine Thimmesh. Houghton.

2006 ***Secrets of a Civil War Submarine: Solving the Mysteries of the*** H. L. Hunley by Sally M. Walker. Carolrhoda.

2005 ***The Voice That Challenged a Nation: Marian Anderson and the Struggle for Equal Rights*** by Russell Freedman. Clarion.

2004 ***An American Plague: The True and Terrifying Story of the Yellow Fever Epidemic of 1793*** by Jim Murphy. Clarion.

2003 ***The Life and Death of Adolf Hitler*** by James Cross Giblin. Clarion.

2002 ***Black Potatoes: The Story of the Great Irish Famine, 1845–1850*** by Susan Campbell Bartoletti. Houghton.

Other Notable Book Awards

International Board on Books for Young People Honour List

Sponsored by the International Board on Books for Young People (IBBY), this biennial list is composed of three books (one for text, one for illustration, and one for translation) from each IBBY National Section to represent the best in children's literature published in that country in the past two years. The books selected are recommended as suitable for publication worldwide.

New York Times Best Illustrated Children's Books of the Year

Sponsored by the *New York Times,* this list of 10 books appears annually in November in the *New York Times.* A three-member panel of experts chooses the books.

Notable Books for a Global Society

This annual list of 25 books is selected by the Children's Literature and Reading Special Interest Group of ILA, for outstanding K-8 fiction and nonfiction that enhance children's understanding of people and cultures throughout the world.

Notable Children's Books in the Language Arts

This annual list of 30 books is named by the Children's Literature Assembly of NCTE, for fiction and nonfiction that deal explicitly with language (word origins, word play, history of language) or demonstrate uniqueness in the use of language or style.

Outstanding International Books

The U.S. Board of Books for Young People sponsors an annual list of 40 books for K–12 to highlight books published and distributed in the U.S. but originally published in another country. The list includes translated books.

State Children's Choice Award Programs

Nearly all states have a children's choice book award program. Usually, a ballot of about 25 titles is generated from children's or teachers' nominations and children from all over the state vote for their favorite title. These programs are sponsored by state library associations.

Appendix B

Professional Resources

Books

Barr, C., & Naidoo, J. C. (2014). ***Best books for children, preschool through Grade 6*** (10th ed.). Santa Barbara, CA: Libraries Unlimited.

Identifies the best fiction and nonfiction books for children, with 30,000 annotations and indexes for quick access by author/illustrator, title, and subject/grade level.

Bedford, A., & Albright, L. (Eds.) (2011). ***A master class in children's literature: Trends and issues***. Urbana, IL: NCTE.

Each chapter focuses on a contemporary issue in children's literature and provides suggestions, strategies, and resources.

Bishop, R. S. (2007). ***Free within ourselves: The development of African-American children's literature.*** Westport, CT: Greenwood.

The evolution of fiction written for black children and by black authors and illustrators within the context of African American social and literary history. Profiles of contemporary African American authors and illustrators.

Clark, E., Flores, B., Smith, H., González, D. (2015). ***Multicultural literature for Latino bilingual children***. New York: Rowan & Littlefield.

Classroom practices for using multicultural children's literature to support the linguistic, cultural, and academic learning of bilingual children.

Copeland, B., & Messner, P. (2013). ***School library storytime***. Santa Barbara, CA: Libraries Unlimited.

Resource for planning storytime activities, including how to read to children and a read-aloud curriculum for a school year.

Cunningham, K. E. (2015). ***Story: Still the heart of literacy learning***. Portsmouth, ME: Stenhouse.

Discusses the importance of story in children's lives and shares ways of integrating story into classrooms; includes many classroom examples and lists of resources.

de Las Casas, D. (2006). ***Kamishibai story theater: The art of picture telling.*** Santa Barbara, CA: Libraries Unlimited.

Practical information on developing a kamishibai program using large illustrated cards based on the street art form seen from the 1920s to 1950s in Japan. See Allen Say's ***Kamishibai Man*** (Houghton, 2005) for a story about an itinerant storyteller.

Duke, N. (2014). ***Inside information: Developing powerful readers and writers of informational text through project-based instruction***. New York: Scholastic.

Shares how to build strategies for reading and writing with different types of informational text through project-based learning.

Duke, N., Caughlan, S., & Juzwik, M. (2011). ***Reading and writing genre with purpose in K–8 classrooms***. Portsmouth, NH: Heinemann.

Identifies the problems in commonly used approaches to teaching genre and shares examples of alternative practices along with five guiding principles for instruction. Provides tools for managing a genre approach in the classroom.

Evans, D. (2008). ***Show & Tell: Exploring the fine art of children's book illustration***. San Francisco, CA: Chronicle.

Examines the work of twelve illustrators to teach the elements of art and composition as they relate to picturebook illustration.

Fox, D. L., & Short, K. G. (Eds.). (2003). ***Stories matter: The complexity of cultural authenticity in children's literature.*** Urbana, IL: NCTE.

Social responsibility of authors, cultural sensitivity and values, authenticity of content and images, and authorial freedom addressed by many contributors, including authors, illustrators, editors, publishers, educators, librarians, and scholars.

Freeman, J., & Bauer, C. F. (2015). ***The handbook for storytellers.*** Chicago: ALA.

Guidelines and practical advice on how, when, where and why to tell stories. Contains folktales and an extensive bibliography of books and websites.

Goldsmith, A., Heras, T., & Corapi, S. (2016). ***Reading the world's stories: An annotated bibliography of international youth literature.*** New York: Rowman & Littlefield.

Includes annotations of international children's books published between 2010 and 2014 first published outside of the U.S. and essays on global literature for children.

Hall, S. (2007). ***Using picture storybooks to teach literary devices: Recommended books for children and young adults***. Phoenix, AZ: Oryx Press.

Offers strategies for using picturebooks to teach complex literary devices.

Layne, S. (2009). ***Igniting a passion for reading***. Portland, ME: Stenhouse.

Ways of engaging students to become readers who love a good book and to create a reading culture in a classroom.

Lehman, B., Freeman, E., & Scharer, P. 2010. ***Reading globally, K–8***. Thousand Oaks, CA: Corwin.

The use of global literature across subject areas with numerous examples of outstanding books and teaching strategies.

Lehr, S. S. (Ed.). (2008). ***Shattering the looking glass: Challenge, risk and controversy in children's literature.*** Norwood, MA: Christopher-Gordon.

Politics, controversial issues, and recent change in the world of children's literature.

Leland, C., Lewison, M., & Harste, J. (2012). ***Teaching children's literature: It's critical***. New York, NY: Routledge.

Practical strategies for a critical approach to engaging children with literature in ways that build from children's lives and cultural knowledge to question the world, explore power relationships, and consider actions to promote social justice.

Lukens, R., Smith, J., & Coffel, C. (2013). ***A critical handbook of children's literature*** (9th ed.). New York: Pearson.

Contains separate chapters on each literary element along with examples from children's books; also focuses on other aspects of literary concepts, such as genres and formats.

Marcus, L. (2008). ***Minders of make-believe: Idealists, entrepreneurs, and the shaping of American children's literature.*** Boston: Houghton.

A 300-year history of children's book publishing, showing the evolution from a local endeavor to an international business.

Marcus, L. (2012). ***Show me a story! Why picture books matter***. Somerville, MA: Candlewick.

Interviews with 21 illustrators of children's picturebooks.

Miller, D. (2013). ***Reading in the wild: Cultivating lifelong reading habits***. New York: Jossey-Bass.

Advice and strategies for how to build the habits essential to children's developing a lifelong love of reading. Includes resources, lesson plans, and lists of books.

Naidoo, J. C. (Ed.) (2010). ***Celebrating cuentos: Promoting Latino children's literature and literacy in classrooms and libraries***. Santa Barbara, CA: Libraries Unlimited.

Strategies and research on integrating Latino children's literature into classrooms and libraries, interviews with Latino authors and illustrators, and information on evaluating and selecting quality Latino literature.

Naidoo, J. C. (2016). ***A world of rainbow families: Children's books and media with lesbian, gay, bisexual, transgender, and queer themes around the globe***. Santa Barbara, CA: Libraries Unlimited.

Provides access to a range of books and materials presenting LGBTQ content to children in books set around the globe, including materials for immigrant populations.

Nichols, M. (2006). ***Comprehension through conversation***. Portsmouth, NH: Heinemann.

Issues and strategies to consider in engaging students in purposeful booktalks to lead them to deeper understandings of fiction and nonfiction. Talk as a way to encourage students to think about text through comprehension, conversation, and collaboration.

Pavonetti, L. (Ed.) (2011). ***Bridges to understanding: Envisioning the world through children's books.*** Lanham, MD: Scarecrow.

A guide to international children's books published in the U.S. from 2005 to 2010, with descriptions of 700 books from more than 70 countries in an annotated bibliography.

Short, K. G., Day, D., & Schroder, J., (Eds.). (2016). ***Teaching globally: Reading the world through literature.*** Portsmouth, ME: Stenhouse.

Each chapter shares the story of how a classroom teacher integrated global literature into the classroom to help children explore their own cultural identities and inquire into global communities. Includes lists of global literature.

Sullivan, M. (2009). ***Connecting boys with books 2: Closing the reading gap.*** Chicago: American Library Association.

A strategic plan for boys and reading through stimulating a sense of excitement in reading.

Thomas, R. (2014). ***A to Zoo: Subject access to children's picture books*** (9th ed.). Santa Barbara, CA: Libraries Unlimited. Also has a 2016 supplement.

Provides easy subject access to 17,000 picturebooks on a broad range of themes and topics.

Trelease, J. (2013). ***The read-aloud handbook*** (7th ed.). New York: Penguin.

Benefits, rewards, and importance of reading aloud along with techniques to make read-alouds effective and annotated book lists.

Vardell, S. M. (2014). ***Children's literature in action: A librarian's guide.*** Santa Barbara, CA: Libraries Unlimited.

Practical information on trends, titles, and tools for choosing the best books and materials for children, as well as planning programs and activities in school and public libraries.

Wadham, R., & Young, T. (2015). ***Integrating children's literature through the Common Core State Standards***. Santa Barbara, CA: Libraries Unlimited.

Defines the CCSS and the role of the school librarian along with tools for collaborative instruction in libraries.

Bibliographies: Annual Lists

CCBC Choices

An annual spring annotated booklist published by and for the members of the Friends of the CCBC, Inc. (Cooperative Children's Book Center). Available on the CCBC website at https://ccbc.education.wisc.edu/.

Children's Choices

This yearly list of newly published books, chosen by young readers themselves, appears in the October issue of *The Reading Teacher* as a project of the International Literacy Association/Children's Book Council Joint Committee.

Notable Books for a Global Society

An annual list of K–12 books that enhance children's understandings of people and cultures throughout the world, a project of Children's Literature Special Interest Group of ILA. Published in *Dragon Lode* and on the CL/R SIG website at http://www.clrsig.org/.

Notable Children's Books

This annual American Library Association list appears in the March issue of *School Library Journal* and also in the March 15 issue of *Booklist.*

Notable Children's Books in the Language Arts (K–8)

This annual list of outstanding trade books for enhancing language awareness among students in grades K–8 appears in each March issue of *Language Arts*.

Notable Social Studies Trade Books for Young People

This list appears in the May/June issue of *Social Education* and at www.socialstudies.org/notable.

Outstanding International Book List

This annual list of outstanding books for K–12 is sponsored by USBBY and highlights books that were first published in another country. Published in February, *School Library Journal.*

Outstanding Science Trade Books for Students K–12

This list appears in the March issue of *Science and Children* and at www.nsta.org/publications/ostb/.

Teachers' Choices

This yearly list includes books recommended by teachers. It appears each November in *The Reading Teacher* and at www.reading.org.

Appendix C

Children's Magazines

The following list includes some of the most popular children's magazines available to young people, organized by primary emphasis.

Drama

Plays, the Drama Magazine for Young People. Scripts for plays, skits, puppet shows, and round-the-table readings (a type of readers' theatre). 6–8 scripts per issue. Ages 6–17. 7 issues/year. Order at www.playsmagazine.com.

Health and Creativity

Humpty Dumpty Magazine (ages 2–6) and *Jack and Jill* (ages 6–12). Order at www.cbhi.org.

History

Cobblestone. Articles about U.S. history. Themed issues. Ages 9–14. 9 issues/year. Order at www.cobblestonepub.com.

Dig Into History. Archeology, paleontology, and earth sciences in a world history context. Ages 9–14. 9 issues/year. Order at www.cobblestonepub.com.

Language

Allons-y!. Topics of interest for 12- to 18-year-olds in French. Information and cultural details of French-speaking countries. Read-aloud plays and language CDs. 6 issues/year. Order at http://classroommagazines.scholastic.com.

Das Rad. Topics of interest for 12- to 18-year-olds in German. Information and cultural details of German-speaking countries. Read-aloud plays and language CDs. 6 issues/year. Order at http://classroommagazines.scholastic.com.

¿Qué Tal? Topics of interest for 12- to 18-year-olds in Spanish. Information and cultural details of Spanish-speaking countries. Read-aloud plays and language CDs. 6 issues/year. Order at http://classroommagazines.scholastic.com.

Language Arts

Scholastic Scope. Plays, short stories, nonfiction, writing exercises, and skill builders. Ages 11–15. 8 issues/year. Order at http://classroommagazines.scholastic.com.

Stone Soup: The Magazine by Young Writers and Artists. Stories, poems, book reviews, and art by children. Ages 8–13. 6 issues/year. Order at www.stonesoup.com.

Storyworks. Focuses on development of grammar, writing, vocabulary, test-taking. Includes read-aloud plays. Ages 8–11. 6 issues/year. Order at http://classroommagazines.scholastic.com.

Literature

Cricket. Fiction, nonfiction, book reviews, activities. Features international literature. Ages 9–14. 9 issues/year. Order at www.cricketmag.com.

Lady Bug. Fiction, poems, songs, and games. Ages 3–6. 9 issues/year. Order at www.cricketmag.com.

Spider. Fiction, poems, songs, and games for the beginning reader. Ages 6–9. 9 issues/year. Order at www.cricketmag.com.

Mathematics

DynaMath. Humorously formatted word problems, computation, and test preparation; careers in mathematics feature. Ages 8–11. 8 issues/year. Order at http://classroommagazines.scholastic.com.

Scholastic MATH. Math problems, computation, statistics, consumer math, real-life applications, career math, critical reasoning. Ages 11–15. 10 issues/year. Order at http://classroommagazines.scholastic.com.

Nature

National Geographic Explorer. Classroom magazines featuring nonfiction and nature photography aligned with science and social studies curriculum. For grades K–6. 7 issues/year. Order at http://ngexplorer.buysub.com.

National Geographic Kids. Nonfiction articles and nature photography. Promotes geographic awareness. Ages 6–14. 10 issues/year. Order at www.kids.nationalgeographic.com/kids.

Ranger Rick. Fiction and nonfiction, photo essays, jokes, riddles, crafts, plays, and poetry promoting the appreciation of nature. Superlative nature photography. Ages 7–12. 10 issues/year. Order at www.nwf.org/kids.

Recreation

Boys' Life. News, nature, sports, history, fiction, science, comics, Scouting, colorful graphics, and photos. Published by the Boy Scouts of America. Ages 7–18. 12 issues/year. Order at www.boyslife.org.

Highlights. General-interest magazine offering fiction and nonfiction, crafts, poetry, and thinking features. Ages 6–12. 12 issues/year. Order at www.highlights.com.

Junior Baseball Magazine. Articles on baseball skills, sportsmanship, safety, and physical fitness. Ages 10–14. 6 issues/year. Order at www.juniorbaseball.com.

New Moon: The Magazine for Girls and Their Dreams. An international magazine by and about girls. Builds healthy resistance to gender inequities. Ages 8–14. 6 issues/year. Order at http://www.newmoon.com.

Nickelodeon Magazine. Nickelodeon television channel entertainment and humor magazine with television-related celebrity interviews, comics, puzzles, and activities. Ages 6–14. 12 issues/year. Order at http://papercutz.com/nickmag.

Sports Illustrated for Kids. Stories about sports and sports celebrities, amateur sports, trivia. Poster included with each issue. Ages 6–10. 12 issues/year. Order at www.sikids.com.

Science

Science World. Articles, experiments, and news to supplement the science curriculum. Ages 11–16. 12 issues/year. Order at http://classroommagazines.scholastic.com.

SuperScience. Science concepts, critical thinking, and reasoning through hands-on activities and experiments; science news stories; interviews with scientists. Themed issues. Ages 8–11. 8 issues/year. Order at http://classroommagazines.scholastic.com.

Social Studies

Faces. Articles and activities exploring world cultures. Ages 9–14. 9 issues/year. Order at www.cobblestonepub.com.

Junior Scholastic. Features U.S. and world history, current events, world cultures, map skills, and geography. Ages 11–14. 16 issues/year. Order at http://classroommagazines.scholastic.com.

Muse. Wide-ranging articles exploring ideas in science, history, and the arts. Ages 9–14. 9 issues/year. Order at www.cricketmag.com.

Skipping Stones: An International Multicultural Magazine. Articles by, about, and for children about world cultures and cooperation. Multilingual. Ages 7–17. 5 issues/year. Order at www.skippingstones.org.

Index to Children's Books and Authors